HEALTH AND DISEASE:
A READER

HEALTH AND DISEASE: A READER

EDITED BY
**BASIRO DAVEY, ALASTAIR GRAY
AND CLIVE SEALE**

Open University Press
Buckingham · Philadelphia

Open University Press
Celtic Court
22 Ballmoor
Buckingham
MK18 1XW

email: enquiries@openup.co.uk
world wide web: www.openup.co.uk

and
325 Chestnut Street
Philadelphia, PA 19106, USA

First edition published 1984
Reprinted 1986, 1988, 1989, 1990, 1992, 1993

Second edition published in 1995
Reprinted 1995, 1996, 1999, 2000, 2001

First published in this third edition 2001

A catalogue record of this book is available from the British Library

ISBN   0 335 20967 X (pbk)   0 335 20968 8 (hbk)

Library of Congress Cataloging-in-Publication Data
Health and disease : a reader / edited by Basiro Davey, Alastair Gray, and Clive Seale.—
3rd ed.
        p. cm. — (Health and disease series)
    Includes bibliographical references and index.
    ISBN 0–335–20968–8 (hb) — ISBN 0–335–20967–X (pbk.)
    1. Public health.   2. Social medicine.   3. Medical care.   I. Davey, Basiro.   II. Gray,
Alastair, 1953–   III. Seale, Clive.   IV. Series.

RA436 .H43 2002
362.1—dc21   2001036256

Typeset in 10/11.5pt Sabon by Graphicraft Limited, Hong Kong
Printed in Great Britain by Biddles Limited, Guildford and King's Lynn

Contents

Part 5   The social context of health care
Introduction

Part 6   Health work
Introduction

Part 7   Prospects and speculations
Introduction

Acknowledgements

1 Abridged selections from *Mirage of Health: Utopias, Progress and Biological Change* by René Dubos published by Rutgers University Press, 1987, Rutgers, The State University. Published by permission of the estate of the late René Dubos.

2 Reprinted from Roy Porter, *The Greatest Benefit to Mankind*, 1997, HarperCollins Publishers, by permission of HarperCollins Publishers.

3 Reprinted from *Culture, Medicine and Psychiatry* 2, 1978, pp. 107–37: 'Feed a cold, starve a fever', Cecil Helman, copyright © 1978 by D. Reidel Publishing Company, Dordrecht, Holland. Reprinted by kind permission of Kluwer Academic Publishers. Reprinted from *New Society*, 5 November 1981, by permission of *New Society*.

4 Reprinted from Mildred Blaxter, *Health and Lifestyles*, 1990, Tavistock Publications. Reproduced by kind permission of Taylor and Francis Books Ltd.

5 Extract from *Illness as Metaphor* by Susan Sontag, Chapter 4, Viking 1979. Reproduced by permission of Penguin Books Ltd.

6 Reprinted from David Armstrong, 'The problem of the whole-person in holistic medicine' in *Holistic Medicine*, 1, pp. 27–36, 1986.

7 Reprinted from Sarah Nettleton, 'Protecting the vulnerable margin: towards an analysis of how the mouth came to be separated from the body', *Sociology of Health and Illness*, 1988, 10(2), pp. 156–69, by permission of Blackwell Publishers.

8 Original article by Mary James © The Open University 1995, by permission of The Open University.

9 Reprinted from Cecil Helman, *Culture, Health and Illness: An Introduction for Health Professionals*, 4th edition, Chapter 10, Arnold 2000. Reprinted by permission of Arnold Publishers Ltd.

10 Reprinted from Greg Philo (ed.). *Message Received: Glasgow Media Group Research 1993–1998*, Chapter 4, Pearson Education 1999. © Pearson Education Limited 1999, reprinted by permission of Pearson Education Limited.

11 Reprinted from Peter Conrad, 'Public eyes and private genes', *Social Problems*, May 1997, **44**(2), pp. 139–55. © 1997 by The Society for the Study of Social Problems. Reprinted from *Social Problems* by permission.

12 Reprinted from Mary O'Hagan, 'Two accounts of mental distress' in Jim Read and Jean Reynolds (eds) *Speaking our Minds: An Anthology*, 1996, The Open University and Macmillan Press. Reproduced with Permission of Palgrave and The Open University.

13 Reprinted from The Sainsbury Centre for Mental Health, *Acute Problems: A Survey of the Quality of Care in Acute Psychiatric Wards*, 1998, London.

14 Extract from Erving Goffman 'The insanity of place', *Relations in Public: Microstudies of the Public Order* (Viking 1961). Reproduced by permission of Penguin Books Ltd.

15 Reprinted from Andrew Nocon and Tim Booth, *The Social Impact of Asthma* published by Joint Unit for Social Services Research, The University, Sheffield.

16 Adapted from *Journal of Medical Ethics*, 1999, 25, pp. 195–9, 'Beyond the disorder: one parent's reflection on genetic counselling' by Ruth McGowan. Reproduced by permission of the BMJ Publishing Group.

17 Reprinted from Sally Macintyre and David Oldman, 'Coping with migraine' in A. Davies and G. Horobin (eds): *Medical Encounters*, Croom Helm, 1977. Reproduced by kind permission of Taylor and Francis Books Ltd.

18 Reprinted from Ursula Sharma, 'Using alternative therapies: marginal medicine and central concerns' in P. Abbott and G. Payne (eds) *New Directions in the Sociology of Health*, Falmer Press, 1990, pp. 140–52. Reproduced by kind permission of Taylor and Francis Books Ltd.

19 Reprinted from Jaber F. Gubrium, 'The social preservation of mind: the Alzheimer's disease experience', *Symbolic Interaction*, 1986, Vol. 9(1), pp. 37–51, by permission. © 1986 by JAI Press. Reprinted by permission of University of California Press.

20 Reprinted from Tony Parker, *The People of Providence*, 1983, Hutchinson & Co., London. © Tony Parker 1983. Reproduced by permission of the author c/o Rogers, Coleridge & White Ltd., 20 Powis Mews, London, W11 1JN.

21 The extract on pages 118–21 from *Pride Against Prejudice: A Personal Politics of Disability* by Jenny Morris, published in Great Britain by The Women's Press Ltd, 1991, 34 Great Sutton Street, London, EC1V 0LQ is used by permission of The Women's Press Ltd.

22 Reprinted from Naomi Pfeffer, 'The stigma of infertility' in M. Stanworth (ed.) *Reproductive Technologies: Gender, Motherhood and Medicine*, Polity Press, Cambridge, 1987.

23 Reprinted from Kathy Charmaz, 'Identity dilemmas of chronically ill men', *The Sociological Quarterly*, May 1994, 35(2), pp. 269–88, © 1994 by JAI Press. Reprinted by permission of Univ. of CA Press.

24 Reprinted from David Finkel, 'Few drugs for the needy: in impoverished Malawi, one man faces the odds,' *The Washington Post*, 1 November 2000, p. A01. © 2000, The Washington Post. Reprinted with permission.
Reprinted, with minor changes, from Thomas Garrett, 'One year on therapy and counting . . . Doses taken: 1,460; Doses missed: 0', from AIDS Care, a publication of Dorrance Company.

25 Reprinted from F. Engels, *The Condition of the Working Class in England*,

translated by the Institute of Marxism-Leninism, Moscow, Panther Books, 1969, by permission of Panther Books and Lawrence and Wishart.

26 Reprinted extract with permission from David E. Bloom and David Canning, 'The health and wealth of nations', *Science*, February 2000, 287, pp. 1207–9. Copyright 2000 American Association for the Advancement of Science.

27 Extract on pages 151–4 from *The Rise and Fall of the Third Chimpanzee* by C. Jared Diamond published by Hutchinson. Used by permission of The Random House Group Limited and HarperCollins Publishers, Inc.

28 Reprinted extract with permission from Paul R. Epstein, 'Climate and health', *Science*, 16 July 1999, 285, pp. 347–8. Copyright 1999 American Association for the Advancement of Science.

29 Reprinted from the Royal College of Physicians Medical Services Study Group, 'Deaths under 50', in *British Medical Journal*, 2, pp. 1061–1062, (1978), by permission of the BMJ Publishing Group.

30 Reprinted from Helen Roberts, Susan Smith and Carol Bryce, 'Prevention is better . . .' in *Sociology of Health and Illness*, 15(1993), pp. 447–463. By permission of Blackwell Publishers Ltd and the Foundation for the Sociology of Health and Illness.

31 Reprinted from *Richard Asher: Talking Sense*, edited by F.A. Jones, 'Malingering', 1986, by permission of the publisher Churchill Livingstone.

32 Reprinted from Francis Notzon *et al.*, 'Causes of declining life expectancy in Russia', *Journal of the American Medical Association*, March 1998, 279(10), pp. 793–800, by permission of the authors.

33 Reprinted from Richard Wilkinson, *Unhealthy Societies – The Afflictions of Inequality*, Chapter 9, pp. 175–92, 1996, Routledge. Reproduced by kind permission of Taylor and Francis Books Ltd.

34 © Jean Drèze and Amartya Sen 1989. Reprinted from *Hunger and Public Action* by Jean Drèze and Amartya Sen (1989) by permission of Oxford University Press.

35 Reprinted from Barry Bogin, 'Why must I be a teenager at all?' in *New Scientist*, 6 March 1993, pp. 34–8. Reproduced by permission of *New Scientist*.

36 Reprinted from James D. Watson, 'Good gene, bad gene', TIME International Winter 1997–1998. © 1998 Time Inc. reprinted by permission.

37 Reprinted extract with permission from James W. Vaupel *et al.*, 'Biodemographic trajectories of longevity, *Science*, 1988, 280, pp. 855–60. Copyright 1988 American Association for the Advancement of Science.

38 Reprinted from P. Laslett, *A Fresh Map of Life*, Chapter 1, 1989, by permission of Weidenfeld and Nicolson, London.

39 Reprinted from T. McKeown, *The Modern Rise of Population*, Edward Arnold, 1976, by permission of Edward Arnold Publishers Ltd.

40 Reprinted from Simon Sretzer, 'The importance of social intervention in Britain's mortality decline', *Social History of Medicine*, 1, 1, (1998), pp. 1–37, by permission of The Society for the Social History of Medicine.

41 Reprinted from *Effectiveness and Efficiency: Random Reflections on Health Services* by A.L. Cochrane, Royal Society of Medicine Press Ltd, 1999.

42 Reprinted from John P. Bunker, 'Medicine matters after all', *Journal of the Royal College of Physicians of London*, March/April 1995, Vol. 29(2), pp. 105–12, by permission of the Royal College of Physicians of London.

43 Reprinted from *The Lancet* and the *British Medical Journal* by permission and *The Guardian* © *The Guardian*.

44 Reprinted from Marc A. Strassburg, 'The global eradication of smallpox' in *American Journal of Infection Control*, **19**, pp. 220–225, with permission from Mosby, Inc.

45 Reprinted from I. Illich, *Limits to Medicine*, Marion Boyars, 1976, by permission of Marion Boyars Publishers Ltd.

46 Reprinted from V. Navarro, *Medicine under Capitalism*, Prodist, 1976, by permission of the author.

47 Reprinted from D.R. Gwatkin, 'Health inequalities and the health of the poor: What do we know? What can we do?' in *Bulletin of the World Health Organization*, 2000, 78(1), pp. 3–17, by permission of the World Health Organization.

48 Adapted from *British Medical Journal*, 1999, **319**, pp. 1353–5, 'Ageism in cardiology' by Ann Bowling. Reproduced by permission of the BMJ publishing group.

49 Adapted from *British Medical Journal*, 1993, **306**, pp. 1047–50, 'Controversies in treatment: should smokers be offered bypass surgery?' by M.J. Underwood, J.S. Bailey and M. Shiu. Reproduced by permission of the BMJ publishing group.

50 Adapted from *British Medical Journal*, 1996, **312**, pp. 71–2, 'Evidence based medicine: what it is and what it isn't', by David Sackett *et al*. Reproduced by permission of the BMJ publishing group. Reprinted from Blair H. Smith, Nigel T. James and Alan Maynard, in *British Medical Journal*, 1996, **313**, pp. 169–71.

51 Reprinted from Ray Fitzpatrick and Deena White, 'Public participation in the evaluation of health care', *Health and Social Care in the Community*, 1997, 5(1), pp. 3–8. Reproduced by permission of Blackwell Publishers.

52 Original article by Andy Alaszewski and Ian Harvey © The Open University 2001, by permission of The Open University.

53 Adapted from *British Medical Journal*, 1999, **319**, pp. 1490–2, 'Improving NHS performance: human behaviour and health policy' by Chris Ham. Reproduced by permission of the BMJ publishing group.

54 Reprinted from *Social Science and Medicine*, **45**, Gerald Bloom and Gu Xingyuan, 'Health sector reform: lessons from China', 1997, pp. 351–60, with permission from Elsevier Science.

55 Reprinted from Rosemary Stevens, *The Evolution of the Health-care Systems in the US and the UK*, by permission of the author.

56 Reprinted from Martin McKee and Judith Healy, 'The role of the hospital in a changing environment' in *Bulletin of the World Health Organization*, 2000, 78(6), p. 803–10, by permission of the World Health Organization.

57 Reprinted from Michael Young and Lesley Cullen, *A Good Death: Conversations with East Londoners*, 1996, Routledge. Reproduced by kind permission of Taylor and Francis Books Ltd.

58 Reprinted from David Field 'We didn't want him to die on his own' in *Journal of Advanced Nursing*, 9, 1984, pp. 59–70. Reproduced by permission of Blackwell Science.

59 Reprinted from Celia Davies, *Gender and the Professional Predicament in Nursing*, 1995, Open University Press.

60 Reprinted from Thurstan B. Brewin, 'Truth, trust and paternalism' in *The Lancet*, **31**, 31 August 1985, pp. 490–2 © by The Lancet Ltd.

61 Reprinted from A. Oakley, *Women Confined*, Martin Robertson, 1980, by permission of the author.

62 Reprinted from Roger Jeffery, 'Normal rubbish: deviant patients in casualty departments' in *Sociology of Health and Illness*, **1** (1979), pp. 90–108. By permission of Blackwell Publishers Ltd and the Foundation for the Sociology of Health and Illness.

63 Reprinted from E. Paterson, 'Food-work' in Atkinson, P. and Health, C. (eds) *Medical Work*, Gower, 1981.

64 Original article by Lesley Doyal and Ailsa Cameron © The Open University 2001, by permission of The Open University.

65 Reprinted from David Werner, 'The village health-worker: lackey or liberator?' in M. Skeet and K. Elliott (eds) *Health Auxilliaries and the Health Team*, Croom Helm, 1978.

66 Adapted from *Journal of Epidemiology and Community Health*, 1998, **52**, pp. 538–9, 'The new globalisation, food and health: is public health receiving its due emphasis?' by Tim Lang. Reproduced by permission of the BMJ Publishing Group.

67 Reprinted extract with permission from Peter Piot, 'Global AIDS epidemic: time to turn the tide', *Science*, February 2000, **288**, pp. 2176–8. Copyright 2000 American Association for the Advancement of Science.

68 Reprinted from Michael Hardey, 'Doctor in the house: the Internet as a source of lay health knowledge and the challenge to expertise' in *Sociology of Health and Illness*, 1999, **21**(6), pp. 820–35. By permission of Blackwell Publishers Ltd and the Foundation for the Sociology of Health and Illness.

69 Reprinted from J. Grimley Evans, 'Ageing and medicine' in *Journal of Internal Medicine*, 2000, **247**, pp. 159–67. By permission of Blackwell Science.

70 Reprinted from Tom Shakespeare, 'Brave New World II', *The Guardian*, 5 January 2000. By permission of the author.

71 Reprinted from Sally Vincent, 'Exists', *The Guardian Weekend*, 19 February 1994. © *The Guardian*.

72 B. Müller-Hill, 'The shadow of genetic injustice'. Reprinted by permission from *Nature*, **362**, 8 April 1993, pp. 491–492. © 1993 Macmillan Magazines Ltd.

73 Reprinted from S. Jones, *The Language of the Genes*, 1993, by permission of HarperCollins Publishers Limited.

74 Nicola Griffith, 'Spawn of Satan?' Reprinted by permission from *Nature*, **402**, 1999, p. 585. © 1999 Macmillan Magazines Ltd.

75 Reprinted from J. Desmond Bernal, *The World, The Flesh and The Devil*, 1929, Jonathan Cape. Reproduced by kind permission of Taylor and Francis Books Ltd.

76 Shulamit Reinharz, Chapter 4 in B. Glassner and R. Hertz (eds): *Qualitative Sociology as Everyday Life*. pp. 31–40, copyright © by Sage Publications. Reprinted by permission of Sage Publications.

Note

permission to publish this material. Any omissions brought to our attention will be remedied in future editions.

The editors express their grateful thanks to Denise Rowe and Joy Wilson of the Open University for their superb assistance in preparing the manuscript of this book.

General introduction

The third edition of this Reader, building on the successful 1984 and 1995 editions, reflects a continuing steady expansion of research and publication relevant to the subjects of health and disease. The increasing diversity of this field means that we can draw on a yet more varied range of authors and commentators. The growth of the disability rights movement, the increased importance of research into human genetics, the creation of new medical therapies, concerns about the environment and health, the changing patterns of mortality associated with social and political changes in some parts of the world, the trend towards 'evidence based' medicine and new thinking about inter-professional responsibilities in health care are a few of the developments whose importance has increasingly been recognized since the last edition of this book, and which are now reflected in our choice of articles.

This Reader contains contributions from most of the major academic disciplines engaged in active research into some aspect of health and disease, together with extracts from official reports, letters, essays, fiction and interviews. Some contributions are deeply embedded in the concepts and viewpoints of a constrained sphere of interest; others bridge traditional disciplinary boundaries and attempt a synthesis of views, or reach into the future to speculate about the shape of things to come. Many difficult decisions had to be made on what to include and what to leave out. In some cases we have kept articles from previous editions, though these may have been re-edited and reduced in length; generally these are 'classic' texts, which are difficult to find in print. Two of the 37 'new' articles in this edition have not been published previously.

The diversity of the material can be exemplified by considering several articles that focus on a single topic, that of genetics. In Part 1, the sociologist Peter Conrad shows how genetic ideas have influenced public perceptions of the causes of human behaviour and capabilities, through their popularization in the mass media. In Part 2, Ruth McGowan describes, from the viewpoint of a parent, how genetic counselling can throw up many ethical and personal dilemmas in the way in which it conveys vital information. The biologist James D. Watson presents an optimistic vision in Part 3 of the promise of genetic science, stressing the desirability of 'banishing genetic disability' through the kinds of screening and counselling programmes that Ruth McGowan experienced. In Watson's vision of the future, genetic progress would also have 'banished' McGowan's sons.

Benno Müller-Hill and Steve Jones, both biologists, take different views of the future in Part 7 – the first envisaging growing 'genetic injustice' in inequitable social arrangements, and the second holding out the prospect of a gradual reduction in the amount of genetically based disease. Finally, the disability activist Tom Shakespeare raises important questions about a 'brave new world' that may be emerging under the influence of genetic science, in which a form of 'disability eugenics' becomes the norm.

Several of these articles make reference to underlying economic factors in genetic science and its application, and to historical studies that shed light on current events, such as the story of the eugenics movement. Thus a number of perspectives and academic disciplines converge on this single topic, as they do for many others represented in this book.

The medical model of disease and the contribution of medicine to health and health care arise in many parts of this Reader – for example, in the classic articles by McKeown, Szreter, Illich, Navarro and Cochrane. The practice of medicine and its interaction with health and social policy are covered by Sackett *et al.*, Chris Ham and Ann Bowling, among many others. Richard Wilkinson questions the medical model and argues for more emphasis on psychosocial causes of ill health.

The investigation of any aspect of health and disease can benefit not only from a multidisciplinary approach, but one that also values the subjective and illuminative as well as the objective and quantifiable. Both qualitative and quantitative approaches are well represented in this Reader. Accounts of the experience of illness in Part 2 often draw on qualitative interviews; by contrast, Mildred Blaxter shows the value of quantifying answers to the question 'What is health?' by analysing the vocabulary and ideas expressed by 900 people in a nationwide survey. Health economists also draw on quantitative methods to answer questions of causation, as can be seen in the contribution by Francis Notzon *et al.* on the factors leading to declining life expectancy in Russia.

Historians and social anthropologists can be found in this edition too – for example, in Roy Porter's account of Hippocratic medicine and Mary James' vivid description of the treatment of hysteria in nineteenth century France; in Jared Diamond's analysis of the health decline following the first agricultural revolution, or Elizabeth Paterson's article on working practices in a hospital kitchen. The biological dimension is prominent in articles on the evolution of longevity by Vaupel *et al.*, on theories of ageing by Grimley-Evans and in the environmental perspective provided by Paul Epstein in Part 3.

Thus the contributions to this Reader differ greatly in style, content, focus and intent. Given this diversity and the broad reach of the selection, the editors have imposed a degree of order by grouping the contributions under seven headings:

Part 1   Cultural aspects of health, illness and healing
Part 2   Experiencing health, disease and health care
Part 3   Influences on health and disease
Part 4   The role of medicine
Part 5   The social context of health care
Part 6   Health work
Part 7   Prospects and speculations.

Each part begins with a short introduction prepared by the editors, which aims to draw the reader's attention to common themes and sharp discontinuities. Within each part the emphasis has been on choosing material that adequately represents the range of disciplines, perspectives and styles of writing. To this end, we have edited the majority of articles to reduce their length from the original texts, thereby enabling us to include a larger selection; in some cases, the editors had the assistance of authors or trustees in carrying out this task. We have also edited the references cited by each article, but have retained the original citation styles. Where substantial and significant parts of a text have been omitted, this has been acknowledged in the note at the end of the article, which also contains a brief description of the author(s) and a full reference to the original source in which the unabridged material was published.

This Reader has been assembled as part of an Open University second-level course for undergraduate study and professional development, entitled '*Health and Disease*' (course code U205), which explores in depth the possibilities of a multidisciplinary approach to a range of health and disease topics. The course consists of this Reader, eight specially prepared distance-teaching textbooks (published by Open University Press), and audiovisual materials. This Reader is indispensable for students taking the course, but it has also been designed to stand alone as a coherent and self-contained collection, accessible to a wide readership, which includes health workers and social workers of all kinds, students of the many disciplines represented here and the general public.

PART 1

Cultural aspects of health, illness and healing

I INTRODUCTION

People at different moments in history, and across different cultures, think about health and disease in different ways. We would not expect a western doctor trained in the biomedical tradition to understand disease in the same way as a doctor trained in traditional Chinese medicine. Neither of these practitioners would subscribe uncritically to the systems of medical knowledge and therapy that applied in their societies several hundred years ago. Additionally, the beliefs held by professional healers may contrast with those held by their patients. Definitions of health and disease are therefore variable, and may be linked with the interests of particular groups, some of whom may have more power than others to impose their definitions.

Thus we can say that health and disease, studied as cultural phenomena, are concepts around which there are often rival explanations, differing practices and few areas of consensus. The articles in Part 1 show that debates in the health care field do not just revolve around how best to promote health or deal with ill health, as if these concepts had some fixed, objective meaning. The very objects of study – health, illness and healing – are contested concepts.

Most societies maintain some myth of a Golden Age which, while usually set in the past, may be considered to be attainable in the future if the appropriate policies and practices are adopted. In 'Mirage of health', the first article in the book, René Dubos argues that the concept of health as arising from a harmony with nature is attractive, but essentially an illusion. It is opposed by a conception of health, represented in Greek mythology by the god Asclepius, which identifies causes of ill health in precisely located malfunctions of the body. Dubos' preferred synthesis rests on the interaction between these two traditions.

The historian Roy Porter, in his account of Hippocratic medicine, describes how ideas about balance and harmony, and of disease as disequilibrium, were implemented in western medical practices in the past. Humoral theory proposed a patient-centred approach to diagnosis and therapy, which focused on the unique circumstances of the individual, in contrast to the modern focus on disease entities, with patients designated as mere 'carriers' of an illness. Porter reveals the importance of the individualized doctor–patient contract in Greek antiquity, which also obliged physicians to develop a code of ethics, formulated as the famous Hippocratic 'oath'.

Modern individuals may feel that humoral theory, with its bleeding, purges and other strange and unscientific therapies, has now been thoroughly discredited by the rise of the Asclepian tradition and its 'magic bullets', surgical interventions, targeted drug therapies and the like. But the anthropologist Cecil Helman, in 'Feed a cold, starve a fever' demonstrates that ordinary people in North London often subscribe to the idea that ill health is due to an imbalance between the person and forces of nature. Thus lay beliefs are placed by Helman firmly within the camp that Dubos earlier identified as that of the Greek goddess Hygeia, who embodied the precept *mens sana in corpore sano* (a healthy mind in a healthy body), founded on the belief that health arose when people lived wisely.

The sociologist Mildred Blaxter in the next article 'What is health?' reports a larger scale study of the health beliefs of ordinary people, showing a greater variety of such 'lay beliefs' than does Helman. Some of these beliefs are quite close to the medical, Asclepian view of health as the absence of disease; others incorporate broader notions of the 'healthy life' which – as for the people studied by Helman – include attributions about morality and character underpinning health. The idea that disease confers a particular quality of character upon a person is also explored by Susan Sontag, who describes the romanticized images of tuberculosis (TB) sufferers in the past, evident in literary and other accounts. Humoral theory did not distinguish mind from body; Sontag observes the same thing going on in attributions of a 'melancholy' character to TB sufferers.

A belief in the value of holistic approaches to diagnosis and therapy is often promoted by advocates of complementary therapies in modern times, and one can see continuities between this and humoral theory. David Armstrong, in 'The problem of the whole-person in holistic medicine' takes a critical view of this. He returns us to themes evident in Dubos' article, presenting a sceptical account of the Golden Age myth. Holism, with its idealized construction of what it is to be 'natural' is, in Armstrong's eyes, an ideological view designed to promote the interests of its practitioners. However, he cautions against being too critical of complementary therapies on the grounds of what harm or good they may do, arguing that the ideas they incorporate offer us new ways of thinking about ourselves and our health.

Armstrong is presenting what sociologists and others who study cultural variability in the forms that knowledge takes like to call a 'constructionist' approach. That is to say, medical knowledge is not necessarily to be seen as an account of 'discovery' in which a single overarching truth is progressively revealed, but instead as a system of beliefs, useful in a certain time or place, but containing a substantial degree of invention. This potentially radical view of knowledge is explored to its logical extreme in Sarah Nettleton's article, 'Protecting a vulnerable margin: towards an analysis of how the mouth came to be separated from the body'. Nettleton applies to the case of dentistry the view that medical knowledge is a social construction, rather than an objective description of external reality. She argues that we are taught to see some events – such as tooth decay – as having an objective physical existence. Toothache appears to have a singular and most pressing meaning to the sufferer, and tooth brushing appears to be an incontrovertibly sensible, rational and inevitable response to conditions in mouths. See if you feel differently about brushing your teeth when you have read Nettleton's article!

Many people find that the constructionist view of knowledge, or if you prefer, the cultural analysis of ideas about health, is somewhat easier to accept in the realm of mental rather than physical illness. The three articles by James, Helman again, and Philo, all explore different aspects of the cultural construction of mental troubles. Mary James takes a historical perspective in her account of the medical view of hysteria in Paris in the nineteenth century. In 'Hysteria and demonic possession' she describes the work of the pioneering physician Charcot in seeking a medical understanding of a phenomenon previously explained by religious ideas about demon possession, but which nowadays has been largely dropped as a psychiatric category. The role that medical power plays in the construction of particular versions of mental illness is illustrated very effectively by this case study; James shows that display of the 'symptoms' of hysteria was encouraged by a subtle process of suggestion by male doctors to their relatively powerless female patients.

In Cecil Helman's second article in Part 1, he demonstrates again how anthropological study can assist in perceiving the influence of culture on medical knowledge as well as revealing patients' understandings of their troubles. He shows that what is considered 'normal' behaviour in one culture may be considered 'abnormal' in another, and attract the label 'mental illness'. Statements of spirit possession, or speaking in tongues, may indicate schizophrenia in one place, but be considered acceptable forms of religious behaviour elsewhere. Cross-cultural diagnosis by psychiatrists is notoriously variable. At the same time, Helman suggests, there may be a core of 'uncontrolled' behaviour which in any society is considered a sign of disturbance, suggesting that there are limitations to the view of endless cultural diversity.

Greg Philo's study of 'Media and mental illness' focuses on the impact on media audiences of the prevalent media stereotype of mental illness involving violent behaviour. This, he argues, is not only inaccurate but also profoundly damaging to the reputations and personal self-esteem of people with mental troubles, who already face a difficult time. Philo, then, wants to see some changes in the culture in which he lives, reminding us that respect for culturally determined beliefs is not always something that needs to be granted. Some 'cultures of illness' have pretty damaging outcomes.

Part 1 ends with 'Public eyes and private genes' by Peter Conrad, who illustrates ways in which beliefs derived from recent research into genetics have influenced popular culture. This continues the theme begun by Philo, on the importance of mass media in framing public perceptions of health issues, and raises similar concerns about the potentially harmful effects of these media representations. Notions that forms of human behaviour considered as culturally 'deviant' – alcoholism, homosexuality – can be explained by genetics (and in time will be 'treated' by genetic therapies) are enthusiastically fostered in the mass media, which nevertheless has remained consistently critical of claims that genetically determined racial differences exist – for example, in educational attainment and IQ. Conrad argues that concerns with the 'new genetics' must be seen in the context of the sorry history of the eugenics movement. In this respect, he foreshadows the article by Tom Shakespeare in Part 7 of this book, on the threat of a new 'eugenics of disability'.

1 | Mirage of health

RENÉ DUBOS

The Gardens of Eden

The illusion that perfect health and happiness are within man's possibilities has flourished in many different forms throughout history. Primitive religions and folklores are wont to place in the remote past this idyllic state of paradise on earth. In the Old Testament the Patriarchs are said to have lived hundreds of years, while their descendants can hardly aspire to more than threescore and ten. The ancient Greeks believed in the existence of happy races, vigorous and virtuous, in inaccessible parts of the earth. According to their legends, the Hyperboreans and the Scythians in the north, the Ethiopians in the south, lived exempt from toil and warfare, from disease and old age, in everlasting bliss like the dwellers in the Isles of the Blest at the edge of the Western Sea.

The return to Nature

Like primitive peoples, men in civilized societies commonly believe in the possibility of an ideal state of health and happiness. But, instead of expressing this belief through legends and folklore, they are apt to rationalize it in the form of philosophical theories and to assert that a healthy mind in a healthy body can be achieved only by harmonizing life with the ways of nature. The latter part of the eighteenth century proved particularly receptive – in theory at least – to the gospel that all human problems could be solved by returning to the ways of nature. Jean Jacques Rousseau asserted that man in his original state was good, healthy, and happy and that all his troubles came from the fact that civilization had spoiled him physically and corrupted him mentally. 'Hygiene,' Rousseau claimed, 'is less a science than a virtue.' Sickness being the result of straying away from the natural environment, the blessed original state of health and happiness could be recaptured only through abiding by the simple order and purity of nature – or, as Voltaire said in maliciously paraphrasing Rousseau, through learning again to walk on all fours.

Since very ancient times the theory that most of the ills of mankind arise from failure to follow the laws of nature has been endlessly reformulated in every possible form and mood, in technical and poetical language, in ponderous treatises and witty epigrams. In particular, the Taoist philosophy which has so profoundly influenced Chinese life and art is pervaded by reverence for nature. Lao-tzu, the Jean Jacques Rousseau of ancient China, was followed by many translators and imitators. Chuangtzu wrote of the time when 'the ancient men lived in a world of primitive simplicity. . . . That was the time when the *yin* and the *yang* worked harmoniously, and the spirits of men and beasts did not interfere with the life of the people, when the four seasons were in order and all creation was unharmed, and the people did not die young.'

Modern man has done many odd things to display his faith in the fundamental goodness of nature. Following in the steps of Rousseau, one hundred million Central Europeans went botanizing in the hope of discovering among lowly flowers both the soul of the universe and natural remedies for chest troubles. More prosaic twentieth-century man tries to re-establish contact with this forgotten biological past in countless country clubs, hunting or ski lodges and beach bungalows, through clambakes in the moonlight and barbecue parties in suburban gardens and picnic groves. Whatever his inhibitions and tastes, Western man believes in the natural holiness of seminudism and raw vegetable juice, because these have become for him symbols of unadulterated nature.

The concept of Nature

It is probable that a few people now and then in limited periods of history have enjoyed relative peace in a fairly constant physical and social environment. But the state of equilibrium never lasts long and its characteristics are at best elusive, because the word 'nature' does not designate a definable and constant entity. With reference to life there is not one *nature*; there are only associations of states and circumstances, varying from place to place and from time to time.

Living things can survive and function effectively only if they adapt themselves to the peculiarities of each individual situation. For some sulphur bacteria, nature is a Mexican spring with extremely acid water at very high temperature; for the reindeer moss, it is a rock surface in the frozen atmosphere of the arctic. The word 'nature' also means very different things to different men. Man, by manipulating the external world, renders 'natural' for his individual taste many kinds of environments which display an astonishingly wide range of moods.

Harmonious equilibrium with nature is an abstract concept with a Platonic beauty but lacking the flesh and blood of life. It fails, in particular, to convey the creative emergent quality of human existence. [For man] the seasons and the soil, the plants and the beasts, the permanent dwellers and the distant visitors with which he came into contact during his long journey, all the factors of his total environment, differed from one place to another, from one period to another, and their temporary association constituted the 'nature' to which he had to adapt in each situation and at each moment.

The doctrine of specific etiology

Until late in the nineteenth century disease had been regarded as resulting from a lack of harmony between the sick person and his environment. Louis Pasteur, Robert Koch, and their followers took a far simpler and more direct view of the problem. They showed by laboratory experiments that disease could be produced at will by the mere artifice of introducing a single specific factor – a virulent microorganism – into a healthy animal.

From the field of infection the doctrine of specific etiology spread rapidly to other areas of medicine; a large variety of well-defined disease states could be produced experimentally by creating in the body specific biochemical or physiological lesions. Microbial agents, disturbances in essential metabolic processes, deficiencies in growth factors or in hormones, and physiological stresses are now regarded as specific causes of disease. The ancient concept of disharmony between the sick person and his environment seems very primitive and obscure indeed when compared with the precise terminology and explanations of modern medical science.

Unquestionably the doctrine of specific etiology has been the most constructive force in medical research for almost a century and the theoretical and practical achievements to which it has led constitute the bulk of modern medicine. Yet few are the cases in which it has provided a complete account of the causation of disease. Despite frantic efforts, the causes of cancer, of arteriosclerosis, of mental disorders, and of the great medical problems of our times remain undiscovered. It is generally assumed that these failures are due to technical difficulties and that the cause of all diseases can and will be found in due time by bringing the big guns of science to bear on the problems. In reality, however, search for *the* cause may be a hopeless pursuit because most disease states are the indirect outcome of a constellation of circumstances rather than the direct result of single determinant factors.

It is true that in a few cases – far less common than usually believed – the search for *the* cause has led to effective measures of control. But it does not follow that these measures provide information as to the nature of the trouble that they correct. While drenching with water may help in putting out a blaze, few are the cases in which fire has its origin in a lack of water. Effective therapies do not constitute evidence for the doctrine of specific etiology.

Darwin and Bernard

By equating disease with the effect of a precise cause – microbial invader, biochemical lesion, or mental stress – the doctrine of specific etiology had appeared to negate the philosophical view of health as equilibrium and to render obsolete the traditional art of medicine. Oddly enough, however, the vague and abstract concepts symbolized by the Hippocratic doctrine of harmony are now re-entering the scientific arena. Hippocratic medicine has acquired a more profound significance from the implications of the discoveries that Darwin and Claude Bernard were making around 1850 – even before Pasteur and Koch had made their contributions to the etiology of disease. Darwinism implies that the individual and species which survive and multiply selectively are those best adapted to the external environment. Claude Bernard supplemented the doctrine of evolutionary adaptation by his visionary guess that fitness depends upon a constant interplay between the internal and the external environment of the individual. He emphasized that at all levels of biological organization, in plants as well as in animals, survival and fitness are conditioned by the ability of the organism to resist the impact of the outside world and maintain constant within narrow limits the physicochemical characteristics of its internal environment. In other words, life depends not only upon the reactions through which the individual manages to grow and to reproduce itself but also upon the operation of the control mechanisms which permit the maintenance of individuality. The dual concept of fitness to the external environment and fixity of the internal environment is the modern expression of the Hippocratic dictum that health is universal sympathy.

The gods of health

The word 'hygiene' now conjures up smells of chlorine and phenol, pasteurized food-stuffs and beverages in cellophane wrappers, a way of life in which the search for pleasurable sensations must yield to practices that are assumed to be sanitary. Its etymology, however, bears no relation to this pedestrian concept. Hygiene is the modern ersatz for the cult of Hygeia, the lovely goddess who once watched over the health of Athens. She was the guardian of health and symbolized the belief that men could remain well if they lived according to reason.

Throughout the classical world Hygeia continued to symbolize the virtues of a sane life in a pleasant environment, the ideal of *mens sana in corpore sano*. Hygeia was not an earthbound goddess of ancient origin. Her name derives from an abstract word meaning health. For the Greeks she was a concept rather than a historical person remembered from the myths of their past. She was not a compelling Jeanne d'Arc but only an allegorical goddess Liberty and she never truly touched the hearts of the people. From the fifth century BC on, her cult progressively gave way to that of the healing god, Asclepius.

To ward off disease or recover health, men as a rule find it easier to depend on healers than to attempt the more difficult task of living wisely. Asclepius, the first physician according to Greek legend, achieved fame not by teaching wisdom but by mastering the use of the knife and the knowledge of the curative virtues of plants. Soon Hygeia was relegated to the role of a member of his retinue, usually as his daughter, some-times as his sister or wife, but always subservient to him.

The myths of Hygeia and Asclepius symbolize the never-ending oscillation between two different points of view in medicine. For the worshippers of Hygeia, health is the natural order of things, a positive attribute to which men are entitled if they govern their lives wisely. According to them, the most important function of medicine is to discover and teach the natural laws which will ensure to man a healthy mind in a healthy body. More skeptical or wiser in the ways of the world, the followers of Asclepius believe that the chief role of the physician is to treat disease, to restore health by correcting any imperfection caused by the accidents of birth or of life.

Hippocratic wisdom

Hippocratic writings occupy a place in medicine corresponding to that of the Bible in the literature and ethics of Western peoples. Just as everyone quotes from the Bible, it is the universal practice to look to Hippocrates for statements that give the sanction of authority and of time to almost any kind of medical views, profound or banal. For twenty-five centuries Hippocrates has personified in the Western world the rational outlook of the philosopher, the objective attitude of the scientist, the practical approach of Ascleplus, and the human traditions of Hygeia.

It is implicit in the Hippocratic teachings that both health and disease are under the control of natural laws and reflect the influence exerted by the environment and the way of life. Accordingly, health depends upon a state of equilibrium among the various internal factors which govern the operations of the body and the mind; this equilibrium in turn is reached only when man lives in harmony with his external environment. [Hippocrates'] writings are pervaded with the concept that the life of the patient as a whole is implicated in the disease process and that the cause is to be found in a concatenation of circumstances rather than in the simple direct effect of some external agency.

The modern public health movement

Despite its vigorous intellectual and social basis, the early nineteenth-century health movement in France and Germany was rather ineffective in the way of practical reforms. The goals of the French and German philosophers and physicians were to a large extent political and therefore difficult to reach except by revolutionary action. Furthermore, their doctrines were presented to the public in somewhat abstract terms. In England, by contrast, the leadership was taken by practical men who succeeded in finding a formula that appealed to elementary emotions and was meaningful to everyone. To a group of public-minded citizens guided by the physician Southwood Smith and the engineer Edwin Chadwick it appeared that, since disease always accompanied want, dirt, and pollution, health could be restored only by bringing back to the multitudes pure air, pure water, pure food, and pleasant surroundings.

This simple concept was synthesized in the movement 'The Health of Towns Association', the prototype of the present-day voluntary health associations throughout the world. Its aim was to 'substitute health for disease, cleanliness for filth, order for disorder . . . prevention for palliation . . . enlightened self-interest for ignorant selfishness and bring home to the poorest . . . in purity and abundance, the simple blessings which ignorance and negligence have long combined to limit or to spoil: *Air, Water, Light.*'

Faith in the healing power of pure air, with much contempt for the germ theory of disease, was also the basis of Florence Nightingale's reforms of hospital sanitation during the Crimean War. 'There are no specific diseases,' she wrote. 'There are specific disease conditions.'

The conquest of epidemic diseases was in large part the result of the campaign for pure food, pure water, and pure air based not on a scientific doctrine but on philosophical faith. It was through the humanitarian movements dedicated to the eradication of the social evils of the Industrial Revolution, and the attempt to recapture the goodness of life in harmony with the ways of nature, that Western man succeeded in controlling some of the disease problems generated by the undisciplined ruthlessness of industrialization in its early phase.

Defining health

Health and disease cannot be defined merely in terms of anatomical, physiological, or mental attributes. Their real measure is the ability of the individual to function in a manner acceptable to himself and to the group of which he is part.

For several centuries the Western world has pretended to find a unifying concept of health in the Greek ideal of a proper balance between body and mind. But in reality this ideal is more and more difficult to convert into practice. Poets, philosophers, and creative scientists are rarely found among Olympic laureates. It is not easy to discover a formula of health broad enough to fit Voltaire and Jack Dempsey, to encompass the requirements of a stevedore, a New York City bus driver, and a contemplative monk.

Among other living things, it is man's dignity to value certain ideals above comfort, and even above life. This human trait makes of medicine a philosophy that goes beyond exact medical sciences, because it must encompass not only man as a living machine but also the collective aspirations of mankind. A perfect policy of public health could be conceived for colonies of social ants or bees whose habits have become stabilized by instincts. Likewise it would be possible to devise for a herd of cows an ideal system of husbandry with the proper combination of stables and pastures. But, unless men become robots, no formula can ever give them permanently the health and happiness symbolized by the contented cow, nor can their societies achieve a structure that will last for millennia. As long as mankind is made up of independent individuals with free will, there cannot be any social status quo. Men will develop new urges, and these will give rise to new problems, which will require ever new solutions. Human life implies adventure, and there is no adventure without struggles and dangers.

René Dubos, microbiologist and experimental pathologist, was formerly Professor at the Rockefeller University of New York City. These extracts are taken from his book *Mirage of Health*, published by Rutgers University Press (1987).

2 | Hippocrates

ROY PORTER

All we know about Hippocrates (*c.* 460–377 BC) is legend. Early hagiographers say he was born on the island of Cos and that he lived a long and virtuous life. The sixty or so works comprising the [Hippocratic] Corpus were penned by him only in the sense that the *Iliad* is ascribed to Homer. They derive from a variety of hands, and, as with the books of the Bible, they became jumbled up, fragmented, and then pasted together again in antiquity. What is now called the Corpus was gathered around 250 BC in the library at Alexandria, though further 'Hippocratic' texts were added later still. Scholarly ink galore has been spilt as to which were authentic and which spurious; the controversy is futile. Appeal to reason, rather than to rules or to supernatural forces, gives Hippocratic medicine its distinctiveness. It was also to win a name for being patient-centred rather than disease-oriented, and for being concerned more with observation and experience than with abstractions.

The cardinal concept in the Hippocratic Corpus was that health was equilibrium and illness an upset. *On Regimen* pictured the body as being in perpetual flux: health was a matter of keeping it within bounds. More commonly, notably in *On The Nature Of Man*, the body was viewed as stable until illness subverted it. Imbalance would produce illness if it resulted in undue concentration of fluid in a particular body zone. Thus a flow (defluxion) of humours to the feet would produce gout, or catarrh (defluxation of phlegm from the head to the lungs) would be the cause of coughing. It was the healer's job to apply his skill to preserving balance or, if illness befell, to restoring it.

What was being kept in balance or upset were bodily fluids or *chymoi*, translated as 'humours'. Sap in plants and blood in animals were the fount of life. Other and perhaps less salutary bodily fluids became visible only in case of illness – for example, the mucus of a cold or the runny faeces of dysentery. Two fluids were particularly associated with illness: bile and phlegm, though naturally present in the body, seemed to flow immoderately in sickness. Winter colds were due to phlegm, summer diarrhoea and vomiting to bile, and mania resulted from bile boiling in the brain. *Airs, Waters,*

Places also attributed national characteristics to bile and phlegm: the pasty phlegmatic peoples of the North were contrasted with the swarthy, hot, dry, bilious Africans. Both were judged inferior to the harmonious Greeks in their ideally equable climate.

Bile and phlegm were visible mainly when exuded in sickness, so it made sense to regard them as harmful. But what of other fluids? Since Homeric times, blood has been associated with life, yet even blood was expelled naturally from the body, as in menstruation or nose-bleeds. Such natural evacuations suggested the practice of blood-letting, devised by the Hippocratics, systemized by Galen, and serving for centuries as a therapeutic mainstay.

The four humours – blood, yellow bile, black bile and phlegm – proved wonderfully versatile as an explanatory system. They could be correlated to the four primary qualities – hot, dry, cold and wet; to the four seasons, to the four ages of man (infancy, youth, adulthood and old age), to the four elements (air, fire, earth and water), and the four temperaments. They thus afforded a neat schema with vast explanatory potential. On the assumption, for example, that blood predominated in spring and among the young, precautions against excess could be taken, either by eliminating blood-rich foods, like red meat, or by blood-letting (phlebotomy) to purge excess. The scheme (which finds parallels in Chinese and Indian medicine) could be made to fit with observations, and afforded rationales for disease explanation and treatment within a causal framework.

The Hippocratics specialized in medicine by the bedside, prizing trust-based clinical relations. Their therapeutic stance was 'expectant': they waited and watched their patients, talking, winning trust and giving a helping hand to the 'healing power of nature'. Surgery was regarded as an inferior trade, the work of the hand rather than the head. Hippocratic surgical texts were thus conservative in outlook, encouraging a tradition in which doctors sought to treat complaints first through management, occasionally through drugs and finally, if need be, by surgical intervention.

Drug therapy too was cautious. The preferred Hippocratic treatment lay in dietary regulation. But diet meant more than food and drink – *dietetica* (dietetics), the cornerstone of the healing art, involved an entire lifestyle. Ancient authors linked this therapy to athletic training, and to the well-regulated life as urged by philosophers. *On Regimen* gave advice on taking exercise, so important to the culture of free-born Greeks, and also on sex, bathing and sleep. In winter, for instance, 'sexual intercourse should be more frequent . . . and for older men more than for the younger'.

Hippocratic healing was patient-oriented, focusing on 'dis-ease' rather than diseases understood as ontological entities. But observation identified certain illness patterns. To the Hippocratics, the paradigm acute disease was fever, and its model seems to have been malaria, the seasonal onset and regular course of which allowed it to be documented and explained in terms of humours and times of the year. Though ignorant of the role played by mosquitoes, Hippocratic physicians had a shrewd grasp of the connections between fever and weather, season and locality. *Airs, Waters, Places* observed that if the rains occurred normally in autumn and winter, the year would be healthy, but if they were delayed until spring, many fever cases would occur during the summer, 'for whenever the great heat comes on suddenly while the earth is soaked by reasons of the spring rains . . . the fevers that attack are of the acutest type'.

Hippocratic physicians posited a broad correlation between humours and times of the year. In each season, one humour was thought to predominate. Bodily phlegm increased during the winter because, being cold and wet, it was akin to the chilly and rainy weather of a Mediterranean winter; colds, bronchitis and pneumonia were then more prevalent. When spring came, blood increased in quantity, and diseases would follow from a plethora of blood, including spring fever outbreaks (primarily benign tertian malaria), dysentery and nose-bleeds. By summer, the weather was hotter and drier, yellow bile (hot and dry) increased, and so the diseases resulting from yellow bile would multiply, that is severe fevers (falciparum malaria). With the cooler weather at the end of summer, fevers waned, but many would display the consequences of repeated fever attacks, their skins showing a dirty yellowish tinge and their spleens enlarged. The autumnal decline of fevers indicated to the Hippocratic physician that yellow bile had diminished while black bile was increasing.

The art of diagnosis involved creating a profile of the patient's way of life, habitation, work and dietary habits. This was achieved partly by asking questions, and partly by the use of trained senses:

> When you examine the patient, inquire into all particulars; first how the head is ... then examine if the hyponchondrium and sides be free of pain, for ... if there be pain in the side, and along with the pain either cough, tormina or bellyache, the bowels should be opened with clysters ... The Physician should ascertain whether the patient be apt to faint when he is raised up, and whether his breathing is free.

Hippocratic doctors cultivated diagnostic skills, but the technique they really prized was *prognosis* – a secular version of the prognostications of earlier medicine:

> It appears to me a most excellent thing for the physician to cultivate Prognosis; for by foreseeing and foretelling, in the presence of the sick, the present, the past, and the future, and explaining the omissions which patients have been guilty of, he will be the more readily believed to be acquainted with the circumstances of the sick; so that men will have confidence to entrust themselves to such a physician.

This skill had a social function: prognostic flair created a favourable impression, setting the gifted healer above quacks and diviners. To be able to tell a patient's medical history and prospects displayed acuity. And by declaring, if need be, that death was impending, a healer escaped blame for apparent failure.

Hippocratics made no pretence to miracle cures, but they did undertake that they would first and foremost do no harm (*primum non nocere*) and presented themselves as the friends of the sick. This philanthropic disposition attested the physician's love of his art – above fame and fortune – and reassured anxious patients and their relatives. Such concerns are addressed in the Hippocratic Oath (see box).

For all its later prominence, little is known about the Oath's origins, though it dates from between the fifth and third centuries BC. It certainly did not set general standards of conduct, for the sanctity it accords to human life is anomalous to classical moral thought and practice, abortion and infanticide being familiar practices, condoned by Plato and Aristotle.

The Oath foreshadowed the western paradigm of a profession (one who *professes* an oath) as a morally self-regulating discipline among those sharing craft knowledge and committed to serving others. But it was equally an agreement between apprentice and teacher. As it makes clear, Hippocratic medicine was a male monopoly, although male physicians might cooperate with midwives and nurses.

The Oath

I swear by Apollo the healer, by Aesculapius, By Health and all the powers of healing, and call to witness all the gods and goddesses that I may keep this Oath and Promise to the best of my ability and judgement.

I will pay the same respects to my master in the Sciences as to my parents and share my life with him and pay all my debts to him. I will regard his sons as my brothers and teach them the Science, if they desire to learn it, without fee or contract. I will hand on precepts, lectures and all other learning to my sons, to those of my master and to those pupils duly apprenticed and sworn, and to none other.

I will use my power to help the sick to the best of my ability and judgement; I will abstain from harming or wronging any man by it.

I will not give a fatal draught to anyone if I am asked, nor will I suggest any such thing. Neither will I give a woman means to procure an abortion.

I will be chaste and religious in my life and in my practice.

I will not cut, even for the stone, but I will leave such procedures to the practitioners of that craft.

Whenever I go into a house, I will go to help the sick and never with the intention of doing harm or injury. I will not abuse my position to indulge in sexual contracts with the bodies of women or of men, whether they be freemen or slaves.

Whatever I see or hear, professionally or privately, which ought not to be divulged, I will keep secret and tell no one.

If, therefore, I observe this Oath and do not violate it, may I prosper both in my life and in my profession, earning good repute among all men for all time. If I transgress and forswear this oath, may my lot be otherwise.

Hippocratic medicine had its weaknesses – it knew little of the inner workings of the body – but its striking innovation lay in perceiving sickness as a disturbance in the health of the individual, who would then be accorded devoted personal attention. 'Life is short, the art long, opportunity fleeting, experience fallacious, judgement difficult', proclaims the first of the Hippocratic aphorisms, outlining the arduous but honourable labour of the physician.

The significance of Hippocratic medicine was twofold: it carved out a lofty role for the selfless physician which would serve as a lasting model for professional identity and conduct, and it taught that understanding of sickness required understanding of nature.

This article is an extract from Roy Porter's book *The Greatest Benefit to Mankind* (HarperCollins 1997). The author is Professor of the Social History of Medicine at the Wellcome Trust Centre for the History of Medicine at University College London.

3 | Feed a cold, starve a fever

CECIL HELMAN

The National Health Service was designed to bring the best of scientific medicine to the whole population. Much of the ill-health that had previously been borne, as one writer put it, in 'the imposed silence of poverty,' was now accessible to free health care. But what has been the impact of health education, television programmes about health, and easy access to doctors and hospitals, on traditional beliefs about illness? Whatever happened to folk remedies and old wives' tales? A study I conducted on medical folklore in a north London suburb suggests that these folk beliefs about illness and health *can* survive the impact of scientific medicine, and in some cases may even be reinforced by this contact. This is important because in Britain the majority of ill-health – especially minor complaints – is dealt with outside the formal health care system.

How patients perceive ill-health and its treatment, both before and after seeing a doctor, depends on lay beliefs about what causes illness. There is an increasing amount of research into this; my own study tackled folk beliefs about some common, minor ailments – 'chills', 'colds' and 'fever'. As both an anthropologist and a GP I was trying to find out the concepts underlying the often-heard aphorism, 'Feed a cold, starve a fever.' It arises from a folk model, or scheme of classification, of illness which is widely accepted by the patients; and it relates to those conditions of impaired well-being which the patients perceive as disequilibrium, and regard as 'illness', and which concern perceived changes in body temperature – either 'hotter' than normal, or 'colder'. In general, these feelings of abnormal temperature change are purely subjective; they bear little or no relation to biomedical definitions of 'normal' body temperature as 98.4°F or 37°C, as measured orally on a thermometer. The conditions where the patient 'feels hot' are classified as *Fevers*, those where he 'feels cold' in his body are classified either as *Chills* or *Colds*. Both Fevers and Colds/Chills are states of being – both classified as abnormal – which, in the folk model have different causes, different effects, and thus require different treatments.

There are two important principles underlying this folk classification of 'illness-misfortune': (1) the relation of man with *nature*, i.e. with the natural environment, in

	HOT	COLD
	(1) *Ear, Nose, and Throat* FEVER + NASAL CONGESTION OR DISCHARGE	(1) *Ear, Nose, and Throat* COLD + NASAL CONGESTION OR DISCHARGE, WATERY EYES, 'SINUS' CONGESTION
	(2) *Chest* FEVER + PRODUCTIVE COUGH	(2) *Chest* COLD + NON-PRODUCTIVE COUGH
WET	(3) *Abdomen* FEVER + DIARRHOEA AND ABDOMINAL DISCOMFORT	(3) *Abdomen* COLD + LOOSE STOOLS AND SLIGHT ABDOMINAL DISCOMFORT
	(4) *Urinary System* FEVER + URINARY FREQUENCY AND BURNING	(4) *Urinary System* COLD + SLIGHT URINARY FREQUENCY BUT NO PAIN
	(5) *Skin* FEVER + RASH + NASAL DISCHARGE OR COUGH	
DRY	FEVER + DRY SKIN, FLUSHED FACE, DRY THROAT, NON-PRODUCTIVE COUGH	COLD + SHIVERING, RIGOUR, MALAISE, VAGUE MUSCULAR ACHES

Figure 3.1 The folk classification of common 'hot' and 'cold' symptoms.

Colds and Chills, and (2) the relation of man to man, which exists within human *society*, in Fevers.

To a large extent the area covered by the folk model – which I have set out schematically in Figure 3.1 – corresponds to that area of disorders which biomedicine classifies as Infectious Diseases: that is, acute or chronic inflammatory conditions where the causative agent is known to be either a virus or a bacterium. These disorders, which occur very commonly in general practice, include disorders known as: upper respiratory tract infections; influenza; coryza; bronchitis; pneumonia; sinusitis; urinary tract infections; gastroenteritis; childhood fevers (e.g. rubella); and several others. This classification overlaps, to some extent, the area covered by the folk model but as will be described there are significant differences. Illnesses associated with temperature change are common in all sections of the population, as are the often associated symptoms of cough or rhinitis. Cough is apparently the commonest symptom complained of in general practice, and it is common even among those who do not consult the doctor: in Dunnell and Cartwright's study[1] 32 per cent of adults reported 'cough, catarrh, or phlegm' in a sample two-week period, while 18 per cent had suffered from 'cold, influenza, or rhinitis'. To describe the folk model it is necessary to adopt a diachronic approach: what follows is mainly the folk classification reported by older patients; those born during or since World War Two, while sharing the basic underlying classification, have introduced new elements, particularly with regard to the germ theory.

	HOT	COLD
	HOT	COLD
WET	WET	WET
	HOT	COLD
DRY	DRY	DRY

Figure 3.2

Structural analysis of the folk system

In Figure 3.1 I have listed the common groups of symptoms which relate to, or are accompanied by, perceived changes in body temperature. There are four diagnostic categories in all (see Figure 3.2); the basic division is between '*Hot*' and '*Cold*' conditions, but in addition there is a further division into '*Wet*' and '*Dry*' conditions. 'Wet' conditions are those where the temperature change is accompanied by other symptoms, and with a seemingly abnormal amount of 'Fluid' being present – either still within the body, or else emerging from its orifices; this 'Fluid' includes sputum, phlegm, nasal and sinus discharge, vomitus, urine, and loose stools. The symptoms here include nasal congestion or discharge, sinus congestion, productive coughs, 'congested' chests, diarrhoea, and urinary frequency. 'Dry' conditions are those where the abnormal temperature change is the only, or the paramount symptom – such as a subjective feeling of being cold, shivering or rigours on one hand – and a feeling of being 'hot', perhaps with a dry throat, flushed skin, slight unproductive cough, and possibly delirium, on the other. Skin rashes usually occur on the 'Hot' side of the classification. Other subsidiary symptoms – including pain – may occur in one form or another on both sides of the temperature division.

Thus there are four basic compartments into which common symptoms relating to temperature change can be fitted (see Figure 3.3): 'Hot/Wet' (Fever plus Fluid), 'Hot/ Dry' (Fever), 'Cold/Wet' (Cold plus Fluid), and 'Cold/Dry' (Cold). Obviously these compartments are not watertight; there is always some overlap between divisions. In addition, not all conditions associated with abnormal temperature changes have been included; only the commonest, as encountered in general practice.

'Colds' and 'fevers' relate to two bodily states both perceived as being abnormal. The first is where you feel 'colder', the other 'hotter', than usual. But, in fact, both are subjective feelings, unconnected to actual measurements on a thermometer. Both can occur in a 'dry' form (the abnormal temperature change alone), or in a 'wet' form (where temperature change is associated with excess fluid). 'Wet' symptoms would include nasal congestion, 'runny noses', 'congested chests', coughing up mucus, diarrhoea or urinary frequency.

In *chills* and *colds*, the abnormal temperature change is usually seen as a by-product of one's personal battle with the natural environment – particularly with areas of lowered temperature. In this view, damp or rain ('cold/wet' conditions), or cold winds or draughts ('cold/dry'), can penetrate the boundary of the skin, and cause similar conditions within the body. A cold, rainy day causes one to feel 'cold', with a runny nose. Sitting in a cold wind ('a draught') causes a feeling of coldness, though often without the excess fluid.

	HOT	COLD
WET	FEVER + FLUID	COLD + FLUID
DRY	FEVER	COLD

Figure 3.3

Wind at body temperature is not dangerous, and is merely 'fresh air'. Night air, however, is often considered dangerous by older patients. And 'the children get sick if you leave the bedroom windows open at night.' Some areas of skin are seen as more vulnerable than others to penetration by environmental cold – particularly the top of the head, the back of the neck, and the feet. I found that 'colds' occurred when these areas were inadvertently exposed to draughts or damp – for example: 'getting your feet wet', 'walking around with damp hair', 'going out into the rain, without a hat on', or 'stepping into a puddle'. Elderly men, in particular, reported an increased vulnerability to 'head colds' after a haircut – when the back and top of the head are unprotected by their normal covering of hair.

Temperature changes between hot and cold environments were considered dangerous, especially the intermediate zone between the two temperatures – for example, 'going into a cold room after a hot bath', 'walking on a cold floor when you have a fever'. Changes in season were also risky – autumn, for example, where the 'hot' summer is changing to 'cold' winter. It was explained to me that 'summer colds' are more common since cheap air flights returned people suddenly from 'hot' Spain or Italy to 'cold' Britain, with disastrous results.

Cold, once it has entered the body, can move around. From damp feet it can migrate to cause a 'stomach chill', or it can shift even further upwards to cause 'a head cold' or 'sinus cold'. In general, *chills* occur below the waist ('stomach chill', 'bladder chill', 'kidney chill'), and *colds* above it ('a head cold', 'a cold in the sinuses', 'a cold in the chest').

Unlike fevers, cold and chills are more one's own responsibility. They are the result of carelessness, or lack of foresight – if 'you don't dress properly', 'allow your head to get wet', 'wash your hair when you don't feel well'. Colds are caused, as one middle-aged patient explained seriously, 'by doing something abnormal'.

So folk remedies for colds emphasise the return to 'normal' temperature and equilibrium, by treating 'cold' with 'hot'. Hot drinks, hot food, rest in a warm bed, and generating your own bodily heat by 'tonics' or food ('feed a cold . . .') were frequently advised. Other remedies stress the return from the 'wet' state to the 'dry' one: drying up the excess fluid by a variety of traditional remedies (goose fat was commonly used at one time), or patent decongestants bought from a chemist.

By contrast, *fevers* are thought to be due to invisible entitles known – interchangeably – as 'germs', 'bugs' or 'viruses'. Some of these terms may be borrowed from modern medicine, but they are used and conceptualised in an entirely different way.

For example, 'germs' are described as living, invisible and malevolent entities. They have no free existence in nature, it seems, but exist only in or among people. They are thought of as occurring in a cloud of tiny particles, or as a tiny invisible 'insect'. They travel through the air between people, entering the body of their victim by one of the orifices (usually the mouth, or the nose, but also the ears, urethra, and so on). They signal their presence by causing a 'fever'. The germs that cause stomach upsets are more 'insect-like' than others ('a tummy bug'), and apparently larger in size.

Germs have personalities. These reveal themselves, or are expressed in, the sorts of symptoms they cause. 'I've got that germ, doctor, you know – the one that gives you the dry cough and the watery eyes,' or 'the one that gives you diarrhoea, and makes you bring up.' The germs are amoral in their selection of victims, but they can only cause harm once they do attack. There are no 'good' germs: *all* germs are bad, and patients do not differentiate between 'germs', 'bugs' and 'viruses'.

Once a germ enters the body, and causes a fever, it can move or expand to attack several parts of the body simultaneously. 'It's gone to my lungs', 'I can feel it in my stomach', 'It's moved to my chest', or, as one patient with a peptic ulcer said, 'I got the flu, but then it flew to the ulcer and that blew up'.

Because germs, unlike colds (at least to older patients), originate in other *people*, rather than in the natural environment, germ infection implies some sort of social relationship of whatever duration. Infection is an inherent risk in all relationships, though neither party is to blame if one 'picks up a germ'.

Cough up the muck

In that case, the victim is less blameworthy than in the case of a cold, and more able to mobilize sympathetic friends or relatives around him. One of the obligations of close relationships is to risk infection, if necessary, in looking after another person.

'Fevers' particularly attack the weak, the old, and the poor. This vulnerability of the poor is often explained away by their association with the dirt and disorder of poverty. 'Dirt' is seen as concentrated, or condensed, germs.

Like colds and chills, fevers can occur in the 'dry' ('feeling feverish', with a flushed skin, dry mouth) or 'wet' form (accompanied by excess catarrh, phlegm, urine). Folk remedies for fevers aim to return the victim from the 'hot' state to normal temperature; but also to move him (with the aid of *fluids* which 'flush out' or 'wash out' the germ) from the 'dry' state to the 'wet' state.

Fluids of one sort or another are used to 'wash out' the germ from the chest, so that a 'dry' cough can 'loosen', bringing with it the offending germ. A variety of fluids, like tea, hot water, and now patent cough mixtures, are used for 'getting it off your chest', 'coughing up the muck', 'getting it out of your system'. Patients complain that a dry cough 'hasn't broken', or 'hasn't loosened', so that they can 'cough it off my chest'. 'I gargled with salt water to get the catarrh out,' one man said, 'and I always swallow a bit of it to loosen the cough.'

Fluids are also used as folk treatments for other hot/wet conditions, like diarrhoea, vomiting, or urinary frequency accompanied by a fever, to flush out the offending germ. Other folk remedies induce sweating, allowing you to 'sweat it out' of your system – in this case through the skin itself. Antibiotics are seen as powerful chemicals that kill germs *in situ*, with the body being the battlefield of this great clash. Both 'germs' and 'viruses' are seen as vulnerable to the effects of antibiotics.

Most people who use the words 'germs' or 'viruses' have never *seen* either of these entities. They have no perceptual evidence for their existence. So that they can be thought of more as hypotheses, or theories of causality. There is some similarity between these western ideas of 'germs', and the invisible, malign 'spirits' said to cause illness by people in non-western and non-industrialised societies.

There is a marked difference in lay views of colds and fevers between older patients, and those born since the second world war – who constitute the world's first 'antibiotic generation'. Younger patients are more likely to ascribe both fevers and colds to 'germs' or 'viruses'.

The Germ Theory is one example of a medical concept that has gradually influenced patients' ways of thinking about illness. 'Germs', as a cause of illness, have gradually spread to include many of the 'cold' conditions as well. Instead of 'a chill on the bladder', you have 'a germ in the water'; instead of 'a cold in the head', you have 'picked up a virus'.

One result of this is that the amount of personal responsibility for illness (as in old-fashioned 'colds') seems to have gradually declined. If more and more conditions are due to 'germs', then the victims are increasingly blameless, and more able to mobilise a caring community around themselves. Illness seems to have become more *social* in its origin, effects and even treatment. Where you have 'germs' as a believed cause for illness, then you have a greater need of doctors and their remedies. There is also the slight sense of increased danger in social relationships – the threat of infection. Young mothers – more often than their own mothers would have – now ask, 'My child's got a cold; can she mix with other children?'

The metaphor of 'germs' as invisible forces 'out there' which cause suffering to the innocent, seems to have become a pervasive social metaphor. Pollution, radiation, and social changes 'of epidemic proportions', are all expressions of this.

The GP and the folk model

The main meeting place between lay health beliefs and the medical profession, is usually the GP's surgery. In the surgery, both doctor and patient have to agree on what is wrong with the patient, and what should be done about it. This involves a process of 'negotiation', whereby each party tries to influence the other about the outcome of the consultation, and the treatment to be given. One aspect of this is that, in order to get their patients' cooperation, GPs have to couch their diagnoses and treatment in concepts that *make sense* in terms of the patients' view of ill-health. This, in turn, may reinforce those same ideas.

A patient who presents a list of symptoms is often given a diagnosis couched in the everyday idiom of the folk model: 'You've picked up a germ,' 'You've got a flu bug,' 'It's a viral infection,' 'It's just a tummy bug – there's one going around,' 'You've got a germ in the water,' 'I'm afraid it's gone to your chest,' or 'Oh yes, is that the one where you've got a runny nose, watery eyes, and you lose your voice? I've seen a dozen already this week.'

More precise medical diagnoses are less commonly given, especially to uneducated patients. In many cases, these conditions are trivial, and self-limiting. They won't get worse; they will soon go away of their own accord; and no one else will catch them. A precise 'technical' diagnosis may be unnecessary, and in fact impossible. Not every cough and cold can be subjected to complex and expensive laboratory tests to identify the precise virus or bacteria causing it. The four-to-seven minute GP consultation time also makes more precise diagnoses impractical.

Many doctors do not, or cannot, differentiate between bacteria and viruses. So neither do patients. Bacteria *are* treatable by antibiotics but viruses are not. The distinction, however, has become blurred. Doctors reinforce this when they over-prescribe antibiotics generally – and particularly when they prescribe them for viral illnesses. This blurring strengthens the lay view that all 'germs' are bad; all are similar in nature; and all of them therefore susceptible to antibiotics. It also increases dependence on the doctor for prescribed treatment, even for minor complaints.

Doctors' receptionists, who do a great deal of health counselling over the surgery telephone, can also help the process of reinforcing folk beliefs. As one receptionist was heard to say to a patient with diarrhoea and vomiting: 'Yes, there is a tummy bug going around. Starve yourself and take only sips of water for 24 hours. Otherwise, the more you feed it [the bug], the more it'll enjoy itself and cause diarrhoea and sickness.'

Not everything which GPs do in order to meet their patients' need to 'make sense' of the treatment given can be 'scientifically' justified. For example, it's been estimated that *six million gallons* of cough mixtures are prescribed in Britain every year under the NHS. (This excludes the vast amount bought over the counter.) Yet most medical textbooks cast doubt on the scientific efficacy of these preparations. Part of this ocean of cough mixture must represent the subtle pressure of patients' expectations on GPs to prescribe – in a modern form – the *liquids* believed to 'wash out' or 'flush out' the infection from one's chest.

We need to know more about how people understand their sickness, how they deal with it, and how they interpret medical treatment they are given. Because self-treatment and 'non-compliance' are so common, we also need to know what happens to health and illness *outside* the NHS.

Free access to GPs, and health education on the media, does not seem to have altered some of the traditional folk beliefs about illness. Obviously, medical concepts like the Germ Theory of disease are widely known to the lay public. But they may be understood in entirely a different way, and often in terms of a much older folk view of illness.

Reference

1. Dunnell, K. and Cartwright, A. *Medicine takers, prescribers and hoarders*, Routledge and Kegan Paul, London, p. 11 (1972).

Cecil Helman has been a general practitioner and is a social anthropologist in the Department of Primary Care and Population Sciences, University College London Medical School. This article is made up from one published in *New Society*, 221–224 (5 November 1981) and an extract from an article of the same title published in *Culture, Medicine and Psychiatry* 2, 107–137 (1978).

4 | What is health?

MILDRED BLAXTER

What do people mean when they talk of 'health'? A dichotomy has traditionally been seen between the biomedical or scientific model of health and a looser, more holistic model. These are sometimes falsely regarded as 'medical' and 'non-medical' ways of looking at health. Crudely, medical knowledge is seen as based on universal, generalizable science, and lay knowledge as unscientific, based on folk knowledge or individual experience. The lay concepts discussed here are not, however, being presented as necessarily or essentially different from medical concepts. In western societies, an intermixing is inevitable: lay people have been taught to think, at least in part, in biomedical terms. Nor is modern medicine entirely wedded, in practice, to a narrowly-defined biomedical science: holistic concepts are also part of medical philosophy. Lay concepts are, of course, sometimes less informed or expert than those of medical professionals. In other ways, however – since health must in part be subjectively experienced – they may be better informed. As other studies have found, they are often complex, subtle, and sophisticated.

The concepts of health discussed here are derived from answers to two questions asked in a survey of 9,000 individuals carried out by an interdisciplinary team at the University of Cambridge Clinical School: (1) Think of someone you know who is very healthy. Who are you thinking of? How old are they? What makes you call them healthy? (2) At times people are healthier than at other times. What is it like when you are healthy? The replies – sometimes quite long and thoughtful – were written down verbatim.

The discussion and analysis in this article is based on a random 10 per cent sample of respondents, in which it was possible to examine in a more qualitative way the precise vocabulary used and the combinations of ideas which each individual expressed. First, those people who found themselves unable to offer any definition of health will be considered.

'Negative' answers

Almost 15 per cent of the respondents could not think of anyone who was 'very healthy', and over 10 per cent said in reply to the question about health for themselves, 'I just don't think about it', 'I can't answer that'. A proportion of this group, especially among the elderly, were expressing pessimism about their own health status 'I'm never healthy so I don't know', 'It's so long since I was healthy that I can't tell you what it's like'.

However, higher proportions, especially of men under 60, were expressing the idea that health is the norm, is just 'ordinary', and so is difficult to describe:

> I don't think I know when I'm healthy, I only know if I'm ill (office worker, aged 28).

> How do you describe it? I don't know. I think if you are healthy you don't think about it. You only think about ill health (wife of a tractor driver, aged 51).

This group of people tended to be among those who, in other parts of the survey, did not rate health very highly as a value. They were also likely, among the elderly, to see their own health as poor. Whether old or young, they were commonly people who expressed a lack of concern for 'healthy' behaviour.

Health as not-ill

The more explicit description of health as not being ill – as not suffering any symptoms, never having anything more serious than a cold, never seeing the doctor, having no aches and pains – has also sometimes been seen as a 'negative' concept, in opposition to the positive concept of fitness. It was a more popular definition of health in another person rather than oneself, offering an easy way of 'proving' that the person was healthy:

> She's healthy because she never seems to suffer with her chest. She has an occasional cold but she's never been seriously ill (woman 70, with severe bronchitis herself, speaking of her daughter).

For oneself, more frequently than for others, 'not-ill' was expressed in terms of experienced symptoms, rather than recourse to medical services, though the nature of the symptoms naturally tended to vary with age:

> Health is when you don't have a cold (man of 19).

> You don't have to think about pain – to be free of aches and pains (woman of 78).

It has sometimes been suggested that a definition of health as 'not-ill' (or without disease) is characteristic of people in poorer circumstances, and to lack a positive view of health as fitness is a mark of general social deprivation (Blaxter and Paterson 1982). Though the latter may be true, there was little sign in this large sample of any social differentiation in the use of the concept 'not-ill': it seems possible that the previous finding may demonstrate one of the pitfalls of small-scale surveys. Because a 'negative' definition is found to be common among working-class respondents, it is assumed to be in some way associated with their social position. The 'not-ill' description of health was very markedly associated with the speaker's own state of health. At all ages, but particularly among the elderly, those who themselves were in poor health; or suffering from chronic conditions were less likely to define health in terms of illness.

The 'not-ill' description of health was found to be more frequently used by the better educated and those with higher incomes. It was also very markedly associated with the speaker's own state of health. At all ages, but particularly among the elderly, those who themselves were in poor health or suffering from chronic conditions were less likely to define health in terms of illness.

Health as absence of disease/health despite disease

It is not always easy, in the respondent's replies, to distinguish illness – the experience of symptoms or malfunctioning – from a more clearly biomedical definition of disease. Disease was specifically mentioned rather rarely, whether for others or oneself, though phrases such as 'never had to go to hospital', 'don't have any really serious illnesses', 'never had any big illnesses', might be held to represent this concept. To have no (chronic or serious) disease is certainly one dimension of health, though not one commonly expressed by these respondents.

Certainly, however, there were expressions of a concept of health despite disease. Many people said of themselves 'I am very healthy although I do have diabetes', or 'I am very healthy apart from this arthritis' (crippled and housebound woman of 61). The concept of health as overcoming or coping with disease could be extended to include misfortune also:

> Although he has TB he's been aware of his problems and has got over them. Though he was made redundant, since then he's done his own thing, just worked the way and when he wanted to. He didn't worry about being redundant, and he hasn't taken on too much in the size of house and garden. He enjoys life (man of 64 explaining why he calls a friend of the same age healthy).

Health as a reserve

The idea of 'healthy though diseased' often had some affinity with the 'reserve of health' noted by Herzlich (1973). Someone is healthy because 'when he is ill he recovers very quickly', 'he has had an operation and got over it very well', or even because he takes risks and suffers no consequences: as one respondent said, 'he goes out on the drink but he never gets a hangover or a headache'. Occasionally, respondents expressed the idea of an inborn reserve of health:

> He never goes to the doctors and only suffers from occasional colds. Both parents are still alive at 90 so he belongs to healthy stock (woman of 51 talking of her husband).

Health as behaviour, health as 'the healthy life'

'The healthy person' (but rarely oneself) was rather frequently defined in terms of their 'virtuous' behaviour. He or she is a vegetarian, or a non-smoker and non-drinker, or goes jogging, or does exercises:

I call her healthy because she goes jogging and she doesn't eat fried food. She walks a lot and she doesn't drink alcohol (woman of 50 about her neighbour).

For these respondents, health was identical with the healthy life: the non-smoker, non-drinker must be healthy, though no evidence about their health could be offered. These respondents were also more likely to be those who, throughout the rest of the interview, stressed the role of 'bad habits' in the causation of disease and the importance of self-responsibility. As one lady said:

Why do I call her healthy? She leads a proper respectable life so she's never ill.

Health as physical fitness

Among younger people, physical fitness was very prominent. When thinking of 'the healthy person', young men in particular stressed strength, athletic prowess, the ability to play sports: 'fit' was by far the most common word used in their descriptions of health by men under 40. The 'healthy other' was, for them, likely to be either a well-known athlete or sportsman, or a personal acquaintance who ran marathons, played squash, engaged in karate or judo, or 'trained every week'. Weight-lifting and body-building were very frequently mentioned as a source of, and a proof of, fitness. Older men also mentioned sportsmen, though less frequently. Young women, too, commonly expressed a concept of health (in others) that involved sports and physical fitness.

This is one reason why the sex of the 'person thought of as healthy' was predominantly male. Among those who offered any answer, whatever concept of health they were expressing, 80 per cent of males mentioned a man, and 57 per cent of females also mentioned a man. Few women athletes appeared as role models.

Women rarely mentioned sports or specific physical leisure pursuits. They did, however, frequently define physical fitness in terms of its outward appearance. They commonly mentioned being (or feeling) slim. To be fit was to have a clear complexion, bright eyes and shining hair:

Being healthy is when my skin is good and my hair isn't greasy and I can do all the things I want to without feeling tired (woman of 30).

Health as energy, vitality

The last quotation combines the notions of an appearance of fitness with a feeling of energy or vitality. 'Energy' was in fact the word most frequently used by all women and older men to describe health, and for younger men it came a close second to 'fitness'. Sometimes physical energy was clearly meant, and sometimes a psycho-social vitality which had little to do with physique: most often, the two were combined.

The words used to describe this were 'lively', 'alert', 'full of get up and go', 'full of life', 'not tired', 'not listless' As one young man said:

Health is when I feel I can do anything. I jump out of bed in the morning, I wash my car in the cold without a thought. I feel like doing things. Nothing can stop you in your tracks (engineer of 28).

Many young men, like this one, mentioned getting up early, or not going to bed so early at night: 'it's easier to get out of bed', 'I feel like getting up in the morning', 'I don't spend all morning in bed', 'You can afford to sleep less at night'. Even as a description of the healthy 'other', not staying in bed appeared to mark really positive healthiness:

> He regularly wakes up early in the morning, gets up, doesn't watch a lot of TV (man of 21).

For older men, the same concept of energy and vitality was most often expressed as enthusiasm about work:

> I can give myself to work a hundred per cent. Work is a pleasure. Work's not a problem (Council engineering employee, aged 49).

> You feel ready to get on with anything that needs doing. You feel that you can tackle any physical work (man of 74).

Women, too, very commonly defined healthiness in terms of energy and enthusiasm for work. It was notable, however, that few of any age, whether or not they had a job outside the home, mentioned paid work. The symbol of energy for women was 'going right through the house', 'cleaning the house from top to bottom': 14 per cent of all women under 60 mentioned enthusiasm about housework. For elderly women, being *able* to do housework might be a mark of health, but for the younger, who took their everyday work for granted, *enjoyment* of housework indicated special energy. Certain less popular jobs were singled out:

> I clean the windows and rush round like a mad thing. When I'm not healthy is when I want to sit in front of the box (single-handed mother, kitchen assistant, aged 29).

> When I'm healthy I feel like tackling the cooker and getting it clean (female teacher, aged 47).

Health as a social relationship

A notable difference between men and women was that women were considerably more likely to define health in terms of relationships with other people.

> She goes around looking after friends and shopping for them. She's active, her mind's alive. She paints and she's a member of the theatre club and a lot of other groups (woman of 51 speaking of her mother of 77).

For younger women, health was commonly defined in terms of good relationships with family and children – 'having more patience with them', 'coping with the family', 'enjoying the family'. For the older, serving other people, being in a position to help other people, having sufficient energy to care for other people, were often cited as the marks of good health.

Health as function

Both health as energy, and health as social relationships, are concepts which overlap with the idea of health as function – health defined by being able to do things, with less stress upon a description of feelings. This was more likely to be expressed by older people: for the young, of course, the ability to cope with the tasks of life might be taken for granted, and it is only later in life that health may be seen as a generally restricting factor.

For men below retirement age, and especially those who did manual work, health for oneself or for others could be defined as being able to do hard work. Many women who identified a man (usually their husband) as 'someone who is very healthy' also gave as their reason the physically demanding nature of his work, or the fact that he was able to work long hours. Although women were chosen as a 'healthy other' because of their general social, family and community activity, it was notable that neither sex often chose women because of their demanding work, whether within the house or outside it.

However, many elderly men and women were identified as 'someone I know who is very healthy' because they were able to work despite an advanced age:

> She's 81 and she gets her work done quicker than me, and she does the garden (woman of 63).

Health as psycho-social well-being

The concept of health as psycho-social well-being is often close to or combined with the notions of health as energy, health as social relationships, or health as function, which have been discussed. In this analysis the category was reserved, however, for expressions of health as a purely mental state, instead of, or as well as, a physical condition. Often, these were embedded in a very holistic view of health:

> She's a person with a spiritual core. She's physically, mentally and spiritually at one (single woman, aged 45, living in a religious community).

For health in oneself, psycho-social health was stressed at all ages, and for those in the middle years was the most popular concept. It tended to be used rather more frequently by women than by men, and by those with more education rather than less. 'Health is a state of mind' or 'health is a mental thing more than physical' were common statements. 'Feel like living life to the full', 'on top of the world', 'full of the joys of spring', were phrases very commonly repeated.

> I've reached the stage now where I say isn't it lovely and good to be alive, seeing all the lovely leaves on the trees, it's wonderful to be alive and to be able to stand and stare! (farmer's widow, aged 74).

Conclusions

Firstly, the way in which health is conceived of differs over the life course, in not unexpected ways. Younger men tend to speak of health in terms of physical strength and fitness, and commonly cite athletes as the 'healthy other'. Young women, though they also talk of fitness or its appearance, favour ideas of energy, vitality, and ability to cope. In middle age, concepts of health become more complex, with an emphasis upon total mental and physical well-being. Older people, particularly men, think in terms of function, or the ability to do things, though ideas of health as contentment, happiness, a state of mind – even in the presence of disease or disability – are also prominent.

Secondly, there are clear sex differences. At all ages women, in general, gave more expansive answers than men, and appeared to find the questions more interesting. Women of higher social class or higher educational qualifications, in particular, expressed many dimensional concepts. Many women, but few men, included social relationships in their definition of health.

References

Blaxter, M. and Paterson, E. *Mothers and Daughters: A Three-Generational Study of Health Attitudes and Behaviour*, Heinemann, London (1982).
Herzlich, C. *Health and Illness: A Social Psychological Analysis*, Academic Press, London (1973).

Mildred Blaxter is Honorary Professor of Medical Sociology, at the School of Social and Economic Studies, University of East Anglia. This article is a heavily edited extract from Chapter 3 of her book *Health and Lifestyles*, published by Tavistock-Routledge, London (1990).

5 | Illness as metaphor

SUSAN SONTAG

It seems that having TB had already acquired the association of being romantic by the mid eighteenth century. In Act I, Scene I of Oliver Goldsmith's satire on life in the provinces, *She Stoops to Conquer* (1773), Mr Hardcastle is mildly remonstrating with Mrs Hardcastle about how much she spoils her loutish son by a former marriage, Tony Lumpkin:

Mrs H: And I am to blame? The poor boy was always too sickly to do any good. A school would be his death. When he comes to be a little stronger, who knows what a year or two's Latin may do to him?

Mr H: Latin for him! A cat and fiddle. No, No, the alehouse and the stable are the only schools he'll ever go to.

Mrs H: Well, we must not snub the poor boy now, for I believe we shan't have him long among us. Any body that looks in his face may see he's consumptive.

Mr H: Ay, if growing too fat be one of the symptoms.

Mrs H: He coughs sometimes.

Mr H: Yes, when his liquor goes the wrong way.

Mrs H: I'm actually afraid of his lungs.

Mr H: And truly so am I; for he sometimes whoops like a speaking trumpet – [TONY *hallooing, behind the Scenes*] – O there he goes – A very consumptive figure, truly.

This exchange suggests that the fantasy about TB was already a received idea, for Mrs Hardcastle is nothing but an anthology of clichés of the smart London world to which she aspires, and which was the audience of Goldsmith's play.[1] Goldsmith presumes

---

1. Goldsmith, who was trained as a doctor and practiced medicine for a while, had other clichés about TB. In his essay 'On Education' (1759) Goldsmith wrote that a diet lightly salted, sugared, and seasoned 'corrects any consumptive habits, not unfrequently found amongst the children of city parents.' Consumption is viewed as a habit, a disposition (if not an affectation), a weakness that must be strengthened and to which city people are more disposed.

that the TB myth is already widely disseminated – TB being, as it were, the anti-gout. For snobs and parvenus and social climbers, TB was one index of being genteel, delicate, sensitive. With the new mobility (social and geographical) made possible in the eighteenth century, worth and station are not given; they must be asserted. They were asserted through new notions about clothes ('fashion') and new attitudes toward illness. Both clothes (the outer garment of the body) and illness (a kind of interior décor of the body) became tropes for new attitudes toward the self.

Shelley wrote on July 27, 1820 to Keats, commiserating as one TB sufferer to another, that he has learned 'that you continue to wear a consumptive appearance.' This was no mere turn of phrase. Consumption was understood as a manner of appearing, and that appearance became a staple of nineteenth-century manners. It became rude to eat heartily. It was glamorous to look sickly. 'Chopin was tubercular at a time when good health was not chic,' Camille Saint-Saëns wrote in 1913. 'It was fashionable to be pale and drained. Princess Belgiojoso strolled along the boulevards . . . pale as death in person.' Saint-Saëns was right to connect an artist, Chopin, with the most celebrated *femme fatale* of the period, who did a great deal to popularize the tubercular look. The TB-influenced idea of the body was a new model for aristocratic looks – at a moment when aristocracy stops being a matter of power, and starts being mainly a matter of image. ('One can never be too rich. One can never be too thin,' the Duchess of Windsor once said.) Indeed, the romanticizing of TB is the first widespread example of that distinctively modern activity, promoting the self as an image. The tubercular look had to be considered attractive once it came to be considered a mark of distinction, of breeding. 'I cough continually!' Marie Bashkirtsev wrote in the once widely read *Journal*, which was published, after her death at twenty-four, in 1887. 'But for a wonder, far from making me look ugly, this gives me an air of languor that is very becoming.' What was once the fashion of aristocratic *femmes fatales* and aspiring young artists became, eventually, the province of fashion as such. Twentieth-century women's fashions (with their cult of thinness) are the last stronghold of the metaphors associated with the romanticizing of TB in the late eighteenth and early nineteenth centuries.

Many of the literary and erotic attitudes known as 'romantic agony' derive from tuberculosis and its transformation through metaphor. Agony became romantic in a stylized account of the disease's preliminary symptoms (for example, debility is transformed into languor) and the actual agony was simply suppressed. Wan, hollow-chested young women and pallid, rachitic young men vied with each other as candidates for this mostly (at that time) incurable, disabling, really awful disease. 'When I was young,' wrote Théophile Gautier, 'I could not have accepted as a lyrical poet anyone weighing more than ninety-nine pounds.' (Note that Gautier says lyrical poet, apparently resigned to the fact that novelists had to be made of coarser and bulkier stuff.) Gradually, the tubercular look, which symbolized an appealing vulnerability, a superior sensitivity, became more and more the ideal look for women – while great men of the mid and late nineteenth century grew fat, founded industrial empires, wrote hundreds of novels, made wars, and plundered continents.

One might reasonably suppose that this romanticization of TB was a merely literary transfiguration of the disease, and that in the era of its great depredations TB was probably thought to be disgusting – as cancer is now. Surely everyone in the nineteenth century knew about, for example, the stench in the breath of the consumptive person. (Describing their visit to the dying Murger, the Goncourts note 'the odor of rotting flesh in his bedroom.') Yet all the evidence indicates that the cult of TB was not simply an invention of romantic poets and opera librettists but a widespread attitude, and that the person dying (young) of TB really was perceived as a romantic personality. One must suppose that the reality of this terrible disease was no match for important new ideas, particularly about individuality. It is with TB that the idea of individual illness was articulated, along with the idea that people are made more conscious as they confront their deaths, and in the images that collected around the disease one can see emerging a modern idea of individuality that has taken in the twentieth century a more aggressive, if no less narcissistic, form. Sickness was a way of making people 'interesting' – which is how 'romantic' was originally defined. (Schlegel, in his essay 'On the Study of Greek Poetry' [1795], offers 'the interesting' as the ideal of modern – that is, romantic – poetry.) 'The ideal of perfect health,' Novalis wrote in a fragment from the period 1799–1800, 'is only scientifically interesting'; what is really interesting is sickness, 'which belongs to individualizing.' This idea – of how interesting the sick are – was given its boldest and most ambivalent formulation by Nietzsche in *The Will to Power* and other writings, and though Nietzsche rarely mentioned a specific illness, those famous judgments about individual weakness and cultural exhaustion or decadence incorporate and extend many of the clichés about TB.

The romantic treatment of death asserts that people were made singular, made wore interesting, by their illness. 'I look pale,' said Byron, looking into the mirror. 'I should like to die of a consumption.' 'Why?' asked a friend, who was visiting Byron in Athens in October 1810. 'Because the ladies would all say, "Look at that poor Byron, how interesting he looks in dying."' Perhaps the main gift to sensibility made by the Romantics is not the aesthetics of cruelty and the beauty of the morbid (as Mario Praz suggested in his famous book), or even the demand for unlimited personal liberty, but the nihilistic and sentimental idea of 'the interesting.'

Sadness made one 'interesting.' It was a mark of refinement, of sensibility, to be sad. That is, to be powerless. In Stendhal's *Armance*, the anxious mother is reassured by the doctor that Octave is not, after all, suffering from tuberculosis but only from that 'dissatisfied and critical melancholy characteristic of young people of his generation and position.' Sadness and tuberculosis became synonymous. The Swiss writer Henri Amiel, himself tubercular, wrote in 1852 in his *Journal intime*:

> Sky draped in gray, pleated by subtle shading, mists trailing on the distant mountains; nature despairing, leaves falling on all sides like the lost illusions of youth under the tears of incurable grief . . . The fir tree, alone in its vigour, green, stoical in the midst of this universal tuberculosis.

But it takes a sensitive person to feel such sadness; or by implication, to contract tuberculosis. The myth of TB constitutes the next-to-last episode in the long career of the ancient idea of melancholy – which was the artist's disease, according to the theory of the four humors. The melancholy character – or the tubercular – was a superior one: sensitive, creative, a being apart. Keats and Shelley may have suffered atrociously from the disease. But Shelley consoled Keats that 'this consumption is a disease particularly fond of people who write such good verses as you have done . . .' So well established was the cliché which connected TB and creativity that at the end of the century one critic suggested that it was the progressive disappearance of TB which accounted for the current decline of literature and the arts.

But the myth of TB provided more than an account of creativity. It supplied an important model of Bohemian life, lived with or without the vocation of the artist. The TB sufferer was a dropout, a wanderer in endless search of the healthy place. Starting in the early nineteenth century, TB became a new reason for exile, for a life that was mainly travelling. (Neither travel nor isolation in a sanatorium was a form of treatment for TB before then.) There were special places thought to be good for tuberculars: in the early nineteenth century, Italy; then, islands in the Mediterranean, or the South Pacific; in the twentieth century, the mountains, the desert – all landscapes that had themselves been successively romanticized. Keats was advised by his doctors to move to Rome; Chopin tried the islands of the western Mediterranean; Robert Louis Stevenson chose a Pacific exile; D. H. Lawrence roamed over half the globe.[2] The Romantics invented invalidism as a pretext for leisure, and for dismissing bourgeois obligations in order to live only for one's art. It was a way of retiring from the world without having to take responsibility for the decision – the story of *The Magic Mountain*. After passing his exams and before taking up his job in a Hamburg ship-building firm, young Hans Castorp makes a three-week visit to his tubercular cousin in the sanatorium at Davos. Just before Hans 'goes down,' the doctor diagnoses a spot on his lungs. He stays on the mountain for the next seven years.

By validating so many possibly subversive longings and turning them into cultural pieties, the TB myth survived irrefutable human experience and accumulating medical knowledge for nearly two hundred years. Although there was a certain reaction against the Romantic cult of the disease in the second half of the last century. TB retained most of its romantic attributes – as the sign of a superior nature, as a becoming frailty – through the end of the century and well into ours. It is still the sensitive young artist's disease in O'Neill's *Long Day's Journey into Night*. Kafka's letters are a compendium of speculations about the meaning of tuberculosis, as is *The Magic Mountain*, published in 1924, the year Kafka died. Much of the irony of *The Magic Mountain* turns on Hans Castorp, the stolid burgher, getting TB, the artist's disease – for Mann's novel is a late, self-conscious commentary on the myth of TB. But the novel still reflects the myth: the burgher *is* indeed spiritually refined by his disease. To die of TB was still mysterious and (often) edifying and remained so until practically no-body in Western Europe and North America died of it any more. Although the incidence of the disease began to decline precipitously after 1900 because of improved hygiene, the mortality rate among those who contracted it remained high; the power of the myth was dispelled only when proper treatment was finally developed, with the discovery of streptomycin in 1944 and the introduction of isoniazid in 1952.

---

2. By a curious irony,' Stevenson wrote, 'the places to which we are sent when health deserts us are often singularly beautiful . . . [and] I daresay the sick man is not very inconsolable when he receives sentence of banishment and is inclined to regard his ill-health as not the least fortunate accident of his life.' But the experience of such enforced banishment, as Stevenson went on to describe it, was something less agreeable. The tubercular cannot enjoy his good fortune: 'the world is disenchanted for him.'

Katherine Mansfield wrote: 'I seem to spend half of my life arriving at strange hotels . . . The strange door shuts upon the stranger, and then I slip down in the sheets. Waiting for the shadows to come out of the corners and spin their slow, slow web over the Ugliest Wallpaper of All . . . The man in the room next to mine has the same complaint as I. When I wake in the night I hear him turning. And then he coughs. And after a silence I cough. And he coughs again. This goes on for a long time. Until I feel we are like two roosters calling each other at false dawns. From far-away hidden farms.

If it is still difficult to imagine how the reality of such a dreadful disease could be transformed so preposterously, it may help to consider our own era's comparable act of distortion, under the pressure of the need to express romantic attitudes about the self. The object of distortion is not, of course, cancer – a disease which nobody has managed to glamorize (although it fulfils some of the functions as a metaphor that TB did in the nineteenth century). In the twentieth century, the repellent, harrowing disease that is made the index of a superior sensitivity, the vehicle of 'spiritual' feelings and 'critical' discontent, is insanity.

The fancies associated with tuberculosis and insanity have many parallels. With both illnesses, there is confinement. Sufferers are sent to a 'sanatorium' (the common word for a clinic for tuberculars and the most common euphemism for an insane asylum). Once put away, the patient enters a duplicate world with special rules. Like TB, insanity is a kind of exile. The metaphor of the psychic voyage is an extension of the romantic idea of travel that was associated with tuberculosis. To be cured, the patient had to be taken out of his or her daily routine. It is not an accident that the most common metaphor for an extreme psychological experience viewed positively – whether produced by drugs or by becoming psychotic – is a trip.

In the twentieth century the cluster of metaphors and attitudes formerly attached to TB split up and are parcelled out to two diseases. Some features of TB go to insanity: the notion of the sufferer as a hectic, reckless creature of passionate extremes, someone too sensitive to bear the horrors of the vulgar, everyday world. Other features of TB go to cancer – the agonies that can't be romanticized. Not TB but insanity is the current vehicle of our secular myth of self-transcendence. The romantic view is that illness exacerbates consciousness. Once that illness was TB; now it is insanity that is thought to bring consciousness to a state of paroxysmic enlightenment. The romanticizing of madness reflects in the most vehement way the contemporary prestige of irrational or rude (spontaneous) behaviour (acting-out), of that very passionateness whose repression was once imagined to cause TB, and is now thought to cause cancer.

Susan Sontag is a leading American critic and essayist, who has also published novels and stories. The extract above is the whole of Chapter 4 of her book, *Illness as Metaphor*, which was originally published in 1979 by Viking, reproduced by permission of Penguin Books Ltd.

6 | The problem of the whole-person in holistic medicine

DAVID ARMSTRONG

Being so recent, holistic medicine has hardly had time to establish a coherent account of its historical origins, but nevertheless it cannot for long exist in a temporal vacuum. Indeed one of the first tasks of any new discipline is the construction of a history which will explain the inevitability of its arrival, justify its existence and promote its future.[1]

A 'tradition' is important because it helps sidestep the awkward question of 'why now?' Holistic medicine is so 'obvious' that if it were in fact to be only recent it would be difficult to explain how preceding times failed to grasp its inherent truth, particularly as the whole-person has had universal existence. The advent of holistic medicine must therefore be construed as simply one event in a long process of gradual enlightenment and progress. The evocation of tradition is no doubt of assistance in promoting and establishing the recent growth of holistic medicine. But the endorsement of a 'tradition' in holistic medicine carries with it a significant explanatory difficulty, namely the historical ascendency of reductionist medicine.

From within holistic medicine (hospital based) medicine is criticized as 'reductionist' because it attempts to reduce all illness to a single intra-corporal lesion and thereby reduces the body – and the whole-person – to a collection of separate systems, organs, tissues and cells. But if holistic medicine is somehow rooted in tradition, how was it possible for pathological medicine, the apparent antithesis of holistic medicine, to gain ascendency? The liberationist explanation holds that there was a period of holistic medicine in the past but this tradition was repressed with the ascendency of reductionist medicine. Recently however that period of subjugation has been lifted by the rediscovery of traditional holistic practices. In effect the historical triumph of reductionist medicine is claimed to be an aberration and modern holistic medicine presented as a means of liberation from error. Yet this leaves unresolved how holistic medicine has only now begun to throw off the repression of reductionist medicine and, perhaps more importantly, it fails to explain how reductionist medicine triumphed in the first place over a medicine which was the natural and traditional attendant of the whole-person.

The social control thesis

Critics from without, however, have advanced an analysis which challenges the liberationist claims of holistic medicine. That there might be an unconscious danger in allowing medicine an extended position in social control was first pointed out by Zola in the early 1970s.[2] Though not attacking holistic medicine by name he pointed to the increasing intervention of doctors into all sorts of different facets of people's lives. A reductionist medicine which only monitored a component of the body had limited control functions over people's bodies, but a medicine which took a broader interest in the whole-person and offered advice and support on diet, exercise, stress, anxiety, etc., carried with it the incipient danger that the social control functions of medicine were getting out of hand and invading areas of people's lives to their ultimate detriment. While the stated claim of holistic medicine might be the enhancement of personal autonomy, its actual practical effect was to undermine it.

Marxists have argued that the modern industrial state has had to develop complex systems of medical control.[3] Thus a homeless patient has a problem in their environment, not in the politics which denies them homes; a depressed patient is drugged or counselled so that they can cope with their moods rather than being encouraged to challenge the system which made them depressed; and so on. From this point of view holistic medicine might claim to be radical but it is only radical chic; its proponents might be well-meaning but they are the unwitting advance guard of medical hegemony or the lackeys of a capitalist system; their wider concerns with the whole-person simply means that the whole-person must be brought into visibility and into control.

Political anatomy

The argument that medicine is inherently an agency of social control and that holistic medicine is simply another manifestation of this function certainly offers a more coherent explanation for the rise of holistic medicine than holistic medicine itself offers. The difficulty with the social control argument however is that it tends to assume a conspiratorial or malevolent medicine; and yet the avowed and no doubt sincere intentions and practice of most advocates of holistic medicines is to provide a humanist medicine which truly serves the interests of the whole person. In this way the intentions, actions and probably effects of most of those within holistic medicine seem completely opposed to the charges of repression.

There is a third explanation for the rise of holistic medicine which manages both to accept the sincerity and goals of holistic medicine and to incorporate some of the key features of the social control argument. This third position is not a compromise one but a radical solution to the historical puzzle of holistic medicine: it starts with the rejection of the core assumption of both holistic and social control arguments that the whole person is a 'universal' being. Instead it argues that the patient is an 'invention' or construction.

Both holistic and social control perspectives tend to assume a golden age of medicine in the past, sometimes specified – perhaps Hippocratic medicine or pre-capitalism – more often left vague. No evidence is offered to support the existence of a golden age beyond a faith that it must have existed. It is important to note the historical context of these claims: they are certainly made about the past but only from the perspective of the last two decades. Does whole-person medicine therefore belong to the past or is it backward projection of the present? And if the whole-person has no immutable identity then he or she can neither be liberated nor repressed, in effect they can only be 'constructed'.

Pathological medicine first emerged at the end of the 18th century when disease became located to specific anatomical structures and hence illness could yield to a reductionist analysis. Pathological medicine treated the patient's body as a machine, as an object. This fundamentally new approach is one of the principal points of attack for holistic medicine which decries this new corporal positivism, this strategy which objectified 'real' people. But alternatively, the objectification of the individual can be seen as the first step in the actual creation of the individual whole person. The constructivist position is that reality does not exist independently of perception, thus the new medicine created its own reality and pathological medicine far from being repressive and negative was creative and positive.

The end of the 18th century and beginning of the 19th, which saw the birth of this new medicine, was a watershed period in Western history. The 'objectified' individual appeared for the first time in medicine but also in the school, the prison, the workshop and the barracks.[4] New techniques for examining individuals were devised; dossiers and case histories for the first time recorded the actions and states of ordinary individuals; the novel, which documented the lives of ordinary people, made its appearance; and the word 'individualism' entered the language.[5]

What existed before pathological medicine is difficult to know. It was a different world; there are no criteria by which it can be judged a golden age or not. What is more certain is that it was only since this period over the last two centuries that the 'whole-person' has had some form of rudimentary existence. It was not therefore a new 'dark ages', rather it was a period during which the reality of the body as an analysable object was slowly constituted, a period in which a new 'political anatomy' was forged and when the human sciences made their first appearance.[4] Before the advent of reductionist medicine bodies were not explored: doctors did not physically examine their patients, post-mortems were not conducted and case histories were not written because the body itself contained no secrets, no truth to be revealed. The ascendency of reductionist medicine therefore established the body as the material core of a new individuality and ushered in a new realm of humanist concerns.

In 1935 Brackenbury published a book on whole-person medicine.[6] To be sure the patient as viewed by Brackenbury was less than complete, being a rather passive object, but it was in the first few decades of the 20th century that a new analysis of the nature of the patient and illness was commenced. As before, when at the end of the 18th century a certain analysis constructed a particular object, so too the identity of the patient began to be transformed by a new medicine which sought to explore the social and conceptual spaces surrounding the individualized body.[7]

From the beginning of the 20th century medicine began to focus on 'social' diseases which were in some way linked to the social contact of one body with another and as it did so the old public health gave way to a new discipline of social medicine. The body became seen as inhabiting a social as well as physical space; in consequence it became a social as well as physical phenomenon. For example, in the 19th century psychiatric disease had been virtually restricted to insanity and its precursors; in the 20th century medicine 'discovered' the neuroses. When the mind had been restricted to a faculty of rationality, madness was its only disease. When, on the other hand, the mind was seen as the interface between body and outside world then it became the faculty of 'coping' and the neuroses could be invented to identify failure and difficulty with the management of affect.[8]

Since the 1950s these elements of an extended patient identity have been reinforced and extended. Certainly reductionist medicine continues to fabricate a discrete and analysable body but the mind and social context of that body have been interrogated to construct a psycho-social identity for patienthood. How was it possible for the placebo effect only to be extensively recognized from the 1950s? How was it possible that the 'problem' of doctor–patient relationship could only be identified during the 1950s and 1960s? How was it that the importance of 'the patient's view' had to wait until the 1970s?[9] That the psychological adjustment of the dying patient could only be recognized from the 1960s?[10] And so on. In the last three decades medicine has investigated a series of new phenomena and problems which have as their common goal and assumption the existence of the patient as a subjective 'whole-person': the actual practice of medicine has presupposed and reinforced the independent existence of a particular patient identity. The whole-person is therefore a construction of this new perspective in medicine, as is its supposed 'universal' status.

References

1. Kuhn, T.S. *The Structure of Scientific Revolutions*, Chicago (1962).
2. Zola, I.K. 'Medicine as an institution of social control', *Sociological Review*, 20, 487–504 (1972).
3. Ehrenreich, J. (ed.) *The Cultural Crisis of Modern Medicine*, Monthly Review Press (1978).
4. Foucault, M. *Discipline and Punish; the Birth of the Prison*, Tavistock (1977).
5. Lukes, S. *Individualism*, Blackwell (1973).
6. Brackenbury, H.B. *Patient and Doctor*, Hodder & Stoughton (1935).
7. Armstrong, D. *Political Anatomy of the Body: Medical Knowledge in Britain in the 20th Century*, Cambridge University Press (1983).
8. Armstrong, D. 'Madness and coping', *Sociology of Health and Illness*, 2, 293–316 (1980).
9. Armstrong, D. 'The patient's view', *Social Science and Medicine*, 18, 737–744 (1984).
10. Arney, W.R. and Bergen, B. *Medicine and the Management of Living*, Chicago University Press (1982).

David Armstrong is a Senior Lecturer at London King's College, Department of Primary Care and Public Health. This article is an edited version of the original which appeared in *Holistic Medicine*, 1, 27–36 (1986).

7 | Protecting a vulnerable margin: towards an analysis of how the mouth came to be separated from the body

SARAH NETTLETON

Introduction

In 1841 George Waite published the document *An Appeal to Parliament; the Medical Profession and the Public on the present state of Dental Surgery*, in which he argued that the legislature should recognize dental surgery as a legitimate branch of medicine. Eighteen years later the London School of Dental Surgery was established, followed by the first Dental Act in 1878 which created a dental register and the founding of the British Dental Association in 1880 to uphold this Act.[1] Finally, in 1921 the Dentists Act abolished unregistered practice and dentistry became a recognizable organized occupation with state support.[2]

These developments represented the appearance of a new knowledge: a knowledge of the mouth containing the teeth. That the mouth should come to be the focus of a new profession with a distinct body of knowledge presents a sociological puzzle. Identified as an object of knowledge in the mid-nineteenth century, it became by the end of that century and throughout the twentieth century the focus of a whole new system of beliefs and associated practices.

Conventional historical accounts have assumed that people in the population increasingly experienced dental disease during and towards the end of the nineteenth century.[3,4] This has been associated with an increase in sugar consumption.[5,6] Those suffering pain sought the services of the local barber-surgeon. With time these surgeons became increasingly aware of their skills, and so grouped together to make demands that their expertise be recognized. Political pressure groups were established, for example the College of Dentists in England and the Odontological Society. In 1921 their demands were finally met and dentistry established as a profession.[7]

[In these accounts] no consideration has been given to the object of dental knowledge. The appearance of the dental profession, it has been assumed, took place only in response to diseased mouths. This paper however, argues that to assume the mouth as a discrete entity, which suffered from increasing amounts of dental disease, does not permit an adequate analysis of the appearance of dentistry.

A discourse on public health

In the nineteenth century, the numbers of the poor and the sick who were seen to be suffering from communicable diseases, for example cholera, were growing.[8] Indeed the whole population was at risk from epidemics. The sources of disease were seen to lie in the natural environment; in the water, soil, air and food. Increasingly however throughout the twentieth century the public health movement influenced by 'discoveries of bacteriology' has shifted from the environment to the individual.[9]

Disease by the turn of the century was seen to arise from

> . . . people and their points of contact. It was people who carried health from the natural world into the social body and transmitted it within.[10]

Writing in his Annual Report of 1910 the Chief Medical Officer wrote:

> . . . the fact emerges that the centre of gravity of our public health system is passing in some degree from the environment to the individual and from problems of outward sanitation to the problems of personal hygiene.[11]

With reorientation of public health from the environment as the source of danger and the individual being perceived as the victim, to the person as the transmitter of disease, the surveillance of all bodies came to be of utmost importance. The points of contact between people came to be crucial in the control of bodies. A regulation of the mouth however did not so much involve the repression of the population but rather produced a new knowledge of it.

Certainly when we look to the medical texts of the end of the nineteenth, and beginning of the twentieth centuries we can see the evidence of 'points of contact' that came to be significant. It was argued that a healthy body was only possible with a healthy mouth, for example a school medical officer reported:

> . . . with such dreadful oral conditions and constant absorption of septic materials the chances of a healthy childhood are small in most infants.

The Medical Officers Association reported on the care of children's teeth and in 1910 wrote that:

> . . . it is a peculiarity of dental disorders that they bring innumerable evils in their train, not least of which is lowering the body's vitality and thus opening wide a door for other diseases to enter.[12]

Further, Wallis, an active figure in the development of the dental service, was anxious to point out in 1908:

> . . . it has been proved by actual practice that the health of children has been markedly raised through dental treatment, and dental treatment aids in the prevention of disease and in the war against tuberculosis.[13]

Wheatly (1912) suggested that prevention of dental disease would do 'more for the improvement of the health of the people than the extermination of any other disease, even TB'.[14] It was suggested [in 1929] that

> . . . if your children are to enjoy the blessing of a firm and intelligent countenance, see to it that their mouths have unremitting, careful attention.[15]

In 1920, in *Practical Preventive Medicine*, Boyd described the significance of the 'portals through which infective agents enter the body':

> The principal body orifices play an important part 'particularly' the orifices of entrance, rather than those of exit . . . the mouth and the nose are the portals of entrance of the greatest importance from the standpoint of the number of infective agents which are introduced through them.[16]

The mouth was conceived of as the boundary between the internal body and the external sources of pollution. Specified or unseen matter, which crossed the boundary of the mouth was indeed 'matter out of place'. The mouth then was to be rigorously protected from the pollutants that lay 'out there'. Hyatt wrote in 1929 that:

> We are zealously taught and trained from our earliest years to guard against and repel visible foes external to our bodies. How much more important it is to exercise the utmost vigilance to see that the more insidious foes . . . do not gain access to the marvellous and delicate organs that compose the hidden mechanism of the human body. By far the greatest number of germ infections that assail us gain their entrance by the mouth. Air breathed in through the nose is comparatively innocuous, physicians state, because the hairs in the nose serve as traps for bacteria, and by far the largest proportion of those that try to get in are ejected with succeeding exhalation.[15]

The use of common drinking cups and utensils was discouraged [by Boyd in 1920] and it was important to avoid the mouths of persons who 'laugh and talk loudly in an explosive manner'.[16]

A discipline of the mouth

Once the mouth was established as a socially significant object, it was deemed necessary to find the 'truth' about it; to analyse, describe and to understand it. The focus towards the mouth took place in a wider process in which attention was being directed towards individual bodies and populations. The individual, it has been suggested [by Foucault 1985], was part of the machinery of power, a power that creates the body, isolates it, explores it, breaks it down and rearranges it.[17] A knowledge of the body therefore required a mechanism of discipline; that is, a machinery of power that was part of the production of knowledge. Discipline was the 'political anatomy of detail', that is to say the body became known and understood as a series of useable parts which could be manipulated, trained, corrected and controlled. The outcome was to be a cumulation of increasingly detailed observations which simultaneously and inescapably produced knowledge of individuals.

Foucault has argued that this mechanism of discipline required and developed three conditions for its implementation.[17] First it was cellular, in that it referred to the space into which individuals were located, they were isolated into individual units. For example in the school [of 1910]:

> basins should be provided with water taps over them and unbreakable cups, a toothbrush for *every* child with its own number, racks where they may be placed with names and numbers on. The 'toothbrush drill' will then be a reality instead of a farce and this wholesome recreation will save much money in the future.[12]

A second condition of discipline concerned the control of activity, exemplified by the timetable. Behaviours were allocated to strict temporal regimes: teeth were brushed in the morning and before bed. Harvey (1928) wrote a text on the *Care of the Mouth and Teeth* in which he detailed for various age groups the precise times when these children should eat and the nature of their food.[18]

A third dimension of discipline was 'the correct use of the body, which makes possible the correct use of time' (Foucault 1985); for example, the correct way to brush teeth was described to the finest detail. An extract from a lengthier description [written in 1921] of a method of brushing reads:

> With the bristles of the brush pointing upward and the end of the thumb on the back of the handle, brush the roof of the mouth and the inside gums and surfaces of the teeth with a fast in-out-stroke, reaching back on the gums as far as you can go. Go back and forth across the roof of the mouth with this in-and-out stroke at least four times. Hold the handle of the toothbrush in your fist with the thumb lying across the back of the handle and brush the gums and teeth with an in-out-stroke, using chiefly the tuft end or the toe of the brush. Reach back in the mouth on the gums below the last tooth on both sides and brush with a fast, light in-and-out stroke.[19]

People were trained and supervised to control their own mouths, individuals were recruited to the 'army' to fight the 'ravages of decay',[20] children had to practise their 'toothbrush drill', for example:

> The drill proper is given when the children are seated, while the assistants pass up and down the aisles helping the children to hold the brushes correctly. There are four positions for holding the brush and two movements in each drill. The children brush to a count in a stereotyped form, it being intended to teach merely the correct form of brushing, and not meant for the actual cleaning of teeth . . . the children repeat the drill standing, and brushes are wrapped in waxed paper to be taken home.[19]

This is what Foucault referred to as the art of 'composing forces in order to obtain an efficient machine' that is 'the individual body becomes an element, that may be placed, moved and articulated on others.'[17] There was no space for idiosyncrasies, each individual was part of a greater whole; a 'body segment in a whole ensemble over which it is articulated . . . the body is constituted as a part of a multisegmentary machine'.[17]

By drawing on Foucault's concept of the disciplinary regime we can better appreciate how the mouth came to be policed. It was policed not by the dominator controlling the dominated but through the operation of examining (the dental check up) measuring and comparing (dental epidemiological records) and normalizing the mouth. The toothbrush drill was an example of the micro-mechanisms of power that since the late eighteenth century have played an increasing part in the management of people's lives through direct action on their bodies.

The regular dental examination is perhaps one of the more readily tangible illustrations of the disciplinary regime. Foucault wrote of the examination that 'in this slender technique are to be found a whole domain of knowledge, a whole type of power.[17] Each mouth was to be subjected to systematic examination, a neglected mouth would inevitably result in disease. Cunningham (1905) said the case for bringing the doctor and dentist into the school for regular inspections was unanswerable.[21] The regular dental examination placed the patient in a situation of perpetual observation and facilitated a knowledge of the population. Knowledge was extracted from the patient by the dentist and documented, recorded, classified and compared. A record of each individual's teeth was kept in the dental case notes. Each tooth, and each tooth surface (palatal, buccal, mesial, distal, occlusial and lingual) was recorded and arranged for epidemiological data. The examination, wrote Foucault, of all the mechanisms of power is highly ritualized because:

> In it are combined the ceremony of power and the form of experiment, the deployment of force and the establishment of truth. At the heart of the procedures of discipline it manifests the subjection of those who are perceived as objects and the objectification of those who are subjected.[17]

The examination of the individual which provided a knowledge of the population was part of a technique of knowledge; the epidemiological survey. In this way it established over individuals a visibility through which mouths were measured, compared and distributed. Epidemiology acted as a process of 'normalization', every mouth could be placed in relation to every other, no mouth could escape categorization.

The mouth had emerged as a discrete object at the same time as the invention of the child as an object of medical attention. The mouth was but one of other areas of the body that was to be used, manipulated and subjected to surveillance. As Armstrong (1983) noted:

> At the same time as the body of every child was subjected to educational surveillance through the introduction of compulsory education the child entered medical discourse as a discrete object with attendant pathologies.

The Chief Medical Officer's Annual Report of 1915 announced that, in 1914, 130 of the 317 education authorities had established dental clinics for the examination of school children's teeth.[22] The dentist could be added to the list of 'experts' who generated a knowledge of increasingly diversified categories associated with the child's body and mind.[23]

Conclusion

Dentists did not emerge simply as an outcome of an increasing demand for the relief of toothache. The increasingly skilled dentist did not merely draw the tooth from the suffering patient, but rather a population of bodies produced a dental knowledge as they were caught up in the machinery of dentistry. The mouth became an object of surveillance, a subject of the mechanisms of discipline which were inherent in the twentieth century public health movement. It was then that dentistry could become established as an accepted profession, the largest specialized sub-branch of medicine peering intently into the mouths of the population. It was then that knowledge of the mouth and teeth could be accumulated in texts and journals and transmitted in specialized schools. It was only at this moment that oral and dental hygiene could become embedded in the routinized and everyday practices of the whole population.

References

1. Bennett, N.G. 'The BDA: its origins, progress and advance', *British Dental Journal*, **51**(11), 565–587 (1930).
2. Richards, N.D. 'Dentistry in England in the 1940s: the first movements towards professionalisation', *Medical History*, **12**, 137–152 (1968).
3. Gelbier, S. and Randall, S. 'Charles Edward Wallis & the rise of London's school service', *Medical History*, **20**, 395–404 (1982).
4. Norman, H.D. 'Public health dentistry before 1948', *Dental Public Health: An Introduction to Community Dentistry*, John Wright & Sons, Bristol (1981).
5. Quick, A., Sheiham, H. and Sheiham, A. *Sweet Nothings*, Vol. 3, Health Education Council, London (1981).
6. Hardwick, J.L. 'The incidence and distribution of caries throughout the ages in relation to the Englishman's diet', *British Dental Journal*, **108**, 11–12 (1960).
7. Freidson, E. *The Profession of Medicine*, Dodd Mead, New York (1970).
8. The occurrence of disease was recorded in reports throughout the country. The most often quoted is Chadwick's *Report on the Enquiry into Sanitary Conditions of the Labouring Population in Great Britain* (1850). The General Health Board produced many reports, for example the *Report on the Epidemic of Cholera of 1848–1849* (1850).
9. Starr, P. *The Social Transformation of American Medicine*, see pp. 189–194, Basic Books, New York (1982).
10. Armstrong, D. *The Political Anatomy of the Body*, Cambridge University Press, Cambridge (1983).
11. Newman, G. *Annual Report of the Chief Medical Officer of the Board of Education for 1908*, London (1910).
12. Denson Redley, R. *The Care of Teeth During School Life*, Medical Officers Association, Churchill, London (1910).
13. Wallis, E. *The Care of Teeth in Public Elementary Schools with Special Reference to what is done in Germany*, Medical Officers Association, London (1908).
14. Wheatly, J. 'Dental caries as a field of preventive medicine', *Public Health*, **25**, 406–414 (1912).
15. Hyatt, T.P. *Hygiene of the Mouth and Teeth*, Brooklyn Dental Publishing Co., New York (1929).
16. Boyd, M.F. *Practical Preventive Medicine*, W.B. Saunders & Co., London (1920).
17. Foucault, M. *Discipline and Punish: The Birth of the Prison*, Penguin Books, London (1985).
18. Harvey, J. *Care of the Mouth and Teeth*, Burkhard, London (1928).
19. Turner, C.L. *Hygiene, Dental and General*, Kimpton, London (1921).
20. Militaristic words and phrases like these are used frequently throughout the dental literature.
21. Cunningham, G. 'The teeth and physical deterioration', *British Dental Journal*, **26**(17), 817–825 (1905).
22. Chief Medical Officer Board of Education *Annual Report*, London Cd. 8055 (1915).
23. Foucault (1985) notes that 'judges of normality are present everywhere. We are in a society of the teacher-judge, the doctor-judge, the educator-judge, the social worker-judge; it is on them that the universal reign of the normative is based.' To this list we could add the dentist-judge.

This article is a heavily edited version of a much longer text, which was originally published in 1988, under the same title, in the journal *Sociology of Health and Illness*, volume 10 (No. 2), pages 156–169. At the time of writing, Sarah Nettleton was a researcher at King's College School of Medicine and Dentistry in London, and is now a Senior Lecturer in Social Policy and Social Work at the University of York. This article was further developed in her book, *Power, Pain and Dentistry*, published in 1992 by Open University Press.

8 | Hysteria and demonic possession

MARY JAMES

Introduction

Jean-Martin Charcot (1825–1893) was a figure of major importance in French medicine at the end of the nineteenth century. In 1856, when he first took a post at the vast and ancient Salpêtrière hospital in Paris, doctors and students alike were reluctant to work there. Charcot, however, was quick to recognize the enormous potential this institution held for medical research. Its population of some 5,000 old and ailing women suffered from a great variety of chronic illnesses, especially diseases of the nervous system, which had yet to be classified and diagnosed.

In 1862, as head of one of the hospital's largest sections, Charcot embarked upon the enormous task of methodically examining every one of his patients, completing his clinical notes, where possible, by correlating symptoms with lesions at postmortem. Charcot's special talent in this field was to produce most fruitful results. By the late 1860s virtually all the most chronic neurological diseases on his wards had been systematized. By the time of his death, in 1893, he had constructed the basic framework of modern neuropathology and the Salpêtrière had been transformed into one of the world's leading teaching hospitals.

Although Charcot studied a number of different diseases, by 1872 hysteria had become his main area of interest, especially in its convulsive form which he termed *la grande hystérie* (major hysteria). The Paris Medical Faculty, at that time, considered hysteria to be unsatisfactorily defined as a disease because of its highly variable manifestations for which no cause could be found. Charcot, however, was confident that the method responsible for his neurological achievements could be extended to explain hysteria as a disorder of the nervous system. By prolonged clinical observation the seemingly formless attacks of *la grande hystérie* were schematized into four distinct stages occurring with various degrees of intensity according to the patient.

The aims of this article are twofold. The first is to explore Charcot's concept of *la grande hystérie* by looking closely at his description of the four stage classical attack.

It will then be possible to examine how this diagnosis was used at the Salpêtrière to reinterpret certain historical accounts of supernatural phenomena as instances of hysterical pathology.

Implicit in Charcot's project of reinterpretation was the rejection of religious and metaphysical explanations of phenomena. His view that only systematic observation and experiment were capable of yielding genuine knowledge was informed by the positivist tradition of scientific explanation. The belief that one can only have knowledge of observable phenomena and the law-like relations between them was well established in Charcot's day. It exerted a profound influence on many branches of intellectual activity and was crucial to his understanding of hysteria.

Given this, Charcot needed to demonstrate the law-governed regularity of hysteria before this condition could be satisfactorily explained. This meant that Charcot needed evidence that *la grande hystérie* was not limited to any specific time or place. As proof that it existed in former times Charcot used various historical paintings and written accounts of saints in ecstasy and the demonic possessed. By making meticulous, point by point comparisons with his *grandes hystériques* (major hysterics) he was able to highlight significant similarities that lent support to his claim. This process of identifying historical instances of hysteria was known as *retrospective diagnosis*.

In order to examine more closely how this was done at the Salpêtrère and to bring to light the conceptual and methodological difficulties that it entailed, the second part of this paper focuses on the case history of one of his *grandes hystériques*, Geneviève, known by the doctors at the Salpêtrière as 'La Succube' (that is a female demon supposed to have sexual intercourse with sleeping men). Her photographically illustrated case history was published in 1877–78 in the *Iconographie Photographique de la Salpêtrière*.[1]

This case is interesting for a number of reasons. Most importantly it illustrates how, at the Salpêtrière, clinical and religious interpretations became intertwined. It also offers a rich source for insights into the relationship between hysterical symptoms and socio-cultural context in which they occur.

La grande hystérie

When, in 1870, Charcot first turned his attention explicitly towards hysteria, considerable controversy surrounded its diagnosis. Convulsive hysteria, on account of its resemblance to epileptic fits, was known as hystero-epilepsy and many doctors believed it to be a combination of the two disorders. Charcot, however, held that where epileptic fits seemed to occur simultaneously with the symptoms of convulsive hysteria the condition was in fact only very severe hysteria. Although Charcot decided to retain the term hystero-epilepsy, he preferred the designations *la grande hystérie* or hysteria major, as they were less likely to arouse confusion.

Influenced by Pierre Briquet's study of hysteria in 1859, Charcot showed that *la grande attaque hystérique* (attack of major hysteria) in its most perfect form could be reduced to a very simple formula. In the complete attack four distinct phases succeeded one another with mechanical regularity. However, the concept of a *pure type* of hysteria was an abstract one to which patients, in reality, only very rarely conformed. Nevertheless Charcot believed that any inconvenience that arose from this was compensated by its potential for imposing order on the chaos of seemingly random hysterical manifestations.

According to the degree of intensity of any one of the stages of the *grande attaque*, different varieties were identified. At the Salpêtrière each aspect of patients' hysterical attacks was observed, documented, photographed and sketched in minute detail. The multiplicity of observations recorded were interpreted in the framework of the four stage model.

The classical *grande attaque* began with a warning *prodrome* or *aura*, usually of only a few minutes duration. This was generally marked by excessive sensitivity around the ovaries with the sensation of a ball rising from the abdomen to the throat, causing a feeling of suffocation. Other characteristic signs were palpitations of the heart, beating at the temples and whistling in the ears, often accompanied by mental excitation and sometimes by hallucinations.

The attack proper commenced with the stage designated *épileptoid* because of its similarity to an epileptic fit. Involuntary muscular contractions contorted the patient's face and body. Typically the eyeballs convulsed upwards, respiration was snorelike and foam appeared at the mouth. This stage was estimated to continue for about four minutes in all.

Next came the stage termed *grandes mouvements* (great movements) on account of the immense struggling purposelessness that it entailed. Beginning after a moment of calm, it was said to be motivated by an exaggerated expenditure of muscular force, enabling the patient to perform feats of staggering strength and agility. The bizarre postures and contortions of this period were known as *attitudes illogiques* (illogical postures), in which no overall rhythm or order could be identified. It was described as a fit of rage in which the subject, howling like a wild beast, tore or broke anything within reach, and attacked anyone who tried to approach.

The third stage to occur was the *période des attitudes passionnelles* (period of postures denoting strong emotion). In this phase the patient experienced hallucinations, the content of which was expressively acted out in mime. A certain sentiment, either cheerful (*gaie*), or sad (*triste*) was said always to predominate and sometimes patients switched from one to the other in succession. Romantic or religious joy were usually the subject of *hallucinations gaies*, whilst fires, wars, revolutions and murders were most often the basis of the *tableaux tristes* (mimes portraying sadness). Sometimes expressive poses were adopted in which the patient appeared as a living statue. Charcot said that this phase was generally short and might not occur at all.

The attack drew to a close with the fourth or terminal period. The patient came back to self-awareness, but only in part, often being prey to deliria and to symptoms very similar to those of the initial aura. The four-part attack generally lasted for around a quarter of an hour, but it could recur to constitute a series sometimes of two hundred or more attacks.

Retrospective diagnosis and the *attaque démoniaque*

Meticulous clinical observation at the Salpêtrière revealed the *attaque démoniaque* (demonic attack) to be a frequently occurring variation of the classical *grande attaque hystérique* that has just been described. It consisted in the predominance of the second stage of *grandes mouvements*. Charcot drew a close parallel between the bizarre contortions and violent outbursts of this period and the behaviour which had historically been understood as demonic possession. For instance, In both cases the superhuman muscular strength and agility of seemingly frail women often astounded spectators.

To establish this point historical literature on demonic possession was sometimes quoted at length in the case histories of hystero-epileptics. Works such as *La Piété Affligée*, published in 1700 by the exorcist involved in occurrences of possession at a convent in Louviers, and *L'Histoire des Diables de Loudun*, an eyewitness account by a protestant minister of possession in a convent in Loudun, published in 1693, were used to confirm the similarity between the *attaque démoniaque* and all the major characteristics of demonic possession.

Works of art were also subjected to medical scrutiny. For instance, a sketch of a person possessed by devils, by the Flemish painter Rubens (1577–1640), was used to illustrate the case of the *grande-hystérique*, Celina.[2] Analogies were drawn between the sketch and photographs of her in the throes of a 'demonic' attack.

Retrospective diagnosis served a dual purpose. The fact that the classical symptoms of hysteria, as enumerated by Charcot, had already been fully described hundreds of years before was taken as proof that *la grande hystérie* was objectively real and could not be the result of suggestion (this is a covert or inadvertent influence) proceeding from any current medical theory. It also meant that supernatural accounts of demonic possession could be replaced by reference to natural causes alone, thereby extending the boundaries of scientific knowledge. This approach to diagnosis was, however, problematic in several respects, not least because Charcot's focus of attention on superstitious beliefs brought them to the fore, making the Salpêtrière itself into a kind of 'theatre of possession'.[3,4] Once the concept of the *attaque démoniaque* had been set in place not only were doctors more likely to identify and emphasize those characteristics which could be subsumed within this category, but patients, in turn, became more inclined to supply them with good cause. At the Salpêtrière the results of a complex process of suggestion, autosuggestion and expectation were subtle and far-reaching.

Geneviève – *La Succube*

The demonic connotations of hysteria are especially interesting and intricate in the case of Geneviève. The second part of her case history, entitled *Succube*, was compiled in 1878 by Charcot's colleague and former student D. M Bourneville (1840–1909). He stated that less than two centuries ago she would have been thought of as possessed by a demon.[5] This identity was attributed to her, not on account of her hysterical crises, which did not conform to the *attaque démoniaque*, but because of her generally bizarre and unruly behaviour and the strange hallucinations she experienced. The seventeenth century accounts of demonic possession at the convents in Loudun and Louviers were referred to throughout to illustrate the point. For Bourneville, Geneviève was 'living proof' that the nuns had been hysterics.

Geneviève's case history records that she was first taken into hospital in 1851, when she was eight years old. She could not, however, remember why. Throughout the rest of her childhood and adolescence many periods were spent as a hospital patient. Although she received no formal schooling, nursing nuns taught her to read religious texts. When not in hospital she lived with a foster family and worked on their farm.

At the age of fourteen, she was courted by a young man named Camille. Eighteen months later she was devastated when he died of brain fever. Her foster family tried to prevent her from attending his funeral, but she escaped and attempted to throw herself in the grave. This experience left her depressed and angry and she often refused to speak. The following year, when her foster mother died, her condition deteriorated and she was taken back into hospital at Poitiers.

Six months later, in better health, she took work as a chamber-maid in the town. Soon her employer began to make sexual advances and although she tried to defend herself her feelings towards him were ambivalent. It was in this frame of mind that she suffered her first convulsive attack. She was taken back to the hospital and for the next five or six months had attacks every day.

By the time Geneviève became one of Charcot's patients, in March 1872, she was twenty nine years old and had already spent a considerable amount of time at the Salpêtrière. She first went there in 1864 as a psychiatric patient, and then, as her condition improved, stayed on as a nursing assistant. In 1865 she was taken to the section for epileptics, but after being granted permission to go into town with a nurse, had escaped and run to the house of a lover she had met in Paris.

Over the next fifteen months she moved from one hospital to another, her status oscillating between patient and nursing assistant. However in July 1866, after violently assaulting the *chef du service* (chief of staff) at La Pitié hospital in Paris, she was sent back to the section for the insane at the Salpêtrière. Later that year she was transferred to an asylum at Toulouse, but, having gained the confidence of the nursing nuns, she soon absconded. For the next three months, dressed in hospital uniform and clogs, she made her way back to Paris on foot, sleeping rough and begging for alms. Upon her return she went to join her lover and in August 1867 gave birth to a daughter at the Salpêtrière.

Bourneville's account of Geneviève's history clearly depicts her as rebellious and recalcitrant both to medical control and diagnosis. As a patient of Charcot's she often tried to run away by climbing on the roof and jumping over the fence, sometimes accompanied by the 'demonic' Celina. Behaviour of this kind was used to draw comparisons with the nuns of Loudun whose exploits in the acrobatic field included shinning up trees and climbing onto the convent roof.

However, what is perhaps most significant about the demonic interpretation of Geneviève's hysteria is that she was born in Loudun and grew up in that area. Throughout her childhood and adolescence she was in close contact with nursing nuns who, because of her boisterous and headstrong character, frequently beat and punished her. Whilst supplying these details, Bourneville did not acknowledge that they may have influenced her 'demonic' behaviour.

The demonic possession at the Ursuline convent is perhaps Loudun's only claim to fame, and stories of the nuns' bizarre and often lewd behaviour were well known. Until 1861, when Geneviève first came to Paris, she had been immersed in this milieu of possession. Whilst Bourneville recognised the influence of convent life upon her marked religiosity (for instance she spent much time kneeling in prayer in front of a large crucifix which she kept constantly by her), it was supposed that her unruly outbursts shed light on the strange conduct of the possessed nuns of the seventeenth century rather than vice versa.

The numerous comparisons drawn between Geneviève and the demonic possessed were intended to show not just that the nuns were hysterics, but that Geneviève's hysteria was objectively real. Most notably, Geneviève's hallucinations, in which she received nocturnal visits of a sexual nature from a Dr X, were said to have an historical counterpart. The possessed nuns had claimed that they had been necromantically seduced by Urbain Grandier, Loudun's handsome, young parish priest. He was, consequently, tried and burned at the stake as a sorcerer in 1634.

Geneviève's extravagant antics before and after attacks were also likened to those of demoniacs. In particular, her insensitivity to cold and pain and her tendency to take off all her clothes and cavort about naked in all weathers, were said to resemble in every detail descriptions of the Ursuline Mother Superior, Madame de Belfiel, one of Grandier's accusers.

Ostensibly it was on account of these resemblances to *les possédées* (the possessed) that Geneviève was referred to as 'La Succube'. This terminology is interesting in two respects. Not only does it make medical and historical discourse interchangeable, but it subtly distorts the issue at hand. Geneviève believed Dr X visited her in her hospital bed in order to have sexual intercourse. However by naming *her* La Succube she is misleadingly represented as the female demon which folk lore characterizes as having sexual intercourse with sleeping men.

This inversion of meaning not only attributes to her a demonic identity that is inappropriate under the circumstances, it also suggests that she is sexually culpable. This implication is amplified by the connotation of prostitution that the term carries from the Latin *succuba* (i.e. prostitute). Thus this label had moral as well as medical significance, stereotyping the sexually unconventional Geneviève as a whore. (The idea that an actual seduction by Dr X might have occurred did not enter the question and is now beyond the reach of time.)

Conclusion

Charcot's method of retrospective diagnosis, whilst it brought many interesting comparisons to light, was nevertheless seriously flawed in its deployment of the evidence. Historical depictions of demoniacs, on the one hand, were taken as evidence of the authenticity of certain hysterical phenomena witnessed by Charcot and his colleagues. On the other hand contemporary manifestations of 'demonic' behaviour were 'living proof' that the demoniacs of former times were actually hysterics. This strategy entails the uncomfortable consequence of explanatory reciprocity, that is to say the 'objective' evidence supporting either claim was itself defined in terms of the condition it was intended to guarantee.

At the Salpêtrière, two systems of representation, the clinical and the religious, were constantly intermingling and contaminating one another. The medical discourse drew heavily on the religious superstitions it was trying to dispel, often becoming entangled and confused in the process. The unintended result was the accentuation of the very demonic connotations that the positivist approach aimed to counteract. Ironically the demonic phenomena exhibited at the Salpêtrière arose from and were closely related to Charcot's main clinical objective, namely to provide a scientific explanation for hysteria as an objectively real, law-governed phenomenon, on the basis of clinical observation.

References

1. Bourneville, D.M. and Regnard, P. *Iconographie Photographique de la Salpêtrière*, Vol. 1, Observation IV (1876–7), Vol. 2, Observation IV (1878). Progrès Médical, Delahaye and Lecrosnier, Paris.

2. Plate XI in Volume 1 of Bourneville and Regnard (1877).
3. Page 501 in Carroy-Thirand, J. 'Possession, extase, hystérie au XIXe siècle'. *Psychanalyse à l'université*, 5(19), pp. 499–515 (1980).
4. Chapter 5 in James, M. The *Therapeutic Practices of Jean-Martin Charcot (1825–1893) in their Historical and Social Context*. Ph.D. thesis, University of Essex (1989).
5. Page 202 in Volume 2, Part II of Bourneville and Regnard (1878).

Further sources for this article

Charcot, J.-M. *Lectures on Diseases of the Nervous System*, Vols 72, 90, 128. Translated and edited by George Sigerson, New Sydenham Society, London (1877–89).
Charcot, J.-M. and Richer, P. *Les Démoniaques dans l'Art*, Delahaye and Lecrosnier, Paris (1887).
Didi-Huberman, G. 'Charcot, l'histoire et l'art', postface to J.-M. Charcot and P. Richer, *Les Démoniaques dans l'Art* (1887), Macula, Paris, 1984.

This article was first published by the Open University in 1994 as a supplementary article to *Medical Knowledge: Doubt and Certainty*, for students studying the second-level course *U205 Health and Disease*. Mary James wrote her doctoral thesis on the work of the French doctor, Jean-Martin Charcot, who described various specific aspects of hysterical manifestations in his writings with the French terms used in this article (since no corresponding English terms exist in most cases, a rough translation only has been given in brackets). Mary James fomerly lectured in the Department of History at the University of Essex.

9 | Cross-cultural psychiatry

CECIL HELMAN

Definitions of 'normality', like definitions of 'health', vary widely throughout the world: and in many cultures, these two concepts overlap. Displays of behaviour that are 'abnormal' by the standards of everyday life, must be seen against the background of the culture in which they appear. In many cultures, especially in the non-industrialized world, individuals involved in interpersonal conflicts, or who are experiencing feelings of unhappiness, guilt, anger or helplessness, are able to express these feelings in a standardized language of distress. This may be purely verbal, or involve extreme changes in dress, behaviour or posture. To the Western-trained observer, some of these languages of distress may closely resemble the diagnostic entities of the Western psychiatric model. For example, they may involve statements such as, 'I've been bewitched', 'I've been possessed by a spirit (or by God)', or 'I can hear the voices of my ancestors speaking to me'. In a Western setting, people making this type of statement are likely to be diagnosed as psychotic, probably schizophrenic.

However, it should be remembered that in many parts of the world people freely admit to being 'possessed' by supernatural forces, to having 'spirits' speak and act through them, and to having had dreams or visions that conveyed an important message to them. In most cases this is not considered by their communities to be evidence of mental illness. One example of this is the widespread belief, especially in parts of Africa, of spirit possession as a cause of mental or physical ill-health.

Another form of controlled abnormal behaviour is *glossolalia*, or speaking in unknown tongues. To those who believe in it, it is thought to result from a supernatural power entering into the individual, with 'control of the organs of speech by the Holy Spirit, who prays through the speaker in a heavenly language'.[1] It is a dissociative, trance-like state in which the participants 'tend to have their eyes closed, they may make twitching movements and fall; they flush, sweat and may tear at their clothes'. It is a feature of religious practices in parts of India, the Caribbean, Africa, Southern Europe, North America and among many Pentecostal churches in the UK (including those with West Indian congregations). There are believed to be about two million practitioners of glossolalia in the USA in various denominations, including some Lutheran, Episcopalian and Presbyterian churches. Glossolalia usually takes place in a specified context (the church) and at specified times during the service. It can be seen as a form of 'controlled abnormality' which, to a Western-trained psychiatrist, might seem evidence of a mental illness.

In every society there is a spectrum between what people regard as 'normal' and 'abnormal' social behaviour. However, there is also a spectrum of 'abnormal' behaviour, from *controlled* to *uncontrolled* forms of abnormality. It is behaviour at the *uncontrolled* end of the spectrum that cultures regard as a major social problem, and that they label as either 'mad' or 'bad'. As Foster and Anderson[2] put it 'there is no culture in which men and women remain oblivious to erratic, disturbed, threatening or bizarre behaviour in their midst, whatever the culturally defined context of that behaviour'.

In one study by Edgerton,[3] lay beliefs about what behaviour constitutes madness or psychosis were examined in four East African tribes: two in Kenya, one in Uganda and one in Tanzania (Tanganyika). It was found that all four societies shared a broad area of agreement as to what behaviours suggested a diagnosis of 'madness'. These included such actions as violent conduct, wandering around naked, 'talking nonsense' or 'sleeps and hides in the bush'. Edgerton notes how this catalogue of abnormal behaviours is not markedly at variance with Western definitions of psychosis, particularly schizophrenia.

Where the mentally ill people come from a cultural or ethnic minority, they often have to utilize the symbols of the dominant majority culture in order to articulate their psychological distress and obtain help.[1] That is, they have to internalize (or appear to internalize) the value system of the dominant culture, and to utilize the vocabulary that goes with these values. This process is illustrated in the following case history.

Case study: 'Beatrice Jackson'

Littlewood[4] describes the case of 'Beatrice Jackson', a 34-year-old widow, daughter of a black Jamaican Baptist minister, who had lived in London for 15 years. She lived alone with her son, and worked at a dress factory far from home. She was often lonely and depressed, and felt guilty about her long estrangement from her father back in the Caribbean. She was very religious and frequently attended church. After her father died she became increasingly guilty, constantly ruminating over her past life. She developed pain in her womb, and persuaded a gynaecologist to do a hysterectomy, so 'clearing all that away'. The pains now shifted to her back, and she continued to ask for further operations to remove the trouble. Her psychotic breakdown was precipitated by her son's criticism of the white police during a riot, which she bitterly contested. The following day she was admitted to a mental hospital, talking incoherently and threatening to kill herself, shouting that her son was not hers because he was black, and that black people were ugly although *she* was not as she was not black. In hospital she became more attached to the white medical and nursing staff, helping them as far as she could and taking their part against the patients in any dispute. By contrast, she kept on getting into arguments with the West Indian staff, refusing to carry out requests for them which she readily agreed to if asked by a white nurse.

Closer analysis of the case revealed that she saw the world literally in black and white terms. According to Littlewood, she had internalized the dominant racialist symbolism of both colonial Jamaica and of the England she had encountered, where 'black' represented badness, 'sin, sexual indulgence and dirt'. In her religion, black also represented hatred, evil (evil people were 'black-hearted'), devils, darkness and mourning. By contrast, 'white' was associated with 'religion, purity and renunciation'; it also stood for purity and joy, and both brides and angels are dressed in white. In the Caribbean, popular magazines often advertise skin lightening creams and hair straighteners, and a lighter coloured skin is a highly valued social asset. She had internalized this dichotomy, and had hoped to become 'white inside' by strict adherence to religious values, but could not match this by social acceptance from the white world outside. She felt that part of her remained 'black' (and therefore evil, unacceptable) and located the trouble in her sexual organs, blaming these for the carnal feeling which 'is in conflict with that part of her which seems to have managed to become white'. Her son's repudiation of the police, the representatives of white society, seemed to threaten her category of white = good, black = bad and she could no longer reconcile her inner symbolic system, the outer social reality, and her emotional relationships. Thus 'her system collapsed'.

Cultural influences on psychiatric diagnosis

Before psychological disorders can be compared they have to be diagnosed. In recent years a number of studies have indicated some of the difficulties in standardizing psychiatric diagnoses, particularly among psychiatrists working in different countries. Variations in the clinical criteria used to diagnose schizophrenia, for example, have been found between British and American psychiatrists and British and French psychiatrists, and among psychiatrists working within these countries. Some of the diagnostic categories in French psychiatry – such as 'chronic delusional states' (*délires chroniques*) and 'transitory delusional states' (*bouffées delirantes*) – are significantly different from the diagnostic categories of Anglo-American psychiatry.[5] A further example was the diagnostic category 'sluggish schizophrenia' in Soviet psychiatry, which was virtually limited to the former USSR.[6] All of these discrepancies in diagnostic behaviour among psychiatrists are important, since they affect both the treatment and prognosis of mental illness, as well as the reliability of comparing morbidity statistics for these conditions between different countries.

Part of the reason for these differences lies in the nature of psychiatric diagnosis, and the categories into which it places psychological disorders. Unlike the diagnosis of medical 'diseases', there is often little evidence of typical biological malfunctioning, as revealed by diagnostic technology. Where biological evidence does exist, it is often difficult to relate this to specific clinical symptoms. Most psychiatric diagnoses are based on the doctor's subjective evaluation of the patient's appearance, speech and behaviour, as well as performance in certain standardized psychometric tests. The aim is to fit the symptoms and signs into a known category of mental illness, by their similarity to the 'typical' textbook description of the condition. However, according to Kendell,[7] the way that psychiatrists learn how to do this may actually make diagnostic differences among them more likely. He suggests that

> diagnostic concepts are not securely anchored. They are at the mercy of the personal views and idiosyncrasies of influential teachers, of therapeutic fashions and innovations, of changing assumptions about aetiology, and many other less tangible influences to boot.

In their study of mental illness among immigrants to the UK, Littlewood and Lipsedge[1] also suggest that psychiatry can sometimes be used as a form of social control, misinterpreting the religious and other behaviour of some Afro-Caribbean patients (as well as their response to discrimination) as evidence of schizophrenia. By contrast with the high rate of schizophrenia among Afro-Caribbeans, depression is rarely diagnosed, and the authors suggest that

> whatever the empirical justification, the frequent diagnosis in black patients of schizophrenia (bizarre, irrational, outside) and the infrequent diagnosis of depression (acceptable, understandable, inside) validates our stereotypes.

In dealing with immigrants and the poor, they warn against psychiatry's role in 'disguising disadvantage as disease'.

Other researchers, however, while agreeing that ethnic and racial prejudices do exist among UK psychiatrists, dispute that this alone leads to an over-diagnosis of schizophrenia among Afro-Caribbeans. Lewis et al.[8] for example, in their study of 139 British psychiatrists, *did* find evidence of stereotyping and 'race-thinking' towards Afro-Caribbean patients – judging them as potentially more violent, less suitable for medication, but more suitable for criminal proceedings than white patients. Presented with identical vignettes of black and white patients, they were more likely to diagnose cannabis psychosis and acute reactive psychosis among the black patients, but *less* likely to diagnose schizophrenia. Thus, while confirming the role of prejudice in psychiatric diagnosis, they found no evidence of a 'greater readiness to detain patients compulsorily or to manage them on a locked ward merely on the grounds of "race"'.

Thomas et al.,[9] in a study of compulsory psychiatric admissions in Manchester, found that second-generation (UK-born) Afro-Caribbeans had nine times the rate of schizophrenia of whites. However, this could largely be explained by their greater socio-economic disadvantage, with poor inner-city housing and higher rates of unemployment – all of which have been correlated with high rates of schizophrenia – rather than by psychiatric misdiagnosis. They therefore suggest that

> efforts aimed at improving social disadvantage and the provision of employment for ethnic minority groups may improve the mental health of such groups.

Wesseley et al.,[10] also, found higher rates of schizophrenia among Afro-Caribbeans in South London, irrespective of their place of birth, compared to other groups, but these differences could also mostly be explained by the greater social adversity they suffered, rather than by their ethnicity. Some of the differences in diagnosis between psychiatrists in different Western countries, and within a single country, are illustrated in the following case studies.

Case study: Differences in psychiatric diagnosis in the UK and the USA

Katz et al.[11] examined the process of psychiatric diagnosis among both British and American psychiatrists in more detail. The study aimed to discover whether disagreements among these diagnoses were a 'function of differences in their actual perception of the patient, or patients on whose symptoms and behaviour they are in agreement'. Groups of British and American psychiatrists were shown films of interviews with patients, and asked to note down all pathological symptoms and to make a diagnosis.

Marked disagreements in diagnosis between the two groups were found, as well as different patterns of symptomatology perceived. The British saw less pathology generally, and less evidence of the key diagnostic symptoms 'retardation' and 'apathy', and little or no 'paranoid projection' or 'perceptual distortion'. On the other hand, they saw more 'anxious intropunitiveness' than did the Americans. Perceiving less of these key symptoms led the British psychiatrists to diagnose schizophrenia less frequently. For example, one patient was diagnosed as 'schizophrenic' by one-third of the Americans, but by none of the British. The authors conclude that 'ethnic background apparently influences choice of diagnosis and perception of symptomatology'.

Case study: Differences in psychiatric diagnosis within the UK

Copeland et al.[12] studied differences in diagnostic behaviour among 200 British psychiatrists, all of whom had at least 4 years in full-time practice, and possessed similar qualifications. They were shown videotapes of interviews with three patients, and asked to rate their abnormal traits on a standardized scale, and to assign the patients to diagnostic categories. There was fairly good agreement on diagnoses among the sample, except that psychiatrists trained in Glasgow had a significant tendency to make a diagnosis of 'affective illness' in one of the tapes, where the choice of diagnosis was between affective illness and schizophrenia.

In addition, psychiatrists trained at the Maudsley Hospital, London, gave lower ratings of abnormal behaviour on the patients than the rest, while older psychiatrists and those with psychotherapeutic training rated a higher level of abnormalities than did younger psychiatrists. The authors point out that rating behaviour as 'abnormal' is 'likely to be affected by the rater's attitude towards illness and health and what is normal and abnormal'. The survey illustrates therefore that differences in these attitudes are associated with differences in postgraduate psychiatric training, as well as with age.

Conclusion

[I have] illustrated some of the complexities in making cross-cultural psychiatric diagnoses, and especially the problems of defining 'normality' and 'abnormality' in the members of other cultures. A further problem is that clinicians may *over*emphasize 'culture' as an explanation for patients' behaviour, and thus ignore any underlying psychopatholgy.[13] In making cross-cultural diagnoses therefore, the clinician should always be aware of:

- The extent to which cultural factors affect some of the diagnostic categories and techniques of Western psychiatry.
- The role of the patients' culture in helping them understand and communicate their psychological distress.
- How the patients' beliefs and behaviour are viewed by other members of their cultural group, and whether their abnormality is viewed as beneficial to the group or not.

- Whether the specific cluster of symptoms, signs and behavioural changes shown by the patients are interpreted by them, and by their community, as evidence of a 'culture-bound' psychological disorder.
- Whether the patients' condition is indicative or not of mental illness, but rather of the social, political and economic pressures on them.

References

1. Littlewood, R. and Lipsedge, M. (1989) *Aliens and Alienists*, 2nd edn. London: Unwin Hyman, pp. 174–81, 207, 218–42, 249–54.
2. Foster, G.M. and Anderson, B.G. (1978) *Medical Anthropology*. New York: Wiley, pp. 81–100.
3. Edgerton, R.B. (1977) Conceptions of psychosis in four East African societies. In: Landy, D. (ed.), *Culture, Disease and Healing: Studies in Medical Anthropology*. New York: Macmillan, pp. 358–67.
4. Littlewood, R. (1989) Anthropology and psychiatry: an alternative approach, *Br. J. Med. Psychol.*, **53**, 213–25.
5. Pichot, P. (1982) The diagnosis and classification of mental disorders in French-speaking countries: background, current views and comparison with other nomenclatures, *Psychol. Med.*, **12**, 475–92.
6. Merskey, H. and Shafran, B. (1986) Political hazards in the diagnosis of 'sluggish schizophrenia', *Br. J. Psychiatry*, **148**, 247–56.
7. Kendell, R.E. (1975) *The Role of Diagnosis in Psychiatry*. Oxford: Blackwell, pp. 70–1.
8. Lewis, G., Croft-Jeffreys, C. and David, A. (1990) Are British psychiatrists racist? *Br. J. Psychiatry*, **157**, 410–15.
9. Thomas, C.S., Stone, K., Osborn, M., Thomas, P.T. and Fisher, M. (1993) Psychiatric morbidity and compulsory admissions among UK-born Europeans, Afro-Caribbeans and Asians in Central Manchester. *Br. J. Psychiatry*, **163**, 91–9.
10. Wesseley, S., Castle, D., Der, G. and Murray, R. (1991) Schizophrenia and Afro-Caribbeans: a case-control study. *Br. J. Psychiatry*, **159**, 795–801.
11. Katz, M.M., Cole, J.O. and Lowery, H.A. (1969) Studies of the diagnostic process: the influence of symptom perception, past experience, and ethnic background on diagnostic decisions, *Am. J. Psychiatry*, **125**, 109–19.
12. Copeland, J.R.M., Cooper, J.E., Kendell, R.E. and Gourlay, A.J. (1971) Differences in usage of diagnostic labels among psychiatrists in the British Isles, *Br. J. Psychiatry*, **118**, 629–40.
13. Lopez, S. and Hernandez, P. (1976) How culture is considered in evaluations of psychotherapy, *J. Nerv. Ment. Dis.* **176**, 598–606.

This edited extract comes from Chapter 10, 'Cross-cultural psychiatry' of the fourth edition of Cecil Helman's book, *Culture, Health and Illness: An Introduction for Health Professionals* (London, Arnold, 2000). The author is Senior Lecturer in the Department of Primary Care and Population Sciences, Royal Free and University College Medical School, and Associate Professor of medical anthropology in the Department of Human Sciences, Brunel University.

10 | Media and mental illness

GREG PHILO

This chapter reports on research by the Glasgow Media Group on press and television treatment of mental health issues. It looks at the negative impact that such coverage can have on popular understanding, and examines possible strategies for achieving a more positive response from media in this area. The research included a content analysis of press and television output, plus a series of focus group interviews to analyse the processes by which audiences received and understood messages in this area (for a more detailed account of the sample and methods *see* Philo, 1996). The results show clearly that ill-informed beliefs on, for example, the association of schizophrenia with violence can be traced directly to media accounts.

The content sample focused on television news and press reporting, plus popular magazines and children's literature as well as fictional TV such as soap operas, films and drama, for a period of one month. This yielded a total of 562 items whose content fell into five main categories: violence to others; harm to self; prescriptive/advice; criticism of accepted definitions of mental illness; and 'comic' images. As an example of the last category, the Ruby Wax show offered a 'comic' presentation of the rehabilitation of Joanna Lumley:

> *Wax*: We have someone here with us tonight who recently joined the ranks of the chronically barking . . . I know you are going to be kind because if you are not she may pull a knife . . . back from the abyss, Miss Joanna Lumley!
> (BBC, 22 April 1992)

Overall in the coverage, the category of 'violence to others' was by far the most common, outweighing the next most common ('advice') by a ratio of almost four to one. We also found that items linking mental illness and violence tended to receive 'headline' treatment, while more sympathetic items were largely 'back page' in their profile, such as problem page letters or health columns.

The audience reception study used 70 people, divided into focus groups, who were asked to work through a programme of exercises and interviews. In the exercises, sub-groups of two or three people were asked to write news reports prompted by copies of original headlines from newspapers. They were also asked to write dialogue for an episode of ITV's *Coronation Street*, prompted by still photographs from the programme. Following this, each member of the group gave written replies to questions. In writing their own stories, the audience groups demonstrated a remarkable ability to reproduce the style and language of both television and the press. We also found that some group members could reproduce detailed and accurate scripts from *Coronation Street*, months after the relevant scenes had been transmitted. The photographs which they used related to a story line in which a mentally ill person has an erotic fixation for the husband of one of the regular characters. These scenes had apparently generated an intense hostility towards the mentally ill character among the majority of the group members who had seen them. We asked how they would have reacted to her and received many responses such as 'killed her', 'battered her bloody mouth in', 'kicked hell out of her' and 'I would have killed the cow'. A much smaller number suggested that she needed psychiatric help – a judgement which was made mostly on the basis of their own professional or personal experience in the area. But even here, the judgement could be accompanied by a list of other things which had to be 'done' to the woman first:

> [I would have] thrown her out of the house, denounced her in public and with Martin [the husband] by my side, let the whole world know what she was up to. Then suggested to her that she needed psychiatric help.

Media presentations were also a very powerful influence on beliefs about the nature of mental illness. For example, the character of Trevor Jordache in the soap opera *Brookside* was presented as alternating between being an amiable loving family man and making violent threats to his wife: 'You won't tell anyone, because if you do I'll kill you, do you understand?' (17 April 1993).

In the popular press, he was referred to as 'psycho Trevor' (*Daily Star*, 19 April 1993) and in our group interviews, he was spontaneously referred to as being 'what a mentally ill person was like'. As one female interviewee commented: 'in *Brookside*, that man who is the child-abuser and the wife-beater, he looks like a schizophrenic – he's like a split personality, like two different people'.

The important point is that beliefs derived from fictional accounts clearly affected attitudes in real life. One interviewee gave her views about the mentally ill as: 'They could be all right one minute and then just snap – I'm kind of wary of them . . . That *Fatal Attraction* she was as nice as ninepence and then . . .' Such comments can reveal very deep levels of fear. Another interviewee wrote in her reply that mentally ill people were 'quite likely to be violent – split personality usually tend to be violent'. She went on to write that, 'I would tend to be more wary as some mentally ill people can be very clever and devious'. The source of her views was given as 'probably from TV and newspapers, I think!' She went on in her interview to comment that: 'Hungerford, that type of thing – anything you see on the news, it's likely to be violent when it is connected with mentally ill people'. It was apparent from this that 'factual' accounts could also strongly affect attitudes.

One of the key issues explored in the research was whether serious mental illness was believed to be associated with violence. Forty per cent of the people in the general sample believed this to be so, while giving the media as the source of their beliefs. The depth of the anxiety is so great in this area that some media accounts can apparently exert great power. In other research programmes, we have studied many different areas of media content. We have normally found that personal experience is a much stronger influence on belief than the messages which are given by media. But in this research we found cases where this pattern was reversed. We found a number of cases (21 per cent of the general sample) where people had non-violent experiences which were apparently 'overlaid' by media influences. These people traced their beliefs mostly to violent portrayals in fiction or to news reporting. An example of these was given by a young woman who lived near Woodilee Hospital just outside Glasgow. She wrote that she had worked there at a jumble sale and mixed with patients. Yet she associated mental illness with violence and wrote of 'split/double personalities, one side violence'. She then went on to say:

> The actual people I met weren't violent – that I think they are violent, that comes from television, from plays and things. That's the strange thing – the people were mainly geriatric – it wasn't the people you hear of on television. Not all of them were old, some of them were younger. None of them were violent – but I remember being scared of them, because it was a mental hospital – it's not a very good attitude to have but it is the way things come across on TV, and films – you know, mental axe murders and plays and things – the people I met weren't like that, but that is what I associated them with.

In a further example, one interviewee had visited a hospital in Glasgow many times to see a relative who had been a patient there for 25 years. She associated mental illness with violence and cited 'TV films' as the source of her beliefs. '*Texas Chainsaw Massacre, Freddy's Revenge, Nightmare on Elm Street, Psycho* – I watch a lot of them, I like all them ones'. She was asked specifically if the feeling about violence came from the films rather than what she had seen when visiting. She replied: 'Oh aye – every day I was up visiting, I never saw any violence and he was in a big open ward'.

We also found clear links between media representations and public attitudes to policies such as community care. An interviewee related her own beliefs about violence and mental illness to 'Hollywood film and television drama'. She then commented that: 'I feel that government policies in Britain of putting mentally ill people in the "care of the community" is dangerous'.

Another area of crucial importance is how media images may affect the beliefs of users of the mental health service, and the responses of their families and other carers. For example, if the association of schizophrenia with violence is so widespread in popular belief, then what does this say to the families of people with such an illness? There are very few 'positive' images in the media, in the sense that such people can recover, achieve or be active in their own right.

The new research investigated this area through a series of interviews with 32 users of services (at locations such as 'drop-in' centres in Glasgow, Manchester and Aberdeen). The most powerful negative effect seemed to be in the area of self-definition and the stigma developed and reinforced by media portrayals. As one interviewee put it: 'You see a programme and it shows a very bad image of what it feels like yourself and then you think, "What are my neighbours going to think of it?"' Another group member described to us in detail his feelings when he was given the label of being schizophrenic:

> When I was told I was schizophrenic, I was very intimidated by it – I thought I was some sort of monster. I didn't actually feel like a monster, but when they said I was schizophrenic, I just couldn't believe it . . . It's just such a hell of a word, you

know, and it has got a hell of a stigma . . . I just thought it was Jekyll and Hyde.
I was just one of those people I'm characterising this morning [for having incorrect
beliefs about mental illness] . . . but you're really more likely to hurt yourself –
what was blasting through my head was, 'You'll never get a job, you'll never get
a sick line, you'll have nowhere to live.' It was just going through my head, 'Kill
yourself.'

This group member was asked about where his original ideas on mental illness had
come from. He replied:

Jane Eyre was my mother's favourite programme and I think I got it from her.
We watched it faithfully every Saturday night. She [a character in the story] was
insane and she ran around screaming and shouting and burnt the house down –
and that instilled real fear in me . . . 'They'll burn the house down, they'll stab you,
they'll kill you.' – that is what I thought myself, until I realised I had a problem
myself.

He also described the changes in his social relationships:

When my neighbours knew that I was schizophrenic, they were worried about
getting into the lift with me – they didn't want to be in a confined space with me,
and they wouldn't open the door to me . . . My window cleaner asked me: 'Would
you not hit me over the head with a hammer?' – I had to reassure him that 'Look
mate, I'm not violent.' – and he was telling the neighbours. It rots you, it just rots
you.

The Glasgow research shows clearly the climate of fear that surrounds the subject of
mental illness. One organiser at a drop-in centre for users of services told us how the
assumed link between violence and mental illness affected enquiries that they received:

I had one woman asking me if [she] was safe living in [her] own house – 'Am I
going to get my throat cut?' – She said she loved her son . . . but she was terrified,
she wanted to know if her daughter would be safe. Her son was on medication
and he was due to come home. He had no history of violence . . . and this is
common.

Many of those who work in the area of mental health have experience of the damage
caused by this climate of fear. They believe that the media is in part responsible for this
and should be confronted with the consequences of its own actions. Those concerned
with mental health should not be reluctant to insist that it is a major social issue and
that some media coverage of it is a serious problem. In other areas, such as in coverage
of black and gay people, this has already been done. After long campaigns to challenge
traditional images and stereotypes both press and television did in some respects change.
We have not found the same level of interest in mental health. Yet the code of conduct
drawn up by the Press Complaints Commission, agreed by newspaper editors, clearly
specifies that there should be no discrimination in press reporting relating to physical
or mental illness. The code of practice states that: '*the press must avoid prejudicial or
pejorative reference to . . . any physical or mental illness or disability*'.

Our research findings showed that in the past the provisions of this code of practice
have been frequently broken. The new code was of course designed for the press, but
it is hard to see how broadcasters could argue that they do not intend to respect its

guidelines and ethos in their own practice. A combination of new research and collective pressure from the organisations concerned with mental health could now produce the changes in media coverage that so many people wish to see.

Media stereotypes, and the stigma that they carry, distort a fundamental truth about mental distress as experienced by very many people. As David King recently put it: 'It's a human condition, you can experience, you can recover and you can resume normal functioning' (King, 1995). Those who make media products can be made more aware of the problems that they are creating. But the demands for change cannot be left simply to mental health professionals. Users of mental health services, their families and supporters should be actively involved. The media will not change until there is a movement that demands it.

References

King, D. (1995): *Prevention: lessons learned from taskforce experiences.* Unpublished paper.
Philo, G. (ed.) (1996): *Media and Mental Distress.* London: Longman.

Gregory Philo is the Research Director of the Glasgow University Media Unit. This is an edited extract from Part 1 of his *Message Received: Glasgow Media Group Research* 1993–1998, published by Pearson Education in 1999.

11 | Public eyes and private genes

PETER CONRAD

The emergence of social constructionism over the past three decades has transformed the sociological analysis of social problems. A constructionist orientation urges us to take public conceptions of social problems seriously, at least as fodder for the ascent, decline and characterization of particular problems. Social problems in the public eye are not constant. Public conceptions of social problems have histories and shift over time and place. Professional definitions are only one source of problem designations but they often serve to legitimize and frame what constitute the character and nature of the problem. The dominion of particular lenses may wax and wane over time; in the last decade a genetic lens has ascended as a frame for understanding and explaining human problems. It is increasingly common to see behavioural problems explained as resulting from genetic sources, with attributions to chromosomes, genes, and the DNA. This can especially be seen in the media's reporting of genetic findings about behaviour; for most people, the reality of science is what they know from the press.

Rise of the genetic paradigm

In the wake of the discovery of the structure of DNA and innovations in identifying and cloning genes, a new genetics has emerged in recent decades that now stands on the cutting edge of science. Significant discoveries include genes for cystic fibrosis, Huntington's disease, Fragile X Syndrome, Duchenne muscular dystrophy, and types of breast and colon cancer. Many of these received widespread notice in the news media. The Human Genome Project, the largest biological project in history, is a 15-year international research initiative mapping the entire 3 billion base pairs of the human genetic structure. The avowed purpose of the genome project is to find the chemical or genetic basis for the 4000 or so genetic diseases that affect humans, as well as identify genetic linkages with other diseases, with the ultimate hope of producing new preventions and cures. As the project proceeds, new claims about genetic associations and linkages with diseases, conditions and behaviours will be announced at an accelerated pace over the next decade.

The mapping of the human genome has been the object of several provocative metaphors, including the search for the 'holy grail' (Gilbert 1992), investigating 'the essence of human life', and decoding 'the book of life'. James Watson, co-discoverer of the double helix structure of DNA and former head of the genome project declared, 'We used to think our fate was in our stars. Now we know, in large part, it is in our genes' (cited in Horgan 1993, p. 123). These are not humble images. Others have suggested that the gene is becoming a cultural icon in American society (Nelkin and Lindee 1995), invested with almost mystical powers. Critics contend that the 'geneticization' of human problems has expanded beyond scientific knowledge (Lippman 1992), and that a kind of 'genetic fatalism' – the assumption that a genetic association is deterministic and implying such a trait or behaviour is unchangeable – underlies much public discourse about genetics (Alper and Beckwith 1993).

The genetic paradigm has considerable appeal. It promises primary causes, located on a basic level of biological reality. Genes are often depicted as an essence, what one is really made of. This gives genetic thinking almost a mystical quality. While the older genetics relied on correlations and twin studies, we now can be tempted by the lure of specificity, associating specific genes with particular problems. Identifying specific genes seems so much neater than complex, messy epidemiological and social analyses. This specificity feeds hopes for genetic 'magic bullets' to alleviate human problems. While the genetics of social problems is not a central concern of the genome project or molecular biology, it seems clear that with the huge scientific industry exploring for differences in DNA, we are likely to continue to see more genetic explanations for human problems. We will see new claims that genetic research might help eliminate problems like homelessness, drug abuse and violent crime.

In the shadow of eugenics

To assess concerns with the new genetics it is necessary to understand them in the context of the old eugenics. The term eugenics was coined by Frances Galton in 1883 and defined as 'the science of improvement of the human race germplasm through better breeding'. We can see eugenics as promoting a dual-pronged program; the genetically fit should be encouraged to have more children while the genetically unfit should be compelled to have fewer. What is important to my line of analysis is both the potentials of new forms of eugenics and the prevailing image of eugenics that remains with us. The old eugenics, which focused on populations, was political and manifestly coercive; the new genetics focuses on individuals and emphasizes genetic counselling and individual choice, yet social anxieties over eugenic potentials still remain. Disability rights activists have been outspoken about the potential of eugenic outcomes as a result of prenatal screening for Down's syndrome, spina bifida, and other potentially disabling conditions. In the extreme, they fear genetic testing could lead to a disability genocide.

Genetics and behaviour in the news

Three examples of social problems where proposed genetic explanations have received significant press coverage [are] alcoholism, sexual orientation, and race and inequality.

Alcoholism

The idea that alcoholism may be hereditary is not new. Over the past two decades, scientists have reported twin and adoption studies that suggest a component of biological heredity, but the first actual genetic link was reported in April 1990 in the *Journal of the American Medical Association* (*JAMA*; Blum *et al.* 1990). The authors concluded they had found a marker for a specific gene at a specific location that 'confers susceptibility to at least one form of alcoholism' (p. 2055). The study was widely reported in the news. All five major newspapers in my study and all three newsmagazines reported it. The newspapers presented it as front page news or in a prominent location. Headlines announced 'Alcoholism is Linked to Gene' and 'Scientists Link Alcoholism to a Gene Defect'. *The New York Times*, among others, reported it as a major breakthrough. The newspaper stories were very positive and optimistic, citing the growing conviction of the importance of heredity in alcoholism and the potential emergence of new treatments.

Eight months later, *JAMA* published a study that essentially found no significant differences between alcoholics and controls (Bolos *et al.* 1990). The disconfirmation received much less attention from the press than the Blum *et al.* study. While several of the newspapers carried some notice of the disconfirmation, none of the newsmagazines did. The disconfirmation reports were considerably shorter than those for the original study and were located in less prominent places. Frequently the stories were written in a form that still affirmed a genetic basis for alcoholism.

This case is not unique; in recent years there have been reports of genes for manic-depression and schizophrenia that were disconfirmed. The pattern is similar; prominent, headline reports of the gene's discovery, and limited or nonexistent reporting of the disconfirmation. This amplifies the impression that genes for particular problems are being discovered, but is unlikely to correct that view when a disconfirmation occurs. [This] ultimately presents an over-optimistic view of the role of genetics in social problems and misinforms public knowledge.

Homosexuality and 'gay genes'

For at least a century, scientists and physicians have offered theories about the hereditary predisposition or congenital nature of homosexuality. [But] with the rise of the gay liberation movement, the demedicalization of homosexuality, and the emergence of open homosexual and lesbian 'lifestyles' there was little research and public discussion of the heritability of homosexuality in the 1970s and early 1980s. This all changed in the 1990s. Between 1991 and 1993, five studies that implicated genetics in the development of homosexuality were published in scientific journals (see Conrad and Davidson 1995). These studies were widely covered by the press, with many featured as page one stories. I want to focus on one story and its sequelae.

In July 1993, Dean Hamer, a neurogeneticist at the National Institutes of Health, published an article in *Science* reporting the discovery of a genetic marker associated with homosexuality (Hamer *et al.* 1993). Hamer's research was widely reported. It was on the front page of five of the six newspapers we studied. All three newsmagazines covered the story, including a nine-page cover story in *Newsweek*.

With the reports of Hamer's study, the press for the first time began occasionally using the term 'gay gene' to describe the findings (even though Hamer explicitly noted that it is unlikely a single gene is responsible for homosexuality); the text of most articles did not use the term. But within two years the term 'gay gene' had become much more common. When Hamer and a journalist co-authored a book about the research, the subtitle was *The Search for the Gay Gene and the Biology of Behavior* (Hamer and Copeland 1994). Clearly terms like 'gay gene' are catchy and adopted as journalists short cuts – easier than saying, more accurately, a marker for a gene associated with homosexuality. Neither Hamer nor any other researcher claims this or any other gene is likely to be *the* cause of homosexuality, yet calling it *the* gay gene suggests that it is the cause. Not all gay men have the [genetic] marker (probably most do not), so there are other causes, be they environmental, pyschological or other genes. Is it still 'the gay gene' if individuals who have it are not homosexual?

The lesbian and gay community is divided about whether finding genetic links to homosexuality is good, bad, or irrelevant. Some suggest that genetic linkage shows a homosexual orientation is 'natural' and implies that gays should not be blamed, stigmatized, or discriminated against for their genetic make-up. On the other hand, there are people in the gay community who are much less sanguine about a genetics of homosexuality. They are concerned about the slippery slope leading to a remedicalization of homosexuality, testing and aborting fetuses with the implicated genes, potential 'treatments' for the 'defect', and possibly even eugenic interventions.

As yet, 'the gay gene' is more a social construction than a biological reality. Nevertheless, its designation influences the public image of homosexuality, and may affect how we think about homosexual orientation and how we treat people who are gay.

Inequality, race and IQ

The publication of Arthur Jensen's (1969) article, 'How Much Can We Boost IQ and Scholastic Achievement?' in the *Harvard Educational Review* ignited a firestorm in the press over issues of intelligence, race and heredity. Arguing that intelligence was inherited and biological differences accounted for IQ differences between different 'racial' groups, Jensen proposed that compensatory and early childhood education had failed to boost achievement because intelligence was heritable and essentially immutable. The same year, physicist William Shockley received considerable media attention when he made public statements arguing that Blacks were intellectually inferior to Whites and proposed monetary incentives to those with low IQs to undergo sterilization. The American press widely covered what has been called the 'IQ Controversy'.

In 1994, [Harvard psychologist] Richard Herrnstein and political scientist Charles Murray published *The Bell Curve: Intelligence and Class Structure in American Life*. The authors asserted that differences in IQ among social classes and races are genetically based and that intelligence determines such attributes as income, employment, divorce, welfare dependency, and violence. As in 1969, the press responded to *The Bell Curve* with a barrage of feature stories, interviews, editorials, and opinion pieces.

Despite some subtle and interesting differences, the news responses in [the] two periods a quarter-century apart were remarkably similar. While the views of Jensen, Shockley, Herrnstein and Murray are given considerable attention, the press is consistently *critical* of claims regarding the hereditary basis of intelligence and IQ differences between racial groups, particularly in the avalanche of commentary pieces (Martin and Conrad 1995). This contrasts markedly to the fundamentally *supportive* tone the press has taken to research relating genetics to issues like homosexuality, alcoholism, mental illness and obesity.

It is possible that the extensive coverage of *The Bell Curve*, notwithstanding its critical tone, may have amplified the book's importance in the public eye and given unintended credence to the book's message. The media response to *The Bell Curve* thus had an irony to it. The media attention given to the critique of the book's race, genes and IQ analysis also served to disseminate the authors' ideas far beyond the book reading public. The critical vigilance of the news media may have inadvertently amplified the importance of the book and reinfused an updated version of the 'genetic inferiority' hypothesis into the culture.

Public eyes and private genes

Until recently, the genetic code was a secret locked in the twists of double helix deep in our cell structure. The genetic revolution is rapidly unearthing information about our DNA, raising concerns and alarms about privacy and individual rights. Genetic knowledge is becoming a public issue. The allure of simple, technical and inexpensive solutions to difficult social problems captivates politicians and the public. At the moment, the viability of the genetic paradigm is more troubling to me than its validity.

The new genetics is here to stay. Even if it does not lead to specific eugenic policies, it will have an enormous impact on how we think about disease and human problems in the foreseeable future. A danger looms that the seductions of the genetic paradigm could shape public conceptions in such ways that alternatives no longer seem viable. The news media will continue to showcase genetic research, amplifying the role of genetics in social problems. At the dawn of the age of genetics, we need [to] remain vigilant and resist those who would overemphasize the power of the genetic paradigm and the notions that the source of all social problems resides in the secrets of the DNA.

References

Alper J.S. and Beckwith J., 1993, Genetic fatalism and social policy: The implications of behavior genetics research, *Yale Journal of Biology and Medicine*, **66**: 511–524

Blum K., Noble E.P., Sheridan P.J., *et al.*, 1990, Allelic association of human Dopamine D2 receptor gene and alcoholism, *JAMA*, **263**: 2055–2060

Bolos A.M., Dean M., Lucas-Derse S., *et al.*, 1990, Population and pedigree studies reveal the lack of association between the Dopamine D2 receptor gene and alcoholism, *JAMA*, **264**: 3156–3160

Conrad P. and Davidson B., 1995, Genes and homosexuality: Contrasting images in the news. Paper presented at the meetings of the Society of Social Problems.

Gilbert W., 1992, A vision of the grail, pp. 83–97 in Kevles D and Hood L (eds), *The Code of Codes*, Cambridge: Harvard University Press

Hamer D., Hu S., Magnuson V.L., *et al.*, 1993, A linkage between DNA markers on the X chromosome and male sexual orientation, *Science*, **261**: 321–327

Hamer D. and Copeland P., 1994, *The Science of Sexual Desire: The Search for the Gay Gene and the Biology of Behavior*, New York: Simon and Schuster

Herrnstein R.J. and Murray C., 1994, *The Bell Curve: Intelligence and Class Structure in American Life*, New York: Free Press

Horgan J., 1993, Eugenics Revisited, *Scientific American*, **269** (June): 122–131

Jensen A., 1969 How much can we boost IQ and scholastic achievement? *Harvard Educational Review*, **39**: 1–123

Lippman A., 1992, Led (astray) by genetic maps: The cartography of the human genome and
   healthcare, *Social Science and Medicine*, **35**: 1469–1476
Martin N. and Conrad P., 1995, The IQ controversy revisited: Press coverage of IQ, race and
   behavioral genetics, 1969–95. Paper presented at meetings of the Society for the Study of
   Social Problems.
Nelkin D. and Lindee S.M., 1995, *The DNA Mystique: The Gene as a Cultural Icon*. New
   York: W.H. Freeman.

The edited extract reproduced here comes from the Presidential Address to the Society for the
Study of Social Problems, given on 16 August 1996, and subsequently published in revised form
in the journal *Social Problems*, 44(2): 139–55, May 1997. Peter Conrad is the Harry Coplan
Professor of Social Sciences and Chair of the Department of Sociology at Brandeis University,
Waltham, Massachusetts, USA.

Experiencing health, disease and health care

| INTRODUCTION

In the second part of the book we focus on the individual's experience of illness and health care. The mixed bag of prejudices and beliefs about the nature of illness that was revealed in Part 1 is shown, in many of the accounts in Part 2, to have profound effects on personal experience, over and above coping with physical manifestations of disease. Additionally, contacts with providers of health care often reveal considerable discrepancies between inner experience and professional views. This is illustrated most dramatically in the first of three articles about the experience of mental illness. Mary O'Hagan's 'Two accounts of mental distress' juxtaposes the diary she kept to record her time as a patient in a psychiatric ward with the notes written by the doctors and nurses who treated her. Looking back, she feels that it is hard to see how the two accounts can refer to the same person.

'Being there' reports on a 1998 survey by the Sainsbury Centre of the quality of life in acute psychiatric wards, in which the gap between the ideas of patients and staff about the patients' problems is further illustrated. While various problems were identified with life in such wards – boredom, occasional violent episodes, unmet social needs – it is also clear that wards can be places of 'asylum' for many, and that distressing symptoms do reduce during hospitalization. The third account, 'The insanity of place' by the sociologist Erving Goffman, stresses the impact of mental illness in families. As long as the sick person is recognizably 'themselves' – as is usually the case with a physical ailment – he or she can maintain their habitual place in the family. But the whole structure of the family may be threatened when one member becomes mentally disturbed, as 'the family is turned inside out'.

The impact of illness on families is demonstrated in a number of other articles in Part 2. Andrew Nocon and Tim Booth, in 'The social impact of childhood asthma', catalogue the multiple sources of anxiety for parents of an asthmatic child. Not only do they experience the worry of their child's episodic illness, but parents must also stay vigilant in the face of a world filled with potential triggers for an attack. From the child's point of view, this parental activity appears largely unnoticed, the illness itself seeming no more than an occasional inconvenience in an otherwise active life.

Parents' dilemmas over their children's health are also reflected in the next piece, by Ruth McGowan, 'Beyond disorder: one parent's reflection on genetic counselling'. McGowan records her personal concerns about the values that guide genetic counselling, which she feels focus excessively on technical issues, failing to address the ethical and emotional dimensions that can have a major impact on families going through the process of genetic testing and its aftermath.

'Coping with migraine' also raises the issue of childhood experience, and how parents' reactions to illness may affect how people cope later on. Through a comparison of their experiences of migraine, Sally Macintyre and David Oldman show two very different approaches. It is clear that Oldman's successful strategies for managing episodes were taught first to him by his mother, who herself had experience of the condition. Sally Macintyre, on the other hand, without such 'wise' advice, suffered considerable anxiety as a result.

Macintyre's experience of gathering often conflicting explanations from a variety of doctors is mirrored in the experiences of patients reported by Ursula M. Sharma in her study of 'Using alternative therapies'. Dissatisfied with the directive approach of orthodox doctors and fearful of the harmful effects of some medical therapies, people seek alternatives in the more democratic relationship offered by acupuncturists, chiropractors, homoeopaths and herbalists. Sharma's own view, that such alternatives address central problems in modern medicine, is clearly stated.

Jaber F. Gubrium's account of 'The social preservation of mind: the Alzheimer's disease experience' raises the intriguing, if also disturbing, possibility that 'illness experience' may sometimes only be knowable through the minds of others. This study of carers of people with Alzheimer's disease, a condition in which there is a 'demise of mind', shows in poignant detail how close family members (most often spouses) struggle to preserve a sense of the sufferer as a thinking, feeling subject. The accounts also remind us that an illness experience is not always confined to the sufferer alone, since 'second victims' may be family members who act as carers.

The next three articles illustrate the experience of people who are healthy, but are often treated as though they are diseased. Old age is not an illness, as we are forcefully reminded by Mrs Williams, a woman of 87 interviewed by Tony Parker. Mrs Williams isn't ill and she doesn't need much help, but she wishes the council would stop sending round 'Some bloody do-gooding cow' to see if she will accept meals on wheels or a card to display in the window to call for help. When she uses the card, no one sees it for three days. Mrs Williams' health problems (with vision and mobility) are clearly bound up with her shrinking social circle – a common experience of older people who live alone in a society where exclusion from participation in mainstream social life increases in old age.

Like old age, disability need not be seen as an illness, but it can also involve a sense of exclusion and stigma, as Jenny Morris's article, 'Pride against prejudice: "lives not worth living"' points out. A common media interpretation of the occasional expression of a wish to die by people with physical impairments is that this is an 'understandable' reaction to an 'intolerable' condition. Morris argues instead that such suicidal depression can be caused by the social rejection that denies disabled people the high level of support necessary to deliver a tolerable quality of life.

People who are infertile are often characterized as though they are suffering a sickness; in reality their physical impairment is only revealed if they attempt to procreate – they are otherwise healthy. In Naomi Pfeffer's article 'The stigma of infertility', it becomes clear that culturally sanctioned attitudes may profoundly affect the experience of childlessness. Pfeffer identifies medical interests in explaining why infertility is so often characterized as a desperate state requiring medical intervention.

Pfeffer's research involves a feminist analysis of medicine, and issues of gender are to the fore in Kathy Charmaz's account of 'Identity dilemmas of chronically ill men'. This study makes it clear that culturally inspired ideas about appropriate masculine behaviour are influential determinants of the experience of illness. Assumptions about male mastery and dominance become threatened if it becomes hard to do the ordinary things associated with 'being a man', and a variety of strategies to deal with these threats to masculine identity are adopted. Some men adopt aggressive stances towards their illness, others may, in public settings, cover up the restrictions it places on them. The stresses and strains that this can place on marriages are made clear.

Part 2 ends with two contrasting experiences of HIV infection and AIDS. In 'Costs of treating AIDS in Malawi and America', two people who are rather similar in so far as they are both middle class and educated men in their own countries, have very different experiences. Their stories demonstrate that cross-cultural variation in the experience of illness does not always have much to do with systems of belief, or generally held attitudes, but the brutal facts of economic life that determine the availability of treatment. Even as a successful Malawian businessman, Yasaya's prospects of paying an annual $10,000 for the drugs that may keep him alive are slim, as David Finkel describes. Conversely, Thomas Garrett's account of his life on combination anti-retroviral therapy in America shows the strain of sticking to a rigorous drug regime that for him, as for many others in the wealthier countries of the world, is life-preserving.

12 | Two accounts of mental distress

MARY O'HAGAN

This is a 'cut and paste' of excerpts from my journal and hospital file written during one of my episodes of mental distress. I wrote most of the journal entries during my last stay in hospital while I crouched in the safety of a locked toilet. With enormous effort I created coherent sequences of words out of the chaos inside me and recorded them in tiny faint handwriting. This was one of the most intense and profound experiences of my life – but down the other end of the long polished corridor, others recorded their own version of my distress in the course of a very ordinary day's work. My journal entries are in italics. The psychiatrist's and nursing notes are in plain text.

The accounts

Today I went to see a psychiatrist. He is a little man with a beard and glasses and he wrote his notes in small, tidy handwriting. He stared right through me. I kept thinking he could see into every corner of my mind. Every time I moved – the way I sat, where I put my hands – I thought would be used as evidence of my badly diseased mind. I was afraid he had the power to trick me into letting out my biggest secrets. I was too terrified to talk to him.

Mary is a 25 year old Caucasian university student who has a history of Manic Depressive Psychosis. Now appears to be entering a depressive phase. Withdrawn and quiet. Dresses unconventionally. Not an easy patient to relate to. She plays her cards very close to her chest.

I stand alone, unable to move inside a dark bubble. I have no face or hands or feet. My veins are broken and my blood has nowhere to travel. Outside the bubble it is day. A rainbow appears but I cannot see it. I remain in the bubble, broken and hidden from the life around me.

Mary has an inadequate and confused sense of identity. She also has a long-standing picture of being an isolate; tending to live in her own world and always finding it difficult to fit in. In this way she presents a schizoid personality picture.

Today I saw the psychiatrist again. I wanted to cry out and collapse against the wall to show him the pain I am in but I couldn't. I wanted him to show from the core of his being that he understood my pain but he didn't. Instead we had a rational discussion. I asked him:

(DIALOGUE STARTS)

What do you think is a well functioning human being?

Why do you ask that question? I think you're worried that I will judge you.

Yes, I am worried about that. I want to know if your ideas on human beings are compatible enough with mine for us to be able to talk about me. How do you ensure that your values don't impose on mine?

Let me assure you, it's not my job to judge you. I'm here to help you know yourself better.

But what if you judged me without knowing it?

That was below the belt. You need a high degree of control in your relationships don't you?

(DIALOGUE ENDS)

Then, somehow we got on to sex. The whole time he just kept gazing into me. I felt terribly uncomfortable and was trying desperately to hide it. The sex talk stripped me right back to the raw. Now all I want to do is shrink back into myself. He had all the power.

Requesting my views on life, sex, religion etc.

1. Why she needs to know my views? Feeling of powerlessness that she knows little about me and my beliefs. Theme of control in relationships and how vulnerable she feels when she cannot label people.
2. Problems with sex relationships – feels loss of control.
3. For further discussion – importance of her control issues.
4. Blood levels satisfactory.

Today I wanted to die. Everything was hurting. My body was screaming. I saw the doctor. I said nothing. Now I feel terrible. Nothing seems good and nothing good seems possible. I am stuck in this twilight mood where I go down like the setting sun into a lonely black hole where there is room for only one.

Flat, lacking motivation, sleep and appetite good. Discussed aetiology. Cont. Licarb. 250mg qid. Levels next time.

I am lying face down behind a chair in the waiting room of the hospital. I am full of red hot blame at myself for everything. I cannot bear being so thoroughly bad. I am carrying hell around inside of me.

On arriving on the ward – spent the entire day curled up on the waiting room floor behind a chair. Could not talk. Impression of over dramatization but with underlying gross psychological turmoil. She is difficult to engage and to that effect I have admitted her for a period of two weeks to consolidate her working relationship with us.

A nurse came to me and said 'Go to supper'. I said 'No'. She growled at me for not making an effort, but all my effort is going into making these thoughts and writing them down. The nurse punished me, saying, 'Well, I'm not bringing you any supper, you know'.

Sitting in ladies' lounge with her head in her hands. Very difficult to involve in conversation. Not responding to activity around her. Is attending the dining room with firm encouragement and eating small meals. Remains very withdrawn but occasionally gives vent to an incongruous sustained laugh – although says she isn't happy. Rx Chlorpromazine BD & Nocte as appears to be preoccupied with thoughts – hopefully medication will break the chain.

Last night they came to me with Chlorpromazine. I refused it. I am afraid medication will dull my mind and the meanings in there will escape forever.

Refusing medication. States she hasn't been taking it because it doesn't do her any good. Not persuaded by explanations or reassurance.

During the night between sleeps I felt bad. I was on the rack. Every thought set off a shrieking alarm in my head. My body would jerk and go rigid as if electric shocks went through me every few seconds. I nearly didn't make it through the night. I nearly asked for Chlorpromazine.

Awake at frequent intervals during the night. Found whimpering and thrashing around on her bed at 2.15 a.m. saying 'No, leave me alone.' Said she was frightened. Kept holding and massaging her head.

Every morning the night nurses pull off my blankets. They are rough. I can't fight back. Even their softest touches bruise me. A nurse said to me 'Face the world.' But I am facing the pain inside me. I cannot face both ways at once.

Mary is not to hide away in her bed. She is to be encouraged to get up for breakfast and engage in ward activities.

My back is hard like a shell. My front is soft like jelly. I hate to stand because I cannot shield my front from the jabbing gaze of the world. I must lie curled up or front down.

Lying in bed under blanket. Face covered by hands. Wouldn't leave bed to talk – 'not safe'. Brief whispered conversation from under her hands. Sleeps worse than usual – can't eat – too frightened – body aching all over.

Everything hurts. I am burning. All the life in me blazing out from the core of me is getting stuck. I can feel it trying to burn through my skin. I am almost on fire.

Experiencing frightening hallucinations, burning sensations, also brightly coloured shapes when eyes shut. Request Sunnyside notes of EEG. Repeat EEG to exclude Temporal Lobe Epilepsy.

I have lost my self. What is my name? I have no name. All I am is shape and weight, rapid shallow breathing and a black space inside my head.

Misinterpreting at times. Obsessed with the feeling of not wanting to be in her body – wanted to be a speck of dust. Also concerned as to her purpose of being alive. Describing feelings of 'emptiness'. Sleep poor, appetite poor.

My mind is a pile of broken up smudgy thoughts. I am searching for one that is clear enough to have meaning. But as soon as I find a thought it gets sucked into the blackness. Before, my thoughts were sliding off into nonsense. This terrified me so I tried to make some sense of things by taking bits out of nonsense and putting them into a story.

An old woman and her grand-daughter lived by a great ocean. Every day the old woman went fishing. She yelled in awe to the ocean 'Let me take the life out of you with my net.' She always returned with fish and cooked them for herself and her grand-daughter. One day she gave some of the fish to her grand-daughter and said 'Cook these for yourself.' The girl wailed 'I can't.' The old woman replied 'You must find your own power.' But the girl didn't understand and went to bed hungry. That night the girl woke from her dreams to a booming voice from the sky: 'You have the power of the old woman and the great ocean flowing into the core of you. Now, take meaning from the rawness of life and cook it for yourself without fear.'

Remains psychotically depressed. Reported hearing voices but no other bizarre symptoms noted. Thoughts still coming in 'fragments'. Unable to complete them. Still spending most of time on bed. On 150mg Doxepin nocte.

Sometimes a speck of light gets into my black hole. The speck is a thought that has come back into focus. I am coming up a bit but I feel all weak and wobbly from being on my bed for days. Before I looked up. This took courage. It was like coming out of a cocoon; the light was strong; it was strange. The next thing I did was walk around and say hello to people. It feels good to be halfway back and looking up.

Is beginning to interact. Says she is feeling much better. Asked permission to go out which was refused. Accepted this well. Enjoyed a game of Scrabble, giggling at times but this was mostly appropriate, e.g. at mildly humorous antics of other patients.

Mary is to be discharged. The family have intimated that they would be glad if I continued to manage Mary. I will be ready to step in if she has any further psychotic breaks and needs the control of this ward.

This slightly edited version comes from an article originally published in *Speaking our Minds: An Anthology* (The Open University and Macmillan Press 1996), edited by Jim Read and Jill Reynolds. Mary O'Hagan is a New Zealander who has been active in campaigning on behalf of users of mental health services in her own country and internationally.

13 | Being there

THE SAINSBURY CENTRE FOR MENTAL HEALTH

How successful are today's acute psychiatric wards at addressing people's needs? Success can be measured in various ways – in outcomes such as relief of symptoms, meeting social and psychological needs, or in process terms, i.e. what actually happens on wards such as time spent with staff, activities and medication. The study evaluated these different factors through weekly assessments of each of 215 patients alongside that of the primary nurse, and using medical notes, care plans and progress notes. The aim was to build up a comprehensive picture of the care provided on nine wards. The study also measured user satisfaction with the wards.

In general terms, most patients leave acute wards in a better condition, both subjectively and objectively, than when they came in. The average severity of user's symptoms (measured by the Brief Psychiatric Rating Scale) nearly halved from admission to discharge. The improvement was observed in users across all nine wards, and is statistically significant. It is not clear however, whether this is due to psychiatric crises being self-limiting or what, if any, attributes of acute care alleviate a psychiatric crisis.

Acute wards deal with many emergency psychiatric needs. However, since nearly half of the patients return in less than a year, it is likely that many of the problems apart from symptoms that may have contributed to breakdowns in the first place – such as housing, finance, social relations, daily occupation or stigma – are not being tackled satisfactorily. It is questionable whether staff on acute wards have the resources or skills to address these problems, or whether other agencies or support systems are being involved sufficiently to assist with these non-medical problems in an attempt to break the cycle of readmission. Expertise on these issues is concentrated in community teams, yet there is little evidence of their skills being deployed effectively during inpatient stays.

Patients' problems were assessed by asking both patients and nurses to complete a checklist of 22 possible areas of need at admission and discharge. These problems ranged from psychiatric symptoms to basic needs like accommodation and food. (See box 1.)

> **Box 1: Assessment of patients' needs (using the Camberwell Assessment of Need)**
>
> Basic needs: Accommodation, food, daytime activities
>
> Health needs: Physical health, psychotic symptoms, distress, drugs, alcohol, self-harm, risk to others
>
> Social needs: Company, relationships, sexual expression
>
> Functioning needs: Looking after home, self-care, child-care, basic education, money
>
> Service needs: Information, access to telephone, transport, benefits.

Both patients and nurses agreed on a similar total number of needs at admission – roughly an average of five per patient. There were, however, some disagreements between staff and patient perceptions. Patients and staff differed in their judgement about the profile of the patients' needs on admission and how well those needs had been met at discharge. Looking at the five different sub-groups, the patients rated their needs at admission as slightly higher than staff did in every area, except health, where the staff rated patients' needs higher than the patients themselves. Obviously there may be difficulties in these assessments. Nurses focus on psychiatric rather than social needs when admitting patients with acute mental health problems, and patients may find it difficult to assess their own mental health – or indeed any other – needs at this point in time dispassionately. However, if staff pay insufficient attention to social needs identified by patients, this could be perpetuating the revolving door pattern. This is highlighted by the fact that patients in socially deprived areas rated themselves as having more basic problems with areas such as accommodation and food, yet staff assessments showed no such relationship.

The divergence of views was also clear at discharge. Patients believed they had fewer total needs when they left than when they arrived. They saw an improvement in their needs across all areas, social and medical, although with only a minor reduction in basic and service needs. Staff, however, only regarded health needs as improved and believed patients' needs in all other areas had increased. Staff interviewed felt that patients' social and other non-medical problems had not been addressed by the end of their stay.

The reasons for these differences over time and between patients and staff are not clear. It may simply be that staff only become aware of a patient's wider needs as they get to know them better during their stay. On admission they may concentrate on psychiatric symptoms, and ignore social problems, which are not considered a priority at that time. For the patient, a respite from their social problems – the traditional role of 'asylum' – may temporarily diminish them. Success in treating a patient's acute symptoms may also raise the relative importance of their wider needs, especially with discharge approaching. The difference of perception may also highlight the lack of information communicated from community services to acute wards at the time patients are admitted. The strong implication is that communication with other services is essential and that community teams need to be involved in care planning at the earliest possible stage if discharge is to be timely and follow-up successful.

Patients appear to leave acute psychiatric wards feeling better than when they arrived. But what actually happens to them during their stay, and are the interventions responsible for the changes in medical, psychological and social profile? There is surprisingly little research to guide staff as to selecting the most effective interventions for this group of increasingly unwell and disturbed patients (Olfson *et al.*, 1993). Much emphasis is placed on the role of multi-professional teams in today's acute hospitals. Research in the U.S. has shown that multi-disciplinary treatment with clear aims, well defined roles for staff, and discharge plans leads to more effective care of mental health patients on acute wards (Hargreaves and Shumway, 1990). Other U.S. studies suggest the most effective acute wards provide high levels of staff and patient interaction (Ellsworth *et al.*, 1979; Collins *et al.*, 1985).

Our study found that the multi-disciplinary approach was absent for the majority of patients on acute psychiatric wards. Patients had remarkably few contacts with staff, apart from doctors and nurses. Obviously, when compared to nurses on the wards, social workers, occupational therapists and psychologists are fewer in number. They are not always available on a ward and, when they are available, their specialised skills are not necessarily used to their full potential. It seems fair to state that these professions could be more involved in therapy and care. Contacts with nursing staff were not included in the research, since they are around constantly, and specific interventions are difficult to distinguish from routine care. However, patients did identify lack of availability of nurses as one of the factors they would most like to change on the wards in the user satisfaction survey discussed later. We also know from other work that presence of staff on wards and the amount of direct patient contact is often low (MHAC, 1997). The implication is that although nurses are present within the overall care setting there is little in the way of specific therapeutic intervention.

All patients had contact with nurses and a psychiatrist during their episode of care, but interactions with other staff groups were very low. The majority of patients had at least one visit during their stay from a relative or friend. Only 11 per cent had no visits but those from more deprived areas had significantly fewer visitors, highlighting the social isolation in these inner-city areas.

An even stronger picture of the poverty of care emerges when frequency of contacts is considered. Patients' most frequent staff contacts if nursing involvement is excluded were with psychiatrists. During their average 38-day stay, patients averaged nearly 11 contacts with psychiatrists. But contact with all other staff – including those who work outside the hospital – averaged less than one per patient during their stay.

Psychiatric wards can be dull places, with little happening apart from ward rounds and meals. Organised activity is important, not only therapeutically or to maintain interest and engagement, but also because of research showing that activities which are disorganised and unpredictable lead to increased rates of violence on psychiatric wards (Katz and Kirkland, 1990). While most wards offered patients some creative activities, there were surprisingly few therapeutic interventions available and what was on offer varied widely between hospitals. A worryingly high proportion of patients in the study – a total of 40 per cent – passed their stay without taking part in any social or re-creational activity, while 30 per cent were not engaged in an activity of any form, whether therapeutic or recreational.

The low activity rate is not totally surprising, since therapeutic interventions, such as psychological therapies and social skills training, were rare or absent on the wards. Patients were more likely to be offered some form of social or recreational activity, although even this was hardly provided in abundance. Less than half of all patients took part in creative therapies such as art and craft groups, while a third joined in social activities such as playing games. However, there was little evidence of organisation around such activities. Nurses tended to set up recreational sessions when they could find the time and they were therefore often run on an ad hoc basis without any formal schedule. This led to patients spending much time in their bedrooms or watching television to pass the day. It was not clear whether activities were geared to the needs of individual patients or whether patients attending different sessions were those most likely to benefit. Boredom was obviously a major factor on the wards.

A variety of forms of medication are in use on acute psychiatric wards. Most patients received anti-psychotic medication. However, nearly a fifth of all patients in the study passed their stay with no medication whatsoever. Male patients were more than twice as likely to be treated without medication. Patients with shorter stays were also more likely to receive no medication.

The use of seclusion to manage patients with temporarily disturbed behaviour varied considerably. Five of the nine wards did not use seclusion at all, while nearly a fifth of patients in one suburban ward spent some time in a seclusion room. In total 11 patients – five per cent of the total – were secluded at some time during their stay. More than half of the patients were put under an increased level of observation during their stay, staff checking their movements at 15-minute intervals ('specialling'). More than a fifth spent at least one period under constant observation.

Violence and aggression is a source of concern to both staff and patients on acute psychiatric wards. Incidents involving violence are reported to be on the increase (Warren and Beadsmoore, 1997). The study uncovered a small, but serious, risk of violence to staff and patients on the acute wards. There were 18 incidents of violence which did not cause detectable injury (first degree) and a further ten incidents which caused minor injuries, such as cuts and bruises (second degree) during the study. There were also 69 incidents of non-physical aggression. There were no violent incidents causing major injury (third degree).

In total nine per cent of patients carried out assaults either on other patients or staff without causing injury. One in 20 patients (five per cent) carried out an assault causing minor injury. Although a relatively small percentage, this nevertheless represents a real risk to the safety of patients and staff and must heighten tension on wards. Nearly a third of all patients displayed some form of non-physical aggression which staff recorded during their stay.

There were 16 incidents where patients harmed themselves seriously enough to require medical attention during their stay. This involved eight per cent of patients – slightly more than the proportion causing injury to others – suggesting that patients are more likely to be a risk to themselves than to other people.

Real lives: the acute ward experience

David

David stayed 15 days on ward H. Staff defined his needs as medication and day-time activities. He identified no needs of his own. During this time he was observed every 15 minutes – according to ward policy. During his stay he was given major and minor tranquillisers. At first he was withdrawn but immediately prior to discharge exhibited few psychiatric symptoms. He saw a psychiatrist seven times in all and was assessed by an OT once during his final week. He had no other interventions.

Dorothy

After admission to ward C under Section 136 of the MHA [Mental Health Act], Dorothy was transferred onto a Section 2, which was lifted after six days. Staff identified help with basic daily living under social needs and it was agreed that this would be tackled by her case manager. She spent 31 days on the ward. After her second week she took leave to attend her college course and was frequently away from the ward. She saw a psychiatrist twice a week and her case manager once on the ward. She occasionally attended art therapy but only for short spells. Her drugs included depot medication and major tranquillisers taken orally, as well as drugs to control side effects.

Mohammed

Mohammed spent nine days on ward H before leaving when his Section 2 was lifted. After 17 days he was readmitted, again under Section 2, after being apprehended by police. He then stayed for a further 36 days. Staff identified several social needs. He had lost his job, was living with his parents, not claiming benefit and had inadequate day-time activity. On his first night he was secluded for violent behaviour and attempting to leave, when he was given a fast-acting injection of a major tranquilliser. He was then placed under constant observation for four days. He saw a psychiatrist ten times during this period. He was prescribed other major and minor tranquillisers along with drugs to control side effects. He attended some creative and recreational activities in the OT department. After readmission, for reinstatement of his medication, he was diagnosed as having a psychotic episode. He was given further doses of major tranquillisers and drugs for side effects and saw the psychiatrist on average twice a week. He attended no activities during this second stay. He absconded twice, once for ten minutes and later for more than eight hours. He appealed against his section under the MHA but this was rejected. However, when it lapsed he stayed on as a voluntary patient for a further 8 days.

Carol

Carol spent 149 days in hospital initially but 7 days after her first discharge she attempted to commit suicide and was readmitted to ward 1 under Section 3 of the MHA for a further 76 days. During the first part of Carol's admission, staff identified that she had housing problems and that she was in danger of losing her job. Her feelings of anxiety and guilt increased before reducing but no diagnosis was made at this time. She was prescribed anti-depressants. She spent more time on leave than on the ward, only attending for appointments with her psychiatrist. She was encouraged but failed to attend art therapy sessions. Staff considered she no longer needed to be on the ward but three months into her first stay she started being disruptive, returned to stay on the ward and disclosed childhood sexual abuse. She attended family therapy sessions. After being allowed home on leave again she was discharged for the first time. Carol was readmitted after 7 days when she tried to commit suicide. She was placed in seclusion because she was abusive, and tried to leave (she was detained under the Mental Health Act). At this time staff considered she no longer needed to be on the ward but could not be discharged except to supported accommodation. She was now diagnosed as having a schizophrenic episode.

References

Olfson, M., Glick, I. and Mechanic, D. (1993) Inpatient treatment of schizophrenia in general hospitals. *Hospital and Community Psychiatry*, **44** (1):40–44.

Hargreaves, W. and Shumway, M. (1990) Effectiveness of mental health services for the severely mentally ill. In Taube, C. *et al.*, *New Directions for Mental Health Services*, London: Hemisphere, 253–284.

Ellsworth, R. *et al.* (1979) Some characteristics of effective psychiatric treatment programmes. *Journal of Consulting and Clinical Psychology*, **47**, 799–817.

Collins, J. *et al.* (1985) Treatment characteristics of psychiatric programs that correlate with patient community adjustment. *Journal of Clinical Psychology*, **41**, 299–308.

Mental Health Act Commission and the Sainsbury Centre for Mental Health (1997) *The National Visit*. The Sainsbury Centre.

Katz, P. and Kirkland, F.R. (1990) Violence and structure on mental hospital wards. *Psychiatry*, **53** (3): 262–277.

Warren, J. and Beadsmoore, A. (1997) Preventing violence on mental health wards. *Nursing Times*, 8 August, 1997 (93), 34.

This article is an edited extract from Chapter 3 of the Sainsbury Centre's 1998 report, *Acute Problems: A Survey of the Quality of Care in Acute Psychiatric Wards*. The Sainsbury Centre is affiliated to King's College London. Its core aim is to improve the quality of life for people with severe mental health problems by enabling the development of excellent mental health services, which are valued by users, carers and professionals.

14 | The insanity of place

ERVING GOFFMAN

The interesting thing about medical symptoms is how utterly nice, how utterly plucky the patient can be in managing them. There may be physical acts of an ordinary kind he cannot perform; there may be various parts of the body he must keep bandaged and hidden from view; he may have to stay home from work for a spell or even spend time in a hospital bed. But for each of these deviations from normal social appearance and functioning, the patient will be able to furnish a compensating mode of address. He gives accounts, belittles his discomfort, and presents an apologetic air, as if to say that in spite of appearance he is, deep in his social soul, someone to be counted on to know his place, someone who appreciates what he ought to be as a normal person and who is this person in spirit, regardless of what has happened to his flesh. He is someone who does not will to be demanding and useless. Tuberculosis patients, formerly isolated in sanitaria, sent home progress notes that were fumigated but cheerful. Brave little troops of colostomites and ileostomites make their brief appearances disguised as nice clean people, while stoically concealing the hours of hellish toilet work required for each appearance in public as a normal person. We even have our Beckett player buried up to his head in an iron lung, unable to blow his own nose, who yet somehow expresses by means of his eyebrows that a full-fledged person is present who knows how to behave and would certainly behave that way were he physically able.

And more than an air is involved. Howsoever demanding the sick person's illness is, almost always there will be some consideration his keepers will *not* have to give. There will be some physical cooperation that can be counted on; there will be some task he can do to help out, often one that would not fall to his lot were he well. And this helpfulness can be *absolutely* counted on, just as though he were no less a responsible participant than anyone else. In the context, these little bits of substantive helpfulness take on a large symbolic function.

Now obviously, physically sick persons do not always keep a stiff upper lip (not even to mention appreciable ethnic differences in the management of the sick role); hypochondriasis is common, and control of others through illness is not uncommon.

But even in these cases I think close examination would find that the culprit tends to acknowledge proper sick-role etiquette. This may not only be a front, a gloss, a way of styling behaviour. But it says: 'Whatever my medical condition demands, the enduring me is to be dissociated from these needs, for I am someone who would make only modest reasonable claims and take a modest and standard role in the affairs of the group were I able.'

The family's treatment of the patient nicely supports this definition of the situation, as does the employer's. In effect they say that special licence can temporarily be accorded the sick person because, were he able to do anything about it, he would not make such demands. Since the patient's spirit and will and intentions are those of a loyal and seemly member, his old place should be kept waiting for him, for he will fill it well, as if nothing untoward has happened, as soon as his outer behaviour can again be dictated by, and be an expression of, the inner man. His increased demands are saved from expressing what they might because it is plain that he has 'good' reasons for making them, that is, reasons that nullify what these claims would otherwise be taken to mean. I do not say that the members of the family will be happy about their destiny. In the case of incurable disorders that are messy or severely incapacitating, the compensative work required by the well members may cost them the life chances their peers enjoy, blunt their personal careers, paint their lives with tragedy, and turn all their feelings to bitterness. But the fact that all of this hardship can be contained shows how clearly the way has been marked for the unfortunate family, a way that obliges them to close ranks and somehow make do as long as the illness lasts.

Now turn to symptoms of mental disorder as a form of social deviation. In our society, what is the nature of the social offence to which the frame of reference 'mental illness' is likely to be applied?

The offence is often one to which formal means of social control do not apply. The offender appears to make little effort to conceal his offence or ritually neutralize it. Mental symptoms are not, by and large, *incidentally* a social infraction. By and large they are specifically and pointedly offensive. As far as the patient's others are concerned, the troublesome acts do not merely happen to coincide partly with what is socially offensive, as is true of medical symptoms; rather these troublesome acts are perceived, at least initially, to be intrinsically a matter of wilful social deviation.

It is important now to emphasize that a social deviation can hardly be reckoned apart from the relationships and organizational memberships of the offender and offended, since there is hardly a social act that in itself is not appropriate or at least excusable in some social context. The delusions of a private can be the rights of a general; the obscene invitations of a man to a strange girl can be the spicy endearments of a husband to his wife; the wariness of a paranoid is the warranted practice of thousands of undercover agents.

Mental symptoms, then, are neither something in themselves nor whatever is so labelled; mental symptoms are acts by an individual which openly proclaim to others that he must have assumptions about himself which the relevant bit of social organization can neither allow him nor do much about.

It follows that if the patient persists in his symptomatic behavior, then he must create organizational havoc in the minds of members. This havoc indicates that medical symptoms and mental symptoms are radically different in their social consequences and in their character. It is this havoc that the philosophy of containment must deal with. It is this havoc that psychiatrists have dismally failed to examine and that sociologists ignore when they treat mental illness merely as a labelling process. It is this havoc that we must explore.

Mental hospitals can manage such diffusions and distortions of identity without too much difficulty. In these establishments much of the person's usual involvement in the undertakings of others and much of his ordinary capacity to make contact with the world are cut off. There is little he can set in motion. A patient who thinks he is a potentate does not worry attendants about their being his minions. That he is in dominion over them is never given any credence. They merely watch him and laugh, as if watching impromptu theatre. Similarly, when a mental hospital patient treats his wife as if she were a suspect stranger, she can deal with this impossible situation merely by adjusting downward the frequency and length of her visits. So, too, the office therapist can withstand the splotches of love and hate that the patient brings to a session, being supported in this disinvolvement by the wonderfully convenient doctrine that direct intercession for the patient, or talk that lasts more than fifty minutes, can only undermine the therapeutic relationship. In all of these cases, distance allows a coming to terms; the patient may express impossible assumptions about himself, but the hospital, the family, or the therapist need not become involved in them.

Matters are quite different, however, when the patient is outside the walls of the hospital or office – outside, where his others commit their persons into his keeping, where his actions make authorized claims and are not symptoms or skits or something disheartening that can be walked away from. Outside the barricades, dramatically wrong self-identification is not necessary in order to produce trouble. Every form of social organization in which the patient participates has its special set of offences perceivable as mental illness that can create organizational havoc.

The maintenance of the internal and external functioning of the family is so central that when family members think of the essential character, the perduring personality of any one of their numbers, it is usually his habitual pattern of support for family-organized activity and family relationships, his style of acceptance of his place in the family, that they have in mind. Any marked change in his pattern of support will tend to be perceived as a marked change in his character. The deepest nature of an individual is only skin-deep, the deepness of his others' skin.

In the case of withdrawals – depressions and regressions – it is chiefly the internal functioning of the family that suffers. The burden of enthusiasm and domestic work must now be carried by fewer numbers. Note that by artfully curtailing its social life, the family can conceal these disorders from the public at large and sustain conventional external functioning. Quiet alcoholism can similarly be contained, provided that economic resources are not jeopardized.

It is the manic disorders and the active phases of a paranoid kind that produce the real trouble. It is these patterns that constitute the insanity of place.

The beginnings are unclear and varied. In some cases something causes the prepatient – whether husband, wife, or child – to feel that the life his others have been allowing him is not sufficient, not right, and no longer tenable. He makes conventional demands for relief and change which are not granted, perhaps not even attended. Then, instead of falling back to the *status quo ante*, he begins his manic activity. As suggested, there are no doubt other etiologies and other precipitating sequences. But all end at the same point – the manic activity the family comes to be concerned with. We shall begin with this, although it is a late point from some perspectives.

The manic begins by promoting himself in the family hierarchy. He finds he no longer has the time to do his accustomed share of family chores. He increasingly orders other members around, displays anger and impatience, makes promises he feels he can break, encroaches on the equipment and space allocated to other members, only fitfully displays affection and respect, and finds he cannot bother adhering to the family schedule for meals, for going to bed and rising. He also becomes hypercritical and derogatory of family members. He moves backward to grandiose statements of the high rank and quality of his forebears, and forward to an exalted view of what he proposes soon to accomplish. He begins to sprinkle his speech with unassimilated technical vocabularies. He talks loudly and constantly, arrogating to himself the place at the centre of things this role assumes. The great events and personages of the day uncharacteristically evoke from him a considered and definitive opinion. He seizes on magazine articles, movies, and TV shows as containing important wisdom that everyone ought to hear about in detail right now.

In addition to these disturbances of rank, there are those related to the minor obligations which symbolize membership and relatedness. He alone ceases to exercise the easy care that keeps household equipment safe and keeps members safe from it. He alone becomes capricious in performing the little courtesy-favours that all grown members offer one another if only because of the minute cost of these services to the giver compared to their appreciable value to the recipient. And he voices groundless beliefs, sometimes in response to hallucinations, which imply to his kin that he has ceased to regulate his thought by the standards that form the common ground of all those to whom they are closely related.

The constant effort of the family to argue the patient out of his foolish notions, to disprove his allegations, to make him take a reasonable view – an argumentation so despaired of by some therapists – can similarly be understood as the family's needs and the family's effort to bring the patient back into appropriate relationship to them. They cannot let him have his wrong beliefs because they cannot let him go. Further, if he reverses his behaviour and becomes more collected, they must try to get him to admit that he has been ill, else his present saneness will raise doubts about the family's warrant for the way they have been treating him, doubts about their motivation and *their* relationship to him. For these reasons, admission of insanity has to whose terms activity ought to be organized, the family begins to turn outward, first to the patient's kinsmen, then to friends, to professionals, to employers. The family's purpose is not merely to obtain help in the secretive management of the patient, but also to get much needed affirmation of its view of events. There is a reversal of the family information rule. Acquaintances or other potential sources of aid who had once been personally distant from the family will now be drawn into the centre of things as part of a new solidarity of those who are helping to manage the patient, just as some of those who were once close may now be dropped because apparently they do not confirm the family's definition of the situation.

Finally, the family finds that in order to prevent others from giving weight to the initiatory activity of the patient, relatively distant persons must be let in on the family secret. There may even be necessity for recourse to the courts to block extravagances by conservator proceedings, to undo unsuitable marriages by annulments, and the like. The family will frankly allow indications that it can no longer handle its own problems, for the family cat must be belled. By that time the family members will have learned to live exposed. There will be less pride and less self-respect. They will be engaged in establishing that one of their members is mentally ill, and in whatever degree they succeed in this, they will be exposing themselves to the current conception that they constitute the kind of family which produces mental illness.

The family's conspiracy is benign, but this conspiracy breeds what others do. The patient finds himself in a world that has only the appearance of innocence, in which small signs can be found – and therefore sought out and wrongly imputed – showing that things are anything but what they seem. At home, when his glance suddenly shifts in a conversation, he may find naked evidence of collusive teamwork against him – teamwork unlike the kind which evaporates when a butt is let in on a good-natured joke that is being played at his expense. He rightly comes to feel that statements made to him are spoken so as to be monitored by the others present, ensuring that they will keep up with the managing of him, and that statements made to others in his presence are designed and delivered for his overhearing. He will find this communication arrangement very unsettling and come to feel that he is purposely being kept out of touch with what is happening.

In addition, the patient is likely to detect that he is being watched. He will sense that he is being treated as a child who can't be trusted around the house, but in this case one who cannot be trusted to be frankly shown that he is not trusted. If he lights a match or takes up a knife, he may find as he turns from these tasks that others present seem to have been watching him and now are trying to cover up their watchfulness.

In response to the response he is creating, the patient, too, will come to feel that life in the family has become deranged. He is likely to try to muster up some support for his own view of what his close ones are up to. And he is likely to have some success.

The result is two collusive factions, each enveloping the other in uncertainties, each drawing on a new and changing set of secret members. The household ceases to be a place where there is the easy fulfilment of a thousand mutually anticipated proper acts. It ceases to be a solid front organized by a stable set of persons against the world, entrenched and buffered by a stable set of friends and servers. The household becomes a no-man's land where changing factions are obliged to negotiate daily, their weapons being collusive communication and their armour selective inattention to the machinations of the other side – an inattention difficult to achieve, since each faction must devote itself to reading the other's furtive signs. The home, where wounds were meant to be licked, becomes precisely where they are inflicted. Boundaries are broken. The family is turned inside out.

Acknowledgement

I am much indebted to Edwin Lemert and Sheldon Messinger and to Helen and Stewart Parry for help in writing this paper.

Erving Goffman, late Professor of Sociology at the University of Pennsylvania, was author of *Asylums, Stigma* and *The Presentation of Self in Everyday Life*. This article consists of edited extracts from an article that originally appeared in *Psychiatry: Journal for the Study of Interpersonal Processes*, XXXII, No. 4 (November 1969).

15 | The social impact of childhood asthma

ANDREW NOCON AND TIM BOOTH

Asthma affects large numbers of people of all ages. One child in ten suffers from some form of asthma before the age of ten. In most cases, the asthma disappears before the child reaches adulthood but, for about one adult in twenty, it will reappear later in life.

A good deal of research has been, and continues to be, carried out on the causation and control of asthma. Less is known about the way that asthma affects sufferers' everyday lives. Nevertheless, asthma is responsible for time lost from school and from work, it can restrict sufferers' social lives and the lives of the people they live with, and it can affect sufferers' personal well-being and family relationships.

The focus of this report is on the social impact of asthma on sufferers and their families. It describes [part of] a research study carried out with asthma sufferers in Sheffield. [Interviews were conducted with the parents of 32 children, all but one of whom was under 10 years old, who had all been admitted to a Sheffield hospital in the previous year as a result of their asthma.]

Restrictions on general activities

While some respondents experienced difficulties at all times, others only had problems when their asthma was bad. For the children, walking uphill caused the greatest degree of difficulty, affecting 28 per cent of the children most of the time. Some types of sport caused some difficulty most of the time for six of the 14 school-age children, while a further two had difficulties when their asthma was worse: most of these children experienced some difficulty with running. In another case, a child was unable to do any horse-riding because of an allergy to horses. A total of nine (64 per cent) of the school-age children thus experienced some degree of difficulty with some sport because of their asthma. However, as will be seen below, none of the children were in fact prevented by their asthma from taking part in sports activities at school. Outside school, some children were not always able to keep up with their friends, and one boy in the cubs had to do some physical activities in stages rather than all at once. Another child sometimes developed asthma if she went on a jumping castle.

Smoke in the atmosphere could trigger asthma attacks in some children and therefore made it difficult (or indeed impossible) for them to visit some relatives or friends of the family or to use some public transport (though the latter restriction was now less frequent as no smoking areas were generally available). One four-year-old boy had to keep well away from bonfires (and had to stay in on bonfire night); he also had to avoid fireworks and the smoke from birthday cake candles. Four children had to avoid places where animals might trigger their asthma, one could not go to parks with flowers or into hothouses where there was dense greenery; another could not paddle or play in cold water. A two-year-old child with severe and easily triggered asthma was unable to attend a playgroup (because excitement set off her asthma), play outside in spring or autumn (when the weather could turn cold), and her parents had to ensure they brought her back home early in the evening if they went out (as she was otherwise liable to become tired and wheezy); her parents also adopted precautionary measures such as keeping her away from bonfires.

Household arrangements

[A] number of respondents [had] made practical changes around the home because of asthma. The most common change was the replacement of bedclothes, usually of feather pillows and duvets with synthetic ones. The parents of two children said that they adopted a generally more health-conscious approach to food because of their child's asthma; [the parents] of 22 per cent of the children avoided particular foods because they provoked allergic response.

Some respondents noted that, while they had been advised to make some changes in their living arrangements, they had not done so. Two respondents, for instance, had been advised to remove bedroom carpets in order to reduce the potential sources of asthma triggers but they had decided against this: the mother of a four-year-old girl said that she did not want the bedroom to seem 'clinical'. Another mother said she had been told to avoid a large number of potential triggers and her son's bedroom had been left very bare. This, though, had had little or no effect on his asthma: his bedroom had been gradually brought back to normal, with no harmful effects.

As with all potential triggers, the presence of pets could provoke asthma in some people but not in others. The parents of one young child had to get rid of some rabbits and a hamster almost as soon as they had bought them because they set off their son's asthma. Other parents, though, refused to give up a cat despite medical advice because they were certain that it was not a factor in their own child's asthma. Two respondents pointed out that it was not just a question of getting rid of any pets they might already have: their children wanted to have a pet and it hurt the parents not to allow them to have one.

In cases where a household member smoked, [less than a quarter of smokers gave] up smoking because it might make the asthma worse. However, many parents of asthma sufferers said that they did not smoke if their child was in the room. Others said that they would not allow visitors to smoke in the house.

Fifteen parents of children with asthma also said they did more housework because of their child's asthma. This typically involved additional cleaning and dusting.

School

Fourteen of the children attended school. Only three of them had not missed any time off school in the past year because of asthma; the average number of days missed from school because of asthma was 6.6. The reasons given by parents for keeping their children off school included bad wheezing, breathlessness and bad coughing.

Eight of the children had suffered from asthma while at school. However, none of the children suffered any restrictions in the classroom and all were able to take part in sports and PE. In only three instances did children sometimes have to finish early when taking part in sports or PE: the activities mentioned in this context were running and circuit training.

One child did not have any medication at school, six were responsible for their own medication, and in six other cases the medication was kept and supervised by school staff. Most parents said there were a number of other children with asthma at school and the staff were used to handling the medication. In one case, though, this issue caused a major problem. Staff at the school in question said they did not want the responsibility for handling or supervising medication; they added that they did not have enough staff to take this on anyway. The child's parents complained that the staff did not realise how important it was for him to take his medication regularly; one staff member had allegedly queried whether he even needed to take any drugs at all. Although this (five-year-old) child's medication was kept by a care assistant at the school, it was then up to the boy's seven-year-old brother to collect the medication each lunchtime and to give it to him.

The parents said that this was a very unsatisfactory state of affairs but they had been unable to find any other solution.

Asthma rarely affected children's relationships with others at school. One child had lost friends in the past because of his frequent admissions to hospital, but this was no longer a problem. Two others were unable to keep up with other children when they were running about. One parent said her son was picked on because of his asthma, though no specific examples were mentioned. With the one exception above, teachers were generally praised for being helpful and caring: only one teacher was said to be a little over-protective.

Practical effects on carers' lives

Two parents had been taking a lot of time off work [because of their child's asthma] and felt they could not keep up their jobs; one child's aunt had been looking after him during the day but then became afraid she would not know what to do if he had an attack; the father of another young child gave up a job that involved a lot of time away from home and took a less well-paid job in order to help his wife with the care of their daughter. Two mothers wanted to go back to work, now that their children had started school, but they had decided not to do so just yet: they felt there should be someone at home in case there was a problem at school or if their children had to come home during the day.

For over half of the parents, asthma meant that they themselves had occasional bad nights' sleep: most of them consequently felt exhausted the next day. Seven of the parents experienced such exhaustion at least once a week. The mother of a three-year-old child noted that 'the worst thing about the asthma is the sleepless nights': other parents similarly referred to feeling exhausted through lack of sleep.

Six parents said that the asthma sometimes stopped them from going out socially. For most people, this only happened infrequently.

For [some] respondents, taking time off work had resulted in a loss of income: this varied from an occasional day's earnings to a total loss of wages or salary where people had given up work completely. In addition, asthma had involved extra costs. These were sometimes one-off costs such as for non-allergenic bedding, more suitable curtains or floor-coverings, vaporisers and nebulisers. More regular costs included travel costs to hospital [and] extra heating.

Some respondents had received additional income because of the asthma, though the amounts were often small. One parent had previously received a weekly addition under the former Supplementary Benefit scheme, as well as a grant for a vacuum cleaner. Three parents had received small payments from a private health care scheme when their children were admitted to hospital. However, the parents of one child mentioned that they had been unable to obtain private health cover for their daughter.

Worry

The parents of four children said the asthma did not worry them at all. However, some of them pointed out that there had been times in the past, especially soon after onset, when it had caused them considerable worry; but they had now learned to live with it. The remaining respondents said that the asthma continued to cause them some degree of worry; the parents of two children [said] it was the cause of 'a lot' of worry. Respondents mentioned a large number of reasons for feeling worried. Many parents said they were aware that asthma can kill and had sometimes wondered whether their children would manage to recover from severe attacks.

Many parents said their main worry was whether their children would have further attacks, how serious those attacks would be, and whether appropriate help could be provided quickly enough. A quarter of the parents expressed serious worries about the future. Two parents were concerned how their children would manage once they started school. Five others were worried about possible long-term effects of the medication.

Effects on family life

The worry caused by a child's asthma frayed many parents' nerves; frequent attacks could lead to tiredness and to short tempers; family holidays were ruined; arguments erupted about appropriate levels of medication; parents disagreed about whether or not to take the child to hospital; and admissions to hospital added to the tensions already present. One mother said the family had to adjust its lifestyle around the asthma, and this caused problems. Other family members sometimes resented the attention the child received and, for one family, the asthma was a further cause of stress in an already tense atmosphere.

However, respondents also said that crises brought families closer together and everyone tried to help out more. One mother said that the asthma had given her family a sense of 'togetherness' and had made them aware of the importance of the family as a unit. Another explained how it made her appreciate her daughter more: it helped her to realise how precious the children were. Several parents found that talking and sharing offered them a means of coping with the worries caused by the asthma: they needed to keep each other going.

Twenty-six of the children with asthma had brothers or sisters. In 11 (42 per cent) of these families, parents stated that asthma did not have any effect on relationships between the children. None of the parents felt that any of their other children 'picked on' the child with asthma. However, three said that one or more of their other children were jealous of the attention given to the child with asthma. The brothers of a young boy objected to him being allowed to get away with misbehaviour without being punished. One young girl was said to be jealous of her brother being able to go to hospital; another child became particularly distressed when her mother stayed in hospital with her sister. The sisters of a young boy who was allergic to horses initially resented having to give up horse-riding: even a few horse-hairs on their clothing could trigger off severe asthma attacks. Additional problems could arise if children shared a bedroom: two parents mentioned that this led to their other child being woken up and not getting enough sleep.

However, in one of these instances a young girl's sister would make a point of listening out for signs of asthma and then calling her parents. In all, nine of the parents said their other children were very understanding towards their brother or sister's asthma. One boy tried to stop other children from making his sister run around too much. Another was said to 'torment her brother less' because of his asthma. Other children generally tried to help out.

Effects on children with asthma

Only one of the 16 children with an inhaler was embarrassed by using it. Indeed, using an inhaler was often seen by children as something special: something which children who did not have asthma often wanted to do as well!

Eighteen parents felt that asthma affected their children's behaviour in some way, mainly when they were unwell. At such times, several children were reported to become bad-tempered, though two became particularly quiet. One child was said to be very naughty when in hospital, another on coming home after a spell in hospital. The mother of a young boy admitted that she had molly-coddled him a little and that he now wanted his own way. Another mother said that her five-year-old son was allowed to get away with more than the other children because of his asthma.

However, only three children were said to try to 'use' the asthma to their own advantage. One breathed heavily in order not to have to go to school – though his parents said this did not work! The others feigned symptoms of asthma in order to get their own way, though in both cases the parents said this rarely happened now.

Emotional effect on parents

Three parents were angry that their children should suffer from asthma. Other parents referred to the disruption it had caused within their families, for instance when they had to return home early from holidays. One mother said she became angry if her child showed signs of a cold, especially if they were on holiday, as this could signal the onset of an attack. Another voiced her anger at the exhaustion she experienced when her child had bad asthma. One person said her son wanted constant attention when he had asthma: this prevented her from getting on with other work. One mother said she tried desperately to do everything she could to avoid her daughter having to go into hospital – and felt angry when she nonetheless had to be admitted.

Two parents said they felt guilty because they might themselves have contributed to their children's asthma. One said she had started smoking two months before her daughter was born; in the other case the child was born prematurely and was admitted to a special care unit. In neither case, though, had these factors been formally identified as causes of asthma. Two other parents felt guilty that they could not prevent their children from getting asthma. Another felt guilty when the family was on holiday and everyone except her daughter were enjoying themselves. Three parents mentioned the effect on their other children. One parent said he had felt guilty in the past that his Christian faith was not strong enough for his son's asthma to be healed.

The majority (29) of parents felt confident in handling their child's asthma. Three, though, said they sometimes felt unsure what to do for the best when their child had a bad attack. One of these felt unable to do much herself and tended to panic, as did one of the other parents. Another commented that only a doctor could really know what to do: she herself relied on guesswork. An issue mentioned by several parents concerned the difficulty they experienced in deciding whether or not to seek medical help. Many doctors had themselves suggested that parents should seek medical assistance if they were in any doubt. But although most parents preferred to err on the side of caution, they did not want to be criticised for wasting doctors' time.

Asthma often imposed a considerable emotional strain on families. One mother stated that 'last year was just a nightmare' and she felt she had simply been 'working on overdrive': she had seen a doctor herself because of the strain she was under. Another said 'you live your life perpetually tired' and 'you never have a rest from an asthmatic'. When the other children also fell ill, she felt she just could not cope. A third noted that 'anxiety gets the better of you'. She felt very frightened when her two-year-old daughter had attacks and she stated that asthma 'affects you in some way most of the time'. The strain caused by asthma compounded the problems of one child's parents and brought them close to splitting up.

When they were at their wits' end, parents wanted someone to talk to, someone who could sit and listen while they aired their grievances or anxieties. This should be a professional person: they felt that other parents, for all their understanding and helpfulness, might not preserve the same degree of confidentiality.

The physical dimension of asthma does not fully account for its overall social impact on the lives of sufferers and their families. It is only through taking full account of the various emotional and practical aspects that make up a person's life that the impact of a condition such as asthma can be comprehensively assessed.

This article is a heavily edited extract from a report, *The Social Impact of Asthma*, commissioned by the Sheffield Asthma Society; the research was carried out by Andrew Nocon and Tim Booth in the Department of Sociological Studies at the University of Sheffield, and published by the Department in 1990. The original report also covers the social impact of asthma on adult asthma patients.

16 | Beyond the disorder: one parent's reflection on genetic counselling

RUTH McGOWAN

'Mummy, if you're really special God picks you to have ALD!' my little boy said after I had just explained that some people are special and have to eat different food from others. Two of my three sons have adrenoleukodystrophy (ALD), an hereditary condition depicted in the 1992 film 'Lorenzo's Oil'.[1] We now take nothing for granted, such as the simple hopes that our sons will become teenagers or adult men.

Until the beginning of 1998, our lives had been blissfully ignorant of the genetic time bomb I am carrying but now we live in the shadow of never quite knowing when it may go off. There had been no previous diagnosis of ALD within my immediate or extended family. It is X-linked, can affect the central nervous system white matter and adrenal cortex, and is associated with the build up of very-long-chain fatty acids due to the impaired ability to degrade these substances.[2] So far my sons remain neurologically normal, although it seems that about one third of boys with the gene will die as a result of progressive neurological damage before they are teenagers.

Finding out

December 1997, my five-year-old son was diagnosed with Addison's disease, which finally explained why in the previous 12 months he had suffered from severe gastro-enteritis, requiring three hospital admissions. After this initial diagnosis my husband and I were adjusting to the fact that our son would be on steroid-replacement medication for life when we were also advised that an appointment had been arranged for us to see the genetic counselling unit; an off-hand remark that filled me with foreboding. Following the shattering news that our eldest son had ALD our adjustment began to the possible impacts of this condition on my family. It was three more weeks before we were scheduled to see the genetic counselling service. Three long weeks of hell, waiting to find out the terms of our sentence and wondering if either of my two younger sons carried the gene for ALD, barely sleeping or eating and fearful whenever one of my children tumbled in the yard – was the fall because of normal childhood clumsiness or 'it'? The fear and grief was at times overwhelming.

Experiences of genetic counselling

Reflecting on my experiences as a client of genetic counselling I found that the service could be more aptly named a genetic *information* service rather than genetic *counselling*, which tends to have connotations of compassion in today's therapy-focused world. The counselling aspects of dealing with the grief, anger and how to cope were second-ary to the emphasis on the information, which covered genetic theory on X-linked inheritance, prenatal testing for termination of an affected fetus and who in my family would be at risk. Genetic counselling was useful in that I found out more about ALD and had some of my questions answered. However, I was left to cope with other issues resulting from this knowledge with little warning of what to expect, and little assistance and advice. Complex issues were either not discussed or sidelined, in a service that seemed to value choice as the guiding principle to the exclusion of a frank discussion of the possible consequences of this right.

The value of choice inherent in prenatal screening is good for some and indeed welcomed but this key aspect of genetic counselling was not immediately going to make my life any easier and as a mother this choice challenges the loyalty I feel towards my sons. I do not plan to become pregnant again as I cannot imagine taking the path offered by prenatal screening. I would find it extremely difficult to terminate an ALD-affected pregnancy and to separate that decision from my love for my sons with ALD. After listening to a genetic counsellor explain prenatal screening, I also think only a very brave parent would knowingly choose to bring a child with a flawed gene into the world.

Family reactions

As the bearer of bad news the onus was on me to inform others who might be affected. It would have helped if the genetic counsellor had given me an authoritative letter to give to people about ALD, which included details on how to contact a local genetic counsellor. Some of my siblings and relatives wanted to know immediately if they could get tested for ALD and asked me about carrier testing and options for prenatal screening.

While acknowledging that my female relations have a right to access technology in order to make an informed choice, it was upsetting to be in the position of having to explain that they could choose to terminate an ALD-affected pregnancy. I answered their questions by explaining what I had heard from the genetic counsellor about prenatal testing options, but all I could think of was 'they want to know how to stop babies like my sons from being born'. When I raised my ambivalence about a possible consequence of choice and the link to what it says about my sons, the genetic counsellor suggested I must 'learn to separate the issues'. It is extremely difficult for me to learn how to do this, and I would have liked the genetic counsellor to have acknowledged this dilemma, and to have taught some skills to deal with it.

The diagnosis of an inherited condition can drop a bombshell into family relation-ships. Some of my siblings have chosen not to be tested to determine their carrier status. This reaction must be common in the experiences of genetic counsellors. I am worried for my sisters who remain untested and their young children but I am unsure how to approach this sensitive issue with them.

Personal reactions

My own status as a carrier who could possibly suffer health problems from ALD, was not addressed by the genetic counsellor. Although the risk of the carrier of the ALD gene suffering some neurological involvement is low, it can impact later in life. In fact, I have met two women carriers who are confined to wheel-chairs and another who has constant pain in her legs and back. Perhaps this risk was unknown or was seen as too low to address, or maybe it was avoided because the priorities of genetic counselling lie with prevention?

As a carrier I feel some guilt for having passed on this condition to my sons. I fear having to nurse my sons through slow, painful deaths from something I gave them, albeit unintentionally. This fear is leading me to try and do everything I can for them – within limits. Bone-marrow transplants are a risky but possible therapy option for my sons if they became symptomatic. Both my affected sons have identical bone-marrow types but there is no other match within the family, reducing the odds of a successful transplant. People have asked me if I would consider having in vitro fertilisation (IVF) and selecting a female embryo, with the chance of finding a bone-marrow match for my sons. At this stage, my husband and I have rejected such options as we feel it is not right for us to have a child for such reasons. I hope I won't regret this decision but I really believe that people should be valued for more than just their genes.

Genetic counselling: what kind of service?

As a client of genetic counselling I found the emphasis was more on what was wrong within a family (the heritable gene) rather than on what is right (my parenting skills). Perhaps this is understandable, but this negative focus fuelled my fear as I tried to survive those months following the diagnosis.

One of the questions we were asked in our first genetic counselling session was about the type of contraception we were using. This is not just an issue of semantics: the way such a question is asked typifies the paradigm of genetic counselling which seems to emphasis prevention (the genetics) rather than the compassionate (counselling) aspects.

I felt that some of the language used by health care professionals objectified my sons by classifying them as unfortunate case studies or freaks, instead of real people. This feeling was exacerbated by the terminology used to describe ALD, which does not recognise that there is so much more order than disorder in my son's lives. I would like the health care professionals I deal with also to have hope for my sons as that is an important basis for a trusting relationship.

Genetic counselling provided me with information that was interesting and useful but it could have done more. As a trained scientist I know how easy it is to define information in terms of the technical language of research results, analysis and probabilities but the values and objectivity of science are of little use to me in facing the ethical issues raised by the diagnosis of my sons and the implications for family relationships. The challenge for genetic counsellors is to focus beyond the science to provide a service which acknowledges and responds to the ethical dilemmas raised and takes on the responsibility of working with the client in dealing with the consequences of this information. My sons are special people and it is love not science that puts meaning in our lives.

References

1. *Lorenzo's Oil*, a film directed by George Miller, starring Nick Nolte and Susan Sarandon, 1992, and made at Universal City Studios.
2. Moser H.W. Adrenoleukodystrophy: phenotype, genetics, pathogenesis and therapy. *Brain* 1997 **120**: 1485–1508.

Ruth McGowan is an agricultural scientist living in Melbourne, Australia, with her husband and three sons, two of whom have adrenoleukodystrophy (ALD). This edited extract comes from a much longer article with the same title, previously published in the *Journal of Medical Ethics*, 1999, 25: 195–9.

17 | Coping with migraine

SALLY MACINTYRE AND DAVID OLDMAN

The main emphasis in the following accounts is on the acquisition of our knowledge of migraine. In these two accounts we introduce the idea of knowledge as developing in a series of discrete *stages* concerned with experiencing the complaint, identifying it as migraine, and finally acquiring a repertoire of methods for coping with it. All migraine sufferers pass in turn through these stages. The forms of the repertoire of coping may change over time through a series of *phases*, each phase characterised by an emphasis on one or another cell in a typology of treatments. Shifts between these phases do not have any necessary sequence.

Sally Macintyre's account

The first stage of my career as a migraine sufferer we characterise as being an anomic stage. My first migraine attack, which I distinctly remember, occurred when I was twelve. During the following five years I had further attacks ranging in frequency from every six weeks to six months. I was unable to name, predict or account for these experiences, and did not possess the appropriate vocabulary with which to describe them to others. I did not know what these attacks were or what they implied. Was I 'just tired', developing a serious illness, about to have a stroke, epileptic, or mad? I had no means of predicting attacks and I had no means of establishing how best to cope with them when they happened. They were thus inexplicable, unpredictable, not amenable to rational means of coping, and apparently alien to everyone else's experience.

The second stage was an identificatory stage, occurring when I was seventeen and lasting for several months. The trigger for this stage was my collapsing in public during an attack. Having been trying for five years unsuccessfully to explain to others that I had 'funny turns', this public manifestation forced a recognition of this account and the process of diagnosis was set in motion. After a number of diagnostic tests arranged by my GP I was admitted to a hospital in London for investigation. The whole of this identificatory stage was characterised by negative diagnosis, i.e. identifying and eliminating what I had *not* got. Thus, the tests I underwent were designed to examine the possibilities of a brain tumour (skull X-rays, angiogram, radioactive tracing tests), epilepsy (EEGs) and other CNS disorders (reflex tests, lumbar puncture). I was finally told, 'Well, you'll be relieved to hear that you haven't got a brain tumour after all – it's only migraine.'

Immediately after the diagnosis my emphasis was on the physicalist/ameliorative aspect of migraine. I accepted myself, and was so accepted by others, as a basically normal person who periodically experienced transient physical disturbances. These disturbances were regarded as being separable from me as a social being with a particular biography, personality and social environment: I was merely a host for occasional physical disturbances. The propensity to attacks was regarded as a morally neutral matter, a definition which I suspect was enhanced by the fact that the diagnosis was conducted through the high technology and high prestige of a neurological department, rather than, for example, a psychiatric department. Coping consisted of handling the attacks, once they occurred, with Cafergot-Q, and learning how to recognise the onset of an attack and how to judge the most efficacious dosage. My knowledge about these techniques derived only secondarily from my GP, mainly stemming from personal experience and trial and error.

On arrival at university my attention shifted to the 'personal/social' and 'preventive' cell. The student health service doctors were oriented towards patients as 'social beings in their total environment'. Rather than providing repeat prescriptions of Cafergot-Q, these doctors recommended recognition and avoidance of stressful situations, a reduction in ambition and competitiveness, and mild sedation at the onset of an attack. The prevailing etiological theory was that migraine was typical of over-conscientious, neurotic and intelligent women; role conflicts (e.g. degree versus marriage); and stressful life events (exams). I was redefined from a blameless, passive host to an active producer of migraines. I learnt and developed strategies for coping with the problem of being a 'migrainous person', mainly by stressing the assumed flattering correlations (conscientious, intelligent, sensitive), avoiding situations in which an attack would be disruptive, and exploiting the definition of myself as neurotic.

This phase of regarding migraine as a personal attribute reached a crisis when I moved to another university for a year and registered with the student health service there. My new GP believed that migraine was the result of deep-seated personality conflicts. When I declined to enter a course of psychoanalysis he refused to provide any further advice or chemotherapy. He variously informed me that my migraine resulted from my not having a boyfriend, sublimating my desire for children for postgraduate studies, and having over-strong internalised guilt and achievement-strivings. When I became depressed lest all these analyses were true, the migraine was attributed to depressive tendencies. These theories were to me highly unwelcome and on one level I rejected them. On another level I suspected that they might be true.

During this time I experienced an attack while on the top of a London bus, and found the experience of social and mental incompetence in such a situation to be deeply disturbing. I developed a fear of having an attack, which after a few months developed into acute anxiety states about travelling by public transport, eating in restaurants, attending seminars and other public meetings. My GP felt that my agoraphobia confirmed his previous character analysis of me, and attempted to refer me to another psychiatrist. When I was unable to keep the appointment, my plea that agoraphobia had prevented me from travelling across London was rejected as a rationalisation.

An acquaintance commented on my rather sorry state at this time, and when I explained the situation arranged for me to see her GP husband. He prescribed Valium. I began to conquer the phobias, started to eat properly again, found the frequency and severity of migraine attacks reduced, and ceased feeling panicky about the possibility of having attacks. I sought out information about the physical correlates of attacks, learned to stop eating certain foods, and wore dark glasses in bright sunlight. Over exams the GP put me on the Pill, which I found made a great improvement in the attacks previously correlated with the two days before a period. I thus moved out of the 'personal/social' phase back into a 'physicalist' phase, but this time one with the main focus on prevention. Having obtained what to me was satisfactory evidence that physical prophylaxis 'worked', I totally rejected the psychoanalytic interpretations of my previous GP, which I had in any case found injurious to my self-image.

When I moved to another part of the country I registered with a group practice and discovered that the practitioners espoused widely differing theories about migraine and its proper treatment. While registered with one doctor I continued regularly to consume Valium with his approval. He was interested in migraine, would discuss various new theories about it and tried out some of the new prophylactic drugs on me. When he left and I applied to another doctor for a repeat prescription I was scolded for taking dihydroergotamine and was refused further prescriptions. The next doctor spent six months weaning me off Valium; the fourth partner in the practice said that he himself was a sufferer, and found that Valium was the best way of managing it.

I registered with a new practice, and informed the new GP of the regimen I preferred. I now regard myself as an 'expert' patient, knowing exactly what I want and using the GP partly as a resource to supply me with those drugs that I want, but which are on prescription.

David Oldman's account

The first significant point about my own career as a migraine sufferer is that I cannot remember my first attack. Fairly regular attacks began somewhere around the age of nine, but the anomic and identificatory stages took up no more than an hour or two of my life. My mother had experienced frequent attacks during childhood and adolescence and was presumably able to normalise my first encounter with the complaint. I have a dim recollection of my mother prescribing by her actions what became for me the standard organisation of an attack – bed, a darkened room, hot-water bottle, bowl within easy reach for the attacks of vomiting, and Lucozade as the only liquid I could tolerate. So, from the start I not only had the complaint identified, but was also given the elements of a therapeutic routine which changed little for twenty years.

The imposition of identification and routine has not necessarily been as helpful as one might expect. If it is done early in life it may prove very hard to alter, and may take on a ritualistic quality which may even hamper the possibilities of more effective prevention and relief. I sweated my way through every attack in childhood surrounded by at least two hot-water bottles and never quite managed to convince myself that I suffered less when chilled – a 'fact' to which I now subscribe. More seriously, on four occasions in thirty years of attacks I have been caught in situations in which it was impossible to withdraw from ongoing social routines. In three cases I was able to get by, with much distress but not necessarily any more than I would normally have felt in the comfort of my own bed. Indeed, on the two occasions when I started an attack on top of a Scottish mountain, the effort of walking at least six miles to safety distracted me from the pain. Occasionally I have wondered whether withdrawal during an attack is either necessary or beneficial.

The very imposition of routine during my school years contained the seeds of liberation. My attacks were then almost invariably associated with the relief of tension *after* two classes of event – exams and rugby matches. The frequency and unpredictability of rugby matches made them loom largest in the production of migraine. I suddenly found myself in a position of control, for when I left school I stopped playing rugby and reduced my migraines to two attacks in five years!

Over the past thirteen years, during which period I have been regularly employed, residentially stable and suitably married, my relationship with the medical profession has been one in which I am invited to speculate on the causes and consequences of migraine as a 'normal' member of society – indeed, one of rather high status. Provided that I remain within the boundaries of legitimate migraine pharmacology I can discuss the effects of drugs and even request some rather than others. My current diet of dihydroergotamine and Migril resulted from an egalitarian discussion with my GP. The fact that I top this up with Stemetil and Valium for an actual attack is unknown to him, and is only possible by 'borrowing' these drugs from friends and relatives.

These ways of coping are not merely the result of achieving a 'normal' social status in the lay sociology of the GP, but are also a result of a definite attempt on my own part to 'medicalise' migraine given that, over the last thirteen years, I have lost the power to correlate my attacks with features of my own life style. I get about three attacks a year and if they correlate with anything at all, it is with quite major events such as moving house or changing jobs – not aspects of one's life that can be stepped around. I now have no way of avoiding migraine – I can only treat the attacks.

So far, then, my career as a migraine sufferer has been a prolonged attempt to find improved physical methods of preventing, and particularly treating, attacks. My 'way of life' has never seemed amenable to change in ways that would affect my migraines. As a child I had no power over my social routines; as an adult my routines have been regarded as too desirable to warrant change. The only development in my methods has been an increasing awareness that I could dictate the physical treatments and, at the same time, an increasing divergence from accepted and acceptable pharmacology.

Discussion – the development of personal theories of migraine

The most striking difference between our two accounts is the different length of time it took us to pass through the anomic and identificatory stages – 5½ years compared with at most a few hours. We attribute this to the respective absence and presence of fellow-sufferers or 'wise' persons in our immediate social environments. We suggest that it is not surprising that migraine 'runs in families', if the quickest identifier is a fellow-sufferer. Subsequent to her own diagnosis, Macintyre 'identified' classical migraine in her brother and sister.

When fellow-sufferers are available as identifiers, symptoms may rapidly be interpreted and named as being migraine, and we suggest that the learning process may be a didactic one of imparting received wisdom both about etiology and coping. In the absence of a pool of fellow-sufferers such symptoms may have to be interpreted by the medical profession. Such medical identification may rely more on the negative diagnosis described above – the successive elimination of alternative and more serious diagnoses – and may present the sufferer with fewer practical recipes for coping. Given this lack of practical advice or the outlining of etiological theories, the sufferer may then more actively search for knowledge from which to construct useful theories, and his knowledge may differ from that of a sufferer socialised by fellow-sufferers.

Another consequence of our differing experiences of identifying migraine is that it appears that Macintyre found the 'anomic' stage deeply disturbing and that this has left a greater residue of anxiety about the topic than that experienced by Oldman, with his relatively unproblematic and matter-of-fact introduction to migraine, mediated by 'wise' family members.

In general, Macintyre's experience more closely approximates the models of illness behaviour posited by medical sociologists than does Oldman's – an initial period of disorganised symptomatology, a 'trigger' for seeking medical help, diagnosis and treatment offered by the medical profession, and reappraisal of doctors' actions.[1,2,3,] We suspect that it is Macintyre's experience which is atypical, and that the experience of illness behaviour, diagnosis and coping, without contact with the medical profession, is a more ubiquitous and frequent phenomenon than is often implied in the medical sociological literature.

References

1. Rosenstock, I.M. 'Why people use health services', *Milbank Memorial Fund Quarterly*, Vol. LXIV, No. 3, Part 2 (1966).
2. Mechanic, D. *Medical Sociology: A Selective View*, Free Press, New York (1968).
3. Stimson, G. and Webb, B. *Going to See the Doctor: The Consultation Process in General Practice*, Routledge and Kegan Paul, London (1975).

Professor Sally Macintyre is Director of the MRC Social and Public Health Sciences Unit at Glasgow University. At the time of writing this article, David Oldman was a medical sociologist at Aberdeen University. This is an edited extract from a chapter with the same title which originally appeared in the book *Medical Encounters*, edited by A. Davis and G. Horobin and published by Croom Helm, London (1977).

18 | Using alternative therapies: marginal medicine and central concerns

URSULA M. SHARMA

Who uses alternative medicine? A hypothesis which seems to have informed some research, either explicitly or implicitly, is the idea that users of alternative medicine are possibly marginal *people* as well as users of marginal *medicine*.

The study which I undertook in 1986 was not designed to compare users of alternative medicine with non-users, but to discover the routes by which patients came to use it. I interviewed thirty people in the Stoke-on-Trent area who had used at least one form of alternative medicine in the past twelve months. The sample was largely obtained by inviting readers of the local newspaper to volunteer their experiences of alternative medicine. We cannot draw any conclusions about the representativeness of such a self-selected sample in terms of demographic or socio-economic characteristics, but this was not the purpose of the research.

The interviews were structured to the extent that they covered some standard questions and elicited a corpus of comparable data, but as far as possible I encouraged respondents to deliver this information in the context of their own 'story' of how they had come to use alternative medicine. This left them free to include in their accounts much that I would not have elicited through standardized questions in a set order. For most of the respondents the 'story of how they had come to use alternative medicine' was a narrative with a point, even a moral, which they wished to convey. In many cases the interviewee was describing a process which was by no means complete.

Using alternative medicine is therefore part of a *process*. While some interviewees could pinpoint predisposing factors in their family background (e.g. usage of herbal medicine by parents, horrific experiences of orthodox medical treatment by a close relative) most took as their starting point their own experience of some chronic disorder and their own subsequent dissatisfaction with the treatment they received for this under the NHS. All had consulted their GP about this illness in the first place and several had seen specialists in connection with diagnosis or treatment. I did not encounter any who had used alternative medicine because they had been brought up to do so, because it was the norm in their ethnic/religious group or for other 'cultural' reasons, apart from one woman whose parents had been ardent adherents of naturopathy, though a larger sample might well identify cases of this kind of usage.

It is important to discuss users' sources of dissatisfaction with orthodox medicine at some length because many of them do not relate straightforwardly to conventional medicine's failure to 'cure' disease so much as to its failure to 'cure' disease on terms that are acceptable to the particular patient. Two individuals did report a conflictual relationship with their GP, but in most cases dissatisfaction was not focused on the perceived incompetence of individual doctors or consultants. The problems with orthodox medicine as offered under the NHS which interviewees mentioned could be grouped as follows.

The claim that conventional medicine fails to get at the 'root cause' of chronic illness or fails to take a preventative approach, and can therefore only treat the symptoms. For example, a young man suffering from chronic depression had been referred to a psychiatrist and had received anti-depressant drugs which had some temporary effect. But he felt that the basic cause of his state had not been discovered and that therefore he would continue to be liable to periods of depression, a prospect which he did not wish to accept. The experience of acupuncture described by friends who had used it suggested to him that this therapy might effect a long term change in his condition. When he had tried acupuncture it so fascinated him that he decided to train as an acupuncturist himself, and whilst his depression has not entirely ceased to be a problem, the periods of disability are shorter and less frequent.

This is not to say that patients always required a detailed diagnosis or a technical description of what the healer saw as the problem; patients varied very much as to the degree of interest they took in the actual rationale or theory of the forms of healing used. What was more often reported was relief that their dissatisfaction with sympto-matic 'cures' had been acknowledged as legitimate and reasonable, and an appreciative sense that the healer was tackling the problem at a more fundamental level than conventional doctors had managed to do.

The fear of drugs which might become habit forming, or the dislike of side effects of particular drugs. Sometimes this took a rather diffuse concern about drugs that are too 'strong' – an imprecise fear of the body being interfered with too drastically. Sometimes there was general anxiety that prolonged or frequent use of drugs would interfere with the body's ability to react to drugs in acute situations, especially with regard to the use of antibiotics for childhood ailments. In other cases the dissatisfaction was based on a very specific experience. For instance, one interviewee's consultant had prescribed drugs for high blood pressure which, she said, made her feel exhausted and weak, 'like an old woman'. When she discovered a herbalist who could treat her she was relieved to be offered medicine which, she said, controlled her condition with no side effects whatsoever. The same interviewee expressed concern over the state of health of her sister who suffered from arthritis and who, she said, had been given ever stronger drugs to control the condition without any real improvement.

Fear or dislike of forms of treatment which are seen as too radical or invasive. A middle-aged woman who suffered from back pain had been offered surgery under the NHS without, however, any guarantee that her condition would be cured. Indeed, she had been told that there was a slight risk that it might become worse. A major operation which did not have any certain outcome seemed to her too drastic a step to take and the risk of a deterioration dismayed her as her work required her to move and lift inmates in an old people's home. She visited a chiropractor at the suggestion of a colleague of her husband and after a fairly lengthy (and at first painful) course of treatment reported an almost complete recovery.

The perceived inability of conventional medicine to cope with the social and experiential aspects of illness. There is now more awareness of the need for personal support in severe or terminal illness, yet even apparently trivial conditions like eczema pose a need for personal support when they are chronic (as patients' self-help groups recognize). The sufferer needs to feel that the healer (of whatever kind) appreciates and does not dismiss the forms of distress or inconvenience which the illness causes. Some interviewees emphasized a desire for practical advice in the day-to-day management of their illness (useful adjustments to diet, suggestions for patterns of rest and exercise, stress management techniques etc.). It is not by any means the case that all conventional doctors are unable to offer this personal interest and support, nor is it the case that all sufferers found alternative healers willing to provide it. Many healers, however, allow for much longer consultation times than do GPs, especially for a first consultation which may (especially in systems like homoeopathy) involve taking a very detailed case history. A time-consuming form of treatment may be acceptable to the sufferer if s/he feels it is producing some lasting effect.

Dissatisfaction with the kind of relationship between doctor and patient which interviewees feel that conventional medicine requires or presupposes. In many of the interviews, patients communicated a conscious appreciation of the more active role they felt able to play in the management of their illness or the general pursuit of health. Usually this feeling of being in control was described as a by-product of their experiences rather than as the goal they had been seeking in the first place. A woman who had suffered from asthma for many years described her encounters with conventional and numerous forms of alternative medicine by saying:

> I am not criticizing other people . . . but I think that very often they go to the doctor and they just accept what the doctor says. I would advise anybody to go to the doctor first, but now I would always use alternative medicine to get a second opinion and treatment if you are not satisfied.

Many took an explicitly consumerist approach; one young man who had recently begun to consult an iridologist and to use herbal medicine described his and his wife's attitude to conventional medicine thus:

> If we need to, then we do go to our GP – we are not totally blinkered. We aim to get the best out of both systems.

Yet some interviewees recognized that this active, critical and perhaps eclectic approach to health care might be incompatible with the model of the doctor–patient relationship in which the doctor has total responsibility for the treatment and the patient has only to trust and comply. Most interviewees had avoided telling their GPs about any alternative treatment they had received because they intended to continue to use the GP's services and did not wish to be seen to violate this model of the GP–patient relationship.

Most interviewees in the sample described the initial decision to use alternative medicine as prompted by a recommendation to a specific practitioner by a specific member of their network (see Table 18.1). Table 18.1, however, refers to the *first* experience of alternative medicine, and many patients had used more than one form of alternative medicine, either for the same disease at different times, or more usually,

Table 18.1 How respondents heard about the 'alternative' healer they used first

Source of information	Number of respondents
'Public' sources	
Advertisements/Yellow Pages	3
GP's recommendation	1
Local association/organization	1
'Private' sources	
Friends/acquaintances/colleagues	23
Relatives	2
Total	30

Table 18.2 Number of types of alternative medicine used by respondents (either serially or simultaneously)

Types of alternative medicine used	1	2	3	4	4+	
Number of respondents	9	8	4	7	2	(total 30)

for different diseases. If we include sources of information used for all consultations (not just the first) we find more diverse sources of information, with cultural and political organizations playing a greater part (for example, the Soil Association, vegetarian cookery classes, feminist groups).

Most patients, however, seemed to have gained the confidence to approach a non-orthodox healer in the first place after hearing some kind of success story about that healer from a relative, friend or colleague, and only used information from more impersonal sources once a personal recommendation had yielded some kind of useful experience.

What is striking about the interviewees' stories is that initial usage of one form of alternative medicine is often followed by use of other forms, either serially or simultaneously, for the same or for different illnesses. Some patients had used as many as five types in as many years (see Table 18.2). In only one case was this due to continued failure to obtain any relief. A young man who had a skin condition affecting his scalp and had seen a consultant dermatologist, but without any significant improvement, announced to me his dogged intention of trying as many different forms of medicine in turn until he found one which had some effect. What seemed more common was that some degree of satisfaction (not necessarily total) with the particular form of alternative medicine first sampled led to a more experimental attitude and eventually to trials of other kinds of healing.

In many cases this change to a more eclectic approach to health care was one which affected the whole family. This could happen in several ways. In some cases the interviewee had recommended a form of treatment which s/he had used to other members of the family or had used it for children. In other cases the treatment involved the family indirectly insofar as the patient had to observe some regime (usually dietary) which

Table 18.3 Types of usage of alternative medicine

Conflictual relationship with GP plus occasional or regular use of alternative medicine	2
'Experimental' or eclectic use of alternative medicine	12
Stable and regular use of one form of alternative medicine	9
'Restricted' use of one form of alternative medicine (for a single illness)	7
Total	30

affected the family. A woman who used a particular kind of diet recommended by a herbalist in treating chronic arthritis said that whilst she could not insist that her family eat the diet prescribed for herself, it was convenient to plan meals so that her work was not unnecessarily duplicated. Her family had accepted these changes in family eating patterns, indeed had come to appreciate them. In other cases the regime presented more problems, but only one patient reported downright uncooperative or dismissive attitudes on the part of household members to their usage of alternative medicine. In a few cases patients reported that a spouse or children had regarded their usage of alternative medicine in the light of an eccentric aberration but had not put any obstacles in the way of the interviewee's sticking to the regime prescribed.

When looking at the effects of use of alternative medicine on family health care practices it is important to place these changes in a broader context. Some of the dietary changes and shifts in lifestyle reported by patients as stemming from the recommendations of alternative healers are changes which are being recommended by many other sources of medical authority or information (GPs, popular medicine journals, health promotion campaigns) and are by no means peculiar to alternative medicine 'sub-cultures'. Reduced consumption of animal fats, high fibre diets, regimes of exercise and use of relaxation techniques might be examples. Such changes should be seen as part of more general shifts in thinking about personal and family health care voiced particularly effectively, but not exclusively, by holistic healers.

More significantly, there is little evidence that users of alternative medicine cease entirely to use orthodox medicine, though they may use it less, or for different purposes, or more critically. A sceptical attitude to orthodox medicine did not lead to its abandonment. Usually patients used alternative medicine for specific illnesses or problems and GPs for others. Interviewees had not abandoned the NHS even though dissatisfied with it. In Table 18.3 I have tried to summarize some of the main patterns of usage which I found among the individuals I interviewed. Most interviewees could think of occasions during the past twelve months when they had consulted their GP for themselves or for other members of their family, and could envisage other times in the future.

One very widespread idea which seems to me to be a misconception is that users of alternative healing are naively attracted by the ideological claims of alternative medicine. Jonathan Miller suggested in a recent newspaper article[1] that

> much alternative medicine on offer – acupuncture or homoeopathy, for example – appeals to soft primitivism

a concept which he defines as

> a belief that there was a time when men were harmonious and happy – the myth of the Golden Age – and possessed with wisdoms we are foolish to ignore and idiotic to forget (Miller, 1989).

Possibly this is so: certainly such ideas are frequently expressed in a variety of quarters. But this would not in itself suffice to explain the increasing use of alternative medicine, which seems related to quite pragmatic objectives such as obtaining a cure for a specific illness or leading a more active and healthy life. Only a very few of the people I interviewed gave explicitly ideological reasons for their initial attraction to alternative medicine, though some, as I have indicated, have altered their way of looking at care of the body and mind as a result of their encounter. So ideological commitment might explain why some people *continue* to use alternative medicine having once used it successfully, insofar as they are convinced by what they learn about it from practitioners, but it would not account for the initial resort to unorthodox medicine itself.

Yet most patients using alternative medicine would seem to be (negatively) dissatisfied with the service offered by orthodox medicine, coming on the whole from its areas of notable failure, rather than (positively) attracted by any alternative world view the former may claim to offer. Two themes recur very frequently in the interviews, and receive widespread mention in the literature on the subject:

1. The demand that the patient's experience and understanding of his or her disease should be acknowledged and treated with respect. Not all interviewees spoke in terms of a more 'equal' relationship with the doctor or healer, but many wanted to be better informed so that they could exercise more control in the management of their illness. Where alternative practitioners took the trouble to explain the rationale of treatment to the patient this was appreciated, and often contrasted with the failure of orthodox doctors to take time to provide information about treatment, or to take account of the patients' experience of his/her illness.
2. The demand for what could loosely be called a more holistic approach on the part of doctors. Patients do not always use the term holism, and when they do, they do not always refer to exactly the same thing. However, a recurrent theme in the interviews was the desire that the personal context of illness should be taken into account. The treatment by drugs, which is all that many patients can obtain under the NHS, was often seen as too narrow even where it was 'effective' in terms of sheer relief of symptoms.

Use of alternative medicine is still a minority choice, but from what I have said here, it will be clear that it is not a marginal issue. Though some patients do change their expectations about what doctors or healers should do, or about how illness is caused, as a result of their encounters with alternative medicine, most cannot be said to belong to a separate cultural group; where they express unease over the way in which orthodox medicine delivers its services, they are generally voicing anxieties which they share with many who do not use alternative medicine. Users of alternative medicine are making certain kinds of consumer choice, albeit choices which may have radical consequences for the entire household's lifestyle and habits. As with other patients, their choices derive from the interaction between the nature or their illnesses (chronic, difficult for orthodox medicine to treat) and the nature of their lay referral networks (access to information about specific healers, cultural and political resources).

Alternative medicine therefore is 'marginal' medicine in the obvious sense that it is still used by a minority (albeit a substantial one), and in the political sense that it has limited recognition by the state. Its study has raised issues concerning changes in household health care practice, consumer eclecticism and sources of dissatisfaction with orthodox medicine which should be of central concern to the medical professionals and social scientists alike.

Reference

1. Miller, J. 'Neither fish, fowl nor red herring', the *Independent*, 7 January (1989).

This article is an edited version of a longer text, which was originally published in 1990, under the same title, in *New Directions in the Sociology of Health*, edited by P. Abbott and G. Payne, Falmer Press. Ursula M. Sharma is a Professor in the School of Education and Social Science at the University of Derby.

19 | The social preservation of mind: the Alzheimer's disease experience

JABER F. GUBRIUM

Called 'the disease of the century' Alzheimer's or senile dementia is now considered to be the single most devastating illness of old age. There is a progressive decline in mental functioning in which victims experience confusion, forgetfulness, depression, disorientation, and agitation. The inability to plan and organize actions leaves one unable to complete the simplest tasks of daily living. While in the early stages, a patient can lead a moderately independent life, severe dementia virtually disables its victim such that one, for example, no longer recognizes the once-familiar faces of a spouse or child and is rendered incapable of managing routine activities like eating, voiding and grooming. However severe the cognitive decline, the victim may be remarkably physically fit. Primarily a custodial problem, the Alzheimer's disease patient becomes the virtual ward of those upon whom he/she is dependent – frequently family members. This combination of conditions has meant that Alzheimer's disease virtually has 'two victims' – the person afflicted and the caregiver. Its so-called living death devolves into a caregiving problem, not a medical one.

A hidden mind

A persistent question for all concerned is 'What significance is assigned the patient's gestures and expressions?' For most caregivers, it is evident that the patient, to paraphrase a widely used slogan, at one time had a bright mind, now dimmed by the disease. The victim was once intelligible, fully in command of wit and wisdom. As another slogan puts it, the disease seems to steal that mind away. Yet, while the victim's outward gestures and expressions may hardly provide a clue to an underlying humanity, the question remains whether the disease has stolen it all or only the capacity to express it, leaving an unmanifested, hidden mind.

Caregivers and concerned others commonly deliberate over, share information, and offer each other practical advice about how to maintain whatever remains of the

Alzheimer's victim's mental life. Because it is hidden – if not completely stolen – by the disease, others are charged with its realization. A common sentiment, it is said to be 'up to us' to look and listen carefully for what the Alzheimer's victim is really trying to communicate. A familiar claim, only those who truly love the person, who may hate the disease, can make the difference between the continued realization of the victim's person as opposed to his/her loss to the 'mere shell' of a former self.

The following exchange is drawn from the proceedings of one of the support groups observed [in the author's research study], comprised mainly of the elderly spouses of Alzheimer's patients. Attention is centered on the mental status of a particular patient. The patient's spouse (call her Rita), asks what to think about her husband's very demented condition of late.

> I just don't know what to think or feel. It's like he's not even there anymore, and it distresses me something awful. He doesn't know me. He thinks I'm a strange woman in the house. He shouts and tries to slap me away from him. It's not like him at all. Most of the time he makes sounds but they sound more like an animal than a person. Do you think he has a mind left? I wish I could just get in there into his head and see what's going on. Sometimes I get so upset that I just pound on him and yell at him to come out to me. Am I being stupid? I feel that if I don't do something quick to get at him that he'll be taken from me altogether.

Immediately responding to Rita, another participant, Sara explains:

> We all have gone through it. I know the feeling . . . like, you just know in your heart of hearts that he's in there and that if *you* let go, that's it. So you keep on trying and trying and trying. You've got to keep the faith, that it's him and just work at him, 'cause if you don't . . . well, I'm afraid we've lost them. That's Alzheimer's. It's up to the ones who care because they [the victims] can't do for themselves.

In the exchange, mind is both individual and social. It is an entity possessed by the victim; yet the possession is also a gift allocated faithfully toward its subsequent realization. It is evident that, in practice, Rita, Sara and their co-participants, are literally 'doing' mind in order to realize it. Rather than presenting mind as a secured individual property, the Alzheimer's disease experience repeatedly raises the question of how to define it as such. Although essentially hidden, when mind is faithfully assigned, it is an entity, a structure, articulated as much by those concerned as by those for whom there is concern. All are equally mind's agents.

A difficult task confronts the caregivers and concerned others who seek the Alzheimer's victim's mind: to read outward signs of mind bereft of common meaning. The disease is said to destroy the victim's capacity to communicate by gesture or expression. Left with little or no memory, muddled speech, erratic movement, or other unintelligible activity, in diverse combinations, the usual route to mind is virtually non-existent.

The demise of mind

For some participants, the function of support groups is to teach one to realize, as a veteran put it, 'that there comes a point where to keep thinking that they're still sensible and lucid underneath it all is ridiculous and blind'. The attitude is not necessarily uncaring but realistic, for, just as those who claim to find definitive evidence of mind and heart in the conduct of their patients, others become equally convinced of their absence. As a daughter explained:

> When all is said and done, for all the finagling they do trying to figure out Mother's strange speech and erratic ways, Mother's just not there anymore. You might just as well be talking to a wall. It's a plain fact as clear as day. All that listening and all the clues in the world are not going to tell you that that brain's still working up there. Everyone should realize that sooner or later. If you ask me, it's more in *their* [caregivers'] minds than in the patient's.

The comment brings us face to face with the social nature of mind and minding. It informs us that, as entities, heart and mind are objects-for-us. The sentiment is that minding should in due course cease, for it eventually represents no conscious thing, nothing. Continued, unrestrained minding itself becomes an affliction – pathological denial – further victimizing the 'other patient' of the disease, the victim's caregiver.

The interpersonal relations of the patient and the caregiver are sometimes said to have a natural history. In veteran [caregivers] and professional judgement, it is only natural for, say, the wife of a recently diagnosed spouse to eagerly search for a cure or some other means of sustaining his 'once bright mind'. Indeed, the search and hope might last for years, well into the most debilitating stages of the disease. For some, the search virtually outlives the victim, as the former caregiver retrospectively attempts to regain the semblance of what the patient 'really must have [meant or] felt even though he couldn't even remember his own name, where he'd been, or where he was going'. Yet, as those who claim to know from experience or from being expert in such matters, there comes a point when it's only natural to begin closing off one's affairs with the hopelessly demented.

The professional rationalization of intervention is crystallized around a developmental-stage view of the human closure process. Discussions and advice columns in newsletters and the human service literature of the disease show that Kübler-Ross' (1969) well-known formula of five stages of dying has been adapted to Alzheimer's disease counterparts. A familiar concern is where the caregiver or a support group 'is at'. *Is at* refers to some point in the natural history of concern. For example, in regard to a particular caregiver, it may be said that he/she is at the stage of denial or in the acceptance phase, respectively, meaning that he/she refuses to close off his affairs with the person behind the disease or comes to accept the need for closure with what is now only the shell of a former self.

Support groups also are said to progress naturally through stages of concern. A group comprised of novice caregivers is likely to dwell on the cure that will again reveal the minds of those who were once so bright. A group of experienced participants is more likely to have confronted, discussed, and perhaps come to terms with mental demise. Indeed, support groups are described as more or less mature depending on whether they are, as a geriatrician put it, 'still preoccupied with cure or are getting their own lives in order'.

While in theory, the natural history view is a linear vision of closure, even veteran caregivers and mature support groups, on occasion, confront that persistent question: 'How do I know . . . behind all that . . . [he's not] trying to reach out?' Sometimes, the question rushes ahead of its own deliberation, the fact of having raised it in the first place taken to be callous and uncaring, the assumption made that, 'of course' the victim still has feelings, if not the ability to rationally express them. In the circumstance, closure may be transformed into urgent preservation, with former hard evidence of total mental demise, of so-called brain failure, becoming previously unrecognized clues of the living person behind the disease. There are support group sessions where ongoing shifts in the discourses of articulation and closure serve to construct, deconstruct, and reconstruct the victim's mind. As such, mind experientially dies and is reborn time and time again, in and through formal and informal concern, an ongoing achievement.

Reference

Kübler-Ross, E. (1969), *On Death and Dying*. New York: Macmillan.

The extract reproduced here is a highly edited version of an article with the same title, which originally appeared in *Symbolic Interaction* (1986) JAI Press Inc. Professor Jaber F. Gubrium (known as Jay) is a leading medical sociologist; he is Professor in the Department of Sociology, University of Florida.

20 | 'Some bloody do-gooding cow'

TONY PARKER

An interview with Mrs Williams

Her blue eyes blank with cataract, she sat in an old armchair with her two rubber ferruled sticks leaning against the arm of it and a pink ribbon in what remained of her wispy grey hair. When she heard the front door close she leaned forward slightly, listening.

'Has she gone dear, that young woman? There's just you and me here is there? I can about make out your shape if you're right in front of me, but I couldn't tell you what you look like. Are you a young man dear, you sound as though you are? Well that's young to me. I'm eighty-seven, so to me you're no age at all are you, goodness I've got grandchildren your age nearly.

And who are you dear, who are you from, what have you come to see me about? It's not that thing they call meals on wheels, is it? Because if it is, I don't want to sound rude dear but I don't want anything to do with it, you're wasting your time.

I was left a widow when I was thirty, with five children to bring up: the eldest girl was twelve, then there were four boys, the youngest of them one year old. My husband worked on the railway, they came and knocked on my door one day and said he'd been run over by a train.

In those days there wasn't the social security and the other things what there is nowadays, so I just had to get on with it. I took people's washing in for them, I went and did cleaning in shops round about, I went on Sundays to help them if they wanted things carrying. I did everything that anybody would offer me, to bring money in. I would never tell anyone I couldn't manage, they'd have taken the children off of me if I had and put them in a home. I wasn't going to let that happen.

Being the eldest, my daughter had to stop at home and help me. She didn't get much schooling but that couldn't be helped: with me out at work till all hours there had to be somebody at home to fend for the boys. None of them got much of a schooling either, they had to leave as soon as they were old enough and get jobs. Things were very hard in those days.

Not being an educated person I couldn't get a regular job myself either: not until I was well past forty, then I was a cook at a road-haulage depot canteen in the docks. I got that job about the time when my youngest boy was old enough to leave school and earn his keep, which was when I didn't really need a steady job any more. But I took it and I stayed there more than twenty years. When I left they gave me a big party and a clock and there were speeches and they said "Our dear Mrs Williams".

After that I lived with my married daughter for a while. But her and me have never really what you might call got on. Her and her husband, they're very interested in one of these religious things, they go out knocking on people's doors and giving them leaflets and trying to convert them to their way of thinking. They say they're doing the Lord's work but I don't hold with it myself.

She told me one day she'd seen they were building these flats and she'd been and inquired off of the GLC if they had any old people's accommodation in them. The GLC told her yes they had, there were these ground-floor flatlets and if I'd like one they'd see what they could do. So that's how I got this place, and I've been here ever since.

What I live on is my state pension, but I don't like it because I don't like having to have charity. Now and again one of my sons will come over to see me and when he's gone there's a five-pound note left on the table: it makes me cross, but I think it'd make them cross if I gave it back to them so I use it for the electric because that's such a terrible expense now. This flat is all electric and it eats more money than I eat food. I used to have a gas stove for doing my cooking on, but as my eyesight started to go I couldn't tell when I wanted to turn the gas down if I hadn't turned it out. Sometimes it would be on and I hadn't lit it, and there was matches with a chance of a dangerous explosion, so they came and turned me into all electric. I think it was from the social, some bloody do-gooding cow interfering like they do: I can't stand these people knocking on your door saying they've got some form or another that's got to be filled in, how much is your rent, what do you do about your washing and all the rest of it. You're not from the social people are you dear? No I thought not, you don't sound like you are.

There's a lady comes in on a Tuesday and a Friday, she's one of the what they call home helps. Her name's Matty, she's been coming for seven years, and if it was left to me she might just as well not bother only the problem is I don't know how to get rid of her. All she does is as soon as she comes she says she'll put the kettle on and make a cup of tea. And then when she's done that, she sits and chats for two hours. She used to be very good, but now she doesn't do a blind thing except have a quick run round with a duster, ask me if I want any shopping bringing in, go and get it, and then she's off and I don't see her till next time. Once in a while she'll take my washing to the launderette, but it's God's honest truth that's all she does mostly, spends all her time talking to me. Not talking with me, or letting me talk to her: that wouldn't be so bad, but talking to me all the time, do you know how I mean? A lady came from somewhere once and asked me was everything all right, was I satisfied with the home help. I said I was. Well you have to don't you when it's somebody's job, you can't complain about them because they might lose it and nobody wants to put somebody out of work do they? I mean not except this Tory government we've got, they enjoy doing that, they're wicked; but nobody else would.

There's somebody called a voluntary visitor or something, she comes in as well. I think she's an old age pensioner who's got nothing else to do with her time, she comes about once a month. I don't know her name; but she's another of them, she wants to tell you what she's been doing, her ideas about this that and the other, she's another one gets on my nerves. Apart from her, that's the lot for my visitors. Mr Cross might call in now and again and make me a cup of tea if he happens to be passing, but no one else.

A typical day for me would be that I usually wake up about six o'clock, and I have my wireless on the table by the bed there and listen to that till about half past eight or nine. Then I get up and get dressed. I've got this very bad rheumatism in my hips and arms, so usually it'll take me an hour and a half to two hours to get dressed. I have to keep stopping for a rest. Then if it's the day for the home help she comes, and if it's not I'll make myself a cup of tea and start making my dinner. I don't like these things you get in packets, I don't think there's any nourishment in them: I'd sooner have a few potatoes and carrots with a bit of gravy. I might have a piece of meat, a sausage or something of that sort, or an egg, but not every day. In the afternoon I listen to the wireless again, I might have a doze until it's my tea time. Then I have something on toast as a rule. I like cheese or sardines or a tomato. Round about seven o'clock I'll have a cup of cocoa and a biscuit, then I go to bed and usually I drop off to sleep about nine.

But it's no use us going on talking about that subject, because I don't care what you say, I'm not having those meals on wheels. I think they're disgusting – all that white sauce over everything so you can't see what you're eating. I had one once six or seven years ago. I don't mean to be rude dear but if you go on until you're blue in the face I shan't change my mind. I'm not having them.

Last night I had a dream, I dreamed I was out shopping. I was along the precinct there at Robins Walk, I was walking about and people were coming up and speaking to me and chatting, it was lovely. Then when I woke up and found it was all a dream, I started to cry. It's five years, no it must be more than that now, since I've been along there or anywhere else on the estate.

Sometimes one of my sons will come for me on a Sunday if it's a nice day in the summer and take me out for a little ride in his motor car. There's two of them live near enough to do that. The other two, one's in America and the other one I don't know where he is, I haven't seen him for years. The two that do come, Michael and Charlie, they're good boys but they've got wives and families and children of their own, they don't want to be bothered with an old woman and you can't blame them, not really.

The vicar used to come, but he seems to have dropped off lately. He told me off once for swearing, I do say "bloody" and that; that might be why he doesn't come. Sometimes the chiropodist comes, she's another one spends all her time talking, I can't be doing with people like that. I don't know why people can't leave you alone; if they don't want me to talk to them, I'd sooner they didn't come and talk to me.

The person I like best is my neighbour next door, the one who goes and gets my pension from the post office for me. She comes and knocks on the door every two weeks for my book. She never says anything apart from "Good morning" and she's never away more than half an hour because she knows I worry. Then she comes back and comes in and puts the money on the table and says "Good morning" again, and then out she goes. That's it then, and I don't see her again for another two weeks.

It does get lonely sometimes, and I do sometimes I do have a bit of a cry about it. But I think to myself "Well Clara" I think, "Well Clara there's no use crying about it, you're getting to be an old woman now and you can't expect any different." I used to be such an active person you see, never had a day's illness, brought up all my kids on my own, never asked anything from them since they was grown up and with families of their own. It's not as though I've been used to being a person who couldn't get about until these last years.

One of my boys, Charlie I think it was, he came to me one day and he said him and Michael and their wives had all been having a talk and they all thought it would be a good idea if I had a telephone. He said then if there was ever anything wrong any time, I could ring up and they'd come over; or if I like wanted the doctor I could call him. So they had this telephone put in for me.

It was, it was bloody awful. I said I didn't care if they were paying for it, it was more trouble then it was worth and they were to have it taken away. One thing was they used to ring up and tell me they couldn't come over at the weekend to see me, so they'd rung up for a chat instead. You can understand it, it made things a lot easier for them. But it got to be none of them came for weeks on end – as soon as I heard the phone ringing on a Friday night I knew who it was, it was either Michael or Charlie or their wife to say they were sorry they couldn't come.

The other thing would happen would be you'd be on the toilet or something and the bloody phone would start ringing. It always did it: I knew for sure if I went to that toilet the phone would ring. It was never anybody proper – it'd always be someone like the electricity people ringing up to say they were checking everything was all right, did I have any problems; or the home help woman would ring up, "It's all right Mrs Williams it's only me, I thought I'd ring up to see how you are since I'm not going to be coming in tomorrow." I used to feel like shouting I'd been all right till she rang up, why the hell didn't she push off. Only I didn't say push off, I used another word I won't say to you.

And a couple of times, this happened without a word of a lie, this is God's honest truth this is – twice it started ringing in the middle of the night. I switched my light on to see what time it was, and if I hold my alarm clock under the lamp and put my face right to it, I can see what time it is: and both times it was two o'clock. I didn't have my name in the telephone book, so where they'd got my phone number from I don't know: but it was a man, or it could have been a boy even, a young man. In all my life I've never heard anything like it, he said such dirty filthy things, over and over he kept on repeating them. I didn't know what to say so I didn't say anything, I couldn't think. You know you should put the phone down, but somehow at the time when it happens you stand there and you can't move. I nearly fainted with it. I let go of the hand thing, what do they call it, receiver, and I was, I was trembling so much I could scarcely get back to my bed.

I didn't dare put my light out and I don't think I slept any more. But I sort of drowsed off some time though, because the next thing I knew it was daylight and the telephone was making that whirring noise it makes when you haven't got it put down properly. I was very frightened but I didn't tell anybody, I didn't ring up my sons or anything. I wished I had, because the next night I've gone to bed again and the same thing happens, in the middle of the night it starts ringing again at two o'clock. I thought if I didn't switch my light on and didn't answer it, they might think I'd gone away and there was no one here. So I left it, I let it ring and ring. I don't know how long it went on, it seemed like hours but I swore I was never going to answer a telephone again, and I didn't.

Next morning I rang them up, the telephone people at the post office or wherever it is. I said I was an old woman on my own and I was frightened of electricity and they were to come straightaway that day and take it away. I don't remember if they did come that same day or not, but they did cut it off for me there and then until they could come and remove it. I never told them the real reason it was all about, and I never told my sons. I don't know who it was, for all I know it might have been the telephone people – but then somebody told the social I wasn't having the phone no more, so the next thing is they came round to see what was the matter and what it was all about. I never told them either.

That woman from the social, she was another of them, another bloody do-gooding cow. She said how was I going to let anybody know if I felt ill any time and needed help. I said if I did I'd shout; but oh no she said, that wouldn't do, I must have one of their cards to put up at that window there. It had got "Help Wanted" in big letters on it so everyone could see it and come to help me. That's the sort of thing they do these people, they think up ideas and tell you to do this that and the other, and then they're surprised when you've no time for them afterwards.

What happened you see was that a few days after she'd give it me I did feel a bit queer, so I thought I'll ask someone if they'd go to the doctor for me and get me some medicine. I put the card up behind the curtain there against the window where anyone passing could see it, then I went and lay on my bed and waited for someone to come. Well no one came, did they? I dozed off, I went to sleep, and when I woke up in the morning there was nothing wrong with me so I carried on as normal. Only I'd forgot to take the card down: a day went by, two days, and I'd still forgotten all about it. Then on the third day in the afternoon I'm sitting in my chair having a doze, and there's a hammering and a banging on that door, and people climbing up on the ledge outside and trying to get their hand inside the window and open it. I was frightened out of my life. This is God's honest truth, I thought it was a gang of burglars or something trying to break in and kill me and steal my money.

After that I threw the card away. I thought if anything happened to me I'd sooner lie there on the floor I would for a couple of days, rather than something like that. That's the social for you.'

This interview is taken from *The People of Providence*, a collection of personal accounts about life on a London housing estate, first published by Hutchinson & Co. (1983). Tony Parker spent five years researching and writing this book and the accounts he has reproduced are taken from his tape recorded interviews with people living in or working on the estate. Mrs Williams is one of the many residents who spoke to him.

21 | Pride against prejudice: 'lives not worth living'

JENNY MORRIS

In May 1990, a 31-year-old man, Kenneth Bergstedt, petitioned the Las Vegas courts for permission to 'end his painful existence'. The press reported that he was 'a 31-year-old quadriplegic hooked to a respirator for more than 20 years' for whom 'life was no longer worth living'. A psychiatrist backed up his application by telling the **court that** 'The quality of life for this man is very poor, moderated only by momentary distraction, but forever profaned by a future which offers no relief.'[1]

This case is but one of an increasing number which have occurred in the USA over the last few years. The first one to be taken up by the disability movement was that of Elizabeth Bouvia, who had cerebral palsy. Dr Paul Longmore, a historian who is also disabled wrote:

> A 26-year-old woman, attractive and educated, checks herself into a hospital psychiatric unit announcing her wish to commit suicide. She reports that she has undergone two years of devastating emotional crises: the death of a brother, serious financial distress, withdrawal from graduate school because of discrimination, pregnancy and miscarriage and, most recently, the breakup of her marriage.
>
> She also has a serious physical disability, which she says is the reason she wants to die.
>
> Three psychiatric professionals ignore the series of emotional blows, concluding that she is mentally competent and that her decision for death is reasonable. They base their judgement on one fact alone – her physical handicap.[2]

The judge who heard the Bouvia case pronounced '. . . she must lie immobile, unable to exist except through the physical acts of others' and expressed the hope that her case would 'cause our society to deal realistically with the plight of those unfortunate individuals to whom death beckons as a welcome respite from suffering'.[2]

A key question for the American courts in these cases has been whether the person petitioning for 'assisted suicide' is taking a rational decision, that is, whether their wish to die is determined by emotion or impulse, or whether it is a reasonable judgement based on a realistic assessment of their situation.

As disability activists like Paul Longmore and Mary Johnson have pointed out, this assessment is made by people who often have no experience of disability, are certainly not disabled themselves and who find it inconceivable that someone who is completely (or almost completely) paralysed and who may have to use a respirator even to breathe, can experience a life which is worth living.

It seems to be relatively easy for the non-disabled world to judge that people who require physical assistance to such a high degree are making a rational decision when they say they want to die. It has been left up to other disabled people to examine the social and economic context in which such decisions are made. The case of Larry McAfee, whose case hit the American press in 1989, illustrates the way in which it is not the physical disability itself but the social and economic circumstances of the experience which can lead to a diminished quality of life.[3]

McAfee was aged 34 when a motorcycle accident resulted in complete paralysis and the need to use a ventilator. His insurance benefit (of $1 million) enabled him to employ personal care attendants in his own home for a period after his accident but when this ran out he was forced to enter a nursing home. He decided life wasn't worth living and tried turning his respirator off but couldn't cope with the feeling of suffocation. So he petitioned the courts to be allowed to be sedated while someone else unplugged his breathing apparatus.

In the event, he acquired a delay mechanism which would allow him to turn off the respirator himself and still allow for sedation, and the court ruled that he could not be stopped from doing so. Throughout the case and the publicity accorded to him, the general assumption was that McAfee's decision was a rational one based solely on the extent of his physical disability.

Yet when, as a result of the publicity, McAfee received an outpouring of support from disability activists, he decided to delay the decision to take his own life. What he really wanted was to live in his own home and to get a job. A disability organization arranged for him to receive training in voice-activated computers and he received tentative offers of employment. However, at this point, his Medicare benefits (the more generous part of the American health benefit system) ran out and the less-generous Medicaid would not pay for his place at the nursing home which was equipped for people who use a respirator. The Georgia Medicaid regulations did not allow Medicaid benefits to be used on home care but McAfee, together with disability activists and organisations, tried to get a waiver to the regulations to allow him to hire care attendants in his own home.

The type of nursing home which was equipped for McAfee's needs cost between $475 to $650 per day (a level which could be paid by Medicare but not Medicaid). McAfee calculated it would cost $265 per day to pay for attendant services in his own home but Medicaid paid only $100 per day for residential care. The Georgia Department of Medical Assistance therefore rejected his proposal. McAfee was then admitted, temporarily and on a voluntary basis, to a psychiatric hospital. Anyone in his situation must be extremely depressed and upset.

The social and economic context of Kenneth Bergstedt's desire to die is also clear. His case was brought into the limelight when his 65-year-old father presented the Las Vegas court with an affidavit from his son that he 'had no encouraging expectations to look forward to from life, receives no enjoyment from life, lives with constant fears and apprehensions and is tired of suffering'.[4] But were these feelings about his life a result of his physical disability or a result of the situation in which he lived? Bergstedt was being looked after by his father who was disabled himself (he had lost a leg in an industrial accident), had high blood pressure and was scared of getting cancer or having a heart attack. Bergstedt was said to be worried that if anything happened to his father he would either die if left on his own in an emergency or be forced into residential care. The court ruled that Bergstedt's wish to die was rational given the level of his physical disability, with no consideration as to whether, if the context in which he experienced his physical disability were changed, his attitude to dying might have been very different.

The question is, in such a context, is the wish to die a so-called rational response to physical disability? Or is it a desperate response to isolated oppression? As Ed Roberts, head of the World Institute on Disability, said, 'It's not the respirator. It's money.' He explained, 'I've been on a respirator for 26 years and I watch these people's cases – they're just as dependent on a respirator as I am; the major difference is they know they're going to be forced to live in a nursing home – or they're already there – and I'm leading a quality life'.[5]

In America, the debate is couched in terms of civil rights. Elizabeth Bouvia received the help of the American Civil Liberties Union lawyers who were intent on winning for her the legal right to assisted suicide.[2] It is also couched in terms of humanitarianism, of concern for the individual and their quality of life.

In Britain, where such cases rarely reach the courts, public opinion has also been concerned with the issue of quality of life for physically disabled people. There has been a similar willingness to accept that a high level of paralysis necessitates an unacceptable quality of life. One example of this involved James Haig, who was tetraplegic as the result of a motorbike accident. During the year following his injury he tried to adjust. Journalist Polly Toynbee wrote in *The Guardian*, 'He tried writing but football had been his great interest before the accident and he found he could not adapt. He was told he could never have any kind of job.' She wrote, 'He looked down at his immobilised and wasted arms and legs. "Suicide is the sensible answer for someone like me," he said'. Toynbee invited the reader to agree with Haig, arguing how wrong it was that it was against the law for anyone to help Haig in his wish to kill himself: 'What Arthur Koestler could do for himself, with dignity and, one hopes, without pain, or panic, the law forced James Haig to do to himself brutishly and cruelly.' Haig set fire to his bungalow and died in the flames.[6]

Steven Bradshaw, director of the Spinal Injuries Association and himself tetraplegic, responded to Toynbee's article. 'We are concerned that she has . . . suggested that suicide is a logical response to tetraplegia.' He could also have pointed out the inappropriate analogy which Toynbee drew between Arthur Koestler who was terminally ill and was merely choosing the form of his death which was inevitable soon, and Haig, who was not ill, who could have lived for 50 more years and whose decision was not about the form of his death but a rejection of his life.

Instead of encouraging the idea that physical disability in itself means an unacceptable quality of life, why didn't Toynbee ask why our society causes young men to think that if they can't play football then life isn't worth living? Or ask why Haig had been told he would never work again?

A liberal humanist approach to euthanasia may insist that individuals should be able to choose the manner and time of their death; that if someone genuinely feels that their life is not worth living then they should not be forced to endure pain and suffering and unhappiness. But individuals do not exist within a vacuum. We are all influenced by the values of the society in which we live. Our society not only values physical ability and perfection; it devalues and discriminates against those who do not conform to the physical norm. The prejudices against disabled people do not just exist out there in the public world, they also reside within our own heads, particularly for those of us who become disabled in adult life.

Given the level of prejudice against disabled people, we cannot realistically expect non-disabled journalists or the medical profession, or the legal profession, to mount a challenge to the assumption that a physical disability means a life not worth living. We have to challenge it ourselves. We have to question the way in which, while it is commonly assumed that a non-disabled person who is not terminally ill but who commits suicide, does so while 'the balance of their mind is disturbed', the suicide of a disabled person is often treated as rational behaviour. No mental disturbance or emotional trauma is deemed necessary to explain the rejection of life by a disabled person. Instead their physical disability is taken as sufficient grounds to want to die.

References

1. p. 16 in Johnson, M. 'Unanswered questions', *Disability Rag*, September/October issue (1990).
2. p. 195 in Longmore, P. 'Whose life is this anyway?' In Maddox, S. (ed.) *Spinal Network*, Sam Maddox, Colorado, USA (1987).
3. pp. 11–12 in *Disability Rag*, July/August issue (1990).
4. pp. 18–19 in Johnson, M. 'Unanswered questions', *Disability Rag*, September/October issue (1990).
5. p. 21 in *Disability Rag*, September/October issue (1990).
6. Toynbee, P. *Guardian*, 25 April (1983).

Jenny Morris is a freelance writer and former lecturer, who broke her back in a fall. This article is an edited extract from Chapter 2 'Lives not Worth Living' in her book *Pride Against Prejudice: A Personal Politics of Disability*, published by The Women's Press, London (1991).

22 | The stigma of infertility

NAOMI PFEFFER

The controversy over the new methods of overcoming involuntary childlessness has focused on the ethical aspects of the techniques. A focus on ethical considerations effectively excludes any discussion of the social and historical context of the condition of infertility. Consequently, none of the many different and often opposing reasons given for the recent interest in new techniques to overcome infertility can be challenged persuasively. Furthermore, this absence of a social and historical context has had an unfortunate consequence for infertile men and women, which is that in the course of considerable public exposure given to infertility, the stigma of infertility has been compounded. Providing a social context has therefore another and to me a more important purpose; that purpose is to deconstruct the stigma of infertility.

Besides their involuntary childlessness there is one characteristic which the infertile are said to share, that of desperation. The word desperation or some such synonym appears so frequently in conjunction with infertility that sometimes it appears that what troubles infertile men and women is not the absence of a child as such but some form of emotional disorder related to their failure. Desperation combined with infertility appears to produce a particularly potent mix; one that forces fecund women to lease their womb, sends infertile men and women scouring the world for orphans to adopt and incites some doctors into developing new techniques that subject people to many indignities.

Does infertility lead inevitably to unremitting desperation? Infertility is a very negative experience and at times most infertile men and women probably will feel desperate. But desperation is only one of many different emotions that infertility can arouse, and not all of these are negative. There are positive aspects to childlessness which are rarely mentioned, or which are glossed as selfishness. Furthermore, desperation may not be a result of the condition of infertility but of the insensitive and humiliating treatment sometimes received at the hands of medical and other authorities, the very people who claim to be interested in rescuing the infertile from desperation. Focusing on desperation to the exclusion of all other emotions serves not to explain but to make a caricature of infertile men and women.

Physical infertility is not synonymous with involuntary childlessness. It is generally forgotten that some men and women are childless because of social and not physical impediments.[1] The litmus test of physical fertility is conception and the safe delivery of a live baby. With few exceptions, no one knows in advance of trying to conceive whether they are fertile or not. Those people rendered sterile by their genes or through disease may not in fact want children; indeed, they may regret the loss of their fertility as a potential but they may not grieve the absence of a child. It is in the attempt to conceive that one discovers whether one is fertile or not. The decision to embark on parenthood, to undertake a major change in social status, antedates the attempt to conceive, particularly today when more effective means of fertility control are available. This decision is the result of processes that are shaped by social and historical forces, the impact of which are shared by the fertile and infertile alike; there is nothing peculiar about the motivation for parenthood of those who later find themselves infertile.

Scientists and doctors do not agree about what is the normal length of time it takes to get pregnant. Hence infertility is a self-imposed definition. At some point during an attempt at conception, frustration is acknowledged; a problem emerges that may require some sort of solution. Not everyone who acknowledges a fertility problem takes that problem to a doctor. Indeed, seeking medical advice is only one of the many options available. These options include denial, applying for a child to adopt or foster, changing partner, finding a new job, moving home, going on a long holiday or grieving the loss of a potential relationship, that of parent and child.[2] The choice of options is shaped by social factors such as class, gender, race, age, marital status, education, social isolation, etc., none of which feature in the discussion about the needs of the infertile.

There is no evidence that the involuntarily childless who take their problem to a doctor are more desperate to have a child than those men and women who choose other solutions to their childlessness. The only factor that distinguishes them is their decision to seek a specifically medical solution to their infertility. It is often claimed that the problem of infertility is growing in scale so that it sometimes appears as though the cumulative desperation of the infertile threatens to engulf the fertile majority. It may be that the number of people seeking a medical solution to their infertility is on the increase, but as statistics are not collected on such issues (and would be very difficult to collect) we have no way of knowing this for sure. Nevertheless, we cannot assume that once in the surgery these people will countenance uniformly the whole panoply of invasive investigations and treatments on offer. There is copious evidence which shows that not all patients concur with their doctors' recommendations.[3,4] Men and women have clear limits beyond which they will not venture. Some will not consider artificial insemination using donor semen, others refuse in-vitro fertilization whilst yet others reject adoption. Such limits are not evidence that some people's motivation for parenthood is insufficiently strong. Rather, these limits highlight the real social differences that exist amongst infertile women and men.

Fleshing out the real and complex experience of infertility leads us to ask who benefits from the pervasive caricature of the infertile as desperate people. Not the infertile themselves, who cannot be helped by the reduction of a complex set of changing emotions and needs to a single negative word. Infertile women are not, I suggest, helped by a description of any distress they may feel as that of a 'barren woman's suffering' (p. 47).[5] These words are Robert Edwards's, the embryologist who, with his collaborator the gynaecologist Patrick Steptoe, pioneered the technique of in-vitro fertilization and embryo transfer.

Who then benefits from this caricature? There is a false assumption frequently made that professionals and their clients share the same goals. In this context, the professionals are the gynaecologists and embryologists and their clients are the infertile men and women who seek their help. For both, the aim is indeed the birth of a child, but their reasons for wanting this child clearly differ. Gynaecologists and embryologists who champion these new techniques have made their views known through articles in newspapers and television documentaries which portray them in heroic terms. We know that these doctors and scientists want to be able to continue to offer in-vitro fertilization and embryo transfer. These professionals have claimed that the new methods for assisting reproduction are indispensable in their endeavours to help their infertile patients. And we know from opinion research that a majority of the population of Britain wish them to be allowed to do so.[6] What we do not know is if this same desire is shared by the majority of men and women who are infertile, most of whom will *not* undergo in-vitro fertilization and embryo transfer.

Little information is available on what infertile people in general want. One survey (the only one of its kind and a little out of date) may provide us with some clues. In 1977, the members of the National Association of the Childless, a voluntary organization which offers support and advice to the infertile, were asked to state the single thing that they felt would most improve the medical treatment they had received. Admittedly, this survey was conducted before the birth of Louise Brown, the first test-tube baby. Nevertheless, its findings are of interest. Only 2 per cent of the respondents stated that more up-to-date techniques would have been beneficial. Of much greater importance to these infertile men and women were improvements in both the organization of the clinics they attended and in the attitude of the doctors they saw. Specifically, they complained about the length of time it took to reach some sort of diagnosis of their condition. This delay was caused by the infrequency of clinics which meant long gaps between each appointment, and when they did see a doctor, many complained of how difficult it was to get an adequate account of their problem. These difficulties in communication were compounded by patients rarely seeing the same doctor throughout the course of a treatment.[7]

These findings have an all-too-familiar ring about them; many patients, whatever their condition, level similar criticisms at their doctors. But in the recent debate about new approaches to the treatment of infertility, these well-rehearsed complaints have disappeared; the hearts and minds of even the most intransigent critics of doctors appear to have been won over. It is now common currency that those same doctors whose attitudes in the past provoked the complaints that I cited above are today concerned solely with the interests of their infertile patients. This is, I suggest, a simple and naïve rendering of an institution as complex as medicine.

References

1. Porter, M. 'Infertility: the extent of the problem', *Biology and Society*, **1**, 128–35 (1984).
2. Woollett, A. 'Childlessness: strategies for coping with infertility', *International Journal for Behavioural Development*, **8**, 473–82 (1985).
3. Stimson, G.V. 'Obeying doctor's orders: a view from the other side', *Social Science and Medicine*, **8**, 97–104 (1975).
4. Cartwright, A. *Patients and Their Doctors*, Routledge and Kegan Paul, London (1967).

5. Steptoe, P. and Edwards, R. *A Matter of Life*, Hutchinson, London (1980).
6. *The Times*, 11 October (1982), p. 2.
7. Owens, D. and Read, M.W. The Provision, Use and Evaluation of Medical Services for the Subfertile: An Analysis based on the Experience of Involuntary Childless Couples, SRU Working Paper 4, University of Cardiff, Cardiff (1979).

Naomi Pfeffer is a social historian and Professor of Social and Historical Studies of Health at the University of North London. She has written extensively about the medicalization of infertility, contraception and assisted conception, most recently *The Stork and the Syringe: A Political History of Reproductive Medicine*, Polity Press, Cambridge (1994). This article is an edited extract from her chapter 'Artificial insemination, in-vitro fertilization and the stigma of infertility' which appeared in *Reproductive Technologies: Gender, Motherhood and Medicine*, Stanworth, M. (ed.), Polity Press, Cambridge (1987).

23 | Identity dilemmas of chronically ill men

KATHY CHARMAZ

Serious chronic illness threatens men's taken-for-granted masculine identities and leads to identity dilemmas that can recur again and again. Men's identity dilemmas include the following oppositions: risking activity vs. forced passivity, remaining independent vs. becoming dependent, maintaining dominance vs. becoming subordinate, and preserving a public persona vs. acknowledging private feelings. Whichever direction a man takes has costs. For example, a man may take enormous risks with his health to remain active, independent and dominant. What is it like to be an active, productive man one moment and a patient who faces death the next? What is it like to change one's view of oneself accordingly? Which identity dilemmas does living with continued uncertainty pose for men? How do they handle them? When do they make identity changes? When do they try to preserve a former self?

This research explores these questions by looking at four major processes in men's experiences of chronic illness: (1) awaking to death after a life-threatening crisis, (2) accommodating to uncertainty as men realize that the crisis has lasting consequences, (3) defining illness and disability, and (4) preserving self to maintain a sense of coherence while experiencing loss and change.

Awakening to death

Awakening to death comes as an unbelievable shock when a man sees himself as too young to die, defines himself as exceptionally healthy, or has had no earlier episodes or heralding symptoms. [One man] recounted his heart attack at age 42:

> I was on my bicycle going on just a routine ride for me and I just went down. I didn't know what happened . . . So I had no indication that I [was having a heart attack] – no chest pains, no shortness of breath, no typical [symptoms of] how you feel. I couldn't even tell you what it feels like.

This man awoke in the hospital to find himself to be partly paralyzed. The paralysis did not faze him but he became furious when his doctor told him that he had had a heart attack. When I asked him what raised his fury, he juxtaposed the finality of heart disease with the injustice of having paid his dues already by stopping smoking, limiting drinking, getting in shape, and losing weight. All this work and then, the biggest injustice, 'It's just I'm too young . . . Why me?'

Several men who had had bypass surgery or other circulatory procedures questioned whether they should participate in a study of experiencing chronic illness. They believed their surgery had effected the necessary repairs. For them, not only the threat of death was over, but also the illness. A referral to my study, especially if by their nurse, undermined their construction of illness as an acute episode.

Eventually, men's routine interactions and unforeseen daily obstacles turn early glimmers of awareness into growing cognizance that illness remains. Everyday routines become much more arduous and time-consuming than before. [This] can challenge men's assumptions about male mastery and competence, thereby leading them into depression. Inability to solve these problems undermines their personal identity. A forty-five year old man with heart disease disclosed that for six months, 'I thought my life was over. Cardiac Cripple.'

[But] awakening to death can also result in direct, positive consequences. During crisis and its immediate aftermath, most married men felt tremendous affirmation of their valued identities in the family as they awakened to death. They received an outpouring of care, comfort, and love from their wives and families. These men often bragged about how supportive and helpful their wives had been. [This] implicitly affirmed their gender identities as men in the household. Supports for single and divorced men, however, usually were much less available. They weathered crises largely on their own.

Accommodating to uncertainty

In which ways do men define and handle uncertainty? [By] 'bracketing' (Husserl, 1970) the event which elicited it, setting apart this event by putting a frame around it and treating it as something separate and removed from the flow of life. Through bracketing, men define uncertainty as having boundaries – those limited to crisis. To the extent that men put boundaries on uncertainty and limit it to flare-ups and crises, they avoid letting it permeate their thoughts and alter their identities.

Eventually most men realize that their bodies have changed. When men acknowledge continued uncertainty, their reappraisals bring reflection and self-appraisal. Men who had attended much more to work than to their families decided to devote more time to them. Men who described themselves as driven by their 'Type A' behaviour believed that they had to relinquish it before it killed them. The man above who had viewed himself as a cardiac cripple for six months saw his heart attack quite differently two years later. He said,

> I would say 'thank you, thank you,' type of thing. But you know, had it not been for my heart attack – I'm grateful it happened now, 'cause it changed my life considerably and so [I] have a lack of words [to describe it]. Yeah, I thank my heart attack for that. In one way I'm grateful.

After awakening to death and defining uncertainty, lifestyles, and also habits, rapidly change – at least for a while. Men quit working, change jobs, renegotiate their work assignments, or retire early. They follow a regimen, lose weight, stop smoking, and reduce drinking. Making permanent changes, however, means *acknowledging* uncertainty and treating its consequences as lasting. Several men with diabetes disclosed that they hadn't attended to their conditions until shocked by a diabetic crisis. One middle-aged manager previously had ignored his diet, his doctor's warnings, and his wife's nagging. After a harrowing struggle against death followed by the loss of his foot, he not only acknowledged his own uncertain future, but also tried to instruct unaware relatives and friends about the negative consequences of their lifestyles . . .'because, look what happened to me.'

Defining illness and disability

These men viewed their conditions in four major ways as: an enemy, an ally, an intrusive presence and an opportunity. At different points in time, a man may hold each definition. Viewing one's illness as an enemy objectifies and externalizes it and thus distances and separates it from identity. Viewing illness as an ally emphasizes subjectivity and identification with it and thus, integrates it with identity.

Images of enemies and allies are present, although sometimes implicit, in the competitive discourse of victories and losses that middle-aged and younger men frequently invoke when talking about their illnesses. Norman Cousins (1983) titles his chapter on dealing with his heart attack, 'Counter-attack'. Lee Foster (1978, p. 526) states, 'The record for longevity on a kidney machine, the last time I checked, was fourteen years, and if I stay on dialysis I aim to break the record.' [Some] men changed their definition from illness as an enemy or an intrusive presence to an experience with positive consequences. [One man said]

> It's an enemy that I've made an ally of. Really, I don't think I'd still be here, if I hadn't been diabetic. It's like the paradox of the return of the prodigal son. It kicked me out of Eden alright, having to, you know, be on my best behaviour so much and think about when to shoot up and all that. But it was what I needed.

By making illness an ally, men can use it as an opportunity for reflection and change. Arthur Frank (1991, p. 1) refers to illness explicitly as 'an opportunity, though a dangerous one'. He writes,

> Illness takes away parts of your life, but in doing so it gives you the opportunity to choose the life you will lead as opposed to living out the one you have simply accumulated over the years. (p. 1)

Whether men treat their conditions as enemies, allies, intrusions, or opportunities, their definitions are seldom mutually exclusive or static. That is, a man who sees illness as an ally because it led him to set priorities can still see it as an intrusive, even ominous presence in his life. Similarly, a man can treat his illness as an ally for a number of years only to redefine it as an increasingly intrusive presence if it steadily limits his activities.

Preserving self

Although certain major identities change, such as that of worker to part-time retiree, men with chronic illnesses try to lead normal lives. In doing so, they implicitly, and often explicitly, devote much effort to preserving aspects of a self known and valued in the past. They aim to reclaim the same identities, the same lives that they had before illness. Nothing less will do. They lapse into invalidism and despondency if they cannot recapture their past selves. Trying to recapture the past self does provide strong incentives to fight illness and to stave off death. When men believe in their doctors and in their treatment, their resolve to struggle maintains their hope. A middle-aged father of young sons commented about having cardiac bypass surgery,

> I felt – I was going to do everything I did before: otherwise it wasn't worth having the surgery . . . I wanted to be just the same as before. And, like for these children, it would be really devastating to them if I were to go ahead and say, 'Well, I can't do this because of my heart; I can't do that,' you know. You don't want to teach young children to be like that.

Despondency about not recapturing the past self increases and renders preserving valued aspects of self more arduous. A middle-aged man with heart disease felt overwhelmed, immobile, and depressed, when he compared his present precarious physical, financial, and marital statuses with his past fitness, financial security, and stable marriage. He said,

> I'd say I hit rock bottom about October, November last year. I got to where I don't care what happens to me, you know; I don't care what happens to anybody.

To the extent that a man takes for granted that masculinity is imbedded in power, the more likely he will tighten his control within the household as access to other arenas decreases. For example, as a retired bartender became house-bound, his scrutiny of his wife's day increased and he became more critical and controlling. She could incur his wrath by failing to anticipate or satisfy his dictates about the smallest household or personal care task. Such men want to be in control. Rather than give up old habits, these men may flaunt them. If they cannot control their health, they may try to control someone else's response. To do this, they will take risks – often many of them and, likely, cast their wives and physicians into the role of adversaries to outwit. In this way, they maintain their assumed status in the hierarchy of men and simultaneously exert dominance over women. At this point, they also risk being identified as obstreperous, unmotivated, and mentally unstable by their practitioners. Wives and partners may find themselves anxiously trying to protect shreds of their husbands' former identities while feeling overwhelmed by the escalating demands placed upon them.

In contrast, possibilities of expanding identities foster hope and support desire to stave off disability and death. The self to be preserved is a developing self, ripe with the potential for new, positive identities. For example, one man had recently won an award in his field which brought him substantial recognition and travel, in addition to renewed friendships. For him, the world was opening up, not closing down upon him. Quite spontaneously, he disclosed, 'I don't want to die, I'm just a baby, a fifty-two year-old baby boy. I'm just starting; I don't want to die.'

Some men claim public identities that reaffirm their pasts and demonstrate continuity with that past. They may have to devote vast amounts of energy to keeping the illness contained and disability invisible or less obvious (cf. Charmaz, 1991). A man struggled to use crutches for far longer than his condition permitted because he wanted to remain in the 'manly' position of being on his feet, rather than in a wheelchair. A man with diabetes could not manage both his wheelchair and a tray in the cafeteria. He could not bring himself to ask his co-workers for help and skipped lunch. He risked a coma rather than request help.

Ironically, the independent public man can transform himself into a dependent patient at home. This stance allows the tyranny of the sickroom, promotes self-pity, and encourages physical dependence. Even when men do not become overly dependent, wives add hours to their day as they manage or collaborate in care by preparing special diets, assisting in bathing, dressing, grooming, [and] completing the daily medical care regimen.

When they needed to keep working, men attended closely to ways they could quite literally preserve themselves to do so. One middle-aged man with renal failure worked in a maintenance crew for the county. He refused his supervisor's offers to reassign him to prove that he could still do the strenuous work. An executive masked leaving the office early for his dialysis treatments by 'attending meetings out of the office.' Not even his secretary knew he was a dialysis patient. He believed that knowledge of his illness in the business community would reduce his stature as an aggressive competitor in the hierarchy of businessmen. A salesman completed his sales calls in the morning when he felt and looked fresher, and did paperwork at home in the afternoons when he could take rest breaks.

Discussion

Traditional assumptions of male identity, including an active, problem-solving stance, emphasis on personal power and autonomy, and bravery in the face of danger, form a two-edged sword for men in chronic illness. On the one hand, these assumptions encourage men to take risks, to be active, and to try to recover, which certainly can prompt recreating a valued life after serious episodes of illness and therefore bolster self-esteem. On the other hand, these assumptions narrow the range of credible male behaviours for those who subscribe to them. Hence, they foster rigidity in stance and set the conditions for slipping into depression.

Thus, an uneasy tension exists between valued identities and disparaged, that is denigrated or shameful, ones. A man can gain a strengthened identity through experiencing illness or can suffer a diminished one. These are not mutually exclusive categories. Men often move back and forth depending on their situations and their perceptions of them. The grieving process in men may be negated or cause those who witness it such discomfort that they cannot give comfort. Men may express their grieving in fear and rage as well as in tears and sorrow. But for many men who experience progressive illness and disability, grieving, instead of being a process, sinks into becoming a permanent depression. Life becomes struggling to live while waiting to die.

What are the conditions that shape whether a man will reconstruct a positive identity or sink into depression? Certainly, whether or not a man defines having future possibilities makes an enormous difference. The men in my study primarily founded their preferred identities in action. Subsequently, if they could define no valued realm of action open to them and no way to preserve a valued self, the likelihood that they would slip into depression increased.

References

Charmaz, K. 1991, *Good Days, Bad Days: The Self in Chronic Illness and Time*, New Brunswick, NJ: Rutgers University Press.

Cousins, N. 1983, *The Healing Heart: Antidotes to Panic and Helplessness*, New York: Avon.

Foster, L. 1978, *Man and Machine: Life Without Kidneys*, pp. 522–526 in Schwartz, H.D. and Kart, C.S. (eds) *Dominant Issues in Medical Sociology*, Reading, MA: Addison-Wesley.

Frank, A. 1991, *At the Will of the Body*, New York: Houghton-Mifflin.

Husserl, E. 1970, *The Crisis of the European Sciences and Transcendental Phenomenology*, Evanston, IL: Northwestern University Press.

This edited extract comes from Chapter 2 in Strauss, A and Corbin, J. (eds) (1997) *Grounded Theory in Practice*, published by Sage, London. The article originally appeared in *The Sociological Quarterly*, 35(2): 269–88. Kathy Charmaz is Professor of Sociology in the Department of Sociology, Sonoma State University, California, USA, where she undertakes qualitative research on illness experience, using grounded theory methodology.

24 | Costs of treating AIDS in Malawi and America

DAVID FINKEL AND
THOMAS GARRETT

In impoverished Malawi, one man faces the odds

David Finkel

BLANTYRE, Malawi – The surprise in this diseased and dying place isn't the man with AIDS, it's the sheets on his hospital bed. They're clean. They're ironed. They're a pleasant design of pastels. And most important, they're soft, giving immeasurable comfort to the 50-year-old man who is tucked in between them, listening in silence as his doctor explains what it will take for him to become one of the luckiest people in Malawi.

'So there are two issues you would have to be clear on' the doctor, Jack Wirima, is saying. 'The first one is the duration of the treatment. It would have to be taken for a long time.' 'For life?' asks the man, whose first name is Yasaya, whose voice is faint, whose arms are well on their way to bones. 'Yes. For the rest of your life. That's the first. And the second is the cost' Wirima goes on, explaining that the price for the treatment works out to about $10,000 a year. The treatment involves three drugs that, taken in combination, can prolong the life of an AIDS patient significantly. In the United States, where the treatment has become standard, the AIDS-related mortality rate fell 75 percent in three years. But in Malawi, which is one of the poorest countries in the world, and one of the sickest, the treatment isn't standard at all. The number of people who are HIV-positive in Malawi: more than 1 million. The number on triple-drug therapy, according to interviews and records of drug inventories: 30. 'So' says Wirima. 'Let me know.' 'Thank you' Yasaya says quietly and settles into his pillow, which matches the bedspread, which matches the sheets, wondering how he will be able to become number 31.

It will take several days for him to sort this through. He will have to decide what to say to his wife, who prays for his health, and sleeps in a chair next to the hospital bed, and tidies him up after he vomits, and has yet to be told he tested positive for HIV, the virus that causes AIDS. He will have to decide what to tell his employer, who he fears won't want to pay for his care, and maybe will no longer want him as an employee if his diagnosis is disclosed (which is why he asked to be identified only by his first name). He will have to decide what to say to his children, and he will have to decide how much of his income he is willing to spend before staying alive becomes, in his own mind, an act of selfishness.

The place isn't only Malawi but sub-Saharan Africa, and the catastrophe, by now, has been well documented. Of the 34 million HIV/AIDS cases in the world, 24 million, or 70 percent, are in Africa. Life expectancies are down dramatically. The number of orphans has surpassed 10 million. The number of AIDS-related deaths is estimated at 5,500 a day, according to the United Nations. And so it is in Malawi, a small, densely populated country of 10 million people in south-central Africa. The United Nations reports that HIV/AIDS caused 70,000 deaths here last year alone, has created 400,000 orphans since the first case was noted in 1984, has reduced life expectancy from 47 years for a baby born in the mid-1980s to 36 for a baby born now, and has, to this point, infected 16 percent of the adult population.

But even in the poorest, most devastated places, possibilities exist, and in Malawi they can be found in a 64-bed hospital in Blantyre that is surrounded by a tall iron fence and has a sign above the front door that says 'Right of Admission Reserved.' This is Mwaiwathu Private Hospital, and as the name makes clear, and the sign makes clear, and the fence makes clear, and the guards at the entry gate make clear, it is not for everyone. Rather, as Wirima puts it, 'If you can pay, you can come here' and those who do include government officials, and the Malawian business executives whose medical insurance allows them access to a kind of care that most Malawians simply can't imagine.

Yasaya is one of those businessmen. Unlike most Malawians, who live in villages, in hand-built huts that have neither plumbing nor electricity, Yasaya lives in a house with several bedrooms and bathrooms and, dominating the living room, a large TV connected to a satellite dish. Because the town they live in is near Lake Malawi, there are plenty of mosquitoes around, and at first Yasaya suspected malaria. But it turned out to be tuberculosis. Followed by malaria. Followed by illness after illness, and weight loss, and weakness, and lethargy, and a constant cough, and a continuous fever, which is why he wasn't surprised when an AIDS test came back positive.

But even a year of sickness didn't prepare him for how ill he was to become. Late one night when he couldn't stop shaking, he went to the emergency room at the government-run hospital. Like all public hospitals in Malawi, it is severely overcrowded. Patients not only fill every bed, they sleep on the floor. Nurses are scarce. Only the most basic drugs are in stock. And on this night no doctor was available, so Yasaya, still shaking, went home. And the following morning came to Mwaiwathu Private Hospital. Where there are flowers in the foyer. Where the hallways, upon instructions from the hospital administrator, always smell of pine spray. Where, in a country in which the annual per-capita income is less than $200, the charge for a bed, just the bed, not the doctors, not the lab tests, not the drugs, is $50 a day.

Yasaya is explaining how he might have become infected, saying maybe it was the time he had to carry his dying brother, who was bleeding and too weak to walk. 'Or it could be the condom that broke. Or it could be the hospital. Maybe they reuse syringes.' He looks at himself. He is on an IV. He is catheterized. He is, for the moment, alone. His wife is out in the hallway. She is his only wife, even though men are allowed several in Malawi, just as they're allowed girlfriends, which is one of the reasons the infection rate among women aged 25 to 29 is 32 percent. 'It was sex, basically' he says after a while. 'But I don't know who.'

What he also doesn't know is very much about anti-retroviral drugs, which, though not a cure for AIDS, have had a dramatic effect on mortality and morbidity rates in developed countries, especially the United States, where the drugs have become a $1 billion-a-year business. He doesn't know about the ongoing debate over worldwide access to these drugs in which certain aid organizations are saying that anything less than full access in even the poorest countries is unconscionable, and drug companies are saying there has to be a balance between charity and business, and any number of studies are saying that even if the drugs were available, there are plenty of other problems that would prohibit their administration, from a shortage of trained health care workers to a lack of passable roads.

A one-month supply of Crixivan, a protease inhibitor, that has offered the most hope for HIV/AIDS patients costs about $500. Five hundred dollars is what he earns a month, after taxes. What he does know is that there is a house to pay for, and food to buy, and his children's school tuition is coming due. He wants the drugs – of course he wants the drugs – but if his company doesn't pay for the treatment, 'I would have to abandon it. It would be too costly.' Meaning? 'I would die. Sooner than later. But sometimes dying is not the end' he says. 'I would just relieve myself of certain obligations. If I live, the expectations of my family are very high.' Such are the unsentimental calculations of one man in a hospital bed – and, on a much wider scale, of Malawi itself.

Unlike in other countries, the Malawian government at least has acknowledged the scope of AIDS, even producing an official 'strategic framework' for dealing with the disease over the next several years. Should there be more AIDS testing? Yes. Should there be more education? Yes. Should there be more 'hope, faith, compassion and a spirit of acceptance of the reality of HIV/AIDS among Malawians'? Yes. But while the plan focuses on prevention, it pays hardly any attention to those already infected. What about them? 'Well, they'll be dying at various rates' says Wesley Sangala, the health official who oversaw the development of the government's plan. How much of a priority is their treatment? 'In reality, we cannot entertain it' he says, sounding resigned. 'It is just too expensive to contemplate. So all we are saying, unfortunately, is that they have to die.'

This article is an edited version of 'Few drugs for the needy: in impoverished Malawi, one man faces the odds', which appeared in *The Washington Post* on 1 November 2000, p. A01. The author, David Finkel, is a staff writer with the newspaper.

America: one year on therapy and counting

Thomas Garrett

I am what is referred to as a highly motivated and compliant patient. I am highly motivated to stay alive and healthy, and I know that the way to maintain my health is to comply, conscientiously and consistently, with the multi-drug regimen my doctor has prescribed for me. In my first year on therapy I didn't miss a single one of the 1,460 doses I was supposed to take. Here's how I did it.

Two years ago I had what physicians call 'advanced' HIV disease. If someone had told me that I would one day be on an anti-retroviral regimen that required me to take pills four times a day, some of those pills with food, some of those pills on an empty stomach, and all of those pills at fixed intervals throughout the day – and that I would adjust to this demanding schedule without missing a single dose – I would have told them they were crazy. Today, if someone were to tell me that it is okay to miss an occasional dose, I would tell them they are crazy.

When, in the early summer of 1996, the doctor told me I had full-blown AIDS, the diagnosis brought twelve years of denial to an abrupt end. I'd known I was HIV-positive since 1984, but I managed to push this unwelcome information into a back corner of my consciousness. There was no effective treatment for HIV infection in 1984, so I saw no point in acknowledging my seropositivity. Like many others who discovered that they were HIV-positive in the early days of the epidemic, I reasoned that admitting I had HIV would, in a sense, empower the virus to cause disease – in the same way that believers in voodoo give it its magic.

And for twelve years I was able to tell myself that this strategy of mine was working, because I had no obvious signs or symptoms of HIV disease. I moved through life as if HIV did not affect me, as if it would not, could not, touch me. I got my degree; I got my first job; I got my first 'grown-up' apartment. I fell in love. And out of love. Then, in the early summer of 1996, I developed chronic bronchitis – which was bad enough that it eventually brought me to the emergency room. During a follow-up visit I learned that I no longer simply had HIV. I had AIDS.

My doctor immediately prescribed all of the medications that were then being given to someone with advanced HIV disease. I sat stunned and speechless. Although I'd had twelve years to prepare myself for this moment, I found that I was utterly unready for it. And, as I soon discovered, I was woefully ill-equipped to make decisions about my own health care. Worse still, even though I'd known for more than a decade that I had HIV, even though I knew that I would eventually get AIDS, I had no health insurance. I excused myself from the doctor's office, made an appointment with the hospital's AIDS clinic, went home, and cried.

Having lived in New York City since the beginning of the AIDS crisis, I had seen firsthand the pain and frustration of people living with, and dying of, HIV. I had heard all the horror stories, and I had heard the repeated refrain 'The treatment is worse than the disease.' So I was decidedly unenthusiastic about beginning any kind of anti-retroviral regimen. Most people with HIV have gone through this same process. And most of us have come through it in much the way I did: we recognize that our apprehensions about anti-retroviral therapy are irrational. For me, beginning anti-retroviral therapy meant admitting, finally, that I was HIV-positive. That's what made it such a hurdle. I saw it as the first step of what, I was sure, would be my final steps – and so my drugs sat on a shelf of my medicine cabinet for weeks before I could bring myself to begin taking them. I wasn't ready to begin what I thought of as the end game. And given that I couldn't even manage to take vitamins on a regular basis, I legitimately wondered how I could possibly comply with the rigorous dosing schedule imposed by combination therapy, a schedule that I would probably have to be on for the rest of my life.

As I began to educate myself about HIV and treatment, I encountered the same advice over and over again: If you want to retard, and possibly even prevent, the emergence of drug-resistant strains of HIV, you have to remain completely compliant with your drug regimen. In theory, at least, if I stick to my assigned regimen, drug resistance will never have the chance to emerge, and I can keep HIV at bay indefinitely. That is what my doctor tells me. That's the theory. And so, armed with this hope, I have learned to incorporate my drug regimen into my daily life. And I am proud to report that in my first full year on therapy I never missed a single dose.

I have achieved this track record for one simple reason: fear is a very powerful motivator. The thought of missing a dose fills me with such dread that I would much rather interrupt whatever I am doing to swallow a handful of pills than risk missing a dose. On the rare occasions when I leave home without the medications I will be needing while I am gone, I turn around and go back for those pills – even if it means that I'll be late for my appointments. After all, I can make excuses to clients for my tardiness, but HIV does not accept excuses.

Like practically everyone on anti-retroviral therapy, I do experience some unpleasant side effects from my cocktail. I had to stop taking AZT, for example, because it made me feel so rotten. I had such terrible headaches that I actually cried out in pain – but I kept on taking my scheduled doses until I could see my doctor, explain the problem, and get him to change my regimen. I tried the non-nucleoside analog nevirapine (Viramune®) next, but I had an allergic reaction to that drug, as a small percentage of patients do. When I switched to my current regimen, I had to adjust my doses of Norvir to minimize the diarrhoea. I seem to have the side effects under control at this point but some days I feel as if I have no energy. At such times I remind myself that my goal was not zero side effects but minimal, manageable side effects – side effects I can live with.

The part of pill-taking that was hardest for me – as it is for most people with HIV – was learning how to time my doses throughout the day. Ideally, I should be taking each dose exactly 12 hours after the previous dose, to keep the amount of drug in my bloodstream as level as possible. Because it isn't always possible to take my drugs at precise 12-hour intervals, since Videx must be taken on an empty stomach – and all my other medications must be taken with food – I have to remember to take my meds at four different times during the day. Furthermore, I have to time my meals so that I end up taking my Videx no less than one hour before, or two hours after, a meal.

And so it goes, every day, day after day, dose after dose, without fail. I make sure my prescriptions are filled on time; I set aside time on Sunday to count out the pills for the week; and every time I look in my refrigerator and see those little bottles, I am reminded to take my meds. At this point pill-taking is as routine to me as eating or brushing my teeth. Those pills are doing their job – because I am doing mine – and my future, which only a year ago seemed very dim indeed, now seems brighter than it has at any time in the 14 years since I first tested seropositive. I am living with HIV. And I am living, quite successfully, with the dosing demands of combination therapy. I thought all the pill-taking might overwhelm me, but complying with therapy proved to be nothing more than another of life's adjustments.

This edited extract comes from a personal perspective by Thomas Garrett, which appeared on the Internet on *The Body* website in June 1998, under the title 'One year on therapy and counting . . . Doses taken: 1,460; Doses missed: 0'. *The Body* is an AIDS and HIV information resource, funded by major pharmaceutical companies, which has won several awards for 'best health website'. It can be accessed at http://www.thebody.com/index.shtml

Influences on health and disease

| INTRODUCTION

What factors influence patterns of health and disease? The answers to this question reflect many viewpoints: a particular historical or political perspective; the frame of reference provided by an academic discipline; the relative importance attached to biological factors, particularly human genes; the role of individual actions and personal responsibility; or the impact of social processes and social relationships. The articles in Part 3 reflect the variety of possible answers and illustrate the many ways in which the question is posed, and the nature of the evidence is considered.

For Friedrich Engels, revolutionary communist and close colleague of Karl Marx, the question followed on from his analysis of nineteenth-century English society. Cities like Manchester were being dramatically transformed by industrialization, producing explosive rates of urban growth and stark extremes of wealth and poverty. Engels set about the systematic documentation of the consequences of this upheaval for that part of the population – the majority – to whom the benefits of industrialization must have seemed far from obvious. In 'Health: 1844' he portrays the squalor of existence and the disparities between social classes in death and disease. What marks out his portrait as unique, however, are not the facts themselves (which in large part were culled from official reports), but his repeated stress on the nature of the society that could produce these conditions. The bourgeoisie, 'interested in maintaining and prolonging this disorder', has created these victims and stands accused by Engels of deliberate 'murder'. Although Engels' political conclusions are as disputed now as in the 1840s, his description is generally accepted as a valuable historical document.

Observing the process of economic development one and a half centuries after Engels, the economists David Bloom and David Canning describe much more benign consequences of industrialization in 'The health and wealth of nations', in particular the powerful positive association between development measured by average income and life expectancy. However, where this correlation is conventionally explained in terms of higher incomes permitting better nutrition, public health and health services, they argue that the direction of causality runs at least in part in the opposite direction – health can influence wealth. Healthier populations are more productive, have more incentive to invest in their education and their future and accelerate the demographic transition, all of which can lead to higher rates of income growth. On this analysis, investing in health becomes an explicit development tool, rather than a hoped-for consequence of economic growth.

The physiologist and evolutionary biologist Jared Diamond is also concerned with the links between development and health, but for him the decisive moment in human history was the transition from hunting and gathering to agriculture, around 10,000 years ago. Diamond does not claim that some Golden Age has been lost, but in 'Agriculture's two-edged sword' he argues convincingly that the influences on health of the shift to agriculture were far-reaching and often deleterious, and that humankind has not yet solved the problems that came in its wake. The power of his argument derives in large measure from his efforts to apply science to the study of history, where biology provides the scientific framework, evolution is the concept and paleopathology yields the evidence.

Another increasingly apparent consequence of industrialization and economic development is global climate change and the impact this may have on human health – the subject of 'Climate and health' by Paul R. Epstein. While the fact of climate change has become incontrovertible, the precise form it will take and its consequences for human health are much less certain. Epstein suggests a number of mechanisms likely to affect the range and severity of infectious diseases, but also notes the possible effects on nutrition and food security, and the direct consequences of floods, hurricanes and extremes of heat and cold. Ultimately, however, as Epstein notes, it is the overall impact of climate change on atmosphere, oceans and forests that is likely to have the most profound and unpredictable consequences for human health as the twenty-first century unfolds.

While economic development, industrialization and climate change can all be traced back to human actions, it is easy to lose sight of the influences on health of individual actions and consequences. The Medical Services Study Group of the Royal College of Physicians gaze unrelentingly on individual behaviour. Of the 250 patients whose 'Deaths under 50' were examined by the Group, in their view almost 40 per cent could be held as largely 'to blame' for their own death – by choosing to smoke, drink, overeat, ignore medical advice or not comply with treatment, or by taking a more direct path to 'self-destruction' – suicide. The extent to which these patients are held personally responsible is indicated by the Study Group's implicit view that the demands placed by such patients on health services are unreasonable and wasteful.

In 'Prevention is better . . .', Helen Roberts, Susan Smith and Carol Bryce explore one major cause of ill health (accidents) at one point in the life course (childhood). Where the Medical Services Study Group give primacy to the influence of individual behaviour on health, these authors argue that it is only one factor in a complex story. Their research found that individual parents have a detailed knowledge of the risks in their physical environment, and undertake a wide range of preventive activities to reduce these risks to their children. The analysis by Roberts, Smith and Bryce also has a social dimension, in that the environmental hazards are in many ways related to the poor housing and poverty in the area of Glasgow they studied. Their conclusion has important implications for health promotion, which they argue has adopted a misconceived focus on 'deficient parenting' and behavioural changes inside the home, rather than on enacting policies to improve the unsafe environments in which parents strive to keep their children safe.

One implication of the Medical Services Study Group's report is that patients should allow their doctors to have a greater influence on their health, noting the 'psychopathic' attitude to doctors attributed to many of the patients in their sample. Doctors are thereby allotted a central influence in defining and legitimating the existence of disease. Richard Asher, a British physician, describes a situation in which doctors are faced with this dilemma by patients who are 'malingering' – deliberately faking ill health. What influences a person to display this form of 'illness'? Asher identifies fear, desire or escape, and observes the ingenuity of, for example, prisoners of war in faking illness. However, there is also a 'borderland of malingering', where the purpose is not evident and the motives obscure. Munchausen's syndrome, which is perhaps the most spectacular example provided by Asher, calls into question the ease with which a dividing line can be drawn between 'real' and 'fake' illness.

The analysis by Notzon and colleagues of influences on the decline in life expectancy in Russia during the early 1990s – an unprecedented experience for an industrialized country – also addresses issues of 'poor personal health behaviours', but again within a more complex setting. It seems clear that alcohol abuse, smoking, suicide, homicide and vehicle accidents were all implicated in Russia's health problems, but the background was the enormous social and economic dislocation following the break-up of the Soviet Union. The details of this painful episode are still being pieced together, and there is some evidence that the deterioration in health was halted in the later 1990s. But the broader lesson the authors draw is that no industrialized country can take its current levels of life expectancy for granted: changed circumstances can provoke rapid and substantial declines.

One striking feature of Russian society in the 1990s was the emergence of gross inequalities in income and wealth. The relation between inequality and health has been at the core of Richard Wilkinson's research, and in 'The psychosocial causes of illness' he sets out his hypothesis that the psychosocial effects of relative inequality may well have as big an effect on health as the material effects of absolute deprivation. His assertion that 'stress' is a more important factor in the aetiology of disease than is generally allowed has provoked much debate; so too has its corollary, that social cohesion and supportive relationships are protective. Such complex interactions can ultimately only be proved or disproved by evidence from well-designed epidemiological studies. However, as Wilkinson acknowledges, there are innumerable possible causal mechanisms underlying his hypothesis, and this greatly complicates the task of designing and interpreting such studies.

Inequality is also at the heart of the research by the economists Jean Drèze and Amartya Sen into the characteristics and economic context of mass hunger. Drèze and Sen argue that conventional explanations for famines, often focusing on food supply, are usually misleading. Instead, they argue that the system of entitlement relations, which dictates whether or not people can command a right to available food, is much more important. In 'Entitlement and deprivation' they illustrate this with examples of famines occurring in situations where food supply was above average. The policy implications of their work are clear, pointing towards issues of equity and distribution rather than an exclusive focus on increasing food production.

For social analysts such as Wilkinson, biological features of humans such as adrenal glands and immune systems are primarily mechanisms linking a social context to a health consequence. Barry Bogin, an American anthropologist, extends this viewpoint further by arguing that the biological evolution of puberty has co-evolved with the development of gender roles. Bogin is concerned with adolescence, that period of spectacular biological change accompanying the transition from childhood to adulthood. The human adolescent growth spurt is unique among mammals, and Bogin explores what evolutionary advantages this biological trait may confer. In 'Why must I be a teenager at all?' he concludes that adolescence offers maturing boys and girls an ideal opportunity to learn their adult social roles – girls while infertile but perceived as mature, boys while fertile but perceived as immature – and that this in turn has allowed humans to be more reproductively successful than other primates.

The Nobel prizewinner James D. Watson, forever linked with Francis Crick for their pioneering work to identify the structure and role of DNA, was also closely involved in the development of the Human Genome Project. In 'Good gene, bad gene' he starts from the premise that our genetic heritage is the fundamental influence on our health, and then puts the argument for embracing genetic knowledge and using it to the full to minimize the impact of genetic disease. In this account, 'bad genes' are simply random tragedies that we should prevent as vigorously as possible. Watson sees 'controlling our children's genetic destiny' as a 'truly moral way for us to proceed'. Elsewhere in this Reader, other authors resoundingly reject this position.

Our genetic attributes are also an essential part of the analysis by James W. Vaupel and colleagues of 'Biodemographic trajectories of longevity' – the slowing down of death rates that occurs in old age. They see no immediate limit to further declines in mortality rates in older age groups, but explanations for this phenomenon are still obscure, as evolutionary theory predicts short post-reproductive life spans. The biodemographic concepts they draw on to resolve this paradox are difficult and not fully formed, but hold the promise of disentangling the genetic and non-genetic factors that influence our mortality trajectories, as individuals, societies and as a species.

Peter Laslett, best known for his path-breaking history of English social structure, *The World We Have Lost*, is also concerned with increases in longevity. In 'A new division of the life course', he examines some implications of the vastly increased numbers of people now experiencing old age. Laslett argues that the 'biological' is only one of several dimensions to a life course, and that age has a range of meanings that may be ambiguous and contradictory. He suggests that the historical association of old age with 'dependence and decrepitude' permeates our language, culture and social policies, but has been rendered hopelessly inaccurate by demographic changes which have resulted in large numbers of active and healthy people beyond the current retirement age. The result is a damaging depreciation of the talents and experience of a large part of the population. Laslett's objective is to displace this dissonant perception of old age by offering an ordering of the life course in which the period between earning and saving, and dependence and death – what he terms the Third Age – is seen as an era of personal fulfilment.

The articles in Part 3 represent a wide range of views on what influences health and disease. Some are irreconcilable with others, and some are differentiated largely by the rather arbitrary demarcations of academic disciplines. Overcoming these demarcations would not remove all conflicts of view, but would make the substance of such conflicts much clearer.

25 | Health: 1844

FRIEDRICH ENGELS

When one individual inflicts bodily injury upon another, such injury that death results, we call the deed manslaughter; when the assailant knew in advance that the injury would be fatal, we call his deed murder. But when society places hundreds of proletarians in such a position that they inevitably meet a too early and an unnatural death, one which is quite as much a death by violence as that by the sword or bullet; when it deprives thousands of the necessaries of life, places them under conditions in which they *cannot* live – forces them, through the strong arm of the law, to remain in such conditions until that death ensues which is the inevitable consequence – knows that these thousands of victims must perish, and yet permits these conditions to remain, its deed is murder just as surely as the deed of the single individual; disguised, malicious murder, murder against which none can defend himself, which does not seem what it is, because no man sees the murderer, because the death of the victim seems a natural one, since the offence is more one of omission than of commission. But murder it remains.

The manner in which the great multitude of the poor is treated by society today is revolting. They are drawn into large cities where they breathe a poorer atmosphere than in the country; they are relegated to districts which, by reason of the method of construction, are worse ventilated than any others; they are deprived of all means of cleanliness, of water itself, since pipes are laid only when paid for, and the rivers so polluted that they are useless for such purposes; they are obliged to throw all offal and garbage, all dirty water, often all disgusting drainage and excrement into the streets, being without other means of disposing of them; they are thus compelled to infect the region of their own dwellings. Nor is this enough. All conceivable evils are heaped upon the heads of the poor. If the population of great cities is too dense in general, it is they in particular who are packed into the least space. As though the vitiated atmosphere of the streets were not enough, they are penned in dozens into single rooms, so that the air in which they breathe at night is enough in itself to stifle them. They are given damp dwellings, cellar dens that are not waterproof from below, or garrets that leak from above. Their houses are so built that the clammy air cannot escape. They are supplied bad, tattered, or rotten clothing, adulterated and indigestible food. They are exposed to the most exciting changes of mental condition, the most violent vibrations between hope and fear; they are hunted like game, and not permitted to attain peace of mind and quiet enjoyment of life. They are deprived of all enjoyments except that of sexual indulgence and drunkenness, are worked every day to the point of complete exhaustion of their mental and physical energies, and are thus constantly spurred on to the maddest excess in the only two enjoyments at their disposal. And if they surmount all this, they fall victims to want of work in a crisis when all the little is taken from them that had hitherto been vouchsafed them.

How is it possible, under such conditions, for the lower class to be healthy and long lived? What else can be expected than an excessive mortality, an unbroken series of epidemics, a progressive deterioration in the physique of the working population? Let us see how the facts stand.

That the bad air of London, and especially of the working-people's districts, is in the highest degree favourable to the development of consumption, the hectic appearance of great numbers of persons sufficiently indicates. If one roams the streets a little in the early morning, when the multitudes are on their way to their work, one is amazed at the number of persons who look wholly or half-consumptive, pale, lank, narrow-chested, hollow-eyed ghosts, whom one passes at every step, these languid, flabby faces, incapable of the slightest energetic expression.

In competition with consumption stand typhus, to say nothing of scarlet fever, a disease which brings most frightful devastation into the ranks of the working-class. This fever has the same character almost everywhere, and develops in nearly every case into specific typhus. According to the annual report of Dr Southwood Smith on the London Fever Hospital, the number of patients in 1843 was 1,462, or 418 more than in any previous year. Many of the patients were working-people from the country, who had endured the severest privation while migrating, and, after their arrival, had slept hungry and half-naked in the streets, and so fallen victims to the fever. These people were brought into the hospital in such a state of weakness, that unusual quantities of wine, cognac, and preparations of ammonia and other stimulants were required for their treatment; $16\frac{1}{2}$ per cent of all patients died.

In Edinburgh and Glasgow it broke out in 1817, after the famine, and in 1826 and 1837 with especial violence, after the commercial crisis, subsiding somewhat each time after having raged about three years. In Edinburgh about 6,000 persons were attacked by the fever during the epidemic of 1817, and about 10,000 in that of 1837, and not only the number of persons attacked but the violence of the disease increased with each repetition.

But the fury of the epidemic in all former periods seems to have been child's play in comparison with its ravages after the crisis of 1842. One-sixth of the whole indigent population of Scotland was seized by the fever, and the infection was carried by wandering beggars with fearful rapidity from one locality to another. It did not reach the middle and upper classes of the population, yet in two months there were more fever cases than in twelve years before. In Glasgow, 12 per cent of the population were seized in the year 1843; 32,000 persons, of whom 32 per cent perished, while this mortality in Manchester and Liverpool does not ordinarily exceed 8 per cent.

When one remembers under what conditions the working-people live, when one thinks how crowded their dwellings are, how every nook and corner swarms with human beings, how sick and well sleep in the same room, in the same bed, the only wonder is that a contagious disease like this fever does not spread yet farther. And when one reflects how little medical assistance the sick have at command, how many are without any medical advice whatsoever, and ignorant of the most ordinary precautionary measures, the mortality seems actually small.

Another category of diseases arises directly from the food rather than the dwellings of the workers. The food of the labourer, indigestible enough in itself, is utterly unfit for young children, and he has neither means nor time to get his children more suitable food. Moreover, the custom of giving children spirits, and even opium, is very general; and these two influences, with the rest of the conditions of life prejudicial to bodily development, give rise to the most diverse affections of the digestive organs, leaving lifelong traces behind them. Scrofula is almost universal among the working-class, and scrofulous parents have scrofulous children, especially when the original influences continue in full force to operate upon the inherited tendency of the children. A second consequence of this insufficient bodily nourishment, during the years of growth and development, is rachitis, which is extremely common among the children of the working-class. The hardening of the bones is delayed, the development of the skeleton in general is restricted, and deformities of the legs and spinal column are frequent, in addition to the usual rachitic affections. How greatly all these evils are increased by the changes to which the workers are subject in consequence of fluctuations in trade, want of work, and the scanty wages in time of crisis, it is not necessary to dwell upon. Temporary want of sufficient food, to which almost every working-man is exposed at least once in the course of his life, only contributes to intensify the effect of his usually sufficient but bad diet.

Besides these, there are other influences which enfeeble the health of a great number of workers, intemperance most of all. All possible temptations, all allurements combine to bring the workers to drunkenness. Liquor is almost their only source of pleasure, and all things conspire to make it accessible to them. The working-man comes from his work tired, exhausted, finds his home comfortless, damp, dirty, repulsive; he has urgent need of recreation, he *must* have something to make work worth his trouble, to make the prospect of the next day endurable. Drunkenness has here ceased to be a vice, for which the vicious can be held responsible; it becomes a phenomenon, the necessary, inevitable effect of certain conditions upon an object possessed of no volition in relation to those conditions. They who have degraded the working-man to a mere object have the responsibility to bear.

Another source of physical mischief to the working-class lies in the impossibility of employing skilled physicians in cases of illness. English doctors charge high fees, and working-men are not in a position to pay them. They can therefore do nothing or are compelled to call in cheap charlatans, and use quack remedies, which do more harm than good. An immense number of such quacks thrive in every English town, securing their *clientèle* among the poor by means of advertisements, posters, and other such devices. Besides these, vast quantities of patent medicines are sold, for all conceivable ailments: Morrison's Pills, Parr's Life Pills, Dr Mainwaring's Pills, and a thousand other pills, essences, and balsams, all of which have the property of curing all the ills that flesh is heir to. It is by no means unusual for the manufacturer of Parr's Life Pills to sell twenty to twenty-five thousand boxes of these salutary pills in a week, and they are taken for constipation by this one, for diarrhoea by that one, for fever, weakness, and all possible ailments. As our German peasants are cupped or bled at certain seasons, so do the English working-people now consume patent medicines to their own injury and the great profit of the manufacturer. One of the most injurious of these patent medicines is a drink prepared with opiates, chiefly laudanum, under the name Godfrey's Cordial. Women who work at home, and have their own and other people's children to take care of, give them this drink to keep them quiet, and, as many believe, to strengthen them. They often begin to give this medicine to newly-born children, and continue, without knowing the effects of this 'heart's-ease', until the children die. The less susceptible the child's system to the action of the opium, the greater the quantities administered. When the cordial ceases to act, laudanum alone is given, often to the extent of fifteen to twenty drops at a dose. The Coroner of Nottingham testified before a Parliamentary Commission that one apothecary had, according to his own statement, used thirteen hundred-weight of laudanum in one year in the preparation of Godfrey's Cordial. The effects upon the children so treated may be readily imagined. They are pale, feeble, wilted, and usually die before completing the second year. The use of this cordial is very extensive in all great towns and industrial districts in the kingdom.

The result of all these influences is a general enfeeblement of the frame in the working-class. They are almost all weakly, of angular but not powerful build, lean, pale, and of relaxed fibre, with the exception of the muscles especially exercised in their work. Nearly all suffer from indigestion, and consequently from a more or less hypochondriac, melancholy, irritable, nervous condition. Their enfeebled constitutions are unable to resist disease, and are therefore seized by it on every occasion. Hence they age prematurely, and die early. On this point the mortality statistics supply unquestionable testimony.

According to the Report of Register-General Graham, the annual death-rate of all England and Wales is something less than $2^1/4$ per cent. That is to say, out of forty-five persons, one dies every year. This was the average for the year 1839–40. In 1840–41 the mortality diminished somewhat, and the death-rate was but one in forty-six. But in the great cities the proportion is wholly different. I have before me official tables of mortality (*Manchester Guardian*, 31 July 1844), according to which the death-rate of several large towns is as follows: In Manchester, including Chorlton and Salford, 1 in 32.72; and excluding Chorlton and Salford, 1 in 30.75. In Liverpool, including West Derby (suburb), 31.90, and excluding West Derby, 29.00; while the average of all the districts of Cheshire, Lancashire, and Yorkshire cited, including a number of wholly or partially rural districts and many small towns, with a total population of 2,172,506 for the whole, is 1 death in 39.80 persons. How unfavourably the workers are placed in the great cities, the mortality for Prescott in Lancashire shows; a district inhabited by miners, and showing a lower sanitary condition than of the agricultural districts, mining being by no means a healthful occupation. But these miners live in the country, and the death-rate among them is but 1 in 47.54, or nearly $2^1/2$ per cent, better than that for all England. All these statements are based upon the mortality tables for 1843. Still higher is the death-rate in the Scotch cities; in Edinburgh, in 1838–39, 1 in 29; in 1831, in the Old Town alone, 1 in 22. In Glasgow, according to Dr Cowen, the average has been, since 1830, 1 in 30; and in single years, 1 in 22 to 24. That this enormous shortening of life falls chiefly upon the working-class, that the general average is improved by the smaller mortality of the upper and middle-classes, is attested upon all sides. One of the most recent depositions is that of a physician, Dr P. H. Holland, in Manchester, who investigated Chorlton-on-Medlock, a suburb of Manchester, under official commission. He divided the houses and streets into three classes each, and ascertained the following variations in the death-rate:

First class of Streets. Houses			I. class.	Mortality	1 in	51
,,	,,	,,	II. ,,	,,	,,	41
,,	,,	,,	III. ,,	,,	,,	36
Second	,,	,,	I. ,,	,,	,,	55
,,	,,	,,	II. ,,	,,	,,	38
,,	,,	,,	III. ,,	,,	,,	35
Third	,,	,,	I. ,,	Wanting	–	–
,,	,,	,,	II. ,,	Mortality	,,	35
,,	,,	,,	III. ,,	,,	,,	25

It is clear from other tables given by Holland that the mortality in the *streets* of the second class is 18 per cent greater, and in the streets of the third class 68 per cent greater than in those of the first class; that the mortality in the *houses* of the second class is 31 per cent greater, and in the third class 78 per cent greater than in those of the first class; that the mortality in those bad streets which were improved, decreased 25 per cent. He closes with the remark, very frank for an English bourgeois:[1]

When we find the rate of mortality four times as high in some streets as in others, and twice as high in whole classes of streets as in other classes, and further find it is all but invariably high in those streets which are in bad condition, and almost invariably low in those whose condition is good, we cannot resist the conclusion that multitudes of our fellow-creatures, *hundreds of our immediate neighbours*, are annually destroyed for want of the most evident precautions.

The death-rate is kept so high chiefly by the heavy mortality among young children in the working-class. The tender frame of a child is least able to withstand the unfavourable influences of an inferior lot in life; the neglect to which they are often subjected, when both parents work or one is dead, avenges itself promptly, and no one need wonder that in Manchester more than 57 per cent of the children of the working-class perish before the fifth year, while but 20 per cent of the children of the higher classes, and not quite 32 per cent of the children of all classes in the country die under five years of age.

Apart from the diverse diseases which are the necessary consequence of the present neglect and oppression of the poorer classes, there are other influences which contribute to increase the mortality among small children. In many families the wife, like the husband, has to work away from home, and the consequence is the total neglect of the children, who are either locked up or given out to be taken care of. It is, therefore, not to be wondered at if hundreds of them perish through all manner of accidents. Nowhere are so many children run over, nowhere are so many killed by falling, drowning, or burning, as in the great cities and towns of England. Deaths from burns and scalds are especially frequent, such a case occurring nearly every week during the winter months in Manchester, and very frequently in London, though little mention is made of them in the papers. I have at hand a copy of the *Weekly Dispatch* of 15 December 1844, according to which, in the week from 1 December to 7 December inclusive, *six* such cases occurred. These unhappy children, perishing in this terrible way, are victims of our social disorder, and of the property-holding classes interested in maintaining and prolonging this disorder. Yet one is left in doubt whether even this terribly torturing death is not a blessing for the children in rescuing them from a long life of toil and wretchedness, rich in suffering and poor in enjoyment. So far has it gone in England; and the bourgeoisie reads these things every day in the newspapers and takes no further trouble in the matter. But it cannot complain if, after the official and non-official testimony here cited which must be known to it, I broadly accuse it of social murder.

Reference

1. Report of Commission of Inquiry into the State of Large Towns and Populous Districts, First Report, 1844. Appendix.

Friedrich Engels, son of a German textile manufacturer, came to Manchester in 1842 to work in his father's factory. In 1845, aged 25, he published *The Condition of the Working Class in England* in Leipzig. The first British edition did not appear until 1892. The extract reproduced here is drawn from the translation of the full work by the Institute of Marxism–Leninism, Moscow, published by Panther Books, London, 1969.

26 | The health and wealth of nations

DAVID E. BLOOM AND DAVID CANNING

The positive correlation between health and income per capita is one of the best-known relations in international development, [and] is commonly thought to reflect a causal link running from income to health. Higher income gives greater command over many of the goods and services that promote health, such as better nutrition and access to safe water, sanitation, and good quality health services.

Recently, however, another intriguing possibility has emerged: that the health–income correlation is partly explained by a causal link running the other way – from health to income. Several mechanisms, falling into four main categories, could account for this relation:

Productivity. Healthier populations tend to have higher labor productivity, because their workers are physically more energetic and mentally more robust. They suffer fewer lost workdays from illness or the need to care for other family members who have fallen ill.

Education. Healthier people who live longer have stronger incentives to invest in developing their skills, because they expect to reap the benefits of such investments over longer periods. Increased schooling promotes greater productivity and, in turn, higher income. Good health also promotes school attendance and enhances cognitive function.

Investment in physical capital. Improvements in longevity create a greater need for people to save for their retirement. Insofar as increased savings lead to increased investment, workers will have access to more capital and their incomes will rise. In addition, a healthy and educated workforce acts as a strong magnet for foreign investment.

'Demographic dividend'. The transition from high to low rates of mortality and fertility has been dramatic and rapid in many developing countries in recent decades. Mortality declines concentrated among infants and children typically initiate the transition and trigger subsequent declines in fertility. An initial surge in the numbers of young

dependents gradually gives way to an increase in the proportion of the population that is of working age. As this happens, income per capita can rise dramatically, provided the broader policy environment permits the new workers to be absorbed into productive employment.[1]

All these mechanisms offer plausible ways in which health improvements can lead to income growth. However, examining the data allows evaluation of how important these mechanisms are. Recent economic analysis indicates that health status (as measured by life expectancy) is a significant predictor of subsequent economic growth.[2] This effect is above and beyond other influences on economic growth, emerges consistently across studies, and is strikingly large.[3]

Suppose we compare two countries that are identical in all respects, except one has a 5-year advantage in life expectancy. On the basis of studies in several countries, real income per capita in the healthier country will grow 0.3% to 0.5% per year faster than in its less healthy counterpart. This represents a sizable boost to growth, given that, from 1965 to 1990, countries experienced an average per capita income growth of only 2% per year. Moreover, a gain of 5 years in life expectancy is well within the reach of most developing countries – since 1950, for example, life expectancy worldwide has increased by about 20 years.

As these health improvements fortify the economy, they also alleviate poverty. Economic growth is an exceedingly powerful way to reduce poverty among the 1.3 billion people living on less than US$1 per day. Available evidence indicates that increases in average income translate – percentage point for percentage point – into increases in the income of the poor. In addition, health improvements are disproportionately beneficial for the poor, as they depend on their labor power more than any other segment of the population.

Just as the direct effects of life expectancy on economic growth are important, so too are the indirect effects of improvements in health status that operate via demographic change. In East Asia, for example, the working-age population grew several times faster than the dependent population between 1965 and 1990. The whole process seems to have been triggered by declining child and infant mortality, itself prompted by the development of antibiotics and antimicrobials, the use of DDT, and classic public health improvements related to safe water and sanitation.[4] Health improvements can therefore be seen to be one of the major pillars upon which East Asia's phenomenal economic achievements were based, with the demographic dividend accounting for perhaps one-third of its 'economic miracle'.[4,5]

By contrast, poor health can slow the demographic transition and inhibit growth. In Sub-Saharan Africa, for example, a seemingly intractable disease burden induces many families to dissipate their resources among large numbers of children, creating a high-fertility, high-mortality poverty trap that impedes economic growth.[6]

Patterns of energy use also mediate the interactions between health, demography, and income. The rural poor rely heavily on wood, dung, and other biomass. The resulting smoke and particulates are detrimental to human health and can diminish people's productivity. Across countries, there is a strong association between demographic and health indicators and the use of biomass in traditional ways. Infant and child mortality rates are elevated, and life expectancy is diminished, particularly for women who undergo higher exposure to smoke while cooking. Fertility rates are also high, partly to ensure enough children for firewood collection.[7] These effects appear to be quite large. For example, a 40% increase in traditional fuel use (which corresponds to the difference between Vietnam and Malaysia) translates, on average, into one extra birth per woman over her lifetime, and a full percentage point rise in the population growth rate. Slow income growth is the end result.

Mutual reinforcement

Traditionally, economists have treated health like any other consumer good and have assumed that the direction of causality was from income to health. We now have good reasons and strong evidence for believing that health improvements also stimulate economic development. These two views are, of course, compatible. The development process is inherently dynamic – with health improvements promoting economic growth, which in turn promotes better health. This 'virtuous spiral' can transform an impoverished, disease-prone country into one that offers its people a much higher quality of life. Compelling examples of such a transformation can be found in East Asia and Ireland, and in the economic history of several wealthy industrial countries.[8]

Health improvements and economic growth can be mutually reinforcing in another way. As rising incomes cause fertility to decline, there are consequent benefits to the health of mothers and children, via longer breast-feeding, less stress on women's reproductive systems, more opportunities for them to work outside the home, and increased resources for each child's upbringing. In turn, declines in fertility promote economic growth by allowing more of society's resources to be devoted to urgently needed investments in physical capital, infrastructure, and educational quality.

Regrettably, the mutual reinforcement between health and income can also operate in reverse. Declines in health status in some parts of the world are having staggering impacts on economic well-being. The AIDS epidemic in Africa is perhaps the most prominent example. About 8% of African adults are now HIV positive, with 56% of Sub-Saharan Africans not expected to reach age 60.[9] The economic burden imposed by HIV/AIDS is enormous. The required costs of detecting and treating the infection and its clinical manifestations are well in excess of per capita public expenditures on health care in Sub-Saharan Africa. With more than 80% of global AIDS mortality occurring among people of working age, the income and output losses associated with the epidemic are daunting. A number of economic studies conclude that the AIDS epidemic is slowing the pace of economic growth and depleting the wherewithal to deal with other diseases – such as diarrhea, hepatitis, malaria, and tuberculosis – that are also ravaging health in many countries.[10]

Russia provides another example. Its transition to a market economy, which began in the early 1990s, coincides closely with a precipitous fall in life expectancy, accounting for 1.4 to 1.6 million premature deaths during 1990–95, including disproportionately large numbers of working-age men. There are many reasons to believe that Russia's economic and political instability and plummeting incomes are to blame for this health crisis, which left the life expectancy of Russian males in the mid-1990s below the average for developing countries. Among the factors that link falling incomes to the worsening of Russians' health are a further deterioration of the already poor Russian diet, increased alcohol consumption, mental stress, and the related surge in accidents and injuries. Negative income growth took a major toll on public spending on health care, and many parts of the Russian medical system have descended into chaos as a result. The health crisis is now having an impact on Russia's catastrophic economic performance. The effects are currently modest, but are indisputably negative and likely to worsen as the vicious spiral picks up momentum.[11]

Health-led development

A revolution in economic thinking has taken place over the past few decades, putting human capital, particularly educated workers, on a par with physical capital as an input into production. We would argue that increased health is another aspect of human capital that also enters into production. In addition, long life expectancy may be the fundamental force that creates the demand for education and encourages the domestic saving that is a key determinant of economic growth. This perspective offers an exciting new possibility in international development: investing in health to help stimulate development. A focus on health cannot be the sole approach to improving living standards, nor may it even be the best. However, the evidence for viewing health as one of the more effective arrows in the development quiver is surely growing stronger.

References

1. D.E. Bloom and D. Canning, in *Population Does Matter: Demography, Growth, and Poverty in the Developing World*, N. Birdsall, A.S. Kelley, S. Sinding (eds) (Oxford University Press, New York, in press).
2. World Health Organization, *World Health Report 1999: Making a Difference* (WHO, Geneva 1999).
3. J. Strauss and D. Thomas, Health, nutrition, and economic development, *Journal of Economic Literature*, **36** (2), 766–817 (1998).
4. D.E. Bloom and J.G. Williamson, Demographic transitions and economic miracles in emerging Asia, *World Bank Economic Review*, **12** (3), 419–455 (1998).
5. D.E. Bloom, D. Canning, P.N. Malaney, *Population Development Review* (in press).
6. D.E. Bloom and J.D. Sachs, Geography, demography, and economic growth in Africa, *Brookings Papers on Economic Activity*, **2**, 207–295 (1998).
7. D.E. Bloom, P. Craig, P.N. Malaney, *The Quality of Life in Rural Asia* (Oxford University Press, USA, 2000).
8. R.H. Steckel and R. Floud, (eds) *Health and Welfare During Industrialization* (University of Chicago Press, Chicago, 1997).
9. D.E. Bloom, A. Rosenfield, River Path Associates, *A Moment in Time: AIDS and Business* (American Foundation for AIDS Research, New York, 1999).
10. World Bank, *Confronting AIDS: Public Priorities in a Global Epidemic* (Oxford University Press, New York, 1997).
11. C.M. Becker and D.E. Bloom, The demographic crisis in the former Soviet Union: Introduction, *World Development*, **26** (11), 1913–1919 (1998).

This article is a slightly shorter version of the original, which appeared in February 2000 under the same title in the journal *Science*, 287: 1207–9. David Bloom is Professor of Economics and Demography at Harvard University's School of Public Health, Boston, USA. David Canning is Professor of Economics at the Queen's University, Belfast, Northern Ireland.

27 | Agriculture's two-edged sword

JARED DIAMOND

We are accustomed to assuming that the transition from the hunter–gatherer lifestyle to agriculture brought us health, longevity, security, leisure, and great art. While the case for this view *seems* overwhelming, it is hard to prove. How do you actually show that lives of people 10,000 years ago got better when they abandoned hunting for farming? That question has become answerable only in recent years, through the newly emerging science of 'paleopathology': looking for signs of disease (the science of pathology) in remains of ancient peoples (from the Greek word *paleo* meaning 'ancient', as in paleontology). In some lucky situations, the paleopathologist has almost as much material to study as does a pathologist. For example, archaeologists in the deserts of Chile found well-preserved mummies whose medical condition at time of death could be determined by an autopsy, just as one would do on a fresh corpse in a hospital today. Faeces of long-dead Indians who lived in dry caves in Nevada remained sufficiently well-preserved to examine for hookworm and other parasites.

Usually, though, the only human remains available for paleopathologists to study are skeletons, but they still permit a surprising number of deductions about health. To begin with, a skeleton identifies its owner's sex, and his/her weight and approximate age at time of death. Thus, with enough skeletons, one can construct mortality tables like those used by life insurance companies to calculate expected lifespan and risk of death at any given age. Paleopathologists can also calculate growth rates by measuring bones of people of different ages, can examine teeth for cavities (signs of a high-carbohydrate diet) or enamel defects (signs of a poor diet in childhood), and can recognize scars that many diseases such as anaemia, tuberculosis, leprosy, and osteo-arthritis leave on bones.

One straightforward example of what paleopathologists have learned from skeletons concerns historical changes in height. Paleopathologists studying ancient skeletons from Greece and Turkey found the average height of hunter–gatherers in that region towards the end of the Ice Age was a generous 5 foot 10 inches for men, 5 foot 6 inches for women. With the adoption of agriculture, height crashed, reaching by 4000

BC a low value of only 5 foot 3 inches for men, 5 foot 1 inch for women. By classical times, heights were very slowly on the rise again, but modern Greeks and Turks have still not regained the heights of their healthy hunter–gatherer ancestors.

Another example of paleopathologists at work is the study of thousands of American Indian skeletons excavated from burial mounds in the Illinois and Ohio River valleys. Corn, first domesticated in Central America thousands of years ago, became the basis of intensive farming in those valleys around 1000 AD. Until then, Indian hunter–gatherers had skeletons 'so healthy it is somewhat discouraging to work with them' as one paleopathologist complained. With the arrival of corn, Indian skeletons suddenly became interesting to study. The number of cavities in an average adult's mouth jumped from less than one to nearly seven, and tooth loss and abscesses became rampant. Enamel defects in children's milk teeth imply that pregnant and nursing mothers were severely undernourished. Anaemia quadrupled in frequency; tuberculosis became established as an epidemic disease; half the population suffered from yaws or syphilis; and two-thirds suffered from osteoarthritis and other degenerative diseases. Mortality rates at every age increased, with the result that only one per cent of the population survived past the age of fifty, as compared to five per cent in the golden days before corn. Almost one-fifth of the whole population died between the ages of one and four, probably because weaned toddlers succumbed to malnutrition and infectious diseases. Thus, corn, usually considered among the New World's blessings, actually proved to be a public health disaster. Similar conclusions about the transition from hunting to farming emerge from studies of skeletons elsewhere in the world.

There are at least three sets of reasons to explain these findings that agriculture was bad for health. Firstly, hunter–gatherers enjoyed a varied diet with adequate amounts of protein, vitamins, and minerals, while farmers obtained most of their food from starchy crops. In effect, the farmers gained cheap calories at the cost of poor nutrition. Today just three high-carbohydrate plants – wheat, rice, and corn – provide more than fifty per cent of the calories consumed by the human species.

Secondly, because of that dependence on one or a few crops, farmers ran a greater risk of starvation if one food crop failed than did hunters. The Irish potato famine is merely one of many examples.

Finally, most of today's leading infectious diseases and parasites of mankind could not become established until after the transition to agriculture. These killers persist only in societies of crowded, malnourished, sedentary people constantly reinfected by each other and by their own sewage. The cholera bacterium, for example, does not survive for long outside the human body. It spreads from one victim to the next through contamination of drinking water with faeces of cholera patients. Measles dies out in small populations once it has either killed or immunized most potential hosts; only in populations numbering at least a few hundred thousand people can it maintain itself indefinitely. Such crowd epidemics could not persist in small, scattered bands of hunters who often shifted camp. Tuberculosis, leprosy, and cholera had to await the rise of farming, while smallpox, bubonic plague, and measles appeared only in the past few thousand years with the rise of cities.

Besides malnutrition, starvation, and epidemic diseases, farming brought another curse to humanity – class divisions.

Only in a farming population could contrasts between the disease-ridden masses and a healthy, non-producing, elite develop. Skeletons from Greek tombs at Mycenae around 1500 BC suggest that royals enjoyed a better diet than commoners, since the royal skeletons were two or three inches taller and had better teeth (on the average, one instead of six cavities or missing teeth). Among mummies from Chilean cemeteries around 1000 AD, the elite were distinguished not only by ornaments and gold hairclips, but also by a four-fold lower rate of bone lesions stemming from infectious diseases.

These signs of health differentials within local communities of farmers in the past appear on a global scale in the modern world. To most American and European readers, the argument that humanity could on the average be better off as hunter–gatherers than we are today sounds ridiculous, because most people in industrial societies today enjoy better health than most hunter–gatherers. However, Americans and Europeans are an elite in today's world, dependent on oil and other materials imported from countries with large peasant populations and much lower health standards. If you could choose between being a middle-class American, a Bushman hunter, and a peasant farmer in Ethiopia, the first choice would undoubtedly be the healthiest one, but the third choice might be the least healthy.

Farming may also have exacerbated sexual inequality already in existence. With the advent of agriculture, women often became beasts of burden, were drained by more frequent pregnancies, and thus suffered poorer health.

Thus, with the advent of agriculture an elite became healthier, but many people became worse off. A cynic might ask how we got trapped by agriculture despite its being such a mixed blessing. The answer boils down to the adage, 'Might makes right.' Farming could support far more people than hunting, whether or not it also brought, on the average, more food per mouth. As population densities of hunter–gatherers slowly rose at the end of the Ice Age, bands had to 'choose', whether consciously or unconsciously, between feeding more mouths by taking the first steps towards agriculture, or else finding ways to limit growth. Some bands adopted the former solution, unable to anticipate the evils of farming, and seduced by the transient abundance they enjoyed until population growth caught up with increased food production. Such bands outbred and then drove off or killed the bands that chose to remain hunter–gatherers, because ten malnourished farmers can still outfight one healthy hunter. It is not that hunter–gatherers abandoned their lifestyle, but that those sensible enough not to abandon it were forced out of all areas except ones that farmers did not want. Modern hunter–gatherers persisted only in scattered areas useless for agriculture, such as the Arctic, deserts, and some rainforests.

At this point it is ironic to recall the common complaint that archaeology is an expensive luxury, concerned with the remote past, and offering no lessons of present relevance. Archaeologists studying the rise of farming have reconstructed for us a stage where we made one of the most crucial decisions in human history. Forced to choose between limiting population growth or trying to increase food production, we opted for the latter and ended up with starvation, warfare, and tyranny. The same choice faces us today, with the difference that we now can learn from the past.

Hunter–gatherers practised the most successful and long-persistent lifestyle in the career of our species. In contrast, we are still struggling with the problems into which we descended with agriculture, and it is unclear whether we can solve them. Suppose that an archaeologist who had visited us from outer space were trying to explain human history to his fellow spacelings. The visitor might illustrate the results of his digs by a twenty-four-hour clock on which one hour of clock-time represents 100,000 years of real past time. If the history of the human race began at midnight, then we would now be almost at the end of our first day. We lived as hunter–gatherers for nearly the whole of that day, from midnight through dawn, noon, and sunset. Finally, at 11:54 pm we adopted agriculture. In retrospect, the decision was inevitable, and there is now no question of turning back. But as our second midnight approaches, will the present plight of African peasants gradually spread to engulf all of us? Or, will we somehow achieve those seductive blessings that we imagine behind agriculture's glittering facade, and that have so far eluded us except in mixed form?

This article is an edited extract from Professor Diamond's book, *The Rise and Fall of the Third Chimpanzee* (Vintage Books, 1992, pp. 166–72). Jared Diamond is Professor of Physiology at the University of California School of Medicine in the USA.

28 | Climate and health

PAUL R. EPSTEIN

Extreme weather events – unusually heavy rainfall or long periods of drought – have a profound impact on public health, particularly in developing countries, and the aftershocks are rippling through economies worldwide.[1] For example, Hurricane Mitch – nourished by a warmed Caribbean – hit Central America in November 1998, killing more than 11,000 people and causing damage exceeding US$5 billion. The intense precipitation and flooding associated with the hurricane spawned a cluster of disease outbreaks, including cholera, a water-borne disease (>30,000 cases), and malaria and dengue fever, transmitted by mosquitoes that flourish under these conditions (>30,000 and >1,000 cases, respectively). If more frequent and intense extreme weather events continue to be a primary manifestation of climate change, then harnessing climate data to better forecast future disease outbreaks should enable preventative action to be taken.

Linthicum et al.[2] examine links between periods of heavy rainfall in East Africa between 1950 and 1998 and outbreaks of Rift Valley fever, a mosquito-borne viral disease that infects both domestic animals and humans (see Figure 28.1 overleaf). In the Horn of Africa, records since 1950 indicate that Rift Valley fever outbreaks follow periods of intense precipitation. During the 1997–1998 El Niño event, the Horn received up to 40 times the average rainfall, isolating villages, obliterating roads, and precipitating a cluster of diseases: tens of thousands of new cases of cholera and malaria and 89,000 cases (with nearly 1000 deaths) of Rift Valley fever.[3] Linthicum and colleagues show that by tracking sea surface temperature anomalies of the Pacific and Indian oceans and combining these data with vegetation changes detected by remote sensing satellites,[2] they were able to forecast Rift Valley fever epidemics 5 months in advance of outbreaks. Such early warnings would give sufficient time for interventions, such as vaccination of livestock and treatment of mosquito breeding sites. Using climate data to project conditions that are conducive to disease outbreaks will be invaluable in combating the burden of extreme weather events on public health.

Connections between climate and disease are not new. Climate constrains the range of many infectious diseases, and weather affects the timing and intensity of outbreaks.[4]

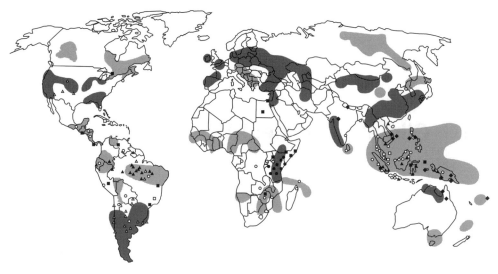

Extreme weather events
June 1997 to May 1998
▨ dry ■ wet

Associated disease outbreaks
○ cholera   ◆ encephalitis   ■ malaria   ▵ hantavirus pulmonary syndrome
● Rift Valley fever   ▫ dengue fever
▲ respiratory illness related to fire and smoke

Figure 28.1 Predicting disease outbreaks. The map shows regions of heavy rainfall and drought during 1997–98 and the associated clustering of outbreaks of emerging infectious disease. Extreme weather events have resulted in a surge in epidemics, particularly in tropical regions. Using climate data to predict the arrival of conditions that are likely to favour disease outbreaks can facilitate public health interventions, such as vaccination and preparations at treatment facilities.

Reappraisal of these associations is aided by increased understanding of the Earth's climate system, in particular how land and sea surface temperatures and pressure gradients drive winds and weather. The atmosphere holds 6 per cent more water vapour with each 1°C rise in temperature. The resulting increase in evaporation and greater residence time for water vapour in the atmosphere boosts humidity and heat indices, fuels storms, and reinforces the greenhouse effect (the trapping of heat by atmospheric gases such as carbon dioxide). An increase in the cloud cover blocks outgoing heat, contributing to disproportionate warming at night and during the winter – conditions that are unhealthy for humans but advantageous for insects that transmit infectious diseases. A moisture-laden atmosphere also generates more tropical-like downpours that create breeding grounds for mosquitoes, propel rodents from burrows, and flush nutrients, chemicals, and micro-organisms into waterways.

Sudden weather changes and sequential extremes can also yield surprises. Droughts suppress predators, whereas heavy rains boost food supplies – a synergy that can spark rodent population 'explosions'. A large increase in the deer mouse population in the South Western United States in 1993 resulted in the emergence of Hantavirus Pulmonary Syndrome.[5] In Honduras, drought-sustained wildfires consumed 11,000 km² of forest during the summer preceding hurricane Mitch,[3] widening the deforestation that magnified the flooding and devastation from the hurricane.[1,6]

Understanding the evolution of such weather anomalies will require integrating data from the El Niño–Southern Oscillation (ENSO; the anomalous warming or cooling of the Eastern Pacific) with local sea surface temperatures[2] and, eventually, with decadal-to-centennial cycles in climate variability and human influences. Changes in atmospheric chemistry may have so altered Earth's heat budget that natural climate modes such as ENSO have been modified. Studies suggest that the ocean is becoming warmer at intermediate depths and around both poles. If the world's oceans are a long-term heat sink for this century's global warming, then this has profound implications for marine life and terrestrial weather patterns.

Historically, periods of accelerated social transition have often been accompanied by the re-emergence of infectious diseases. The current resurgence[7] can be attributed to changes at three levels – social (economic disparities and untoward practices such as excessive use of antibiotics and pesticides), ecological (habitat loss and simplification), and global (alterations in climate and stratospheric ozone). Ecological integrity is central to health. Habitat mosaics (for example, wetlands and forests) absorb floodwaters and support the genetic, species, and functional group diversity that ensures resilience to stress and resistance to pests and pathogens.[8]

Extended droughts and thawing during warmer winters renders northern forests vulnerable to infestations with insect pests. Parched agricultural lands attract aphids, locusts, and virus-bearing white flies, and fungi flourish after floods. Warming and 'CO_2 fertilization' causing enhanced plant growth may also encourage leaf-eating pests, favour weeds, and promote pollen production. Already, 35 to 42 per cent of growing and stored crops are lost to pests, pathogens, and weeds, costing US$244 billion worldwide annually.[9] Increased climate variability could substantially alter future food security and global nutrition.[10]

Emerging diseases associated with algal toxins, bacteria, and viruses are affecting a wide range of marine species: fish, shorebirds, and mammals.[11] Of great concern are diseases that attack coral and sea grasses, essential habitats that sustain mobile aquatic species. Corals are already endangered: high sea surface temperatures in the 1990s have resulted in bleaching, perhaps the most disturbing biological sign of global warming.

With disproportionate warming in the winter, at higher latitudes and high elevations, most summit glaciers are in retreat. Polar researchers suspect that melting at the base of the Greenland ice sheet may be sculpting fault lines that could diminish its stability.[12] Shrinking of Earth's ice cover (cryosphere) has implications for water (agriculture, hydropower, and health) and for climate stability. The impacts of warming and changing weather patterns on forests, agriculture, marine life, and water may hold the most profound consequences for global health.

The cost of extreme weather events and associated emerging infectious diseases is mounting. Trade, travel, and tourism can be affected. In 1998, livestock exports were blocked from East Africa because of Rift Valley fever, and Europe refused seafood imports because of cholera outbreaks in the same region. Indonesian forest fires (the extended drought compounding hazardous land-clearing practices) resulted in widespread acute and chronic respiratory illnesses and plummeting rice yields.[1] The 1998 floods in China killed 3700 individuals, displaced 223 million people, and cost US$30 billion. All told, weather-related losses – combining growth of coastal settlements, ecological vulnerabilities, and extreme weather – grew exponentially from the 1980s to the 1990s; losses of US$89 billion in 1998 (11 months) eclipsed the losses of US$55 billion for the entire decade of the 1980s.[13]

There are several solutions to combating the increased burden of emerging infectious diseases. Greater surveillance of and response to outbreaks is essential. Health early-warning systems based on climate forecasting and remote sensing, such as the system developed by Linthicum and colleagues for Rift Valley fever, can complement famine early-warning systems. Prevention is possible if the underlying social and environmental causes are addressed.

Contemporaneous changes in greenhouse gas concentrations, ozone levels, the cryosphere, ocean temperature, land use, and land cover challenge the stability of our epoch, the Holocene – a remarkable 10,000-year era that followed the retreat of the great ice sheets from temperate zones. High-resolution ice-core records suggest that greater variance from climate norms may indicate greater climate instability, increasing the potential for rapid shifts between stable climate states.[14]

In the 1980s, health considerations helped forge international agreements banning ozone-depleting chemicals and atmospheric nuclear testing. Today, concerns for our health in the face of global change necessitate ecological restoration and development of non-polluting energy sources.

Clean energy helps to stabilize the climate and also can be used to power health facilities, pump water for irrigation, and purify it for consumption. Renewable and energy-efficient technologies may become the new engine of economic growth, driving improvements in public health. Ultimately, we must shed inherited economic burdens and adopt new financial mechanisms – incentives, subsidies, and funds – to reverse environmental assaults on public health, preserve the global commons, and achieve healthy, clean and equitable development in the coming century.

References

1. International Federation of Red Cross and Red Crescent Societies, *World Disasters Report 1998* (Oxford University Press, New York, 1998), p. 198.
2. K.J. Linthicum *et al.*, *Science* **285**, 396 (1999).
3. P.R. Epstein, (ed.), *Extreme Weather Events: The Health and Economic Consequences of the 1997/98 El Niño and La Niña* (Center for Health and the Global Environment, Harvard Medical School, Boston, MA, 1999) (Available at http://chge2.med.harvard.edu/enso/disease.html).
4. P.R. Epstein *et al.*, *Bull. Am. Meteorol. Soc.* **78**, 409 (1998).
5. P.R. Epstein, *Am. J. Pub. Health* **85**, 168 (1994).
6. J. Hellin, M. Haigh, F. Marks, *Nature* **399**, 316 (1999).
7. *The World Health Report 1996: Fighting Disease Fostering Development* (World Health Organization, Geneva, 1996).
8. P.D. Coley, *Science* **284**, 2098 (1999); P. Wilf and C.C. Labandeira, *ibid.*, p. 21153.
9. D. Pimental (ed.) in *Techniques for Reducing Pesticide Use* (Wiley, New York, 1997), pp. 1–11.
10. C. Rosenzweig and D. Hillel, *Climate Change and the Global Harvest* (Oxford University Press, New York, 1998), pp. 191–122.
11. P.R. Epstein, (ed.), *Marine Ecosystems; Emerging Diseases as Indicators of Change* (Health, Ecological and Economic Dimensions of Global Change, Center for Health and the Global Environment, Harvard Medical School, Boston, MA, 1998) (available at http://heed.unh.edu).
12. W. Krabill *et al.*, *Science* **283**, 1522 (1999).
13. J.N. Abramovitz and S. Dunn, *Record Year for Weather-Related Disasters, Vital Signs Brief 98–5* (World-Watch Institute, Washington, DC, 1998) (available at http://www.worldwatch.org).
14. K. Taylor, *Am. Sci.* **87**, 320 (1999).

This article is reproduced from *Science*, **285**: 347–8, and was originally published in this form on 16 July 1999. Professor Epstein is Associate Director of the Center for Health and the Global Environment, Harvard Medical School, Boston, USA.

29 | Deaths under 50

MEDICAL SERVICES STUDY GROUP OF THE
ROYAL COLLEGE OF PHYSICIANS OF LONDON

Summary and conclusions

The Medical Services Study Group has started a collaborative study in the Mersey, West Midlands, and Grampian regions to examine the causes of death among medical inpatients aged 1 to 50. The cause of death was determined from the case notes and the consultant's opinion. The rate of ascertainment of cases was initially low, though it is increasing; despite this limitation an analysis of the first 250 cases showed one important finding. No fewer than 98 patients contributed to their own deaths through overeating, drinking, smoking, or not complying with treatment.

Introduction

The consultants in hospitals in the Merseyside and West Midlands regions were visited and told about the study. The project put forward was a broad one – namely, to look in detail at the causes and circumstances of all deaths of patients aged 1 to 50 years in medical wards. For this the information contained in the case notes and the consultant's opinion on the patient were needed.

After it had started the physicians in the Grampian Region asked to participate.

Ascertainment

The total population of the three regions under investigation is around 8 million – that is, about a sixth of the population of England and Wales. We would expect about 1,000 sets of case notes on medical patients dying in hospital each year.

From October 1977 to September 1978 over 400 were submitted. At present the rate of ascertainment is therefore about 50 per cent though there has been great variation between hospitals that promised support, some sending us all their deaths and some very few or none.

Results of analysis

Table 29.1 overleaf shows the causes of death in the first 250 patients. Through studying the case notes in detail we have been able to assess the background to each case; in no fewer than 98 cases the patients contributed in large measure to their own deaths.

The 98 cases of 'self-destruction'
Eight patients died from deliberate self-poisoning. In one there was no evidence of any previous psychiatric illness, but of the other seven, one had schizophrenia, one had a psychopathic personality, one was hopelessly dependent on alcohol, and the other four were depressives. Fashions in suicidal agents change and three used paraquat to kill themselves. One who died from barbiturate poisoning had had every conceivable treatment for schizophrenic depression: had been admitted for self-poisoning on three previous occasions; had slashed her wrists in an attempt to kill herself; and in her final illness had spent ten days in an intensive care unit. During her time in the intensive care unit she underwent 94 laboratory tests and 8 radiographic examinations – a sad example of the frequent inescapable commitment of skills and resources to patients beyond hope of being saved or restored to any worthwhile life.

Six of the 98 died from alcoholic cirrhosis of the liver, and another, whose liver disease was not primarily alcoholic in origin, accelerated his death by a high intake of alcohol. Though this group is small they exemplify the difficulty of helping alcoholics and the enormous demand they make on the health and social services. One 24-year-old man, who suffered cardiac arrest and irretrievable brain damage during acute alcoholic intoxication, occupied a bed in a teaching hospital for four months before he died, though it was clear from the outset that no recovery was possible.

Thirteen patients who died from carcinoma of the bronchus were strongly addicted to cigarettes, some smoking as many as 60 a day. Three other heavy cigarette smokers died from chronic airway obstruction and one from bronchopneumonia.

Among those whose death was attributable to myocardial infarction there were 25 with one or more causal factors within their own control. Twelve were grossly overweight; 22 smoked large numbers of cigarettes; two diabetics and two hypertensives did not comply with their treatment; and three others had had symptoms for a long time before they consulted a doctor.

Nine of the 98 patients delayed in seeking medical advice and in four this probably cost them their lives, for two died from gastroenteritis, one from meningococcal infection, and one from myxoedema. The patient with myxoedema had been ill for many years but had refused to see a doctor. Two of the other five might have survived and the remaining three lived longer had they sought help earlier.

Thirty-seven of the 98 patients refused admission to hospital, were unwilling to submit to investigation, discharged themselves from hospital, defaulted from diabetic clinics, or did not co-operate in taking medication. These attitudes were often encouraged by their spouses. It is impossible to quantify this factor, but certainly in many cases it was to some extent responsible for the fatal issue, while in others it hastened death. An anxious and nervous temperament was responsible in many instances but in others

Table 29.1 Summary of cause of death in the 250 patients surveyed

Causes of death		No. of cases
Malignancies:		47
Carcinomas (primary site):		
Ampulla of Vater	1	
Breast	5	
Bronchus	14	
Colon	2	
Stomach	3	
Undetermined	2	
Sarcomas	2	
Gliomas	4	
Myelomatosis	3	
Leukaemias	7	
Lymphomas	4	
Haematological conditions		7
Cardiovascular conditions		96
Myocardial infarction	31	
Cerebrovascular accidents	51	
Thromboembolic disease	7	
Miscellaneous	7	
Respiratory conditions		14
Asthma	6	
Respiratory failure	8	
Alimentary conditions		7
Crohn's disease	2	
Small intestine gangrene	4	
Oesophageal perforation	1	
Neurological conditions:		4
Multiple sclerosis	3	
Muscular dystrophy	1	
Infections:		25
Pneumonia	6	
Acute laryngoepiglottitis	3	
Encephalitis	6	
Meningitis	5	
Bacterial endocarditis	2	
Gastroenteritis	3	
Hepatic failure:		12
Cirrhosis	10	
Acute hepatic necrosis	2	
Renal failure		11
Chronic	8	
Acute	3	
Diabetes		2
Congenital abnormalities, brain damage at birth, etc.		10
Self-poisoning (1 accidental)		9
Others		6
Total		250

lack of co-operation seemed to stem from fecklessness or a psychopathic attitude to life and to doctors in particular. There was little to indicate that lack of intelligence played any significant part.

Discussion

Our initial finding will come as no surprise to the profession. Doctors have been saying for years that the causes of many of the killing diseases of middle life are not mysteries, but are contributed to by overeating, excess alcohol, and tobacco. Doctors' pronouncements tend not to be popular – some are contradictory and some are frankly disbelieved, and the disbelief is reinforced by the fact that the 'patient' often feels quite well. Health education is often derided ('It won't happen to me'), but there is an astonishing statistic which can stand much repetition. In 1930–32 the standard mortality ratio for ischaemic heart disease in social class I was 237 (normal 100). Over the next four decades it gradually fell to 88, but from 1951 to 1971 the crude mortality rate from ischaemic heart disease in all males almost doubled. Much the most likely explanation for this is that people in social class I do heed such advice whereas other groups do not.

The 'deaths under 50' project may be criticised on statistical grounds, but any bias in ascertaining the cases of 'self-destruction' is probably in the direction of under-reporting. The study's great merit lies in the fact that the information on causes of death is obtained from case notes and the clinicians' expert opinions, whereas in many surveys where the rate of ascertainment is better this information comes from death certificates.

'Deaths under 50' formed part of a report prepared by the Medical Services Study Group of the Royal College of Physicians of London and was compiled by Sir Cyril Clarke, director of the study group, and Dr George Whitfield, assistant director. A number of clinicians participated in the study. The full article was published in the *British Medical Journal*, **2**, 1061–1062 (1978).

30 | Prevention is better. . . .

HELEN ROBERTS, SUSAN SMITH AND CAROL BRYCE

As the leading cause of death to children after the age of one in the United Kingdom and elsewhere in the developed world, child accidents are a legitimate focus of preventive activity. In the UK for instance, the majority of deaths to the under-fives are the result of an accident in the home, and to older children the result of a road traffic accident.

The main thrust of accident prevention directed towards children and their parents continues to make heavy use of advice, safety campaigns and competitions for children to design posters, all punctuated with reminders to mothers that the main responsibility is theirs. Health education programmes in child safety which have been evaluated have been disappointing, or have concentrated on inappropriate outcome measures. There is little point in knowing that every health visitor working in a certain area has put a leaflet into the hand of every mother of an under-five, and given personalised advice, if we do not know whether the accident rate is reduced, increased or unchanged by these measures. And we cannot take it for granted that health education messages have no adverse effects. The generation of anxiety in otherwise healthy populations, in the absence of any measurable health gain may be an undesirable consequence of vigorous and enthusiastic health education.

The Corkerhill study

In what follows, we describe some findings from a study set in a Glasgow housing estate and designed to identify factors predisposing children to be at risk of, and protected from, accidents. Fieldwork comprised group interviews with four 'citizens' groups and one group of 'professionals', a household survey and a series of case studies of successful and unsuccessful accident prevention strategies identified during the survey. For the purposes of this paper, we describe some differences in professional and parental perspectives on accidents and their preventability which became evident during the group interviews.

In the course of the household survey, we sought to identify all accidents in the previous year to a child of 14 or under resulting in hospital admission, a trip to the Accident and Emergency (A&E) department, a visit to the GP or dentist, or treatment at home. We also sought details of near-misses and averted accidents.

Corkerhill is a post-war housing scheme of 580 dwellings in Glasgow. When we carried out our work it had a chip shop, a newsagent, a pub, and as community premises, a community 'shop' (in effect, a meeting room) and a tenants' hall. The estate is bounded to the north by a railway line and railway yard, to the south by a river, and to the west by a busy trunk road with a dual carriageway. In contrast, there is an area of parkland immediately to the east of Corkerhill. The single environmental asset in Corkerhill is shortly to be cut off from the community by a major new road. This is unlikely to be of major benefit to Corkerhill where almost 60 per cent of households do not have access to a car or a van. Well over a third of the families in Corkerhill are headed by a lone parent, and most of the families live in conditions of considerable hardship.

What is an accident?

We found little support for the existence of a fatalistic view of accidents, although conceptually, there are clear differences between the views of the parent and professional groups on what comprised an accident. The parents see accidents as just one element of insecurity and one further hazard for people living in damp, cold houses. Thus in discussing risk factors for accidents, parents relate their children's asthma and other respiratory problems to damp housing and chemicals used to treat the mould associated with the damp. 'Your house is damp . . . Your house isn't safe . . .' (Group interview). 'I had to go to my mother's house [because of damp] and every time we came back, my wee boy had diarrhoea and the inspector told me not to cover the dampness' (Case study).

This broad view of what accidents are underpins a related conviction that many events labelled accidents are not accidents at all. Parents felt that many risks in their environment render accidents foreseeable, and with known causes. In what sense, argued the parents, are incidents arising from known hazard accidents? The fact that many of the tenements have balconies with a gap at crawler's eye level just wide enough for a small child to creep through was identified by parents not so much as an accident risk as a frank disregard for child safety on the part of planners, builders and architects. Similar views were expressed about kitchen design; the lack of adequate play facilities; the fact that the housing scheme with its low car ownership was designated a free car parking area for other people's cars; the electrical wiring system in the houses (many plugs were of the old fashioned three holes in the wall type with no switch) and the old fashioned immersion heaters where it was difficult to adjust the heat of bath water at source. It was suggested to us in all the parents' groups that factors such as these do not lead to 'accidents'. It can be foreseen that they will lead to injury, so that the risks that they entail are not accidental at all: 'They're no designed with safety in mind at all, and yet they call them family houses . . .' (Group interview). 'These windows, the weans can open them no bother . . .', 'Then they say [dampness is caused by] lack of ventilation so you go around opening all your windows, and it is freezing' (Case studies).

Professionals had a rather narrower conception of accidents. Not surprisingly, they (like us) did not refer to asthma or respiratory ailments in their discussion of accidents, and kept rather closer to conventional definitions of what an accident is. In discussing accidents in general, they drew on their professional knowledge. Reference was made to the work of a local senior registrar in public health medicine whom some of the group had heard describe the epidemiology of accidents in Glasgow: 'For pre-fives, the incidence of home accidents was much higher . . . But even within the home, I think the main one, the main category, was burns and scalds . . .' Accidents were thus described in terms of the injuries which were caused rather than risks or hazards which led to them, and in terms of the patterns which had become clear to them as health workers, police officers or road safety officers. In this sense, the professionals were far more likely to conceptualise accidents in terms of their sequelae (injury or damage) than in terms of their antecedents.

What are the risk factors for child accidents in Corkerhill?

Parents and teenagers apparently carry clear mental maps of risk factors and risky areas. Road works, pavements dug up, and building works were identified as evident hazards: '. . . they dug up a bit of pavement and just went away home and left it like that . . . and if you didn't have somebody with you and you had a pram, you couldn't get across because you needed someone to help you over' (Group interview). The playpark was identified as unsafe by the teenagers: 'There was four swings between about all the kids. . . . The grass is a mess, it's just all broken glass and things like that.' Broken glass was a recurring theme: 'When the glaziers come to replace the windows, they smash out the old window into the garden' (Case study). Some of the parents meanwhile identified nearby playing fields as a no-go area as children had to cross a fast main road in order to get there: 'Some wee weans are banned from Nethercraigs [the play area] because they have tae cross the road, and the parents havnae always got the time to go with them and wait with them until they come back' (Group interview). An unmanned railway station adjacent to Corkerhill was identified as a danger: 'There's a hole in the fence roon the side and it wis seen being done and it wis actually the workmen who were clearing up the railway taking a short cut to the chippie. That's the kind of thing that the kids would get blamed for . . .' (Group interview).

The professional group saw risk in terms of the characteristics of the children: 'for that age group, 0–4, the main risks are in the home . . .' Only the health visitor made a comment on two specific risk factors in Corkerhill. The first was related to burns: 'There's no heating in some of the houses so a lot of the parents use electric fires so you get a lot of accidents with the smaller kids from the electric fires.' The second related to needlestick injuries: '. . . drug abusers with needles, kids picking up needles in the streets and the closes . . .' When the group was pressed by the interviewer on other specific hazards and risks, none were offered and the discussion was moved on by a participant referring to work in another part of the city associating chip pan fires with drunkenness.

Some risks which parents had raised were downplayed by the professionals: '. . . there is a general perception that the cars are travelling faster than they actually are . . .' and 'if you look at the roads and the amount they get used, and the complexity of them, they're not really that dangerous.' The theme of popular perceptions of external risk being mistaken was taken up by another group member who suggested a sign saying: ' "You are now entering the most dangerous place in the world – your home". And that's about the size of it. I mean we've got a saying in the Fire Brigade that there's only three causes of fires and generally it's men, women and children, and that's the sad fact of it . . .'

Responsibility for safety

Both the 'citizens' and the 'professional' groups were exercised by the question of responsibility for accidents. All of the groups agreed that the maintenance of safety is a parental (or more usually maternal) responsibility. The parents described their commitment to the positive exercise of individual and collective responsibility: 'You've got to watch them constantly and make sure they don't dae anything . . . you're constantly on the alert . . . you're constantly moving things'. There was a recognition that mistakes were made: 'I am fairly safety conscious. It is quite difficult in this kind of house . . . your safety awareness comes by things which nearly happen, just managing to avert them . . . Unfortunately, sometimes they do happen' (Case study). A small percentage of families was viewed as irresponsible: 'One per cent unsocial tenants in this scheme, but they're the people you hear about all the time. You don't hear about the folk who look after their kids' (Group interview).

This view was acknowledged by the professionals who agreed that the community is a good one. Where the parents' and professional groups diverge is in their views on the responsibility which people or institutions *other* than parents have for safety. The parents, while recognising their pivotal place in the maintenance of child safety expressed the view that the regional council, the roads department, the local housing office, workmen coming into the area and British Rail, among others, have a responsibility for child safety in Corkerhill. 'With the amount of scaffolding that is in the scheme, you would think they would have a watchman of some description.' 'It was the company [repairing the pavements]. Sometimes they would go away on a Friday and come back on a Monday, and the pavements would be left just as they were' (Case studies). An ability to identify the hazards and risks which led to accidents by no means meant that parents absolved themselves from blame: 'I am going to murder the person who left that [socket] cover off, and it was probably me . . . because I am usually the last person using it.' 'I blame myself, I should have been more careful,' 'You feel it is your fault' (Case studies).

The professional group, which recognising a *generalised* social responsibility for accidents was less inclined to link specific problems for specific hazards with specific bodies whose responsibility it is, or should be, to reduce those hazards. As one of the professional group bluntly put it: 'The house is there and there's no money to change [in] terms of safety. We couldn't look at that at all. We look at family composition in terms of nuisance and everything else, but we don't look at the insides because there just isn't the money'.

How can accidents be prevented in Corkerhill?

The final week of the 'citizen' interviews, and the final part of the interview with professionals specifically addressed the preventability of accidents, asking the groups what might be done with low funds, no funds or more substantial funds. In other words, what their priorities were for preventive measures given different levels of resources. There was virtual unanimity among the parents' groups that housing was the place to start. 'Raze them to the ground, and make wee front and back doors' '. . . Upstairs, downstairs, back and front garden . . .' 'Aye, that's everybody's ideal isn't it?' 'Window frames, insulation, oh there must be aboot a hundred things you should do in the house – get started with a wee drawing . . .' 'Outside the house: I'd start with a play area, and a one way street.' 'And sleeping policemen in the street.' 'And limited times when they're allowed to come in 'cause it's a play area 'cause there's so many kids.'

With less money to spend, priorities would include re-wiring (many electric sockets in Corkerhill have no on/off switches), a high cupboard in the kitchen, smoke alarms and funds for the sort of community business which would tackle safety issues. Also suggested were thermostats on the water tanks, and gas fires provided with guards ready fixed rather than as an optional extra. The teenagers group would improve the play area. Among the 'no cost' preventive measures were a 10mph speed limit within the housing scheme, shared childcare, passing on equipment, changing routines for the bin men (who at the time came to the housing scheme as children were leaving for school, with the consequence that pavements piled high with black bags were impassable).

The professionals were more modest in their preventive ambitions and focussed solidly on education. 'Even if we had the money to put all these things right, education needs to be done as well,' and 'it's a bit more than making sure equipment is available' were remarks received with nods and murmurs of agreement. There was no such thing as a no cost solution for the professionals. They rightly pointed out that: '. . . if you're going to try and change what people do at home, then that's going to cost something.' But low cost solutions included advice on the use of chip pans, and 'just basic things like that and things like when you're running a bath, don't run scalding water first.' Another possibility was 'Having ongoing videos and displays [in mother toddler groups].' Higher cost solutions were also educational: 'A scheme of paid instructors for training child pedestrian skills . . .' Although the interviewers suggested moving on to specific features within the home which might be changed, the message from the professionals was much the same: 'We have to educate them that the home is really the most unsafe place you can be.'

Discussion

The educational approach to accident prevention invokes a deficit model of parents, for instance posters that work on the exhortation principle (showing two mothers outside a school – 'Meet them: Don't let them die on the roads'). An educational approach of this kind flies in the face of the study reported in this paper. In a low income, high risk council estate, we found little evidence from the group interviews, the household survey or the case studies that knowledge and awareness were lacking.[1] With the exception of a good knowledge of first aid, general knowledge about accidents is high in the community, and specific knowledge about local hazards and risks is quite considerably more detailed among the citizens than among the professionals.

It was clear from the group of interviews that parents already exercise a wide range preventive activities. In relation to building works in the street, one mother said: 'I went away in and I kicked up merry hell aboot the fact that there wasnae a board or anything put over it and it ended up two workmen came oot and lifted the pram over the hole and then left somebody there on guard . . . By the time I got back, they had a workman standing on it, they had boards across it, and by the next morning it was all cemented. So I think part of the thing we have tae dae is to be more voluble – is to shout and to say, "C'mon, get the finger oot, it's time something was done."' Plans were made for an equipment loan scheme (which failed as the local health promotion department was unable to provide any support, offering instead a specially commissioned – and thus not inexpensive – poster). Meanwhile old cots were cut down to make safety gates or playpens. In brief, parents were using the resources they had to hand to try and create a safer environment.

Much health promotion appears to ignore this kind of achievement, and to underestimate the difficulties associated with 'standard solutions' such as the purchase of safety goods. A number of the mothers we spoke to therefore experienced health promotion messages about constant vigilance and the importance of having a variety of safety goods as itself anxiety-provoking (and in that sense, a health hazard). 'You can get really depressed and think about the things your children should have – things that you're told all the time, all this equipment you should have and it can end up, "I'm no bringing my child up properly. I don't have this and I don't have that" and add that to all the other stresses you've got – living in bad housing or poverty and you can get depressed and distracted and that's when accidents are more likely to happen – when you're under stress' (Group interviews).

Currently, education is the cornerstone of accident prevention policy. However, while education is one of the less costly options in the reduction of accidents, there is little evidence that it results in a decrease in injury. This work indicates that parents have a good understanding of the causes of accidents in general, clear views on hazards and risks in their own environments, and that they are effective most of the time in keeping children safe in unsafe conditions. However cheap it may be when compared with other public health measures, to 'educate' parents and children, if it is not effective, then it cannot be cost effective.

Just as the introduction of child resistant containers for medicine has been associated with a steep drop in childhood poisonings, our work indicates a number of areas where preventive efforts based on environmental rather than (though in association with) behavioural change might usefully focus. Further, our view is that to base preventive work on injury and death data is misconceived. A focus on risks and hazards may be more productive, since these provide the context in which parents negotiate their everyday safe keeping behaviour.

Outcome studies of preventive work tend to be poorly conceived, concentrating on delivery or reception of the health message rather than health gain. It is unclear what part, if any, educational health promotion messages have played in the reduction of accidents. Our study suggests one reason for this is the markedly different views held by professionals and 'their' public on the character of accident and accident risk, and the nature of safekeeping.

Reference

1. Roberts, H., Smith, S.J. and Bryce, C. *Safety as a Social Value*, Final report to the Scottish Office Home and Health Department, Public Health Research Unit, University of Glasgow (1993).

Helen Roberts and Carol Bryce were employed at the Public Health Research Unit of the University of Glasgow, and Susan Smith was at the University of Edinburgh when the fieldwork for this research was carried out. Helen Roberts is currently Professor of Child Health at City University, London. The article, an edited extract of which appears here, was originally published in *Sociology of Health and Illness*, 15, 447–463 (1993).

31 | Malingering

RICHARD ASHER

I define malingering as the imitation, production or encouragement of illness for a deliberate end. The patient is quite conscious of what he is doing and quite cognisant of why he is doing it. With that definition, pure malingering – the planned fraudulent faking of illness – is, in my experience, a very rare condition. Either that, or else I am a very gullible physician. I know I have been mistaken before now and it is possible that many malingerers have deceived me without being suspected.

True malingering is best classified by motives rather than by techniques – the principal prime movers being Fear, Desire and Escape.

Fear: fear of call-up, fear of overseas duty, fear of warfare.

Desire: desire for compensation, desire for a comfortable pension, desire for revenge against a surgeon for some (usually imagined) wrong. Desire for the comforts of hospital life. Desire to stay in the ward longer because one has fallen in love with the staff nurse.

Escape: escape from a prisoner-of-war camp by incurable disability, escape from prison by transfer to hospital, escape from an impending court case, escape from battle.

Malingering by prisoners of war has evolved a variety of ingenious techniques, even to the extent of passing borrowed albuminuric urine, secreted in a false bladder and passed in the presence of a suspicious German doctor, through a hand-carved and hand-painted penis of life-like verisimilitude.

It is well known that opposing forces try to weaken the enemy's army by dropping pamphlets persuading them to malinger. A particular pamphlet dropped in large numbers early in 1945 on English troops in Italy is worthy of your attention. Neatly produced in book-match form (to make it easy to hide), it opens with Three Golden Rules for Malingering which I do not think could be beaten:

1. You must make the impression you hate to be ill.
2. Make up your mind for one disease and stick to it.
3. Don't tell the doctor too much.

There is only time to give details about one of those. Here is how to have tuberculosis – according to the instruction book:

'First you must smoke excessively to acquire a cough. Then tell the doctor that you have lost weight, you do not feel well and that you cough a great deal. Say that sometimes you cough up streaks of blood. Sometimes you wake drenched with sweat. Stick to those symptoms, do not invent any new ones.'

Mental as well as physical disease can be simulated. Those with little experience of mental disease may learn with surprise that it is very hard to pretend to be mad. For instance, the peculiar distorted thinking of the schizophrenic is something a sane person cannot manage. An experiment was done in which twenty normal people were asked to feign insanity; they, and twenty genuinely psychotic patients, were interviewed by psychiatrists (who had no other means of telling which was which). The psychiatrists were able to pick out the malingerers in nearly 90 per cent of the cases.

I now pass to those cases of illness which, though self-produced or prolonged, do not constitute malingering. They do not have so definite a purpose. I have grouped them together as The Borderland of Malingering.

The Borderland of Malingering
A. Illness as a comfort
    (a) Hysteria.
    (b) The Proud Lonely Person (Lucy's disease).

B. Illness as a hobby
    (a) The Grand Tour Type (rich hypochondriac).
    (b) The Chronic Out-Patient (poor hypochondriac).
    (c) The Eccentric Hypochondriac (faddist).
    (d) The Chronic Convalescent (daren't recover).

C. Illness as a profession
    (a) Anorexia Nervosa.
    (b) The Chronic Artefactualists.
    (c) Munchausen's Syndrome.

Hysterics differ from malingerers because, although they may produce illness and enjoy it, they are unaware of what they are doing. They possess a capacity for self-deception; they can wall off part of their mind so that it is impervious to self-scrutiny. This process, dignified by psychiatrists with the term 'dissociation', is colloquially called 'kidding yourself'. Some cases of hysteria are very close to malingering. Others start as malingerers, and as they become better at kidding others, they finally succeed in kidding themselves, and become hysterics.

I have seen very little proven hysteria and I diagnose the condition only with diffidence. A fair proportion of 'hysterics' turn out to have organic disease, as many of us know to our cost.

Notice that among illness as a comfort I have put the proud, lonely person. Allow me to explain this. This pathetic type of case usually occurs in later life when praise and companionship are hard to come by. To lonely people a medical consultation may represent an event of great importance. It supplies that need to be noticed that exists in all human beings. A visit from the doctor allows them the illusion of seeking medical advice rather than companionship. A patient may be too proud to complain of loneliness, but there is no loss of pride in complaining of symptoms. Lonely people miss, not only companionship, but also the advice and criticism that go with it.

Turning to the hypochondriacs, first we have the rich hypochondriac. I call this one The Grand Tour Type, because she spends much of her time touring the larger cities in Europe visiting consultants. She always carries a large dossier, opinions from consultants, X-rays and laboratory reports; and usually a list of her own symptoms which she has carefully written out. During her tour she may have persuaded surgeons to remove some of her less essential organs. She has usually had her gall bladder and a quota of her pelvic organs removed by the time she reaches one's consulting room. To the consultant in private practice they are a familiar, tedious and lucrative burden.

The poor hypochondriac (or perpetual out-patient). Every hospital has a number of out-patients who have attended for many years. Whenever they are discharged from one department they turn up in another, thus acquiring a very large collection of documents, rivalling that of the rich hypochondriac although written on less luxurious writing paper and penned by less illustrious names. Though some have genuine chronic illness, many of them attend because they like the companionship of hospital; instead of going to the local public house for a glass of beer and a chat with the landlord, they go to the local hospital for a bottle of medicine and a chat with the other patients. One enlightened doctor tried the experiment of arranging outpatient sessions where the patients did not see the doctor at all unless they asked for him. It was a great success.

The eccentric hypochondriacs. These people like peculiar or unorthodox treatments. They believe with apostolic fervour in nature cures, osteopaths, astrologers and herbalists. Their preoccupation is more with treatment than with illness and they are harmless and often entertaining.

The chronic convalescent. When a patient has had longstanding organic disease for many years it becomes so familiar to him that it is almost a friend. If the illness is suddenly cured, he may feel deserted and friendless. He misses the familiar pain, the sympathetic enquiries of his friends and the security of his medical routine. He does not really want to get well; he has become a hypochondriac.

Now the last group: Illness as a profession. First, I consider anorexia nervosa. The reason why these people go to such lengths to avoid eating is rarely clear. They will resort to a variety of artifices to avoid food. They will hide food in their bed lockers, pour milk into their hot-water bottles and insist on starving in the midst of plenty.

The next group is that of the chronic artefactualists, who may spend years in self-mutilation or the production of spurious fevers. Skin diseases are most favoured by the sufferers from chronic autogenous disease, but various other forms of self-damage are reported.

Lastly, Munchausen's syndrome. This is the strangest and rarest form of chronic autogenous disease. The patient with this syndrome is nearly always brought into hospital by police or bystanders, having collapsed in the street or on a bus with an apparently acute illness, supported by a plausible and yet dramatic history. Though his history seems most convincing at first, later his story is found to be largely false, and his symptoms and signs mostly spurious. He is discovered to have attended and deceived an astounding number of other hospitals. At several of them he may have been operated upon, and a large number of abdominal scars is often found. So skilfully do these people imitate acute illness that the diagnosis may be quite unsuspected until a passing doctor, ward sister or hospital porter says 'I know that man – we had him in St Quinidines last September. He says he's an ex-fighter pilot shot in the chest, in the last War, and he coughs up blood; or sometimes he's been shot through the head in the last war and has fits.'

Common varieties are:

(a) The abdominal type: laparotomophilia migrans.
(b) The bleeding type: haemorrhagica histrionica, colloquially called haematemesis merchants, haemoptysis merchants, and so on.
(c) The type specialising in faints, fits, convulsions and paralysis (neurologica diabolica).

These people differ from other chronic artefactualists in their constant progression from one hospital to another, often under a variety of false names, but nearly always telling the same false story, faking the same fictitious symptoms and submitting to innumerable operations and investigations. It seems that nothing can be done to prevent their continuing clinical depredations. Most doctors are so pleased if they succeed with detection and ejection they never think about protection. Though serious psychiatric studies of these people have been made, nobody can yet answer the two fundamental questions:

(a) Why do they do it?
(b) How can we stop them doing it?

All that can be said about them, and indeed about the whole subject of malingering, are these words of Robert Burns:

> But human bodies are such fools
> For all their colleges and schools
> That when no real ills do perplex them
> They make enough themselves to vex them.

The best explanation for all this self-manufactured disease is simply this: That human beings are such fools.

Richard Asher was a leading British physician who worked both in public health and hospital medicine from 1934 to 1963. This article is an extract from the book *Talking Sense*, a collection of his papers edited by Sir Francis Avery Jones, originally published by Pitman Medical (1972).

32 | Causes of declining life expectancy in Russia

FRANCIS NOTZON, YURI KOMAROV,
SERGEI ERMAKOV, CHRISTOPHER SEMPOS,
JAMES MARKS AND ELENA SEMPOS

Russia (officially known as the Russian Federation) has been undergoing unprecedented political, economic, and social change during the last several years. All aspects of the society have been affected, including the health status of the population. There have been dramatic outbreaks of infectious diseases and decreases in the availability of health services. The most noticeable effect, however, has been an unprecedented decline in life expectancy.[1]

It has been widely recognized that key public health indicators have been worsening since the 1960's. For example, cardiovascular mortality rates increased by about 26% between 1960 and 1985.[2] However, until recently the extent to which conditions had been degrading was not well understood because of the lack of published data. It is in the context of declining trends in health that the phenomenal changes of the late 1980's through the present are overlaid.

The purpose of this article is to compare and contrast mortality trends in Russia with the United States, with the goal of understanding the impact of major mortality determinants on the decline in life expectancy.

Trends before 1990

The rapid rise in mortality since 1990 in Russia has been extensively reported in the press and in some scientific articles. However, the recent rise in deaths is best understood in the context of long-term health trends in Russia. Health outcomes in Russia have not experienced any long-term improvement for several decades, as measured by life expectancy. In fact, male life expectancy went through two decades of gradual decline, from the mid-1960's to the mid-1980's; female life expectancy stagnated over the same interval. The United States life expectancy was only slightly higher than Russia's in the mid-1960's, but the gap has increased steadily since 1970.

The remarkable rise in Russian life expectancy in the 1980's requires careful examination. Between 1985 and 1987, male life expectancy increased by more than 2 years, and female life expectancy rose by more than 1 year. No such sharp increase took place in the United States. There was no major improvement in Russian living standards, access to medical care, or quality of care that might help to explain the sudden rise in life expectancy in both sexes.

However, two aspects of life changed dramatically at that time: the sudden drop in per capita alcohol consumption, brought about by Gorbachev's anti-alcohol campaign, and the period of perestroika that introduced the notion of social democratization and inspired hopes for a better future. The anti-alcohol campaign reduced consumption by raising the price of alcoholic beverages, reducing the production of alcohol, and limiting access by restricting the hours of state liquor stores.[3] The campaign resulted in a rapid drop in alcohol consumption that correlated very well with the temporal rise in life expectancy. An analysis of the changing composition of causes of death has shown that most of the rise in life expectancy was due to a sharp decline in external causes of death, particularly for men, as well as a decrease in deaths due to cardiovascular diseases.[3] The impact of perestroika on mortality levels is more speculative but has been mentioned as a factor in the sharp drop in suicide deaths in the Soviet Union from 1985 to 1988.[4]

Trends 1990 to 1994

Russia experienced a significant rise in mortality between 1990 and 1994. In that 5-year period, the annual number of deaths rose by almost 650,000, or about 39%. Combined with a sharp drop in the annual number of births, the mortality increase led to a significant excess of deaths over births in Russia, beginning in 1992. The Russian age-adjusted mortality rate, already high in 1990 as compared with the United States and most industrialized countries, rose almost one third by 1994, with increases of 36% for the male death rate and 23% for the female rate (Table 32.1).

Similar data for the United States showed a decline in age-adjusted mortality between 1990 and 1994. The negative trend in Russian life expectancy quickly erased the gains of the 1980s and then continued downward. Overall, male life expectancy fell by more than 6 years, from 63.8 years in 1990 to 57.7 years in 1994, while female life expectancy declined by more than 3 years to 71.2 years in 1994. The male–female differential in life expectancy of 10.6 years in 1990, already the highest in Europe, rose to 13.5 years in 1994.

From 1990 through 1994, mortality rates rose sharply for every sex and age group. For both men and women, the largest increases were in the middle-aged groups; the death rate for men aged 35 to 44 years increased almost 100%. United States mortality rates for most sex and age groups fell from 1990 to 1994, with the largest declines among the very young.

Between 1990 and 1994, mortality rates increased by 100% or more for 'other alcohol-related causes' [deaths attributable to alcohol intoxication], pneumonia and influenza, and homicide. Sharp increases also were noted for major causes of death such as diseases of the heart (40% increase) and stroke (20% increase). Thus, in 1994 almost all the Russian cause-specific death rates were substantially higher than the US rates: 2 times higher for diseases of the heart, 3.4 times higher for homicides, 3.5 times

Table 32.1 Age-adjusted mortality rates and life expectancy, Russia and the United States, 1990 and 1994.*

	Age-adjusted mortality rates			Life expectancy at birth		
	1990	1994	% change	1990	1994	Change
			Russia			
Total	1192.7	1581.6	32.6	69.2	64.1	−5.2
Male	1688.4	2290.5	35.7	63.8	57.7	−6.1
Female	892.2	1098.4	23.1	74.4	71.2	−3.2
			United States			
Total	803.4	784.7	−2.3	75.4	75.7	0.3
Male	1035.3	996.4	−3.8	71.8	72.4	0.6
Female	628.8	621.8	−1.1	78.8	79.0	0.2

* Data are from Goskomstat in Russia and the National Center for Health Statistics, Centers for Disease Control and Prevention in the United States. Deaths are per 100 000 population, and rates are age adjusted to World Health Organization European standard population.

higher for suicides, 6 times for stroke and other injuries, and 16 times higher for other alcohol-related causes. However, the neoplasm death rate remained roughly equal to the US rate. For all causes combined, the Russian mortality rate was almost exactly double the US rate (Table 32.1).

A more accurate way to summarize the overall impact of these changes in age- and cause-specific rates is by measuring their contribution to changes in life expectancy. For both men and women, the bulk of the change takes place in the middle ages, in particular for ages 25 to 64 years. The contribution of infant mortality to the decline in life expectancy is small for both sexes, less than 0.1 years for both men and women. Among men, mortality change in the ages 35 to 54 years led to a drop in life expectancy of 2.9 years or almost half of the total decline for men. For women, the age pattern was similar but with a larger contribution from the older age groups than for men.

The same partitioning method was used to assess the contribution of each cause of death to changes in life expectancy. The largest contributors to the decline in life expectancy between 1990 and 1994 were diseases of the heart (26% of the total decline) and other injuries (18%). Other major contributors were stroke, other alcohol-related causes, homicides, and suicides.

Reasons for the rise in mortality

No plausible statistical or reporting factors explain the rapid rise in Russian mortality from 1990 to 1994, [but] evidence clearly exists of a broad-based and substantial deterioration in survival. Russia is not alone in experiencing drops in life expectancy; all the nations created from the breakup of the Soviet Union have reported a decline in life expectancy since 1990, although none has been as large as in Russia.[5] Several hypotheses may explain the rapid rise in Russian mortality. We will discuss each one in turn, although many may have occurred simultaneously.

Economic and Social Instability There is no doubt that Russia is undergoing a painful social and economic transition: average per capita real income declined by almost two thirds between 1990 and 1995, and the number of families living in poverty rose from 2% in 1987 to 38% in 1993.[10] Per capita income is an extremely important factor in determining health outcomes, and long-term improvements in health status depend heavily on income growth and distribution. Increasing poverty and the dissolution of social controls may have played a key role in the rising levels of homicide and suicide in Russia.

Alcohol The rise in alcohol consumption since the late 1980's has resulted from the decline in government controls, rising stress, and other forces of instability. Declining living standards have not reduced alcohol consumption for two reasons. First, an increasing proportion of alcohol consumed is produced at home. Second, the price of alcohol has risen much less than most other consumer prices since 1990.[3] The increase in alcohol consumption has contributed to the rise in deaths due to alcohol poisoning, included in 'other alcohol-related causes'. The declining quality of alcoholic beverages, i.e. the rise in toxic substances contained in alcohol, is an important factor in alcohol poisoning deaths.[3] Alcohol consumption may also contribute to components of the 'other injury' group, including occupational injuries and drownings. The role of alcohol in deaths due to homicides and suicides is no doubt substantial. Finally, chronic alcoholism undoubtedly plays a role in increasing chronic disease mortality, e.g. stroke mortality.

Tobacco The prevalence of smoking among adults in Russia has long been high.[7] The prevalence for men was above 60% in the 1990's and near 10% for women. There is some evidence of an increase in smoking rates since 1985. The level of tobacco imports has risen sharply since 1990, but it is uncertain whether this is due to increased smoking or to a substitution of foreign tobacco for domestic production. Therefore, the level of smoking is another factor explaining historically high mortality levels in Russia, but insufficient to account for more than a part of the post-1990 rise in mortality.

Nutrition Government and private surveys indicate that the declining standards of recent years required families to spend an increasing proportion of their income on food and also led to a reduction in consumption of certain foodstuffs, such as meat.[6] However, the Russian diet in the latter stages of the Communist era could not be considered healthy; it became increasingly high in fat and, in particular, rich in animal food products with little consumption of fresh vegetables or fruit. Although vegetable and fruit consumption has dropped further since 1990, at the same time there has been a considerable reduction in the percentage of energy derived from fat.[8]

Stress and depression Recent research in the United States and other countries has shown that stress, anxiety, and depression contribute to chronic diseases, such as hypertension, heart disease, and myocardial infarction. These psychosocial factors, along with growing hopelessness in the face of increasing unemployment, negative economic growth, and social strife, may in turn underlie the rapid growth in per capita alcohol consumption.

Health care system The deteriorating economic situation has seriously impaired the ability of the health care system to respond to rising health problems. There have been numerous reports of the crumbling of the health care system, increasing demands for payments 'under the table' for care provided, and the virtual disappearance from the market of certain essential pharmaceutical drugs.[6] Nevertheless, the deterioration did not begin in 1990; it has in fact been going on for some time and probably accounts for only a small part of the recent decline in life expectancy.

Major contributors to the decline in life expectancy

More than half of the recent decline in life expectancy can be assigned to two major cause groups: the *cardiovascular diseases* (CVDs, e.g., heart disease and stroke) and *injuries* (motor vehicle crashes, suicides, homicides, and other injuries).

External causes of death   The recent rise in homicide and suicide deaths has been an important component in the growth of the injury group. Possible contributors to the rapid rise include diminishing social controls, a large increase in alcohol consumption, and growing economic instability. The rise in suicides may be due in part to growing hopelessness in Russian society.

Little is known about the magnitude of deaths due to acts of war. Although war-related deaths may have contributed to the rise in mortality due to 'other injuries', the largest recent outbreak of fighting – in Chechnya – did not begin until December 1994. The annual number of deaths in Russia rose by about 650,000 [between 1990–94] – far in excess of the estimated loss of life in Chechnya.

CVD mortality   Because heart diseases and stroke develop over an extended period, mortality from these diseases is not believed to be subject to rapid change. However, a review article on rapid mortality change due to chronic diseases indicates a rapid change in CVD mortality is most likely to occur in the younger middle ages, in part because younger individuals are more likely to modify their behaviour.[9] Another contributor to the long-term rise in CVD in Russia is the absence of public health programs designed to reduce risk factor prevalence. The unavailability of pharmaceuticals, such as blood pressure medication, may also account for some of the rising death rate due to CVD.

Future trends   The rapid growth in Russian mortality may be coming to an end. Data from 1995 indicate an increase in life expectancy for both men and women, to 58.3 and 71.7, respectively.[10] It is too soon to tell if this is the beginning of a return to the lower mortality levels of the recent past or simply the levelling-off of mortality rates at an extremely high level.

Conclusion

The rapidity and scale of the Russian mortality increase exceed those of any other industrialized country in recent memory. From 1990 to 1994 age-adjusted mortality rose by one third, resulting in a decline in life expectancy of more than 6 years for men and more than 3 years for women. The pattern of diseases and mortality have particularly affected the young and middle-aged adult population, that is, those aged 25 to 64 years.

Returning Russian life expectancy to the level of 1990 will require substantial and long-term efforts to improve the economy, social order, and health care systems of Russia. The lesson for the Russian health care system is the same as for the health care system of the United States or other industrialized countries: current levels of life expectancy should not be considered permanent. Life expectancy can decline and, under unusual circumstances, those declines can be rapid and substantial.

References

1. National Center for Health Statistics. Vital and health statistics: Russian Federation and United States, selected years 1980–93. *Vital Health Stat 5.* 1995; 5, pp. 1–28.
2. Deev A.D., Oganov R.G. Trends and determinants of cardiovascular mortality in the Soviet Union. *Int J Epidemiol.* 1989; 18(suppl 1), p. S137–S144.
3. Skolnikov V., Nemtsov A. The anti-alcohol campaign and variations in Russian mortality. In: Bobadilla J.L., Costello C.A., Mitchell F., eds. *Premature Death in the New Independent States.* Washington, DC: National Academy Press; 1997, pp. 239–261.
4. Varnik A., Wasserman D. Suicides in the former Soviet republics. *Acta Psychiatr Scand.* 1992; 86, pp.76–78.
5. Haub C. *Population Change in the former Soviet Republics.* Vol. 49. Washington DC: Population Reference Bureau; 1994. Population Bulletin.
6. Chen L.C., Wittgenstein F., McKeon E. The upsurge in mortality in Russia: causes and policy implications. *Popul Dev Rev.* 1996; 22, pp. 517–530.
7. Prolhorov A.V. Cigarette smoking and priorities for tobacco control in the New Independent States. In: Bobadilla J.L., Costello C.A., Mitchell F., eds. *Premature Death in the New Independent States.* Washington, DC: National Academy Press; 1997, pp. 275–286.
8. Popkin B., Zohoori N., Kohlmeier L., *et al.* Nutritional risk factors in the former Soviet Union. In: Bobadilla J.L., Costello C.A., Mitchell F., eds. *Premature Death in the New Independent States.* Washington, DC: National Academy Press; 1997, pp. 314–334.
9. Berkelman R.L., Buehler J.W. Public health surveillance of non-infectious chronic diseases: the potential to detect rapid changes in disease burden. *Int J Epidemiol.* 1990; 19, pp. 628–635.
10. Goskomstat of Russia. *The Demographic Yearbook of Russia: Statistical Handbook.* Moscow, Russia: Goskomstat; 1996.

This edited extract is from an article with the same title originally published in March 1998 in the *Journal of the American Medical Association* (*JAMA*) 279(10): 793–800. The authors come from the USA (the National Centers for Disease Control and Prevention, US Department of Health and Human Services, the Mid-Atlantic Kaiser Permanente Medical Group, and the National Institutes of Health) and the Russian Federation (MedSocEconomInform and the Ministry of Health of Russia).

33 | The psychosocial causes of illness

RICHARD WILKINSON

We no longer have to evoke images of voodoo death to argue that psychosocial stress can kill. Fortunately there is now a great deal of epidemiological and experimental evidence which removes any doubt that psychosocial factors can exert very powerful influences on physical health – both morbidity and mortality. A brief sketch of the evidence shows the enormous range of possibilities for such links. The problem is not so much that there is a shortage of potential pathways, but that there are a vast number of possibilities which are all quite plausible in the light of what is already known. The work which is needed to rule out some and confirm the importance of others will take some years.

The importance of income distribution implies that we must explain the effect of low income on health through its social meanings and implications for social position, rather than through the direct physical effects which material circumstances might have independently of their social connotations in any particular society. This is not to say that bad (or even non-existent) housing and an inadequate diet do not affect the health of a minority (though still a large number) of people in developed societies: they clearly do. What it means is that the direct material effects of factors such as these are not the main explanations of why national standards of health are related to income distribution. Nor does this mean that we shall ignore the health of the poorest in society. The poor suffer the psychosocial effects of deprivation as well as its direct material effects. Indeed, it is important to recognise that as well as the greatest material deprivation, those at the bottom of the social hierarchy also suffer the greatest social, psychological and emotional deprivation, and this may well have a greater impact on their health than the more direct effects of material deprivation.

Even among those living in what must by any standards have been absolute material poverty, Sapolsky has provided remarkable evidence of the physiological marks of the unremitting nature of the socioeconomic stress they lived with (Sapolsky 1991). After describing how almost all of the dead bodies used to teach anatomy in London medical schools in the century 1830–1930 came from poorhouses, Sapolsky says that the adrenal gland was thought to be much larger than is now regarded as normal. When anatomists saw the occasional adrenal gland from someone richer, they noted it was oddly smaller and invented a new disease – *idiopathic adrenal atrophy* – to explain it. This 'disease' flourished in the early twentieth century until physicians realised that the smaller adrenal glands were the norm and the disorder was transformed into an 'embarrassing footnote' in medical texts. The enlarged adrenals of the poor were the result of prolonged socioeconomic stress.

Hence, even in historical periods when the main problem was absolute rather than relative poverty for a much larger proportion of the population, the physical impact of the extreme psychosocial and emotional stress which came with it should not be underestimated. The material insecurity is itself a source of stress: it is a constant threat and source of worry which often gives way to despair.

Another approach to thinking about the comparative importance of psychosocial and direct material pathways in the link between income and health, is to consider housing. Although people in bad housing have much higher rates of the main cancers and heart disease, almost no one suggests that physical aspects of bad housing make an important direct contribution to these causes of death. However, there is evidence that damp housing contributes directly to the excess of respiratory disease via the increase of mould spores in the air. But first, such respiratory illnesses are a very small part of the burden of increased ill-health associated with bad housing; and second, surveys of housing conditions suggest that perhaps as little as 7 per cent of the total population live in damp housing (Ineichen 1993).

One of the clearest indications that relative deprivation affects health through psychosocial channels has come from studies of the health effects of unemployment. Evidence from factory closures showed that much of the deterioration in health started, not when people actually became unemployed, but before that – when redundancies were first announced. It now turns out that a large part of the link between health and unemployment is related to job insecurity and the anticipation of unemployment. This provides powerful evidence that one of the clearest categories of deprivation in modern societies affects health predominantly through psychosocial channels. These results are also interesting because the problem of job insecurity is much more wide-spread than unemployment itself. Job insecurity is presumably only one among several other categories of financial or material insecurity.

There have also been tightly controlled experiments demonstrating the underlying link between physical health and stress from a variety of sources. In one example volunteers completed a standard psychological questionnaire designed to measure their stress levels and were then randomly allocated between two groups (Cohen *et al.* 1991). In this blind randomised control trial, people in one group were given nasal drops of distilled water containing five varieties of cold virus; those in the control group were given nasal drops containing only pure distilled water. The results showed that there was a gradient in the proportion who developed colds which rose from 27 per cent among low-stress people to 47 per cent among those with high levels of stress. This suggests that high levels of stress may increase the chances of catching a cold by 75 per cent. The association remained even after controlling for age, sex, education, allergic status, weight and season. Nor were the differences accounted for by possible 'stress-illness mediators' such as smoking, alcohol consumption, exercise, diet or sleep loss.

Despite controlling for factors such as these, it might be argued that high- and low-stress people differed from one another in some other way which accounted for the differences in infection rates. However, a number of studies show signs of weakened immunity and poorer health associated with a clearly identifiable environmental source of stress. For example, a study which examined throat swabs from medical students during exams found that comparisons of swabs showed that exam stress weakened their immunity (Kennedy *et al.* 1988). The [same study found] evidence that the stress of marital breakdown and dysfunction can affect the immune system. The effects were found to be stronger the more recent the marital breakdown and the greater the attachment to the ex-partner.

Progress has also been made in identifying psychosocial characteristics of work which affect health. For most workers in the developed world, certainly for all office workers, the social organisation of work is now likely to be the most important occupational health hazard. Research trying to explain socioeconomic status differences in health in relation to the working environment has also come up with results which indicate the importance of psychosocial processes. Karasek and Theorell (1990) drew attention to the deleterious health effects of having little control over one's work, low social support from managers or colleagues in the workplace, and a fast pace of work. The three were independently related to cardiovascular symptoms and a number of other health problems.

Marmot *et al.* (1991) have found similar relationships contributing to the threefold differences in mortality in the Whitehall study. Although the seniority of the level of employment within the Civil Service is closely related to the amount of control people have over their work, control over work was significantly related to health, even after controlling for employment grade and a number of other risk factors. Conflicting job demands and, in the absence of control, a heavy workload, were also associated with poorer health in this study.

In many ways money is a key to the ability to control one's life. The more money, the greater one's options, the more choice and the more easily most problems can be overcome. Indeed, problems of job or housing insecurity may be seen as instances of a more general category of financial insecurity where important areas of control are lost. The importance of social support also transfers to the world outside work.

A number of studies have shown the beneficial health effects of more, and better quality, social contact between people at home or in the community. It seems likely that social support may be important in changing the way people respond to stressful events and circumstances. Lack of a confiding relationship with a close friend, relative or partner is associated with poorer health, but so also is less involvement with wider social networks, community activities, etc. Berkman (1995) emphasises that the effects of a lack of social contact extend to a wide range of causes of death and influence both the incidence of disease and case-fatality rates. Indeed, she cites evidence of threefold differences in case-fatality rates after a heart attack according to whether or not patients had good social support. Several possible causal pathways linking the effects of social relations to health have been identified involving both the immune and the neuroendocrine systems.

Many of the most important sources of stress in our lives are likely to come from the socioeconomic environment and will be exacerbated by relatively low incomes. A sense of desperation, anger, bitterness, learned helplessness or aggression are all wholly understandable responses to various social, economic and material difficulties. Prolonged stress from any of these sources is often all it takes to damage health. Income distribution is an important determinant of the psychosocial welfare of a society. The importance of knowing that social cohesion is likely to be improved by narrower income differences is that it gives policy-makers a way of improving important aspects of the life of our society. Where people had previously only been able to throw their hands up in despair, it may now be possible to take practical steps to improve matters. Because income distribution is powerfully affected by government policy, governments may be able to improve the psychosocial condition and morale of the whole population.

Conclusions

How does all this fit together? Evidence from a variety of sources [shows] the potential of psychosocial processes to affect health directly. Many of the sources of psychosocial difficulties are likely to be related to low relative income and to be more common in societies with low social cohesion. Most directly related to cohesion were the health effects of social networks and social participation. It may be that the epidemiology which shows the importance to health of close personal relations and wider social networks, is really showing a more fundamental way in which people need to live through and in relation to one another to find essential sources of self-confirmation.

In any estimation of the relative importance of different factors affecting population health, it is not simply the size of the additional health risk to exposed individuals which counts. It is also the proportion of the population exposed. Perhaps the consideration which above all others makes psychosocial factors stand out as likely to be the most important determinants of population health in developed countries is simply the high proportion of the population exposed to various forms of psychosocial stress.

References

Berkman, L.F. (1995) The role of social relations in health promotion, *Psychosomatic Research*, 57, pp. 245–54.

Cohen, S., Tyrrell, D.A.J. and Smith, A.P. (1991) Psychological stress and susceptibility to the common cold, *New England Journal of Medicine*, 325, pp. 606–12.

Ineichen, B. (1993) *Homes and Health: How housing and health interact*, Spon, London.

Karasek, R. and Theorell, T. (1990) *Healthy Work: Stress, productivity and the reconstruction of working life*, Basic Books, New York.

Kennedy, S., Kiecolt-Glaser, J.K. and Glaser, R. (1988) Immunological consequences of acute and chronic stressors: mediating role of interpersonal relationships, *British Journal of Medical Psychology*, 61, pp. 77–85.

Marmot, M.G., Davey Smith, G., Stansfield, S. *et al.* (1991) Health inequalities among British civil servants: the Whitehall II Study, *Lancet*, 337, pp. 1387–93.

Sapolsky, R.M. (1991) Poverty's remains, *The Sciences*, 31, pp. 8–10.

This edited extract comes from Chapter 9 of Richard Wilkinson's book *Unhealthy Societies – The Afflictions of Inequality* (Routledge, 1996, pp. 175–92). The author is Professorial Research Fellow in the Trafford Centre for Medical Research at the University of Sussex, Brighton, UK.

34 | Entitlement and deprivation

JEAN DRÈZE AND AMARTYA K. SEN

Deprivation and the law

In a private ownership economy, command over food can be established by either growing food oneself and having property rights over what is grown, or selling other commodities and buying food with the proceeds. There is no guarantee that either process would yield enough for the survival of any particular person or a family in a particular social and economic situation. The third alternative, other than relying on private charity, is to receive free food or supplementary income from the state. These transfers are, as things stand now, rather rare and limited.

For a large part of humanity, about the only substantial asset that a person owns is his or her ability to work, i.e. labour power. If a person fails to secure employment, then that means of acquiring food (e.g. by getting a job, earning a wage, and having food with this income) fails. If, in addition to that, the laws of the land do not provide any social security arrangements, e.g. unemployment insurance, the person will, under these circumstances, fail to secure the means of subsistence. And that can result in serious deprivation – possibly even starvation and death.

It should also be added that even a person who is engaged in growing food and who succeeds in growing more (even, much more) than enough food for survival may not necessarily survive on this basis, and may not even have the legal right to do so. In many famines the majority of the victims come from the class of agricultural labourers. They are often primarily engaged in growing food. However, the legal nature of their contract, which is often informal, basically involves a wage payment in exchange for employment. The contract typically includes no right to the output grown by the person's own labour – no entitlement to the food output which could be the basis of survival for that person and his or her dependants.

Even if a person is lucky enough to find employment and is paid a certain sum of money for it as a wage, he or she has to convert that into food by purchase in the market. How much that wage commands would, of course, depend on the price of food. If food prices rise very rapidly, without money wages rising correspondingly, the labourers who have grown the food themselves may fail to acquire the food they need to survive. The food grown belongs to the employer (typically the owner of the land), and the wage payment is the end of the grower's right to the produce, even if that wage does not yield enough to survive.

Similarly, a person who acquires food by producing some other commodity and selling it in the market has to depend on the actual ability to sell that product and also on the relative price of that product *vis-à-vis* food. If either the sale fails to materialise, or the relative price of that product falls sharply *vis-à-vis* food, the person may again have no option but to starve.

It is also important to realise that uncertainty and vulnerability can be features of subsistence production (involving 'exchange with nature') as well as of market exchange. This precariousness is particularly visible in African famines, where a substantial proportion of the victims often come from the ranks of small farmers who are hit *inter alia* [among other things] by a collapse of their 'direct entitlement' to the food they normally grow. It would be a misleading simplification to regard self-provisioning as synonymous with security. The peasant farmer, like the landless labourer, has no guaranteed entitlement to the necessities of life.

Entitlement failures and economic analysis

If a group of people fail to establish their entitlement over an adequate amount of food, they have to go hungry. If that deprivation is large enough, the resulting starvation can lead to death. There is nothing particularly novel in the recognition that starvation is best seen as a result of 'entitlement failure'. Since the aggregate food supply is not divided among the population through some distributive formula (such as equal division), each family has to establish command over its own food. Even though this fact is elementary enough, it is remarkable that food analysis is often conducted just in terms of production and total availability rather than taking note of the processes through which people establish their entitlements to food.

Entitlement analysis has been used in recent years to study various famines, e.g. the Bengal famine of 1943, the Malawi (in fact, Nyasaland, as it was then called) famine of 1949–50, the Sahel famines of the 1970s, the Bangladesh famine of 1974, the Ethiopian famines of 1973–85, and also a number of historical and recent cases of widespread starvation.

Just as there have been major famines in private ownership economies without state guarantee of basic subsistence rights, there have also been famines in socialist countries with their own systems of legality (e.g. in Ukraine in the early 1930s, in China during 1958–61, in Kampuchea in the late 1970s). The entitlements guaranteed by the law have, on those occasions, failed to provide the means of survival and subsistence to a great many people. In some cases, e.g. in the Ukrainian famines, state policy was in fact positively geared to undermining the entitlements of a large section of the population.

In analysing the causation of famines and in seeking social changes that eliminate them, the nature of entitlement systems and their workings have to be understood and assessed. The same applies to the problem of regular hunger and endemic undernourishment. If people go hungry on a regular basis all the time, or seasonally, the explanations of that have to be sought in the way the entitlement system in operation fails to give the persons involved adequate means of securing enough food. Seeing hunger as entitlement failure points to possible remedies as well as helping us to understand the forces that generate hunger and sustain it. In particular, this approach compels us to take a broad view of the ways in which access to food can be protected or promoted, including reforms of the legal framework within which economic relations take place.

Since food problems have often been discussed in terms of the availability of food without going into the question of entitlement (there is a substantial tradition of concentrating only on food output per head, going back at least to Malthus's famous *Essay On the Principle of Population* of 1798), it is particularly important to understand the relevance of seeing hunger as entitlement failures. Such failures can occur even when food availability is not reduced, and even when the ratio of food to population (on which Malthus concentrated) goes up rather than down. Indeed, the relentless persistence of famines and the enormous reach of world hunger, despite the steady and substantial increase in food availability per head, makes it particularly imperative for us to reorientate our approach away from food availability to entitlements.

This can be done without losing sight of the elementary fact that food availability must be *among* the factors that determine the entitlements of different groups of people, and that food production is one of the important determinants of entitlements.

Availability, command and occupations

The links between food availability and entitlements are indeed numerous and often important. First, for some people, the output of food grown by themselves is also their basic entitlement to food. For example, for peasants engaged mainly in growing food crops, the output, availability, and entitlement of food for the family can be much the same. This is a matter of what may be called 'direct entitlement'. Second, one of the major influences on the ability of anyone to purchase food is clearly the price of food, and that price is, of course, influenced by the production and availability of food in the economy. Third, food production can also be a major source of employment, and a reduction in food production (due to, say, a drought or a flood) would reduce employment and wage income through the same process that leads to a decline in the output and availability of food. Fourth, if and when a famine develops, having a stock of food available in the public distribution system is clearly a major instrument in the hands of the authorities to combat starvation. This can be done either by distributing food directly (in cooked or uncooked form), or by adding to the supply of food in the market, thereby exerting a downward pressure or a moderating influence on possibly rocketing prices. For these and other reasons, food entitlements have close links with food availability and output. It would be amazing if such links were absent, since the physical presence of food cannot but be an influence on the possibility of acquiring food through direct ownership or exchange.

However, as was discussed earlier, the actual command over food that different sections of the population can exercise depends on a set of legal and economic factors, including those governing ownership, production, and exchange. The overall availability of food is thus a very poor guide to the fortunes of different socioeconomic groups.

The inadequacy of the availability view is particularly important to note in the context of the making of economic policy. Indeed, an undue reliance – often implicit –

on the availability view has frequently contributed to the development or continuation of a famine, by making the relevant authorities smug about the food situation. For instance, there have been famines, e.g. in Bengal in 1943 and in Ethiopia in 1973, when the absence of a substantial food availability decline has contributed to official smugness.

The possibly contrary nature of the availability view and the entitlement view can be illustrated by considering the food availability picture during the Bangladesh famine of 1974. The availability in 1974 – the year of the famine – was higher than in any other year during 1971–6. And yet the famine hit Bangladesh exactly in that year of peak food availability! The families of rural labourers and other occupation groups who died because of their inability to command food were affected by a variety of influences (including loss of employment, the rise in food prices etc.), and this occurred despite the fact that the actual availability of food in the economy of Bangladesh was at a peak.

The failure of the availability view of famine can be further brought out by comparing different districts of Bangladesh in terms of their food availability in 1974 *vis-à-vis* their experience of famine.

It turns out that among the nineteen districts of Bangladesh, one of the famine districts (Dinajpur) had the *highest* availability of food in the entire country, and indeed all four of the famine districts were among the top five in terms of food availability per head. Even in terms of change in food availability per head over the preceding year, *all* the famine districts without exception had a substantial increase, and three of the four were among the top six in terms of food availability increase among all the nineteen districts.

The entitlement failure of the famine victims in Bangladesh related to a variety of factors, over and above output and availability of food. The floods that afflicted Bangladesh (particularly the famine districts) caused some havoc during June to August of 1974. The availability of food in the economy, however, remained high since the primary crop of Bangladesh (the *aman* crop, which tended to contribute substantially more than half of the total food output of the country) is harvested during November to January, and this had been high in the *preceding* year (i.e. harvested in November 1973 to January 1974). The floods that hit Bangladesh did, of course, reduce the harvest in late 1974, including the primary *aman* crop. The famine, however, developed and peaked much before those reduced harvests arrived, and indeed by the time the primary crop (*aman*) was harvested, the famine was over and gone. During the famine months, the physical availability of food per head in Bangladesh thus remained high. And this was especially so for the famine districts, since they happened to have had rather good crops earlier, boosting the 1974 availability, even though the floods would eventually affect the availability of food in these districts in the *following* year (1975).

Among the influences that led to the collapse of entitlements of a large section of the population of Bangladesh in 1974 was the loss of employment as a result of the floods, which affected the planting and particularly the transplanting of rice, traditionally carried out in the period following the one in which the floods occurred. This would reduce the food output later, but its impact on employment was immediate and vicious.

The disruption of the economy of Bangladesh as a result of the floods was not, however, confined only to the decline of employment. The effect of the floods on the future output and availability of food and therefore on the expectation of food prices also played a major part. The poor and chaotic functioning of rice markets, fed by alarmist anticipations, led to price explosions following the flood, resulting in a collapse of food entitlements for those who found the already low purchasing power of their earnings further undermined.

The failure of the government to institute a suitable stabilising response also contributed to the unstable behaviour of the rice market. Rural labourers found a sharply diminished ratio of food command per unit of employment, and on top of that many had, in fact, lost employment as a result of floods, especially in the famine districts.

There is, therefore, no paradox in the fact that the Bangladesh famine of 1974 occurred at a time when the physical availability of food in the economy was at a local peak. It is the failure of large sections of the population, particularly of the labouring families, to command food in the market that has to be examined in order to understand the causation of that major catastrophe.

The terrible story of the Bangladesh famine of 1974 brings out the folly of concentrating only on the physical availability of food in the economy, and points to the necessity of investigating the movements of food entitlements of the vulnerable occupation groups and the causal influences (including market operations) that affect these movements. Similar lessons can be drawn from other famines as well.

The 'food crisis' in sub-Saharan Africa

Alarm has often been expressed at the possibility of a decline in the amount of food available per person in the modern world. Indeed, there is a good deal of discussion centring on prospects of disaster, based on modern variants of Malthusian fears. As a matter of fact, however, there has not been any declining trend in food availability per head for the world as a whole in recent decades (nor, of course, any such trend since Malthus's own days). Obviously, any such future gazing is hard to do, but it seems unlikely that the real dangers in the near future can lie in the prospect of food output falling short of the growth of population.

Table 34.1 presents the trends in food output per head over the last half decade and the last decade (i.e. from 1981–3 to 1986–8, and from 1976–8 to 1986–8) for some of the major regions in the world.

The fact that the trend of food output per head is so sharply upward for developing economies in particular is, naturally a source of comfort. But it could he false comfort. In fact, different developing economies have done very differently over the last few decades. Specifically, Africa has been plagued by production problems – in addition to other problems – over nearly two decades now. The aggregate picture for the developing economies put together is thus, quite misleading.

This having been said, we must, however, resist the oversimplified suggestion that Africa's recent problems of hunger arise simply from declines in food output and supply. While food production and availability are undoubtedly among the more important influences in the determination of food entitlements, the connections are complex and there are also other matters involved (such as the performance of industries and non-food agriculture, and the general role of employment and economic participation).

It must be borne in mind that food production is not only a source of food supply, it is also a major source of income and livelihood for vast sections of the African population. As a result, any reduction in food output per head in Africa also tends to be associated with a reduction in overall income for many occupation groups. However, the observed decline in food output per head in Africa need not have resulted in

Table 34.1 World trends in food output per head

Region	The last half decade: 1986–8 average over 1981–3 average	The last decade: 1986–8 average over 1976–8 average
All developed economies	up 2%	up 3%
All developing economies	up 5%	up 11%
Europe	up 5%	up 13%
USA	down 7%	up 7%
Africa	down 2%	down 8%
South America	unchanged	up 2%
Asia	up 8%	up 17%

Source: Calculated from data obtained from *FAO Production Yearbook 1988*, Table 4 and *FAO Quarterly Bulletin of Statistics*, vol. i, pt 4, 1988.

a collapse of food entitlements, if that decline had been compensated by an expansion of alternative incomes usable to acquire food from other sources, e.g. through imports from abroad.

Several economies elsewhere have experienced comparable or even greater declines in food output per head (in some cases as large as 30 or 40 per cent), without having any problems of the kind which have afflicted these African countries. This is so both because food production is a less important source of income and entitlement in these other economies, and also because they have achieved a more than compensating expansion of *non-food* production with favourable effects on incomes and entitlements. What may superficially appear to be a problem of food production and supply in Africa has to be seen in the more general terms of entitlement determination.

One important implication of this perspective is that even though current problems of hunger and famines in sub-Saharan Africa are undoubtedly connected *inter alia* with the decline of food production, remedial action need not necessarily take the form of attempting to reverse that historical trend. Other avenues of action, such as the diversification of economic activities and the expansion of public support, deserve attention as well.

Amartya K. Sen is Lamont University Professor of Economics and Philosophy at Harvard University and Jean Drèze is a freelance development economist. This article is an edited and amended extract from Chapter 3 of their book, *Hunger and Public Action*, Clarendon Press, Oxford, 1989.

35 | Why must I be a teenager at all?

BARRY BOGIN

What biological characteristics set us apart from other animals? The answer seems easy enough. To start with, we have a large brain, or more precisely, a large cerebral cortex. Then comes bipedality, a complex material culture and our decidedly peculiar reproductive biology (where else in nature do you find permanent breasts, concealed ovulation, a conspicuous penis and continuous sexual receptivity in both sexes?). Those in the know might add to this list our unique combination of large molar and small incisor and canine teeth. Yet the chances are that few biologists and anthropologists would mention the adolescent growth spurt.

This is an odd omission. For no other mammals, primates included, experience the equivalent period of growth, and at no other time in our lives do our physical and social attributes change quite so dramatically. Indeed, the uniqueness of our adolescent dash for maturity makes for some challenging puzzles, not least concerning its evolutionary origins. Why did adolescence evolve only in humans and not other primates? What, if any, advantage did it offer our ancestors?

We must first be clear about what adolescence is and where it falls within the human life cycle. Infancy starts at birth and ends when the child is weaned, which in pre-industrial societies occurs most often at 18 to 24 months. Childhood is defined as the period following weaning, when the youngster still depends on older people for feeding and protection. It usually spans the ages of two to eight years, whereupon the child becomes a juvenile. In girls, the juvenile period ends at about the age of 10, two years before it usually ends in boys; the difference reflects the earlier onset of puberty in girls. The adolescent stage begins with puberty, marked by some visible sign of sexual maturation such as pubic hair. Adolescence ends with the attainment of adult stature, which occurs at about age 17 in girls and 21 in boys.

The clearest evidence for these developmental stages comes from studies of human growth rates. During infancy growth rate plummets, to be followed by a period of slower decline during childhood and the juvenile stage. The onset of adolescence is marked by a sudden and rapid increase in growth rate, which peaks at a level unequalled since early infancy.

Most other mammals progress from infancy to adulthood seamlessly, experiencing no childhood and no adolescent growth spurt. Indeed, animals such as mice, guinea pigs, rabbits and cattle all reach sexual maturity with their growth rates in decline: puberty follows hard on the heels of weaning. This trend is broken only by the most social mammals – primates, wolves, elephants and so on – which follow infancy with a period of juvenile growth and behaviour, when they no longer need parental care but are not yet sexually mature. But in these animals, too, puberty occurs while the rate of growth is still decelerating and there is no detectable growth spurt.

That this is true even in our closest living relatives, the apes, makes the evolutionary origins of adolescence all the more puzzling. Why did our ancestors evolve the growth spurt? The conventional theory rests on the observation that humans alone require prolonged stages of infant, childhood and juvenile growth to learn the complex technical and social skills that make up human culture. The growth spurt, so the theory goes, evolved because at the end of this period our ancestors were left with proportionately less time for procreation than most mammals, and therefore needed to attain sexual maturity quickly. In an age when life was 'brutish and short', youngsters who matured and reached adult size quickly would have produced more offspring than their more sluggish cousins.

So genetic traits encouraging an adolescent growth spurt emerged in humans not because of any intrinsic value but to compensate for time 'lost' to learning in early life. In a sense, childhood begot adolescence: that, at least, is the idea.

Growing up ain't easy

But surely this cannot be the whole story. For one thing, the argument that adolescence evolved to compensate for a prolonged childhood does not explain its timing. Girls experience the growth spurt before becoming fertile, but for boys the reverse is true. Why the difference? More fundamentally, the conventional theory assumes a simple, cosy relationship between adult stature and fertility, and between fertility and reproductive success. The reality is more complex: there is much more to raising a child than fertilising an egg, and body size is not linked in a simple way to sexual development.

The complexity of the links between adolescence, fertility and body size suggests that the human growth spurt has its own intrinsic value, and is not just a by-product of slow pre-pubertal development. In short, it evolved because it somehow made our ancestors better equipped to reproduce.

Human beings are a reproductive success story. Even people lacking the benefits of modern medicine raise half their infants to adulthood (chimpanzees manage to rear less than 36 per cent of their offspring to adulthood). The physical roots of this reproductive prowess undoubtedly lie in our capacity for learning complex behaviours and survival skills – language, cooperation, hunting, tool making and so on. And these, in turn, depend in part on the dramatic growth of the brain early in life. Yet the question remains: when and how do young people learn all those exclusively adult behaviours related to sex and child rearing?

As children and juveniles, perhaps. The problem here is that pre-pubescent boys and girls look very similar in terms of size and the amount of muscle and fat that they carry. Not looking like reproductive beings, they are unlikely to be treated as such by adults. Moreover, pre-pubescents have very low levels of testosterone and oestrogens – hormones thought to play an essential part in priming a young person's interest in adult sexual and social behaviour. Pre-pubescents are ill-placed to learn from adults the social behaviours that underpin reproductive success.

Even with the onset of puberty, when girls and boys become hormonally and physically attuned to sexual behaviour, the road to reproductive maturity is long and winding. In girls, the first outward sign of puberty is the development of the breast buds and wisps of pubic hair. This is followed by the laying down of fat on the hips, buttocks and thighs, the growth of more body hair, the adolescent growth spurt and, finally, menarche – the onset of menstruation. Menarche is usually followed by a period of one to three years of adolescent sterility, in which menstrual cycles occur but without ovulation. So it is often not until a young woman is 14 or more years old that she becomes fertile.

Fertility, however, does not necessarily imply reproductive maturity. Becoming pregnant is only a part of the business of reproduction. Maintaining the pregnancy to term and raising offspring to adulthood are equally important. In Western countries today, the risk of spontaneous abortions and complications of pregnancy for girls under 15-years-old is more than twice as high as that for women of 20 to 24 years. Babies born to American mothers under 15 years of age are more than twice as likely to be of 'low birth weight' than infants born to women aged 25 to 29.

A mother's age, of course, is not the only factor affecting her baby's survival prospects: low socioeconomic status, smoking, a failure to put on weight during pregnancy and ethnic origins are important, too. However, holding all these other factors constant still leaves the teenage mother and her infant at risk.

Why? Part of the answer lies with basic biology. A decade ago Marquisa LaVelle, a physical anthropologist now at the University of Rhode Island, uncovered evidence of a physical reason for the high percentage of small babies born to teenage mothers. Examining pelvic X-rays from a group of healthy girls, LaVelle noticed that their pelvic inlets – the bony opening of the birth canal – reached adult size only when the girls were 17 or 18-years-old, four or five years after menarche. The implication was as unexpected as it was profound. The adolescent growth spurt does not influence the size of the girl's pelvis. Rather, the pelvis has its own slow pattern of growth which continues for several years after a girl has reached adult stature.

The fact that women must wait up to a decade from the time of menarche to reach full reproductive maturity suddenly begins to make sense. So, too, does the observation that the average ages at which women in cultures as diverse as the Kikuyu tribe of Kenya and urban North America marry and have their first child all tend to cluster around 19 years. Yet the slow development of the female pelvis raises questions as well as answering them. Why should evolution have selected a developmental trait that hinders successful childbirth for teenage girls?

The answer may lie with the need to learn social skills. A mother-to-be must acquire information about pregnancy and experience in adult sociosexual relations and child care. And this, in my view, is where adolescence comes into play.

The dramatic physical changes that girls experience during adolescence serve as efficient advertisements for their sexual and social maturation – so efficient that they stimulate adults to include adolescent girls in their social circles and encourage the girls themselves to practise adult social interactions: male–female bonding, 'aunt-like' caring for children and so on. As anthropological research shows, girls in every human culture, on reaching adolescence, display a surge of interest in the sexual behaviour of adult women.

In our female ancestors, then, adolescence evolved because it enabled girls to learn how to be more reproductively successful as young women. But is there any direct evidence for this? Some support comes from the fact that first-born infants of monkeys and apes are more likely to die than those of humans. Studies of yellow baboons, toque macaques and chimpanzees show that between 50 and 60 per cent of their first-born offspring die in infancy. By contrast, in hunter-gatherer human societies, such as the !Kung of southern Africa, only about 44 per cent of first-born children die in infancy.

Life-saving experience

Furthermore, studies of wild baboons by Jeanne Altmann of the University of Chicago show that although the rate of infant mortality for the first-born is as high as 50 per cent, it drops to 38 per cent for the second infant, and 25 per cent for the third and fourth infants. This improvement in infant survival is in part due to the experience the mother gains with each birth – experience girls accumulate during adolescence. The initial human advantage may seem small, but it means about 16 more people than baboons or chimpanzees survive out of every 100 first-born infants – more than enough over the vast course of evolutionary time to make human adolescence an overwhelmingly beneficial adaptation.

A further evolutionary advantage may accrue from female adolescence. By priming girls to help their older siblings rear children, adolescence enables women to give birth to more infants than primates can. The primatologist Jane Goodall finds that female chimpanzees have their first baby at about 13 years and must wait an average of 5.6 years between successful births, because each infant is totally dependent on its mother. As a result, few chimpanzee females produce more than three offspring. In traditional human societies, by contrast, women usually have their first baby at 19 and then go on to produce an infant every two to four years. This means they can easily have six or more children.

So much for adolescence in girls; what of boys? Boys become fertile well before they assume adult size and the physical characteristics of men. The little fertility research done on boys suggests that they begin producing sperm at an average age of 14.5 years. Yet the cross-cultural evidence is that few boys successfully father children before their late teenage years. 'When Carol Worthman, now at Emory University in Atlanta, Georgia, lived with the Kikuyu tribe in Kenya, she found that it is customary for the men to defer marriage and fatherhood until the age of about 25, though they become sexually active following their circumcision rite at around 18. The National Center for Health Statistics in the US reports that only four per cent of all births in the US are fathered by men under 20-years-old.

Why the lag between sperm production and fatherhood? One explanation may be that the sperm of younger adolescents do not swim well enough to reach an egg cell in the woman's fallopian tubes. But it could be that the average boy of 14.5-years-old is only beginning his adolescent growth spurt. In terms of physical appearance, physiological status and psychosocial development, he is still more a child than an adult. Young men display the opposite developmental trend to that of girls in that they experience a delay between reaching reproductive maturity and *later* advertising this maturity with an increase in physical size, body hair, muscularity and other secondary sexual characteristics.

To trace the evolutionary advantage of this delay, one must turn to the subtle psychological effects of testosterone and the other androgen hormones released from the male gonads during early adolescence. In effect, these hormones 'prime' boys to be receptive to their future roles as men. Over the past three decades, studies on a cross-section of youths in Europe, North America and Japan have established that as blood levels of testosterone begin to increase, but before the growth spurt reaches its peak, there is an increase in psychosexual activity. Nocturnal emissions begin and masturbation, dating and infatuation all intensify, as do feelings of guilt, anxiety, pleasure and pride. At the same time boys become more interested in adult activities, adjust their attitude to parental figures, and think and act more independently. In short, they begin to behave like men.

However – and this is where I believe the survival advantage lies – they still look like boys. Because their adolescent growth spurt occurs late in sexual development, young males can practise behaving like adults before they are actually perceived as adults. The socio-sexual antics of young adolescent males enable boys to fine-tune their sexual and social roles before either their lives, or those of their offspring, depend on them. In many traditional societies, for example, competition among males for women can be fierce, even fatal, and older men usually come off best. In such circumstances, the 'cute', childlike appearance of an adolescent male may be life-saving.

My argument, then, is this. Girls best learn their adult social roles while they are infertile but perceived by adults as mature; boys best learn their adult social roles while they are fertile but not yet perceived as such by adults. Without the adolescent growth spurt this unique style of social and cultural learning could not occur. And this is why adolescence deserves to stand alongside our large cerebral cortex, bipedality and unique sexual behaviour as a factor defining us as human. Indeed, all these characteristics stem from the same underlying biological trait: our uniquely human pattern of growth.

Barry Bogin is Professor of Anthropology at the University of Michigan, USA. He is the author of, amongst other things, *Patterns of Human Growth* (Cambridge University Press, 1988) and 'The evolution of human childhood' (*BioScience*, January, 1991). This article is an edited extract from a longer text, which was first published in *New Scientist*, 6 March (1993) pp. 34–38.

36 | Good gene, bad gene

JAMES D. WATSON

Genes too often get a bad press. This is not surprising because there are 'bad' genes as well as 'good' ones, and bad news grips readers more than good news. Bad genes are actually mutated good genes that, because of altered DNA messages, do not function normally. One particularly bad gene leads to Huntington's disease, which progressively destroys key nerve cells. Most of an individual's genes, however, are inherently good. Collectively, they are the instruction book for our bodies. Without the right instructions from our genes, we could not develop into functioning adults. And fortunately, many bad genes – like that for cystic fibrosis – have no immediate consequence because they are expressed only when copies are inherited from both the father and mother. Carriers possessing only one copy of this gene are much more common (around one in 25) than individuals with the disease (around one in 2300).

Until recently, there was no way to isolate and characterize bad genes. They were known only by their consequences: disease. Today, however, thanks to the development of powerful new ways for studying DNA, there is a flood of information about the faulty genes implicated in virtually every major human disease, including diabetes, cancer, and asthma. Every week or so a new disease gene is discovered.

But with almost routine ways now available to test DNA samples for the presence of specific mutant genes, there is increased anxiety that an individual's genetic heritage may be vulnerable to unwanted prying. The DNA from a single human hair, for example, may be sufficient to alert a prospective employer or health insurer to a person's genetic predisposition to disease. Broad privacy laws must therefore be enacted to forbid genetic tests without the informed consent of the individual involved. But even with such laws, dilemmas will arise when individuals do not realize the significance of the proposed genetic screening. These tests warn of impending disease, but do not cure. And how many people would want to have certain knowledge that they will contract a disease for which there is no cure?

Banishing genetic disability must therefore be our primary concern. We would not worry about testing for a predisposing gene for Alzheimer's disease if we already had the cure. In this case, knowing that an individual is seriously predisposed might allow drug therapy to begin before brain functioning is irreversibly diminished. The recent discovery of several genes whose malfunctioning leads to Alzheimer's disease provides the pharmaceutical industry with important molecular targets for drug development. Only through the discovery of these kinds of genes can biomedical research stop this most pernicious cause of human senility.

We must never, however, live under the misconception that we will ever effectively control the majority of genetic diseases. Many are likely to prove intractable to drug therapies or gene therapies, in which good genes are introduced into cells to compensate for bad ones. It will be particularly difficult to compensate for genes that malfunction during fetal development. If key genes controlling the networking of brain cells don't come into action in the womb, no drug or gene therapy procedure will be able to correctly rewire the brain later.

There is a great difference of opinion as to whether steps should be taken to prevent the birth of genetically impaired children. Many are opposed for religious reasons to trying to control the genetic destinies of children. Others, recalling Germany's eugenic practices, have an equally strong abhorrence of genetic-based reproductive decisions. These people fear a more powerful eugenic practice, whereby the crude racial and class prejudices of earlier eugenicists are replaced by scientific demonstrations of genetic inequality.

But the possibility of controlling our children's genetic destiny strikes me as only good. It is grossly unfair that some families' lives are dominated by the horrors of genetic disease. As a biologist, I know that people suffering from genetic disease are the victims of unlucky throws of the genetic dice. Mutation has been – and always will be – an essential fact of life, because it is through mistakes in gene replication that the positive genetic variants arise which are the lifeblood of evolution. If the gene-copying process were perfect, life as it now exists never would have come about. Genetic disease is the price we pay for the extraordinary evolutionary process that has given rise to the wonders of life on Earth.

Thus I do not see genetic diseases in any way as an expression of the complex will of any supernatural authority, but rather as random tragedies that we should do everything in our power to prevent. There is, of course, nothing pleasant about terminating the existence of a genetically disabled fetus. But doing so is incomparably more compassionate than allowing an infant to come into the world tragically impaired. There is, of course, the question of who should have the authority to make decisions of this kind. Here the message of past eugenic practices is clear. Never let a government, no matter how benign, into the process. The potential mother should have this authority. It is she who is likely to be most involved with the upbringing of the child.

I am aware that some will argue that the fetus has an inalienable right to life. But the process of evolution never regards any form of life, be it adult or fetal, as an inalienable right. It's better to see humans as wonderful social animals having *needs* (for food, health, sex, for example), *capabilities* (for thought and love, among others) and *responsibilities* (including that to work with other human beings to see that everyone's needs are adequately met). Working intelligently and wisely to see that good genes – not bad ones – dominate as many lives as possible is the truly moral way for us to proceed.

James Watson, with Frances Crick, published the molecular structure of DNA in 1953 and proposed a mechanism by which DNA could replicate, so beginning the 'genetic revolution' that led to the publication of the complete DNA sequence of the Human Genome in 2001. Professor Watson was one of the leaders of this project. He is now President of Cold Spring Harbour Laboratory. This short chapter is reproduced in its entirety from his book *A Passion for DNA: Genes, Genomes and Society* published in 2000 by Cold Spring Harbour Laboratory Press/ Oxford University Press. 'Good gene, bad gene' originally appeared in TIME International Winter 1997–1998.

37 | Biodemographic trajectories of longevity

JAMES W. VAUPEL, JAMES R. CAREY, KAARE CHRISTENSEN *ET AL.*

Humanity is aging. The social, economic, and health-care consequences of the new demography will drive public policy worldwide in coming decades. Growth of the older population is fueled by three factors. Baby-boom generations are growing older. The chance of surviving to old age is increasing. And the elderly are living longer – because of remarkable, largely unexplained reductions in mortality at older ages since 1950. Biodemography, the mating of biology and demography, is, we argue, spawning insights into the enigma of lengthening longevity.[1]

Increases in old-age survival

For Sweden, accurate statistics on mortality are available going back for more than a century. Female death rates at older ages have fallen since 1950, with large absolute reductions at advanced ages. The pattern is similar for males, although from conception to old age males suffer higher death rates than females, and progress in reducing male mortality has generally been slower than for females. Consequently, most older people in Sweden – and nearly all other countries – are women.

For other developed countries, trends in mortality since 1900 have been roughly similar to those in Sweden. For example, old-age survival has also increased since 1950 for female octogenarians in England, France, Iceland, Japan, and the United States. If there were an impending limit to further declines in death rates at older ages, countries with low levels of mortality would tend to show slow rates of reduction. There is, however, no correlation between levels of mortality and rates of reduction. In most developed countries the rate of reduction has accelerated, especially since 1970. Japan, which enjoys the world's longest life expectancy and lowest levels of mortality at older ages, has been a leader in the quickening pace of increase in old-age survival. Since the early 1970's female death rates in Japan have declined at annual rates of about 3% for octogenarians and 2% for nonagenarians.

The reduction in death rates at older ages has increased the size of the elderly population considerably. In developed countries in 1990 there were about twice as many nonagenarians and four to five times as many centenarians as there would have been if mortality after age 80 had stayed at 1960 levels. Reliable data for various developed countries indicate that the population of centenarians has doubled every decade since 1960, mostly as a result of increases in survival after age 80.

The decline in old-age mortality is perplexing. What biological charter permits us (or any other species) to live long post-reproduction lives? A gerontological belief posits genetically determined maximum life-spans. Most sexually reproducing species show signs of senescence with age, and evolutionary biologists have developed theories to account for this. The postreproductive span of life should be short because there is no selection against mutations that are not expressed until reproductive activity has ceased.

The logic of this theory and the absence of compelling counter theories[2] have led many to discount the evidence of substantial declines in old-age mortality. Often it is assumed that the reductions are anomalous and that progress will stagnate. Only time can silence claims about the future. And empirical observations are not fully acceptable until they are explicable. We have therefore focused on testing hypotheses and developing new concepts.

Mortality deceleration

A key testable hypothesis is that mortality accelerates with age as reproduction declines. We estimated age trajectories of death rates for *Homo sapiens*, *Ceratitis capitata* (the Mediterranean fruit fly), *Anastrepha ludens*, *Anastrepha obliqua*, and *Anastrepha serpentina* (three other species of true fruit fly), *Diachasmimorpha longiacaudtis* (a parasitoid wasp), *Drosophila melanogaster*, *Caenorhabditis elegans* (a nematode worm), and *Saccharomyces cerevisiae* (baker's yeast). To peer into the remote realms of exceptional longevity we studied very large cohorts.

The trajectories differ greatly. For instance, human mortality at advanced ages rises to heights that preclude the longevity outliers found in medflies. Such differences demand explanation. But the trajectories also share a key characteristic. For all species for which large cohorts have been followed to extinction, mortality decelerates and, for the biggest populations studied, even declines at older ages. A few smaller studies have found deceleration in additional species.[3] For humans, the insects, and the worms, the deceleration occurs at ages well past normal reproductive ages.

If older individuals contribute to the reproductive success of younger, related individuals, then they promote the propagation of their genes. Hence, in social species, the effective end of reproduction may be much later than indicated by fertility schedules. The deceleration of human mortality, however, occurs after age 80 and the leveling off or decline after age 110, ages that were rarely if ever reached in the course of human evolution and ages at which any reproductive contribution is small.

Biodemographic explanations

It is not clear how to reconcile our two key findings – that mortality decelerates and that human mortality at older ages has declined substantially – with theory about aging. Three biodemographic concepts – mortality correlation, heterogeneity in frailty, and induced demographic schedules – point to promising directions for developing theory.

Mortality correlation. Demographers have long known that death rates at different ages are highly correlated across populations and over time. In addition to environmental correlation, there may be genetic correlation: mutations that raise mortality at older ages may do so at younger ages as well, decreasing evolutionary fitness. A pioneering *Drosophila* experiment found mortality correlation and no evidence of mutations with effects only at late ages.[4] Post-reproductive life-spans might be compared with post warranty survival of equipment. Although living organisms are vastly more complex than manufactured products, they too are bound by mechanical constraints that may impose mortality correlations. The trajectory of mortality for automobiles decelerates, suggesting the possibility that both deceleration and mortality correlation are general properties of complicated systems.

Heterogeneity in frailty. All populations are heterogeneous. Even genetically identical populations display phenotypic differences. Some individuals are frailer than others, innately or because of acquired weaknesses. The frail tend to suffer high mortality, leaving a select subset of survivors. This creates a fundamental problem for analyses of aging and mortality: as a result of compositional change, death rates increase more slowly with age than they would in a homogeneous population.

The leveling off and even decline of mortality can be entirely accounted for by models in which the chance of death for all individuals in the population rises at a constant or increasing rate with age. A frailty model applied to data on the life-spans of Danish twins suggests that mortality for individuals of the same genotype and with the same non-genetic attributes (such as educational achievement and smoking behaviour) at some specified age may increase even faster than exponentially after that age.[5] On the other hand, mortality deceleration could result from behavioural and physiological changes with age.

Induced demographic schedules. A key construct underlying evolutionary theory is the Lotka equation, which determines the growth rate of a population (or the spread of an advantageous mutation) given age schedules of fertility and survival. The simplistic assumption in the Lotka equation that fertility and survival schedules are fixed is surely wrong for most species in the wild: environments in nature are uncertain and changing. Many species have evolved alternative physiological modes for coping with fluctuating conditions, including hibernation. In social insects the same genome can be programmed to produce short-lived workers or long-lived queens. That is, alternative demographic schedules of fertility and survival can be induced by environmental conditions.

To reproduce, medflies need protein – and this is only occasionally available in the wild. Medflies fed sugar and water can survive to advanced ages and still reproduce when fed protein. Regardless of when medflies begin reproducing, their subsequent mortality starts low and rises rapidly. This is a striking example of how, depending on the environment, organisms can manipulate their age-specific fertility and survival. Rodents raised on restricted diets have extended life-spans and increased resistance to environmental carcinogens, heat, and reactive oxidants.[6] These findings suggest that stress-related genes and mechanisms may affect longevity across a broad range of species.

In sum, induced physiological change can lower mortality substantially. An individual does not face fixed fertility and survival schedules as the environment and the individual's capabilities change. Although simplistic, the Lotka equation captures a fundamental insight: It is reproductive success that is optimized, not longevity. Deeper understanding of survival at older ages thus hinges on intensified research into the interactions between fertility and longevity.

Survival attributes

The concepts of mortality correlation, heterogeneity in frailty, and induced demographic schedules can be tied together by a general question: How important are an individual's survival attributes (that is, persistent characteristics, innate or acquired, that affect survival chances) as opposed to current conditions in determining the chance of death? For humans, nutrition and infections in utero and during childhood may program the development of risk factors for several important diseases of middle and old age. Conflicting evidence suggests that current conditions may affect old-age survival chances much more than conditions early in life.

A frailty model applied to Danish twin data sheds some even-handed light on this controversy.[5] The model suggests that about 50% of the variation in human life-spans after age 30 can be attributed to survival attributes that are fixed for individuals by the time they are 30; a third to a half of this effect is due to genetic factors and half to two-thirds to non-genetic survival attributes (related to, for example, socioeconomic status or nutritional and disease history). The model suggests that the importance of survival attributes may increase with a person's life expectancy. For persons who at age 30 can expect to survive into their 90s, more than 80% of the variation in life-span may be due to factors that are fixed by this age.

How many survival attributes account for most of the variation in life-spans? Research over the next decade may resolve this question. For nematode worms and yeast, the mutation of a single gene can result in a qualitative change in the age trajectory of mortality. For other species, including *Drosophila* and humans, no genes with such radical demographic effects have yet been discovered, but some polymorphisms, such as ApoE alleles in humans, alter substantially the chance of surviving to an advanced age.[7] The emerging field of molecular biodemography seeks to uncover how variation at the microscopic level of genetic polymorphisms alters mortality trajectories at the macroscopic level of entire populations.

Analysis of data on Danish twins and other populations of related individuals indicate that 20 to 25% of the variation in adult life-spans can be attributed to genetic variation among individuals; heritability of life-span is also modest for a variety of other species. The possibility that genetic polymorphisms may play an increasing role with age is supported by evidence of increases with age in the genetic component of variation in both cognitive and physical ability.

Although genes and other survival attributes are fixed for individuals, their distribution in a cohort changes with age as the frail die. Hence, it is possible to develop survival attribute assays based on demographic analysis of changes with age in the frequency of fixed attributes. In longitudinal research in progress, we are gathering information on lifestyle and environmental conditions as well as DNA from 7000 Chinese octogenarians and nonagenarians, 3000 Chinese centenarians, and 14,000 elderly Danes.

Survival-attribute assays applied to these data may uncover a suite of genetic and non-genetic determinants of longevity.

Experiments with insects, worms, yeast, and other organisms permit alternative approaches for discovering survival attributes. That genes can alter mortality trajectories is now certain; research on the mechanisms will shed new light on aging and longevity. The importance of diet, stress, and reproduction in inducing alternative mortality schedules has been demonstrated, but the potential of such studies to clarify causal relationships is just beginning to be tapped. The emerging dialogue between biologists and demographers is changing the terms of discourse and opening new vantage points for research on aging.

References

1. K.W. Wachter and C.E. Finch, Eds., *Between Zeus and the Salmon: The Biodemography of Longevity* (National Academy Press, Washington, DC, 1997).
2. L. Keller and M. Genoud, *Nature* **389**, 958 (1997).
3. M. Tatar, J.R. Carey, J.W. Vaupel, *Evolution* **47**, 1302 (1993); D.L. Wilson, *Mech. Aging Dev.* **74**, 15 (1994).
4. S.D. Pletcher, D. Houle, J.W. Curtsinger, *Genetics* **148**, 287 (1998).
5. A.I. Yashin and I.A. Iachine, *Demography* **34**, 31 (1997).
6. E.J. Masoro and S.N. Austard, *J. Gerontol.* **51A**, B387 (1996); S.M. Jazwinski, *Science* **273**, 54 (1996).
7. F. Schächter *et al., Nature Genet.* **6**. 29 (1994); G. De Benedictis *et al., Hum. Genet.* **99**, 312 (1997); J. Maynard Smith, *Nature* **181**, 496 (1958).

This edited extract comes from a much longer article entitled 'Biodemographic trajectories of longevity', originally published in 1998 in *Science*, **280**: 855–60. The 14 authors, headed by James Vaupel of the Max Planck Institute for Demographic Research in Germany, come from research establishments in the USA, Denmark, Mexico and China.

38 | A new division of the life course

PETER LASLETT

Dividing life experience into numbered stages is as old as the study of age and ageing, and the various usages are often to be met with in our literature. William Shakespeare, for example, was following a commonplace, a threadbare literary tradition when he put the speech about the seven ages of man into the mouth of Jaques in *As You Like It*. Large numbers of titles and principles of division have been suggested. The phrase which has been the most recent to arrive is the *Third Age*. The *Third Age* has not as yet been employed at all systematically, that is in relation to a First Age, a Second Age and perhaps a Fourth Age. Here however it will be taken as belonging to a numerical order of the whole life course, and the quadripartite division can be justified as follows.

First comes an era of dependence, socialization, immaturity and education; second an era of independence, maturity and responsibility, of earning and of saving; third an era of personal fulfilment; and fourth an era of final dependence, decrepitude and death. Such a fourfold numbered system has many precedents and many rivals. The present scheme differs from its predecessors in several ways, one of them quite radical.

In this analysis of life experience the divisions between the four ages do not come at birthdays. Moreover the life career which is divided into these four modules has its culmination in the Third Age, the age of personal achievement and fulfilment, not in the Second Age and emphatically not in the Fourth. It follows logically enough that the ages should not be looked upon exclusively as stretches of years, and the possibility has to be contemplated that the Third Age could be lived simultaneously with the Second Age, or even with the First. Since the Third Age is identified here as that during which the apogee of personal life is achieved, anyone who reaches the goal at the same time as money is being earned and accumulated, a family founded and sustained, a successful career brought to a pitch of attainment, could be said to live the Third Age alongside the Second. No passage from one to the other need occur, for an individual with these characteristics is doing his/her own thing from maturity until the final end. Artists, the consummate artists, are the best examples. An athlete, on the other hand, usually has to attain his peak during the First Age, and so live part of the Third Age then.

The ageing both of populations and of societies can be effectively analysed in this way, with some slight inconsistencies which have yet to be resolved. It does provide, however, clear and definite ideas for individuals thinking about their own ages, those of their spouses, children and friends.

There can be no doubt whatever that dependence and decrepitude have always been inseparably associated with becoming old, however active, useful and healthy many people have been at the high, higher, and even highest calendar ages. Such an association can never have been more than partially justified as a general description of a particular calendar age. The effect of failing to make the distinction implied in the phrase the Third Age, therefore, must have fastened upon the senior members of all societies, past and present, inappropriate and damaging descriptions of their physical and mental states. This obstinate unwillingness to see the Third Age apart from the Fourth has sanctioned the exclusion of those in the Third Age from activities, especially earning activities, for which nearly all of them have been perfectly well suited, has debased their status in the eyes of their juniors, and above all has devalued them in their own estimation of themselves. To live as you wish to live after your sixty-fifth, seventieth and especially your eightieth birthday, you still have to have something of the quality ascribed to Shakespeare by Matthew Arnold. *Self-school'd, self-scanned, self-honour'd, self-secure.*

Now that a fifth and more of the whole of our population is classed as retired, the results of this seemingly deliberate mass depreciation scarcely bear contemplation. The waste of talent and experience is incalculable. The fact that those who write off the elderly are also writing off themselves, as they will be in a decade or two's time, defies understanding. The only explanation offered here calls upon the somewhat unsatisfactory terms of cultural lag, even of false-consciousness.

The physical dependence of failing individuals in their final years, and sometimes their mental depreciation too; the dilemma of younger persons obliged to look after them, and frequently to look after other dependants as well; the burdens on the social services; the difficulties of the social workers; the poverty of the working class elderly and the intensification of social divisions which come with age; the problems presented by residential homes for the great and growing numbers of those in the Fourth Age and their horrendous cost – all these are extremely serious issues and they are pre-eminently issues of our time. So is the question of how British society will be able to meet the costs of supporting the elderly and of providing ever more expensive medical care. It is easy to see why nearly all the writings about ageing are about need and dependence, and it is understandable, if deplorable, that an effect of this preponderance is to intensify the conviction that the older population is a problem.

Rearranging these facts by redividing the life course and giving its most important component, from the elderly point of view, a somewhat novel name, may not go very far. But something can be done in this way to make it clear that the challenges are interesting as well as difficult, in human as well as intellectual terms. It is indeed, as I believe, an entirely new world which has opened up and beckoned us within.

If it is necessary to be clear and careful about the terms which have to be used for whole divisions of the course of life, it is also necessary to keep watch on the rest of the language which is used in reference to ageing, even down to the similes and metaphors which have worked themselves into the language. For the subject of this essay, growing old, teems with tired metaphors, unthinkingly applied. Figures of speech derived by analogy from many of the characteristics of the natural world, and the implied comparison of the time of day and the season of the year with the stages of life, are prominent amongst them. Such analogies were natural enough in a traditional society, close to the land and the vicissitudes of the seasons. But they still pervade the jocularity, the sentimentality, the sententiousness which are so often found in discussions of later life, devices no doubt to try to ensure that the more menacing themes shall be kept in the wings. Being old is not in fact at all like evening or like winter, for the good reason that the day and the year are not at all like human life itself. Whiteness, snowy whiteness, no more justifies the vaguely comforting description of being old as the winter of life, than the colour of the light from the declining sun justifies the excruciating description 'golden oldies'. Thinking by analogy and relying upon metaphor makes for muddle: a consistent, realistic vocabulary is imperative if we are to get the fact and circumstance of ageing clear.

Even the word *age* itself has a range of meanings. We shall distinguish five separate senses for the age of a person: calendar age will be seen to differ from biological age, from social age, from personal age and from subjective age. You may think yourself to be young, or old, in any of these senses, and others may judge you in a similar way. But there can be ambiguities. Consider for a moment what may be meant by the remark, 'she is young for her age'.

[For] someone in the Third Age it is natural that he should see things from the senior point of view and defend what he sees to be the interests of the elderly, as they now are and as they will inevitably be. It has not been often that the older part of society has spoken in its own voice in such a way: championship has usually come from younger sympathizers.

Nevertheless, I should not wish it to be thought that I myself had a previously fixed opinion on the gravest of all the questions raised by the subject of ageing, the most demanding and the most intriguing to the intellectual enquirer. This is the issue of justice between age groups, both contemporary age groups, those living alongside each other, and those now separated by death, inter-generational equity as it is coming to be called.

There is a suspicion that those about to succeed to the status of the Third Age have been privileged by time, enriched in comparative terms to an extent never attained by their predecessors and not being accorded to those who will be their successors. If such can be demonstrated, we are faced with the first recognized and defined opportunity for providing against victimization by lottery of the date of birth. Since they are the only age group in society who can be identified as trustees for the future, those in the Third Age must do all they can to elaborate the principles of intergenerational equity, and make whatever provision is open to them to see that justice will be done, even if this is to some extent at their own expense. This is not the only challenge which arises out of taking account of the need to be our age.

Peter Laslett is a social historian and Fellow of Trinity College, Cambridge. This article is an edited version of Chapter 1 of his book *A Fresh Map of Life: The Emergence of the Third Age*, published in 1989 by Weidenfeld and Nicolson, London.

The role of medicine

| INTRODUCTION

In the first half of the nineteenth century, the effectiveness and humanity of medicine came under systematic and vehement criticism from both inside and outside the medical profession. This was the first era of 'therapeutic nihilism'. After that period, with the growth of a more scientific medicine, the prestige of the profession rose to previously unattained heights. But over the past 40 years the role of medicine has once again been questioned, as the articles in Part 4 illustrate. The critics have included epidemiologists and economists, feminists and sociologists, doctors and moral philosophers, social historians and theologians. They have focused on two particular issues – the effectiveness of medicine and the wider role of doctors in society.

Assessment of the effectiveness of medicine has taken two main forms – historical analysis and evaluation of contemporary practice. The leading exponent of the former has been Thomas McKeown, a British doctor and demographer, who has argued that medicine played only a minor role in the dramatic decline in infectious diseases and in the growth of population in the UK since the seventeenth century. For McKeown, these changes resulted instead largely from improvements in nutrition and other social conditions. 'The medical contribution' summarizes his evidence and conclusions.

McKeown's views have been so immensely influential that they have almost become a new orthodoxy. Simon Szreter, a medical historian, does not dispute McKeown's core argument that medicine played a very limited role in the decline of mortality. But he does take issue with McKeown's conclusion that the decline in mortality can be attributed instead to nutritional improvements and rising living standards. In 'The importance of social intervention in Britain's mortality decline *c*. 1850–1914: a reinterpretation of the role of public health', he bases his case on a close reading of the same evidence used by McKeown. Szreter argues that McKeown was methodologically suspect, and also misinterpreted the evidence on the contribution of different diseases to declining mortality, and on the chronology of the decline. Medicine's role may have been small, concludes Szreter, but the contribution of public health measures in improving the urban environment has been underestimated.

Scepticism about the value of *contemporary* medical practice gained widespread attention, at least in the UK, with the publication in 1972 of a book entitled *Effectiveness and Efficiency*, by the epidemiologist and doctor Archie Cochrane; an extract is included in this part of the book. His work was strongly influenced by his experiences in the Second World War, when he was captured and put in charge of medical care for his fellow prisoners. He had almost no medicines and yet, to his surprise, most of his patients made a full recovery. In his later work he went on to explore the dangers of simply assuming that medicine was necessarily effective in combating illness, and argued strongly for the systematic collection and review of evidence on effectiveness, particularly by means of randomized controlled trials. One legacy of his work has been the development, during the 1990s, of a worldwide Cochrane Collaboration, aiming to perform systematic reviews of existing evidence on health interventions.

The fruits of the randomized controlled trial industry are put to use in John P. Bunker's assessment of the contribution of medicine to health. Drawing wherever possible on evidence from trials, he tabulates the effect of a series of preventive and treatment interventions on life expectancy, and concludes that at least 5 of the 30 years of increased life expectancy in the UK and USA in the twentieth century are attributable to clinical preventive and curative services. In 'Medicine matters after all' Bunker concedes that his data, methods and results could be greatly refined, but as he observes in his concluding remarks, they are much firmer than any available for the health effects of intervening in non-medical areas such as education and housing.

Randomized controlled trials, for all their virtues, are not without problems. Some of the ethical and indeed practical issues they raise are illustrated by the collection of articles, editorials and letters entitled 'Ethical dilemmas in evaluation – a correspondence', concerning trials to investigate the effect of vitamin supplements in preventing the occurrence of neural tube defects (such as spina bifida). Initial evidence of such an effect was questioned and a trial proposed, but a trial was itself considered either impractical or unethical by many at the time. In the event, as the final contributions to this collection show, a randomized controlled trial was eventually performed and cleared many if not all uncertainties.

Marc A. Strassburg takes as his subject a health programme of absolute effectiveness, 'The global eradication of smallpox'. As a result of the interventions that Strassburg describes, smallpox was eradicated from Europe and North America by the 1970s, but a number of major reservoirs of the virus still existed. By 1980 the World Health Organization declared the world to be free of smallpox, a feat that had been achieved through the application of medical knowledge and technology by a global organization, based on elaborate economic, political and social coordination. If smallpox can be eradicated, will a future world be free of other major infectious diseases? The answer is probably no. Smallpox was a prime candidate because much was known of the process and progress of the disease, it had no hosts other than humans, and an effective vaccine was available. A similar programme to eliminate malaria has not been successful, largely because it meets none of these criteria.

Many of the assessments of the effectiveness of medicine considered so far have given little formal consideration to the role of doctors *per se*. But some critiques of the role of medicine have started from the power relationship between doctors and lay people which, it is argued, has enabled doctors to perpetuate a hierarchy of advantaged and disadvantaged in society. At their most extreme, these critiques have argued that doctors not only perpetuate existing social structures, but actually cause harm (iatrogenesis, or doctor-made disease). Probably the best known example of such an analysis is the work of Ivan Illich, an Austrian theologian. In 'The epidemics of modern medicine' Illich argues that the ills of society result from individuals' loss of self-reliance, which in turn is a consequence of industrialization. Thus, just as education becomes the province of the teacher so, equally undesirably, health has become the responsibility of doctors who now tyrannize lay people, causing more harm than good.

While Illich sees the basic struggle as one in which individuals must 'regain' their self-reliance and liberty from the oppressive nature of industrialization, Vicente Navarro views it as a struggle against a particular mode of industrial society – capitalism. Navarro, an American doctor originally from Spain, is one of the leading Marxist critics of modern medical care. In 'The mode of state intervention in the health sector' he argues that doctors aid the capitalist process by promoting the view that illness results from decisions made by individuals. This, he argues, is far from the reality of most people's lives, in which the opportunities to exercise free choice are severely circumscribed. In this situation, doctors are seen as an integral support for capitalism and therefore for the health-damaging nature of such an economic and social system. In the extract from his book *Medicine Under Capitalism*, with which we end Part 4, Navarro argues that increasing state intervention in health care is made necessary by the damage done to people's health by a capitalist system that produces great social inequalities.

Thus, the mirror held up to 'medicine' holds many reflections: at one extreme it makes a major contribution to human health and has greatly increased human life spans; at the other, it is a malign instrument of social control. Between these two, medicine is seen as an essentially positive influence on human health, even if perhaps less critical than its practitioners would like to believe.

39 | The medical contribution

THOMAS McKEOWN

Until recently it was accepted, almost without question, that the increase of population in the eighteenth century, and by inference later, was due to a decline of mortality brought about by medical advances. They included expansion of hospital, dispensary and midwifery services; notable changes in medical education; advances in understanding of physiology and anatomy; and introduction of a specific protective measure, inoculation against smallpox. Taken together these developments seemed impressive, and it is scarcely surprising that most who considered the matter should have concluded that they contributed substantially to health.

This conclusion, however, results from failure to distinguish clearly between the interests of the doctor and the interests of the patient, a common error in the interpretation of medical history. From the point of view of a student or practitioner of medicine, increased knowledge of anatomy, physiology and morbid anatomy are naturally regarded as important professional advances. But from the point of view of the patient, none of these changes has any practical significance until such time as it contributes to preservation of health or recovery from illness. It is because there is often a considerable interval between acquisition of new knowledge and any demonstrable benefit to the patient, that we cannot accept changes in medical education and institutions as evidence of the immediate effectiveness of medical measures. To arrive at a reliable opinion we must look critically at the work of doctors, and enquire whether in the light of present-day knowledge it is likely to have contributed significantly to the health of their patients.

The obvious way to do this is to assess the contribution which immunization and therapy have made to the control of the infectious diseases associated with the decline of mortality. Since this can be done reliably only from the time when cause of death was certified, I shall examine the influence of medical measures in the post-registration period.

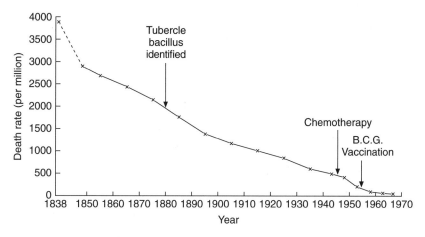

Figure 39.1 Respiratory tuberculosis: death rates, England and Wales

Airborne diseases

Tuberculosis

Figure 39.1 shows the trend of mortality from respiratory tuberculosis in England and Wales since 1838. This is the disease which, if any, was critical for the fall of the death rate. It was much the largest single cause of death in the mid-nineteenth century, and it was associated with nearly a fifth of the total reduction of mortality since then.

The time when effective medical measures became available is not in doubt. The tubercle bacillus was identified by Koch in 1882, but none of the treatments in use in the nineteenth or early twentieth century had a significant influence on the course of the disease. The many chemotherapeutic agents that were tried are now known to have been ineffective, as was also the collapse therapy practised from about 1920. Effective treatment began with the introduction of streptomycin in 1947, and immunization (BCG vaccination) was used in England and Wales on a substantial scale from 1954. By these dates mortality from tuberculosis had fallen to a small fraction of its level in 1848–54; indeed most of the decline (57 per cent) had taken place before the beginning of the present century. Nevertheless, there is no doubt about the contribution of chemotherapy, which was largely responsible for the rapid fall of mortality from the disease since 1950. Without this intervention the death rate would have continued to fall, but at a much slower rate.

Whooping cough

The trend of mortality from whooping cough is shown in Figure 39.2 (overleaf), based on mean annual death rates of children under 15 in England and Wales. Mortality began to decline from the seventh decade of the nineteenth century, and the disease contributed 2.6 per cent to the reduction of the death rate from all causes.

Treatment by sulphonamides and, later, antibiotics was not available before 1938 and even now their effect on the course of the disease is questionable. Immunization was used widely after 1952; the protective effect is variable, and has been estimated to

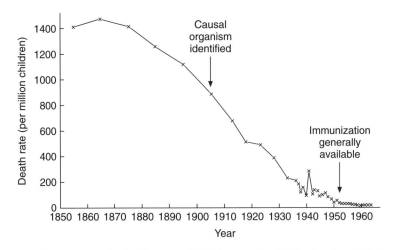

Figure 39.2 Whooping cough: death rates of children under 15, England and Wales

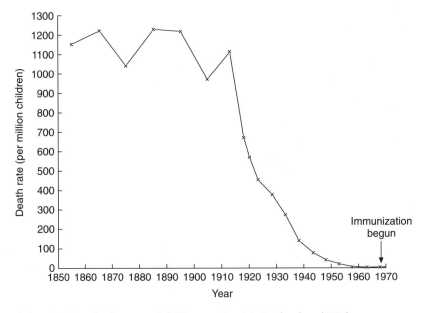

Figure 39.3 Measles: death rates of children under 15, England and Wales

be between less than 20 and over 80 per cent. Clearly almost the whole of the decline of mortality from whooping cough occurred before the introduction of an effective medical measure.

Measles

Again Figure 39.3 is based on deaths of children under 15 in England and Wales. The picture is among the most remarkable for any infectious disease. Mortality fell

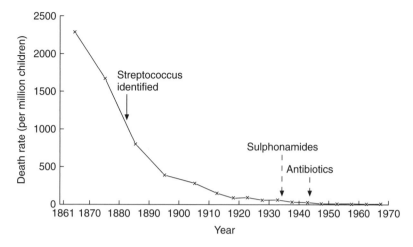

Figure 39.4 Scarlet fever: death rates of children under 15, England and Wales

rapidly and continuously from about 1915. Effective specific measures have only recently become available in the form of immunization, and they can have had no significant effect on the death rate. However, mortality from measles is due largely to invasion by secondary organisms, which have been treated by chemotherapy since 1935. Eighty-two per cent of the decrease of deaths from the disease occurred before this time.

Scarlet fever

Because scarlet fever was grouped with diphtheria in the early years after registration of cause of death, the trend of mortality from the disease in children under 15 is shown from the seventh decade in Figure 39.4. There was no effective treatment before the use of prontosil in 1935. But even by the beginning of the century mortality from scarlet fever had fallen to a relatively low level, and between 1901 and 1971 it was associated with only 1.2 per cent of the total reduction of the death rate from all causes. Approximately 90 per cent of this improvement occurred before the use of the sulphonamides.

Diphtheria

Figure 39.5 (overleaf) is based on the mean annual death rate of children under 15, from the eighth decade of the nineteenth century. It is perhaps the infectious disease in which it is most difficult to assess precisely the time and influence of therapeutic measures. Antitoxin was used first in the late nineteenth century and has been the accepted form of treatment since then. It is believed to have reduced the case fatality rate, which fell from 8.2 per 100 notifications in 1916–25 to 5.4 in 1933–42, while notifications remained at an average level of about 50,000 per year.

It is tempting to attribute much of the decline of diphtheria mortality between 1900 and 1931 to treatment by antitoxin and the rapid fall since 1941 to immunization. Nothing in British experience is seriously inconsistent with this interpretation. However, experience in some other countries is not so impressive; for example there are

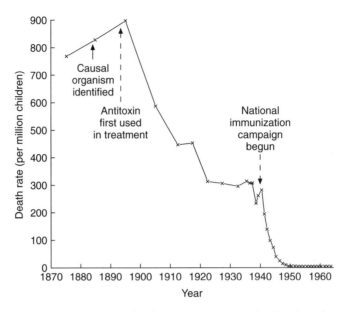

Figure 39.5 Diphtheria: death rates of children under 15, England and Wales

American States where the reduction of mortality in the 1940s did not coincide with the immunization programme. Moreover, several other infections, particularly those that are airborne, declined in the same period in the absence of effective prophylaxis or treatment. While therefore it is usual, and probably reasonable, to attribute the fall of mortality from diphtheria in this century largely to medical measures, we cannot exclude the possibility that other influences also contributed, perhaps substantially.

Smallpox

The death rate from smallpox in the mid-nineteenth century was a good deal smaller than that of the infections already discussed, and the somewhat erratic trend of mortality since then is shown in Figure 39.6. Vaccination of infants was made compulsory in 1854 but the law was not enforced until 1871. From that time until 1898, when the conscientious objector's clause was introduced, almost all children were vaccinated. Most epidemiologists are agreed that we owe the decline of mortality from smallpox mainly to vaccination. Since the mid-nineteenth century the decrease has been associated with only 1.6 per cent of the reduction of the death rate from all causes.

Infections of ear, pharynx and larynx

Together these diseases also were associated with only a small part (0.8 per cent) of the decrease of deaths. The main therapeutic influences have been chemotherapy and, in some ear infections, surgery. It is difficult to give a time from which surgical intervention can be said to have been beneficial, but in view of the small contribution made by these diseases it is perhaps not very important to assess it more precisely than by

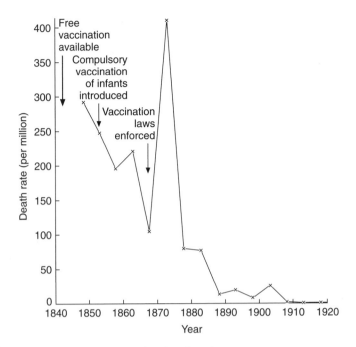

Figure 39.6 Smallpox: death rates, England and Wales

saying that one-third of the decline (0.3 per cent of mortality from all causes in this century) occurred before the use of sulphonamides in 1935.

In summary, the airborne diseases accounted for two-fifths of the reduction of mortality from all causes from the mid-nineteenth century to 1971. Vaccination against smallpox was the only medical measure which contributed to the fall of deaths before 1900, and this disease was associated with only a small part (1.6 per cent) of the decrease of the death rate from all causes. In this century antitoxin probably lowered mortality from diphtheria, and surgery may have reduced deaths from ear infections, but together these influences had little effect on total deaths. With these exceptions, effective medical intervention began with the chemotherapeutic agents which became available after 1935, particularly the sulphonamides and antibiotics. By this time mortality from airborne infections had fallen to a small fraction of its level in the mid-nineteenth century; and even after the introduction of chemotherapy, with the important exception of tuberculosis, it is probably safe to conclude that immunization and therapy were not the main influences on the further decline of the death rate.

Water- and food-borne diseases

Cholera, diarrhoea and dysentery

In the mid-nineteenth century cholera was grouped with other diarrhoeal diseases in the Registrar General's classification; however, the last epidemic in Britain was in 1865, so from that time the contribution of cholera was negligible. Mortality from the diarrhoeal diseases fell in the late nineteenth century; it increased between 1901 and 1911 but then decreased rapidly.

It is unlikely that treatment had any appreciable effect on the outcome of the diseases before the use of intravenous therapy in the nineteen thirties, by which time 95 per cent of the improvement had occurred. For the main explanation of the decline of mortality we must turn to the hygienic measures which reduced exposure.

Non-respiratory tuberculosis

Non-respiratory tuberculosis was an important cause of death in the nineteenth century. Although mortality fell quite rapidly after 1901, there was still a considerable number of deaths in England and Wales (197) in 1971.

Interpretation of this trend is complicated by the fact that non-respiratory tuberculosis is due to both human and bovine infections. The human types can be interpreted in the same terms as the pulmonary disease, but a different explanation must be sought for the bovine infection. It is unlikely that treatment contributed significantly to the fall of mortality, since the level was already low when streptomycin – the first effective measure – was introduced in 1947.

Typhoid and typhus

Mortality from typhus fell rapidly in the late nineteenth century and there have been few deaths in the twentieth. It can be said without hesitation that specific medical measures had no influence on this decline.

The decline of the enteric fevers was also rapid, and began before the turn of the century, somewhat earlier than the fall of deaths from diarrhoea and dysentery. Effective treatment by chloramphenicol was not available until 1950, but by that time mortality from enteric fever was almost eliminated from England and Wales. Although immunization was used widely in the armed services during the war, its effectiveness is doubtful and it can have had little influence on the number of deaths.

In summary, the rapid decline of mortality from the diseases spread by water and food since the late nineteenth century owed little to medical measures. Immunization is relatively ineffective even today, and therapy of some value was not employed until about 1950, by which time the number of deaths had fallen to a very low level.

Other diseases due to micro-organisms

Convulsions and teething

Most of the deaths included under these unsatisfactory terms were due to infectious diseases of childhood, for example to whooping cough, measles, otitis media, meningitis and gastro-enteritis. These infections are mainly airborne, and the general conclusions concerning the time and influence of immunization and therapy on airborne diseases may be accepted for them. That is to say, it is unlikely that medical measures had any significant effect on the frequency of death before the introduction of sulphonamides and antibiotics, and even after that time they were probably less important than other influences.

Syphilis

Although syphilis was associated with only 0.3 per cent of the reduction of mortality from the mid-nineteenth century to 1971, it remained an important cause of sickness and death until about 1916, when salvarsan was made available free of charge to medical practitioners. From this time the number of deaths fell, and it was quite low in 1945 when penicillin largely replaced the arsenical preparations.

The decline of syphilis since its introduction to Europe in the fifteenth century was not due mainly to therapy, for after several centuries of exposure of the population the disease had changed to a milder form. Nevertheless it seems reasonable to attribute the reduction of mortality since 1901 essentially to treatment. It should of course be recognized that effective treatment, as in the case of tuberculosis, not only benefits those affected by the disease, but also reduces the number of persons who spread the infection. It seems right to regard this secondary effect as a further contribution of medical measures.

Appendicitis, peritonitis

Mortality from these causes increased slightly during the nineteenth and early twentieth centuries – probably because of more accurate certification of cause of death – but declined after 1921. This improvement, which accounted for 0.4 per cent of the fall of death rate from all causes, can be attributed to treatment.

Puerperal fever

The death rate from puerperal fever declined from the beginning of this century, but more rapidly after the introduction of the sulphonamides (1935) and, later, penicillin. It seems probable that the initial fall was due mainly to reduced exposure to infection, as the teaching of Semmelweis in the previous century began to improve the practice of the developing midwifery services; but from 1935 these services were greatly reinforced by chemotherapy. Both influences can be credited to medical interventions.

Other infections

The 'other conditions' are a miscellaneous group, including some well recognized infectious diseases which caused few deaths, either because they were uncommon in this period (as in the case of malaria, tetanus, poliomyelitis and encephalitis) or because although common they were not often lethal (as in the case of mumps, chicken pox and rubella). They also include some relatively uncommon certified causes of death which are ill defined.

These infections were associated with 3.5 per cent of the fall of mortality between the mid-nineteenth century and 1971. In view of their varied aetiology it is not possible to assess accurately the major influences, but it is unlikely that therapy made much contribution before 1935. More than half of the reduction of deaths occurred before this time.

To summarize: except in the case of vaccination against smallpox (which was associated with 1.6 per cent of the decline of the death rate from 1848–54 to 1971), it is unlikely that immunization or therapy had a significant effect on mortality from infectious diseases before the twentieth century. Between 1900 and 1935 these measures contributed in some diseases: antitoxin in treatment of diphtheria; surgery in treatment of appendicitis, peritonitis and ear infections; salvarsan in treatment of syphilis; intravenous therapy in treatment of diarrhoeal diseases; passive immunization against tetanus; and improved obstetric care resulting in prevention of puerperal fever. But even if these measures were responsible for the whole decline of mortality from these conditions after 1900 – which clearly they were not – they would account for only a very small part of the decrease of deaths which occurred before 1935. From that time the first powerful chemotherapeutic agents – sulphonamides and, later, antibiotics – came into use, and they were supplemented by improved vaccines. However, they were certainly not the only influences which led to the continued fall of mortality. I conclude that immunization and treatment contributed little to the reduction of deaths from infectious diseases before 1935, and over the whole period since cause of death was first registered (in 1838) they were much less important than other influences.

Thomas McKeown was Professor of Social Medicine at the University of Birmingham from 1945 to 1977. This article is taken from Chapter 5 of his book *The Modern Rise of Population*, published by Edward Arnold, London (1976).

40 The importance of social intervention in Britain's mortality decline *c.* 1850–1914: a re-interpretation of the role of public health

SIMON SZRETER

The belief that directed human agency informed by medical and sanitary science was the principal source of improvement in the nation's health, has been apparently conclusively deflated and debunked by the historical epidemiological research project of Professor Thomas McKeown and associates. The main purpose of this article will be to argue that McKeown's analysis of the empirical data has been misleading. It will be urged that the public health movement working through local government, rather than nutritional improvements through rising living standards, should be seen as the true moving force behind the decline of mortality in this period.

Professor Thomas McKeown's book, *The Modern Rise of Population*, was published in 1976 as an accessible summary of over two decades of painstaking empirical work. It effectively demonstrated that those advances in the science of medicine which form the basis of today's conventional clinical and hospital teaching and practice, in particular the immuno- and chemo-therapies, played only a very minor role in accounting for the historic decline in mortality levels. McKeown simply and conclusively showed that many of the most important diseases involved had already all but disappeared in England and Wales before the earliest date at which the relevant scientific medical innovations occurred.

However, in addition to this *negative* finding that the forward march of modern 'scientific medicine' cannot be given the credit for the historical fall in mortality, McKeown also propounded a *positive* explanatory thesis. He claimed that his analysis of the epidemiological evidence showed that the major factor responsible was 'a rising standard of living, of which the most significant feature was improved diet'.

McKeown believed that his empirical work on the nineteenth-century evidence had conclusively established this in two ways. First, that part of the mortality decline supposedly attributable exclusively to increased nutrition was claimed to have occurred earliest, whereas public health measures came along relatively late in the day, when the momentum of declining mortality was already established. Secondly, that on aetiological grounds, according to the available epidemiological records tracking changes in the incidence of different causes of death, sanitary measures could only have had at the maximum the potential to eliminate roughly a quarter of all deaths, whereas rising nutritional standards had probably been responsible for about twice that proportion. Thus, nutritional improvements were unequivocally presented as the prime moving and primary sustaining forces in accounting for the Victorian mortality decline. However, it is shown below that neither of these arguments can be sustained on a careful re-examination of the historical evidence.

The 'McKeown thesis'

The analysis of death-rates in nineteenth- and twentieth-century Britain which was presented by McKeown *et al.* is based on a uniquely detailed historical source material. These are the returns of deaths classified by age and certified cause of death which are available for the entire population of Britain, excluding Scotland, from July 1837 onwards. Details about the numbers dying from each disease by age and sex were combined with comparable information regarding the total population alive at each of the national censuses taken every ten years to produce a series of age-specific, cause-specific death-rates, published decennially by the Registrar-General in a special supplement.

McKeown grouped the individual diseases into four broad etiological categories, according to what modern medical science understands to be the main pathways of transmission involved in the spread of each particular disease. Three of McKeown's four categories relate to diseases which are due to the invasion of the human host by a micro-organism, meaning usually bacteria or a virus. First, there is the airborne category of diseases, where the microbes in question can simply float about in suspension in the air usually associated with tiny droplets of water vapour or saliva spray from the exhalations of infected victims or carriers. Secondly, there are the diseases caused by water- and food-borne microbes. Thirdly, there is a small residual category of other diseases also attributable to micro-organisms, where the vector of transmission is neither air- nor food- nor water-borne. These include strictly contagious diseases, that is, those passed by direct contact between animals and humans (e.g. plague, typhus) or just between humans (e.g. sexually transmitted diseases). Finally, there is the category of afflictions which are not micro-biotically caused, such as congenital defects and the degenerative diseases which are associated with the normal processes of ageing (subject, of course, to modification by lifestyle, diet, and overall environment). These include cancers and coronary heart diseases as the most significant examples.

With this simple but very useful classification system established, McKeown went on to argue that any observed fall in the incidence of a disease must be due to one of the following causes:

(i) an autonomous decline in the virulence of the micro-organism itself;
(ii) an improvement in the overall environment so as to reduce the chances of initial exposure to potentially harmful organisms. This could either be:

    (a) as a result of scientific advances in immunisation techniques;

    (b) through a public health policy designed to sanitise the urban environment – McKeown calls this 'municipal sanitation' or 'hygiene improvements';

(iii) an improvement in the human victims' defensive resources *after* initial exposure to hostile organisms. This could occur either:

    (a) through the development of effective scientific methods of treating symptoms;

    (b) via an increase in the level and quality of the exposed population's average nutritional intake, that is better and more abundant food, thereby improving the individual's own natural defences.

McKeown's strategy in presenting his argument was to assess each of these candidate 'causes' of mortality decline in turn, regarding their possible proportionate contributions to the overall observed fall in mortality levels.

First, he dealt with (i) the possibility that there might have been a spontaneous change in the virulence of some of the infective micro-organisms. McKeown was willing to allow that two of the airborne diseases, scarlet fever and influenza, probably declined spontaneously in this manner. However, the impression was given, by taking a wider sweeping perspective including the eighteenth and twentieth centuries as well, that this factor was relatively insignificant and could be more or less ruled out as a significant component of the mortality decline.

McKeown next dealt with what was called the medical contribution (iia and iiia), by which was meant, first, scientific advances in protective immunisation and, secondly, scientific advances in chemotherapy and hospitalised treatment of sufferers. Hospitals were dismissed outright. He then proceeded to demonstrate for each of the major diseases in turn that, with the exception of smallpox and diphtheria, the dates at which either effective immunisation procedures or scientific medical treatments first became available were often far too late in time to be able to account for all but the last few percentage points of the overall decline of the disease. This was certainly true of respiratory tuberculosis, measles, and scarlet fever, and broadly true for whooping cough and the bronchitis, pneumonia, and influenza group.

Having eliminated in this fashion both aspects of advances in medical science, McKeown was now left with just two possible causal factors out of the original list, to account between them for the lion's share of the decline in mortality. The argument presented was as follows. It can only have been the water- and food-borne diseases which could have been controlled by (iib) municipal sanitation and similar preventive public health measures in the nineteenth and early twentieth centuries. Airborne diseases by contrast could not be prevented in this way from spreading or from occurring. It was admitted that isolation of individuals with symptoms might have some net effect, but then the efficacy of the hospitals had already been roundly dismissed, whilst it was pointed out that many airborne diseases could be carried and spread by persons not even manifesting symptoms. McKeown argued, therefore, that any real decline in the incidence of mortality from the airborne category of diseases could *only* be the result of (iiib) improvements in the potential victim's resistance to the disease by virtue of an improved nutritional and dietary status, since the chances of initial exposure to the disease could not be affected by public health preventive measures.

Using this *a priori* argument, McKeown's data apparently showed that the airborne category of diseases was responsible for about twice the percentage share of the total reduction in death-rates in both periods, before and after 1901. Accordingly, this constituted irrefutable evidence that above all else it has been improvements in nutritional intake brought about by rising living standards, rather than any other factor – including public health measures – which has been the most important cause of the decline in mortality in Britain.

Critique of McKeown's interpretation

First, as has been pointed out by many others, the weight of presumption in favour of improvements in nutrition as the primary causal factor in the registered mortality decline emerged merely by default, as a result of the sceptical devaluation of other factors including medical intervention, rather than because of any convincing positive evidence in its favour. Secondly, and related to this, the argument by exclusion is only legitimate if *all* the suspects have been correctly identified and are separately examined. But here 'the standard of living' acts very much as a conceptual, residual catch-all, simply subsuming by fiat a variety of other possible factors, which are, therefore, not explicitly addressed in the analysis.

In his interpretation of the data, McKeown was particularly impressed with the importance of the overall long-run decline of the single airborne disease, respiratory tuberculosis (TB). In 1848–54 this had been the most lethal single cause of death, accounting for 13.3 per cent of all deaths occurring at that time. However, if attention is concentrated more closely on the nineteenth century, McKeown's own evidence provides far from unequivocal support either for the contention that a fall in airborne disease is the leading epidemiological feature of the period, or for the derivative conclusion that this could *only* be primarily the reflection of general improvement in dietary standards and nutritional levels.

Apart from respiratory TB, there were two other airborne diseases which declined very significantly in the nineteenth century, scarlet fever and smallpox. However, neither of these can be used to support the nutrition hypothesis, although they are within the airborne category. It has long been recognised that human intervention, in the form of inoculation starting in the eighteenth century and then vaccination, quarantining, and isolation procedures in the nineteenth century, must be granted the major role in the case of smallpox. As for scarlet fever, McKeown is prepared to acknowledge that the epidemiological evidence strongly suggests that this was in all probability a disease which burned itself out spontaneously. But most disconcerting of all for McKeown's general interpretation, is the behaviour of the composite airborne category, 'bronchitis, pneumonia and influenza'. This was the second most important cause of death in 1848–54, accounting for 10.25 per cent of all deaths. It actually registered a very considerable *absolute increase* in mortality of well over 20 per cent down to 1901. By the turn of the century this category was clearly the most important single killer, contributing over 16 per cent of all deaths, a greater proportion of the total than respiratory TB had represented in the mid-nineteenth century.

Thus, McKeown would have us treat the airborne diseases as a single unitary group, which between them accounted for about half of the decline in mortality before 1901 and would have us believe that nutritional improvements, made possible by a rising standard of living, can alone be considered responsible for the large-scale reduction of the group as a whole. Yet, on closer examination, we find that this completely ignores the important contrary trend exhibited by one of the two most lethal disease categories in the group. Furthermore, we find that the nutrition argument applies almost exclusively to only *one* of the several diseases within the group, respiratory TB.

But how strong is McKeown's case that even this one disease's reduction was due to rising living standards and food consumption *alone*? Contrary to McKeown's sweeping assertion, it should be pointed out that overall exposure of the population to airborne diseases would have been affected by the general level of crowding and ventilation in domestic or working environments. Thus incidence of airborne diseases probably was influenced by certain public health and preventive measures.

It would certainly seem presumptuous, therefore, to attribute a long-term reduction in TB mortality to one single factor, such as improving nutritional standards. What, then, were McKeown's grounds for this bold assertion? The critical factor was the apparent empirical finding that the reduction in respiratory TB chronologically led the mortality decline – that it was already falling from the late 1830s and 1840s, before any other major disease and when urban crowding was at a peak. But in fact a careful re-examination of the statistical trend-line invoked by McKeown to back this contention shows no definite fall in TB until the late 1860s. Furthermore, if any important infectious disease can claim chronological priority in its decline, this must be smallpox.

Finally, there still remains to be taken into account the strong counter-trend, already remarked upon, which the increasingly lethal bronchitis group of airborne respiratory diseases exhibited throughout the rest of the nineteenth century. This constitutes the most awkward and serious general caveat on the validity of McKeown's airborne 'nutritional determinism' interpretation, however it is explained.

With the anomalous rise in bronchitis-group fatalities properly acknowledged, the classic sanitation diseases come to the fore in quantitative terms. These two water/food-borne categories would between them be responsible for at least 8 per cent and perhaps 10 per cent of the overall mortality decline. That is one-third part of the nineteenth-century reduction, or over half as much again as that attributable to the airborne combination of TB and the bronchitis group.

Improvement in respiratory TB would, then, no longer appear to have been either chronologically prior or the quantitatively predominant feature of the nineteenth-century mortality decline in England and Wales. According to the logic of McKeown's own arguments, the foregoing would indicate a primary role for sanitary reform and public health measures, rather than rising nutritional levels or living standards.

An alternative interpretation: urban congestion remedied by social intervention

Between 1801 and 1871 the rate of urban growth in Britain was quite unprecedented, both in the provinces and the metropolis. At the commencement of the nineteenth century no provincial town contained as many as 100,000 inhabitants. By 1871 there were seventeen cities over this size on mainland Britain, apart from London.

National aggregate mortality patterns only indirectly reflect the full impact of this period of intensive but chaotic and disorganised urban expansion on the nation's health. According to the best single summary measure currently available, Wrigley and Schofield's series for the expectation of life at birth, average life expectancy at birth rose from around 30 years to about 40 years, then slowed to a halt at the end of the first quarter of the nineteenth century. For about half a century, from the 1820s until the 1870s, there was virtually no perceptible further improvement. Thereafter, a gradual rise to about 47–8 years by the end of the century, followed by a somewhat faster rise, to just over 60 years by 1931. Paradoxically – for McKeown's thesis – it had been almost exactly at this same point in time, when the long eighteenth-century rise in life expectancy had stalled to a halt, that a concomitant eighteenth-century *fall* (or at best stagnation) in national aggregate real wages was reversed and there had begun a trend of continual, although not continuous, improvements in average real wages throughout the rest of the nineteenth century.

The explanation of the inverse relationship is not, however, difficult. It is simply two sides of the same coin that this process could simultaneously engender higher wage-rates for the industrial workers and their families congregating at places where new enterprises were emerging, yet also simultaneously exert a negative influence on their average life expectancy because of the crowded and chaotic living conditions prevalent in the mushrooming towns and cities created by the rapidly expanding employment opportunities.

Whilst increasingly huge populations continued to concentrate ever more intensively in townships growing into cities but lacking the appropriate social overhead capital to preserve – let alone promote – health, then morbidity and mortality risks inevitably proliferated. Equally inevitably, these multiplying and compounding health hazards could only be alleviated through the appropriate social and political responses. For instance, despite its rapid growth and the unhealthy over-crowded conditions which this implied, a mains sewer system for London as a whole, which dumped the waste securely downstream of its population, was not completed until 1865 – the first such large-scale integrated system in the country.

The 1872 Public Health Act obliged local authorities as one of their statutory duties to ensure a pure water supply. In turn, this led to pressure for the 1878 Public Health (Water) Act whereby municipal purchase of private waterworks was made truly financially feasible. Whereas in 1879 only 415 urban local authorities were in charge of their water supplies, by 1905 over two-thirds of the 1,138 urban sanitary authorities then in existence were running the local waterworks, so that the health of the populace was decreasingly left in the hands of the likes of the East London Waterworks Co. Another example is that of the increasingly close regulation of the quality of the urban food supply, which duly resulted from the attention which Medical Officers in the 1860s had begun to pay to adulterated and defective foodstuffs, particularly meat and milk, as a source of disease. The Adulteration of Foods Acts followed in the 1870s leading to the appointment of professional inspectors and public analysts by most local authorities in the 1880s; also Weights and Measures Acts in 1878 and 1889 and a final consolidating Sale of Food & Drugs Act 1899.

The last third of the century was the classic period in which all the hectic activity of the Public Health political and administrative pioneers finally began to bear fruit and to take concrete effect. Of course, all this was only achieved as a result of innumerable unsung local skirmishes between frequently underpaid health officials, often lacking security of tenure, and their local allies – other sanitary officials, the district registrars of births and deaths, perhaps the town's press and occasionally some members of the local councils themselves – as against the parsimonious representatives of the majority of ratepayers. It is precisely the importance and *necessity* of this slow dogged campaign of a million Minutes, fought out of town-halls and the local forums of debate all over the country over the last quarter of the nineteenth century which has been missing in our previous accounts of the mortality decline.

I would argue, therefore, that there is a sound *prima facie* case to be answered that the decline in mortality, which began to be noticeable in the national aggregate statistics in the 1870s, was due more to the eventual successes of the politically and ideologically negotiated movement for public health than to any other positively identifiable factor. The resulting implementation of preventive measures of municipal sanitation and regulation of the urban environment and food market actually arrived on the ground in the many new cities throughout the country during the last third of the nineteenth century and the first decade of the twentieth.

The all but complete eradication by the end of the century of typhoid, cholera, and smallpox each testify in different ways to the importance and effectiveness of various aspects of the large-scale strategic public health measures which were introduced during this period. Provision of a suffcently clean local water supply was essential in the cases of both typhoid and cholera. Due to their epidemic nature, elimination of cholera and smallpox additionally required a properly functioning national system of surveillance to identify and snuff out local outbreaks which could otherwise quickly become major incidents. Port sanitary authorities established by the 1872 Public Health Act, alongside the initiative of the General Register Office in establishing regular communications with foreign authorities so as to gain advance warning of any outbreaks abroad, helped to ensure – in the absence of an entirely secure national water supply – that Britain successfully evaded all three subsequent European visitations of Asiatic cholera in 1873, 1884–6 and 1892–3.

By contrast, the apparent rise in the bronchitis group of airborne respiratory diseases may well be evidence that in those areas of the urban and industrial environment where preventive legislation and action was *not* forthcoming, serious consequences followed. Clean air was one obvious omission from the late nineteenth-century sanitary reform arsenal and one need look no further than the appalling urban smogs to explain such anomalously high levels of respiratory disease in the Victorian period. For instance, male textile workers in the 1890s, a numerically large segment of the factory working class, had a two-and-a-half times higher death-rate from respiratory diseases than agricultural labourers, despite their considerably higher pay and better access to a varied diet – the main factors stressed by McKeown in accounting for secular falls in the incidence of airborne diseases.

Conclusions

In the course of his most brilliant attack on the historical claims of his main target, 'Scientific Medicine', McKeown's detailed historical research work led him to produce an ambitious general interpretation of the causes of mortality decline, which minimalised the role of directed human agency in general, not just that which could be identified as the precursor of modern hospital and clinical practice.

It has been argued here that the historical epidemiological evidence presented by McKeown *et al.* does not in fact offer the conclusive and exclusive support, which it has long been assumed to do, for the contention that rising living standards and associated nutritional improvements have been the predominant source of mortality decline in Victorian and Edwardian Britain.

The revised account indicates a primary role for those public health measures which combated the early nineteenth-century upsurge of diseases directly resulting from the defective and insanitary urban and domestic environments created in the course of industrialisation. Fallible, blundering, but purposive human agency is returned to centre stage in this account of the mortality decline.

Simon Szreter is a demographer and social historian working at St John's College, Cambridge. This article is an edited and amended extract from a very much longer article first published in *Social History of Medicine*, 1, 1, (1988), pp. 1–37.

41 | Effectiveness and efficiency

A. L. COCHRANE

The critical step forward which brought an experimental approach into clinical medicine can be variously dated. At any rate there is no doubt that the credit belongs to Sir Austin Bradford Hill. His ideas have only penetrated a small way into medicine, and they still have to revolutionize sociology, education, and penology. Each generation will, I hope, respect him more.

The basic idea, like most good things, is very simple. The randomized controlled trial (RCT) approaches the problem of the comparability of two groups the other way round. The idea is not to worry about the characteristics of the patients, but to be sure that the division of the patients into two groups is done by some method independent of human choice, i.e. by allocating according to some simple numerical device such as the order in which the patients come under treatment, or, more safely, by the use of random numbers. In this way the characteristics of the patients are randomized between the two groups, and it is possible to test the hypothesis that one treatment is better than another and express the results in the form of the probability of the differences found being due to chance or not.

The RCT is a very beautiful technique, of wide applicability, but as with everything else there are snags. When humans have to make observations there is always a possibility of bias. To reduce this possibility a modification has been introduced: the 'double-blind' randomized trial. In this neither the doctor nor the patients know which of the two treatments is being given. This eliminates the possibility of a great deal of bias, but one still has to be on one's guard.

There are other snags: first a purely statistical one. Many research units carry out hundreds of these so-called tests of significance in a year and it is often difficult to remember that, according to the level of significance chosen, 1 in 20 or 1 in 100 will be misleading. Another snag has been introduced by the current tendency to put too much emphasis on tests of significance. The results of such tests are very dependent on the number in the groups. With small numbers it is very easy to give the impression that a treatment is no more effective than a placebo, whereas in reality it is very difficult indeed to exclude the possibility of a small effect. Alternatively, with large numbers it is often possible to achieve a result that is statistically significant but may be clinically unimportant. All results must be examined very critically to avoid all the snags.

Another snag is that the technique is not always applicable for ethical reasons. There is, of course, no absolute medical ethic but the examples I quote here represent the majority of medical opinion at present, though I do not necessarily agree with them myself. They are: surgery for carcinoma of the lung, cytological tests for the prevention of cervical carcinoma, and dietetic therapy for phenylketonuria. No RCTs have ever been carried out to test the value of these standard therapies and tests. In the first two cases the RCT technique was not available when the surgical and medical innovations were made for carcinoma of the lung and cervix. By the time such RCTs were considered by medical scientists the one-time 'innovations' were embedded in clinical practice. Such trials would necessarily involve denying the routine procedure to half a group of patients and at this stage are nearly always termed unethical. It can be argued that it is ethically questionable to use on patients a procedure whose value is unknown, but the answer is that it is unethical not to do so if the patient will otherwise die or suffer severe disability and there is no alternative therapy. Such trials, it must be accepted, cannot be done in areas where the consensus of medical opinion is against them. This means, on the one hand, that patients' interests are very well protected and on the other that there are sections of medicine whose effectiveness cannot at present be measured and which, *in toto*, probably reduce the overall efficiency of the NHS.

There are other limitations on the general applicability of the RCT. One important area is the group of diseases where improvement or deterioration has to be measured subjectively. It was hoped that the double-blind modification would avoid this trouble, but it has not been very successful in, say, psychiatry. Similarly the assessment of the 'quality of life' in such trials has proved very difficult. A good example is the various forms of treatment attempted for recurrences after operation for carcinoma of the breast. We have so far failed to develop any satisfactory way of measuring quality.

Another very different reason for the relatively slow use of the RCT in measuring effectiveness is illustrated by its geographical distribution. If some such index as the number of RCTs per 1,000 doctors per year for all countries were worked out and a map of the world shaded according to the level of the index (black being the highest), one would see the UK in black, and scattered black patches in Scandinavia, the USA, and a few other countries; the rest would be nearly white. Whatever the cause this limitation to small areas of the world has certainly slowed down progress in two ways. There are too few doctors doing the work and the load on the few is becoming too great. An RCT is great fun for the co-ordinator but can be very boring for the scattered physicians filling in the forms.

In writing this section in praise of the RCT I do not want to give the impression that it is the only technique of any value in medical research. This would, of course, be entirely untrue. I believe, however, that the problem of evaluation is the first priority of the NHS and that for this purpose the RCT is much the most satisfactory in spite of its snags. The main job of medical administrators is to make choices between alternatives. To enable them to make the correct choices they must have accurate comparable data about the benefit and cost of the alternatives. These can really only be obtained by an adequately costed RCT.

If anyone had any doubts about the need for doing RCTs to evaluate therapy, recent publications using this technique have given ample warning of how dangerous it is to assume that well-established therapies which have not been tested are always effective. Possibly the most striking result is Dr Mather's RCT in Bristol[1] in which hospital treatment (including a variable time in a coronary care unit) was compared with treatment at home for acute ischaemic heart disease. The results do not suggest that there is any medical gain in admission to hospital with coronary care units compared with treatment at home. Equally striking are the results of the multi-centre American trial on the value of oral anti-diabetic therapy, insulin, and diet in the treatment of mature diabetics.[2,3] They suggest that giving tolbutamide and phenformin is definitely disadvantageous, and that there is no advantage in giving insulin compared with diet. Dr Elwood, in my unit, has demonstrated very beautifully how illfounded was the general view of the value of iron in pregnant women with haemoglobin levels between 9 g and 12 g per 100 ml in curing the classical symptoms of anaemia.[4]

I have neither the ability, knowledge, time, nor space to classify all present-day therapies. All I feel capable of is a rough classification:

1. Those therapies, with no backing from RCTs, which are justified by their immediate and obvious effect, for example, insulin for acute juvenile diabetes, vitamin B_{12} for pernicious anaemia, penicillin for certain infections, etc.
2. Those therapies backed by RCTs. The best example is the drug therapy of tuberculosis, but there are, of course, many others.
3. Those where there is good experimental evidence of some effect, but no evidence from RCTs, of doing more good than harm to the patient, particularly in the long term. A good example, mentioned above, is the effect of iron on raising haemoglobin levels.
4. Those therapies which were well established before the advent of RCTs whose effectiveness cannot be assessed because of the ethical situation, but where there is some real doubt about the effectiveness.
5. Those therapies where the evidence from RCTs is equivocal. The best example is tonsillectomy.
6. Those therapies under-investigated by RCT, although there are no ethical constraints, which are over-ripe for them. Psychotherapy and physiotherapy are probably the most important members of this group.

If effectiveness has been rather under-investigated, efficiency has hardly been investigated at all.

The most important type of inefficiency is really a combination of two separate groups, the use of ineffective therapies and the use of effective therapies at the wrong time. It is important to distinguish the very respectable, conscious use of placebos. The effect of placebos has been shown by RCTs to be very large. Their use in the correct place is to be encouraged. What is inefficient is the use of relatively expensive drugs as placebos. At the other end of the scale are the therapies for which there is no evidence of effectiveness, but where something has to be done. Simply mastectomy is a case in point for carcinoma of the breast. This I do not consider inefficient, but on present evidence I would not classify the use of radical mastectomy as efficient.

The incorrect place of treatment. This is possibly the least-recognized type of inefficiency, but it seems probable that the increasing cost of hospitalization will force attention to it. There are in general five places where treatment can be given: at the GP's surgery, at home, at the out-patient department, in hospital, or more recently in a 'community' hospital. Traditions have grown up as to the correct place for treatment for particular diseases, and until very recently no one has treated these traditional decisions as hypotheses which should be tested. Weddell has compared the treatment of varicose veins in hospital and in the out-patient department using the RCT technique.[5] No evidence was found of any advantage associated with hospitalization for those cases without skin damage. It is to be hoped that such demonstrations that RCTs are possible and ethical will encourage others to follow suit in this new sphere.

Incorrect length of stay in hospital. It is not surprising, given the economic and psychological facts of the NHS, that the average length of stay in hospital in this country is higher than in some other countries. In addition, evidence has been accumulating of large differences in length of stay between regions and between different consultants when treating the same disease. The most striking evidence (and the most accurate) comes from Heasman and Carstairs[6] from whose paper Figure 41.1 is taken. The extent of the differences is really surprising when hospitalization in a district general hospital is one of the costliest treatments that can be prescribed, and that the majority of patients wish to leave hospital as soon as possible. The only condition in which length of stay has been much investigated is hernia. One group were discharged on the first day post-operatively. [No] serious disadvantages of early discharge [were] noted. Unfortunately this observational evidence does not take us very far. All the consultants cannot be right, but this does not help us to determine the optimum length of stay. This can again be best approached by RCTs, but it will not be easy. The main index will have to be the incidence of complications and as these will in general not be high, very large populations are required to establish an optimum.

I am conscious that I have only scratched the surface of inefficiency. I could have stressed the rising percentage of hospital admissions for iatrogenic diseases; I could have stirred the dirty waters of medical administration, but I think for my limited purposes I have done enough.

An illustrative example: pulmonary tuberculosis

The change in the tuberculosis world between 1944 when I was burying my POW tuberculosis patients in Germany and the present day [1971] when TB deaths in theory should not happen, is one of the most cheering things I have experienced in my life. The way in which the new treatments and preventive measures were introduced can also serve as a model for the introduction of all new treatments in the future. RCTs were used from the very beginning, and through this the correct dosages and combinations of drugs were quickly established; 'resistance to drugs' was quickly identified and means found of preventing it; each new drug was carefully assessed as it came on the market. The result is that there now are effective methods of treatment and prevention for TB. It would have been impossible without the technique of the RCT.

On the efficiency side there is also a great deal to the credit of this branch of medicine. 'Place of treatment' was first investigated by an RCT when hospital and home care for the tuberculous were compared in Madras[7] and various studies in this country and the USA have confirmed the Madras finding that bed rest was unimport-

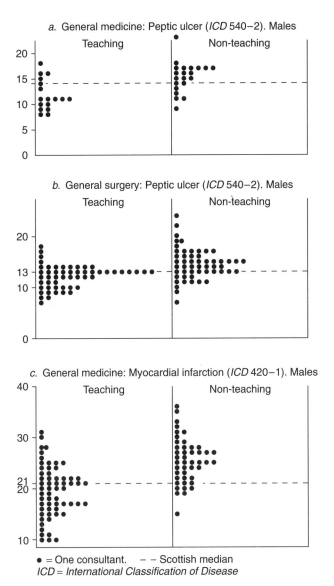

a. General medicine: Peptic ulcer (*ICD* 540–2). Males

b. General surgery: Peptic ulcer (*ICD* 540–2). Males

c. General medicine: Myocardial infarction (*ICD* 420–1). Males

● = One consultant.   – – Scottish median
ICD = International Classification of Disease

Figure 41.1   Median duration of stay in days for two diagnoses for individual consultants in Scotland (data for 1967), in teaching and non-teaching hospitals

ant.[8,9,10] In spite of the striking evidence about the unimportance of bed rest, it is surprising to find how slowly the mean length of stay in hospitals in England and Wales is falling (Figure 41.2, see p. 232), and how much the variation in length of stay seems to depend on individual consultants (Figure 41.3 overleaf). The real problem is how to ensure that patients take their chemotherapy after leaving hospital.

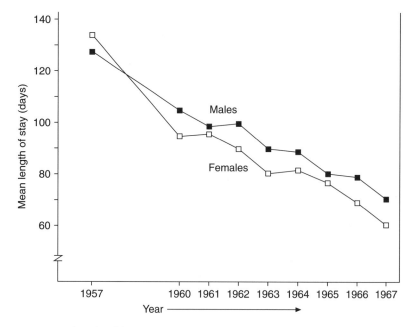

Figure 41.2 Mean length of hospital stay (days) for patients with respiratory tuberculosis (*ICD*, 7th revision, causes 001–008) in England and Wales, 1957–67

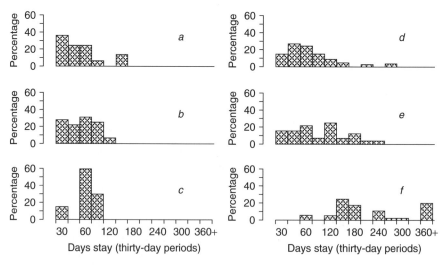

Figure 41.3 Length of hospital stay in thirty-day periods for male patients with pulmonary tuberculosis (*ICD*, 8th revision, cause 011) before discharge home from six selected chest hospitals in 1969

Someone, rather sardonically asked me once how far I was prepared to take this 'randomizing game'. I answered, without thinking, 'You should randomize until it hurts (the clinicians).' In spite of my great admiration for the effective therapy and the efficiency with which it has been applied in this field I still think there is room for improvement. The TB world has not randomized until it hurts.

References

1. Mather, H.G., Pearson, W.G., Read, K.L.Q. *et al.*, 'Acute myocardial infarction: Home and hospital treatment', *Br. Med. J.* 3, 334 (1971).
2. Universities Group Diabetes Program 'A study of the effects of hypoglycemic agents on vascular complications in patients with adult-onset diabetes. II, Mortality results', *Diabetes*, **19**, suppl. 2 (1970).
3. Knatterud, G.L., Meinhert, C.L., Klimit *et al.*, 'Effects of hypoglycemic agents on vascular complications in patients with adult onset diabetes', *J. Am. med. Ass.* **217**, 6, 777 (1971).
4. Elwood, P.C., Waters, W.E., Green, W.J., and Wood, M.M. 'Evaluation of a screening survey for anaemia in adult non-pregnant women', *Br. Med. J.* **4**, 714 (1967).
5. Piachaud, D., and Weddell, J.M. 'The economics of treating varicose veins', *International J. Epid.* **1**(3), 287–294 (1972).
6. Heasman, M.A., and Carstairs, V. 'Inpatient management variations in some aspects of practice in Scotland', ibid. **1**, 495 (1971).
7. Dawson, J.J.Y., Devadatta, S., Fox, W. *et al.*, Tuberculosis Chemotherapy Centre, Madras 'A five year study of patients with pulmonary tuberculosis, *Bull. Wld Hlth Org.* **34**, 533 (1966).
8. Tuberculosis Society of Scotland 'The treatment of pulmonary tuberculosis at work: a controlled trial', *Tubercle. Lond.* **41**, 161 (1960).
9. Spriggs, E.A., Bruce, A.A., and Jones, M. 'Rest and exercise in pulmonary tuberculosis: A controlled study', ibid. **42**, 267 (1961).
10. Tyrell, W.F. 'Bed rest in the treatment of pulmonary tuberculosis', *Lancet*, i, 821 (1956).

A.L. (Archie) Cochrane was Director of the Medical Research Council's Epidemiology Unit in Cardiff before his retirement. These extracts are taken from his book, *Effectiveness and Efficiency: Random Reflections on Health Services*, produced for the 1971 Rock Carling Fellowship, published by Nuffield Provincial Hospital Trust. He has given his name to the Cochrane Collaboration, an electronic database publishing systematic reviews of clinical trials on the Internet (http://www.cochrane.org).

42 | Medicine matters after all

JOHN P. BUNKER

The view that medicine contributes little to health harks back 20 years to the publication of Thomas McKeown's *The Role of Medicine*[1]. McKeown drew his conclusions from an epidemiological analysis of public health data from years prior to 1971. The quarter century that followed has seen an explosion of new medical treatments, many of which have been shown in clinical trials and meta-analyses to result in considerable improvements in health; and at the same time evidence crediting medical care with the extension of life began to appear. The American economist Jack Hadley compared expenditures by the government's Medicare program with regional death rates and calculated that for every 10% increase in expenditure there was a 1–2% fall in mortality[2]. But conflicting data also appeared in which national age-specific death rates were found to be greater in countries with greater numbers of doctors, and presumably more medical care[3]. Efforts to separate the effects of medical care from those of other determinants using aggregate data have been fraught with similar difficulties. Examination of the effect of individual medical interventions, one at a time, has offered a more appropriate approach, and this is the approach we have taken.

For both life-expectancy and quality of life analyses we selected conditions for which strong evidence of efficacy, usually in clinical trials, was available, and whose prevalence is sufficient to create a notable impact when their effect is spread across the entire population. Many less common or rare, but important, conditions were therefore not included.

Outcomes of medical care

Life expectancy

Estimation of months or years of increased life-expectancy attributable to the treatment of a particular condition involved a two-step procedure: estimation of increases in life-expectancy from the decline in diagnosis-specific death rates, and estimation of how much of an improvement could be attributed to medical care specifically. Documentation of the decline in disease-specific death rates was based on annual reports from the National Center for Health Statistics (NCHS) in Hyattsville, Maryland[4]. The proportion of improvement attributable to medical treatment was based, whenever possible, on clinical trials and meta-analyses.

Comprehensive annual reports of death rates have been published by NCHS since 1950. The age-adjusted death rate for the American population fell from 840 per 100,000 in 1950 to 523 per 100,000 in 1989, with a rise in life expectancy of 7.1 years. (Life-expectancy in England and Wales rose by almost exactly the same amount during the same period, and I assume that the break-down by diagnosis was roughly similar in our two countries.) 'Diseases of the heart' were by far the largest contributors to the improvement, their age-adjusted death rate falling from 307 to 156 per 100,000 during the 39 year period, constituting just under half of the fall in death rate from all causes. As a first approximation, we estimated that the fall in death rate from heart disease contributed 3.38 years of improved life-expectancy.

For an estimation of how much of the fall in death rates from heart disease and improved life expectancy to attribute to medical care, we relied heavily on Goldman and Cook's 1984 analysis[5]. They reviewed evidence of the efficacy of medical intervention in heart disease and estimated that 40% of the decline in cardiac death rates for the years between 1968 and 1976 could be attributed to coronary care units, treatment of hypertension, and medical and surgical treatment of ischaemic heart disease. Accepting their analysis, we credited medical care with 40% of the 3.38 years of increased life-expectancy associated with the fall in cardiac deaths for the entire 39 year period. Medical treatment at the beginning of the period, we assume, contributed somewhat less than 40%, but treatment at the end has clearly contributed a good deal more.

Tables 42.1 and 42.2 (overleaf) present our estimates of the gains in life-expectancy credited to clinical preventive and clinical curative services, respectively. We credit curative services with three and a half to four years of increased life-expectancy, with the potential of adding an additional year and a half if efficacious care were made more widely available. We credit clinical preventive services with a current gain in life-expectancy of a year and a half and the potential for an additional seven or eight months.

All told, we estimated that together, clinical preventive and curative services can be credited with about five of the 30 years increased life-expectancy gained in the United States and in Great Britain during this century, i.e. 17 or 18%. This is certainly a good deal more than McKeown was able to identify 24 years ago, but still a relatively small contribution. To place a five year change in life-expectancy in perspective, however, it may be useful to consider that a gain of five years in life-expectancy is roughly equivalent to the loss in life-expectancy that an individual suffers by smoking a pack a day starting at age 20; and it is roughly equivalent to the difference in life expectancy between the top grade and unskilled workers in the Whitehall study of British civil servants[7].

Quality of life

Much of the debate over the contribution of medical services to health has been based on death rates and life-expectancy, since they are relatively easy to measure. The majority of medical care is, of course, devoted to improving the quality of life, or, more accurately, to relief from the poor quality of life associated with many chronic diseases. The need

Table 42.1 Clinical preventive services: estimated numbers at risk and gains in life-expectancy for those receiving selected successful services, with gain in life expectance for the US population and potential gain not yet achieved.

Clinical preventive service	Relevant population	Individuals affected by condition in the absence of preventive service	Gain per individual receiving preventive service	Proportion of those at risk receiving preventive service	Gain in life-expectancy distributed across US population	
					Current	Potential
Screening for hypertension	All over age 3	58 million[a] (10 million moderate or severe)	3 months	50%	1.5–2 months	1.5–2 months
Screening for cancer of the cervix	Adult women	13,000[b]	96 days	60%–90%	2 weeks[c]	1 week[c]
Screening for colorectal cancer	All 50–80 years of age	155,000[b]	2 weeks	Unknown	Unknown	1 week
Counselling to stop smoking	Smokers	Smokers (approximately one-third of population)[a]	3 months	Unknown	Unknown	1 month
Immunisation for diphtheria	All children	40 deaths per 100,000[b]	10 months	73%–85% pre-school; 97%–98% entering school	10 months	
Immunisation for poliomyelitis tetanus	All All	2,500 deaths[b] 2,500 deaths[b]	}3 weeks	73%–85% pre-school; 97%–98% entering school	3 weeks	0

Immunisation for smallpox	All	NA[d]	3–6 months[e]	Almost all before immunisations; almost nobody today	3–6 months	0
Immunisation for influenza	All over 65	10,000–40,000 deaths[b]	3 weeks	30%	1 week	3 weeks
Pneumococcal immunisation	All over 65	400,000 cases[b]	6 weeks	14%	1 week	6 weeks
Hepatitis-B immunisation	All	21,000 cases[b]	1.5–2 weeks	10%	1–2 days	1.5–2 weeks
Hormone replacement	Post menopausal women	8,000 deaths[b]	3 months	50%	3 weeks[c]	3 weeks[c]
Aspirin prophylaxis for heart attack	Men over 40	Approximately 30% of men	Unknown	Unknown	Unknown	Unknown

(Reprinted with permission from the *Millbank Quarterly*[6]).
[a] Prevalence (all cases);
[b] Incidence (new cases per annum);
[c] Double for single sex;
[d] Not applicable following worldwide eradication;
[e] Limited to this century only.

Table 42.2 Clinical curative services: for selected diagnoses, estimated numbers at risk and gains in life-expectancy for those receiving successful treatment, with gain in life-expectancy for the US population and potential gain not yet achieved.

Condition treated	Relevant population	Number at risk	Gain per individual receiving successful treatment (years)	Gain in life expectancy distributed across US population	
				Current	Potential
Cancer of cervix	Adult women	13,000[b]	21[d]	2 weeks[c]	1 week[c]
Colorectal cancer	All	155,000[b]	12[d]	2 weeks	1 week
Peptic ulcer	All	250,000[b]	10[e]	2 weeks	Unknown
Ischaemic heart disease[f]	All	6 million[a]	14[e]	1.2 years	6–8 months
Hypertension	All	58 million[a]	10[e]	3.5–4 months[g]	3.5–4 months[g]
Kidney failure	All	41,000[b]	11[e]	2–3 months	Unknown
Infant respiratory failure	Premature infants	75,000–100,000[b]	20–30[d]	3–4 months	Unknown
Appendicitis	All	273,000[b]	50[d]	4 months	0
Diabetes	All	6 million[a]	25	6 months	Unknown
Pregnancy	Women 15–44	4 million[b]	45	2 weeks[c]	0
Pneumonia and influenza	All	400,000–1 million[b]	9[e]	3 months	0
Tuberculosis	All	27,000 cases[b]	15[e]	3 months[h]	Uncertain[h]
Trauma	All	50–65 million[b]	24–38	1.5–2 months	3–4 months

(Reprinted with permission from *The Millbank Quarterly*[6]).

[a] Prevalence (all cases).

[b] Incidence (new cases per annum).

[c] Double for women.

[d] For cancer of the cervix, colon cancer, infant respiratory distress syndrome, and appendicitis, we have made rough approximations based on mean age at death and life expectancy at that age.

[e] Gain in expectation of life at birth due to eliminating specified cause of death by race and sex, for those who would have died; United States, 1979–87.

[f] Includes coronary-artery surgery, coronary-care units, and medical management of heart disease.

[g] Impact of treatment of hypertension on stroke and heart mortality.

[h] Increased likelihood of poor compliance with treatment regimens and increased frequency of infection with drug-resistant strains of tuberculosis make these estimates speculative and subject to change.

to measure quality of life and to assess its response to therapy has been recognised for a good many years. Sophisticated measurement instruments are now in widespread use in clinical research, but only fragmentary data are yet available by which to determine the impact of medical care on the quality of life at the population level.

As a first approximation I have developed such an inventory, again from secondary sources, of the months and years that an individual, or cohort of individuals, has been spared the lessened quality of life associated with common severe illnesses, mostly chronic, a few acute[8]. I estimate that, on average, an individual has been relieved as a result of medical care from about five years of poor quality [life]. Estimates of increases in the quality of life that I attributed to the treatment of hypertension illustrate how the estimates were made.

The treatment of hypertension contributes to the quality of life by lessening the probability of non-fatal myocardial infarction and non-fatal stroke. Goldman and Cook[5] attributed 8.7% of the fall in fatal ischaemic heart disease that occurred between 1968 and 1976 to the treatment of hypertension. Deaths attributed to diseases of the heart fell, as discussed in the sections on life-expectancy, from 307 to 156 per 100,000 between 1950 and 1989, about two-thirds of which were attributed to ischaemic heart disease[4]. If it is assumed that for every 100 ischaemic heart deaths there were 200 non-fatal ischaemic heart attacks, and if we assume that patients survive on average ten years after a non-fatal ischaemic heart attack, we estimate that there have been approximately 150 fewer years of post-myocardial disability per 100 population in the lifetime of individuals today than there would have been had deaths from ischaemic heart disease remained unchanged from those of 1950. We credited 8.7% of this improvement, 13 years, to the treatment of hypertension. An increase in the medical control of hypertension, above the 50% reported in 1986 by Drizd and associates[9] could further increase this benefit, perhaps to as high as 20 years per 100 population.

The age-adjusted death rate from cerebrovascular disease in the United States declined from 88.6 per 100,000 in 1950 to 28.0 in 1989[4]. The reported death rate for strokes varies between 20% and 33%. We estimated, therefore, that between 120 and 240 fewer non-fatal strokes per 100,000 occurred in 1989 than occurred in 1950. Assuming a five year average survival for patients suffering non-fatal stroke, and there-fore 600 to 1,200 fewer years per 100,000 of survival with stroke, I estimate that there has been a decline in years with stroke of between 45 and 90 per 100 population. Marked increase in medical control of hypertension during this period from less than 10% to approximately 50%[9], and the 45% reduction in stroke observed in randomised trials of anti-hypertensive drugs[10,11] could explain as much as 15–20% of the reduction in stroke morbidity. Accordingly, I credit the treatment of hypertension with a reduction of ten to 20 years of stroke-related poor quality of life per 100 population.

The doctor–patient relationship

What happens between doctor and patient during the medical encounter has a pro-found impact on outcome. Its importance is unquestioned, but it has generally been assumed that it could not be measured. On close examination, however, one can find considerable quantitative evidence of benefits. The assessment and recommendation for or against therapeutic intervention have a profound impact on outcome, the magnitude of which is reflected in two- and three-fold variations in rates of medical and surgical intervention.

Knowledge and belief are also key determinants of a patient's peace of mind. The provision of information can enhance patients' sense of control or 'self-efficacy', and perhaps optimism, each of which is strongly associated with improved health status. The mechanism by which the positive effects of counselling, encouragement, and reassurance are mediated may not be known, but the effect is a large one. The placebo effect that accompanies a wide spectrum of medical and surgical interventions is estimated to be responsible for about a third of their therapeutic effects.

Conclusions

In a time of political ferment when hard choices must be made as to where and how to spend public and private funds, it is important that decisions be made on the basis of the best available information. Our estimates of medicine's contribution to health are more than speculative and less than precise; they are approximations extrapolated from secondary sources. We have urged that better data, analysed with more sophisticated methods, be developed as the basis for a continually updated inventory of life-expectancy and quality of life as improved by medical care[6].

These, or similar data, do not tell decision-makers what choices to make, but they do help to inform the decision process. The public and its representatives in Parliament or Congress must choose among a large spectrum of competing social programmes, only some of which are designed to improve health; and among programmes to improve health, medical care is only one of several. Education, housing, and employment, as the *British Medical Journal* has reminded us[12], also affect health. But if we have been slow to document the effects of medical care, and if our data are less precise than we would like, they are considerably firmer than any that can be presented for the non-medical determinants of health[13].

It is true that education, income, and occupation are strongly associated with health, but, except for occupation, they are not independent determinants; they may, indeed, be proxies for other determinants yet to be identified, and we have only the vaguest idea of the mechanism by which they may affect health. Education, housing, and employment are all highly important goods in their own right, of course, with urgent and valid needs. Let us not, however, imagine that enough is known about their effect on health to divert resources to them for that reason alone.

The association of socioeconomic status with health has been known for a great many years, but governments have been reluctant to take compensatory action. Governmental inaction might reasonably be attributed to the absence of a practical solution; indeed it is still unclear how to correct the disparities in health that have been documented across all income and occupational levels, not merely between the well to do and the poor and unemployed[7]. By contrast, the scientific basis of medicine is increasingly well understood, the outcomes of medical care are being widely documented, and the cumulative benefits to the population can now be tabulated as the basis for political action.

References

1. McKeown, T. *The Role of Medicine: Dream, Mirage or Nemesis?* London: Nuffield Provincial Trust, 1976 (2nd edn. Princeton University Press, 1979). See also Chapter 39 in this Reader.

2. Hadley, J. *More Medical Care, Better Health?* Washington: Urban Institute Press, 1982.
3. Cochrane, A.L., St Leger, A.S., Moore, F. Health service 'input' and mortality 'output' in developed countries. *Journal of Epidemiology and Community Health* 1978; **32**: 200–205.
4. National Center for Health Statistics. *Health, United States 1991*. Hyattsville, Maryland, 1992.
5. Goldman, L., Cook, E.F. The decline in ischemic heart disease mortality rates: an analysis of the comparative effects of medical interventions and changes in lifestyle. *Annals of Internal Medicine* 1984; **101**: 825–36.
6. Bunker, J.P., Frazier, H.S., Mosteller, F. Improving health: measuring effects of medical care. *Millbank Quarterly* 1994: **72**: 225–58.
7. Marmot, M.G., Davey Smith, G., Stansfeld, S., Patel, C. *et al.* Health inequalities among British civil servants: the Whitehall II study. *Lancet* 1991; **337**: 1387–93.
8. Bunker, J.P. The role of medical care in improving the quality of life: an inventory from secondary sources. In: *Proceedings of an international symposium on quality of life and health*. Oxford: Blackwell Scientific Publishing, 1995.
9. Drizd, T., Dannenberg, A.L., Engel, A. Blood pressure levels in persons 18–74 years of age in 1976–80, and trends in blood pressure from 1960 to 1980 in the United States. In: *Vital and health statistics* (Series 11, No. 234 DHHS pub. No. (PHS) 86–1684). Washington: National Center for Health Statistics, 1986.
10. MacMahon, S., Peto, R., Cutler, J., Collins, R., *et al.* Blood pressure, stroke, and coronary heart disease: Part 1, prolonged differences in blood pressure; prospective observational studies corrected for the regression dilution bias. *Lancet* 1990; **335**: 827–38.
11. Collins, R., Peto, R., MacMahon, S., Hebert, P., *et al.* Blood pressure, stroke, and coronary heart disease: Part 2, short-term reductions in blood pressure: overview of randomised drug trials in their epidemiological context. *Lancet* 1990; **335**: 827–38.
12. Smith, R. Medicine's core values, *British Medical Journal*, 1994; **309**: 1247–8.
13. Frank, J.W., Mustard, J.F. The determinants of health from a historical perspective, *Daedalus*, 1994; **123**: 1–9.

This article is an edited extract from an original with the same title, which appeared in the March/April 1995 issue of the *Journal of the Royal College of Physicians of London*, 29(2): 105–12. The data and their interpretation are presented in greater depth, and the role of medicine is discussed in the broader context of other determinants of health in a monograph, *Medicine Matters After All* by John P. Bunker, published in 2001 by the Nuffield Press, London. John, P. Bunker is now a visiting Professor in the Department of Epidemiology and Public Health, Faculty of Clinical Sciences, the Royal Free and University College Medical School.

43 | Ethical dilemmas in evaluation
A CORRESPONDENCE

The following (edited) article appeared in *The Lancet* on 16 February 1980.

Possible prevention of neural-tube defects by periconceptional vitamin supplementation

R.W. Smithells, S. Sheppard, and C.J. Schorah
Department of Paediatrics and Child Health, University of Leeds

M.J. Seller
Paediatric Research Unit, Guy's Hospital, London

N.C. Nevin
Department of Medical Genetics, Queen's University of Belfast

R. Harris, and A.P. Read
Department of Medical Genetics, University of Manchester

D.W. Fielding
Department of Paediatrics, Chester Hospitals

Summary

Women who had previously given birth to one or more infants with a neural-tube defect (NTD) were recruited into a trial of periconceptional multivitamin supplementation. One of 178 infants/fetuses of fully supplemented mothers (0.6 per cent) had an NTD, compared with 13 of 260 infants/fetuses of unsupplemented mothers (5.0 per cent).

Introduction

The well-known social-class gradient in the incidence of neural-tube defects (NTD) suggests that nutritional factors might be involved in NTD aetiology. A possible link between folate deficiency and NTDs in man was first reported in 1965.[1] More recently, significant social-class differences in dietary intakes in the first trimester,[2] and in first-trimester values for red cell folate, leucocyte ascorbic acid, red-blood-cell riboflavin, and serum vitamin A have been reported,[3] dietary and biochemical values being higher in classes I and II than in classes III, IV, and V. Furthermore, seven mothers, of whom six subsequently gave birth to NTD infants and one to an infant with unexplained microcephaly, had first-trimester mean values for red cell folate and leucocyte ascorbic acid that were significantly lower than those of controls.

These observations are compatible with the hypothesis that subclinical deficiencies of one or more vitamins contribute to the causation of NTDs. We report preliminary results of an intervention study in which mothers at increased risk of having NTD infants were offered periconceptional multivitamin supplements.

Patients and methods

Women who had one or more NTD infants, were planning a further pregnancy, but were not yet pregnant were admitted to the study. All women referred to the departments involved in the study and who met these criteria were invited to take part. Patients came from Northern Ireland, South-East England, Yorkshire, Lancashire, and Cheshire. One hundred and eighty-five women who received full vitamin supplementation (see below) became pregnant.

The control group comprised women who had had one or more previous NTD infants but were either pregnant when referred to the study centres or declined to take part in the study. Some centres were able to select a control for each supplemented mother, matched for the number of previous NTD births, the estimated date of conception, and, where possible, age. There were 264 control mothers. The numbers of fully supplemented (S) and control (C) mothers in each centre were as follows: Northern Ireland S 37, C 122; South-East England S 70, C 70; Yorkshire S 38, C 35; Lancashire S 31, C 27; Cheshire S 9, C 10.

All mothers in supplemented and control groups were offered amniocentesis. Six mothers in Northern Ireland (three supplemented; three controls) declined amniocentesis and their pregnancies continue. They are not included in the figures above or in the accompanying table. All mothers with raised amniotic-fluid alpha-fetoprotein (AFP) values (one supplemented, eleven controls) accepted termination of pregnancy.

Study mothers were given a multivitamin and iron preparation ('Pregnative Forte F' Bencard), one tablet three times a day for not less than twenty-eight days before conception and continuing at least until the date of the second missed period, i.e. until well after the time of neural-tube closure.

Results

One hundred and eighty-seven control mothers have delivered 192 infants (including five twin pairs) without NTDs, and a further thirty-eight have normal amniotic-fluid

Table 43.1 Outcome of pregnancy in fully supplemented and control mothers

	Fully supplemented	Controls
Infant/fetus with NTD	1	12
Infant without NTD	140(3)	192(5)
Subtotal (1)	141(3)	204(5)
Normal amniotic AFP	26	38
Subtotal (2)	167(3)	242(5)
Spontaneous abortions		
Examined, NTD	0	1
Examined, no NTD	11	17
Subtotal (3)	178(3)	260(5)
Not examined	10	9
Total	188(3)	269(5)

All numbers relate to infants/fetuses.
Figures in parentheses indicate numbers of twin pairs included.
AFP = alpha-feto protein, which is often elevated in the amniotic fluid surrounding a fetus affected by a neural tube defect

AFP values (see Table 43.1). Thirteen mothers have been delivered of NTD infants/fetuses. Seventeen fetuses of a further twenty-six control mothers who aborted spontaneously were examined and had no NTD. The provisional recurrence-rate of NTDs is 5.0 per cent (13 in 260), consistent with those previously reported and widely adopted in genetic counselling.

One hundred and thirty-seven fully supplemented mothers have given birth to 140 babies (including three twin pairs) without NTD, twenty-six have normal amniotic-fluid AFP values and their pregnancies continue, and one has had a further affected infant. Eleven fetuses of twenty-one mothers who aborted spontaneously were examined; none had an NTD. The provisional recurrence-rate in the supplemented group is therefore 0.6 per cent (1 in 178).

Comparison of NTD frequencies in the supplemented and control groups by Fisher's exact test showed significant differences ($p < 0.01$) for subtotals (1), (2), and (3) (Table 43.1).

Discussion

Despite problems with choosing controls, the control women in this study have shown recurrence-rates for NTDs entirely consistent with published data. By contrast the supplemented mothers had a significantly lower recurrence-rate. Possible interpretations of this observation include the following:

(1) *A group of women with a naturally low recurrence risk has unwittingly selected itself for supplementation.* Apart from geographic and secular variations there is no evidence to suggest that any particular sub-group within populations, whether by social class or any other division, has a higher or lower recurrence risk. In genetic counselling clinics it is customary to quote the same risk for all mothers after one

affected child. We cannot exclude the possibility that women who volunteered and cooperated in the trial might have had a reduced risk of recurrence of NTD.

(2) *Supplemented mothers aborted more NTD fetuses than did controls.* The proportion of pregnancies ending in spontaneous abortion is similar in the two groups (supplemented 11.4 per cent, control 9.6 per cent). If the supplemented mothers have aborted more NTD fetuses, they must have aborted fewer other fetuses or had a lower initial risk of abortion. Eleven of twenty-one abortuses of supplemented mothers have been examined and none had an NTD. Eighteen of twenty-seven abortuses of control mothers were examined and one had an NTD. An explanation based on selective abortion of fetuses with NTD seems improbable.

(3) *Something other than vitamin supplementation has reduced the incidence of NTDs in the treated group.* This is an almost untestable hypothesis, but if anything has reduced the incidence of NTDs it needs to be identified urgently.

(4) *Vitamin supplementation has prevented some NTD.* This is the most straightforward interpretation and is consistent with the circumstantial evidence linking nutrition with NTDs. If the vitamin tablets are directly responsible, we cannot tell from this study whether they operate via a nutritional or a placebo effect.

We hope that the data presented will encourage others to initiate similar and related studies.

References

1. Hibbard, E.D. and Smithells, R.W. 'Folic acid metabolism and human embryopathy', *Lancet*, i, 1254–56 (1965).
2. Smithells, R.W., Ankers, G., Carver, M.E., Lennon, D, Schorah, C.J. and Sheppard, S. 'Maternal nutrition in early, pregnancy', *Br. J. Nutr.* 38, 497–506 (1977).
3. Smithells, R.W., Sheppard, S. and Schorah, C.J. 'Vitamin deficiencies and neural tube defects', *Arch. Dis. Childh.* 51, 944–50 (1976).

The three following letters appeared in *The Lancet* on 22 March 1980.

Possible prevention of neural-tube defects by periconceptional vitamin supplementation

Sir, Professor Smithells and others believe they have observed a preventive effect of periconceptional vitamin supplementation on the recurrence of neural-tube defect (NTD). Their conclusions are based on the observation that the incidence of NTD in 185 fully supplemented women was significantly lower than that in 264 unsupplemented or control women.

Such an interpretation of the data rests upon the assumption that both the supplemented and the control women were, initially, at equal risk of conceiving a further affected fetus. A geographical analysis of the total sample shows that this was probably not so. In the accompanying Table (Table 43.2 overleaf) the study subjects are charac-

Table 43.2 Geographical distribution of supplemented and control mothers

	Relatively high risk areas No. (%)	Relatively low risk areas No. (%)	Total No. (%)
Supplemented mothers	77 (41.6)	108 (58.4)	185 (100)
Control mothers	159 (60.2)	105 (39.8)	264 (100)

terised as falling into one of two groups – a 'relatively high risk' group, residing in Northern Ireland, Lancashire, and Cheshire; and a 'relatively low risk' group residing in south-east England and Yorkshire. (The varying geographical risk of NTD is well established.) It is clear that the supplemented sample is as heavily biased towards 'relatively low risk' areas as the control sample is towards 'relatively high risk' areas. The higher incidence of recurrent NTD in the control group is therefore hardly surprising.

Why, I wonder, did Professor Smithells and his co-workers not evaluate their interesting hypothesis by means of a randomised controlled trial, which would have been eminently practicable, would have minimised selection bias, and would have been more likely to convince the sceptics?

David H. Stone
University of Glasgow, Social Paediatric and Obstetric Research Unit, Glasgow

Sir, with the wisdom of hindsight, we should have stated in our preliminary communication that our original intention had been a double-blind controlled study for which placebo tablets had already been prepared, but that the protocol was rejected by three separate hospital research ethics committees, and we had to resort to a less satisfactory design.

The number of fully supplemented (S) and 'control' mothers (C) was almost identical in all centres except Northern Ireland which had an excess of controls (Northern Ireland S 37, C 122; S-E England S 70, C 70; Yorkshire S 38, C 35; Lancashire S 31, C 27; Cheshire S 9, C 10). The recurrence rate of NTDs in the controls was in keeping with earlier reports. The excess of controls in Northern Ireland does not alter the fact that there was only one recurrence among the progeny of 185 fully supplemented mothers.

The geographical variation in the *incidence* of NTD is well recognised. What is relevant to our study is geographical variation in *recurrence* rate, about which little is known.

Dr Stone makes reference to what we 'believe', to our 'conclusions', and to 'an interpretation'. In our paper we subscribe to no belief, reach no conclusions, and offer four possible interpretations, of which the first covers the point Dr Stone raises.

We are not trying 'to convince the sceptics', among whom we count ourselves. We present some observations (which will be fully detailed in a later paper) and would welcome further studies to assist in their interpretation.

R.W. Smithells, S. Sheppard

Sir, Professor Smithells and his colleagues have opened the next chapter in the saga of neural-tube defects. Since a deficiency of some nutrient has been proposed as the source of nearly every ailment since antiquity, why not propose another? An unfortunate effect of this form of communication is that women will be induced to self-administer large quantities of vitamins, some of which may be teratogenic. I hope that future studies will incorporate properly selected controls treated with placebos and that nutritional assessment of the mother, before and during therapy, will be done.

Paul M. Fernhoff

Department of Pediatrics, Emory University School of Medicine, Atlanta, Georgia

---

The following extract is from an editorial which appeared in *The Lancet* on 17 May 1980.

Vitamins, neural-tube defects and ethics committees

Some years ago Renwick[1] suggested that a specific teratogen present in blighted potatoes might be the causal agent. The plausibility of Renwick's hypothesis did draw attention to the possibility of maternal nutritional factors in the aetiology of neural-tube defects. An investigation reported in *The Lancet* in February suggests that subclinical maternal vitamin deficiency may be one of these factors.

At a time when the reduction in birth incidence of neural-tube defects rests largely on alpha-fetoprotein screening and selective abortion, this is an exciting finding. However, the study by Smithells *et al.* depends critically on the assumption that the vitamin-supplemented group and their controls were equally at risk of conceiving a further affected fetus. On this point there must be some doubt.

The vitamin-supplemented group were recruited on the basis of their ability to adhere to a fairly stringent regimen of tablet-taking while the controls were those who could not or would not adhere to the required protocol. Thus, selection was based on self-motivation and self-discipline, and one suspects that such women will have better-than-average outcome of pregnancy. A randomised control trial would have been more appropriate. But, as Professor Smithells[2] explains, such a study was proposed by the investigators and rejected by three separate hospital research ethics committees. As a result a far less satisfactory design was chosen.

How much does this matter? The results achieved by Smithells *et al.* are so striking that they provide a strong argument for the immediate vitamin supplementation of all mothers who are at risk of bearing a child with a neural-tube defect. If vitamins were completely harmless one could perhaps extend this argument to all mothers. But already there is evidence that at least one of the components of the multivitamin preparation, vitamin A, is a teratogen in rodents.[3,4] Doctors are thus faced with a dilemma; if they ignore the results of the Smithells study they may be allowing the conception of infants with neural-tube defects whose malformations might have been prevented. If they advise vitamin supplementation to all would-be mothers they may be contributing to the induction of a different range of congenital abnormalities whose appearance may not be recognised for some time.

The problem would probably be best resolved by a large randomised controlled trial on a general population of mothers, with vitamins being administered to one group and placebos to the other. But if this design has already been rejected by an ethics committee, it is even less likely to be acceptable now that the results of the Smithells trial are known. This raises the question of accountability. Research workers are quite properly called upon to explain and justify any investigation involving patients, both directly to an ethics committee and indirectly in the publication of their results. Ethics committees are less subject to scrutiny. They may explain their decision to individual workers, but many researchers find these arbitrary and lacking the coherence necessary to stand up to public examination. Perhaps the time has come to devise a system for making those ubiquitous committees more accountable.

References

1. Renwick, J.H. 'Anencephaly and spina bifida are usually preventable by avoidance of a specific unidentified substance present in certain potato tubers', *Br. J. Prev. Soc. Med.*, **26**, 67–88 (1972).
2. Smithells, R.W. and Sheppard, S. 'Possible prevention of neural tube defects by periconceptional vitamin supplementation', *Lancet*, **i**, 647 (1980).
3. Seller, M.J., Embury, S., Polani, P.F. and Adinolphi, M. 'Neural tube defects in curly-tail mice. II Effect of maternal administration of vitamin', *Proc. Roy. Soc. Lond. B.*, **206**, 95–107 (1979).
4. Nakamura, H. 'Digital anomalies in the embryonic mouse limb cultured in the presence of excess vitamin A', *Teratology*, **14**, 195–202 (1977).

The following letter appeared in *The Lancet* on 14 June 1980.

Vitamins, neural-tube defects, and ethics committees

Sir, As a result of the study by Professor Smithells and his colleagues there is now a suggestion that periconceptional multivitamin supplementation may reduce the incidence of fetal neural tube defect (NTD). This possibility is of great interest in Ireland where the incidence of NTD is high.

Some of the shortcomings of the research design used by Smithells *et al.* have been discussed in your editorial and in your correspondence columns. The essential problem is the lack of comparability of the supplemented and non-supplemented mothers: we do not know whether the favourable outcome in the fully supplemented mothers is greater than might be expected for such a highly selected group.

You emphasise, as do your correspondents, need for a randomised controlled trial but suggest that such a design is even less likely to be acceptable to research ethics committees now in the light of the Smithells study. If this is so, then it is a matter for concern. Perhaps the most serious consequence of not testing this hypothesis with the most appropriate research design is the possibility that millions of mothers-to-be may take multivitamin preparations around the time of conception in the as yet unproven belief that to do so significantly reduces the risk of having a baby with NTD. Furthermore there is the important question of possible teratogenic effects. How certain are we that the ingestion by mothers of considerable quantities of this multivitamin, iron, and calcium preparation ('Pregnative Forte F') during the period of most rapid fetal organogenesis is safe? By rejecting randomised controlled trials, ethics committees are sanctioning what amounts to a situation of uncontrolled experimentation on mothers and their babies. In so doing can they be said to be carrying out their function of protecting the welfare of patients?

The weight of medical scientific opinion is that only a large randomised controlled trial will permit us to say with confidence whether periconceptional multivitamin supplementation reduces the incidence of NTD, and whether such regimes are free from teratogenic effects. Our professional duty would seem to be clear – to conduct such a trial as soon as possible.

Peadar N. Kirke
Medico-Social Research Board, Dublin, Ireland

The following (edited) article appeared in the *British Medical Journal* on 9 May 1981.

Double-blind randomised controlled trial of folate treatment before conception to prevent recurrence of neural-tube defects

---

K.M. Laurence, DSC, FRCP(E), professor of paediatric research and clinical geneticist
Nansi James, MB, MRCP, fieldworker
Mary H. Miller, MB, DCH, fieldworker
Department of Child Health, Welsh National School of Medicine, Cardiff

G.B. Tennant, MSC, senior scientific officer
Department of Haematology, Welsh National School of Medicine

H. Campbell, FRCP, FRSS, professor
Department of Medical Statistics, Welsh National School of Medicine

Abstract

A randomised controlled double-blind trial was undertaken in South Wales to prevent the recurrence of neural-tube defects in women who had had one child with a neural-tube defect. Sixty women were allocated before conception to take 4 mg of folic acid a day before and during early pregnancy and 44 complied with these instructions. Fifty-one women were allocated to placebo treatment. There were no recurrences among the compliant mothers but two among the non-compliers and four among the women in the placebo group. Thus there were no recurrences among those who received supplementation and six among those who did not; this difference is significant (p = 0.04).

It is concluded that folic acid supplementation might be a cheap, safe, and effective method of primary prevention of neural-tube defects but that this must be confirmed in a large, multicentre trial.

Subjects and methods

Women resident in Glamorgan and Gwent who had had a pregnancy complicated by a fetal neural-tube defect (anencephaly, encephalocele, and spina bifida cystica) between

1954 and 1969 were traced. Those under 35 years of age at the time of study were visited in their homes by medically qualified fieldworkers.

During the home visit a questionnaire was completed giving details of the woman's diet during the interpregnancy period and during her previous pregnancies. A simple diet sheet was used that provided a general pattern for meals and a check list showing the amount of food consumed during the average week and listing first-class proteins, dairy products, fresh vegetables and salads, cereals, and refined carbohydrates, paying special attention to those items rich in folic acid. Diets were judged as good, fair, or inadequate, those that were poor or fair but deranged by an excessive amount of fat and refined carbohydrates being judged as inadequate.[1] A sample of blood was taken from all women who were planning to have further children for estimation of serum and red-cell folic acid concentrations. Those willing to cooperate were asked to take twice a day a tablet containing either 2 mg of folic acid or placebo starting from the time contraceptive precautions were stopped. Women were allocated to receive treatment or placebo by random numbers and did not know the content of the tablets; we were also unaware of the treatment prescribed. Women were instructed to report to us within six weeks of a missed period and were revisited as soon as possible thereafter. Inquiries were made about the quality of the diet during the current pregnancy and about any anorexia or vomiting, drugs, or illness, and a further sample was taken for folate estimation and other investigations. The women were revisited at six months and again at the end of pregnancy, when details of the outcome of the pregnancy were available.

Results

Altogether 905 women who had had a child with a neural-tube defect were seen by the fieldworkers, of whom 111 (12.3 per cent) agreed to take part in the prophylactic randomised controlled trial and achieved a subsequent pregnancy. Of these, 60 had been randomised to receive folate supplementation and 51 placebos.

Compliance in taking the folate tablets was monitored at the sixth to ninth week of estimated gestation; if the serum folate concentration at this stage was higher than 10 µg/l the woman's account of taking the tablets during the earlier part of the pregnancy could be accepted as valid. If the serum folate concentration was below 10 µg/l the woman was classified as a non-complier. None of the placebo group had a serum folate concentration above 12 µg/l. There were 16 non-compliers (27 per cent) among the 60 women allocated to receive folate treatment (Table 43.3). Compliance was not tested among the controls.

Table 43.3 Outcome of pregnancy by treatment group

Outcome of pregnancy	Folate groups		Placebo group
	Compliers	Non-compliers	
Normal fetus	44	14	47
Fetus with neural-tube defect	0	2	4
All cases	44	16	51

Table 43.4 Numbers of women taking good, fair, or inadequate diets classified according to whether they received folate treatment and whether fetus was normal or had a neural-tube defect

Diet	Received folate		Did not receive folate		All cases
	Normal	Neural-tube defect	Normal	Neural-tube defect	
Good	17	0	26	0	43
Fair	17	0	24	0	41
Inadequate	10	0	11	6	27
All cases	44	0	61	6	111

Table 43.5 Mean ±SD red-cell folate concentration (µg/l red blood cells) by treatment group and quality of diet

Diet	Folate groups		Placebo group
	Compliers	Non-compliers	
Good	618 ± 60 (n = 17)	277 ± 44 (n = 5)	278 ± 25 (n = 21)
Fair	847 ± 60 (n = 17)	292 ± 23 (n = 6)	298 ± 34 (n = 18)
Inadequate	761 ± 85 (n = 10)	193 ± 34 (n = 5)	250 ± 26 (n = 12)
All cases	738 ± 42 (n = 44)	256 ± 22 (n = 16)	278 ± 16 (n = 51)

Six pregnancies resulted in a fetus with a neural-tube defect (Table 43.3): none in the compliers, two in the non-compliers, and four in the placebo group.

Table 43.4 shows the number of women taking a good, fair, or inadequate diet classified by outcome of pregnancy and whether they had received folate treatment. The proportion of women with inadequate diets was similar in the two treatment groups: 10 out of the 44 compliers and 17 out of the 67 non-compliers and women in the placebo group. All six of the recurrences of fetal neural-tube defects occurred in women taking an inadequate diet.

Table 43.5 shows the mean red-cell folate concentration in each treatment group by the adequacy of the diet. In each dietary group the compliers had a mean concentration at least twice that in the placebo group, and these differences were significantly different (p < 0.001).

Discussion

None of the 44 women who received treatment had a recurrence, whereas there were six recurrences among 67 untreated cases. The probability of such a distribution, using Fisher's exact test with a single tail, was p = 0.04.

The specific effect of folate has to be separated from the non-specific effect of diet. There were no recurrences among the 84 women who received good or fair diets, but there were six recurrences among the 27 women receiving a poor diet (p < 0.0001, Fisher's exact test). As we have shown,[2] women who take poor diets are at an extremely high risk of a recurrence of fetal neural-tube defects. Within this high-risk group of women, however, there were no recurrences in the 10 who had taken folate supplementation but six recurrences in the 17 who had not taken supplementation (p = 0.04, Fisher's exact test). Thus although there may have been some bias owing to women who were receiving an inadequate diet also failing to comply, yet within this group receiving an inadequate diet the preventive effect could still be detected. We conclude that women receiving a poor diet who are at high risk of a recurrence of fetal neural-tube defects can reduce their risk either by improving their diet or by taking folate supplements.

The use of folate as an effective prophylactic regimen to prevent neural-tube defects in high-risk groups, communities with a high incidence of such defects, or even all women at risk of pregnancy should be further tested in a larger controlled trial conducted at several centres. Such a trial would be ethical as we found a probably biological beneficial effect, but the problem might be to consider an alternative regimen. A placebo could be justified by the argument that it is not normal practice to begin supplementation before conception is confirmed. As a result of the study by Smithells et al.[3] Pregnative Forte F without folate would seem to be a suitable alternative. With an expensive blunderbuss preparation of that type, which includes several agents in addition to folate, the specific beneficial agent and the hazards that might arise from the other constituents should be identified.

References

1. Laurence, K.M., James, N., Miller, M. and Campbell, H. 'The increased risk of recurrence of neural tube defect to mothers on poor diets and the possible benefit of dietary counselling', *Br. Med. J.*, **281**, 1542–4 (1980).
2. Tennant, G.B. and Withey, J.L. 'An assessment of work simplified procedures for the microbiological array of serum vitamin B12 and serum folate', *Medical Laboratory Technology*, **29**, 171–81 (1972).
3. Smithells, R.W., Sheppard, S., Schorah, C.J. *et al.* 'Possible prevention of neural tube defects by preconceptional vitamin supplementation', *Lancet*, i, 339–40 (1980).

The following (edited) letter appeared in the *British Medical Journal* on 30 May 1981.

Trial of folate treatment to prevent recurrence of neural tube defects

Sir, We have been extremely interested to read the recent papers by Dr K.M. Laurence and others. We are puzzled by their use of the term 'double-blind' in their more recent paper, which can only have applied until six to nine weeks of gestation, when blood folate levels were estimated and 'non-compliers' were identified. The high rate of non-compliance must also have disappointed the authors. We entirely endorse their view that further studies are needed, directed towards the following ends:

1. To provide further confirmation that vitamin prophylaxis is effective.
2. To define further the role of folic acid and other vitamins.
3. To study carefully mothers who are enrolled for supplementation but who comply only in part.

There is considerable urgency. The medical correspondent of *The Times* has advocated (8 May) vitamin supplementation on the basis of our series and those of the Cardiff group. It can no longer be assumed that mothers not given vitamin supplements by research workers necessarily have none. There is also a danger of 'do-it-yourself' supplementation by mothers obtaining over-the-counter vitamin preparations, none of which contains folic acid.

R.W. Smithells, Sheila Sheppard, C.J. Schorah, N.C. Nevin, Mary J. Seller

---

The following (edited) article appeared in *The Guardian* on 10 December 1982.

Specialists voice fear that some doctors and patients will boycott scheme to test vitamin theory

Women to act as guinea-pigs in spina bifida trials, by Andrew Veitch

The controversial plan to find out whether vitamin supplements prevent mothers from having spina bifida babies is to go ahead, the Medical Research Council said yesterday. It involves denying the vitamins to hundreds of mothers known to be at risk.

Specialists said yesterday that it might be doomed from the start because not enough women or doctors would volunteer to take part.

The public controversy about the proposals – which reached a peak two weeks ago when the MRC secretary, Sir James Gowans, was accused of suppressing debate – and the mass of evidence of the merits of folic acid which had accumulated in the past two years, meant that few mothers would be prepared to volunteer for a trial in which they faced a one-in-two chance of not having folic acid and a one-in-four chance of receiving no vitamins at all.

Medical teams in Manchester, Leeds and Belfast have declined to take part in the trial. Teams in Liverpool and Chester are thought likely to follow suit. So the area with the highest incidence of spina bifida – the North-west – will not be represented.

Professor Norman Nevin, head of medical genetics at Queen's University Belfast, said that the MRC was not justified in giving some women a placebo. The trial was also condemned yesterday by the National Childbirth Trust. 'It is not ethical to withhold vitamins from some women', said the Trust's secretary, Ms. Hanna Corbishley.

The following (edited) article appeared in *The Guardian* on 13 December 1982.

Wasted years, damaged lives

After two years of dithering the Medical Research Council has finally decided to go ahead with its plan to establish conclusively whether vitamin supplements prevent spina bifida in babies. In view of the large controversy these trials have generated, however, it is hard to see how they can now produce any evidence worth having. Medical teams in Manchester, Leeds and Belfast are refusing to take part, and it seems likely that Liverpool and Chester will follow suit. Moreover, it is hard to see how any woman would want to take part in these trials in the first place. Surely, any woman who has already had a spina bifida baby will reply that if there is even a slim chance that vitamins and folic acid will reduce the likelihood of another damaged child – and such supplements have no known toxic effects – then she would very much like to have them, please, and no, she wouldn't be prepared to run the slightest extra risk.

It is said that the Department of Health is reluctant to fund a national programme of vitamin and folic acid supplements until conclusive proof is provided. This means that, for the next five years, these supplements will not be available automatically to women at risk of producing a spina bifida baby – because of a trial whose conclusions are likely to be as dubious as its ethics.

The following (edited) letter appeared in *The Guardian* on 14 December 1982.

Spina bifida: a new trial

Sir, I oppose the proposed trial both on ethical and practical grounds, and consider that it is unlikely to produce a more conclusive answer than is already available from the admittedly imperfect trials conducted by Professor Smithells and his colleagues.

Nevertheless, the results are so promising that to deprive women of a totally harmless vitamin cocktail seems unethical. I would find it difficult to persuade the mothers of any of my patients to have a placebo, when they could have something which is likely to be helpful.

It is true that we do not know which vitamins, or which combination of them, is likely to decrease the incidence of neural-tube defects, but I see no evidence that folic acid alone has shown itself to be of benefit. The data relating to this are based on very few pregnancies.

There is, however, an alternative and totally ethical way in which the question could be settled without difficulty. It is known that the incidence of neural-tube defects is 5 per cent after the birth of a baby with spina bifida or anencephaly. If, therefore, all women at risk are offered vitamin supplementation starting some three months before pregnancy is contemplated, within a very short time it will be apparent whether vitamin supplementation is helpful or not. It does not really matter which of the vitamins or their combination is helpful.

John Lorber
(Emeritus Professor of Paediatrics), Sheffield

The following abstract (i.e. summary) is taken from a detailed report of a major clinical trial, which was published in full in *The Lancet* in July 1991.

Prevention of neural tube defects: results of the Medical Research Council vitamin study

MRC Vitamin Study Research Group

Abstract

A randomised double-blind prevention trial with a factorial design was conducted at 33 centres in seven countries to determine whether supplementation with folic acid (one of the vitamins in the B group) or a mixture of seven other vitamins (A, D, B_1, B_2, B_6, C, and nicotinamide) around the time of conception can prevent neural tube defects (anencephaly, spina bifida, encephalocele). [In anencephaly, the brain does not develop. In spina bifida, the spinal cord is not fully enclosed in the bones of the spine. In encephalocele, the skull bones enclosing the brain do not join together properly.] A total of 1817 women at high risk of having a pregnancy with a neural tube defect, because of a previous affected pregnancy, were allocated at random to one of four groups – namely, folic acid, other vitamins, both, or neither. 1195 had a completed pregnancy in which the fetus or infant was known to have or not have a neural tube defect; 27 of these had a known neural tube defect, 6 in the folic acid groups and 21 in the two other groups, a 72 per cent protective effect (relative risk 0.28, 95 per cent confidence interval [CI] 0.12–0.71). The other vitamins showed no significant protective effect (relative risk 0.80, 95 per cent CI 0.32–1.72). There was no demonstrable harm from the folic acid supplementation, though the ability of the study to detect rare or slight adverse effects was limited. Folic acid supplementation starting before pregnancy can now be firmly recommended for all women who have had an affected pregnancy, and public health measures should be taken to ensure that the diet of all women who may bear children contains an adequate amount of folic acid.

The full article appeared in *The Lancet* on 20 July 1991, **338**, pages 131–7; it reports the work of a large number of investigators in several countries. The overall study co-ordinator, and the main author of the article is the epidemiologist Nicholas Wald, Professor of Environmental and Preventive Medicine at St Bartholomew's Hospital Medical College.

The following editorial appeared in *The Lancet* on 20 July 1991, and refers to the MRC Vitamin Study (1991), the abstract of which precedes this editorial.

Folic acid and neural tube defects

Fifty years ago Gregg's classic observations linked congenital cataract to infection of the mother with rubella during pregnancy.[1] These findings were a huge advance in the difficult and unrewarding task of understanding and preventing birth defects. It could not be a more appropriate anniversary for the publication of the exciting paper in this issue [i.e. the paper whose abstract is reprinted above] which reports the prevention of neural tube defects by folate supplementation in a randomised clinical trial. The arguments over the role of micronutrients in this group of disorders have been to a very large extent resolved, at last.

A prevention trial of periconceptional supplementation with a vitamin and mineral preparation was planned in the 1970s by Smithells, but permission to carry it out was refused by an ethics committee who insisted that the design be altered to a study in which all women at increased risk of having an infant with a neural tube defect were offered the supplement.[2] In the interpretation of the modified study it was impossible to disentangle the apparent benefit of supplementation from possible differences in the risk of having a subsequent affected pregnancy between women who did take the supplement and those who did not.

The intervention of the ethics committee had other adverse effects. Given the findings in that study of a large difference in the recurrence rate of neural tube defects between the supplemented and unsupplemented groups the ethical difficulties of mounting a randomised trial became much greater. Yet the uncertainty about the efficacy of supplementation, and about which was the active component of the preparation, could not be resolved by repetition of the study with the same non-randomised design: the issue was not whether the results could be due to chance but whether they could be due to differences between the groups.

Those who argued for a trial pointed to other instances of apparent benefits in non-randomised studies that could not be detected when the same treatment was formally evaluated with random allocation: there are many examples in the perinatal domain.[3] Opponents believed that a randomised trial was redundant since the effect associated with taking supplements was so large that it was highly unlikely to be attributable to any known or unknown confounders. The arguments of those most closely involved and their comments on one another's views were made available at the time in a fascinating publication.[4] When the current trial was planned the debate became public and acrimonious. The trial was condemned by some as unethical: researchers with an interest in maternal and child health were asked to join the critics in trying to have the trial stopped.

Two factors seem to have been important in this reaction. One was the nature of the preventive agent: a multivitamin preparation was regarded as synonymous with good health. Even if it did not have the hoped for effect, it was perceived as being completely harmless. The term 'experimental drug' was not seen to apply here. Where an intervention is believed to be totally without risk, arguments about the need for certainty before it is widely prescribed are dismissed as academic. The second factor was the original ethics committee decision. If a randomised trial had been regarded as unethical even before the treatment had been tried how much more so was it afterwards? In the long term these factors probably slowed recruitment to such an extent that it took 8 years to accumulate enough participating women and enough pregnancies, despite the involvement of 33 centres. How many affected infants have been born during those years whose abnormalities would have been prevented if the trial had been completed sooner?

Several features of the current trial deserve special mention. The process for informing women about the trial, whereby they had time to consider whether they wished to take part, was careful and sensitive. The factorial design ensured that three-quarters of those taking part received folate or multivitamins or both. Assessments of compliance by counting the number of capsules at the regular prepregnancy and early pregnancy visits suggested that this particular intervention is highly acceptable to women at special risk of having a child with a neural tube defect; only 7 per cent of women stopped taking the capsules before they became pregnant and fewer than 1 per cent of the remaining women took less than half of their assigned capsules. Some commentators had predicted that participants would supplement themselves with folate or multi-vitamins in addition to the capsules given to them in the trial, but measurements of serum folic acid levels showed that this did not happen. The factorial design and the sequential analysis helped to limit the size of the trial, enabling the data monitoring committee to recommend that the trial be stopped after 1195 pregnancies instead of the planned 2000.

Supplementation with 4 mg a day of folic acid did not prevent all neural tube defects and the six unsuccessful cases were not accounted for by unusually low serum folic acid concentrations. This is a reminder of the possibility that the group of disorders may be heterogeneous in aetiology. The overall result was unequivocal. All analyses, whether based on the original allocation of the women (intention-to-treat), or restricted to women who were not already pregnant at the time of randomisation, or repeated after exclusion of women who stopped taking the capsules, showed the reduction in neural tube defects to be substantial with relative risks of the order of 0.28 to 0.17. Even the adjustments to the relative risk necessitated by the early stopping of the trial give a relative risk estimate of 0.33 – a two-thirds reduction – with a 95 per cent confidence interval of 0.06 to 0.80. The reduction was not as large as that found in the non-randomised studies.[5]

Thus the policy implications are clear. Women who have had an affected fetus should be offered folic acid supplements if they intend having another pregnancy and supplementation should begin before conception. Counselling services associated with prenatal diagnosis or the birth of infants with malformations will provide an appropri-ate place and setting for advice and prescription.

The unanswered questions will be less easy to resolve. Is 4 mg a day of folic acid the necessary dose or is the 0.36 mg a day contained in the original multivitamin prepara-tion enough? How long before conception is supplementation needed? Perhaps the population-wide trial of primary prevention of neural tube defects currently under way in China can be modified to take up these two questions. Are there any risks in folic acid supplementation and if so are they the same at the two folic acid dosages? The present trial could not detect a harmful effect of the supplements but its capacity to do so was limited by the size of the groups. The collaborative birth defects monitoring programmes in Europe and worldwide may be able to devise a strategy for taking up the issue. Will the beneficial effect of folic acid be the same in populations with a much lower prevalence at birth of neural tube defects? It has been argued in the past that the determinants in such populations are likely to be different. Will the effect in women who are not at increased risk of having an affected child be the same as in the present trial? The authors argue that benefits can be expected but their magnitude cannot be predicted precisely. Compliance would probably be very different among women with no personal experience of the abnormality. Moreover, the practical difficulties of providing folic acid supplements to all women before pregnancy, and particularly to women before their first pregnancy, are formidable. Can the requisite folic acid be eaten in food instead of given as a supplement? Green leafy vegetables are a good source, although the vitamin will dissolve in water with prolonged boiling; even then, raw green cabbage contains only 90 µg of total folic acid per 100 g. Can culturally appropriate dietary guidelines be prepared as a matter of urgency for all ethnic groups? Providing specific dietary advice about the prevention of malformations to women before pregnancy will be at least as challenging as providing supplementation.

The MRC Vitamin Study was built on almost 20 years of work on the possible role of folic acid and other micronutrients in human malformations[6] and on the increasing willingness of the perinatal community to collaborate in randomised trials to answer important questions of policy and clinical practice. It should lead to major benefits for infants, mothers, and the whole community.

References

1. Gregg, N.M. 'Congenital cataract following German measles in the mother', *Trans. Ophthalmol. Soc. Aust.*, 3, 35 (1941).
2. Smithells, R.W., Sheppard, S., Schorah, C.J., *et al.* 'Possible prevention of neural-tube defects by periconceptional vitamin supplementation', *Lancet*, i, 330–40 (1980).
3. Silverman, W.A., *Retrolental Fibroplasia: A Modern Parable*, Grune & Stratton, New York, p. 85 (1980).
4. Dobbing, J. (ed.) *Prevention of Spina Bifida and Other Neural Tube Defects*, Academic Press, London (1983).
5. Smithells, R.W., Seller, M.J., Harris, R., *et al.* 'Further experience of vitamin supplementation for prevention of neural tube defect recurrences', *Lancet*, i, 648–69 (1983).
6. Hibbard, E.D. and Smithells, R.W. 'Folic acid metabolism and human embryopathy', *Lancet*, i, 1254 (1965).

This editorial is reproduced in its entirety from *The Lancet*, 20 July 1991, **338** pages 153–4.

44 | The global eradication of smallpox

MARC A. STRASSBURG

On 8 May 1980, the 33rd World Health Authority Assembly declared the world free of smallpox. This followed approximately $2^{1}/_{2}$ years after the last documented naturally occurring case of smallpox was diagnosed in a hospital worker in Merca, Somalia. The lessons learned from the smallpox campaign can be readily applied to other public health programs.

To certify a country as smallpox-free, two years had to have elapsed without a case of smallpox being detected by an active and sensitive surveillance system. Almost two years to the day (26 October 1979) after the last case in Somalia, the (WHO) Global Commission for the Certification of Smallpox Eradication confirmed that smallpox also had been eradicated in Ethiopia, Somalia, and Kenya. Eradication efforts had been successful in this last endemic area, despite the ongoing war between Ethiopia and Somalia in the rugged and inaccessible Ogaden desert.

History

The origin of smallpox probably predates written history. Epidemics of smallpox-like illnesses have been described in ancient Chinese and Sanskrit texts. Historical accounts beginning in the sixth century describe pandemics both in Europe and Asia. In the Americas, the disease was probably introduced during the 1500s by slave ships from Africa. Reported fatality rates for smallpox have varied between less than 1 per cent and 50 per cent. Differences in fatality rates were probably related to both the virulence of a particular strain (variola major and variola minor as well as intermediate strains have been described) and the nutritional status of the affected population.

Prior to the eighteenth century, few effective measures for the control of smallpox were known. Although quarantine proved useful for a number of diseases, the procedure had limited success in smallpox control, since the disease was communicable during the prodromal period before the onset of rash. Prior to Jenner's discovery of vaccination, a procedure known as variolation was used to confer immunity. Variolation was accomplished by obtaining material from the pustules of a smallpox patient and scratching the material onto the skin of a susceptible person. Many persons so variolated had symptoms of reduced severity, although they were capable of transmitting fully virulent cases of smallpox to others. Of special concern was that many of the variolated persons did not require bed rest, and thus they promoted a rapid spread of the disease. This practice, which originally had been described by the Chinese in 1000 BC, was still found in a number of countries in the twentieth century.[1]

The vaccine

A major breakthrough in providing an effective measure for the control of smallpox occurred in 1796 when Edward Jenner observed that persons who contracted cowpox, a relatively mild disease, developed immunity to smallpox. Jenner prepared a vaccine consisting of material from cowpox lesions. He fully understood the implication of the discovery of his new vaccine when he predicted that 'the annihilation of smallpox must be the final result of this practice.'

Despite the discovery of such an effective vaccine, it took nearly 200 years to bring about the eradication of smallpox. Several explanations for this delay may be offered. First, it was not until the 1950s that a heat-stable, freeze-dried vaccine was available. This important advance prolonged the viability of the vaccine in parts of the world where strict maintenance of the cold chain was difficult. Second, it was not until the 1960s that the bifurcated needle was developed. The bifurcated needle (used in the multiple-puncture vaccination technique) was easier to use, required less vaccine, and resulted in higher 'take' rates than other methods. Third, even with an improved vaccine and vaccination technique, not all countries were capable of carrying out a successful mass vaccination campaign. Although mass vaccination campaigns had been effective in eliminating smallpox in many Western countries, the limited resources and the organizational problems common to many health service systems in the developing world made complete vaccination coverage nearly impossible.

The World Health Organization's program for eradication

In 1966 the World Health Assembly, which is the controlling body for WHO, voted a special budget ($2.5 million) to begin the global program aimed at eliminating smallpox from the world. Although it would seem that all involved in such a program would be highly motivated, many participants, both at national and local levels, were skeptical that smallpox or any other disease could be eradicated. One possible explanation for this lack of enthusiasm was that the WHO eradication program for another disease – malaria – was not succeeding.

In 1967, when the smallpox campaign began, more than 30 countries were considered endemic, with importations being reported in another 12 countries. At that time four major reservoirs existed: Brazil; Africa south of the Sahara; Asia, including Bangladesh, Nepal, India and Pakistan; and the Indonesian Archipelago. Although only 130,000 cases were reported in 1967, it was estimated that there were closer to 10 million cases.[1]

Of paramount importance to the success of the smallpox eradication program was administrative and logistical support. Under the able leadership of Donald A. Henderson of WHO, precise objectives and goals for each country were established. WHO trained both international and national epidemiologists and was responsible for securing additional supporting funds for the eradication program.

New approach to eradication

A new strategy for smallpox eradication, one which did not rely on mass vaccination, was eventually adopted. This new strategy was called *surveillance and containment* and was developed by smallpox workers in West Africa. The development of this strategy was greatly influenced by a thorough knowledge of the following important elements in the natural history of smallpox.

1. The spread of smallpox was relatively slow, and a case usually infected only from two to five other persons.
2. Smallpox tended to cluster within villages or in a single area.
3. Man was the only reservoir of infection, and no carrier state was known.
4. Immunity was of long duration after either infection or vaccination.

Surveillance consisted of case-finding through systematic searches, improved reporting systems, and active source tracing. Many countries offered cash rewards to persons providing information leading to the discovery of a smallpox case. Containment efforts included isolation of patients and vaccination of all known or suspected contacts. The principal objective of this approach was to seal off outbreaks within specific geographical areas, thereby reducing transmission into unaffected areas. Although large-scale vaccination programs were still conducted, mass vaccination was no longer solely relied upon for control of the disease.

The hospital's role in transmission

Important to the success of this new strategy was the development of effective isolation and quarantine measures. Historically, special huts, 'pest-houses', or isolation hospitals were principally used to remove affected persons from the community. It is probable that many of these early hospitals played major roles in smallpox transmission. This was well documented during the 1950s and 1960s when numerous hospitals were implicated as the principal source of spread in outbreaks. After analyzing 30 epidemics of smallpox in Western countries between 1946 and 1964, Thomas Mack of the Centers for Disease Control reported that, of 516 cases of smallpox, 280 had been hospital-acquired. The last major outbreak of smallpox in the United States, which occurred in January 1947, began after an immigrant with smallpox (from Mexico) was hospitalized at Willard Parker, the communicable diseases hospital in Manhattan. The first secondary cases included another patient and a hospital staff member. A total of 12 secondary cases resulted, and within 1 month over 6 million persons were vaccinated in New York City.[2] Common to many hospital-centered outbreaks was (1) misdiagnosis or late diagnosis of the smallpox case, (2) inadequate isolation of the patient, (3) spread among unvaccinated hospital staff, and (4) spread to the surrounding community.

With the new emphasis on surveillance and containment, the necessity for effective isolation was even more critical to success. During 1975, I worked as a consultant in the Bangladesh Eradication Program in the crowded capital of Dacca City. At the Infectious Diseases Hospital there, it was necessary to post vaccination guards around the clock to vaccinate routinely all persons going into the facility who did not have proof of a recent vaccination. In many countries the practice of hospitalizing smallpox patients was openly discouraged, and the patients remained at home accompanied by a vaccinator until the patient fully recovered.

Between 1967 and 1977 the eradication campaign moved steadily forward, with smallpox successively eliminated in Western and Central Africa, Brazil, Indonesia, Southern Africa, and finally in East Africa.

Still cause for concern?

There are some who believe that smallpox may emerge from some hidden focus of infection, an unknown animal reservoir, or from some old smallpox crusts that are lying dormant somewhere in the world. There may be some who believe that smallpox eradication will not be complete until those strains maintained in laboratory freezers are destroyed. Concern over the maintenance of such a virus was heightened by events in Birmingham, England. There, in August 1978, a photographer who worked above a laboratory housing the smallpox virus contracted the disease. Only one secondary case was reported – the photographer's mother.[3] In 1976, 76 laboratories were known to stock smallpox virus; as of January 1, 2001 there were two laboratories (one in the U.S. and the other in Russia) reporting that they still maintained the virus.

What's next?

Polio is currently targeted for world-wide eradiction, and excellent progress is being made. Meanwhile, many public health workers are looking for another candidate for eradication. Although not everyone agrees on a single definition of the word 'eradication', for smallpox it implied an absence of clinical cases of the disease on a continent, with little or zero likelihood of the disease reoccurring. In the selection of a new candidate for eradication, a number of factors need consideration: (1) the degree of understanding of the natural history of the disease; (2) types of appropriate control measures available; (3) mortality produced by the disease; (4) morbidity, including suffering and disability; (5) availability of adequate funding; (6) the cost–benefit of such an eradication effort; and (7) the probability of success within a given time period.

Many of these factors are interdependent. For example, malaria, which is considered by many as the leading cause of mortality in the World today, may require in excess of one billion dollars for the first years of an eradication program. Similar expenses would accompany attempts to eradicate other diseases transmitted by arthropod vectors (e.g. yellow fever, trypanosomiasis, and onchocerciasis).

Zoonotic diseases are also difficult to eradicate because animal populations serve as principal reservoirs and are difficult to control. Possibly from the group of diseases that, like smallpox, is transmitted chiefly from person to person and for which man is either the principal or only reservoir of infection, a candidate can be found. From this group, measles clearly stands out as a potential candidate for eradication. Although the effect of measles on world mortality and morbidity may not be as great as was that of smallpox, the natural history of measles is well understood, there is a good vaccine (though not as heat-stable as the smallpox vaccine), and man is the only reservoir of infection. Thus measles would require a similar strategy and organization to carry out a successful eradication effort.

References

1. WHO Expert Committee on Smallpox Eradication, World Health Organization Tech. Rep. Ser. No. 493 (1972).
2. Weinstein, I. 'An outbreak of smallpox in New York City', *Am. J. Public Health*, **37**, 1376–1384 (1947).
3. Hawkes, N. 'Smallpox death in Britain challenges presumption of laboratory safety: peer review failed dismally', *Science*, **203**, 855–856 (1979).

Marc A. Strassburg is Chief of Web Informatics and Epidemiology for the Department of Health Services, County of Los Angeles, California. The article is an edited extract from the *American Journal of Infection Control* (**19**, pp. 220–225, 1982), which is published by C.V. Mosby, St Louis, Missouri, USA.

45 | The epidemics of modern medicine

IVAN ILLICH

During the past three generations the diseases afflicting Western societies have undergone dramatic changes. Polio, diphtheria, and tuberculosis are vanishing; one shot of an antibiotic often cures pneumonia or syphilis; and so many mass killers have come under control that two-thirds of all deaths are now associated with the diseases of old age. Those who die young are more often than not victims of accidents, violence, or suicide.

These changes in health status are generally equated with a decrease in suffering and attributed to more or to better medical care. Although almost everyone believes that at least one of his friends would not be alive and well except for the skill of a doctor, there is in fact no evidence of any direct relationship between this mutation of sickness and the so-called progress of medicine. The changes are dependent variables of political and technological transformations, which in turn are reflected in what doctors do and say; they are not significantly related to the activities that require the preparation, status, and costly equipment in which the health professions take pride. In addition, an expanding proportion of the *new* burden of disease of the last fifteen years is itself the result of medical intervention in favor of people who are or might become sick. It is doctor-made, or *iatrogenic*.

After a century of pursuit of medical utopia, and contrary to current conventional wisdom, medical services have not been important in producing the changes in life expectancy that have occurred. A vast amount of contemporary clinical care is incidental to the curing of disease, but the damage done by medicine to the health of individuals and populations is very significant. These facts are obvious, well documented, and well repressed.

Doctors' effectiveness – an illusion

The study of the evolution of disease patterns provides evidence that during the last century doctors have affected epidemics no more profoundly than did priests during earlier times. Epidemics came and went, imprecated by both but touched by neither. They are not modified any more decisively by the rituals performed in medical clinics than by those customary at religious shrines. Discussion of the future of health care might usefully begin with the recognition of this fact.

In England, by the middle of the nineteenth century, infectious epidemics had been replaced by major malnutrition syndromes, such as rickets and pellagra. These in turn peaked and vanished, to be replaced by the diseases of early childhood and, somewhat later, by an increase in duodenal ulcers in young men. When these declined, the modern epidemics took over: coronary heart disease, emphysema, bronchitis, obesity, hypertension, cancer (especially of the lungs), arthritis, diabetes, and so-called mental disorders. Despite intensive research, we have no complete explanation for the genesis of these changes. But two things are certain: the professional practice of physicians cannot be credited with the elimination of old forms of mortality or morbidity, nor should it be blamed for the increased expectancy of life spent in suffering from the new diseases. For more than a century, analysis of disease trends has shown that the environment is the primary determinant of the state of general health of any population: food, water, and air, in correlation with the level of sociopolitical equality and the cultural mechanisms that make it possible to keep the population stable.

Some modern techniques, often developed with the help of doctors, and optimally effective when they become part of the culture and environment or when they are applied independently of professional delivery, have also effected changes in general health, but to a lesser degree. Among these can be included contraception, smallpox vaccination of infants, and such nonmedical health measures as the treatment of water and sewage, the use of soap and scissors by midwives, and some antibacterial and insecticidal procedures. The importance of many of these practices was first recognized and stated by doctors – often courageous dissidents who suffered for their recommendations – but does not consign soap, pincers, vaccination needles, delousing preparations, or condoms to the category of 'medical equipment'. The most recent shifts in mortality from younger to older groups can be explained by the incorporation of these procedures and devices into the layman's culture.

In contrast to environmental improvements and modern nonprofessional health measures, the specifically medical treatment of people is never significantly related to a decline in the compound disease burden or to a rise in life expectancy. Neither the proportion of doctors in a population nor the clinical tools at their disposal nor the number of hospital beds is a causal factor in the striking changes in over-all patterns of disease. The new techniques for recognizing and treating such conditions as pernicious anemia and hypertension, or for correcting congenital malformations by surgical intervention, redefine but do not reduce morbidity. The fact that the doctor population is higher where certain diseases have become rare has little to do with the doctors' ability to control or eliminate them. It simply means that doctors deploy themselves as they like, more so than other professionals, and that they tend to gather where the climate is healthy, where the water is clean, and where people are employed and can pay for their services.

Useless medical treatment

Awe-inspiring medical technology has combined with egalitarian rhetoric to create the impression that contemporary medicine is highly effective. Undoubtedly, during the last generation, a limited number of specific procedures have become extremely useful. But where they are not monopolized by professionals as tools of their trade, those which are applicable to widespread diseases are usually very inexpensive and require a minimum of personal skills, materials and custodial services from hospitals. In contrast, most of today's skyrocketing medical expenditures are destined for the kind of diagnosis and treatment whose effectiveness at best is doubtful. To make this point I will distinguish between infectious and noninfectious diseases.

In the case of infectious diseases, chemotherapy has played a significant role in the control of pneumonia, gonorrhea, and syphilis. Death from pneumonia, once the 'old man's friend', declined yearly by 5 to 8 per cent after sulphonamides and antibiotics came on the market. Syphilis, yaws, and many cases of malaria and typhoid can be cured quickly and easily. The rising rate of venereal disease is due to new mores, not to ineffectual medicine. The reappearance of malaria is due to the development of pesticide-resistant mosquitoes and not to any lack of new antimalarial drugs. Immunization has almost wiped out paralytic poliomyelitis, a disease of developed countries, and vaccines have certainly contributed to the decline of whooping cough and measles, thus seeming to confirm the popular belief in 'medical progress'. But for most other infections, medicine can show no comparable results. Drug treatment has helped to reduce mortality from tuberculosis, tetanus, diphtheria, and scarlet fever, but in the total decline of mortality or morbidity from these diseases, chemotherapy played a minor and possibly insignificant role. Malaria, leishmaniasis, and sleeping sickness indeed receded for a time under the onslaught of chemical attack, but are now on the rise again.

The effectiveness of medical intervention in combatting noninfectious diseases is even more questionable. In some situations and for some conditions, effective progress has indeed been demonstrated: the partial prevention of caries through fluoridation of water is possible, though at a cost not fully understood. Replacement therapy lessens the direct impact of diabetes, though only in the short run. Through intravenous feeding, blood transfusions, and surgical techniques, more of those who get to the hospital survive trauma, but survival rates for the most common types of cancer – those which make up 90 per cent of the cases – have remained virtually unchanged over the last twenty-five years. Surgery and chemotherapy for rare congenital and rheumatic heart disease have increased the chances for an active life for some of those who suffer from degenerative conditions. The medical treatment of common cardiovascular disease and the intensive treatment of heart disease, however, are effective only when rather exceptional circumstances combine that are outside the physician's control. The drug treatment of high blood pressure is effective and warrants the risk of side-effects in the few in whom it is a malignant condition; it represents a considerable risk of serious harm, far outweighing any proven benefit, for the 10 or 20 million Americans on whom rash artery-plumbers are trying to foist it.

Doctor-inflicted injuries

Unfortunately, futile but otherwise harmless medical care is the least important of the damages a proliferating medical enterprise inflicts on contemporary society. The pain, dysfunction, disability, and anguish resulting from technical medical intervention now rival the morbidity due to traffic and industrial accidents and even war-related activities, and make the impact of medicine one of the most rapidly spreading epidemics of our time. Among murderous institutional torts, only modern malnutrition injures more people than iatrogenic disease in its various manifestations. In the most narrow sense, iatrogenic disease includes only illnesses that would not have come about if sound and professionally recommended treatment had *not* been applied. Within this definition, a patient could sue his therapist if the latter, in the course of his management, failed to apply a recommended treatment that, in the physician's opinion, would have risked making him sick. In a more general and more widely accepted sense, clinical iatrogenic disease comprises all clinical conditions for which remedies, physicians, or hospitals are the pathogens, or 'sickening' agents. I will call this plethora of therapeutic side-effects *clinical iatrogenesis*. They are as old as medicine itself, and have always been a subject of medical studies.

Medicines have always been potentially poisonous, but their unwanted side-effects have increased with their power and widespread use. Every twenty-four to thirty-six hours, from 50 to 80 per cent of adults in the United States and the United Kingdom swallow a medically prescribed chemical. Some take the wrong drug; others get an old or a contaminated batch, and others a counterfeit; others take several drugs in dangerous combinations, and still others receive injections with improperly sterilized syringes. Some drugs are addictive, others mutilating, and others mutagenic, although perhaps only in combination with food coloring or insecticides. In some patients, antibiotics alter the normal bacterial flora and induce a superinfection, permitting more resistant organisms to proliferate and invade the host. Other drugs contribute to the breeding of drug-resistant strains of bacteria. Subtle kinds of poisoning thus have spread even faster than the bewildering variety and ubiquity of nostrums. Unnecessary surgery is a standard procedure. *Disabling nondiseases* result from the medical treatment of nonexistent diseases and are on the increase: the number of children disabled in Massachusetts through the treatment of cardiac nondisease exceeds the number of children under effective treatment for real cardiac disease.

Doctor-inflicted pain and infirmity have always been a part of medical practice. Professional callousness, negligence, and sheer incompetence are age-old forms of malpractice. The problem, however, is that most of the damage inflicted by the modern doctor occurs in the ordinary practice of well-trained men and women who have learned to bow to prevailing professional judgment and procedure, even though they know (or could and should know) what damage they do.

The United States Department of Health, Education and Welfare calculates that 7 per cent of all patients suffer compensable injuries while hospitalized, though few of them do anything about it. Moreover, the frequency of reported accidents in hospitals is higher than in all industries but mines and high-rise construction. Accidents are the major cause of death in American children. In proportion to the time spent there, these accidents seem to occur more often in hospitals than in any other kind of place. One in fifty children admitted to a hospital suffers an accident which requires specific treatment. University hospitals are relatively more pathogenic, or, in blunt language, more sickening. It has also been established that one out of every five patients admitted to a typical research hospital acquires an iatrogenic disease, sometimes trivial, usually requiring special treatment, and in one case in thirty leading to death. Half of these episodes result from complications of drug therapy; amazingly, one in ten comes from diagnostic procedures. Despite good intentions and claims to public service, a military officer with a similar record of performance would be relieved of his command, and a restaurant or amusement center would be closed by the police. No wonder that the health industry tries to shift the blame for the damage caused onto the victim, and that the dope-sheet of a multinational pharmaceutical concern tells its readers that 'iatrogenic disease is almost always of neurotic origin'.

Defenseless patients

The undesirable side effects of approved, mistaken, callous, or contraindicated technical contacts with the medical system represent just the first level of pathogenic medicine. Such *clinical iatrogenesis* includes not only the damage that doctors inflict with the intent of curing or of exploiting the patient, but also those other torts that result from the doctor's attempt to protect himself against the possibility of a suit for malpractice. Such attempts to avoid litigation and persecution may now do more damage than any other iatrogenic stimulus.

On a second level, medical practice sponsors sickness by reinforcing a morbid society that encourages people to become consumers of curative, preventive, industrial, and environmental medicine. On the one hand defectives survive in increasing numbers and are fit only for life under institutional care, while on the other hand, medically certified symptoms exempt people from industrial work and thereby remove them from the scene of political struggle to reshape the society that has made them sick. Second-level iatrogenesis finds its expression in various symptoms of social overmedicalization that amount to what I shall call the expropriation of health. This second-level impact of medicine I designate as *social iatrogenesis*.

On the third level, the so-called health professions have an even deeper, culturally health-denying effect insofar as they destroy the potential of people to deal with their human weakness, vulnerability, and uniqueness in a personal and autonomous way. The patient in the grip of contemporary medicine is but one of mankind in the grip of its pernicious techniques. This *cultural iatrogenesis* is the ultimate backlash of hygienic progress and consists in the paralysis of healthy responses to suffering, impairment, and death. It occurs when people accept health management designed on the engineering model, when they conspire in an attempt to produce, as if it were a commodity, something called 'better health'. This inevitably results in the managed maintenance of life on high levels of sublethal illness. This ultimate evil of medical 'progress' must be clearly distinguished from both clinical and social iatrogenesis.

I hope to show that on each of its three levels iatrogenesis has become medically irreversible: a feature built right into the medical endeavour. The unwanted physiological social, and psychological by-products of diagnostic and therapeutic progress have become resistant to medical remedies. New devices, approaches, and organizational arrangements, which are conceived as remedies for clinical and social iatrogenesis, themselves tend to become pathogens contributing to the new epidemic. Technical and managerial measures taken on any level to avoid damaging the patient by his treatment tend to engender a self-reinforcing iatrogenic loop analogous to the escalating destruction generated by the polluting procedures used as antipollution devices.

I will designate this self-reinforcing loop of negative institutional feedback by its classical Greek equivalent and call it *medical nemesis*. The Greeks saw gods in the forces of nature. For them, nemesis represented divine vengeance visited upon mortals who infringe on those prerogatives the gods enviously guard for themselves. Nemesis was the inevitable punishment for attempts to be a hero rather than a human being.

Like most abstract Greek nouns, Nemesis took the shape of a divinity. She represented nature's response to *hubris:* to the individual's presumption in seeking to acquire the attributes of a god. Our contemporary hygienic hubris has led to the new syndrome of medical nemesis.

By using the Greek term I want to emphasize that the corresponding phenomenon does not fit within the explanatory paradigm now offered by bureaucrats, therapists, and ideologues for the snowballing diseconomies and disutilities that, lacking all intuition, they have engineered and that they tend to call the 'counterintuitive behavior of large systems'. By invoking myths and ancestral gods I should make it clear that my framework for analysis of the current breakdown of medicine is foreign to the industrially determined logic and ethos. I believe that the *reversal of nemesis* can come only from within man and not from yet another managed (heteronomous) source dependent once again on presumptuous expertise and subsequent mystification.

Medical nemesis is resistant to medical remedies. It can be reversed only through a recovery of the will to self-care among the laity, and through the legal, political, and institutional recognition of the right to care, which imposes limits upon the professional monopoly of physicians. I do not suggest any specific forms of health care or sick-care, and I do not advocate any new medical philosophy any more than I recommend remedies for medical technique, doctrine, or organization. However, I do propose an alternative approach to the use of medical organization and technology together with the allied bureaucracies and illusions.

Ivan Illich is a theologian and philosopher who lives and works in Cuernavaca, Mexico. He is the author of several books including *Celebration of Awareness* (1969), *Deschooling Society* (1971), *Tools for Conviviality* (1973) and *Limits to Medicine* (1976). This article, which has been edited, originally appeared as the first chapter to the last mentioned book and was published by Marion Boyars, London. The extensive footnotes and references that accompanied the original version have been omitted here.

46 | The mode of state intervention in the health sector

VICENTE NAVARRO

Mechanisms of state intervention

Let us now analyze the specific mechanisms of state intervention in capitalist societies. And let us begin by somewhat arbitrarily dividing those interventions into primarily two levels: one of negative and the other of positive selection.

A. Negative selection mechanisms

By negative selection, I mean that mode of intervention that systematically and continually excludes those strategies that conflict with the class nature of the capitalist society. This negative intervention takes place through (a) structural selective mechanisms, (b) ideological mechanisms, (c) decision-making mechanisms, and (d) repressive coercion mechanisms.

Structural selective mechanisms
These mechanisms refer to the exclusion of alternatives that threaten the capitalist system, an exclusion that is inherent in the nature of the capitalist state. In fact, the overall priority given to property and capital accumulation explains why, when health and property conflict, the latter usually takes priority over the former. For example, the appalling lack of adequate legislation protecting the worker in most capitalist societies (including social democratic Sweden) contrasts most dramatically with the large array of laws protecting private property and its owners.

This structural negative selective mechanism also appears in the implied assumption that all health programs and reforms have to take place within the set of class relations prevalent in capitalist societies. For example, in Britain, Bevan's Labour Party strategy of implementing the NHS (a victory for the British working class) assumed an unalterability of class relations in Britain. Indeed, the creation of the NHS was seen as taking place within the structure of capitalist Britain of 1948, respecting the class distribution of power both outside and within the health sector. Bevan relied very heavily on the consultants, who clearly were of upper class extraction and position, to break the general practitioner's resistance against the implementation of the NHS. As he proudly indicated, 'I bought them with gold.'[1] The strategy of using the nationalization of the health sector to break with the class structure outside and within the health sector, as Lenin did in the Soviet Union, was not even considered.[2]

Moreover, to reassure the medical profession in general and the consultants in particular, they were given dominant influence over the process of planning, regulation, and administration of the health sector.[3]

Ideological mechanisms
These mechanisms insure the exclusion from the realm of debate of ideologies that conflict with the system. In other words, it is not only programs and policies, as indicated before, that are being automatically excluded, but, more importantly, conflicting ideologies as well. This is clearly shown in the lack of attention to and the lack of research in areas that conflict with the requirements and needs of the capitalist system. Reflecting the bourgeois bias of the medical research establishment for example, much priority is given to the assumedly individual causation of disease. One instance, among others, is that most research on heart disease – one of the main killers in society – has focused on diet, exercise, and genetic inheritance. On the study of these etiologies, millions of pounds, dollars, marks, and francs have been spent. However, in a fifteen-year study of aging, cited in a most interesting report prepared by a special task force to the Secretary of Health, Education, and Welfare in the US, it was found that the most important predictor of longevity was work satisfaction. Let me quote from that report:

> . . . the strongest predictor of longevity was work satisfaction. The second best predictor was over-all 'happiness' . . . Other factors are undoubtedly important – diet, exercise, medical care, and genetic inheritance. But research findings suggest that these factors may account for only about 25% of the risk factors in heart disease, the major cause of death. That is, if cholesterol, blood pressure, smoking, glucose level, serum uric acid, and so forth, were perfectly controlled, only about one-fourth of coronary heart disease could be controlled. Although research on this problem has not led to conclusive answers, it appears that work role, work conditions, and other social factors may contribute heavily to this 'unexplained' 75% of risk factors.[4]

But very few studies have investigated these socio-political factors. [. . .] In summary, the exclusion of ideologies which question or threaten the basic assumptions of the capitalist system is a most prevalent mechanism of state intervention, i.e. the exclusion as unthinkable of any alternatives to that system.

Decision making mechanisms
The decision making processes are heavily weighted in favor of certain groups and classes, and thus against certain others. For example, the mechanisms of selection and appointment of members to health planning and administrative agencies in Britain and to the Health System Agencies in the US are conducive to the dominance over those bodies of individuals of the corporate and upper-middle classes, to the detriment of members of lower-middle and working classes.

Repressive coercion mechanisms
The final form of negative selection, repressive coercion mechanisms, takes place either through the use of direct force or, more importantly, by cutting (and thus nullifying) those programs that may conflict with sources of power within the state organism.

B. Positive selection mechanisms

By positive selection, I mean the type of state intervention that generates, stimulates, and determines a positive response favorable to overall capital accumulation, as opposed to a negative selection which excludes anticapitalist possibilities. Offe distinguishes between two types of such intervention – allocative and productive.[5] In the former, the state regulates and coordinates the allocation of resources that have already been produced, while in the latter, the state becomes directly involved in the production of goods and services.

Allocative intervention policies
These policies are based on the authority of the state in influencing, guiding and even directing the main activities of society, including the most important one – capital accumulation. The policies are put into effect primarily (although not exclusively) through laws that make certain behavior mandatory and through regulations that make certain claims legal. In the health sector, examples of the former are laws requiring doctors to register contagious disease with the state health department and for employers to install protective devices to prevent industrial accidents, while an example of the latter is regulations determining that certain categories of people receive health insurance. Both laws and regulations are determined and dictated in the world of politics. As Offe indicates, in allocative functions 'policy and politics are not differentiated'. And, as such, those policies are determined by the different degrees of dominance of the branches of the state by pressure groups and factions primarily within the dominant class.

Productive intervention policies
As I have indicated, productive intervention policies are those whereby the state directly participates in the production of resources, e.g. medical education in most Western capitalist countries, production of drugs in nationalized drug industries, management of public hospitals, medical research, etc.

Both allocative and productive policies have increased dramatically in all capitalist countries since World War II and, along with that increase, a shift has taken place from allocative to productive policies. An example of the latter is the production of medical knowledge, where there has been a shift in state intervention from an allocative function (e.g. subsidies, tax benefits) to actual production: (e.g. nationalization of medical schools and research institutions). Similarly, there is a trend in the health sector to move from national insurance schemes (allocative) to national health services (productive). Britain in 1948, Quebec (Canada) in 1968, and Italy in the 1970s are each examples of that trend. In all capitalist countries, there has been an impressive growth of state intervention, primarily of the productive type of intervention, as measured by either public expenditures or public employment. Moreover, this growth has taken place mainly in the social (including health) services sector.

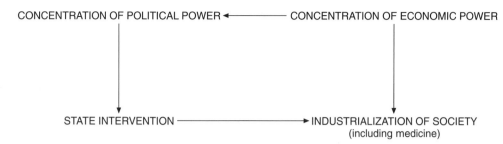

Figure 46.1 The dialectical relationship between concentration of economic power and industrialization of society (including medicine)

The reasons for the growth of state intervention

The growth of the health sector in developed capitalist countries is due to the growth of social needs, which are determined by the process of capital accumulation and by the heightening of the level of class struggle. Let me expand on each.

The growth of social needs as demanded by the process of capital accumulation

A primary characteristic of that process of accumulation is, as indicated earlier, its concentration. Indeed, insurance, banking, manufacturing, and other sectors of economic life are in the hands of an increasingly small number of corporations that, for the most part, control the market in each sector. The consequences of that concentration are many but, among them, the most important is the type of technology and industrial development determined by and intended primarily to serve the needs of that concentration. And determined by that economic concentration and by that type of technological and industrial development are the following:

- *A division of labor, with a continuous demand for specialization* that fragments the process of production and ultimately the producer himself . . . In summary, and as expressed in Figure 46.1, increased economic concentration determines a growing concentration of political power and a greater need for state intervention to facilitate the type of industrialization demanded by that economic concentration – an industrialization that influences and determines the type of specialized medicine that is prevalent today.

    Let me clarify here that I believe the relationship among these categories to be dialectical, not linear, with a pattern of dominance that is expressed by the main direction of the arrow in Figure 46.1.
- *An invasion of all sectors of economic life by corporate capital.* Indeed, it is a tendency of the process of capital accumulation that the search for profits invades all sectors of economic life, including social services such as health, education, transportation, etc.
- *An invasion of the spheres of social life by corporate capital and its process of industrialization,* causing dislocation, diswelfare, and insecurity that state intervention, through social services (including medicine) is in turn supposed to mitigate. The

most important example, of course, is the alienation that the industrialized process of production causes in the working population – an alienation that becomes reflected in psychosomatic conditions which medicine is supposed to care for and cure. Similarly, occupational diseases and environmental damage are, for the most part, also corporately caused, but, according to bourgeois ideology, individually cured through medical intervention.

- *An invasion of corporate capital into the spheres of private life*, with the commodification of all processes of interpersonal relationships, from sex to the pursuit of happiness. Indeed, according to corporate ideology, happiness depends on the amount and type of consumption, i.e. on what the citizen has, not on what he or she does.
- *An increased proletarianization of the population*, including the medical profession. As a result, the health professions have shifted from being independent entrepreneurs to becoming employees of private medical corporations (as in the US) or employees of the state (as in the majority of European capitalist countries). In both cases, that process of proletarianization is stimulated by the state, with the assistance of the corporate segments of the capitalist class.
- *An increased concentration of resources in urban areas*, and deployment of resources to those areas, required and needed for the realization of capital. This process of urbanization necessitates a growth in the allocative functions of the state (e.g. land use legislation and city planning) and of productive functions (e.g. roads and sanitation) so as to support, guide, and direct that process in a way that is responsive to the needs of capital accumulation. It is worth underlining in this context that the majority of infrastructural services are consumed by components of Capital and not by private households. For example, three-quarters of the US water supply is consumed by industry and agriculture (mainly corporate), while private households consume less than one-quarter. Water supply, however, is paid for largely from funds coming from the latter, not from the former.

Moreover, this process of economic concentration, and its concomitant industrialization determines a model of production and distribution in medicine that replicates the characteristics of the overall process of economic production and distribution, i.e. specialization, concentration, urbanization and a technical orientation of medicine. The nature of medicine, then, and its relation to the overall process of production determine in large degree its *characteristics*. And its position within that process of production explains its function, which is to take care of and solve the unsolvable – the diswelfare and dysfunctions created by that very process of production.

The level of class struggle
The tendencies explained in the previous section are the result of the growing needs of capital accumulation which take place within the context of a continuous conflict between Capital and Labor – a conflict primarily between the capitalist class and the working class. Indeed, the working class aims continuously at extracting significant concessions from the state, over and above what the state considers sufficient for the needs of capital accumulation defined in the previous section. For example, it is impossible to understand the creation of the NHS in Britain without taking into account the relationship of class forces in Britain and the wartime radicalization of the working class that had called into question 'the survival of capitalism'. As Forsyth has indicated:

Rightly or wrongly the British Government at the outbreak of war could not be sure that large sections of the working class were entirely satisfied about the reasons for fighting the war . . . For the sake of public morale the Government tried to make it clear that after the war things were going to be very different from the heartbreak conditions of the 'thirties'.[6]

The much heralded consensus on the need for a national health service that existed among Labour and Conservative politicians was the result of the radicalization of the working class on the one hand, and the concern for the survival of capitalism by the capitalist class and the state on the other. Indeed, labor movements have historically viewed social services (including health) as part of the *social wage*, to be defended and increased in the same way that *money wages* are. In fact, Wilensky has shown how the size of social wages depends, in large degree, on the level of militancy of the labor movements.[7] Thus, contrary to popular belief, the size and nature of social benefits in terms of social services is higher in France and Italy than in Scandinavia or even in Britain. And I attribute this to the greater militancy of the unions in those countries and to the existence of mass Socialist and Communist parties (whose platforms are, at least in theory, anticapitalist) that force an increase of social wages upon the state. Another indicator is the percentage of GNP spent on social security which, in 1965, was 17.5 per cent in Italy, 18.3 per cent in France, but only 7.9 per cent in the US. The practical absence of a comprehensive coverage for social benefits in the US is also undoubtedly due to the lack of an organized left party.

In summary, then, the nature and growth of the state in contemporary capitalist societies can be attributed to the increased *social needs of capital* and *social demands of labor*. And in order to understand the nature of any state policy, including health policy, we have to place our analysis within those parameters. Having said that, let me clarify two points. First, there is no single-factor explanation of social policy. Rather, it is explained by the combination of factors already mentioned. And the nature and number of those combinations will depend on the *historical* origins of each factor, the *political* form determining the factor and its relation to others, and its *function* in that specific social formation. Second, there is no clear cut dichotomy between the social needs of capital and the social demands of labor. Any given policy can serve both. Indeed, social policies that serve the interests of the working class can be subsequently adapted to benefit the interests of the dominant class. As Miliband and others have shown so well, the 'bias of the system' has always insured that these policies can be deflected to suit the capitalist class. Indeed, history shows that concessions won by labor in the class struggle become, *in the absence of further struggle*, modified to serve the interests of the capitalist class.

In summary, I have aimed to show that if we are to understand the nature, composition, distribution and function of the medical care sector in Western developed capitalist societies, we must first understand the distribution of power in those societies and the nature, role, and instrumentality of the state. This understanding leads us to realize that (a) the assumedly transcended and diluted category of social class is a much needed category in understanding the distribution of power in our societies; and that (b) class struggle, far from being an outmoded concept of interest only to 'vulgar' Marxists, is most relevant indeed and as much needed today to understand the nature of our societies and of our health sectors as it was when Marx and Engels wrote that 'class struggle is the motor of history'.

Needless to say, this interpretation is a minority voice in our Western academic setting. It is in conflict with the prevalent explanations of the health sector, and this accounts for its exclusion from the realm of debate. Still, its veracity will be affirmed not by its 'popularity' in the corridors of power, which will be nil, but in its verification on the terrain of history. It is because of this that I dedicated this article to all those with whom I share a praxis aimed at building up a society of truly free and self-governing men and women – a society in which, as Marx indicated, the state (and I would add medicine) will he converted 'from an organ superimposed upon society into one completely subordinated to it'.[8]

References

1. See Tudor Hart, J. 'Primary care in the industrial areas of Britain: evolution and current problems', *International Journal of Health Services*, **2**(3), 349–365 (1972) and 'Bevan and the Doctors', *Lancet*, **2**(7839), 1196–1197 (1973).
2. For Lenin's strategy in health services, see 'Leninism and medicine'. In Navarro, V. *The Political Economy of Social Security and Medical Care in the USSR*.
3. For an excellent analysis of the professional dominance in the NHS, see Robson, J. 'The NHS company inc.? the social consequence of the professional dominance in the National Health Service', *International Journal of Health Services*, **3**(3), 413–426 (1973). Also Draper, P. and Smart, T. 'Social science and health policy in the United Kingdom: some contributions of the social sciences to the bureaucratization of the National Health Service', *International Journal of Health Services*, **4**(3), 453–470 (1974).
4. Special Task Force to the Secretary of Health, Education and Welfare, *Work in America*, M.I.T. Press, Cambridge, MA., pp. 77–79 (1973).
5. Offe, C. 'The theory of the capitalist state and the problem of policy formation'. In Lindberg, L. *et al.* (eds) *Stress and Contradiction in Modern Capitalism*, Lexington Books, London, p. 128 (1975).
6. Forsyth, G. *Doctors and State Medicine: A Study of the British Health Service*, Pitman and Sons, London, p. 16 (1973).
7. Wilensky, H.L. *The Welfare State and Equality*, University of California Press, Berkeley and Los Angeles (1975).
8. Marx, K. *Critique of the Gotha Program*, International Publishers, New York (1938).

Vicente Navarro is Professor of Health and Social Policy at The Johns Hopkins University, Baltimore, USA. This article is an edited extract from his book *Medicine Under Capitalism* which was published by Prodist, New York (1976).

PART 5

The social context
of health care

| INTRODUCTION

Just as the concept of health means different things to different people in different places (see the variety of conflicting perspectives in the articles chosen for Part 1 of this book), so the content, objectives and organization of health care varies tremendously, being influenced by history, social circumstances and cultural preferences. The articles in Part 5 reflect some of this diversity.

D.R. Gwatkin, Director of the World Bank's International Health Policy Program, provides a useful starting point in 'Health inequalities and the health of the poor: what do we know? What can we do?' As he notes, health policy has tended to oscillate between the two broad objectives of efficiency and equity, at some times being primarily concerned with the efficient organization and use of health care resources, at others placing more emphasis on the degree to which health systems and health policy are in line with concerns for fairness. Gwatkin acknowledges that the health care sector may not be the most important mechanism for tackling inequalities, but suggests that health professionals do have a comparative advantage in that sector and should at least identify what can be done within it. However, his central point is that different strategies for health improvement may have radically different distributional implications, underlining the need to move away from the emphasis on national averages when measuring health.

Ann Bowling is also concerned about inequalities in health care, with a focus on the way in which a patient's age may be used as a basis for deciding whether and how to treat particular health problems such as cardiovascular disease. There is fairly clear evidence that this happens, but as Bowling notes in 'Ageism in cardiology' there are very different views on this: some analysts suggest that using age as a basis for rationing is reasonable as the elderly have had a 'fair innings', while others reject this as prejudiced, unethical and ageist. Such an atmosphere is not conducive to cool analysis and recommendation, but without it we may find ourselves with a health system that is neither equitable nor efficient.

Similar issues are raised by Underwood and Bailey's proposition that coronary bypass surgery should not be offered to people who smoke, partly on the grounds that they are more likely to have complications, longer hospital stays and generally a poorer outcome than non-smokers, and partly because doing so reduces the resources available to treat non-smokers who would derive more benefit. Implicit in this argument is the view that smokers bear some personal responsibility for their ill-health, which should be taken into account when allocating scarce resources. Matthew Shiu's response, contained in the same chapter, illustrates some of the difficulties inherent in this approach: if smokers are penalized for failing to stop smoking, what about patients with high cholesterol who fail to adhere to therapy, or patients with sexually transmitted diseases from unprotected encounters, or those involved in road traffic accidents while drunk? And what if it would be cheaper in the long run to treat such patients than to refuse them and unleash other consequences?

One framework within which such difficult questions might be handled is the 'evidence based medicine' approach, as advocated by David Sackett and colleagues. The 'EBM' project is an attempt to bring best clinical evidence systematically to bear on individual patient care. Even within its own terms of reference this is no small task, bearing in mind the difficulties of identifying and synthesizing external research evidence, and the complexities of facilitating the timely and appropriate use of this evidence by clinicians. Within this framework, it is hard to see ageism or other prejudices thriving, as care decisions would be based on maximizing quality and quantity of life for individual patients. However, the authors state that 'good doctors' also use individual clinical expertise, arguing that the best available external evidence cannot identify which treatment protocol is appropriate for an individual patient's needs. As the correspondence provoked by this article indicates, the concept of evidence based medicine is keenly contested. Some critics are primarily concerned that the way evidence is defined is too circumscribed, or that the appeal to individual clinical expertise gives doctors an opt-out from following EBM's dictates; others, such as Alan Maynard, accuse EBM's advocates of ignoring the need to consider costs as well as effectiveness.

Ray Fitzpatrick and Deena White explore another aspect of health care's evidence base: the frequent failure to involve patients in evaluating the contents and outcomes of health care. For them, patient involvement goes far beyond measuring patient satisfaction and preferences, or giving them health status and quality of life questionnaires. Ultimately, they argue, what is required is a means of translating patient preferences into the way health care is planned and delivered.

There are similarities in the conclusion of Andy Alaszewski and Ian Harvey's review of the way health technologies are adopted. In this account, the medical profession has increasingly seized control of the process of technical innovation, with motives that are not entirely disinterested. They suggest one consequence has been a decline in the willingness of the public and patients to trust the judgements and assessments of professionals concerning the risk of these technologies. Only by greater public participation in decision making, they argue, will this trust be restored.

Chris Ham is also concerned with the motivations of decision makers and clinicians, but for him the key question is the assumptions politicians make about these motivations when diagnosing health care problems and designing policy solutions. In particular, Ham highlights the contrast between policies that assume health professionals can and should be closely directed from the centre, policies which relied on professionals responding predictably within carefully designed incentive systems and policies that characterize professionals as obstructive 'forces of conservatism' who need to be confronted and reformed. Perhaps not surprisingly, Ham concludes that an amalgam of policy mechanisms is required that is not tied to a single simplistic view of motivation, but does support and reward professionals committed to innovation and good practice.

'Health sector reform: lessons from China' by Gerald Bloom and Gu Xingyuan illustrates some of Ham's concerns on a very much larger scale. From a centrally controlled, hierarchical and closely directed health system, China has moved since the 1980s towards a 'socialist market economy' in which the health system has become more individualistic, decentralized, unplanned, market-led and unequally provided. The authors concede that there is as yet no evidence that health has been adversely affected by these changes, which have taken place in a context of very rapid economic growth. But the clear implication is that the health needs of the rural poor are no longer a political priority, and that in time this will be reflected in health inequalities. The broader conclusion is that the health system usually reflects and seldom leads the broader prevailing political agenda.

Differences and similarities in 'The evolution of the health-care systems in the United States and the United Kingdom' also illustrate the importance of social context, as the social historian Rosemary Stevens' analysis makes clear. She traces the point of divergence to the social structure of the two countries in the nineteenth century, using as an example the degree to which medical practice is separated into specialties. In the UK there are numerous general practitioners (GPs), whose profession originated in the trade guilds of earlier centuries; today their earnings derive from the state, they govern primary care and act as 'gatekeepers', referring patients to hospital specialists. Thus, the separation of primary and secondary care in the UK preserved the role of the GP while allowing the increasing specialization of hospital consultants and services. By contrast, in the USA, the generalist family practitioner had all but disappeared by the First World War. Medical practitioners in the USA had specialized early on (the system was based on competition), and patients have long had direct access to individual specialists. The consequences of this divergence are still evident in the twenty-first century.

The influence of the past on the future is also one of the themes taken up by Martin McKee and Judith Healy in the final chapter in Part 5, 'The role of the hospital in a changing environment'. Hospitals are one of the core institutions of most health care systems, yet they are difficult to adapt to changing circumstances. Their physical configuration reflects the concerns and needs of the period in which they were built, and they are often staffed by élites who are well equipped to oppose unwelcome reforms. One striking feature of McKee and Healy's review is the extent to which hospital policy – for example, towards centralization or decentralization of services – has been unsupported by convincing evidence. Another theme also found elsewhere in Part 5 is the wide range of belief systems and philosophies underlying attempts to improve hospital performance. Looking into the future, the only certainty is that the role of the hospital, and of the health care system in its entirety, will continue to be profoundly influenced by its social context.

47 | Health inequalities and the health of the poor: What do we know? What can we do?

D.R. GWATKIN

The setting: renewed concern for health inequalities

The interest of the international community in health inequalities has varied greatly in recent years. It was high from around the mid-1970s to mid-1980s. It was then displaced by greater concern for health system efficiency and sustainability. More recently, the interest in equality, equity, and the health of the poor has begun to rise again.

While all this is encouraging for those concerned with health equity and the health of the poor, it remains far from enough to guarantee significant improvements in the current situation. The serious problems presented by inadequate health among the neediest require far more than a few policy pronouncements, statistical studies, and international meetings to combat successfully.

Although the health sector is not necessarily the most important channel for dealing with inequalities, it is the field in which health professionals have the greatest expertise and thus a comparative advantage. This provides a rationale for health professionals to devote at least some of their time and energy to the health sector, to see what they can do within it to support the struggle for a more equal society. This paper therefore concentrates on the health sector, and suggests two initial steps which health professionals might take, as part of the far broader effort that will be required in this direction – that is, towards increasing the degree and the effectiveness of the health sector's concern for health inequalities.

Establishing objectives: coming to terms with the poverty-equality-equity distinction

The first step is to think more clearly about objectives. This means, in the first instance, coming to terms with three streams of thought existing within the international community concerning the most appropriate objective when dealing with the health of disadvantaged population groups. These streams focus on: 1) improving the health of the poor; 2) reducing poor-rich health inequalities; and 3) re-dressing health inequities.

What are the similarities and differences among these three streams? Those concerned with poverty and those more interested in reducing inequality or inequity all share a recognition that in health, as in many other fields, societal averages typically disguise as much as they reveal. Their interest is thus not in health conditions that prevail in society as a whole, but in the condition of different socioeconomic groups within society – especially in that of the lowest or most disadvantaged groups. But within this shared concern lie a number of distinctions. Those who approach health from a poverty perspective are typically concerned primarily with improving the health of the poor alone, rather than with reducing differences between poor and rich. For those oriented towards equality, the principal objective is the reduction of poor-rich health differences. Those concerned with health inequities are concerned with righting the injustice represented by inequalities or poor health conditions among the disadvantaged.

Their shared concern for the distribution of health benefits places advocates of all the approaches described here squarely at odds with the currently predominant school of international thought about health systems. Members of this school are concerned primarily with the efficiency of health systems in bringing about improvements in health conditions prevailing in society at large, and with the reforms required to achieve this objective. Proponents of the alternative, poverty/equality/equity viewpoint, just described, are no less convinced of the need for health system reforms. But the reforms they consider necessary would have a very different objective – to see that the systems are more equitable and reach the poor more effectively, rather than that the systems are more efficient in serving society at large.

Compared with the distinction between overall efficiency on the one hand and poverty-equality-equity on the other, the differences between the poverty-oriented, the equality-oriented, and the equity-oriented health policy advocates approach insignificance. This implies that the advocates of poverty/equality/equity-oriented health systems reform can most productively focus on what unites them rather than on the distinctions between them.

Taking the next step: formulating health policy goals in distributional terms

With the conceptual underbrush cleared away, the next step is to begin thinking operationally. This means, in the first instance, formulating health policy goals with greater attention to specific health problems of the poor, which distinguish them from the rich. Surprisingly, this has rarely been done.

In economic development, the evolution of the 'basic human needs' school of thought gave rise to a tradition of expressing general development goals, not in terms of a society's average per capita income growth, which was the earlier tradition, but in terms of what was happening to the incomes of people in poverty. It also led to the establishment of data collection systems specific to the poor.

But nothing similar happened in health. Those concerned with poverty tended to rely primarily on general humanitarian appeals, which proved quite effective in mobilizing support, without employing the rigorous epidemiological tools to the measurement of poor-rich differentials and of conditions prevailing among the poor. To the extent that rigorous tools were employed, they were applied to the development of overall goals for societies as a whole. The result is a deficiency that has two aspects: a lack of health goals that are relevant for the poor; and a lack of the information needed to track progress towards such goals.

The need for more relevant goals. Only rarely have health goals been expressed in terms relevant for equity enhancement or poverty reduction. Almost inevitably, health goals are stated in terms of some societal average: say, a decline of x% in a country's infant or maternal mortality rate, or an increase of y years in its life expectancy.

A recent, prominent example illustrating this point, and the difference in contemporary thinking about economic and about health goals, is the set of year 2015 targets developed by the Organization for Economic Co-operation and Development (OECD). The economic target is stated in terms that are exclusively distributional. In accord with current economic approaches to poverty lessening, the target is to reduce by at least one-half the proportion of people living in extreme poverty in developing countries.

In contrast, the principal health target makes no reference to the health of those living in poverty. It is stated, rather, in the health equivalent of the earlier tradition of expressing economic goals in terms of raising average per capita income growth. That is, the principal health indicators used are the national infant and child mortality rates, which are societal averages, and which are to be reduced by two-thirds in each developing country.

While achievement of the OECD goals might benefit the poor, it would also be possible to achieve this goal by reducing deaths with significantly larger declines among the non-poor. The existing range of possibilities can be illustrated by considering two very different scenarios by which the OECD target of a two-thirds reduction in infant mortality might be reached.

- A 'top-down' strategy, under which reductions in the upper classes come first, followed by reductions in the middle classes, and only later by improvements in conditions among the poor.
- A 'bottom-up' strategy which, as its name suggests, is the converse of the top-down strategy described. Infant mortality reductions start in the poorest segment of the population, then spread to the next-poorest, and continue up the economic class scale until the OECD target is achieved.

For the present purposes, data from three countries – Bolivia, Côte d'Ivoire, and India – are used to show the range of possibilities that exist. The possibilities are illustrated through a pair of estimates for each country. One estimate shows the results of following an extreme form of the top-down approach just described. The second estimate permits identification of the impact of following the most extreme form of a bottom-up approach.

Table 47.1 presents the infant mortality level that would prevail in each population quintile after achieving the OECD objective through a top-down and a bottom-up strategy. For comparative purposes, information about the infant mortality level currently prevailing in each quintile is also provided. Even a cursory glance at Table 47.1 suffices to show that the distributional situations produced by following a top-down and a bottom-up strategy differ greatly from one another.

Table 47.1   Infant mortality rates[a], by wealth quintile, before and after achieving the OECD goal

	Bolivia			Côte d'Ivoire			India		
	Current level	Level after attaining OECD goal		Current level	Level after attaining OECD goal		Current level	Level after attaining OECD goal	
		'top-down' strategy	'bottom-up' strategy		'top-down' strategy	'bottom-up' strategy		'top-down' strategy	'bottom-up' strategy
Top 20% of population	25.5	7.0	25.5	63.3	7.0	63.3	44.0	7.0	44.0
Next-highest 20%	38.6	7.0	38.6	78.8	7.0	78.8	65.6	7.0	65.6
Middle 20%	75.5	7.0	52.7	86.9	7.0	10.8	89.7	7.0	31.1
Next-lowest 20%	85.0	7.0	7.0	97.3	7.0	7.0	106.3	7.0	7.0
Bottom 20%	106.5	74.4	7.0	117.2	110.3	7.0	109.2	101.5	7.0
Population average[b]	73.5	24.5	24.5	90.9	30.3	30.3	86.3	28.8	28.8

[a] Deaths under one year of age per 1000 live births; [b] Population averages are based on population quintile figures, weighted by the number of births in each quintile.

At present, the infant mortality rate in the bottom population quintile is roughly two to four times higher than it is in the top population quintile. Under the top-down strategy, that ratio would have increased greatly by the time the OECD goal is reached. Specifically, infant mortality would be in the order of eleven to sixteen times higher in the bottom than in the top quintile. Were the bottom-up strategy followed instead, the ratio would be reversed. That is, at the time of reaching the OECD goal, the infant mortality rate would be around four to nine times higher in the top that in the bottom quintile.

To be sure, such large differences result from producing estimates of situations that lie at the two extremes of the range of theoretically attainable possibilities. In the 'real world', the differences resulting from a determined effort to implement one strategy rather than the other, i.e. a top-down or a bottom-up strategy, would no doubt be much smaller than those indicated in Table 47.1. The results are nonetheless of interest for two reasons.

First, the breadth of the range, even though theoretical, is instructive as an indication of just how wide an array of distributional patterns the attainment of the OECD goal can accommodate. The fact that the framers of this goal, whose commitment to poverty reduction is not to be doubted, did not think of expressing the goal in distributional terms suggests that the existence of such a wide range of possible outcomes is not intuitively obvious.

Second, the range can serve as the starting point for speculation about the likely distributional consequences of an effort to reach the OECD goal through initiatives that focus only on the population average infant mortality rate, a focus which the goal's current formulation encourages. Such speculation leads to the suspicion that an outcome closer to that produced in the top-down illustration is at least more likely than that resulting from a bottom-up one. Admittedly, an extreme version of the top-down outcome may well seem improbable. But given the political realities of today's world and the role of political considerations in health policy formation, some variant of it appears considerably less implausible than a bottom-up scenario which would see most of the gains going to the poorest.

To the extent that the suspicion just presented is correct, one would be ill-advised to look to attainment of the OECD or other health goals stated in terms of population averages, to bring major improvements to the health of the poor, and even less to the reduction of poor-rich health inequalities. For the poor to benefit, it will be necessary to work towards goals that are stated in terms much more directly relevant to the disadvantaged.

The need for more relevant information. If correctly stated goals are to be meaningful, information to track progress towards achieving them must be readily available. Here, too, the health field has until recently been weak. Thus, for example, there were no distributional data on health to report in the *1998 World Development Indicators*[1]; and it remains silent about intra-country differences in health conditions. Rather, all health information relates to conditions in countries as a whole. There is information about infant mortality in entire country populations, but not about infant mortality among the poorest 20% of the population. Data are presented on the percentage of births attended by trained health staff; but not about the percentage of births among the poor who receive this service, or about how big the poor-rich difference is in this regard. Figures are provided for overall government health expenditures, but not for how the beneficiaries of these expenditures are distributed across economic classes.

Only now, well over a decade after poverty-orientated economists began collecting the data needed for equitable development, are there signs that this situation is about to change; and that health statisticians may soon begin to catch up in providing the data that policy planners need for poverty- and equality-oriented programmes.

Conclusion: from research to action

Global opinion has begun to shift towards an increased concern for the health of the poor and for a reduction in health inequalities. This interest now provides a better opportunity for movement towards action than has existed for the past decade or more. The priority need at present is to begin applying what is already known in order to obtain a political commitment and develop effective intervention strategies.

This paper proposes two initial actions that professionals can take to begin meeting the need.

- The first is that those concerned with health inequalities and the health of the poor should look beyond the issues that divide them and focus on the much more important beliefs which they share.
- The second is that they work towards the redefinition of health goals, now expressed primarily in terms of population averages, so that the goals refer directly to improving the conditions among the poorer groups and to reducing the differences between those groups and others in society.

The proposed actions remain very modest relative to the total need. They cannot legitimately claim to represent anything more than two early steps in the long journey to be covered if the health of the poor is to be improved and health inequalities lessened. Even small steps can be valuable, however.

Reference

1. World Bank. *1998 World Development Indicators*. Washington DC, The World Bank, 1998.

This article is an edited extract from a much longer original, published under the same title in the *Bulletin of the World Health Organization*, 2000, 78(1): 3–17. The author, D.R. Gwatkin, is Principle Health and Population Specialist, The World Bank, Washington USA.

48 | Ageism in cardiology

ANN BOWLING

Evidence

The ageing of the population is one of the major challenges facing health services. The growing number of older people is likely to place increasing demands on health services for access to effective health technology in cases in which this can enhance the quality, not just the quantity, of life. There is some evidence that age has been used as a criterion in allocating health care[1] and in inviting participation in screening programmes.[2] However the idea that a patient's age may be used as an explicit basis for priority setting has rarely been acknowledged.

Cardiovascular diseases are a common cause of death and disability among older people, and the use of appropriate health technology for diagnosis and treatment is expensive. Despite the slightly higher risks of perioperative mortality [deaths occurring soon after surgery] and morbidity in older people, if they are selected appropriately they are likely to gain substantial health benefits from cardiological interventions.[3–5] Ironically, although cardiac surgeons are increasingly operating on people aged 75 and older, analyses in Europe and the United States which examined both the rates and types of interventions used indicated that age biases exist in cardiology. The argument presented here – that ageism exists in health care – uses research on the equity of access to cardiological services.

[Higher] rates of potentially life saving and life enhancing cardiological interventions occur among younger people than among older people, despite the prevalence of cardiovascular disease being considerably higher among the latter group. Older people, and older women in particular, are less likely to receive appropriate cardiological investigations – from echo-cardiography to measuring cholesterol concentrations.[6] Older people are more likely to have more severe disease and to be treated medically rather than surgically,[7,8] and they are less likely to receive the most effective treatment after acute myocardial infarction [heart attack].[9] The effects of age on access to health care occur independently of sex.

Reasons

It is unknown whether implicitly age-based referrals, investigations, and treatment policies in primary care and secondary care reflect rationing criteria or prejudices against older people. The consequence of both rationing and prejudices are that younger people take priority over older people. In relation to rationing, shortages of resources might lead to discrimination against older patients on the basis of the belief that they are more expensive to treat (for example, they may need longer to recover after surgery), or that they have a shorter life expectancy and therefore resources should be diverted to younger people who would be expected to live longer. Age is frequently discussed as a criterion for rationing. It is defended on the grounds that older people have had their 'fair innings'.[10] It is rejected on the grounds that decision making on the basis of sociodemographic characteristics, without reference to relevant comorbidity and ability to benefit, is unethical.[11,12]

Age biases are likely to be a consequence of different values being attributed to different social groups and to age stereotyping. Any ageism in medicine is simply a reflection of ageist attitudes that exist in the wider society, where youth is given priority over age.

Ageism in medicine may be partly a consequence of lack of awareness of the evidence based literature on the treatment of older people. Variations in clinical decisions made on the basis of the age of the patient might also be caused by the differing thresholds for intervention that exist when a healthcare professional is faced with clinical uncertainty; these variations might also reflect preferences for selecting low risk, rather than high risk, patients to undergo interventions.

That variations in treatment exist is unsurprising given that people aged 65 and older, and certainly those who are 75 and older (most of whom are women), have been largely excluded from major clinical trials. They are therefore significantly under-represented in the evidence base used to determine clinical effectiveness.[13,14] Investigators have traditionally used age limits as cut off points when recruiting patients into clinical trials to minimise analytical problems caused by factors such as comorbidity and an increased risk of loss to long term follow up caused by death. Most of the evidence on the clinical effectiveness of treatments for older people is based on a few smaller trials and cohort studies. This research bias may have led clinicians to be cautious in treating very old people, especially older women.

The collective consequences of these biases, whatever their causes, is that older people may not be treated equitably when it comes to allocating healthcare resources. Moreover, current practice is not necessarily the most efficient for health or social services. Clinical delay or denying older people the benefit of certain interventions may lead to greater spending on 'maintenance' services such as those provided by district nurses, home helps, and 'meals on wheels' programmes. The provision of more invasive treatments could be cost effective if they enabled people to function independently.

Solutions

Patients are not usually in a position to assess the appropriateness of the care they receive, and they trust their doctors to act in their best interests. Ageism in medicine needs to be tackled to preserve – or recapture – this trust within an ageing population.

Clinicians, managers and educationalists need to work together to eradicate it. A wide ranging approach is required if equity in the provision of healthcare by age is to be ensured.

Clinical guidelines should be developed and regularly updated to enable clinicians to make more informed decisions about treating older people, and access to investigations and treatments should be monitored centrally. Educational efforts are needed to increase the awareness of the public and professionals that age stereotyping and ageist attitudes are not acceptable and that ageist stances in clinical and health policy decision making are unethical. The major medical bodies that fund research now specify that exclusion from clinical trials on the grounds of age alone are no longer acceptable without justification. We should empower older people to influence the choices and standards of treatments offered. This could be achieved by publicly disseminating information on treatment alternatives and investigating patients' preferences for treatments.

Finally, recourse to the law to eradicate ageist attitudes and practices could be considered through the enactment of an age discrimination act. Older people would then be less likely to suffer discrimination, particularly if discrimination perpetrated to save money became illegal, as it is under the Race Relations Act. It is only by eliminating ageism in clinical research and practice that valid information on clinical effectiveness can be established and the necessary level of funding for health services can be identified.

References

1. Audit Commission. *Dear to our hearts? Commissioning services for the treatment and prevention of coronary disease.* London: HMSO 1995.
2. Sutton, G.C. Will you still need me, will you still screen me, when I'm past 64? *BMJ* 1997; **315**: 1032–3.
3. Royal College of Physicians. *Cardiological intervention in elderly patients. A report of a working group of the Royal College of Physicians.* London: RCP, 1991.
4. Gilbert, T., Orr, W., Banning, A.P. Surgery for aortic stenosis in severely symptomatic patients older that 80 years: experience in a single UK centre. *Heart* 1999; **82**: 138–42.
5. Cheitlin, M.D. Coronary artery bypass surgery in the elderly. *Clin Geriatr Med* 1996; **12**: 195–205.
6. Bowling, A., Riccardi, G., La Torre, G., *et al.* The effect of age on the treatment and referral of older people with cardiovascular disease [abstract]. *J Epidemiol Commun Health* 1995; **53**: 658.
7. Stone, P.H., Thompson, B., Anderson, H.V., *et al.* Influence of race, sex and age on management of unstable angina and non-Q-wave myocardial infarction. *JAMA* 1996; **275**: 1104–12.
8. Wenger, N.K. Coronary heart disease: an older woman's major health risk. *BMJ* 1997; **315**: 1085–90.
9. McLaughlin, T.J., Soumerai, S.B., Willison, D.J., *et al.* Adherence to national guidelines for drug treatment of suspected acute myocardial infarction. Evidence for undertreatment in women and the elderly. *Arch Intern Med* 1996; **156**: 799–805.
10. Williams, A. Rationing health care by age: the case for. *BMJ* 1997; **314**: 820–2.
11. Grimley Evans, J. Rationing health care by age: the case against. *BMJ* 1997; **314**: 822–5.
12. Rivlin, M.M. Protecting elderly people: flaws in ageist arguments. *BMJ* 1995; **310**: 1179–82.
13. Bugeja, G., Kumar, A., Banerjee, A.K. Exclusion of elderly people from clinical research: a descriptive study of published reports. *BMJ* 1997; **315**:1059.

14. Gurwitz, J.H., Col, N.K., Avorn J. The exclusion of the elderly and women from clinical trials in acute myocardial infarcation. *JAMA* 1992; **268**: 1417–22.

This article is a slightly edited version of an original published under the same title in the *British Medical Journal*, 1999, **319**: 1353–5. Ann Bowling is Professor of Health Services Research, Research Unit on Ageing and Population Studies, Centre for Health Informatics and Multi-professional Education, Royal Free and University College London Medical School, London, UK.

49 | Should smokers be offered coronary bypass surgery?

M.J. UNDERWOOD AND J.S. BAILEY
MATTHEW SHIU

Coronary bypass should not be offered to smokers

M. J. Underwood and J. S. Bailey

Cigarette smoking accelerates the progression of coronary artery disease[1] and is a determinant of early death in patients awaiting coronary bypass surgery.[2] Optimal surgical treatment results in substantial reduction of symptoms with increased exercise tolerance, freedom from angina, and in certain subgroups prolonged survival.

Unfortunately, coronary vein graft disease is a major cause of mortality and morbidity and is responsible for recurrent angina, myocardial infarction, and compromised ventricular function. One in 10 vein grafts undergo thrombotic occlusion within two weeks of operation, and diffuse intimal hyperplasia is a common finding after one year. By five years, frank atherosclerotic lesions are identifiable in many grafts.[3]

Early patency rates may be improved with anti-platelet agents such as aspirin, but this protective effect is greatly reduced in patients who continue to smoke, presumably as a result of increased thrombogenicity and enhanced platelet reactivity, which is well recognised in smokers. Late thrombotic occlusion is also considerably increased in patients who continue to smoke after surgery,[4] and this correlates well with reports of increased graft occlusion in smokers undergoing peripheral vascular reconstruction. The artherosclerotic process in vein grafts is identical to that of native coronary arteries and the risk factors, including smoking, are the same. Not surprisingly, a higher incidence of vein graft atherosclerosis has been reported after surgery in smokers.[5]

Vein graft failure is the major indication for reoperation, and reoperation is nearly twice as expensive as 'first time' coronary surgery, carries twice the mortality,[6] and is associated with a 50% net decrease in the overall rehabilitation status of the patient afterwards. It is in the interest of patients, surgeons, and health departments that, before surgery, patients are carefully assessed to ensure that they will obtain maximum benefit from the operation and that the risk of subsequent reoperation is minimised.

The problems associated with performing coronary surgery on patients who continue to smoke are not confined to risks of vein graft occlusion and reoperation in the future. Immediate postoperative complications are commoner, leading to increased mortality and morbidity; these include pulmonary complications (increased almost fourfold),[7] infection, and consequently a prolonged hospital stay.

Without substantial increases in resources, additional pressure will be put on the already growing waiting lists for coronary surgery. Patients who smoke spend longer in hospital and have poorer results from surgery than non-smokers. Treating them deprives patients who have never smoked or who have stopped smoking of more efficient and effective surgery.

Considerable evidence exists regarding the adverse effect of continued smoking on vein graft patency rates and early operative mortality and morbidity. Subjecting patients who continue to smoke, and for whom the only indication for operation is the relief of angina, to the increased risks of surgery in the face of remediable cause is not justified.

References and Notes

1. Nikutta, P., Lichtlen, P.R., Wiese, B., Jost, S., Dekkers, J., Raffenbeul, W., *et al*. Influence of cigarette smoking on the progression of coronary artery disease within three years: results of the INTACT study. *J. Am. Coll Cardiol* 1990; **15**: 181A.
2. Suttorp, M.J., Kingma, J.H., Vos, J., Koomen, E.M., Tijssen, J.G.P., Vermeulen, F.E.C., *et al*. Determinants for early mortality in patients awaiting coronary artery bypass graft surgery: a case-control study. *Eur Heart J* 1992; **13**: 238–42.
3. Badimon, J.J., Ip, J., Badimon, L., Fuster, V. Thrombosis and accelerated atherosclerosis in coronary angioplasty: implications for therapy. *Coronary Artery Disease* 1990; **2**: 170–9.
4. Solymoss, B.C., Nadeau, P., Millette, D., Inge, B., Campeau, I. Late thrombosis of saphenous vein coronary bypass grafts related to risk factors. *Circulation* 1988; **78**(suppl I): 140–3.
5. Fitzgibbon, G.M., Leach, A.J., Kafka, H.P. Atherosclerosis of coronary artery bypass grafts and smoking. *Can Med Assoc J* 1987; **136**: 45–7.
6. Ivert, T.S., Ekestrom, S., Peterffy, A., Welts, R. Coronary artery reoperations. Early and late results in 101 patients. *Scand J Thorac Cardiovasc Surg* 1988; **22**: 111–18.
7. Warner, M., Offard, K.P., Warner, M.E., Lennon, R.L., Conover, M.A., Jansson-Schumacher, U., *et al*. Role of preoperative cessation of smoking and other factors in postoperative pulmonary complications: a blinded prospective study of coronary artery bypass patients. *Mayo Clin Proc* 1989; **64**: 609–16.

This edited extract comes from a series in the *British Medical Journal*, 1993, **306**: 1047–50, concerning 'Controversies in treatment'. The first contribution (above) was by M.J. Underwood, then a Research Fellow, and J.S. Bailey, a consultant surgeon – both in the Department of Cardiothoracic Surgery, Groby Road Hospital, Leicester, UK. The second contribution follows.

Refusing to treat smokers is unethical and a dangerous precedent

Matthew Shiu

Should cigarette smokers be offered coronary artery bypass graft operations? Some specialists are adamant that they should not unless they promise to give up smoking.

With increasing resource limitations, such views may soon become accepted policy. Some of the argument would seem well founded on several fronts: the known adverse effects of smoking on the use of anaesthetics, the known adverse effects of continued smoking on graft survival and progression of coronary artery disease; and limited resources with ever increasing demand.

There is no doubt that cigarette smoking is harmful to coronary arteries. The medical profession is united in condemning smoking and has been fairly successful. Working as a general practitioner and with a special interest in cardiology, I spend much of my time getting patients off cigarettes. There is, however, a small group of patients who truly cannot give up their habit. All anti-smoking clinics have such examples. The medical profession does not have a satisfactory treatment for true cigarette addiction. So is it right to completely deny this group of high risk patients a recognised form of treatment because they cannot give up smoking? According to a spokesperson at the Medical Defence Union, should a case ever be brought to the court it would be difficult to defend such a stand if treatment was refused solely on those grounds.

The outcome of coronary artery surgery can be compromised by other factors such as hypertension, diabetes, age, female gender, obesity, and hypercholesterolaemia. These are all accepted as deleterious but not absolute overriding contra-indications. Is it right to isolate one risk factor and make a firm policy without taking other issues into consideration? Diabetic patients are operated on – even the ones who cannot stay on a strict diet. Will patients be refused surgery because they cannot stick to a cholesterol-lowering diet?

Resources are limited and will continue to be limited. If we examine the resource issue more closely, however, the argument does not seem so strong. The financial cost of not operating is often much higher than the cost of operating. Patients not given operations are unemployable, need sickness benefits, remain on multiple expensive medication and require repeated hospital admission for chest pains. Money is saved on the surgical units at the expense of the state.

But the real issue is not money but ethics. Limited resources should be a problem for the health care system. Instead of withholding treatment, doctors should use their influence in the proper channel. One surgeon said he would not operate on smokers even with all the resources available on the NHS for he does not wish to construct walls for people who are busy knocking them down. If we accept this argument, then more than half the genitourinary clinics can close down. Asthmatic smokers will not be given nebulisers.

It has been argued that damage caused by smoking is self-inflicted, hence smokers do not deserve treatment. But has self-infliction in any other condition ever barred patients from receiving proper investigation and treatment in Britain? I would like to believe that up to now doctors have always treated patients, irrespective of the degree of culpability of the person concerned. Drunken victims of road traffic accidents are never made to promise total alcohol abstinence before they are given first aid. Patients who attempt suicide are always treated. My view is that once we accept an absolute bar to surgery for smokers, we would next refuse lifesaving treatment to asthmatic smokers and soon may well be on the slippery slope to withholding treatment for the unmotivated and the unfit.

Matthew Shiu is a general practitioner in Birmingham, UK.

50 | Evidence based medicine: what it is and what it isn't

DAVID SACKETT, WILLIAM ROSENBERG, MUIR GRAY,
BRIAN HAYNES AND SCOTT RICHARDSON
With replies by Nigel T. James, Blair H. Smith and
Alan Maynard

Evidence based medicine, whose philosophical origins extend back to mid-19th century Paris and earlier, remains a hot topic for clinicians, public health practitioners, purchasers, planners, and the public. There are now frequent workshops in how to practise and teach it; undergraduate and postgraduate training programmes are incorporating it (or pondering how to do so); British centres for evidence based practice have been established or planned in adult medicine, child health, surgery, pathology, pharmacotherapy, nursing, general practice, and dentistry; the Cochrane Collaboration and Britain's Centre for Review and Dissemination in York are providing systematic reviews of the effects of health care; new evidence based practice journals are being launched; and it has become a common topic in the lay media.

But enthusiasm has been mixed with some negative reaction. Criticism has ranged from evidence based medicine being old hat to it being a dangerous innovation, perpetrated by the arrogant to serve cost cutters and suppress clinical freedom. As evidence based medicine continues to evolve and adapt, now is a useful time to refine the discussion of what it is and what it is not.

Evidence based medicine is the conscientious, explicit, and judicious use of current best evidence in making decisions about the care of individual patients. The practice of evidence based medicine means integrating individual clinical expertise with the best available external clinical evidence from systematic research. By individual clinical expertise we mean the proficiency and judgement that individual clinicians acquire through clinical experience and clinical practice. Increased expertise is reflected in many ways, but especially in more effective and efficient diagnosis and in the more thoughtful identification and compassionate use of individual patients' predicaments, rights, and preferences in making clinical decisions about their care. By best available external clinical evidence we mean clinically relevant research, often from the basic sciences of medicine, but especially from patient centred clinical research into the accuracy and precision of diagnostic tests (including the clinical examination), the power of prognostic markers, and the efficacy and safety of therapeutic, rehabilitative, and preventive regimens. External clinical evidence both invalidates previously accepted diagnostic tests and treatments and replaces them with new ones that are more powerful, more accurate, more efficacious, and safer.

This description of what evidence based medicine is helps clarify what evidence based medicine is not. Evidence based medicine is neither old hat nor impossible to practise. The argument that 'everyone already is doing it' falls before evidence of striking variations in both the integration of patient values into our clinical behaviour and in the rates with which clinicians provide interventions to their patients. The difficulties that clinicians face in keeping abreast of all the medical advances reported in primary journals are obvious from a comparison of the time required for reading (for general medicine, enough to examine 19 articles per day, 365 days per year) with the time available (well under an hour a week by British medical consultants, even on self reports).

The argument that evidence based medicine can be conducted only from ivory towers and armchairs is refuted by audits from the front lines of clinical care where at least some inpatient clinical teams in general medicine,[1] psychiatry, and surgery have provided evidence based care to the vast majority of their patients. Such studies show that busy clinicians who devote their scarce reading time to selective, efficient, patient driven searching, appraisal, and incorporation of the best available evidence can practise evidence based medicine.

Evidence based medicine is not 'cookbook' medicine. Because it requires a bottom up approach that integrates the best external evidence with individual clinical expertise and patients' choice, it cannot result in slavish, cookbook approaches to individual patient care. External clinical evidence can inform, but can never replace, individual clinical expertise, and it is this expertise that decides whether the external evidence applies to the individual patient at all and, if so, how it should be integrated into a clinical decision. Similarly, any external guideline must be integrated with individual clinical expertise in deciding whether and how it matches the patient's clinical state, predicament, and preferences, and thus whether it should be applied. Clinicians who fear top down cookbooks will find the advocates of evidence based medicine joining them at the barricades.

Some fear that evidence based medicine will be hijacked by purchasers and managers to cut the costs of health care. This would not only be a misuse of evidence based medicine but suggests a fundamental misunderstanding of its financial consequences. Doctors practising evidence based medicine will identify and apply the most efficacious interventions to maximise the quality and quantity of life for individual patients; this may raise rather than lower the cost of their care.

Evidence based medicine is not restricted to randomised trials and meta-analyses. It involves tracking down the best external evidence with which to answer our clinical questions. To find out about the accuracy of a diagnostic test, we need to find proper cross sectional studies of patients clinically suspected of harbouring the relevant disorder, not a randomised trial. For a question about prognosis, we need proper follow up studies of patients assembled at a uniform, early point in the clinical course of their disease. And sometimes the evidence we need will come from the basic sciences such as genetics or immunology.

It is when asking questions about therapy that we should try to avoid the non-experimental approaches, since these routinely lead to false positive conclusions about efficacy. Because the randomised trial, and especially the systematic review of several randomised trials, is so much more likely to inform us and so much less likely to mislead us, it has become the 'gold standard' for judging whether a treatment does more good than harm. However, some questions about therapy do not require randomised trials (successful interventions for otherwise fatal conditions) or cannot wait for the trials to be conducted. And if no randomised trial has been carried out for our patient's predicament, we must follow the trail to the next best external evidence and work from there.

Reference

1. Ellis, J., Mulligan, I., Rowe, J. and Sackett, D.L. Inpatient general medicine is evidence based. *Lancet*, 1995: **346**, 407–10.

The edited extract reproduced here was originally published in the *British Medical Journal*, 1996, 312: 71–2. At the time this article was written, the first author, Professor David Sackett was at the NHS Research and Development Centre for Evidence Based Medicine, Oxford; other authors are from the Nuffield Department of Clinical Medicine, University of Oxford; the Anglia and Oxford Regional Health Authority; McMaster University, Ontario, Canada; and the University of Rochester School of Medicine and Dentistry, New York, USA. Six months after this article appeared, the *BMJ* published a series of responses to it – three of which appear below.

Rich sources of evidence are ignored

Blair H. Smith

It is reassuring that David Sackett and colleagues have made two important concessions from their previous extreme position relating to evidence based medicine. Firstly, they have recognised the importance of clinical skill, as distinct from the consideration of scientific evidence; and, secondly, they have allowed other forms of evidence to take a step towards the hallowed position held by the randomised controlled trial.

A contradiction then ensues. Clinical skill is essentially derived from experience and is expressed as judgement in decision making. But the variation in the ways in which different individuals interpret experience and formulate judgements renders this aspect difficult to expose to 'biostatistical ways of thinking'. It is therefore difficult to apportion scientifically the appropriate use of 'best available clinical evidence' in any particular decision process. We are thus led back or on to a wider view of medicine as a humane art that is supported by science. In this view the discipline of evidence based medicine is important for certain aspects of clinical decision making but is a relatively small part of the practice of medicine.

Forms of evidence allowable in evidence based medicine, while now extending beyond the randomised controlled trial, remain heavily numerate. This encourages emphasis on the quantifiable and physical aspects of any clinical dilemma, which may be inappropriate. Denial of social and psychological aspects may be detrimental, and ignoring the less readily measured dimensions may be dangerous. Rich sources of evidence also include the anecdotal, which are so often slated, and the qualitative, which is not mentioned by this lobby yet has developed considerably and provides illuminative results. The search for justification continues.

Scientific method and raw data should be considered

Nigel T. James

Proponents of evidence based medicine claim that it is the conscientious, explicit, and judicious use of current best available external evidence about medical care. What about scientific method and raw data? Scientific method – the fundamental intellectual activity of obtaining data, assessing them by a series of valid arguments, and obtaining a series of conclusions in descending order of likelihood in all subjects – does not seem to merit consideration.

Paradoxically, evidence based medicine seems to avoid all contact with the first hand evidence by replacing original findings with subjectively selected, arbitrarily summarised, laundered, and biased conclusions of indeterminate validity or completeness. It has been carried out by people of unknown ability, experience, and skills using methods whose opacity prevents assessment of the original data.

The new journal *Evidence-based Medicine* makes no reference in its first issue to methodology, experimental design, or statistics. No reason is given for the selection of the 24 papers that are published. No explanation of the sources and techniques of the added manipulations is included. No evidence of authorship within the new journal can be divined. There is no reference to the second-hand methodology, just the quoting of subjectively attractive and unqualified conclusions, fourth hand.

Those who are concerned with validity will examine raw data and access much more extensive databases by standard methods on the Internet on a more comprehensive scale at only second-hand level. Those who are not concerned with validity will find a ready substitute for thought and effort. At best, evidence based medicine is a heuristic method for a lower-level partial abstracting service. There is little new or of merit in this allegedly new discipline. Assessing the raw data and understanding their validity and the means of their creation make up the true evidence based foundation of scientific and academic inquiry.

Evidence based medicine in its present form is inconsistent and incompatible with science, and its lack of soundness is sufficient for us to consider whether it is even ethical. Neither the Renaissance nor the Reformation, during which the direct examination of the human body by Vesalius and Leonardo da Vinci replaced the evidence based teachings of Galen, would have been possible without the abandonment of contemporary evidence based systems. To a scientist, the advent of evidence based medicine creates an unassailable gulf and denies the fundamental tenets of millenniums of thought and philosophy of inquiry. To a university teacher devoted to honest original inquiry, it is a falsehood. And we are going to teach it, as an allegedly new specialty, in the new medical school curriculum recommended by the General Medical Council's medical education subcommittee.

Cost effectiveness and equity are ignored

Alan Maynard

David Sackett and colleagues' editorial on evidence based medicine is confused and inadequate. The authors argue, among other things, that 'doctors practising evidence based medicine will identify and apply the most efficacious interventions to maximise the quality and quantity of life for individual patients.' (Note the use of 'apply' (does the patient have no choice?) and 'efficacious' rather than effective.)

This individual medical ethic has to be traded off against the social ethic of the efficient use of scarce resources. While the individual patient might welcome treatment regardless of cost, any health care system is unlikely to be able to afford or condone such behaviour. Society requires doctors to allocate resources on the basis of knowledge of cost effectiveness. This obliges doctors to deny patients access to efficacious treatments if such interventions are not cost effective. Failure to do this without reasonable cause means that scarce resources are wasted and patients who could benefit from care are left untreated. Such inefficient treatment is unethical and should be construed by employers as prima facie evidence for dismissal in an NHS striving to maximise health benefits from its £40 billion budget.

The necessity to ration or allocate care on the basis of cost effectiveness was recognised by Archie Cochrane nearly 25 years ago:

> Allocations of funds and facilities are nearly always based on the opinions of senior consultants, but, more and more, requests for additional facilities will have to be based on detailed arguments with 'hard evidence' as to the gain to be expected from the patient's angle and the cost. Few can possibly object to this.[1]

Nowadays we would complement Cochrane's position by noting that the goal of efficiency might be mediated by considerations of equity – that is, society might deliberately decide to forgo efficiency (health gains) to discriminate in favour of poor people. It is remarkable that the approach of evidence based medicine ignores such considerations and, in so doing, favours the middle class, which has a greater capacity to benefit from care, rather than poor people, who, if treated, will yield fewer health gains because of their 'mean' condition.

It is a pity that the so-called apostles of Cochrane have yet to understand his gospel of cost effectiveness and be concerned by considerations of equity, which would have been close to his heart.

Reference

1. Cochrane, A.L. *Effectiveness and Efficiency: Random Reflections on Health Services*, London: Nuffield Provincial Hospital Trust, 1972. [An extract appears as Chapter 41 in Part 4 of this Reader.]

The three 'letters to the editor' reproduced here were published (with several others, and a response from Sackett *et al.*) in the *British Medical Journal*, 1996, **313**: 169–71. Blair H. Smith was then a Lecturer in General Practice in the Department of General Practice, University of Aberdeen; Nigel T. James was a Senior Lecturer in the Department of Biomedical Science, University of Sheffield; and Alan Maynard was Secretary of the Nuffield Provincial Hospitals Trust, London.

51 | Public participation in the evaluation of health care

RAY FITZPATRICK AND DEENA WHITE

This paper reviews the main themes that have dominated research in the field of patient satisfaction. The paper also examines arguments to extend the scope and forms of involvement of patients and the community in the evaluation of health services. In addition, it considers some of the barriers and difficulties likely to be encountered by extending the scope of patients' involvement in evaluation and speculates on some solutions.

Patients' involvement in health care evaluation usually is as the occasional respondent to surveys about health services. Alternatively bodies with little or no influence are created to speak for or represent patients, usually without any obvious or convincing mechanisms of representation. In either case, a fairly passive, indirect and ultimately token form of lay involvement, it is argued, reinforces a relative lack of public voice in health care policy (Williams 1994).

Dominant themes in patient satisfaction research

Although consumerism generally has been quite a major force for change, for much of its evolution the NHS experienced a fairly mild version, largely in the form of interest groups representing at local or national level the needs of specific client groups with particular health problems that were neglected by health professionals. However, the striking feature of many consumer-orientated developments in the NHS is that they have top-down paternalist origins (Klein 1995). For example, public funds were used to subsidize MIND (a British mental health charity), to create an additional pressure for reform of mental health services. The most generic voice of patients – the Community Health Council – was again a bureaucratically inspired reform to provide an organized channel of local public opinion (Klein 1995).

In both the USA and Britain the championing of users' concerns by management resulted in particular issues being given salience. Above all attention was given to aspects of service delivery such as access, facilities, waiting times and so called 'hotel' issues for in-patients. This somewhat limited definition of patients' concerns to a large extent stemmed from managers' natural tendency to focus on those issues within the health care system over which they felt some sense of control. The content and quality of medical care were considered outside the sphere of responsibility of management and were regulated almost entirely by traditional professional mechanisms.

The one area of individual health professionals' care that did become subject to managerial scrutiny was inter-personal relations, sometimes referred to as 'humaneness' or 'art of care'. A very substantial body of evidence has been produced showing the importance of the impact of the health professional's behaviour; his or her manner, level of interest in the patient, styles of communication and information giving can all evoke strong responses from patients. This body of work is now beginning to influence the education of health professionals because of evidence that interpersonal relations can influence not only patient satisfaction but adherence to recommendations, readiness to return to the same provider and indeed clinical outcomes such as reassurance and health status (Fitzpatrick 1993).

The neglect of patients' views about outcomes

It is now generally accepted that patients have important and distinct views in relation to a wide range of aspects of the quality of the care that they receive. Patient satisfaction surveys are increasingly multidimensional and address such diverse issues as access, informativeness, costs and continuity of care (Fitzpatrick 1991). In other words it is still unusual to involve patients in judgements about the value or outcomes of care in studies.

The so-called 'outcomes movement' has contributed to a sense that patients' views about the content and outcomes of health care are now adequately addressed by means of the increasingly sophisticated array of health status and quality of life questionnaires. However, they do not permit patients to contribute to an evaluation of health services in relation to needs for knowledge and understanding, hope, reassurance, support, dignity, control and other 'non-specific' outcomes which patients hope for from health care. The outcomes approach to the evaluation of health services, whilst placing far greater emphasis upon patients' perceptions, has yet to develop a methodology for capturing patients' views about this wider range of functions that health services fulfil.

Quite apart from substantial methodological issues that emerge with regard to difficulties of obtaining clear, reliable and representative views, the results of public consultations have shown that public values very substantially differ from those of doctors or public health specialists (Bowling *et al.* 1993).

Analyses of public consultation exercises have concluded that, as members of the public themselves often admit, it is difficult for lay individuals to participate in prioritizing without acquiring more information about health care. The need to raise levels of public understanding regarding outcomes and effectiveness would therefore be a serious issue if attempts were made to increase involvement in decisions about the content, quality and outcomes of health care.

Limited forms of public involvement in evaluation

Another commonly identified problem is that the role of the patient in the evaluation of health services as reflected in patient satisfaction surveys is essentially passive and occasional. Most radically it is argued that the patient's agenda can only truly be pursued by direct representation of patients on the bodies that control providers. In other words solutions range from those that address the validity of assessments of patients' and communities' views to those that begin to raise issues of power and of politics.

Studies that challenge the notion of the patient as active consumer are consistent with a related body of evidence that suggests that patients do not play a very active role in seeking information about their health problems from the doctor or in treatment decisions generally (Beisecker & Beisecker 1990). Most importantly there is evidence that when a serious illness occurs the desire to play an active and leading role in treatment decisions diminishes markedly (Degner & Sloan 1992). Patients anticipate the substantial sense of regret that may occur if they select the 'wrong' option and by handing over responsibility to the doctor, they substantially eliminate the possibility of regretting their own decision. From such patchy evidence one might doubt the scope for extending patients' contributions to health service evaluation.

The other way of extending lay involvement is to involve patients and the general population actively in decisions about health services in more organized and institutionalized forms of consumer representation. [However], where lay involvement in consumer or community bodies is direct and informal, the main criticism of such exercises is that those who become involved tend not be representative of the population as a whole. In Britain, a number of general practices have set up patient participation groups in which patients are involved in the policy discussions of the practice. Participants are overwhelmingly middle-class (Agass et al. 1991).

Where lay or community involvement includes more formal responsibilities, the concept of representation rapidly emerges as problematic. Similar issues arise with the Community Health Council (CHC) in the NHS. The perceived value and effectiveness of CHCs has always been determined by the impact of forceful individuals rather than any power deriving from formal representation of 'the community' by the CHC (Moon & Lupton 1995).

An agenda for the future

Two means of increasing the effectiveness of lay participation in the evaluation [of health care] can be considered. First, managerial control of the research agenda can be balanced by research partnerships with consumer groups. This would in effect provide consumer groups with the expertise and credibility they need. A second possibility for balancing the managerial bias imposed on lay consultation is to dissociate some evaluation research from the applied environment altogether. Rather than being driven by the questions managers asked, it would be driven by hypotheses developed in the light of previous research. [This] suggests that its greatest impact lies in influencing the kinds of questions that managers and planners might ask themselves.

It is sometimes taken for granted that evaluation ensures the quality of services, but this is true only in so far as the results are taken into consideration by those in a position to act upon them. We have no knowledge of the impact of patient surveys on decision-making, nor do we know whether health authorities perceive patient satisfaction surveys, lay evaluations of outcome and active patient participation to be of use. If there is a political interest in empowering consumers, simply knowing their preferences is insufficient. It is equally important to understand how, and to what extent these preferences can and do influence the delivery of health care.

References

Agass, M., Coulter, A., Mant, D. and Fuller, A. (1991) Patients' participation in general practice: who participates? *British Journal of General Practice*; **41**: 198–201.

Beisecker, A. and Beisecker, T. (1990) Patient information seeking behaviours when communicating with doctors. *Medical Care*; **28**: 19–28.

Bowling, A., Jacobson, B. and Southgate, L. (1993) Health service priorities: explorations in consultation of the public and health professionals on priority setting in an inner London health district. *Social Science and Medicine*; **37**: 851–857.

Degner, L. and Sloan, J. (1992) Decision making during serious illness: what role do patients really want to play? *Journal of Clinical Epidemiology*; **45**: 941–950.

Fitzpatrick, R. (1991) Surveys of patient satisfaction: I – Important general considerations. *British Medical Journal*; **302**: 887–889.

Fitzpatrick, R. (1993) Patient satisfaction in relation to clinical care. In R. Fitzpatrick and A. Hopkins (Eds) *The Measurement of Patient Satisfaction*. Royal College of Physicians, London.

Klein, R. (1995) *The New Politics of the NHS*. Longman, London.

Moon, G. and Lupton, C. (1995) Within acceptable limits: health care provider perspectives on community health councils in the reformed British National Health Service. *Policy and Politics*; **23**: 335–346.

Williams, B. (1994) Patient satisfaction: a valid concept? *Social Science and Medicine*; **38**: 509–516.

This edited extract comes from a much longer article, originally published under the same title in *Health and Social Care in the Community*, 1997, 5(1): 3–8. Professor Ray Fitzpatrick is from the Department of Public Health and Primary Care, University of Oxford, UK; Dr Deena White is from the Department of Sociology, University of Montreal, Quebec, Canada.

52 | Health technology and knowledge

ANDY ALASZEWSKI AND IAN HARVEY

In the twentieth century, medicine has become identified with the development, application and promotion of science. In this chapter we explore the social implications of the development of innovative health technologies. Talcott Parsons (1951: 432) argues that medical practitioners are 'applied scientists' who use their expertise to identify and manage the risks and uncertainties associated with disease. He notes that 'Modern medical practice is organized about the application of scientific knowledge to problems of illness and health, to the control of disease'.

Technology, science and the creation of uncertainty

Modern societies are characterized by and differentiated from pre-modern society by the development of scientific knowledge and the expert use of this knowledge through technologies. For example, advances in human genetics appear to open up the possibility of controlling not only infectious diseases but diseases which have a genetic component, such as multiple sclerosis and breast cancer, by identifying and changing the genes responsible for specific diseases.

The development of science and technology is usually seen as part of the process of modernization in which prejudice and superstition are replaced by modern rational systems of thought. This process benefits by providing individuals with greater certainty and order. However, in the twenty-first century it has become apparent that modernization and the development of science and technology actually increase uncertainty and can be seen as threats to individual well-being: 'The more rationally we calculate and the more complex the calculations become, the more aspects come into view concerning uncertainty about the future and risk. Seen from this point of view, it is no accident that the risk perspective has developed parallel to the growth in scientific specialisation' (Luhmann 1993: 28).

What characterizes modern society is not the replacement of irrationality by rationality but the reduction of certainty which increases the scope and necessity of individual decision making. This increase in choice is usually seen as socially beneficial and empowering. Anthony Giddens (1991) notes that in modern society individuals no longer have to accept 'fate', but through their choices shape their own lives and express themselves and their values. However, Abby Lippman (1999: 285) suggests that this choice may be more apparent than real, especially when professionals emphasize the importance of safe and responsible choice: 'with risk increasingly becoming the lens through which choice is filtered – a dangerous synergy between a "tyranny of risk" ... and what has become a "tyranny of choice" is catalysed'. It is clear that the development of knowledge and associated technologies has had a major impact on modern society, increasing both choice and uncertainty.

Experts and technology: creating and managing uncertainty

Doctors are the key decision makers in the development and adoption of innovative health technologies. They provide the link between the suppliers of technology and the final users (the patients), and also play a crucial role in the allocation of funds in health care systems. In the twentieth century, doctors became enthusiastic innovators. The speed with which general surgeons responded to the opportunities that instruments such as laparoscopes created for minimally invasive or keyhole surgery actually overwhelmed the manufacturers (Harvey 1999: 156).

Technological change creates risks and uncertainties which experts exploit to establish control of the technology and a monopoly of its use. This process can be seen in the early developments of X-rays. The medical practitioners laid claim to the technology by emphasizing uncertainty and hazards even though there was no real evidence that they understood and could manage these hazards:

> Arguments about safety in the use of X-rays were quickly put forward to justify the extension of medical control. For example the *BMJ* [in 1905] noted that unsupervised lay use of X-rays was under attack from the medical profession in France ... A Professor Debove was quoted as arguing that Röntgen rays were only safe in medical hands. These claims were advanced considerably in advance of any well-developed understanding of the hazards involved ...
>
> (Larkin 1983: 64)

The relationships within and between the medical profession and other occupational groups was stabilized in the 1920s with the development of medical specialists (radiologists) who interpreted and reported on X-rays, and a subordinate group of paramedical technicians (radiographers) who produced the X-rays. This division of labour excluded non-medical specialists such as engineers and other doctors such as surgeons. Radiologists used their ability to manage uncertainty and ensure safety to justify their control over the technology and its medical applications (Larkin 1983).

A similar pattern can be identified in more recent technological developments, such as magnetic resonance imaging (MRI):

> The radiological community thus seized on [arguments about] the inappropriate use of X-rays, safety issues (excessive radiation) and legal ones ... to argue for the

replacement of X-rays by devices [such as MRIs] which did not cause ionising radiation and the centralisation of diagnostic control in the expertise of the radiologist.

(Harvey 1999: 124)

Uncertainty and risk have repeatedly been manipulated to establish and maintain control over new technologies. This process can itself create further uncertainty and risk, especially for patients. This can be seen in the case of laparoscopic cholecystectomy ('keyhole' surgery to remove the gall bladder). The mass media, relying heavily on experts, manufacturers and surgeons, initially portrayed keyhole surgery as a panacea, a safe technological fix for painful conditions. The reality was rather different. The rapid introduction of the technology has been described as 'the biggest unaudited free-for-all in the history of surgery' as many surgeons were self-taught (Johnson 1997: 633). Evidence rapidly emerged of a 'learning curve' and serious harm to patients. Early media enthusiasm rapidly turned to criticism. Paradoxically, the outcome of these criticisms was to reinforce professional control of the technology. While the Royal College of Surgeons accepted minimally invasive surgery had been introduced too quickly, it persuaded ministers that this 'new' risk should be managed through improved self-regulation (Harvey 1999: 188–9).

The introduction of medical technologies cannot be seen in isolation from the organization and management of health care. While uncertainty and risk are clearly involved in the introduction of technologies, it is not a simple or straightforward process.

Controlling and managing technology

Since innovative health technologies were a major and potentially controllable factor in escalating health expenditure growth, they came under scrutiny from governments in the 1970s and 1980s who were trying to control the level of public expenditure. The Department of Health's contribution took the form of a research and development strategy focusing on the effectiveness and risks of existing and new technology. This programme is so important that the whole of the NHS has become a 'laboratory' for technology assessments (Faulkner 1997: 186). The results of these assessments are then used to inform decision making. Initially the government focused on specific, expensive technologies, which were introduced unless there was an explicit national decision to exclude or control their dissemination. An example of this approach was the limitation of heart transplantation to a number of specially designated and funded national centres. Following the introduction of contracting in the 1990s the approach changed to 'opting in', whereby new technologies would only be introduced if individual health authorities decided to purchase them.

The attempt to control technological innovation has been undermined by the behaviour of the medical profession. Doctors have bypassed financial and other controls by exploiting alternative sources of income, especially for supposed research and development, which may in reality pre-empt decisions about adoption of the technology. In the UK, radiologists played a key role in promoting MRI. In the late 1980s they bypassed central constraints on funding by using a combination of research and charity funding, especially cancer funds. Product champions linked MRI to national campaigns against cancer, emphasizing the potential of MRI for the early identification of soft tissue changes such as tumours. Most early machines were located in teaching hospitals and used for a combination of research and care. Manufacturers contributed by subsidizing the first generation of machines (Harvey 1999).

The government response to initial failures to assess and control technology has been to shift the rationale for controlling technology from costs to safety. While cost control is unpopular, concerns with safety can be presented as self-evidentially good. Thus, while governments promote and proclaim the benefits of technological innovation, especially in health care, they have developed strategies to control both the costs and the risks associated with these technologies. They are concerned to ensure that risks are acceptable to the public and to users of services so that public confidence and trust are maintained. However, the government is primarily concerned with the objective measurement of risk and this approach will only work if the public use the same approach and measures.

Individual perceptions of the risk of technology

In modern society we live and cope with uncertainty. Every day we are reminded of the ever present threat to life from existing and new diseases such as cancer or HIV/AIDS. These anxieties about the threat of illness underpin one of the major paradoxes of modernity: that as individuals who live in developed countries become objectively safer (for example, have longer and healthier lives), they also experience increasing levels of uncertainty and anxiety about their health.

These anxieties are related to the ways in which individuals perceive and assess risk. For example, experts use objective measures of risk derived mainly from routinely collected official sources such as death certificates, while individuals develop subjective perceptions based on information they accept as reliable, such as their own personal experience or the mass media. Research undertaken by psychologists indicates that there is a systematic difference between experts' assessments of risk and individuals' perceptions of risk. When individuals are asked to compare risks (for example, the risk of being killed by botulism or a stroke) they systematically overestimate their chance of being killed by the rare disease, botulism, but underestimate their chance of being killed by a common disease such as a stroke (Pidgeon *et al.*, 1999).

Sir Kenneth Calman, a former chief medical officer, and his colleagues have identified a number of 'fright' factors which increase individuals' sensitivity to risk (Calman *et al.*, 1999: 111). Most of these factors can be linked to modern technologies. These are often experienced as 'threatening' because they act invisibly and/or are difficult to understand; as 'disempowering' because they remove control from the individual; and as 'unfair' because they harm the most vulnerable individuals in society. Ulrich Beck argues that modern technologies are experienced as threatening because their effects are often invisible and global. Technological change affects the whole globe and leads to major technological catastrophes such as the development of strains of malaria resistant to chloroquine and bacteria resistant to antibiotics such as MRSA: '[Modern risks] are risks *of modernization*. They are a *wholesale product* of industrialization, and are systematically intensified as it becomes global' (Beck 1992: 21).

One explanation for the systematic variation between expert assessment and individual perception, is *risk amplification* and in particular the importance of the mass media as a source of information. The mass media tends to concentrate on unusual or low probability events that have major disastrous consequences. Thus, a major aircraft or train accident, or a death from a rare tropical disease is more likely to attract media attention than more common events such as a cancer death.

There is increasing awareness and concern in government about the expert assessment/ lay perception gap. The solution is seen very much in terms of effective risk communication by government. This approach is clearly articulated by Sir Kenneth Calman and a departmental colleague:

> There are plenty of cases in which – even with the benefit of hindsight – both the advice provided and the public response appear sensible enough. But what is clear is that the old-fashioned view of risk communication as a one-way process of drip-feeding expert knowledge onto a supposedly grateful public will no longer do. 'Experts' no longer command automatic deference – no matter how genuine their expertise. Increasingly, people are only prepared to listen if they feel there is some prospect of their own views being heard.
>
> (Bennett and Calman 1999: Preface)

There is little understanding of how individuals and groups assess the risk of health technologies and the trustworthiness of experts using these technologies. An Australian survey of three 'best practice' medical interventions found that patients did not share clinicians' perceptions of risk, and in particular did not view the risk-benefit ratios of the interventions favourably. The authors therefore questioned the extent to which patients were able to provide informed consent (Fitzgerald and Phillipov 2000: 9).

Building trust

Innovative health technologies create a dilemma. They provide both an opportunity to improve individual and collective health, but they generate uncertainty and associated anxieties about health. It is clear that individuals are no longer willing to automatically trust governments and experts, so we need to develop a new relationship. Anna Coote (1998: 126) has argued that this trust can be developed through a genuine commitment by health and welfare agencies, and the professionals they employ, to openness and participation in decision making.

However, Anthony Giddens (1991: 191–4) argues that the general sense of powerlessness and anxiety which individuals in modern society experience can be overcome if individuals question, and if experts are willing to share the information that underpins their judgements and involve lay people in the process of decision making. Professionals will only be fully trusted if lay people understand how and why decisions are made and feel involved in the process.

References

Beck, U. (1992) *Risk Society: Towards a New Modernity*. London: Sage.

Bennett, P. and Calman, K. (1999) Preface, in P. Bennett and K. Calman (eds) *Risk, Communication and Public Health*. Oxford: Oxford University Press.

Calman, K.C., Bennett, P.G. and Coles, D.G. (1999) Risk to health: some key issues in management, regulation and communication, *Health, Risk and Society*, 1: 107–16.

Coote, A. (1998) Risk and public policy: towards a high-trust democracy, in J. Franklin (ed.) *The Politics of Risk Society*. Cambridge: Polity Press.

Faulkner, A. (1997) Strange bedfellows in the laboratory of the NHS? An analysis of the new science of health technology assessment, in M.A. Elston (ed.) *The Sociology of Medical Science and Technology*. Oxford: Blackwell.

Fitzgerald, S.P. and Phillipov, G. (2000) Patients' attitudes to commonly promoted medical interventions, *Medical Journal of Australia*, 171: 9–12.

Giddens, A. (1991) *Modernity and Self-Identity: Self and Society in the Late Modern Society*. Cambridge: Polity Press.

Harvey, I. (1999) Managing the diffusion of medical technologies. PhD thesis, University of Hull.

Johnson, A. (1997) Laparoscopic surgery, *Lancet*, 349: 631–5.

Larkin, G. (1983) *Occupational Monopoly and Modern Medicine*. London: Tavistock.

Lippman, A. (1999) Choice as a risk to women's health, *Health, Risk and Society*, 1: 281–91.

Luhmann, N. (1993) *Risk: A Sociological Theory*. New York: de Grutyer.

Parsons, T. (1951) *The Social System*. London: Routledge & Kegan Paul.

Pidgeon, N., Henwood, K. and Maguire, B. (1999) Public health communication and the social amplification of risks: present knowledge and future prospects, in P. Bennett and K. Calman (eds) *Risk, Communication and Public Health*. Oxford: Oxford University Press.

This article has not previously appeared in print. Professor A.M. Alaszewski is Director and Professor of Health Studies at the Centre for Health Services Studies, University of Kent at Canterbury, UK. Dr Ian Harvey was a PhD student in the same department and is now a research Consultant at the Hull and East Yorkshire Hospitals Trust, UK.

Policy reform

Policies towards the NHS in the post-war period reveal a variety of assumptions on the part of politicians about the motivations of managers and clinicians. For much of this period, the NHS was a classic example of the centralised, bureaucratic organisation in which politicians at the apex sought to control the behaviour of staff at the periphery through a combination of central planning and national directives. The weaknesses of this command and control system led the Thatcher government to introduce radical reforms to the NHS in the 1990s. At the heart of the Thatcher reforms was devolution of control to NHS trusts and general practitioners and the use of competition to improve performance.

The Thatcher government was particularly concerned to tackle the perverse incentives facing hospitals. Specifically, hospitals were penalised for productivity improvements because they operated within fixed budgets that were insensitive to changes in activity. Within the so called internal market, the intention was that money should follow patients in order to reward hospitals and other healthcare providers that offered services which were efficient and responsive to users. In pursuing these policies, the government was emulating trends in other organisations and sectors in which there was delegation to profit centres and business units within a framework that ensured accountability upwards for performance. Consistent with these trends, central control of the NHS was therefore not abandoned by the Thatcher government. Rather, central direction was joined together with delegation and competition in the oxymoron that became known as a politically managed market.[1] The result was an uneasy hybrid in which central control over some areas of the NHS was strengthened while in other areas managers and clinicians were allowed greater freedom to bring about change.

The Labour government that was elected in 1997 has introduced a further set of reforms which claim to be different from both the command and control mechanisms used after the establishment of the NHS and the market oriented policies of this government's immediate Conservative predecessors. Indeed, the Labour government has argued that these reforms represent a 'third way' that goes beyond both planning and markets. In reality, the third way comprises a mixture of policy instruments, embracing elements of planning and competition, directives and incentives, and centralisation and devolution. Furthermore, similar instruments have been applied in other areas of public policy, like education, as politicians seek to modernise government as a whole.

Underlying assumptions

What do these policies reveal about the assumptions made by politicians in relation to the motivation of managers and clinicians? The first way followed the traditional precepts of Weberian bureaucracy. The core assumption was that those at the centre of organisations had the task of securing the implementation of their objectives through specifying these objectives and ensuring that staff at lower levels carried them through into action. There was also an assumption in the first way that those at the top knew better than those at the bottom what needed to be done. It followed that discretion on the part of managers and clinicians was a problem that had to be reduced through central control and supervision of performance within the organisation concerned. Reorganisations of the structure of the NHS during this period were designed with this purpose in mind, the changes occurring in the mid-1970s exemplifying the concern to 'get the organisation right' by detailed definitions of functions and roles and the introduction of a national planning system.

The second way, by contrast, was based on the assumption that planning was likely to be less effective than competition in producing change. According to this school of thought, health service staff, like those in other sectors, respond positively to the structure of incentives with which they are faced. If they are able to enhance the resources of their organisations by competing successfully, then they will do so. Equally, if they are faced with the threat of bankruptcy, merger, or closure by not competing successfully, then they will be motivated to change their behaviour in order to survive. The second way further assumed that there are inherent limits to the ways in which those at the centre can control those at the periphery and therefore it relied more on empowering staff than controlling them.

The third way recognises the limits of both central control and staff empowerment. However, rather than rejecting these approaches, it seeks to combine them in a complex cocktail of policy ingredients.[2] Alongside planning and competition, the third way makes use of other mechanisms, including new forms of inspection, regulation, and the publication of information on comparative performance within the NHS. The implicit assumption of the third way is that human behaviour has more, and more complex, motivations than were recognised by proponents of the first and second ways. Accordingly, policy makers need to have access to a range of instruments if they are to deliver their objectives.

Testing the third way

The question that arises is, how well founded are these different assumptions? Evidence from the first phase of the NHS indicates that central planning and national directives were successful up to a point in addressing the weaknesses of the NHS when it was established. It was through central planning that greater equity was achieved in the distribution of medical staff and that a start was made on the modernisation of hospitals. On the other hand, there continued to be wide variations in performance, and the record of the NHS in implementing national policies was uneven. Equally important, attempts by the centre to tighten its grip on managers and clinicians, like the NHS planning system introduced in 1976, did not succeed in overcoming these problems.

Evidence from the internal market is similarly equivocal. As the most thorough review of the evidence has shown, competition had little measurable impact and where it did make a difference the effects were felt at the margins.[3] As an example, the incentives contained within general practitioner fundholding produced changes in clinical practices in some areas, such as prescribing, and among some practices, but they did not deliver the transformation in performance that was hoped for by the architects of the internal market. While one explanation of the limited impact of empowerment and incentives is that the government did not go far enough in delegating control within the NHS and strengthening the incentives facing managers and clinicians, an alternative view is that markets are no more a panacea than is planning, and although they will achieve some of the objectives of policy makers, they are unlikely to be sufficient.

It is, or course, precisely this rationale that lies behind the third way. Put simply, the architects of the Labour government's approach seem to believe that policy makers are analogous to golfers, requiring a collection of clubs in their bag to enable them to play the most appropriate shot in the circumstances in which they find themselves. To extend the analogy, the success of the third way will therefore depend on the selection of clubs and the execution of shots. It might be added that the advice of the caddy will also be of some significance, not least because of the current influence over health policy of specialist advisers and members of the policy unit at No 10. The next phase of the Labour government will enable the assumptions of the third way to be tested in practice.

Are staff the problem or the solution?

Given the eclectic nature of the [1997 Labour] government's approach, it might seem that all possible means of improving performance in the NHS have already been deployed. There is, however, a lacuna in the government's thinking, and in the longer term it could prove to be a significant omission. One of the assumptions about human behaviour that does not loom large in the third way is that NHS staff are fundamentally well motivated to deliver service improvements and simply need training, development, and support to enable them to realise their potential. Indeed, the prime minister and his senior ministers suggest that the 'forces of conservatism' are blocking the modernisation of public services, and that staff in these services are part of the problem rather than part of the solution.

The argument that public services like the NHS may be run more for the benefit of staff than patients is of course not new. What is unusual is the espousal of this argument by a Labour government and its apparent willingness to challenge the power of its traditional support base in the trade unions and entrenched interests of the health professions, including doctors. Yet if the assumptions that lay behind the first and second way encompassed elements of truth without seeing the whole picture, so too the critique of the 'forces of conservatism' risks turning an accurate perception of part of the problem confronting the NHS into a programme that is applied without discrimination. This would alienate managers and clinicians who support the direction of travel that has been set out by the government and whose continuing commitment is needed to deliver the modernisation agenda.

These observations take on added force because, in the life cycle of governments, Labour is moving away from a preoccupation with policy development to a focus on implementation and delivery. Its impatience to see the delivery of service improvements is manifested in the prime minister's close personal involvement in domestic policy priorities, and the stated commitment of ministers to increase rather than reduce the pace of change. An appeal to the altruism of those working in the NHS, and recognition of the key role they have to play in delivering the modernisation programme, are just as likely to succeed as an attack on their conservatism and, unless this is taken on board, health policy will once more become a battleground between politicians and NHS staff.

Recognising the forces of innovation

What, then, should be done? The priority of the health secretary should be to recognise the forces of innovation within the NHS and provide them with the resources required to implement the government's vision. Delivering NHS modernisation depends fundamentally on ministers acknowledging this fact and not losing the support of those who are committed to providing a modern and dependable service. No amount of guidance from the NHS Executive or hectoring by politicians can substitute for a drive to improve performance that comes from within and is acknowledged and valued by those steering the process of change.

Above all, ministers should champion entrepreneurial managers and clinicians who are leading the modernisation drive within the NHS, and they should support the more rapid dissemination of good practices as they are identified. These measures may not be sufficient but they are certainly necessary in enabling the third way to be realised.

Summary

Policies about managing the NHS reflect changing beliefs about what motivates clinicians and managers. Command and control mechanisms have given way to market forces and now, in Labour's 'third way', to a variety of mechanisms used according to the circumstances. One omission in government thinking is failure to recognise that NHS staff are motivated to deliver improvements and simply need training and support to do so.

References

1. Ham, C., Managed markets in health care: the UK experiment. *Health Policy* 1996; 35: 279–292.

2. Ham, C., The third way in health care reform: does the emperor have any clothes? *J Health Serv Res Policy* 1999; **4**: 168–173.
3. Le Grand, J., Mays, N. and Mulligan, J-A. (eds) *Learning from the NHS internal market: a review of the evidence*. London: King's Fund, 1998.

This is a slightly edited version of an article which originally appeared under the same title in the *British Medical Journal*, 1999, **319**: 1490–2. Professor Chris Ham is the Director of the Health Services Management Centre, University of Birmingham, UK.

54 | Health sector reform: lessons from China

GERALD BLOOM AND GU XINGYUAN

China has been a laboratory for testing models of health sector organisation for many years; first in establishing centrally planned and managed rural health services, and then in changing the organisation of these services radically.

By the late 1970s most of rural China had a highly structured health service. Approximately 85% of villages had a health station staffed by bare-foot doctors who provided basic curative and preventive services; townships had health centres that provided referral services and supervised the bare-foot doctors; and county health bureaus planned and supervised countywide health services. A number of public health campaigns were organised under the technical leadership of the Ministry of Health (MoH) and the political leadership of the Communist Party. Almost the entire rural population had access to essential health services at a reasonable cost. This contributed to a dramatic increase in life expectancy at birth from 39 years during 1946–1949, to 68 in 1981 and 69 in 1990 (data from Yen and Chen, 1991 and the third and fourth census).

The success of China's rural health system strongly influenced the development of the primary health care approach, which dominated international health policy for many years.

Since the early 1980s, China has been evolving into 'a socialist market economy'. This has involved a shift from collective to household agricultural production; the phasing out of price controls; the reform of state-owned enterprises; the creation of a labour market; the development of new forms of ownership of enterprises; and the devolution of tax authority and public sector financial management. The transition has taken place against a background of rapid economic growth, in which the gross national product increased by 9.5% per year, in real terms, between 1978 and 1994 (State Statistical Bureau, 1995).

Changes in the organisation of the rural health sector

China's rural health services have undergone many of the changes commonly associated with health sector reform.

Increased reliance on out-of-pocket payments by users of health services. Prior to the economic reforms the rural health services were funded by government, communes (units of collective agricultural production), and users of services. Between 1981 and 1993 the government's share of national health expenditure (exclusive of subsidised care for government workers) fell from 28% to 14%. During the same period, the communes ceased to provide funds to the health sector. Rural households now have to pay a much greater share of medical costs themselves.

Most village health workers, who were paid by the communes prior to the economic reforms, now generate their own income (Tang *et al.*, 1994). They earn most of it by charging patients, selling drugs and working their plot of land. The government also pays them very modest fees for providing preventive services. In 1992, user charges accounted for over three-quarters of the revenue of county hospitals and township health centres in three poor counties (Gu *et al.*, 1995). These facilities had derived half of their revenue from this source during 1981.

Decentralisation of public sector health services. Prior to the 1980s, the government health services were organised as a centrally planned bureaucracy. The national MoH formulated policies and established targets and the lower levels had to meet these targets. Each level of government had to approve the plans of the levels below it.

Provincial and lower level governments now decide on sectoral allocations. Provincial and county health departments enjoy a great deal of autonomy within the health sector structure and they come directly under the authority of their local governments. Townships have been re-established to perform the administrative tasks previously undertaken by communes (Shue, 1984). They are responsible for the health centres.

Increased autonomy of health facilities. Prior to the economic reforms, managers of health facilities answered directly to government and political authorities. Health facility managers now have more autonomy from government and political structures. This has been reinforced by the fiscal responsibility system under which facilities generate most of their revenue and are allowed to pay bonuses to employees and invest in new equipment out of surpluses they earn.

Increased freedom of movement for health workers and flexibility in pay. Prior to the economic reforms most health workers were guaranteed a job until retirement. Pay was set nationally and people had to work where they were assigned. During the 1960s and 1970s many health workers were posted to rural facilities.

Certain market elements have been introduced into the management of labour. Health facilities now supplement basic salaries with bonuses whose size is linked to revenue generation. Health workers no longer have to stay in their post and many of the better trained ones have left rural facilities to earn more in the urban areas. Private practice has been permitted since 1980 (Liu *et al.*, 1994). In 1990 almost half the village health facilities were private.

Decreased political mobilisation. China's health services had a high political profile during the 1960s and 1970s. Most of the bare-foot doctors were trained and village health stations were built during that period. Entire communities were mobilised to participate in public health campaigns. The ethic of 'serving the people' strongly influenced health work.

Political factors have become less important to the health sector. One reason is a reaction against the intensive political mobilisation which took place during the Cultural Revolution. This reaction has been reinforced by the shift to household agricultural production, which means that rural residents can no longer be forced to participate in public health campaigns. Individuals and institutions now give priority to earning money. This change in ethos is reflected in the emphasis that local political leaders give to economic growth and generation of government revenue. Health's decreased political profile has given health workers considerable freedom from interference. Rural doctors, mostly the former bare-foot doctors, now work as individual practitioners under virtually no supervision.

The impact of structural change on health sector performance

Greater inequality of access to health care. Urban/rural inequalities in access to care have increased. By 1989 urban health services cost five times as much per person as those in the rural areas (Yu, 1992). The differences between rich and poor rural areas have also increased. Tang *et al.* (1994) found that average health expenditure per person was twice as high in rich than in relatively poor counties in 1987. Their sample did not include the poorest counties, where health centres are dilapidated and village level services are provided by poorly equipped part-time health workers (Croll, 1994).

Rises in the cost of care. The cost of rural health care has increased rapidly. This has been due to rises in health worker pay, a growth in drug expenditure and an increasing use of sophisticated medical technologies, particularly in the richer areas. The rise in health care costs has increased the burden on the poor, and severe illness is believed to be an important cause of financial hardship.

Weakening of the preventive services. There are increasing inter-regional differences in preventive services. The incidence of infectious disease has continued to fall in the more developed parts of the country. In these areas the major causes of excess ill health are increasingly related to chronic exposure to risks such as tobacco, alcohol, and environmental pollution. The preventive programmes are less successful in the poorer areas. One sign of this is the resurgence of preventable illnesses such as tuberculosis and schistosomiasis. Infant mortality and maternal mortality are much higher in these areas. One factor is the poor coverage of maternal and child health services.

Summary. Prior to the 1980s the rural health sector was tightly organised to deliver a package of services under the dual authority of the MoH and the Communist Party. These services contributed to substantial improvements in health at a reasonable cost. Now, the structure of the health sector is more diverse. In some parts of the country the changes have been minor and collective bodies have established alternative mechanisms for funding and overseeing health services. The major problem in these areas has been a rapid increase in the cost of health care. In other areas, particularly very poor ones, the rural health services are facing difficulties. Many facilities are suffering from financial hardships and their services have deteriorated. In spite of this, there is no evidence that the population's health has worsened (Liu *et al.*, 1995). This may be due to the lack of reliable data, but it is also related to the rise in most people's standard of living.

Health service regulation

Most health services in advanced market economies have complex arrangements to protect the population from harmful practices. These frequently include regulations that give professionals a monopoly right to provide certain services and protection against criminal charges should a patient suffer ill effects as a result of treatment. In exchange, the organised professions are expected to ensure that members provide an appropriate standard of care. There are no simple criteria defining who has the right to be called a doctor in China. Until recently, health workers could be promoted to the position of doctor, even if they had not graduated from a medical college. One reason for this is that the government perceived professional monopolies as a major constraint to the expansion of health services in the rural areas. The MoH is now exploring measures for improving the quality of service provision, arguing that most of the population has access to some kind of health worker.

Prior to the economic reforms, opportunistic behaviour was constrained by a combination of bureaucratic and political controls, and a powerful moral code. These mechanisms have been weakened since the early 1980s and they have not been replaced by alternative control mechanisms. As a consequence, service providers can respond much more vigorously to economic opportunities.

This is illustrated by the changes in the role of village health workers. Prior to the economic reforms most villages had several part-time bare-foot doctors. Their technical work was supervised by health centre doctors and their service to the public was monitored by local political leaders. They dealt with simple problems (using a small number of drugs) and referred sicker patients to higher levels. Many village health workers are now private practitioners. Their function is not clearly defined in law and they are virtually unsupervised. Village doctors prescribe a wide variety of drugs including steroids and powerful antibiotics, even though most have not been trained to use them. The major factors protecting patients against malpractice are competition from other providers and a residual ethos of public service among village health workers. It is hard to predict how long this ethos will last, as newly trained personnel begin to practice.

Political factors

One of the reasons China succeeded in creating services that addressed the health needs of the rural population at a reasonable cost was that the government and political structures gave this matter high priority. Their priorities have changed since the early 1980s.

The richer regions are resisting transfers of tax revenues to poor areas. This has contributed to the inequalities within the health sector. Demand for sophisticated curative services has increased in areas experiencing rapid economic growth. Hospitals in these areas provide the same style of care as hospitals in advanced market countries. The growth of modern medical care has affected services in poor areas by putting pressure on hospitals to obtain new equipment and contributing to the departure of experienced personnel from inferior facilities.

The increase in inequalities has heightened the struggle for health resources. The pressure to pay wage increases to health workers has made it more difficult for health services to fund operational expenditure or provide funds for village health services in poor areas. Those who can afford to pay receive preferential treatment. Even institutes whose official mandate is to oversee preventive programmes provide services for fee-paying clients. This is diverting resources from the provision of basic services.

Policy-makers need to develop strategies for protecting the interests of the poor in a situation of growing inequality. Unless some mechanisms can be established to ensure that health services meet the needs of the population, the present trend towards increasing inequalities in service delivery will continue.

Conclusions

In some cases, health can play a leadership role in a broader process of economic and institutional reform. This occurred in 19th Century Britain, where the public health movement was instrumental in the establishment of local governments capable of establishing a safe urban environment. Mostly, however, the health sector does not have the power to lead a major government restructuring. On the contrary, it must take factors outside the health sector into account. It needs to identify the major constraints to effective health service delivery and lobby for measures to diminish them.

China's experience underlines the influence of political factors on the pattern of health service delivery. A coalition in favour of reform needs to be constructed (Reich, 1995). The coalition will probably include providers of services for the poor, representatives of users, and local governments in poor areas. Without such a coalition, pressures by the powerful are likely to have a predominant influence on service development.

References

Croll, E. (1994) *From Heaven to Earth: Images and Experiences of Development in China.* Routledge, London.

Gu, X., Bloom, G., Tang, S. and Lucas, H. (1995) Financing Health Services in Poor Rural China: A Strategy for Health Sector Reform. *IDS Working Paper No. 17*, IDS, Brighton.

Liu, G., Liu, X. and Meng, Q. (1994) Privatization of the medical market in socialist China: a historical approach. *Health Policy 27*, 157–173.

Liu, Y., Hsiao, W., Li, Q., Liu, X. and Ren, M. (1995) Transformation of China's rural health care financing. *Social Science & Medicine*, 41(8), 1085–1093.

Reich, M. (1995) The politics of health sector reform: three cases of pharmaceutical policy. In *Health Sector Reform in Developing Countries*, ed. P. Berman, pp. 59–100. Harvard University Press, Boston.

Shue, V. (1984) The fate of the commune. *Modern China*, 10(3), 259–283.

State Statistical Bureau of the People's Republic of China (1995) *China Statistical Yearbook 1995*. China Statistical Information Consultancy Center, Beijing.

Tang, S., Bloom, G., Feng, X., Lucas, H., Gu, X. and Segall, M. (1994) Financing Rural Health Services in China: Adapting to Economic Reform. *IDS Research Report No. 26*, IDS, Brighton.

Yen, R. and Chen, S.L. (1991) *Chinese Population Studies*, 2, 1–10.

Yu, D. (1992) Changes in health care financing and health status: the case of China in the 1980s. *Innocenti Occasional Papers*. Economic Policy Series No. 34, International Child Development Centre, Florence.

This edited extract comes from a much longer paper, published under the same title in *Social Science and Medicine*, 1997, 45(3): 351–60. Gerald Bloom is a Fellow of the Institute of Development Studies, University of Sussex, Brighton, U.K. Gu Xingyuan is in the School of Public Health, Shanghai Medical University, China.

55 | The evolution of the health-care systems in the United States and the United Kingdom: similarities and differences

ROSEMARY STEVENS

I should like to present some ideas about the nature of the health-care systems of the two countries. For in the two systems there are some fundamental differences which long antedate the National Health Service in Britain or more recent Government initiatives here. Basic professional and social assumptions as they have evolved over the centuries, suggest that medical care itself means different things in different places. We are not always using common assumptions, rationalizations, or even definitions.

Specialization: common developments

For 100 years we have been under the spell of a movement toward increased technical specialization in medicine. Now this movement is virtually completed. Specialized departments in hospitals sprang up on both sides of the Atlantic only in the 1870s and 1880s, marking organizational acceptance that specialization was here to stay. St Thomas's Hospital in London set up outpatient departments for ophthalmology in 1871, for otolaryngology in 1882, for dermatology in 1884.[1] Over here, the Massachusetts General Hospital was setting up its own departments of dermatology (1870), neurology (1872), laryngology (1872), ophthalmology (1873), and aural surgery (1886) during the same period.[2] While specialization was accepted reluctantly by leaders of the medical professions in both countries – the first neurologist appointed to the Massachusetts General Hospital was barely dignified by the title of 'electrician' – the movement toward specialization had become inevitable.

By the early 1900s it appeared in America that general practice was moribund, if not dead. While the role of the family doctor as adviser and counselor was idealized as the ultimate in the doctor–patient relationship after 1890, a certain aura of myth and nostalgia surrounded this idealization – as it has, indeed, to the present. The family physician, that 'chum of the old people, the intimate of confiding girlhood, the uncle and oracle of the kids',[3] had largely disappeared by 1915. Outpatient departments of city hospitals provided general services for the indigent masses. The American middle class was already going directly to specialists.

Even in England, where the general practitioner was more readily defined and firmly established, outpatient departments of general hospitals and the rise of special hospitals in the last quarter of the nineteenth century threatened the generalist's position. It has been estimated that, before the National Health Insurance Act of 1911, only 10 to 20 per cent of the British population had family practitioners.[4] Hospitals had become 'temples of research, and the avenues leading to additional medical knowledge'.[5]

By World War I the specialization movement was in full swing. New professions added vertical specialization to the horizontal specialization developing in medicine. Besides the great rise of the nursing profession, there were social workers, optometrists, X-ray technicians, laboratory workers, physical therapists, and (in the American Midwest) nurse-anesthetists. Medicine was no longer a single matter of a conference between two individuals: one patient and one practitioner.

Specialization demanded some response to the questionable relationship between the new specialists and general practitioners – if, indeed, the generalists were to survive. Generalist–specialist relations, transmitted later to questions of primary versus secondary (and tertiary) care, became one set of issues for discussion in the modern healthcare system. A related set of issues concerned the emerging role of the hospital, that center of specialized knowledge and techniques. Was it to be the center of all medical care, the temple of service as well as scientific excellence? Such questions were engaging writers on both sides of the Atlantic well before World War I and became intense in the 1920s and 30s.

Other themes with which we still contend have been apparent over many decades. Problems of cost increases and cost containment in medical care have been discussed, particularly on this side of the Atlantic, for at least six decades. The distribution of medical services – questions of urban–rural distributions and the concentration of specialists in major cities – was already of concern in the 1920s. The medical profession, a rag-bag of individuals with varying training and from varying backgrounds on both sides of the Atlantic in the late nineteenth century, became homogenized, standardized, and middle class in the years between the two World Wars. As the status of the profession rose with its advancing techniques so, from World War I, did the social background of its students.

Yet, while some of the dilemmas of modern medicine are clear – the relationship between generalists and specialists, the role of the hospital, the nature of the 'physician', and the role of medical education – the specific responses to medical specialization in Britain and America have been, and may continue to be, quite different, because of the way each health system has developed.

Professional distinction and social differences

Most of the basic characteristics of British and American medicine existed in embryonic form in the 1870s and were clearly evident by 1914. Differences existed in the relative development of professional patterns of medical practice in the two countries, in professional regulation and medical education, in general social attitudes toward the provision of medical care, and even in the behavior of patients.

A quite conservative student of the hospital scene, Henry Burdett,[6] noted with some criticism: 'Free relief has now become so general that the majority of the population in England consider it not only not a disgrace, but the most natural thing in the world, when they fall ill, to demand and receive free medical treatment without question or delay.'

In contrast, he commented, 'America, owing no doubt to the fact of its being a relatively new country, possessing few endowed charities, and an energetic population consisting largely of those who resort to it in the hope of earning an independence may be regarded as the home of the pay system.'

Most patients in American hospitals occupied pay beds or paying wards, in contrast to the largely charitable English hospital system. Moreover, patients were already characterized as being, in England, relatively passive recipients of medical care, while Americans were both more adventurous and more litigious.

Trying to explain the difference a generation earlier, a leading Californian physician had remarked: 'Patients in old countries are more timid: they are not anxious to be the subjects of experiments. In new countries, they bite at all new medicines.'[7]

But while this adventurousness might appeal to the desires of American physicians to show initiative, it resulted equally in 'serious annoyance' from malpractice claims. Modern Californians may be reassured to learn that malpractice claims similar to those of today were being made 100 years ago: 'A certain class of patients make it a business to extort money in this way, by the aid of a certain class of lawyers who go halves in the speculation'.[7]

There would inevitably have been differences in the type of medical organization developing for the small, densely populated, and relatively homogeneous population of Britain and the diverse population of America, scattered over a vast continent. But coupled with these topographical distinctions and with the more general distinctions between the rough and tumble of life in a rapidly growing country and one with centuries of social stability, there were already marked distinctions in patterns of professional organization in medicine.

Medicine in England grew from centralized professional guilds and from a professional system clearly stratified by social status. Before 1858, there were technically three recognized medical professions in England. The Royal College of Physicians, established in 1518, was the traditional domain of the educated elite. The Royal College of Surgeons, founded in 1800, represented the growing prestige of surgeons – well before the technological revolution in surgery made such a distinction functionally inevitable. Apothecaries formed a third strain. Systematic training of apothecaries for medical practice was achieved through an act of 1815, and the resulting apothecaries' license rapidly became the most popular way to become a licensed practitioner. In fact, the most common way of becoming licensed by the mid-nineteenth century was to become both an apothecary and a surgeon.[8]

The early existence of the guilds of physicians, surgeons, and apothecaries has left an enduring imprint on medical care in England. Physicians, as the elite of the medical profession, were a relatively small – if powerful – body, whose clientele during the nineteenth century was divided into two extraordinarily diverse groups. As private practitioners, members of the Royal College of Physicians catered largely to the upper segments of society, although they might function as general consultants to apothecaries when called upon to do so. Yet at the same time, because physicians had been instrumental in founding the great charitable hospitals of England in the eighteenth century, physicians were also the honorary medical staffs of the most prestigious hospitals – which, in turn, catered largely to the poverty-stricken.

Surgeon-apothecaries, on the other hand, found themselves a growing role during the nineteenth century as practitioners to the middle class in the expanding industrial cities. When the three branches of practice were combined into one medical register under the Medical Acts of 1858 and 1886, the earlier distinctions did not evaporate. There was now one medical profession, with a training supposedly designed for general practice, but distinctions remained at the graduate level. The elite of the profession (members of the Royal College of Physicians and fellows of the Royal College of Surgeons) continued to control major hospital positions. Indeed, the struggle for an honorary appointment could become the dominant motive of a doctor's career. In 1900, when American hospital building was in full swing and hospital appointments tended to be open to most recognized physicians, the British voluntary hospital was controlled by a small number of leading practitioners. Each was usually responsible for an identifiable group of beds in a particular ward and thus for the patients who occupied those beds. Surgeon-apothecaries, meanwhile, were general practitioners who worked almost entirely outside the voluntary hospital system.

National health insurance provided the final endorsement of this system in 1911 by creating a central role for the general practitioner. Members of the working population below a specified income level were now insured for the services of general practitioners, but not for hospital or specialist care.

General or family practice became, and has remained, central to the organization of the British system. It has been bolstered, it is true, by further government action: the National Health Service Act of 1946, which incorporated general practice as the basis of the health-care system, and changes in reimbursement following the profession's 'Doctor's Charter' of 1965, equalizing generalist and specialist incomes. But such actions would have been unthinkable had the earlier traditions not existed.

Modern medical care in Britain relies, in short, on the system of checks and balances which emerged from the prespecialization era. General practitioners control access to the health-care system; salaried hospital staff, the consultants (who are now, of course, all specialists), control access to hospital care. When each round of specialist treatment is completed, the patient returns to his family practitioner. The old social division between the branches of practice have been continued in the separate *functions* of primary and secondary care, and there continue to be far more general practitioners than specialists,

In the United States there were no guilds, no national focus for an elite such as London provided to British practitioners, and until the 1870s there were relatively few hospitals. American medicine was a profession without institutions. If the professional development of British medicine can be characterized as the history of guilds which eventually came together, establishing mutually acceptable positions, the development of American medicine for most of its history has been a search for *itself*, for identity and professional unity. Out of this movement was to come a medical profession committed to university-centered education and technological advancement, organizationally based on an array of specialists.

Defining the practice of medicine

From time to time efforts were made to establish guilds on this side of the Atlantic. John Morgan was one of several Scottish-trained physicians returning to the Colonies who tried before Independence to establish the educated 'physician' as a separate rank of practitioner along British lines. But such efforts were doomed to failure in the competitive and social climate of the day. One continuing theme of American medicine was already evident. Even in the Revolutionary era there were relatively large *numbers* of doctors in America. Clearly medicine was felt to be a desirable occupation.

One estimate for New York in 1750 gives a ratio of one doctor to every 350 members of the population; in Williamsburg in 1730 there was one doctor to every 135 members of the population, relatively a far greater density of doctors than today.[9] It was just not practicable for the American doctor (unless he had considerable private income) to say he would do no surgery and dispense no drugs, but merely be an educated physician. Almost from the beginning, the American doctor has been an individual in a competitive market situation, dependent on his success – not on family connections or institutional affiliations (as is clearly the case of physicians in England), but on the exercise of his own initiative.

Even in the eighteenth century, any suggestion of a guild also suggested the imposition of a potentially dangerous monopoly. Social elitism in medical practice as in other fields has consistently been regarded as un-American. Early licensing laws were repealed in the 1830s and 1840s, leaving the field of medicine open to all comers. (Modern licensing laws date from the 1870s.) The rise of proprietary or profitmaking medical schools during the century added another component for untrammelled competition.

Instead of creating distinctions within the profession, medical societies arose in America to protect all 'regular' practitioners from the common threat of 'irregulars' or quacks.[10] The American College of Surgeons and the American College of Physicians, which followed in 1915, came much too late to direct basic patterns of the medical profession.

Probably the most important early impact of the College of Surgeons was its accreditation and upgrading of the standards of hospitals, which had sprung up like mushrooms from the 1880s in the American doctor's enthusiastic desire to do surgery. The British response to the technological possibilities or relatively 'safe' surgery in the post-asepsis, post-anesthetics era had been to exclude any remaining general practitioners from the staffs of hospitals, restricting operations to the small staff of consulting surgeons. But no such constraints existed in America, and there was a ready market for hospital construction in the expanding cities. Surgery, indeed, was so instantly popular that it was to become a lasting characteristic of American medicine: about a fourth of all American physicians have been surgeons in recent decades, a much larger proportion than in England. While England was consolidating the general practitioner, America was hailing the virtuosity of the surgeon and sometimes criticizing his excesses and deploring his greed.

But in all fields, compared with the individualism, exuberance, and ingenuity of American medical practice at the beginning of this century, medicine in England seemed tame and settled. Abraham Flexner, reporting on England in 1912, found educational standards there low and medical education regarded among clinicians as merely a 'professional incident', with any interest in research mostly missing. The guild system was, he remarked, 'admirably calculated to protect honor and dignity, to conserve ceremony, and to transmit tradition'.[11]

While there were relatively large numbers of doctors in Britain in the first decade of the century, social and ethical structures in Britain precluded out-and-out competition. The British doctor, accustomed to working for the Poor Law and for public health authorities, might welcome National Health Insurance as a means of upgrading his financial status. In America, while there was also discussion of health insurance through the state, the mood was different. Fee-splitting was rife, there were kickbacks, usually from surgeons to referring practitioners. It was acknowledged that fees and services were related: the higher the fee, the better the care. The California state medical journal put forward as its primary objection to contract practice in 1913 *not* the argument that the rates paid were too low, but that patients for whom only 10 cents were paid would get only 10 cents' worth of treatment.[12] Cost and quality were inextricably combined, as indeed they have remained to this day.

Since there was no entrenched social structure for general practice, there was no ethical or other barrier against specialization or direct competition for patients by American physicians. There were both money and social advancement in specialism through private office practice – in contrast to the British system of social advancement through hospital positions. Virginia doctors, even in the 1870s, advertised in such areas as 'Speciality Surgery', 'Diseases of Females', 'Diseases of Urinary Organs', 'Diseases of the Ear and Eye'.[13] A formal social class system for medical education had failed in America; there was now an emergence of a self-proclaimed technological elite, competing directly with generalists for patients.

The standardization movement in American medical practice was well underway at the turn of the century. There was a gradual 'leveling up of the masses of the profession'.[14] The reorganization of the Harvard curriculum in 1870 had been followed by upgrading of standards in other schools, and the foundation of the Johns Hopkins school in 1893 provided a paradigm for the future development of scientific, laboratory-oriented medical schools based on universities.

The American Medical Association, unifying its scattered organization over the same period, rose on the banner of standardization. There was to be one American doctor, produced by medical schools of equivalent quality. While the profession in Britain was grappling with the problems of introducing general practitioner services under National Health Insurance in 1911, American medical education was set on the road to an increasingly scientific emphasis for medicine. The movement was rapid. By 1920, America had replaced Germany as the world leader of scientific medicine. Medical education was based on universities, with a strong research emphasis. It was not surprising that the graduates of these schools would turn increasingly to the specialities. Nor, indeed, was there any social structure such as National Health Insurance to encourage the continuation of general practice as a means of making a reasonable living; nor any ethical arrangement such as the referral system, which existed in England, to establish primary care as a central function of the emerging health system. In America generalists continued to compete with specialists, and one specialist with another.

References

1. McInnes, E.M. *St Thomas's Hospital*, Allen and Unwin, London (1963).
2. Washburn, F.A. *The Massachusetts General Hospital: Its Development, 1900–1935*, Houghton Mifflin Co., Boston (1939).

3. Jacobi, A., quoted by Michael M. Davis 'Organization of medical service', *American Labor Legislation Review*, **6**, 16–20 (1916).
4. Titmuss, R.M. 'Trends of social policy'. In *Law and Opinion in England in the Twentieth Century*, Ginsberg, M. (ed.) Greenwood, London (1959).
5. Kershaw, R. *Special Hospitals: Their Origin, Development, and Relationship to Medical Education*, Pulman, London (1909).
6. Burdett, H.C. *Hospitals and Asylums of the World*, Vol. III, J. and A. Churchill, London (1893).
7. Gibbons, H. Annual Address to the California State Medical Society. *Transactions of the Medical Society of California*, privately printed (1872).
8. Newman, C. *The Evolution of Medical Education in the Nineteenth Century*, Oxford University Press, London (1957).
9. Shryock, R.H. *Medicine and Society in America 1660–1860*, New York University Press, New York (1962).
10. Kett, J. *The Formation of the American Medical Profession: The Role of Institutions 1760–1860*, Yale University Press, New Haven (1968).
11. Flexner, A. *Medical Education in Europe*, Carnegie Foundation, New York (1912).
12. *California State Journal of Medicine*, Editorial, **11**, 41 (1913).
13. Blanton, W.B. *Medicine in Virginia in the Nineteenth Century*, Garrett and Massie, Richmond (1933).
14. Mumford, J.G. *A Narrative of Medicine in America*, Lippincott, Philadelphia (1903).

Rosemary Stevens is in the Department of History and Sociology of Science, University of Pennsylvania, though at the time of writing the article she was at Tulane University in Louisiana. The article has been edited from a longer version that appeared in 1976 in *Priorities in the Use of Resources in Medicine*, Number 40 in the Fogarty International Center Proceedings, published by the US Department of Health, Education and Welfare.

56 | The role of the hospital in a changing environment

MARTIN McKEE AND JUDITH HEALY

Hospitals pose many challenges to those undertaking reform of health care systems. They are, quite literally, immovable structures whose design was set in concrete, usually many years previously. Their configuration often reflects the practice of health care and the patient populations of a bygone era. Their incompatibility with present needs ranges from major design problems, such as a scarcity of operating theatres, to more minor problems, such as the lack of power sockets for the ever expanding number of electronic monitors.

It is not only the physical structure that is difficult to change. Hospital functions are also resistant to change, as illustrated by the persistence of large tuberculosis sanitoria in some countries long after they were required. Hospitals are staffed by the élite members of the medical profession who, in many cases, can use their excellent political connections to oppose changes that threaten their interests. An environment that is technically complex, surrounded by much uncertainty, and which contains information asymmetry, only enhances the mystique of the medical professional and often leaves the outsider confused and perplexed.

Given these barriers to change, it is unsurprising that hospital reform is viewed with trepidation by health policy-makers. Yet hospitals are a very important element of the health care system. Financially, they account for about 50% of overall health care expenditure. Organizationally, they dominate the rest of the health care system. Symbolically, they are viewed by the public as the main manifestation of the health care system, as shown by the enthusiasm with which politicians seek to be photographed opening new hospitals.

The survival of the hospital as an institution reflects two quite different needs. The first derives from the rapid growth of advanced technology and clinical specialization. The resources involved, including humans and equipment, are scarce and expensive. It is simply not tenable to disperse such resources across a large number of small facilities. This situation is analogous to the growth of the factory in the eighteenth century, driven by the spread of the steam engine, that made the earlier cottage industries obsolete.

The second need, to provide care rather than cure, is quite different. Care requires people rather than equipment, and generalists rather than specialists. Centralization of services is not necessary on cost grounds, especially since access may be more important for patients and families. In this complex environment it is essential that policy-makers know which aspects of hospital design and configuration are supported by evidence and which are not.

What should a hospital look like?

The configuration of hospital services in a given setting reflects a tension between two competing objectives: centralization versus dispersion of hospital services. There are two arguments for centralizing hospital services. First, hospitals and clinicians undertaking high volumes of work achieve better outcomes; and second, large hospitals achieve economies of scale. The counter argument for dispersing hospitals is that this improves population access and reduces inequalities. (The major source of evidence on these issues is a systematic review of over 200 studies undertaken in 1996 by the University of York.[1])

Greater volume leads to better health outcomes

The volume of procedures at which optimal results are achieved is often relatively low. In the case of coronary artery bypass grafting, there is no significant improvement in outcome in hospitals undertaking over 200 procedures per year. In most countries, few hospitals undertake such a low volume of cases. Studies that have examined both hospital and physician volume have found a relationship between outcome and hospital volume, but not between outcome and physician volume, suggesting that the collective expertise of the entire surgical team is more important than that of the individual surgeon. This finding is plausible given that surgical patients are more likely to die from post-operative complications than from problems occurring in the operating theatre.

Large hospitals achieve economies of scale

The second argument for concentrating hospitals is on grounds of efficiency, with larger hospitals purportedly achieving economies of scale. This has been examined in detail by Aletras *et al.*,[2] who concluded that economies of scale, assuming the hospital is already operating at maximum efficiency, are exploited at quite low levels of around 200 beds, and diseconomies of scale become important at levels over 650 beds. The data were insufficient to specify an optimal size but suggested it was in the range of 200–400 beds.

Economies of scope should also be considered. The hospital contains a complex set of interrelated functions and one factor driving the growth of modern general hospitals was to gather different specialities together under one roof. There may be strong arguments for creating larger hospital units to facilitate links between related specialities, to strengthen multidisciplinary teams, to ensure optimal use of expensive equipment such as scanners or operating theatres, or to support the training role of the hospital. Here, each case must be considered on its merits.

Although existing research on hospital configurations has limitations, it provides little support for concentrating care in very large hospitals, either on grounds of effectiveness or efficiency, but some concentration may be required to achieve economies of scope, which should then be made explicit. Importantly, where the current pattern of provision is dispersed, there is little evidence to support mergers of existing facilities.

An important argument against concentration of hospitals is that such a policy will reduce access to care. This may be especially important if, as has been suggested in New Zealand, differential access to health care contributes to socioeconomic inequalities in health.[3] Such problems are likely to be greatest in rural areas, as illustrated by a study from France. Patients with colorectal cancer living in rural areas experienced greater delay in obtaining treatment, were less likely to be treated in specialist centres, and also had worse outcomes than those in urban areas.[4] The relationship between distance and access, often characterized as a distance-decay effect, has been reported for preventive, primary and secondary care. For example, in a study of factors influencing uptake of breast cancer screening, distance was the single most important factor.[5] In a study from Northern Ireland, use of emergency services was much greater among those living closer to a hospital.[6] Furthermore, patients already attending hospital may be less likely to remain in a treatment programme if they must travel long distances.[7]

In contrast, several studies have found no effect of distance on utilization of care. The apparently conflicting evidence has been examined in detail by Carr-Hill *et al.*,[8] who noted that the research is subject to several limitations. One is the need for caution when extrapolating from a country such as the United Kingdom, where the distances involved are generally short, to a country like Canada where distances may be vastly greater. Another is the absence, in many studies, of an examination of any differential impact of distance upon different social classes or ethnic groups. The absence of an overall effect, therefore, may obscure important inequalities within particular population groups.

In summary, access is generally more important in relation to primary care, outpatient services, and screening programmes, with inpatient care being relatively less affected. These findings have important implications for hospital planning, since they show that hospital size is only one consideration. For example, the overall mix of functions required to meet the needs of the population served must be decided; and it must then be decided how each function can best establish a critical mass for providing good quality care. It must be recognized that in many places this has not yet been achieved, with multiple small units isolated from other specialities and with duplication of costly equipment. In such cases, major restructuring will be required.

Unpacking the black box

Hospitals have been subjected to systematic efforts to change organizational behaviour over the last few decades. Three main approaches have been used to improve performance: (i) providing incentives for optimizing clinical performance; (ii) changing the organizational environment; and (iii) changing payment mechanisms.

Incentives for optimizing clinical performance

In many countries there is growing evidence that clinical performance in hospitals is sub-optimal. The strategies used to address this problem include quality assurance models, clinical audit and the new concept of clinical governance, in which quality is a shared managerial and clinical responsibility. These are based on the assumption that quality assurance activities and continuing professional development lead to improved quality of care.

Unfortunately, the available evidence, mostly drawn together within the framework of the Cochrane Collaboration, demonstrates that clinical behaviour is quite resistant to change. For example, a review of 99 trials concluded that there was little or no change following conferences or short educational events.[8] Perhaps the most important finding to emerge is that behavioural change is most likely to follow a range of interventions that are mutually reinforcing.[9]

Changing the organizational environment

A second approach to improving the quality of care has emerged from research on the relationship between organizational culture and quality of care.[10] Certain hospitals ('magnet' hospitals) were identified that were widely regarded by nurses as offering a good environment in which to practise nursing (but where patient outcomes were unknown). These hospitals were characterized by greater nursing autonomy and better relationships between doctors and nurses. These hospitals were matched with controls and, after adjustment for severity, the 'magnet' hospitals achieved a significantly lower inpatient mortality rate.

Other work reached similar conclusions, finding tangible benefits to patients from a supportive culture among clinical staff. For example, organizational and professional job satisfaction among nurses is a strong predictor of process measures of quality of care.[11] In intensive care units, the best predictors of better patient outcomes are organizational factors such as a patient-centred culture, strong medical and nursing leadership, effective collaboration, and an open approach to problem solving.[12]

This research has several important implications. First, it helps us understand why some hospitals perform better than others. Second, it highlights the fact that hospitals are complex human service organizations, and not just assemblies of industrial units to be reconfigured at will.

Changing payment mechanisms

The third main approach to quality of care is the use of financial incentives. Payment mechanisms have received considerable attention, but can only be mentioned briefly here. The ideal mechanism would be one that offered incentives for producing effective, efficient and equitable treatment, with no perverse incentives and with minimal transaction costs. In practice, many of the systems fail on one or more of these counts. A perfect system is not of course achievable, since there are inevitable trade-offs. Financial incentives, while good at pushing behaviour in a certain direction, are less good at putting limits upon financial motivation. In each case it is important to identify, on the basis of empirical evidence, the positive and negative effects of each model of payment and then to monitor the effects in practice.

Looking ahead

The environment in which hospitals exist has continually changed and the pace of change is accelerating. The situation is complicated further in that different countries start from very different baselines and face different challenges, both in the demands placed upon them and the resources available to them.

It is, however, possible to speculate about some factors. A key issue will be the continually changing burden of disease, although the effects are difficult to quantify. First, the nature of the change will be different in every country, reflecting differences in, for example, diet, smoking rates, and exposure to risk of injury or infections. Second, it is possible that some previously unknown disease will emerge, as human immunodeficiency virus (HIV)/acquired immunodeficiency syndrome (AIDS) emerged in the twentieth century. Changes in patterns of existing diseases are more amenable to prediction, at least in the short term. In many industrialized countries, for example, rates of some chronic diseases will continue to fall. However, this will be accompanied by increases in degenerative disorders such as Alzheimer's disease, increasing the need for care rather than cure. Rapid increases in smoking-related diseases can be predicted, as well as a continuing growth in AIDS.

The possible consequences of newly emerging diseases are much more problematic, with important consequences for clinical practice and hospital design. An example has been the need to adopt universal precautions to prevent transmission of HIV. In the future, the growth of antibiotic resistance may lead to further changes as diseases that are generally amenable to treatment, such as tuberculosis, become not only effectively incurable but also easily transmissible to staff and other patients. A particular concern in some European countries is the possibility that human forms of bovine spongiform encephalopathy (so-called mad cow disease) could become widespread as the prion agent involved is extremely resistant to sterilization.[13] These drug-resistant and highly infectious diseases could fundamentally challenge the concept of the hospital, rendering them as dangerous as they were in the pre-antibiotic days.

A second set of issues relates to changes in the people who work in hospitals. Some changes will reflect demographic trends and macroeconomic trends, in particular affecting the size of the nursing workforce. Others will reflect changing expectations, such as the willingness to work long and unsocial hours.

A third set of issues arises from developments in technology, with new possibilities for investigation or treatment. Examples include the continuing advances in imaging, fibre-optics and information technology. These advances will lead to changes in professional demarcations as particular tasks cease to be seen as the reserve of a single group. These changes will affect not only the internal organization of the hospital, but also its interface with the outside world, as complex diagnosis and treatment, and thus patients, move into clinics for day surgery and into the primary care sector.

Technology will also bring profound changes in what it is possible to do within the hospital. Early computers occupied whole buildings, yet their processing power was less than a present-day hand-held organizer. The growth in information technology has left few areas of health care untouched, ranging from rapid processing of digital images to an enhanced capacity to monitor and more actively manage patient care. Miniaturization has allowed user-friendly diagnostic kits to replace what would previously have required a complex laboratory. As has already happened with AIDS in many countries, and with peptic ulcers previously, new drugs will reduce demand for inpatient treatment.

What are the implications of these likely changes for the hospital of the future? If a narrow technological perspective is taken, it is possible to argue that the hospital as a concept will no longer be justified. Advances in technology may mean that the hospital is not needed as a means of concentrating expensive equipment. Developments in communications technology and, in particular, telemedicine may mean that the hospital is not needed to concentrate skilled staff. In such circumstances it is conceivable that a virtual hospital could be constructed, in which patients would be diagnosed and treated in local ambulatory care centres, drawing on specialist expertise located remotely where necessary. Conversely, it is arguable that this model ignores other roles of the hospital, in particular its caring role, as well as its role in training and professional development.

The hospital of the future must respond to all of these challenges. It must balance economies of scope with optimal access, drawing on advances in technology as appropriate. It may need fewer beds, but it will need more operating theatres and recovery areas, as well as purpose-built facilities that can offer one-day surgery, or integrated care for common disorders. Most importantly, the hospital will need to be flexible, because the diseases it treats and the ways in which it treats them will be very different from those of today.

References

1. *Hospital volume and health care outcomes, costs and patient access.* York, National Health Service Centre for Reviews and Dissemination, University of York, 1996.
2. Aletras, V., Jones, A., Sheldon, T.A. Economies of scale and scope. In Ferguson, B., Sheldon, T., Posnett, J., eds. *Concentration and choice in health care.* Glasgow, Royal Society of Medicine Press, 1997: 23–26.
3. Marshall, S.W. *et al.* Social class differences in mortality from diseases amenable to medical intervention in New Zealand. *International Journal of Epidemiology*, 1993, **22**: 255–261.
4. Launoy, G. *et al.* Influence of rural environment on diagnosis, treatment and prognosis of colorectal cancer. *Journal of Epidemiology and Community Health*, 1992, **46**: 365–367.
5. Haiart, D. *et al.* Mobile breast screening factors affecting uptake, efforts to increase response and acceptability. *Public Health*, 1990, **104**: 239–247.
6. McKee, C.M., Gleadhill, D.N., Watson, J.D. Accident and emergency attendance rates: variation among patients from different general practices. *British Journal of General Practice*, 1990, **40**: 150–153.
7. Fortney, J.C. *et al.* The effects of travel barriers and age on the utilization of alcoholism treatment aftercare. *American Journal of Drug and Alcohol Abuse*, 1995, **21**: 391–406.
8. Carr-Hill, R.A., Place, M., Posnett, J. Access and the utilization of healthcare services. In Ferguson, B., Sheldon, T., Posnett, J., eds. *Concentration and choice in health care.* Glasgow, Royal Society of Medicine Press, 1997: 37–49.
9. Davis, D.A. *et al.* Changing physician performance. A systematic review of the effect of continuing medical education strategies. *Journal of American Medical Association*, 1995, **274**: 700–705.
10. Aiken, L.H., Smith, H.L., Lake, E.T. Lower Medicare mortality among a set of hospitals known for good nursing care. *Medical Care*, 1994, **32**: 771–787.

11. Leveck, M.L., Jones, C.B. The nursing practice environment, staff retention, and quality of care. *Research in Nursing Health*, 1996, **19**: 331–343.
12. Zimmerman, J.E. *et al*. Improving intensive care: observations based on organisational case studies in nine intensive care units: a prospective, multicenter study. *Critical Care Medicine*, 1993, **21**: 1443–1451.
13. Ghani, A.C. *et al*. Epidemiological determinants of the pattern and magnitude of the vCJD epidemic in Great Britain. *Proceedings of the Royal Society of London. Series B: Biological Sciences*, 1998, **265**: 2443–2452.

This edited extract is from a much longer article, originally published under the same title in the *Bulletin of the World Health Organization*, 2000, **78**(6): 803–10. The article is based upon material from the following book: Martin McKee and Judith Healy (eds) *Hospitals in a Changing Europe*, Open University Press, Buckingham, UK (2002). Martin McKee is a Research Director of the European Observatory on Health Care Systems and Professor of European Public Health, London School of Hygiene & Tropical Medicine, UK. Judith Healy is a Senior Research Fellow in the same department.

Health work

INTRODUCTION

All of us are 'health workers' in one sense or another, and the choice of articles for Part 6 illustrates the variety of meanings, roles and tasks that can be construed as health work. But they do more than simply illustrate the range of people, occupations and locations in which the practice of health care is conducted. Several themes emerge from these articles: the struggle to find ways to 'care' as well as to 'practise'; the issue of relative power between occupational groups and between health care workers and patients, as role boundaries become increasingly blurred; and the striving for recognition as a 'professional' in a fast-changing health service.

Michael Young and Lesley Cullen's account of 'The carer at home' shows the extent of health work that goes on outside the formal health care system. Here we see it under the greatest pressure in households where someone is slowly declining through the later stages of a terminal illness. The strain on carers is immense, but even neighbours are prepared to take on this demanding role where close relatives are absent, and it is clear that the dying person remains a central figure within the caring network, able to exercise choices and negotiate their needs to the very end.

A practical demonstration of Young and Cullen's conclusion that 'death can bring out life-giving qualities' in carers and in recipients is given in the next article, 'We didn't want him to die on his own', by David Field. He describes the emotional attachment that grew between nurses and their dying patients on a busy hospital ward, as the nurses tried to provide care of such a personal quality that it transcended the impersonal bustle around them. Field links the nurses' capacity to do this with a move towards non-hierarchical relationships between health care staff, in which doctors relinquished some control of the information that nurses could share with patients, but he also highlights the expectation that nursing involves 'doing something'.

Celia Davies picks up this theme in her analysis of threats to nursing as a 'caring' profession, in which attending to the needs of patients by listening and 'being there' is supported and valued as much as the scientific knowledge that underpins treatment. The desirability of 'professionalism' is rarely questioned, since it implies in most people's minds a form of behaviour that is both fair and altruistic, placing the needs of patients before those of practitioners. In 'Professionalism and the conundrum of care', Davies argues that nursing benefits from a recognition of its similarities with the kind of informal care described by Young and Cullen and highlighted in Field's account. But the generally lower status of women as health workers means that the 'new' nurses have been keen to appropriate the label 'professional' for the work they do. Davies suggests that striving for the traditional hallmarks of professional status may lead to an 'élite' group of professional nurses, distanced from the hands-on nursing care that nurses say they value. She proposes a new definition of professionalism involving recognition – both by nurses and the policy makers who set pay scales and determine the conditions of nursing work – that nursing is a fusion of labour and love.

The definition of 'caring' takes on another dimension in Thurstan B. Brewin's article 'Truth, trust and paternalism'. Brewin, a cancer specialist, argues that doctors who encourage a trusting and paternalistic relationship with patients are motivated by a desire to give genuine medical care. He maintains that a doctor who tells everything to his dying patient and seeks permission for the decisions he takes is discarding half the value of a consultation. He sees the interaction as one in which the patient benefits from the doctor's experience and judgement.

Ann Oakley's critical account of paternalism in the medical management of childbirth, 'Doctor knows best', presents a radically different interpretation of what she sees as the unequal relationship between doctor and patient. For Oakley, the main effect of paternalism has been to reinforce the oppression of women by a male-dominated medical profession. She argues that doctors in this area of health care too often inflate their professional expertise by questioning the reliability of women's own accounts of their pregnancies and undermining women's authority as experts in managing their own experience.

The disappearance of the patient as an individual in need of care is also apparent in Roger Jeffery's classic account of 'Normal rubbish: deviant patients in casualty departments'. The idea that health workers may have preferences for working with certain kinds of patient, and dislike or even stigmatize and 'punish' others, goes against conventional notions of professional behaviour. In Jeffery's study, casualty staff categorized patients as either 'good' cases, who enabled them to demonstrate or acquire specialist skills, and 'rubbish' – patients whose problems were considered trivial or self-inflicted. (The articles by Goffman in Part 2 and Asher in Part 3 also distinguish between 'deserving' and 'blameworthy' patients.) Jeffery points to the low professional status of casualty work in the medical hierarchy as one reason why staff may attempt to distance themselves from patients by typifications such as these, and claims that prestige among doctors is measured in part by how far removed they are from the interface with the community.

Perhaps the lowest in the hierarchy of hospital work are the ancillary staff, whose position is reflected in low autonomy and pay, and whose contribution to patient care is generally disregarded as 'health work' – as Elizabeth Paterson discovered when she spent time as a participant observer preparing food with the 'Maids in a hospital kitchen'. Just like the staff engaged in direct patient care, the kitchen maids carved out areas of higher and lower status work (preparing macaroni cheese is 'good', washing lettuce is 'bad'), and demonstrated their competence as a means of maintaining self-esteem. And like Jeffery's casualty workers, the kitchen maids distinguished between clients: medical staff and private patients were given the newer, shiny containers; 'ordinary' patients got 'any bashed object'. It remains to be seen whether the status of kitchen staff will change with the recognition that the quality of hospital food contributes to patients' recovery and length of stay.

Another professional group engaged in redefinition of their roles and relationships with other health workers are the PAMs – professions allied to medicine. Over 100,000 state-registered PAMs work in the British National Health Service, including occupational therapists, radiographers and physiotherapists, all rapidly moving towards a graduate workforce with codified professional standards (following the nursing trajectory that concerned Davies). Lesley Doyal and Ailsa Cameron's study of PAMs highlights 'continuity and change in a complex workforce', where innovative roles such as diagnostic radiographer are viewed with suspicion, and potential contributions by PAMs to patient care are overlooked by a management structure in which they are neither represented nor understood. But if a blurring of boundaries between various forms of health work contributes to interprofessional tensions in the short term, it also opens up possibilities for cooperative multidisciplinary work in the future.

Part 6 ends by stepping outside the UK with an account by David Werner of primary health care in Latin America in the 1970s. In 'The village health worker: lackey or liberator?' he maintains the focus on issues of power and professional status by suggesting that health workers should make a political alliance with the people they serve to tackle the social inequalities that lead to ill health. He argues for more widespread use of health workers with a basic training that reflects local needs, and the confidence to serve their communities. Werner says the day must come when we 'look at the primary health worker as the key member of the health team, and at the doctor as the auxiliary', but he identifies health care programmes that oppress communities as well as those that support them. His argument against the concentration of resources in hospitals and at the top of the 'skills pyramid' represented by expensively trained doctors is reminiscent of the articles by Davies, and by Doyal and Cameron, describing a health workforce inspired by non-élitist 'new' professionalism. Werner's ideals are close to the practice observed by Young and Cullen in London homes and by Field in British medical wards. But, as Gerald Bloom and Gu Xingyuan's article in Part 5 records, health sector reform in China – once a leader in the village health worker movement – has led to the 'professionalization' of practitioners with rudimentary training, who were meant to serve their communities but are now carving out their own careers.

57 | The carer at home

MICHAEL YOUNG AND LESLEY CULLEN

[This article is based on a study of the experience of families in the East End of London, where one person was terminally ill.]

'There is no such thing as a baby,' said D.W. Winnicott, the psychologist: for every baby there is a mother. Nor is there any such thing as a patient. You are someone's patient. All our people dearly wanted to hang on to as much independence as they could, but for this they needed help from others. Eight of the patients had a relative living with them – five a spouse, one although unmarried, a partner, one a mother and one a daughter. Four were living on their own but with daughters or sons very much on the scene. Two were living quite alone. It was, as usual for carers, very notable that where there was a principal carer, all but two of them were women. In the sickroom gender-typing of roles is still very marked.

The carers could not avoid a series of adjustments in their own lives and ideas which were almost as far-reaching for them as for their patients. The strain was all the greater on both sides because the patient could change almost as rapidly as a new-born infant at the other end of the age spectrum. The patient was liable to become a different person, especially in the first phases of the illness while still suffering from shock, not only changing physically but also in behaviour, becoming withdrawn, grumpy, demanding, when they had not been like that when well. If this had happened in ordinary times, it could have been openly discussed. But now that the changelings have to be treated with special consideration, the carers' queries and resentments have to be bottled up. So there had to be adjustment all round by patients and carers.

Traditional families

The Chandlers and the Allens: [in these families] the man, at least when he was at home for a long stretch, was dominant and remained so throughout his illness. Even while he was dying, he was the household's undisputed head. Perhaps partly because he was dying, his word was more law than ever. This must have been so over the whole of the fifty years or so of their marriages. Terrible as it was for their wives when their husbands became ill with cancer, at least they did not have to change their role of carer, housekeeper, cook, companion. They did not know in advance how to do the more demanding nursing they now had to do – this had to be learned the hard way, by doing it and failing and taking advice and doing it again; but they did know how to look after a home and make a dying husband not only comfortable but feel as much respected, as loved, as he had ever been. If anyone in East London could choose the setting in which to endure a long-drawn-out illness without too much misery, and with some compensation for the inevitable setback, he would be a man and at home.

In the Barnes family, however, Jennifer had the cancer, not John. To begin with [said Jennifer Barnes], John would not talk at all, partly because she herself was rather tongue-tied as well. He was withdrawn because he felt helpless and guilty because he could not do more. John had always been a loner. She could visualise him, unhappily, unhappy after she had died. 'He'll sit here and not answer the door, I know him.' Gradually, once Jennifer had got over the shock of it she began to encourage her husband to talk a little more openly. He joined in when friends came to find out how she was and did not dry up completely on the subject of her cancer when they had gone. 'So what was taboo at one time isn't taboo any more.'

Their greater openness with each other made it easier to accomplish the reversal of roles. To begin with, the Barnes had continued rather as they had done before. Jennifer did not give up work right away, nor did her husband. [But John] was near retirement and, on the production of a doctor's letter explaining why he was now needed at home, he was allowed to take indefinite sick leave, and then a pension.

Released from his old job, John did not hold back from his new one – not enough as it happened – but threw himself into it with a will. He had always enjoyed cooking – in that respect it was easier for him than it would have been for many men. But he bought too much and cooked too much. He could not believe his partner now had no appetite. Jennifer tried not to disappoint him by eating as much as she could, but there were limits.

> It used to hurt him when I turned it away because he was trying his best, not that I didn't appreciate it but I didn't have the appetite.

He did not want her to do anything except just sit, as though she, who had once been the centre of the family, always on the go, the manager, was now a fragile doll who could not do anything lest she break into pieces. Her problem was not to accelerate the reversal of roles, but to put a brake on it – persuade him that she could still do some of the things she had always done. She wanted to feel she was still of some use, not a doll. After many weeks she won him round. When she announced that 'last Sunday he allowed me to cook dinner' she was as delighted as if she had been promoted at work.

She promised John to stop if she got tired. But now she felt less tired rather than more. 'The space I needed, I'm getting it now. With our understanding of each other, the space has come without really knowing it.' In other ways, too, she did not need to act more as the sick person than she felt. She went out to shop, to visit friends and to church.

> I used to lie on top of the bedclothes. John would tuck me in. He had to do everything. He doesn't have to now. I'm happier and it makes him happier.

No full-time carers

The stock notion of a family is still that it contains a man and a woman and children, even though the children may have left home. But only four people [in the study] were in such a family. All the others were without wives or husbands or other carers who could devote all their time to the new vocation. They had little left of their family of origin or never formed such a family as adults or, if they had, it had left little or no trace on how they were living when we saw them.

Two were in mother–daughter households, with the daughter (Carol Taylor) being the patient in one of them and the mother (Dora Anstey) the patient in the other. Neither Carol nor Dora had husbands living with them. Carol's mother was amazing. She did as much as she could for her daughter. But she gave up one of her three part-time jobs, persevering with the other two in order to bring in enough money for the household. At the age of 76 she managed to combine both her paid job and her unpaid – and this after she had been stricken by a string of family deaths. She had been more attached to another of her daughters than to Carol, and Carol knew that.

Dora Anstey was the other way around, a mother looked after by her daughters, especially by one of them, Jackie. They had not been close to their mother. Both daughters were unable to feel the love their mother was asking of them and guilty because they could not.

Jackie, estranged from her husband, came to live with her mother and looked after her early morning and evening. As Dora became more dependent, another daughter, Debbie, joined in, but she didn't live with them until the very last weeks. Both in full-time work, their caring role put an extra strain on them. They boxed and coxed with each other and with their work, one staying at home while the other went to the office. Their mother's battle with death upset, distressed and exhausted them emotionally, and threatened to undermine the two sisters' own close relationship with each other.

The principle of substitution works in many families. If a spouse is available as a full-time carer, other members of the family matter if only in a supporting role. But if the person who would have been a full-time carer is no more, or never existed, children and other relatives move up to do more.

Neighbours to the fore

[The] people living on their own, such as Jack, Arthur and Walter, were not without some support from relatives. But they needed more than that, and they did, in fact all get help from women neighbours who were more supplements than substitutes for family.

Another three people living on their own when they first got cancer had no children and very little or no contact with any relatives still alive. Dermot was one of them. Dermot's neighbour, Ellen, lived alone on the landing above and he must have known her for about eight years.

> I met Ellen after I moved in. She's Irish. She goes to church every morning. She's a very Christian woman. She's about 80. Every year for the last eight years she's brought in Christmas dinner for me.

Ellen did Dermot's washing; he declined a home help because of her assistance. She came in a couple of times a week and got him a 'bit of stuff – she keeps bringing me in food'. She visited him regularly, several times a week during his last stay in hospital and in his last days in the hospice.

As for our last patient, Julia, her friend Maria used to work in the same hospital. Later she bought a flat near Julia's and they grew closer and closer, like sisters, or more so.

> I haven't done all that much. Julia looked after herself mostly. It's only in the last year that that has become impossible or more difficult. I started by just doing the heavy shopping for her and I've gradually done more.

[***]

Unless countervailing tendencies develop, dying is going to be more miserable in the twenty-first century. Medicine will be that much more sophisticated than the medicine of [the twentieth] century, keeping people alive longer; lingering illnesses could as a result become even more common while the setting in which people linger becomes less and less desirable, especially for older widowed people who cannot be cared for by a spouse. One survey suggested that

> The consequence of all this is that the very old were more likely to be cared for by people, who in retrospect, felt that it would have been better if the old person had died earlier.
>
> (Seale and Addington-Hall, 1995)

Yet we were surprised that the patients living alone, while on that account less fortunate, managed so well. Most of the children of marriages broken by separation or death did not desert their parents. They responded when their father or mother was in such critical need.

Death could be a healing force as well as a destructive one. What we did not expect – and this is perhaps the most striking conclusion – was that the imminence of death could bring out the same kind of solidarity amongst neighbours. Their actions belong more to altruism than duty. Such unselfishness is a continuation of what used to be ordinary neighbourliness in this district. But as well as that, death is not only an extraordinary event for the dying but brings out extraordinary behaviour in other people. The close intimacy between carer and cared for generates its own feelings which both take the place of, and reinforce, obligation. There can also be something very special and love-inspiring about the imminence of death. Death can bring out life-giving qualities.

References

D.W. Winnicott, *Collected Papers: Through Paediatrics to Psychoanalysis*, London, Tavistock Publications, 1958, p. 99.

C. Seale and J. Addington-Hall, 'Dying at the best time', *Social Science and Medicine*, 1995, vol. 40, no. 5, pp. 589–95.

The edited extract reproduced here is taken from Chapter 4 of *A Good Death: Conversations with East Londoners* (Routledge, 1996) by the medical sociologists Michael Young (Lord Young of Dartington) of the Institute of Community Studies, Bethnal Green, London, and Lesley Cullen. Since researching for *The Good Death* study, Lesley Cullen has completed a study of hospices and is now a consultant and council member of the National Funerals College.

58 | 'We didn't want him to die on his own' – nurses' accounts of nursing dying patients

DAVID FIELD

Over half of all deaths in the United Kingdom occur in National Health Service hospitals. While for dying patients and their relatives their experience is unique and problematic, for hospital staff care of the dying is part of their work. As such it is shaped in various ways by the organizational demands and routines of hospital life. The two groups of hospital staff most directly concerned with such work are doctors and nurses, with the everyday care and close contact with the dying falling to the latter. In this paper I look at nurses' accounts of their experiences of nursing dying patients and their attitudes towards nursing the dying. I suggest ways in which the organization of their work influences such experiences and attitudes.

The study was based on interviews with all of the nursing staff working on day, shifts in a 28-bed general medical ward at a general hospital in the Midlands. Nurses received practical and psychological support from other team members when they experienced difficulty in their work, and also received such help from other members of the ward staff. The ward as a whole was run along team lines, with authority delegated widely among the trained nursing staff. For example, charge nurse duty rotated among all qualified staff rather than being based simply on seniority. A policy of 'open disclosure' existed on the ward which meant that nurses could inform patients about their diagnosis and prognosis – including that of terminality – without first having to seek permission to do so from the consultants.

The ward sister, seven qualified nurses, nine nurses in training and two nursing auxiliaries were interviewed. All but two of the nurses were female, and their experience ranged from trainees on their first ward placement to one nurse with 20 years experience of nursing. Most of the nurses (14) were between the ages of 20 and 25 years old.

Awareness contexts

A central concern of the study was to examine nurses' views of various awareness contexts. At one extreme is the situation of 'open awareness' where all parties including the patient, know that the patient is dying and know that such knowledge is shared. At the other extreme is the situation of 'closed awareness' where the doctors know that the patient is dying but the patient does not. Other staff and relatives may also be aware of the impending death. Between these extremes are the self-explanatory 'suspicion' and 'mutual pretence' situations. The majority of nurses who expressed a preference chose 'open awareness';

> *ER*: . . . it's far easier to cope with a patient that's dying and knows they're dying.

For the nurses in training such a view was largely anticipatory, although two of them had experienced 'suspicion awareness' and found this difficult to cope with. They were tentative in their choice, and even for trained staff the preference for 'openness' was not unproblematic, as this experienced staff nurse indicates:

> *DF*: So you have no difficulty talking to them?
> *RL*: Oh no. Sometimes I find it difficult if they don't know they're dying, and the relatives have expressed a wish that they're not to be told and the doctors haven't told them yet. You know, . . . the time when they first get to know, I find that a bit difficult still. It's alright when they know. It's alright if they don't know. It's the in between bit when they're getting to know and they're asking some difficult questions.

As this shows, *getting* to the situation of open awareness may be hard – especially for the unqualified nurse. It was in this phase of their relationship with the dying patient that the qualified staff saw their ward sister as playing an important role as the 'broker' who negotiated the transition to open awareness when they could not do so. (Both the sister and the nursing officer told me that they saw this as an important part of their work.) Despite the difficulties of achieving open awareness all of the qualified nurses indicated that they had developed strategies for 'telling' patients the truth about their terminality.

> *EW*: If the patient asks you outright if they're dying and you know then I think a student nurse or a pupil nurse might sort of hedge 'Of course you're not going to. Ask the doctor'. They may sort of hedge. But, it depends . . . sister does allow us to use our own judgement, but just the same you've got to be very careful what you say.
> *DF*: Can you think of anyone you've actually told?
> *EW*: I've never actually said to someone 'Yes, you are dying'.
> *DF*: But there are ways of saying you're dying.
> *EW*: I remember a lady saying 'Well I'm not going to get better am I?, and then I said 'Well no, I don't think so. But nobody knows for sure' . . . 'If it's left to us, if it's left to our care you will go home'.
> *DF*: So, you always try to be positive?
> *EW*: Yes. You try to be positive as well because nobody can say 'yes, you are going to die' . . . I try not to lie or pretend to them. Try not disguise. I try not to kid them along. I try not to say 'Oh no you're not going to die', try not to do that. That's wrong. They still need the same sort of – they still need nursing. It's just your approach to them. I think you should be as honest as you can. If you can't then I think you should get somebody else to talk to them who can be.

Emotional involvement

Given the strong preference expressed by these nurses for 'open awareness' it is perhaps not surprising that nearly all of them (16) said that they were or had been emotionally involved with dying patients, often to the extent of crying and grieving at their deaths. All of the qualified staff and five of the trainees felt that such involvement was inevitable and unavoidable. For the qualified nurses such involvement was not seen as particularly problematic, and five felt it was positively beneficial and rewarding for them. Unqualified staff were not as positive with five expressing problems. A student nurse gave a very full account of her experience of nursing an 80-year old terminally ill woman with whom she had become very emotionally involved. The woman had died two weeks before the interview and the student had shared the death with the woman's husband. Both of them had cried after the death.

> SH: Well I shouldn't really have done that. I shouldn't have got involved so much probably, but it's hard to draw the line. And – particularly with somebody like her. She was so kind to everybody. And I thought 'well, this isn't a very good example for the younger nurses walking out crying with the husband' but I thought 'well they obviously know it's an upsetting thing even though they weren't involved'. And they said afterwards they were glad they weren't involved at all because it would have made them cry. But I wasn't the only one in tears so I didn't feel so bad. It wasn't as if it was just me who was involved with her.
> DF: Do you feel it is bad to cry when a patient's died?
> SH: Not really. Not if the relative's there and – he said then 'She wasn't just another lady was she?' 'No', I said. 'None of them are. Everybody's an individual here'.

Another indicator of the high level of emotional involvement which these nurses seemed to have with their dying patients was the continued contact which some of them maintained with the relatives of patients who had died and with terminally ill patients who had been discharged. The most dramatic example of such behaviour was provided by the sister. She kept in contact with many relatives even though she didn't always want to:

> Sr: . . . because they are a terrific drain. And very often . . . you want to forget about work and it's forced upon you. I always have this terrible feeling that they expect so much of nurses, that you are representing every nurse. So to be unkind or to be curt, or not to have time would, well have a devastating effect on them. They feel they could be next. And so you're obligated to give them every consideration, and yet I don't always want to . . . You can't nurse a dying patient without – well you *can*, but obviously it isn't desirable to keep them at a distance – and so you *do* get to know them very well. And this is what they're really after. They want to talk about the person, not the death . . . I can never bring myself to cut them off, and they may not be able to do this with anyone else.

Nursing the dying may be satisfying for the nurse because it allows them to fully implement their ideal of nursing care.

> DF: You said you got pleasure from nursing the dying patient.

EW: Well, well perhaps that's the wrong thing – *satisfaction*. I don't mean pleasure: satisfaction. You can *see* results from nursing a patient that's a long term patient or dying. You can see what you're doing for them. . . .

You can make time to sit and talk with them. And obviously if they're dying the physical condition is going to deteriorate so you've got to be that extra bit careful keeping them clean and comfortable, bathing and things like that. And to me that's nursing.

Discussion

What emerges very clearly is a consistent set of predispositions to act in particular ways. Namely; to become emotionally involved with the patients they are nursing (and their relatives), especially if they are long-term patients; to disclose rather than to withhold information about dying when this is sought by the patient; to be honest in their dealings with patients (and relatives); to accept individual responsibility for patients while working as part of a team; to help and support each other. In short a predisposition to provide 'total nursing care' for the 'whole person'. I suggest that these predispositions *are* likely to be acted upon in the ward which was the focus of this study for a number of reasons.

General medical wards differ from other wards in a number of ways with respect to patient flow and rhythms of work, and with respect to the characteristics of their patients. They are generally geared towards less intensive therapeutic intervention than acute surgical wards or coronary care units; their patient turnover is on average lower with a concomitant longer term stay; and their patients are older. Patients are typically mature adults rather than children or teenagers. Further, deaths are usually predictable to nursing staff and relatively infrequent when compared to some other settings. Most patients recover or are discharged in an improved condition. Thus, nurses may have more extended contact with patients and so have a greater chance to get to know them, and are dealing with deaths which are less problematic and less frequent than those found in other settings.

Despite the high level of bed occupancy, the rhythm of work on the ward appeared to be generally relaxed. During the 'slack times' (when most of my visits occurred) nurses could typically be found chatting to patients. The democratic and 'permissive' leadership style of the sister was very evident, and the attitude that nursing work meant *doing* something *to* patients was noticeably absent. Trainees were fully involved with patient care, and were not relegated to performing only routine tasks. The ward very clearly worked as a cohesive team involving all of the nursing staff. The sister's role appeared to be in large part devoted to supporting the rest of her team, facilitating their interpersonal relationships with patients (and trying to develop their skills) where necessary, and mediating between nurses and patients and the medical staff. Her leadership style and strongly expressed attitudes were central to the ethos of patient care enacted on the ward.

Doctor–nurse relationships

A crucial structural characteristic of ward organization is the nature of doctor–nurse relationships. In a previously studied acute surgical ward (Knight & Field, 1981) these were very formal and hierarchical, with consultants and other surgical staff talking only to the sister or charge nurse. This hierarchy was mirrored by a similar formal ranking of the nursing staff. Nurses on this ward were forbidden to disclose their prognosis to dying patients. On the present ward, relationships were much less formal, with nurses allowed a good deal of autonomy. Cases were discussed between medical and nursing staff, and nurses reported that a good relationship existed between them.

> DF: Do you have reasonably good relations with the doctors on this ward?
> ER: Most of the time, yes. It's very friendly, all of the doctors and nurses are on first name terms. If you ask them 'Will you do me a favour? Mr so-and-so wants a chat' – he hasn't asked for the doctor, just got you in a bit of a predicament – and the go off. They are quite good.

With respect to care of the dying, medical staff had less active involvement and might withdraw almost entirely once the transition from 'therapeutic cure' to 'relief care' had been decided upon. Medical staff were willing to accede to nurses' views about the desirability of 'disclosure'. For example, a case was recounted where medical staff felt that a patient should not be informed that she was terminally ill whereas the nursing staff felt that she should be. It was agreed that the sister would tell the patient who, when told, thanked the sister and made arrangements to ensure that a planned holiday occurred whilst she was well enough to go.

The predisposition to care is, one suspects, an important characteristic of entrants to the health care professions. Studies of medical students suggests that it may quite quickly become transformed as they lose their 'idealism' (Becker & Geer, 1958), develop 'detached concern' (Fox, 1957), and in many other ways change their earlier commitment to caring for 'whole people'. A similar process may also affect nurses (Melia, 1972). Such change is not inevitable, but induced during the course of nurse training and early ward experiences as a qualified nurse. The predisposition to care for the 'whole person' and the derivation of satisfaction and reward from such caring nursing can flow from the type of arrangement identified above. This is to the mutual benefit of nurse and patient, and can pertain, it seems, even in such an apparently negative situation as nursing the dying.

> RE: We had a patient who was here over a year – and we were all very close to 'C'. I saw him from when he came in, to getting really better, then going down again. It was awful because there was nothing I could do; I just had to sit and hold his hand. At that time we were all taking it in turns to sit with him as long as we could 'cos we just didn't want him to die on his own. Nobody wanted just to go in and find him dead. Which I think goes for most patients that you know are on their last legs. You *don't* want to leave them on their own. . . . I remember very clearly a patient on geriatrics. I had nursed him on nights, and I went back on to days – he was a double-sided CVA. He was very incoherent. By some miracle could just whisper words. And at night he couldn't sleep because he was so uncomfortable so I used to spend a lot of my nights sitting and talking to him and holding his hand. When I went back on to days I went behind the curtains – and he was really on his last legs. So I just sat with him and held his hand. And I remember the staff nurse coming in and asking me if I had nothing better to do. So I said 'No. Not at this moment, no.' So she said 'would you mind going and finding something to do?' I remember it so clearly.

I really hated her, because this man was dying. I'd been with him all this time, and why should he die alone? All she was content with was giving him BPO's and he still had an enema the day he did die. Well he died that afternoon. I felt awful – this poor little man – and just as I went behind the curtains he just said – he grabbed hold of my arms (he got very little movement in that hand), and he just put his hand on mine and whispered 'I love you'. And then he died in the afternoon. I thought 'well it's all worthwhile' because at least he realized that somebody cared.

References

Becker, H.S. and Geer, B.S. 'The fate of idealism in medical school', *American Sociological Review*, **23**, 50–56 (1958).

Clarke, M. 'Getting through the work'. In *Readings in the Sociology of Nursing* (eds Dingwall, R. and McIntosh, J.) Chapter 5, Churchill Livingstone, Edinburgh (1978).

Fox, R.C. 'Training for detached concern'. In *The Student Physician: Introductory Studies in The Sociology of Medical Education* (eds Merton, R.K., Reader, G.G. and Kendall, P.L.) Harvard University Press, Cambridge, Mass. (1957).

Knight, M. and Field, D. 'A silent conspiracy: coping with dying cancer patients on an acute surgical ward', *Journal of Advanced Nursing*, **6**, 221–229 (1981).

Melia, K.M. ' "Tell it as it is" – qualitative methodology and nursing research: understanding the student nurse's world', *Journal of Advanced Nursing*, **7**, 327–335 (1982).

David Field is a medical sociologist and is Professor, Department of Epidemiology and Public Health at the University of Leicester. This article is an edited version of the original, which appeared in the *Journal of Advanced Nursing*, **9**, 59–70 (1984).

59 | Professionalism and the conundrum of care

CELIA DAVIES

Is it possible for a nurse to argue against professionalism as the model for her work? At first sight the answer has to be no. It is not only that much that a student learns is couched in terms of learning to act in a properly 'professional way' in her encounters with patients and with colleagues and co-workers in health care; it is also that norms for 'professional conduct' are laid down formally and that the nurse is answerable ultimately to the Professional Conduct Committee of the UKCC which has powers to strike her off the Register and remove her source of livelihood in the practice of nursing if she acts in a way that is deemed unprofessional. If we distinguish, however, between:

one, a broad sense of professionalism as probity or integrity of personal conduct, and
two, professionalism/professionalization as a route taken collectively by members of an occupational group who refine and guard their knowledge base, set boundaries around who can enter and what the limits of practice will be, then there is something more to debate and to question.

Jane Salvage (1985), makes just this kind of a distinction, arguing that when leaders call for a 'professional nursing service', when they put forward visions of an all-qualified nursing labour force, it is not professionalism of individual behaviour, but professionalization of an occupation that is at stake. Her questions are of several kinds.

First, there is the sheer unreality of a model of profession of this latter kind. The reality of the staffing of hospital wards, and indeed, we can say too of much community nursing care, is that it is not remotely approaching professionalization; leaders, she says, are exhibiting the 'ostrich syndrome' in looking in this direction.

Second, however, and much more importantly perhaps, since professionalizing entails the limiting of numbers, they are in danger of condoning the notion of nurses not only as highly skilled but also as a small and elite group. Such a group, of course, by definition does not deliver nursing care but manages it and/or provides technical backup through advanced skills. Her discussion (Salvage 1985: see especially pp. 95–101) throws down a number of challenges.

1. *Professionalism is divisive.* In failing to acknowledge that most basic nursing care inside and outside the hospitals is given by untrained people and in identifying with doctors, it damages relationships and lessens the quality of care. Controlling access to knowledge has similar results.
2. *Professionalism seeks to impose a uniform view.* While all share the goal of good nursing care, interests do differ, questions of the exploitation of some groups over others – managers and students for example – get submerged.
3. *Professionalism denies the needs of its workers.* Service to patients is placed as the highest priority, yet there may be times when nurses need to assert their own day-to-day needs and not, for example, rule out completely the possibility of strike action.
4. *Professionalism emphasizes an individual approach.* It stresses individual responsibility for the personal delivery of high quality care; yet can staff be accountable for situations where they have little control? Is it right that the individual nurse should be disciplined for a personal failure when staffing levels are inadequate? Is it reasonable also to put the onus on the individual to keep up to date with developments in professional practice?
5. *Professionalism does not challenge the status quo.* Is more autonomy for the nurse automatically better for the patient? Should we be talking about more radical approaches to the fragmentation of health care, giving a basic training, for example, to more people?
6. *Professionalism does not give strong support to the NHS.* It directs attention to the needs of the professional group rather than to the needs of the health care system as a whole.

The doubts expressed here, about elitism, professional power, accountability and so on, are emerging with growing frequency amongst commentators on nursing. They also, however, find an echo inside other professions, among the public at large and in academic studies of the subject.

For nurses to look to professionalism, is thus to look to a model of practice that is under severe attack. For this reason if for no other, it is wise to begin to cast the net rather more widely, giving attention, not to old-style professionalism as such, but to those who have seen the writing on the wall and are seeking to reshape it.

New professionalism – not enough

A clear agenda for the 'new professions' emerges from the study made by sociologist Margaret Stacey, drawing from her experience as a lay member of the General Medical Council (GMC), of the functioning of that regulatory body (Stacey, 1992). Stacey mounts a strong argument that professionalism as evidenced by the behaviours of the GMC is an outdated nineteenth-century phenomenon – a set of 'collective illusions' that now needs urgently to be set aside. Doctors acting collectively have put 'profession before public' in their emphasis on the exclusive character of their knowledge, their insistence on unity and their preservation and enhancement of their own status. Factors such as these misguide doctors, keeping them on the terrain of restrictive and defensive practices, contributing to an inward-lookingness and arrogance, whereas the need is to rebuild from the ideals of service that were also implicated in the nineteenth-century ideal.

In particular, Margaret Stacey argues, doctors need to relinquish the outmoded idea that theirs is a one-to-one relationship with the patient. They must recognize the contribution of others (including the patient), to health and healing and make consequential adjustments to notions of clinical autonomy, of control over allied professions and of the exclusive right of doctors to sit in judgement over other doctors.

Development requires doctors to move towards a new professionalism which puts patients 'not necessarily first, but equal to and part of the professional interest' and means attending to lay conceptual frameworks as well as to those of medicine (ibid.: 260).

Underpinning much of this thinking is the concept, first developed a decade ago, of the 'reflective practitioner' (Schön, 1983). Professional practice, Schön argued, is not a matter of straightforward rational analysis, of 'instrumental problem-solving made rigorous by the application of scientific theory and techniques' (ibid.: 21); instead it involves a process of reflection on expertise and experience and which draws on the uniqueness and the uncertainty of the specific situation. This type of reflection he calls 'situated' reflection, which he maintains, is actually the core of professional practice, even though it is rarely accepted, even by those who use it, as a legitimate form of professional knowing. Sadly, the move of professions into the universities meant acceptance of rational, scientific thought and of a hierarchy which elevates research over practical problem-solving, downplaying the complexity and uniqueness of specific instances.

But Schön fails to see the gendered division of labour that helps sustain the elite professions through the work of women dealing with the local, the applied and the human dimensions of professional practice, and the acute dilemmas that this adjunct work produces for women who wish to appropriate the label 'professional' for the work that they do. Furthermore, the concept of reflective practice emphasizes reflection as an act for the most part of the practitioner *alone*. For this reason, we can say that Schön fails fully to confront the engagement of the practitioner with the client, hence ignoring the always specific and embodied character of the contribution the professional makes, the commitment to and respect for the client and for co-workers, all with their histories and identities which are to be brought into play if the full pattern of experience and expertise is to be acknowledged and utilized. We need to examine *both* the professional *and* the caring side of professional practice and it is to the question of conceptualizing care, especially nursing care, that we now turn.

Caregiving, carework and professional care

Caring, as Hilary Graham (1983) ably demonstrated in a ground-breaking article 'Caring: a labour of love', is something that slips through the conceptual nets offered by the academic disciplines of the social sciences. Its fusion of 'labour and love' is frustratingly diffuse, hard to capture by means of the usual apparatus of definition and measurement in the disciplines of psychology, sociology and social policy. Practical job analysis techniques such as are employed in organizational settings, with their minute breakdown of tasks, cannot encompass it – since a moment's reflection suggests that all kinds of specific activities can be carried out in the name of care for the other, including apparently no activities at all. Caring can mean just 'being there' for someone, not necessarily listening, not necessarily even being physically present but being known to be available, checking the situation out from time to time and being ready to respond if asked. Caring in this broad sense can be defined as *attending, physically, mentally and emotionally to the needs of another and giving a commitment to the nurturance, growth and healing of that other.* Caring does not involve specific tasks; instead, it involves the creation of a sustained relationship with the other, an ability to reflect on the specifics of that person's history, and an ongoing process of dialogue through which assessments and interventions can be tried, monitored for relevance and adopted or adapted as necessary. It is this business of 'attending' to another, the close observation that a carer undertakes, that attunes her or him to minute differences that are not necessarily available to the more casual or sporadic observer. In the public world of paid health care, the nurse is often, though not always, structurally placed to achieve this, whereas the doctor is rarely so placed.

In-depth interviews with women who are caring for elderly parents and sick and disabled children demonstrate that carers often find it difficult to put into words what it is that they do; they would comment that it was 'natural' that they should care, that they just 'got on with it', sometimes cheerfully, sometimes with resentment. Their commentaries emphasize the importance of bringing previously hidden and taken for granted aspects of women's lives as carers into view, including the hard daily grind of physical labour, the lengthy hours spent with the cared for and the emotional turmoils and moral debates about love, duty and guilt that the work as a carer can evoke.

The care that women give in the home and family setting is governed by values of love and spontaneity, is carried out in isolation from others, is bereft of validation by any source apart from the care recipient. It is rare in this context that anyone puts into words the skills and experience that are brought to bear and distinguishes these from the specifics of the setting and the personalities involved. Arlene Kaplan Daniels is one writer who has emphasized and expanded on this in an important way, making links between domestic caregiving and paid carework. She suggests that as far as women's paid work is concerned, the closer it is to the activities of nurturing, comforting, encouraging and facilitating interaction – features encompassed by the definition of caring given above – the more likely it is to be seen as natural or the expression of women's style in general (Daniels 1987: p. 408).

What happens when the unpaid caregiving described above becomes 'carework', the paid work of public caregiving? The jobs of care assistants of various kinds in the home or in residential care, of home helps, of domestic servants, childminders and so on have a number of obvious characteristics. They remain largely women's work, they exist outside any sustained training framework, they retain a low status and attract low rewards. All this is consistent with a blindness to the skill base which is involved. Equally important, however, is the conflict that such work sets up when incorporated into a regular bureaucratic control system. This has been described particularly vividly in the case of home helps whose work is organized in such a way as to allow them to give flexible and versatile services to a small number of clients in their own homes over a long period. Home helps exhibit strong personal attachment to the clients, and this is the feature that they most enjoy and see as integral to the work.

The work of Norwegian sociologist Kari Waerness, first published in the early 1980s, provides several important links in the chain of understanding carework. Waerness (1992) insists that a fundamental shift in approach is required if we are to bring this work into focus at all, a shift that goes against the mainstream of thinking in the social sciences. The first step is to work with a more rounded notion of the individual as a 'sentient' being, who blends thought and emotion, who not only takes a cognitive, instrumental approach, calculating likely outcomes on the basis of systematic knowledge and the rules which can be derived from this, but also takes account of the particularities of persons and the feelings of all concerned.

Waerness identifies the limited nature of scientific rationality and its embeddedness in a masculinist thinking that stresses a cognitive solution to problems via mastery of knowledge and control of its applications. From this perspective it is possible to begin to lay bare what she calls a 'rationality of caring', an approach that is not driven by blind emotion and sentiment, but which has a describable logic of its own. To operate within a 'rationality of caring' means acknowledging that caring work cannot be entirely contained within and governed by scientific knowledge, accepting that emotions and commitments are part and parcel of the process of effective caregiving and recognizing that flexibility, adaptability and hence uncertainty are entailed by this work.

Where then does professional care – public caregiving that is preceded by systematic formal training – fit into all of this? Waerness provides a pessimistic comment, suggesting that caring values tend to get lost when brought into the public arena and professionalized. She cites empirical work that suggests that formal training suppresses the values of caring and promotes not flexibility but rigidity. She sees nursing as a particular case in point. Its leaders everywhere favour the development of formally acquired knowledge as a route to greater status, but, she comments:

> 'nursing science' is . . . not a solution to the problems of strengthening the values inherent in the rationality of caring, at least as long as this science is based in the generally accepted notions of scientific knowledge and learning.
>
> (Waerness 1992: p. 224)

Nurses do not simply attempt to take on the mantle of old professionalism, however, they also frequently face the issues of reconciling professionalism and caring as dilemmas of daily practice. There is plenty of evidence for this. It is there, for example, in the frustrations of nurses who say that the system does not allow them to nurse, and in the striving to provide individualized care. It is apparent in the way that nursing seems so resistant to clear definition, and in discussions that refer to the 'science and art' of nursing, in the unease yet fascination with books and articles that propose that nursing is 'a form of loving'.

In facing these dilemmas, professional nurses are in the same position as the home helps described earlier – there are no acceptable words for the logic of caring that they are trying to put into practice, the work has not been and cannot be conceptualized without a revolution in the frameworks on offer. This is not simply a matter only of finding words to express negative feelings. When nurses themselves recount their most positive experiences in their work, their words continue to fall outside the professional frame.

It is very clear from this that to bring the terms profession and care together is more than a step in semantics. Much work is already under way, at both a theoretical and practical level, to further clarify and develop this. Still more needs to be done to explore the nature of professional care and to codify our understanding in such a way that we can legitimize and hence embed caring values in nursing practice.

To argue that there is something to be gained for nursing from focusing on unpaid and low-paid carework which so often falls to women – activities such as childcare, eldercare, residential care, home help and so on – may seem anathema to many in the nursing profession and raises many questions. Has nursing not advanced precisely by distinguishing the work of the trained and untrained, distancing 'professional nursing' from the 'nursing' that is done at home? Will there be few incentives and few spaces in a world gendered masculine for a new approach to be heard? Will it take nurses away from the very actions and activities that grant occupations the status they need? Finally, will it lock nursing further into the devaluation it already experiences by association with women's work?

My answer to these questions is two-fold:

- First, an advance into old professionalism is an advance into a cul de sac. There is too much in the model that is directly antithetical to what nurses wish to do. Nurses would be better engaged in joining the growing army of those who wish to build a new professionalism from the ashes of the old.
- Second, while work on the 'rationality of caring' is not yet far advanced, its outlines are sufficiently clear to see that it offers a real potential to reflect back to nurses their subjective understanding of their work, to legitimize the work that nurses do and to give them a new confidence in policy settings.

References

Daniels, A.K. (1987) Invisible Work, *Social Problems*, 34(5), 403–13.
Graham, H. (1983) 'Caring: a labour of love', in J. Finch and D. Groves (eds) *A Labour of Love: Women, Work and Caring*. London, Routledge and Kegan Paul.
Salvage, J. (1985) *The Politics of Nursing*. London, Heinemann.
Schön, D. (1983) *The Reflective Practitioner: How professionals think in action*. London, Temple Smith.
Stacey, M. (1992) *Regulating British Medicine: The General Medical Council*. Chichester: Wiley.
Waerness, K. (1992) 'On the rationality of caring', in A. Showstack Sassoon (ed.) *Women and the State*. London, Routledge (first published in 1984).

This article is an edited extract from Chapter 7 of Celia Davies' book *Gender and the Professional Predicament in Nursing* (Open University Press, 1995). The author is Professor of Health Care in the School of Health and Social Welfare at the Open University, Milton Keynes, UK.

60 | Truth, trust and paternalism

THURSTAN B. BREWIN

Let's be a little more honest about the importance of 'being honest'. We need to strike a balance between 'informed consent' and 'paternalism'. The idea of the first as a great good and the second as a great evil is today in danger of being carried to absurd lengths. Yet few doctors dare say so (at any rate in public) for fear of being called paternalistic, old fashioned, arrogant – or worse.

Communication is of crucial importance in medicine. Partly to inform, explain, and advise. And partly – especially when a patient is frightened, ill, weak, or otherwise vulnerable – to raise morale, give confidence, encourage, and protect. Whether or not we call this 'paternalism', the fact is that to try and abolish it would be a sure way to add greatly to the sum total of human suffering.

Unfortunately, as so often in life, one aim may conflict with the other. To compromise makes us feel uncomfortable. We would prefer to be guided by some noble moral principle. But such principles – pure and inspiring though they seem at first sight – are liable to give contradictory advice. Sanctity of life is a precious concept, but most people feel that it has to be restrained at times, if it is not to cause excessive suffering or distress. The rights of the individual may have to be curtailed in the interests of the community. Similarly, though we all prize truthfulness, there are times when the thought of 'telling someone the truth' – or a particular part of it – may seem so cruel and pointless that most of us (whether doctors or not) will decide against it.

It is easy to denigrate compromise of this kind. But sometimes the only alternative is to embrace one noble principle and murder another. Which seems even worse. So we compromise; but, we hope, in a civilised and humane manner.

Two new books provide good examples of the tendency to stress the first aim of communication at the expense of the second. One, written jointly by a journalist and a doctor,[1] covers all kinds of ethical dilemma (abortion, embryo research, confidentiality, resource allocation, and so on) and is recommended for the fair and thorough way it deals with most of them. However, when it comes to 'informed consent' both this book and the other (written by a journalist on her own[2]) give views which, I would guess, will be judged by future generations to be lacking in balance. The advantages of trying to explain risks and options to all patients are well set out, but the serious limitations and disadvantages are too often played down or ignored.

Here are two uncompromising extracts from the first book:[1]

> Consent is meaningless unless it is informed. And it is not possible for the patient to be informed unless he has been told the whole truth about himself. (p. 144)

> The patient's most important safeguard is for the doctor to tell the truth – not simply never to lie, but not to withhold information . . . for without information there can be no consent to treatment. (p. 173)

This sort of thing sounds fine until we come down to earth and think it through, in terms of practical everyday life. Is consent really to be judged 'meaningless unless it is informed?' What about trust? If I seek the help of an accountant, builder, lawyer, or cobbler, my consent to what he does with my money, my house, my reputation, or my shoes is likely to be based on a blend of information and trust. Of course, I may want to discuss certain options and risks. But the more trust the less need for me to ask a lot of searching questions. Thus saving both his time and mine.

As soon as the expert that I consult sees what the problem is, may I not just trust him to do his best and get on with it? Does he have to keep explaining to every client or customer why he prefers his own particular way of doing things? Or how he has been lately trying out new methods? Or how somebody in a similar situation once finished up worse off instead of better off? And if he 'deliberately conceals' such things (partly because if he tried to explain everything to everybody he could never get on with his work) is he being unethical? Is his failure to tell the whole truth to be judged morally equivalent to telling a lie?

What happens when the element of fear is injected into a non-medical situation? Most people facing death or danger during a hijack, the failure of an aircraft, or some other disaster will feel safer if there is some leadership. A good leader behaves in a very similar way to a good doctor in a medical crisis.[3] Much will depend on his personality, but he must not be too optimistic, nor too pessimistic. He must be blunt enough to get everyone's confidence, but he will often keep to himself certain grim possibilities and certain areas of doubt or confusion. Nearly everyone will see this as part of his job and will not think any less of him for it. Nobody calls him a paternalist just because he uses his discretion. Words of encouragement that cut no ice with people who are not unduly frightened may greatly help those who are. If he does a good job he can improve morale immeasurably. Above all, he does not just blindly dish out 'complete honesty' and tell everybody everything that they 'have a right to know'. It is not that easy. Nor will he – if he has a grain of sense – ask each person to choose if they want to know the full facts or not. What are they supposed to say? And what will be the subsequent state of mind of someone who replies that he prefers not to know? Will he not just feel a coward and worry about what others have been told?

Moreover, trust is a marvellous time saver. Whether we are speaking of medical or non-medical problems, discussions of risks and options may, of course, have a high priority. On the other hand, it does not make sense to allow lengthy low-priority explanations to encroach too far into available time, leading to less work done and fewer people helped. How strange that this obvious and important point regarding priorities is so seldom mentioned by those who urge patients and others not to take so much on trust. They seem to imagine that vast chunks of time can be plucked out of thin air without any damage to general standards of care and efficiency.

Trust also means less risk of those misconceptions that experience teaches us can arise so easily when detailed information is given. Phillips and Dawson, the authors of the first book I am quoting, believe that 'to argue that detail equals confusion is an example of the worst kind of paternalism'. But any doctor who asks a patient or relative at the end of a lengthy interview (or even a brief one) 'what will you say if someone asks you what I have told you?', soon discovers how common are immediate misconceptions – quite apart from how much is remembered later. Evidence confirms it.[4] And this is hardly surprising. Picture a doctor in his own home discussing complicated matters with his plumber. How will he get on if he tries to repeat it all to a friend a week later? And supposing experience has taught the plumber that, although some doctors understand what he is talking about, others don't – and suppose that the plumber (especially when he is busy) says to the customer 'you will just have to trust me to do the best job I can'. Is that arrogant paternalism?

True, there are patients getting too much paternalism and not enough explanation. But when it is the other way round it is much less likely to be reported. No patient is going to complain that he was told too much. Nor that when he was frightened nobody held his hand.

Fortunately for general standards of medical care, a fair amount of trust and a limited amount of information about risks and options still suits many patients very well (including many doctors when they are ill) – at least in the United Kingdom. Others (again including many doctors, who vary just as much as anyone else) prefer a lot of information and are greatly reassured by it. Knowledge can improve morale. So can trust. Sometimes it is right to discuss painful choices with the patient, even though they will distress him. Sometimes it seems better not to. As in ordinary life, only a very insensitive person believes that what is best for one patient is necessarily best for another. Moreover, the very same person may need much more protection (paternalism if you like) at one stage of his illness than at another.[3]

Such a regard for individual variations seems to worry some anti-paternalists almost more than consistent paternalism. All patients should be treated alike, they seem to say. Not to do so is arrogant.

Also very common is a remarkable ambivalence towards this question of whether or not the doctor should use his discretion. Here are some examples from the second book (Faulder[2]). On the one hand we are told that 'The medical consensus . . . is that remote risks do not need to be revealed . . . the patient will be told only what the doctors think it is fit for her to know . . . this outrageous paternalism has been endorsed in case after case in the English courts'. And that, 'Either a moral right [the right to informed consent] exists or it does not. If it does, then it is universal and no-one has the right to deny it to anyone'. Also that, 'Informed consent . . . is neither a concession nor a courtesy to be granted by well disposed doctors as and when they see fit, but an inalienable human right . . .'. Yet on other pages we read that 'A doctor has to tread very carefully. Some information he must volunteer, but if he sees that the patient is shutting herself off from hearing too much, although agreeing to his proposals for treatment, then he is justified in presuming that she is giving her consent . . . this kind of signalling from the patient is usually expressed tacitly'. And elsewhere that 'It is equally a denial of autonomy to force unwanted information on those who have clearly indicated, not necessarily verbally' (my emphasis) 'that they do not want it'. We also read that, 'Doctors argue with some truth that it is all very well for the strong and healthy to cry shame, but paternalism is still what the vast majority of their patients thrust upon them'. And that 'It is far too easy for the outsider to condemn doctors for not telling the truth'.

Phillips and Dawson[1] would presumably disagree with this last comment. 'We feel', they say, 'that the importance of telling the truth cannot be over-estimated.' But, like many other fine principles, we all know in our heart of hearts that this is not so. It can be overestimated. Easily. 'Truth', in fact, can sometimes create havoc. One distinguished American journalist learnt this during his own illness and was not afraid to say so afterwards. 'Most doctors', he said, 'are panic producers without realising it . . . they under-estimate the extent to which their truths become death sentences.'[5]

Many friends and relatives curse the clumsy insensitivity of doctors who needlessly tell patients grim or frightening facts about proposed treatment. 'That stupid doctor', they say, 'why did he have to tell my mother – frightened enough already – about something terrible, if it is very unlikely that it will ever happen?'

Of course, it is another story when those with the benefit of hindsight express indignation that the unfortunate victim of some remote risk was never warned about it. It would be interesting to know how consistent such critics are. When they visit friends or elderly relatives in hospital do they treat them all alike? Do they consistently discourage trust and urge them all to question staff closely in order to make sure that they are fully aware of all remote risks?

We may perhaps speak of 'anti-paternalists' as either extreme or moderate. The moderate group often imagine that they are in conflict with traditional medicine. Their criticism serves a useful purpose, but what they are really doing is little more than tilting at windmills. They ignore the fact that all good medical teachers have always spoken out against arrogance, insensitivity, discourtesy, or failure to take a proper interest in a patient's real problems and lifestyle – which is apparently what they mean by paternalism. What they should really be accusing us of is failing to live up to our ideals.

The extreme anti-paternalist, on the other hand, hates trust. Probably in his private life he is secretly very pleased when somebody trusts him. But he doesn't like to see other people being trusted. It worries him. He is even not too happy about people being given advice. He would prefer them just to be given facts and then to make up their own minds. This is in order to preserve their 'autonomy'. He forgets that if any of us in any situation (medical or non-medical) takes advantage only of an expert's skill and knowledge – not his experience and judgment – we are throwing away half the value of the consultation.

What we need is better communication; more explanation for those who need it, less for those who don't; and greater empathy and understanding of the patient's real needs, fears, and aspirations. What we don't need is unhelpful rhetoric; a wholesale attack on trust; excessive emphasis on 'fully informed consent' and 'autonomy'; and a serious distortion of priorities with a consequent fall in standards of care.

For two reasons there has to be compromise. Firstly, because noble principles often give contradictory advice. Every patient has a right to full information. He also has a right to be treated with compassion, common sense, and respect for his dignity – a respect that is not usually enhanced by asking him, 'Do you want us to be frank about all the risks or not?' Secondly, because we are all the prisoners of time, the more time we spend trying to explain things, the less there is for other aspects of patient care.

Who should make the compromise? Presumably it should be those members of society who have most experience of all the subtle and paradoxical ways in which human beings may react to illness and to fear; and who have had the greatest opportunity of learning, from first hand experience, when to speak out and when to keep silent. In other words, doctors and nurses, rather than philosophers or experts in ethics.

Provided, of course, that we are at least as concerned for the welfare of patients as are the rest of society. Which is not for us to judge. But even Bernard Shaw, in the famous preface to *The Doctor's Dilemma*, observed that 'doctors, if no better than other men, are certainly no worse'.

References

1. Phillips, M. and Dawson J. 'Doctors dilemmas: medical ethics and contemporary science', 230, Harvester Press (1985).
2. Faulder, C. 'Whose body is it? The troubling issue of informed consent', *Lancet*, ii, 75, Virago Press (1985).
3. Brewin, T.B. 'The cancer patient: communication and morale', *British Medical Journal*, ii, 1623–7 (1977).
4. Joyce, C.R.B., Caple, G., Mason, M., Reynolds, E. and Matthews, J.A. 'Quantitative study of doctor-patient communications', *Quarterly Journal of Medicine*, 38, 183–94 (1969).
5. Cushner, T. 'A conversation with Norman Cousins', *Lancet*, ii, 527–8, Virago Press (1980).

This article first appeared, in the form reproduced here, in the 31 August 1985 issue of *The Lancet*, pages 490–492. Until his retirement, Thurstan B. Brewin was a consultant oncologist (cancer specialist) in practice in Scotland, who has published a number of articles in the medical press on communicating 'bad news' to cancer patients.

61 | Doctor knows best

ANN OAKLEY

You decide when to see your doctor and let him confirm the fact of your pregnancy. From then onwards you are going to have to answer a lot of questions and be the subject of a lot of examinations. Never worry about any of these. They are necessary, they are in the interests of your baby and yourself, and none of them will ever hurt you.[1]

These admonitions, from a British Medical Association publication on pregnancy, are intended to console. Their tone is patronizing and their message clear: doctors know more about having babies than women do. (An alternative, and less charitable, construction would be that women are fundamentally stupid and doctors are inherently more intelligent.)

Obstetrics, like midwifery, in its original meaning describes a female province. The management of reproduction has been, throughout most of history and in most cultures, a female concern; what is characteristic about childbirth in the industrial world is, conversely, its control by men. The conversion of female-controlled community management to male-controlled medical management alone would suggest that the propagation of particular paradigms of women as maternity cases has been central to the whole development of medically dominated maternity care. The ideological element, as would be expected, is not part of the agenda in conventional medical histories chronicling the rise of male obstetrics – for example H.R. Spencer's *The History of British Midwifery from 1650 to 1800*.[2] Spencer terminates his discussion in a tone characteristic of the genus when he says:

In conclusion it may be said that during the hundred and fifty years since Harvey published his 'De Generatione Animalium', a great advance had been made in the science and art of midwifery. This was due chiefly to the introduction of male practitioners, many of whom were men of learning and devoted to anatomy, the groundwork of obstetrics.

The achievements of male obstetrics over those of female midwifery are rarely argued empirically, but always *a priori*, from the double premise of male and medical superiority. More recent investigations of this argument are now revealing a different picture, in which the introduction of men into the business of reproductive management brought special dangers to mothers and babies. The easier transmission of puerperal fever in male-run lying-in hospitals is one example; the generally careless and ignorant use of technology another.[3,4] In Britain in the eighteenth and early nineteenth centuries many of the male midwives' innovations were often fatal for both mother and child. The forceps, in particular, which are frequently claimed to be the chief advantage of male medicine, were not used in more than a minority of cases attended by male midwives, and had little effect on infant mortality, except perhaps to raise it further.[4] In the 1920s in America, where female midwifery was to be most completely phased out, doctors had to contend with the fact that midwifery was obviously associated with less mortality and morbidity than the interventionist character of the new obstetrical approach.[5]

Improvements in knowledge and technique do not in retrospect justify male participation in midwifery during the eighteenth and nineteenth centuries, and if they did so at the time it was the ideological power of the claim to greater expertise that had this effect. The success of the claim seems to have had a great deal to do with the propagation of certain notions of womanhood. The nineteenth century was a crucial period both for the evolution of modern woman's position and for the consolidation of the male obstetrical takeover. Medical writing about women's diseases and reproductive capacity during this period was characterized by a curiously strong 'emotionally charged conviction' in relation to women's character.[6] Women were also seen as the 'carriers' of contagion, an intrinsic threat to the health of society. Class intersects with sexism here, for it was working-class women who were seen as 'sickening' in this sense.[7]

'It is almost a pity that a woman has a womb', exclaimed an American professor of gynaecology in the 1860s.[6] This statement neatly summarizes the low regard in which the medical profession held its female patients; through its ideological construction of the uterus as the controlling organ of womanhood, it effectively demoted reproduction as woman's unique achievement to the status of a pitiable handicap. Such a construction presented women essentially as reproductive machines, subject to a direct biological input. It enabled physicians to assert a role in the mechanical management of female disorder, thus justifying the particular techniques of drastic gynaecological surgery and obstetrical intervention, and therefore establishing the 'need' for a male medical ascendancy over the whole domain of reproductive care.

All sorts of claims were made about the womb, and its associates, the ovaries, as the site and cause of female inferiority, from physiological pathology to mental disorder, from personality characteristics to occupational qualification (or, rather, disqualification). It was not simply the process of reproduction that was perceived as disabling, but the possession of the apparatus, which evidenced its presence in a monthly flow of reminders about the incapacity of women to be anything other than slaves to their biology.[5]

Doctors contended that a woman's reproductive organs explained her femininity in a double-bind sense: women were ill because they were women, but also if they tried to avoid being women by choosing to follow masculine occupations. Medicine thus outlined the contours of woman's place – in nature, not culture, safely outside the limits of masculine society.

How and why male medicine came to assume control over the care of women in childbirth in Britain and America over the last hundred years is, of course, a complex question. But its general location is within this framework of medical concerns about the essential character of women. There are important parallels between medical and social ideologies of womanhood, yet medicine plays a particular role as social ideology. The reason for this is that the theoretical foundations of patriarchy lie in the manipulation of women's biology to constitute their social inferiority. Medicine, as the definer of biology, holds the key to its 'scientific' interpretation, and thus its cultural consequences. The power of medical ideology stems from the incorporation of social assumptions into the very language of physiological theories. The sent and received message hence has a holistic appearance.[8] To deduce the ideological component is a difficult exercise.

Ehrenreich and English[9] demonstrate how the exclusion of women from obstetrics followed a long process of staged decline in the female community health care function. They argue that male medical hostility to women is based on a fear of female procreative power – hence the corroding impact of male obstetrics on female midwifery, whether to its virtual extermination, as in North America, or to its definition as a secondary status health profession, as in Britain. Barker-Benfield's thesis is that the assault on midwives, the rise of eugenic interest in women as breeders, and the coterminous development of destructive gynaecological surgery, can only be understood as aspects of 'a persistent, defensive attempt to control and shape women's procreative power'. Among the many pungent anecdotes included in Barker-Benfield's book is his account of how J. Marion Sims 'discovered' the speculum. Sims said 'Introducing the bent handle of a spoon into a woman's vagina I saw everything as no man had ever seen before . . . I felt like an explorer . . . who first views a new and important territory.' And a contemporary commentator caught up the colonial metaphor: 'Sims' speculum has been to diseases of the womb . . . what the compass is to the mariner'. Sims saw himself as a Columbus; his New World, and that of his male gynaecological successors, was the vagina.

The tools used by traditional female midwives lack documentation, but it seems likely that they also used an instrument such as the bent handle of a spoon to examine the vagina and cervix. But the routinization of the speculum-assisted vaginal examination by doctors facilitated an opposition between male medical knowledge of women's bodies and women's own knowledge. Throughout obstetricians' long fight to establish themselves as experts, in possession of *all* the resources necessary to the care and control of women in childbirth, this clash has remained the most vulnerable link in the chain of medical command.

The conflict between reproducer as expert and doctor as expert may have five outcomes: the reproducer may accept the doctor's definition of the situation; the doctor may accept the reproducer's; the reproducer may challenge the doctor's view; the doctor may challenge the reproducer's; or the conflict between them may be manifested in a certain pattern of communication between doctor and patient that indicates the presence of unresolved questions to do with what has been termed 'intrauterine neocolonialism'.[10] In a large series of doctor–patient encounters observed for the Transition to Motherhood study, this latter outcome was much more common than direct confrontation. The woman's status as an expert may be accorded joking recognition:

Doctor: First baby?
Patient: Second.
Doctor: [laughing]: So you're an expert?

Or:

Doctor: You're looking rather serious.
Patient: Well, I am rather worried about it all. It feels like a small baby – I feel much smaller with this one than I did with my first, and she weighed under six pounds. Ultrasound last week said the baby was very small, as well.
Doctor: Weighed it, did they?
Second Doctor [entering cubicle]: They go round the flower shows and weigh cakes, you know.
First Doctor: Yes, it's a piece of cake, really.

But frequently, patients concur in the doctor's presentation of himself (most obstetricians are male) as the possessor of privileged information:

Male Doctor: Will you keep a note in your diary of when you first feel the baby move?
Patient: Do you know – well, of course you would know – what it feels like?
Doctor: It feels like wind pains – something moving in your tummy.

At the same time, a common feature of communication between doctor and patient is a discrepancy between their labelling of significant symptoms. The medical dilemma is that of discerning the 'presenting' symptoms of clinically significant disorders; the patient's concern is with the normalization of her subjective experience of discomfort. Of 677 statements made by patients, 12 per cent concerned symptoms of pain or discomfort, which were medically treated either by being ignored, or with a nonserious response, or through a brief and selective account of relevant physiological/ anatomical data.

Doctor: Feeling well?
Patient: Yes, but very tired – I can't sleep at all at night.
Doctor: Why is that?
Patient: Well, I'm very uncomfortable – I turn from one side to the other, and the baby keeps kicking. I get cramp on one side, high up in my leg. If I sleep on my back I choke myself, so I'm tossing and turning about all night long, which isn't very good.
Doctor: We need to put you in a hammock, don't we? [Reads case notes] Tell me, the urine specimen which you brought in today – when did you do it?

Patient: I've got a pain in my shoulder.
Doctor: Well, that's your shopping bag hand, isn't it?

Patient: I get pains in my groin, down here, why is that?
Doctor: Well, it's some time since your last pregnancy, and also your centre of gravity is changing.
Patient: I see.
Doctor: That's okay. [Pats on back]

Such abbreviated 'commonsense' explanations are one mode in which doctors talk to patients. The contrasting mode is to 'technicalize' – to use technical language as a means of keeping the patient in her place. In maternity consultations this interactive pattern particularly characterizes those encounters in which a patient contends equality with the doctor:

Doctor: I think what we have to do is assess you – see how near you are to having it. [Does internal examination] Right – you'll go like a bomb, and I've given you a good stirring up. So what I think you should do, is I think you should come in.

Patient: Is it possible to wait another week, and see what happens?

Doctor: You've been reading the *Sunday Times*.

Patient: No, I haven't. I'm married to a doctor.

Doctor: Well, you've ripened up since last week and I've given the membranes a good sweep over.

Patient: What does that mean?

Doctor: I've swept them – not with a brush, with my finger. [Writes in notes 'give date for induction']

Patient: I'd still rather wait a bit.

Doctor: Well, we know the baby's mature now, and there's no sense in waiting. The perinatal morbidity and mortality increase rapidly after forty-two weeks. They didn't say that in the *Sunday Times*, did they?

A second classic area of dispute between reproducers and doctors is the dating of pregnancy. Six per cent of the questions asked and 5 per cent of statements made by mothers in the antenatal clinic concerned dates, mothers usually trying to negotiate the 'correct' date of expected delivery with the doctor, who did not see this as a subject for negotiation – as a legitimate area of maternal expertise. The underlying imputation is one of feminine unreliability.

Doctor: Are you absolutely sure of your dates?

Patient: Yes, and I can even tell you the date of conception. [Doctor laughs]

Patient: No, I'm serious. This is an artificial insemination baby.

Doctor: How many weeks are you now?

Patient: Twenty-six-and-a-half.

Doctor [looking at notes]: Twenty weeks now.

Patient: No, twenty-six-and-a-half.

Doctor: You can't be.

Patient: Yes I am, look at the ultrasound report.

Doctor: When was it done?

Patient: Today.

Doctor: It was done today?

Patient: Yes.

Doctor [reads report]: Oh yes, twenty-six-and-a-half weeks, that's right. [Patient smiles triumphantly at researcher]

Perhaps it is significant that increasingly the routine use of serial ultrasound cephalometry is providing an alternative medical technique for the assessment of gestation length. A medical rationale for the inflation of medical over maternal expertise is thus provided. Unbridled medical enthusiasm for new techniques is a general feature of modern medicine and it may be not so much that obstetrics is a special case but that medical attitudes see female reproductive patienthood as a particularly passive and appropriate site for their introduction.

References

1. 'You and your baby, Part 1: From pregnancy to birth', *Family Doctor Publications*, BMA, p. 8 (1977).
2. Spencer, H.R. *The History of British Midwifery from 1650 to 1800*, John Bale, Sons and Danielsson Ltd., London (1927).
3. Oakley, A. 'Wise woman and medicine man: changes in the management of childbirth'. In Mitchell, J. and Oakley, A. (eds) *The Rights and Wrongs of Women*, Penguin, Harmondsworth (1976).
4. Versluyen, M. 'Men–midwives, professionalising strategies and the first maternity hospitals – a sociological interpretation'. Unpublished paper (n.d.).
5. Barker-Benfield, G.J. *The Horrors of the Half-known Life*, Harper and Row, New York (1976).
6. Wood, A.D. ' "The fashionable diseases": women's complaints and their treatment in nineteenth century America'. In Hartman, M. and Banner, L.W. (eds) *Clio's Consciousness Raised: New Perspectives in the History of Women*, Harper and Row, New York (1974).
7. Duffin, L. 'The conspicuous consumptive: woman as an invalid'. In Delamont, S. and Duffin, L. (eds) *The Nineteenth Century Woman: Her Cultural and Physical World*, Croom Helm, London (1978).
8. Jordanova, L. 'Medicine, personal morality and public order: an historical case study'. Paper given at British Sociological Association Medical Sociology Conference, York, 22–41 September (1978).
9. Ehrenreich, B. and English, D. *Witches, Midwives and Nurses*, Glass Mountain Pamphlets, The Feminist Press, New York (1975).
10. Swinscow, T.D.V. 'Personal view', *British Medical Journal*, 28 September (1974).

Ann Oakley is Professor of Sociology and Social Policy at the Institute of Education, London. This article is an extract from her book *Women Confined* which was published by Martin Robertson, Oxford (1980).

62 | Normal rubbish: deviant patients in casualty departments

ROGER JEFFERY

English casualty departments

Casualty departments have been recognised as one of the most problematic areas of the NHS since about 1958. The major criticisms have been that Casualty departments have to operate in old, crowded, and ill-equipped surroundings, and that their unpopularity with doctors has meant that the doctors employed as Casualty Officers [COs] are either overworked or of poor quality. 'Poor quality' in this context seems to mean either doctors in their pre-registration year, or doctors from abroad.

The reasons for the unpopularity of Casualty work amongst doctors have usually been couched either in terms of the poor working conditions, or in terms of the absence of a career structure within Casualty work. Other reasons which are less frequently put forward, but seem to underlie these objections, relate more to the nature of the work, and in particular to the notion that the Casualty department is an interface between hospital and community. Prestige amongst doctors is, at least in part, related to the distance a doctor can get from the undifferentiated mass of patients, so that teaching hospital consultancies are valued because they are at the end of a series of screening mechanisms. Casualty is one of these screening mechanisms, rather like general practitioners in this respect. However, they are unusual in the hospital setting in the freedom of patients to gain entrance without having seen a GP first; another low prestige area similar in this respect is the VD clinic. Casualty has been unsuited to the processes of differentiation and specialisation which have characterised the recent history of the medical profession, and this helps to explain the low prestige of the work, and the low priority it has received in hospital expenditure.

The material on which this paper is based was gathered at three Casualty departments in an English city. These departments would appear to be above average in terms of the criteria discussed above: all were fully staffed; only two of the seventeen doctors employed during the fieldwork period were immigrant; and the working conditions were reasonable.

Typifications of patients

Moral evaluation of patients seems to be a regular feature of medical settings, not merely amongst medical students or in mental hospitals. In general, two broad categories were used to evaluate patients: good or interesting, and bad or rubbish. They were sometimes used as if they were an exclusive dichotomy, but more generally appeared as opposite ends of a continuum.

> [CO to medical students] If there's anything interesting we'll stop, but there's a lot of rubbish this morning. On nights you get some drunken dross in, but also some good cases.

Good patients

Good patients were described almost entirely in terms of their medical characteristics, either in terms of the symptoms or the causes of the injury. Good cases were head injuries, or cardiac arrests, or a stove-in chest; or they were RTAs (Road Traffic Accidents). There were three broad criteria by which patients were seen to be good, and each related to medical considerations.

(i) If they allowed the CO to practise skills necessary for passing professional examinations. In order to pass the FRCS examinations doctors need to be able to diagnose and describe unusual conditions and symptoms. Casualty was not a good place to discover these sorts of cases, and if they did turn up a great fuss was made of them.

(ii) If they allowed staff to practise their chosen speciality. For the doctors, the specific characteristics of good patients of this sort were fairly closely defined, because most doctors saw themselves as future specialists – predominantly surgeons. They tended to accept, or conform to, the model of the surgeon as a man of action who can achieve fairly rapid results. Patients who provided the opportunity to use and act out this model were welcomed.

> But I like doing surgical procedures. These are great fun. It just lets your imagination run riot really [laughs] you know, you forget for a moment you are just a very small cog incising a very small abscess, and you pick up your scalpel like anyone else [laughs].

For some COs, Casualty work had some advantages over other jobs because the clientele was basically healthy, and it was possible to carry out procedures which showed quick success in terms of returning people to a healthy state.

(iii) If they tested the general competence and maturity of the staff. The patients who were most prized were those who stretched the resources of the department in doing the task they saw themselves designed to carry out – the rapid early treatment of acutely ill patients. Many of the COs saw their Casualty job as the first in which they were expected to make decisions without the safety net of ready advice from more senior staff.

> I really do enjoy doing anything where I am a little out of my depth, where I really have to think about what I am doing. Something like a bad road traffic accident, where they ring up and give you a few minutes warning and perhaps give you an idea of what's happening . . . And when the guy finally does arrive you've got a

rough idea of what you are going to do, and sorting it all out and getting him into the right speciality, this kind of thing is very satisfying.

Good patients, then, make demands which fall squarely within the boundaries of what the staff define as appropriate to their job. This is in marked contrast to 'rubbish'.

Rubbish

While the category of the good patient is one I have in part constructed from comments about 'patients I like dealing with' or 'the sort of work I like to do', 'rubbish' is a category generated by the staff themselves.

It's a thankless task, seeing all the rubbish, as we call it, coming through.

I wouldn't be making the same fuss in another job – it's only because it's mostly bloody crumble like women with insect bites.

In an attempt to get a better idea of what patients would be included in the category of rubbish I asked staff what sorts of patients they did not like having to deal with, which sorts of patients made them annoyed, and why. The answers they gave suggested that staff had developed characterisations of 'normal' rubbish – the normal suicide attempt, the normal drunk, and so on – which they were thinking of when they talked about rubbish. In other words, staff felt able to predict a whole range of features related not only to [the patient's] medical condition but also to his past life, to his likely behaviour inside the Casualty department, and to his future behaviour. These expected features of the patient could thus be used to guide the treatment (both socially and medically) that the staff decided to give the patient. The following were the major categories of rubbish mentioned by the staff.

(i) Trivia. The recurring problem of Casualty departments, in the eyes of the doctors, has been the 'casual' attender. Normal trivia banged their heads, their hands or their ankles, carried on working as usual, and several days later looked into Casualty to see if it was all right. Normal trivia treats Casualty like a perfunctory service, on a par with a garage, rather than as an expert emergency service, which is how the staff like to see themselves.

They come in and say 'I did an injury half an hour ago, or half a day ago, or two days ago. I'm perfectly all right, I've just come for a check-up.'

[Trivia] comes up with a pain that he's had for three weeks, and gets you out of bed at 3 in the morning.

(ii) Drunks. Normal drunks are abusive and threatening. They come in shouting and singing after a fight and they are sick all over the place, or they are brought in unconscious, having been found in the street. They come in the small hours of the night, and they often have to be kept in until morning because you never know if they have been knocked out in a fight (with the possibility of a head injury) or whether they were just sleeping it off. They come in weekend after weekend with the same injuries, and they are always unpleasant and awkward.

(iii) Overdoses. The normal overdose is female, and is seen as a case of self-injury rather than of attempted suicide. She comes because her boyfriend/husband/parents

have been unkind, and she is likely to be a regular visitor. She only wants attention, she was not seriously trying to kill herself, but she uses the overdose as moral blackmail. She makes sure she does not succeed by taking a less-than-lethal dose, or by ensuring that she is discovered fairly rapidly.

> In the majority of overdoses, you know, these symbolic overdoses, the sort of '5 aspirins and 5 valiums and I'm ill doctor, I've taken an overdose'.

> By and large they are people who have done it time and time again, who are up, who have had treatment, who haven't responded to treatment.

(iv) Tramps. Normal tramps can be recognised by the many layers of rotten clothing they wear, and by their smell. They are a feature of the cold winter nights and they only come to Casualty to try to wheedle a bed in the warm for the night. Tramps can never be trusted; they will usually sham their symptoms. New COs and young staff nurses should be warned, for if one is let in one night then dozens will turn up the next night.

> [Tramps are] nuisance visitors, frequent visitors, who won't go, who refuse to leave when you want them to.

These four types covered most of the patients included in rubbish, or described as unpleasant or annoying. There were some other characterisations mentioned less frequently, or which seemed to be generated by individual patients, or which seemed to be specific to particular members of staff. 'Nutcases' were in this uncertain position: there were few 'typical' features of psychiatric patients, and these were very diffuse. 'Smelly', 'dirty' and 'obese' patients were also in this limbo. Patients with these characteristics were objected to, but there was no typical career expected for [them].

Rules broken by rubbish

In their elaboration of *why* certain sorts of patients were rubbish, staff organised their answers in terms of a number of unwritten rules which they said rubbish had broken. These rules were in part consensual, and in part ideological. These rules, then, can be seen as the criteria by which staff judged the legitimacy of claims made by patients for entry into the sick role, or for medical care.

(a) Patients must not be responsible, either for their illness or for getting better: medical staff can only be held responsible if, in addition, they were able to treat the illness. The first half of this rule was broken by all normal rubbish. Drunks and tramps were responsible for their illnesses like bronchitis which are a direct result of the life the tramp has chosen to lead. Normal overdoses knew what they were doing, and chose to take an overdose for their own purposes. Trivia *chose* to come to Casualty, and could be expected to deal with their illnesses themselves. All normal rubbish had within their own hands the ability to effect a complete cure, and since there was little the Casualty staff could do about it, they could not be held responsible to treat the illnesses of normal rubbish. Comments which reflected this rule included,

> I don't like having to deal with drunks in particular. I find that usually they're quite aggressive. I don't like aggressive people. And I feel that, you know, they've got themselves into this state entirely through their own follies, why the hell should I have to deal with them on the NHS? So I don't like drunks.

I think they are a bloody nuisance. I don't like overdoses, because I've got very little sympathy with them on the whole, I'm afraid.

The staff normally felt uncertain about the existence of an illness if there was no therapy that they, or anyone else, could provide to correct the state, and it would seem that this uncertainty fostered frustration which was vented as hostility towards these patients. One example of this was in the comments on overdoses, and the distinctions made between those who really tried to commit suicide (for whom there is some respect) and the rest (viewed as immature calls for attention).

It's the same I'm sure in any sphere, that if you're doing something and you're treating it and – say you're a plumber and the thing keeps going wrong because you haven't got the right thing to put it right, you get fed up with it, and in the end you'd much rather hit the thing over the . . . hit the thing with your hammer. Or in this case, to give up rather than go on, you know, making repeated efforts.

(b) Patients should be restricted in their reasonable activities by the illnesses they report with. This rule has particular point in a Casualty department, and trivia who have been able to delay coming to the department most obviously break this rule. However, there is another aspect to this rule, the requirement that the activities being followed should be reasonable, and the obvious offenders against this rule are the tramps.

If a man has led a full productive life, he's entitled to good medical attention, because he's put a lot into society.

[Tramps] put nothing in, and are always trying to get something out.

Obviously the Protestant Ethic of work is alive and well in Casualty departments.

(c) Patients should see illness as an undesirable state. The patients who most obviously offend against this rule are the overdoses and the tramps. The overdoses are seen to want to be ill in order to put moral pressure on someone, or to get attention. Tramps want to be ill in order to get the benefits of being a patient – a warm bed and warm meals.

(d) Patients should cooperate with the competent agencies in trying to get well. The major non-cooperative patients were the drunks and the overdoses. Drunks fail to cooperate by refusing to stay still while being sutured or examined, and overdoses fight back when a rubber tube is being forced down their throats so that their stomachs can be washed out. These are both cases where patients *refuse* to cooperate, rather than being unable to cooperate, as would be the case for patients in epileptic or diabetic fits. Similarly, they refuse to cooperate in getting 'well' because they cannot be trusted to live their lives in future in such a way that would avoid the same injuries.

These four rules seemed to cover the criteria by which normal rubbish was faulted. It can be seen that each of them required quite fine judgement about, for example, whether a patient was uncooperative by choice or because of some underlying illness.

Punishment

Rubbish could be punished by the staff in various ways, the most important being to increase the amount of time that rubbish had to spend in Casualty before completing treatment. In each hospital there were ways of advancing and retarding patients so that they were not seen strictly in the order in which they arrived. Good patients, in general being the more serious, could be seen immediately by being taken directly to the treatment area, either by the receptionist or by the ambulanceman. Less serious cases, including the trivia, would go first to a general waiting area. Patients there were normally left until all serious cases had been dealt with. Sometimes staff employed a deliberate policy of leaving drunks and tramps in the hope that they would get annoyed at the delay and take their own discharge.

The other forms of punishment used were verbal hostility or the vigorous restraint of uncooperative patients. Verbal hostility was in general fairly restrained, at least in my presence, and was usually less forthright than the written comments made in the 'medical' notes, or the comments made in discussions with other staff. Vigorous treatment of patients was most noticeable in the case of overdoses, who would be held down or sat upon while the patient was forced to swallow the rubber tube used. Staff recognised that this procedure had an element of punishment in it, but defended themselves by saying that it was necessary. However, they showed no sympathy for the victim, unlike cases of accidental self-poisoning by children. Drunks and tramps who were uncooperative could be threatened with the police, who were called on a couple of occasions to undress a drunk or to stand around while a tramp was treated.

Punishment was rarely extended to a refusal to see or to treat patients. The staff were very conscious of the adverse publicity raised whenever patients were refused treatment in Casualty departments, and they were also worried by the medico-legal complications to which Casualty departments are prone, and this restrained their hostility and the extent of the delay they were prepared to put patients to. A cautionary tale was told to emphasise the dangers of not treating rubbish properly, concerning a tramp who was seen in a Casualty department and discharged. A little later the porter came in and told the CO that the tramp had collapsed and died outside on the pavement. The porter then calmed the worries of the CO by saying 'It's all right, sir, I've turned him round so that it looks as though he was on his way to Casualty.'

At the time of writing this article, Roger Jeffery was a Lecturer in Sociology in the Department of Sociology, University of Edinburgh. This article is an edited version of one that was originally published in *Sociology of Health and Illness*, 1(1), 90–108 (1979).

63 | Food-work: maids in a hospital kitchen

ELIZABETH PATERSON

What follows is an ethnographic account of how the maids did 'food-work' for all practical purposes, given a variety of organisational and architectural constraints. The paper outlines the routines in which they engaged, some of which proved to be dirty, menial and boring; the common sense assumptions they made about the tasks, the materials used to perform them and the people destined to receive the final product; the 'strain' this type of work placed on the maids' conception of self; and finally the strategies utilised to combat these undesirable effects.

Kitchen maid routine

It was from the daily institutionalised routines that passed as 'maids' work' that the meaning of 'food-work' emerged and description of these processes may lead to some understanding of the everyday assumptions that the maids, and to some extent the other kitchen staff also, made while dealing with the food. The kitchen provided meals for around 700 patients, for the doctors', sisters' and nurses' dining rooms, the service room in the maternity hospital, the staff of the sterilisation department and for the canteen which catered primarily for technical staff.

During observation the maids' routine consisted of a variety of tasks. They emptied food containers from the heated trolleys returned from the wards and placed them in their appropriate storage areas. They prepared carrots for soup-making by processing sackfuls through 'the machine' (skinner), scraping off the remaining black sections, chopping and mincing them. Similar vegetables had to be processed in an equally tedious manner, including the washing of lettuce for salad. Maids also cleaned, battered and coated large boxes of fish. They pared, cored and sliced apples for puddings and prepared any other fruit which appeared on the menu. They removed from chickens any giblets remaining after factory processing and any excess fat, while generally up to the elbows in tepid, greasy water.

Routinely from eight a.m. onwards food was being cooked for lunch in immense vessels, stirred by wooden 'oars', dished into assorted containers and placed in heated trolleys to wait until noon. In addition each meal necessitated a succession of trolley-emptying, dish-washing and plugging-in, the process being repeated continually throughout the day, although by supper time most of the daily maids had gone off duty and had been replaced by others.

When all the food had been processed for that day, and occasionally even before, ingredients were prepared for the *next* day's dishes. Consequently besides regular accepted routines, the week's menu fleshed out the structure of the day. It indicated not only what had to be prepared or cooked immediately, but what had to be prepared that day for the next or even subsequent days.

Working assumptions

From the above description of the grinding forward of a routine day it is clear that food is very much work to those within a kitchen, just as death is work to the staff of a hospital and old people are work to the staff of an old people's home. The need to 'get through the day' has an important effect on how they conceive of what they work upon and around. As a result the typical, common sense ways of thinking about food and its preparation within kitchen walls are different from those outside an area catering for such large numbers and where food is not the object of work. Elsewhere, food is usually considered in small quantities, carefully washed, prepared, cooked to exact times, dished when ready and consumed in small amounts by the person concerned, family or acquaintances. On the other hand, to maids dealing with it in bulk the food became like a factory product and its preparation had meaning in that sense.

As an extension of this type of thinking – food as work – it was categorised in relation to the routines of work and its easy completion. When busy – and during the period of study the maids generally were – foods were typified as 'bad' or 'good', not according to taste but by their relevance for work control.

Washing lettuce for salad was a job which maids tried to avoid. It was a long, boring task and also a back-breaking one, because it necessitated bending over a low sink while holding each leaf under the tap. It had to be performed in such a tedious fashion because lettuce, above most other foods, worried both providers and receivers. Because lettuce is uncooked and tends to lie unadorned on the plate (in the hospital at least), it is patently obvious if it has brown patches, is dirty or is harbouring some wildlife. As a result a maxim about lettuce-washing existed: 'Rather get into trouble for taking a long time than get into trouble for missing slugs'. Hence 'doing lettuce' elicited sympathy from colleagues, a maid was considered brave to tackle it on her own and therefore it was a tactic which led to being classed as a 'good worker'.

On the other hand, 'good' foods were those which required little or no preparation by maids, such as macaroni and cheese, or ones which meant that few boilers or friers had to be washed afterwards. So in this additional way the menu gave meaning to the day's routine, whether it would mean hard work or not, by indicating whether 'good' or 'bad' foods had to be prepared.

'Unexpected' practices

One notable example of 'unexpected' practices concerned cooks rather than maids, but it very clearly illustrates the pervading attitude. Even in an area of patient catering to which one would expect careful attention to be given, special diets, the approach to food was similar.

After consultations about the health and choices of patients, dieticians made out diet sheets for specific diseases and conditions. For salt-free, high- and low-protein and sugar-free diets one would expect that the food would be carefully weighed and prepared. Despite this impression of scientific control, science seemed to be abandoned when the diet sheet left the hands of the dietician. She made frequent visits to the diet's cook, but the latter seemed more concerned with the arrangement and control of work routine than with any desire to achieve accuracy. The cook wanted to receive the diet sheet as early as possible in the morning in order to begin preparing dishes for tea. Any late adjustments meant that the cook's routine was upset; dieticians who were late were invariably labelled 'lazy'. In addition, cooks on diet duty often experienced great difficulty in obtaining from the supervisor the foods indicated on the sheet, so they often had to make do with second (or third) best. Many discovered only too late that a certain food did contain the forbidden salt or sugar.

'Staff' and 'patients'

Up to this point the discussion appears to indicate that the 'unexpected' standards of food production were similar for all categories served by the kitchen. However this was not the case. Standards differed for doctors and sisters, who were considered of high social worth, for nurses and technical staff who were lower in the hierarchy, for private patients who were considered almost as worthy as staff, and for 'ordinary' patients, whose status was considered lowest of all. This was related to the power of the respective categories; their power to demand accounts for food that was deemed unsatisfactory; the power resting in the fact that all groups except 'ordinary' patients could be said to pay for their meals.

Staff also got priority with containers, i.e. they received shiny new ones, or plates and glass dishes as opposed to metal trays, whereas any bashed object that could conceivably hold food was placed in the patients' trolleys. Different maids and cooks prepared staff and patients' meals, the staff side being allocated a larger quota than the patients' side, perhaps indicating the desire to perform staff preparation more thoroughly.

Ward C contained private patients and they often received the same food as staff, except for those patients on special diets. Patients on this ward got personalised extras, such as individual moulds for jelly, parsley in a small container which could be sprinkled on food if desired, sole instead of haddock and so on. They were also likely to receive 'treats' such as strawberry tarts, while these delights were never offered to other patients. However, it must not be overlooked that much of this personalised treatment may have stemmed from the fact that the food was being served for much smaller numbers. So decisions about the worth and financial contributions of clientele in this instance had a quite dramatic effect, especially for bored patients for whom food could have become the only highlight in the day's dull routine.

Implications for maids

Although the impression may have been given that maids performed 'food-work' routines and engaged in dirty and discriminatory practices with equanimity this was not invariably the case. Although much had become taken for granted they frequently reacted unfavourably towards the job and how it affected them as human beings in general and as women in particular. In a large variety of ways the work had implications for their self conception and their general well-being.

Behaviour in the role of bulk food-producer often conflicted with that of food-producer in the home, and this 'role strain' was felt particularly acutely among new-comers or those whose relatives or friends were also patients. A further element of the maids' problem was that since their products seldom reached the consumer direct, there was no one to praise them. They produced only transient things like cleanness and scraped carrots. In addition the maids saw the work as very hard and the allocation of duties as unfair. The job was also dangerous because of the likelihood of falling on the greasy floors, being burned on the multitude of hotplates and ovens, or being cut by knives or other dangerous equipment. Furthermore maids were subordinate to all others in the kitchen hierarchy, low in power and in status.

It was considered a tough and demeaning job even in comparison with being a maid in other sections of the hospital; other maids did not have to wear the unbecoming caps and aprons in addition to their overalls; they were allowed a greater degree of autonomy in organising their work; and they could increase their status by contact with nursing staff. How lowly kitchen maids were considered in hospital eyes was illustrated by the fact that not only had they to queue silently on Friday lunchtime to be handed their pay abruptly 'like a food ration', but kitchen maids received theirs after all other maids and cooks; consequently they had to stand around longer and their half-hour lunch break was reduced considerably.

In sum there were few maids who did not resent the implications of their work for their conception of themselves as clean, attractive, concerned and fairly independent women. As a result of the problems outlined maids utilised a variety of tactics to negate the undesirable effects of the organisational setting, of the dirty, strenuous, repetitive demeaning and unsatisfying work.

Maids' strategies

Making adjustments

Maids tried to 'distance themselves' from their position within the kitchen in an attempt to control the definition of themselves in the situation. To indicate that they did not wish to be classed as a 'skivvy', most expressed the forced nature of their work, i.e. 'this is not the *real* me'. To distance themselves from their subordinate position maids attempted to develop a joking relationship with those cooks considered amenable to this approach. Distance from their position as 'skivvy' was also expressed by sullen replies, biting comments after the superior had departed, or, as happened repeatedly in the kitchen because the facilities were available, by loud banging of containers and equipment. Maids often symbolically rejected being ordered around by appearing aloof, walking slowly and taking an extremely long time to perform a task.

Conversational topics were also part of this comprehensive fabric of behaviour which disassociated their role in menial and dirty tasks from their 'real' selves, the good housewives, the interesting people. Talk not only passed time but gave evidence of the lives these women took part in outside work. Regulating appearance was yet another method used to negate the role. All kitchen maids were forced to wear unattractive nylon caps. The older women with short hair objected to the cap spoiling the style, so they crumpled it into a ball and pinned it at the back. Many of the older maids had their hair styled regularly, and maids and cooks tended to wear a great deal of perfume as if to combat any clinging odours of 'food-work'.

Furthermore, in addition to these distancing tactics, maids worked the system. They would take things from the kitchen as if in compensation for being employed there. They consumed pieces of cooked meat that were lying around; they carefully chose the nicest tomatoes to eat with their toast. Taking food out of the premises was far less common, although it would be fair to say that no kitchen maid's family went short of tomatoes; large turnover and ease of handling made them a popular prey. And although there were continual complaints about the shortage of [cleaning] cloths, most of the married women ensured that they had a constant supply of the better ones for private use. They got the most out of the kitchen as if to compensate for being engaged in a rather demeaning job.

Combating monotony

It has been shown that work was not only subordinate and dirty but that several of its aspects were extremely boring, a factor in many low-status occupations. Hence methods of overcoming the tedium were important for doing 'food-work'.

Most maids took a variety of 'smoke-breaks', generally before breakfast, before lunch and before leaving in the afternoon. These were enjoyed in the toilet due to the scarcity of other 'back regions' or 'free places'. The toilet was one of the few areas almost accepted by senior staff as a place of escape from work routines for short periods of time.

'Floor time', the period when respective 'sides' washed the areas of the kitchen allotted to them, also broke the monotony of work like scraping carrots all morning. In addition they had the more illicit 'tea time', taken apart from the regular breaks, and occurring in the vegetable room, another quite secluded region. In addition the older women went to the refectory each Saturday lunch time for a drink (although the break only lasted half an hour) and on Sunday, when the refectory was closed, they drove to a hotel nearby. For these trips they had to remove their working overalls, and in this way they could step out of their role as maids for a short time at least.

This necessarily truncated description of how maids engaged in some aspects of 'food-work' has outlined the dirty, menial and boring routines which came to be accepted as 'maids' work', and the assumptions they made about that work, the materials involved and the recipients of the final product. This occupation had several undesirable, demeaning effects on the maids' conception of self and led to a variety of strategies or adjustments on their part, many of them tolerated by supervision.

What has been described may disturb those who organise catering in medical (and other) institutions, and is highly relevant to debates concerning the generally poor state of hospital meals and the periodic outbreaks of food-poisoning among patients.

But it has been made clear throughout the discussion that there were numerous practical factors involved in the behaviour displayed; there would be many 'good' organisational reasons for 'bad' hospital food.

At the time of writing this article, Elizabeth Paterson was a Research Fellow and sociologist at the MRC Medical Sociology Unit, Institute of Medical Sociology, Aberdeen. This is an edited version of an article originally published in Atkinson, P. and Heath, C. (eds) *Medical Work: Realities and Routines*, Gower, Farnborough, pp. 152–169 (1981).

64 | Professions allied to medicine: continuity and change in a complex workforce

LESLEY DOYAL AND AILSA CAMERON

Introduction

During the last decade there has been an increasing demand for greater flexibility in the NHS workforce. At provider level this has been reflected in pressures towards 'interprofessional' working as well as reshaping of the work of different professional groups. A number of studies have monitored how these 'new roles' have developed in local settings. While these studies cited personal and professional benefits in increasing the scope of their responsibilities, they also revealed considerable pressures imposed both on individuals and on organizations when these changes were introduced.

The findings presented here highlight the complex and interdependent nature of the NHS workforce and the challenges that will need to be faced if more flexible ways of working are to be achieved (Cameron and Doyal 2000).

Background and policy context

In 1998 there were approximately 105,327 state registered professions allied to medicine (PAMs) compared to a total number of 637,449 nurses (including health visitors and midwives) on the register. The Professions Supplementary to Medicine Act was passed in 1960 in order to regulate the initial training and professional practice of a growing number of allied professions. The Council for the Professions Supplementary to Medicine was set up under the Act to supervise the awarding of qualifications leading to state registration as well as monitor the professional standards of individual practitioners.

Over the past few years there have been significant changes in the education and professional practice of PAMs with a move towards graduate status for all new practitioners. All PAMs now have their own undergraduate education programmes, which are validated jointly by the higher education providers and the professional bodies. As yet, they do not share a common core of education but examples of multi-professional programmes are now beginning to emerge.

The research project

This chapter draws on evidence from the Exploring New Roles in Practice project (ENRiP; SCHARR 1997) which was commissioned by the Department of Health in 1995 as part of its Human Resources Initiative. Its aim was to explore the extent of role development amongst nurses and PAMs working in acute care. For the purposes of the project a 'new' role was one identified by those working in a particular trust as innovative, non-traditional or taking on aspects of care previously performed by a different professional group.

Case studies were carried out on 14 new PAMs' roles: 3 occupational therapists, 7 physiotherapists, 3 diagnostic radiographers and 1 therapeutic radiographer. The posts were based in three acute hospitals (a teaching hospital [Site J], an urban district general hospital [Site L] and a rural district general hospital [Site H]).

PAMs in practice: the challenges of new roles

The range of activities covered by these posts was broad. Some tended towards the 'advanced practice' model of new role development in which clinical practice reaches beyond that of the mainstream profession to new areas. Other posts were much more 'specialist' in their orientation (CSP 1995). Most incorporated a diversity of activities including supervisory, educational, research and management roles as well as clinical responsibilities. For the postholders, these new roles were often complex and demanding and posed major challenges. Many faced very similar organizational obstacles to those described by nurses undertaking innovative work (Doyal *et al.* 1998). However many PAMs reported additional difficulties associated with their small numbers, their lack of representation on trust management teams and the general lack of understanding about their skills and their potential contribution to patient care.

Most participants regarded their new roles as an exciting challenge, commenting positively about what they hoped to achieve both for themselves and the wider profession. The respiratory physiotherapist said: 'I love it, it's not the label. I feel completely fulfilled from a professional point of view . . . there should be more people like me . . .'.

Practitioners valued the greater autonomy the new posts had to offer while also recognizing the increased pressures. At Site L the cardiac rehabilitation physiotherapist summed up the situation very well: 'I am my own boss, I enjoy it, once you get the confidence in what you are doing . . . I like being my own boss and being on my own. On other occasions it's nice to get some support'.

Lack of clarity

Alongside this enthusiasm however, many expressed a lack of clarity about the roles and what was expected of them. Postholders talked about their own confusion and the need to educate colleagues about their roles. As the rheumatology physiotherapist at Site H commented: 'I think consultants' understanding comes with time. General doctors don't know what physios and occupational therapists do, it took quite a long time for Dr X to understand what I could offer the service'.

Accountability and support

Concerns about roles and identity were often exacerbated by confusing patterns of line management and accountability (Dowling *et al.* 1996). Many of the postholders were managed by someone from another profession and this meant that there was often no one to offer support.

All but one of the 14 postholders regarded themselves as professionally account-able to their own profession's senior manager. However, clinical accountability was widely spread. The majority traced their clinical accountability to the consultant with whom they worked and only sometimes to a manager from their own profession. It appeared that practitioners had developed complex matrix arrangements to deal with the varied aspects of their accountability. For those working in more than one role this could be a rather elaborate construction and was often the source of considerable concern.

The complexity of these arrangements was evident from practitioners working at Site L, the urban DGH (district general hospital). The 'clinical physiotherapy specialist' worked in three different roles and saw herself as clinically accountable to the physio-therapy manager when working in pain education and to the orthopaedic surgeon and physiotherapy manager when working in the orthopaedic out-patient clinic. The cardiac rehabilitation occupational therapist was clinically responsible to the cardiac rehabilita-tion physiotherapist, who herself was responsible to the consultant cardiologist. The MRI [magnetic resonance imaging] radiographer on the other hand saw herself as clinically responsible to the radiologist running the particular session and to the business manager who was a radiographer by background.

Training and the assessment of competence

Previous research has identified the ad hoc nature of the training and preparation provided to nurses working in new roles (Doyal *et al.* 1998), and the story was similar for PAMs. When taking up their new roles, all the postholders had identified their educational needs and as a result the majority undertook some further training. How-ever the nature of this process varied significantly. Most was in-house and tailored to the post itself rather than being generic and transferable.

A number of the postholders commented that because they were breaking new ground for their profession no one knew what training they needed. Some resolved this dilemma by contacting colleagues working elsewhere and putting together their own training packages. In general, education and training was a complex and difficult area and the lack of national awards or recognition of skills placed significant constraints on activities of postholders.

Assessments of competence in these new skills were also complex. Most were under-taken by a doctor who would assess a particular skill rather than performance in the role overall. For example the rheumatology clinical specialist received training from the consultant who led the team and was assessed on completing specific procedures such as joint injections, rather than being examined in all aspects of her role.

Being unique

Many of the PAM practitioners constantly returned to what they saw as the challenge of their uniqueness. Sometimes lack of clarity led to a lack of acceptance of the practitioner by their professional colleagues. This was the case for the radiographer who commented that: '. . . because it was a new role and was something they hadn't experienced some people find it hard to accept that a radiographer can do something different than they would traditionally do'.

The debate about changing forms of practice appeared to be less well developed among PAMs than among nurses and this made it difficult for practitioners to get clear advice on professional issues. The respiratory physiotherapist at Site J sought clarity from the Chartered Society of Physiotheraphy (CSP) about the grading of specialist posts. However, she received little help: 'What is the difference between a clinical specialist and physiotherapy practitioner? The CSP didn't know!' Later she reported some progress: 'Good news of the "clinical specialist" and "practitioner" problem. My boss sees me as a clinical practitioner with day to day routine caseload oriented . . . at last some direction! I will photocopy the guidelines and bring them up at our own specialist meetings'.

The representation of PAMs in the trusts

Many of the problems described by respondents could be traced back in part to the overall management arrangements for PAMs, which gave little visibility at board level and their interests often seemed to be neglected. Though the arrangements varied between trusts, all radiographers were managed independently of the other PAMs in separate units and all occupational therapists were represented at senior management level, either formally or informally, by a physiotherapist. The problems created by such arrangements were very evident at Site J. In this teaching hospital, physiotherapists and occupational therapists were based in a therapies directorate and were represented at trust board level by the clinical services director (a physician). Radiographers were based in diagnostic imaging and were also represented at the trust board by the clinical services director. Therapeutic radiographers were based in oncology and represented at executive level by the clinical director of cancer services.

In discussing the effectiveness of these arrangements a number of the respondents emphasised the problem of the relatively small size of their professional group. They also compared the power of PAMs with that of nurses. One therapy manager was particularly bothered that the clinical director was a doctor: 'Doctors don't understand other roles. Therefore they have no concepts to understand [PAMs] with . . . Nursing has accessed the system much better, so there is no room for the rest of us so we are never at the top of her agenda. It doesn't work'.

The clinical services director felt that PAMs were not adequately represented in the trust. She was concerned about inequities between staff groups in their access to development funds and also felt concerned that they did not have easy access to her. She admitted that: '. . . they get forgotten, nurses and doctors have their specific representatives but PAMs don't. I hadn't really thought of myself as the PAMs' executive until you mentioned it'.

The future

The challenges facing PAMs in the new NHS are in many senses unique because of their size, their low visibility and their lack of representation. Though they are subject to many of the same forces for change that other professional groups face, they also have their own particular characteristics both as a group of small professions occupying a specific position within the structure of the NHS and also as individual professions within this larger grouping. These characteristics will have a significant effect on how they are able to respond to current challenges both generally and with respect to the development of new roles.

Occupational therapy

From our observations the group that appears to be most at risk from future developments are occupational therapists. The changing nature of health care has led to radical changes both in the patterns of care delivered by occupational therapists, and in their place of work. As hospital stays have declined and care in the community increased, occupational therapists have experienced a shift away from 'hands on' rehabilitation work towards assessment, evaluation and discharge planning.

Of all the PAMs groups, occupational therapy seems to be furthest from the medical power base. Many occupational therapists are now managed by physiotherapists. This has further weakened their capacity to market their services and determine their own practice. The significance of these developments for the profession has been profound and has marked a fundamental change in their clinical practice (Cameron and Masterson 1998). Their distinctive contribution has often been obscured and their work increasingly overlaps with that of other professional groups.

Physiotherapy

Physiotherapists face similar problems particularly in those areas where new roles have been created that could be occupied by either nurses or physiotherapists. In respiratory medicine and rheumatology, aspects of the therapeutic role are being reconfigured in ways that do not conform with traditional occupational boundaries between physiotherapists, specialist nurses and doctors. However, physiotherapists are probably in a stronger position since they are more likely to be in senior management positions and they appear to have maintained a closer relationship with the medical profession.

Radiography

The situation of the radiography profession seems to be different. Radiography tends to have closer links to medicine and has also managed to maintain its own line management structure. Most radiographers are managed from within their own profession with representation to the board usually being through a doctor. The work of radiographers is more clearly understood by most doctors and they are seen to have a 'harder' and more 'scientific' knowledge than the other PAMs.

In the case of therapeutic radiography however, things look much less certain. The changing nature of oncology practice has posed serious challenges to this very small professional group. For many therapeutic radiographers the main development of their role has been towards a more 'holistic' approach with counselling becoming a major part of their activities. However this moves them away from their technical training and 'scientific' knowledge base to one already colonized by nurses. Thus there is again a blurring of boundaries and a lack of clarity about the implications of new roles for the longer-term professional future of therapeutic radiography.

Diagnostic radiographers have expanded into new roles with greater autonomy. They work independently both in primary care settings and in accident and emergency and are also being given significant responsibilities in the operation of new technologies such as MRI (magnetic resonance imaging) and CT (computed tomography) scanning and ultrasound. However, these developments have high lighted the boundary problem between the work of radiologists and radiographers. While there has been little concern from medical colleagues about radiographers carrying out procedures such as barium enemas, their increasing role in reporting on images has been viewed with suspicion. Diagnostic radiographers as a group are unlikely to face any significant challenge to their position, as diagnostic imaging becomes increasingly central to the practice of acute care.

Conclusion

The national plan for the NHS calls for a new approach to the delivery of health care (Department of Health 2000). Central to this will be a reconfiguration of the health labour force (Doyal and Cameron 2000). However, this will not be easy to achieve. As health care is transformed, some professions are likely to gain power and status while others lose. Indeed some professions may not be sustainable in their current form while other groupings may emerge to meet new needs. Against this background the challenges of 'working together' are likely to be greater than ever before. However, solutions will have to be found if the health service is to meet the challenges that lie ahead.

References

Cameron, A. and Doyal, L. (2000) An invisible revolution within the clinical team: new role development for the professions allied to medicine, in D. Humphries and A. Masterson (eds) *Developing Specialist Practice: A Guide for Health Practitioners*. Edinburgh: Harcourt Health Services.

Cameron, A. and Masterson, A. (1998) The changing policy context of occupational therapy, *British Journal of Occupational Therapy*, 61(12): 556–60.

CSP (Chartered Society of Physiotherapy) (1995) *Specialisms and Specialists*, information paper No. PA23. London: CSP.

Department of Health (2000) *The NHS Plan: A Plan for Investment, A Plan for Reform?* London: HMSO.

Dowling, S., Martin, R., Skidmore, P., Doyal, L., Cameron, A. and Lloyd, S. (1996) Nurses taking on junior doctors' work: a confusion of accountability. *British Medical Journal*, 312: 1211–14.

Doyal, L. and Cameron, A. (2000) Reshaping the NHS workface, *British Medical Journal*, 320: 1023–4.

Doyal, L., Downing, S. and Cameron, A. (1998) *Challenging Practice: An Evaluation of Four Innovatory Nursing Posts in the South and West.* Bristol: Policy Press.
SCHARR (School of Health and Related Research) (1997) *The ENRiP Database.* Sheffield: School of Health and Related Research, University of Sheffield.

This article has not been published previously in this form. Lesley Doyal is Professor of Health and Social Care in the School for Policy Studies, University of Bristol, UK. Ailsa Cameron is a Research Fellow in the same department. The authors would like to thank Abigail Masterson for her contribution to this project and the Department of Health for their financial support.

65 | The village health worker: lackey or liberator?

DAVID WERNER

Throughout Latin America, the programmed use of health auxiliaries has become an important part of the new international push of 'community oriented' health care. But in Latin America village health workers are far from new. Various religious groups and non-government agencies have been training *promotores de salud* or health promoters for decades. And to a large (but diminishing) extent, villagers still rely, as they always have, on their local *curanderos*, herb doctors, bone setters, traditional midwives and spiritual healers. More recently, the *médico practicante* or empirical doctor has assumed in the villages the same role of self-made practitioner and prescriber of drugs that the neighborhood pharmacist has assumed in larger towns and cities.

Until recently, however, the respective Health Departments of Latin America have either ignored or tried to stamp out this motley work force of non-professional healers. Yet the Health Departments have had trouble coming up with viable alternatives. Their Western-style, city-bred and city-trained MDs not only proved uneconomical in terms of cost effectiveness; they flatly refused to serve in the rural area. The first official attempt at a solution was, of course, to produce more doctors. In Mexico the National University began to recruit 5,000 new medical students per year. The result was a surplus of poorly trained doctors who stayed in the cities.

The next attempt was through compulsory social service. Graduating medical students were required (unless they bought their way off) to spend a year in a rural health center before receiving their licenses. The young doctors were unprepared either by training or disposition to cope with the health needs in the rural area. With discouraging frequency they became resentful, irresponsible or blatantly corrupt. Next came the era of the mobile clinics. They, too, failed miserably. They created dependency and expectation without providing continuity of service. The net result was to undermine the people's capacity for self care. It was becoming increasingly clear that provision of health care in the rural area could never be accomplished by professionals alone. But the medical establishment was – and still is – reluctant to crack its legal monopoly.

At long last, and with considerable financial cajoling from foreign and international health and development agencies, the various health departments [began] to train and utilize auxiliaries. In countries where they have been given half a chance, auxiliaries play an important role in the health care of rural and periurban communities. And if given a whole chance, their impact could be far greater. But, to a large extent, politics and the medical establishment still stand in the way.

Rural health projects

A group of my co-workers and I visited nearly forty rural health projects, both government and non-government, in nine Latin American countries (Mexico, Guatemala, Honduras, El Salvador, Nicaragua, Costa Rica, Venezuela, Colombia and Ecuador). Our objective [was] to encourage a dialogue among the various groups, as well as to try to draw together many respective approaches, methods, insights and problems into a sort of field guide for health planners and educators, so we can all learn from each other's experience. We specifically chose to visit projects or programs which were making significant use of local, modestly trained health workers or which were reportedly trying to involve people more effectively in their own health care.

We were inspired by some of the things we saw, and profoundly disturbed by others. While in some of the projects we visited, people were in fact regarded as a resource to control disease, in others we had the sickening impression that disease was being used as a resource to control people. We began to look at different programs, and functions, in terms of where they lay along a continuum between two poles: community supportive and community oppressive.

Community supportive programs or community oppressive programs?

Community supportive programs, or functions, are those which favorably influence the long-range welfare of the community, that help it stand on its own feet, that genuinely encourage responsibility, initiative, decision making and self-reliance at the community level, that build upon human dignity.

Community oppressive programs, or functions, are those which, while invariably giving lip service to the above aspects of community input, are fundamentally authoritarian, paternalistic or are structured and carried out in such a way that they effectively encourage greater dependency, servility and unquestioning acceptance of outside regulations and decisions; those which in the long run are crippling to the dynamics of the community.

It is disturbing to note that, with certain exceptions, the programs which we found to be more community supportive were small non-government efforts, usually operating on a shoestring and with a more or less sub-rosa status. As for the large regional or national programs – for all their international funding, top-ranking foreign consultants and glossy bilingual brochures portraying community participation – we found that when it came down to the nitty-gritty of what was going on in the field, there was usually a minimum of effective community involvement and a maximum of dependency-creating handouts, paternalism and superimposed, initiative destroying norms.

Table 65.1 Primary health workers in Latin America

Auxiliary nurses or health technicians	Health promoters or village health workers
At least primary education plus 1–2 years' training	Average of 3rd grade education plus 1–6 months' training
Usually from outside the community	Usually from the community and selected by it
Usually employed full time	
Salary usually paid by the program (not by the community)	Often a part time health worker supported in part by farm labor or with help from the community
	May be someone who has already been a traditional healer

Primary health workers

In our visits to the many rural health programs in Latin America, we found that primary workers come in a confusing array of types and titles. Generally speaking, however, they fall into two groups (Table 65.1).

In addition to the health workers just described, many Latin American countries have programs to provide minimal training and supervision of traditional midwives. Unfortunately, Health Departments tend to refer to these programs as 'Control de Parteras Empíricas' ('Control of Empirical Midwives') – a terminology which too often reflects an attitude. Thus to Mosquito Control and Leprosy Control has been added Midwife Control. (Small wonder so many midwives are reticent to participate!) Once again, we found the most promising work with village midwives took place in small non-government programs. In one such program the midwives had formed their own club and organized trips to hospital maternity wards to increase their knowledge.

Key questions

What skills can the village health worker perform? How well does he perform them? What are the limiting factors that determine what he can do? These were some of our key questions when we visited different rural health programs.

We found that the skills which village health workers actually performed varied enormously from program to program. In some, local health workers with minimal formal education were able to perform with remarkable competence a wide variety of skills embracing both curative and preventive medicine as well as agricultural extension, village cooperatives and other aspects of community education and mobilization. In other programs – often those sponsored by Health Departments – village workers were permitted to do discouragingly little. Safeguarding the medical profession's monopoly on curative medicine by using the standard argument that prevention is more important than cure (which it may be to us but clearly is not to a mother when her child is sick), instructors often taught these health workers fewer medical skills than many villagers had already mastered for themselves. This sometimes so reduced the people's respect for their health worker that he (or usually she) became less effect-ive, even in preventive measures.

In the majority of cases, we found that external factors, far more than intrinsic factors, proved to be the determinants of what the primary health worker could do. We concluded that *the great variation in range and type of skills performed by village health workers in different programs has less to do with the personal potentials, local conditions or available funding than it has to do with the preconceived attitudes and biases of health program planners, consultants and instructors.* In spite of the often repeated eulogies about 'primary decision making by the communities themselves', seldom do the villagers have much, if any, say in what their health worker is taught and told to do.

The political context

The limitations and potentials of the village health worker – what he is permitted to do and, conversely, what he could do if permitted – can best be understood if we look at his role in its social and political context. In Latin America, as in many other parts of the world, poor nutrition, poor hygiene, low literacy and high fertility help account for the high morbidity and mortality of the impoverished masses. But as we all know, the underlying cause – or more exactly, the primary disease – is inequity: inequity of wealth, of land, of educational opportunity, of political representation and of basic human rights. Such inequities undermine the capacity of the peasantry for self care. As a result, the political/economic powers-that-be assume an increasingly paternalistic stand, under which the rural poor become the politically voiceless recipients of both aid and exploitation. As anyone who has broken bread with villagers or slum dwellers knows only too well: *the health of the people is far more influenced by politics and power groups, by distribution of land and wealth, than it is by treatment or prevention of disease.*

Let us consider the implications in the training and function of a primary health worker. If the village health worker is taught a respectable range of skills, if he is encouraged to think, to take initiative and to keep learning on his own, if his judgement is respected, if his limits are determined by what he knows and can do, if his supervision is supportive and educational, chances are he will work with energy and dedication, will make a major contribution to his community and will win his people's confidence and love. His example will serve as a role model to his neighbors, that they too can learn new skills and assume new responsibilities, that self-improvement is possible. Thus the village health worker becomes an internal agent-of-change, not only for health care, but for the awakening of his people to their human potential . . . and ultimately to their human rights.

However, in countries where social and land reforms are sorely needed, where oppression of the poor and gross disparity of wealth is taken for granted, and where the medical and political establishments jealously covet their power, it is possible that the health worker I have just described knows and does and thinks too much. Such men are dangerous! They are the germ of social change.

So we find, in certain programs, a different breed of village health worker is being molded . . . one who is taught a pathetically limited range of skills, who is trained not to think, but to follow a list of very specific instructions or 'norms', who has a neat uniform, a handsome diploma and who works in a standardized cement block health post, whose supervision is restrictive and whose limitations are rigidly predefined. Such a health worker has a limited impact on the health and even less on the growth of the community. He – or more usually she – spends much of her time filling out forms.

Prevention

We say prevention is more important than cure. But how far are we willing to go? Consider diarrhea: each year millions of peasant children die of diarrhea. We tend to agree that most of these deaths could be prevented. Yet diarrhea remains the number one killer of infants in Latin America and much of the developing world. Does this mean our so-called 'preventive' measures are merely palliative? At what point in the chain of causes which makes death from diarrhea a global problem are we coming to grips with the real underlying cause? Do we do it . . .

   . . . by preventing some deaths through treatment of diarrhea?
   . . . by trying to interrupt the infectious cycle through construction of latrines and
      water systems?
   . . . by reducing high risk from diarrhea through better nutrition?
   . . . or by curbing land tenure inequities through land reform?

Land reform comes closest to the real problem. But the peasantry is oppressed by far more inequities than those of land tenure. Both causing and perpetuating these crushing inequities looms the existing power structure: local, national, foreign and multinational. It includes political, commercial and religious power groups as well as the legal profession and the medical establishment. In short it includes . . . ourselves. As the ultimate link in the causal chain which leads from the hungry child with diarrhea to the legalized inequities of those in power, we come face to face with the tragic flaw in our otherwise human nature, namely *greed*.

Where, then, should prevention begin? Beyond doubt, anything we can do to minimize the inequities perpetuated by the existing power structure will do far more to reduce high infant mortality than all our conventional preventive measures put together. We should, perhaps, carry on with our latrine-building rituals, nutrition centers and agricultural extension projects. But let's stop calling it prevention. We are still only treating symptoms. And unless we are very careful, we may even be making the underlying problem worse . . . through increasing dependency on outside aid, technology and control.

But this need not be the case. *If* the building of latrines brings people together and helps them look ahead, *if* a nutrition center is built and run by the community and fosters self-reliance, and *if* agricultural extension, rather than imposing outside technology encourages internal growth of the people toward more effective understanding and use of their land, their potentials and their rights . . . then, and only then, do latrines, nutrition centers and so-called extension work begin to deal with the real causes of preventable sickness and death.

The village health worker

This is where the village health worker comes in. It doesn't matter much if he spends more time treating diarrhea than building latrines. Both are merely palliative in view of the larger problem. What matters is that he gets his people working together.

Yes, the most important role of the village health worker is preventive. But preventive in the fullest sense, in the sense that he helps put an end to oppressive inequities, in the sense that he helps his people, as individuals and as a community, liberate themselves not only from outside exploitation and oppression, but from their own short-sightedness, futility and greed.

The chief role of the village health worker, at his best, is that of liberator. This does not mean he is a revolutionary (although he may be pushed into that position). His interest is the welfare of his people. And, as Latin America's blood-streaked history bears witness, revolution without evolution too often means trading one oppressive power group for another. Clearly, any viable answer to the abuses of man by man can only come through evolution, in all of us, toward human relations which are no longer founded on short-sighted self-interest, but rather on tolerance, sharing and compassion.

Misconceptions

I shall try to clear up some common misconceptions. Many persons still tend to think of the primary health worker as a temporary second-best substitute for the doctor . . . that, if it were financially feasible, the peasantry would be better off with more doctors and fewer primary health workers. I disagree. After twelve years working and learning from village health workers – and dealing with doctors – I have come to realize that the role of the village health workers is not only very distinct from that of the doctor, but, in terms of health and well-being of a given community, is far more important.

You may notice I have shied away from calling the primary health worker an 'auxiliary'. Rather I think of him as the primary member of the health team. Not only is he willing to work on the front line of health care, where the needs are greatest, but his job is more difficult than that of the average doctor. And his skills are more varied. Whereas the doctor can limit himself to diagnosis and treatment of individual 'cases', the health worker's concern is not only for individuals – as people – but with the whole community. He must not only answer to his people's needs but he must also help them look ahead, and work together to overcome oppression and to stop sickness before it starts. His responsibility is to share rather than hoard his knowledge, not only because informed self-care is more health conducing than ignorance and dependence, but because the principle of sharing is basic to the well-being of man.

Perhaps the most important difference between the village health worker and the doctor is that the health worker's background and training, as well as his membership in and selection by the community, help reinforce his will to serve rather than bleed his people. This is not to say that the village health worker cannot become money-hungry and corrupt. After all, he is as human as the rest of us. It is simply to say that for the village health worker the privilege to grow fat off the illness and misfortune of his fellow man has still not become socially acceptable.

The day must come when we look at the primary health worker as the key member of the health team, and at the doctor as the auxiliary. The doctor, as a specialist in advanced curative technology, would be on call as needed by the primary health worker for referrals and advice. He would attend those 2–3 per cent of illnesses which lie beyond the capacity of an informed people and their health worker, and he even

THE TYPICAL PYRAMID   THE PYRAMID AS IT SHOULD BE

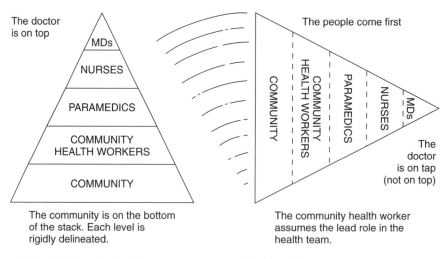

Figure 65.1   Tipping the health manpower pyramid on its side

might, under supportive supervision, help out in the training of the primary health worker in that narrow area of health care called 'Medicine'.

Health care will only become equitable when the skills pyramid has been tipped on its side, so that the primary health worker takes the lead, and so that the doctor is on *tap* and not on *top* (Figure 65.1).

David Werner is an American biologist and at the time of writing was Director of the Hesperian Foundation in California. He spent many years living and working in Mexico. This article previously appeared in *Health Auxiliaries and the Health Team*, edited by Muriel Skeet and Katherine Elliott and published by Croom Helm (1978).

PART 7

Prospects and speculations

| INTRODUCTION

The final part of this Reader illustrates the extraordinary diversity of published material speculating about the global prospects for health, disease and health care, and points to trends that may profoundly change the nature of these processes in the twenty-first century. The editors have chosen 11 articles to represent some of the most pressing global concerns at the start of the new millennium. The styles of writing are more varied here than in earlier parts of this book, as you might expect from an authorship that includes three sociologists with very different perspectives, two geneticists, a geratologist, a physicist turned political scientist, an expert in global food policies, a journalist, a novelist and an assistant secretary general of the United Nations.

The theme of globalization is strongly represented in the first three articles. Part 7 begins with Tim Lang's analysis of the 're-engineering' of the western state from its former role as a provider of welfare and health services to a 'facilitator and safety net of last resort'. In 'The new globalization, food and health', he expresses concern about the growing influence of corporate interests in the supply, pricing and safety of food, and concludes that governments everywhere are compromising their nation's health in favour of international trade and the power of free-market conglomerates. He draws a parallel with pricing policies that deny the new generation of anti-AIDS drugs to the countries that need them most. Lang also points to the meteoric rise in transport of goods around the world, and in international travel, as factors in the increase in food-borne diseases, and he cites the BSE crisis as a disaster made worse by government inaction.

In the second article, 'Global AIDS epidemic: time to turn the tide', Peter Piot, executive director of UNAIDS (the Joint United Nations Programme on HIV/AIDS) attributes the speed of globalization of the AIDS epidemic to the same trends identified by Lang and, like him, accuses the world's governments of reacting too slowly to this unique threat to global health. He argues that the catastrophic loss to AIDS of the educated and skilled adults of developing countries (e.g. Zambia lost the equivalent of two-thirds of its newly-trained teachers in one year) poses a worldwide threat to security and – in the interconnected global economy – renders all nations vulnerable. However, he detects a growing willingness by heads of state to initiate national prevention and treatment programmes that coordinate inputs from health, social and education services and encourage strong community participation.

Participation in a global information exchange is the focus of Michael Hardey's article 'Doctor in the house: the Internet as a source of lay health knowledge and the challenge to expertise'. Hardey identifies AIDS self-help groups as blazing a trail in using the Internet to access expert clinical knowledge and – when it failed to deliver effective treatments – to share experiences and promote alternative therapies. He cites research from around the world which shows that individuals and groups are increasingly challenging the medical profession by accessing research data on the efficacy of pre-scribed treatments, expecting an informed dialogue about their condition, or sidestepping the health service altogether and self-treating, often with products bought via the Internet.

Far from being a tool of the young, Internet use is growing rapidly among the retired populations of high-income countries, with the UK leading the way. When John Grimley Evans calls for a rational reconsideration of 'Ageing and medicine', he focuses primarily on the scientific prospects for delaying ageing and postponing disability, and calls for swifter and more vigorous medical reaction to the onset of health problems in older people. Viewing the ageing population from within the medical model, this leading geratologist advocates a strategy of 'incentives and opportunities' rather than exhortation and pamphlets to persuade people to adopt healthier lifestyles. Extrapolating from Michael Hardey's analysis, affordable Internet access might promote greater autonomy and self-care than the medical profession envisages.

In his newspaper article 'Brave New World II', sociologist Tom Shakespeare asserts that research to combat natural human ageing 'seems like hubris'. He is deeply suspicious of attempts to 'engineer a better human species', which in his view will encourage affluent societies to discard disabled people like himself as mechanical faults. He con-trasts the general support for gene therapy – genetic modification of people – with the furore over GM (genetically modified) food plants and animals, and counsels against 'playing God' in either sphere. In part, his arguments echo points raised earlier by Lang, about addressing inequalities in the global food system rather than attempting to engineer new sources of food that 90 per cent of the world's people cannot afford.

The journalist, Sally Vincent, also fears the direction in which debates about the ageing of populations are going. Her visit to a long-stay geriatric ward confirms the case made by Grimley Evans that health services for society's oldest people are inadequate at best and discriminatory at worst. In 'Exits', Vincent muses on the ambivalence western societies feel towards elderly people whose physical or mental deterioration has left them totally dependent on others. On the one hand, medical technology and the pharmaceutical industry can prolong lives that seem devoid of autonomy or pleasure; on the other, we fear that old people – like the 'imperfect' foetus – may be viewed as having lives not worth living and be identified for dispatch. This debate was given new impetus in 2001, when the Netherlands became the first country in the world to legalize euthanasia.

The consequences of advances in genetics are given different interpretations in the next two articles. In the first, 'The shadow of genetic injustice', Benno Müller-Hill recognizes the threat of discrimination against people deemed to be genetically disadvantaged, who find their way barred when they apply for jobs, a mortgage or insurance. He foresees a future in which everyone carries a 'smart card' imprinted with details of their individual genotype, enabling each person to know their own susceptibilities to avoidable risk factors in the environment and make informed choices about exposure. But unless prohibited by watertight legislation, such knowledge will also enable employers to calculate your chances of staying productive before offering you a job.

Steve Jones, another geneticist, does not expect to see the widespread genetic screening of populations that Müller-Hill predicts, for the pragmatic reason that it would be exceedingly costly. His confidence may be misplaced if Grimley Evans is right and high technology interventions that favour the few continue to be provided, at the expense of cheaper strategies that increase quality of life for the many. Jones directs his attention primarily towards the slowing down of selection pressures that shape human evolution, as falling birth rates coupled with falling childhood mortality enable an increasing proportion of babies to survive and pass on their genes. In theory, this ought to result in a rise in the population prevalence of genetic disorders, but the trend towards globalization of travel that Lang and Piot identified as increasing the spread of infection will counteract this outcome. Jones concludes in 'The evolution of Utopia' that, as intermarriage increases between previously isolated social groups, genetic deficiencies in one partner will be masked by genetic strengths in the other.

The ability to distort evolution by selecting donor eggs and sperm carrying desirable genetic traits is the subject of the short story 'Spawn of Satan?' by novelist Nicola Griffith. The technology for *in vitro* fertilization and 'quality testing' of embryos before implantation already exists and alpha females are advertising their eggs and their exam grades on the Internet, suggesting that Michael Hardey's account of the Internet liberating lay people from dependence on medical experts may have other consequences. In the future imagined by Griffith, widespread egg donation has produced a cadre of super smart, unnaturally well-behaved kids who 'read all the way to school'.

The futures described in the articles up to this point in Part 7 have been rooted in today's realities, but J. Desmond Bernal's vision sees 'The flesh' as an increasingly troublesome encumbrance, from which science will ultimately free the 'cerebral mechanism' to commune with others like itself. Unlike Tom Shakespeare and Benno Müller-Hill, Bernal does not fear the potential outcomes of unrestrained biological wizardry, but looks forward to a time when the individual ceases to exist as an independent entity and is subsumed into a compound mind, where concepts of health, disease, life and death are transcended.

To bring us back down to earth, we end this Reader with a heartfelt complaint by sociologist Shulamit Reinharz about the 'pervasiveness of warnings in everyday life'. She rails against the intrusion of reminders that just about everything is bad for your health – sunshine, butter, salt, eggs, riding in a car, other people's cigarette smoke. She notes that it is impossible to shop and avoid products sponsored by disease charities, enter a public toilet without seeing rape crisis phone lines, or put on your pyjamas without reading a warning to stay away from fire. Among the roots of these proliferating warnings, Reinharz identifies themes that resonate with other articles in Part 7: the medicalization of everyday life, the emergence of political advocacy around illnesses and social problems, and the respect for science. She asks, 'What if it turns out that warnings are stressful and bad for one's mental health?' and concludes 'Enough already!'

66 | The new globalisation, food and health

TIM LANG

Increasingly over the past two decades, governments around the world have been telling their citizens that the old era of looking to the state to resolve public policy problems is over. This experiment in reducing social aspirations has been closely associated with the globalisation process. At its crudest, the argument is that unless citizens work harder and longer, other workforces in unspecified but distant lands will be more competitive than they. Pressure to hold or reduce public spending such as on health and welfare and to increase efficiency quickly follows.

More sophisticated analyses, associated with, but not the prerogative of, the cultural theorists of post-modernity, argue that because barriers between nations are changing, a fundamental restructuring of the state is underway. Far from the state being reduced, as the ideologues of the New Right sought from the 1970s;[1] it is in fact being re-oriented – 're-engineered' to use the vernacular – from being a provider of welfare and health services to become a facilitator and safety net of last resort.[2,3]

Public health specialists should keep close attention on these issues. There are good grounds for concern, and not just about budgets. A restructuring is underway. Food and health policy is a particularly pertinent area to watch. Dietary patterns are already experiencing rapid change. Its most obvious expression is the 'burgerisation' of food culture,[4,5] but behind that is a comprehensive restructuring of world agricultural markets introduced by the 1994 General Agreement on Tariffs and Trade (GATT). In the process, food security, a health goal beloved since the 1974 World Food Summit, is redefined as reliance on farm and world commodity markets rather than maximising local supplies. Another feature is the readiness for public health bodies to be encouraged to work with corporate interests rather than tame them, which was the hallmark of 'old' public health initiatives from John Snow and the Southwark water pump onwards. Thus, health educators now liaise with supermarkets and food companies.

It is true that marketing and branding, associated with media consciousness, now have a remarkable place in people's consciousness and in reinforcing their taste for value added foods, particularly with young people and populations thirsting after a western lifestyle. They have the capacity to change food culture in remarkably short periods. But who is in control of this relationship? Ironically, it is being encouraged just when epidemiological and public health awareness about the growth of degenerative diseases in developing worlds, and their partial dietary aetiology, is consolidating. Major causes of premature death – coronary heart disease and some cancers – are spreading in the developing world as the western diet takes hold, along with other lifestyle changes.[6] This has immense implications both for state budgets and for inequalities in health.

Food policy is a salutary reminder of the complexity that can be lost in an over-glib use of the term globalisation. Food has been traded for millennia. Think only of spices, fruits, wheat, rice, potatoes. These are all grown and consumed thousands of miles from the centres whence they originated. Globalisation is nothing new in food. What is new about the modern period, however, is the pace and scale of change.

The new era of globalisation has been characterised by an astonishingly rapid shift in national boundaries and the meaning of the nation state. The European Union, for instance, introduced the world's largest non-tariff trade area in just five years after the passing of the Single European Act in 1987. Food compositional standards were swept away and in return weak labelling information was supposed to give the consumer power to decide which product to buy: the sausage with 40% meat or one with less.

In the name of removing barriers to trade and ensuing efficiency, national food inspection systems were harmonised and border inspections reduced. Goods were to be judged safe at point of production and sale. A concept of 'due diligence' was introduced under which companies are obliged to be able to show that they have done their best to achieve the highest practicable standards. While these improvements undoubtedly benefit international food traders and companies' expansion, since the BSE debacle of 1996, a sneaking feeling has emerged that public health protection has perhaps been treated too lightly. How can a government really instil a health education message when its budgets are tight (to keep a rein on welfare and to enhance international competitiveness) and when a multinational corporation can spend vast sums on TV advertising to encourage brand recognition?[7]

The question public health proponents need to ask now is: if they were ministers in a cabinet, which brief would take primacy: health or international trade? Until a crisis – as happened with BSE and its apparent transfer to humans – the answer is obvious. Trade and finance carry more clout. But can we afford for public health to be a bolt-on extra? Surely, not. It is time to argue for a better way.

A first task is to accumulate the evidence and to enter the arguments about globalisation with policy makers and, above all, the public. They, after all, are the citizens who vote. In the case of infectious diseases, the case for tough protection is strong. The World Health Organisation (WHO) has long argued the case for concern about diphtheria, cholera and diarrhoeal diseases, tuberculosis, viral hepatitis, AIDS, and more.[8] The baseline is cause for concern enough. Ten per cent of the population of industrialised countries suffer foodborne diseases annually. With tourism on the increase, the 600 million people who travel abroad each year run an estimated 20–50% risk of contracting a foodborne illness.[9] While concern about the health impact of this flow of people is growing, less attention has been accorded to the rapid rise in the distance food travels because of mass food systems. In the UK, for instance, the distance food travels between producer and consumer has risen by 30% in 15 years.[10] A mass food system increases the chance of problems when there is a breakdown in health controls.

A second challenge is public health governance. In most countries, the medical professions have some kudos but even their capacity to influence governments is severely weakened if national governments' role is partly to facilitate removal of public protection powers. One public health person's good regulation is a food magnate's unnecessary burden on business. The 1994 GATT set up the World Trade Organisation (WTO), which has considerable force in relation to national state affairs. The WTO, already distant from world citizenry, now celebrates its proximity to major companies.[11] The processes unleashed by globalisation have increased inequalities. A new world class structure is emerging, where rich and poor within a country may have a lifestyle more in common with that of their equivalents in other countries than with their compatriots. Thirty years ago, the combined incomes of the richest fifth of the world's people were 30 times greater than the poorest fifth. Today their incomes are over 60 times greater. The rise in numbers of billionaires that have benefited from free market deregulation of the global markets is now put at 358. They are collectively worth some $762 billion, which is approximately equivalent to the combined income of the world's poorest two billion – that is, well over a third of world population.

Despite such power, it is possible to achieve modern, tough but fair public health legislation and monitoring. The UK food and health movement has been successful in building pressure to change legislation on food safety, for example. It is possible to win public support for regulation and intervention despite political and commercial opposition.

Globally this task is awesome. The GATT, like many international agreements, was at pains to create a new global system to harmonise food standards. Food standards are now 'influenced' by the Codex Alimentarius Commission, the joint WHO/Food and Agricultural Organisation body. Yet the corporate food giants who already dominate food trade are excessively represented at the decision making table.[12] Who sets standards is now a priority issue for public health. The WTO's disputes procedure, for example, now draws upon Codex when it adjudicates on issues such as whether hormones can be used in beef rearing and, most explosively of all, whether controls over use of genetically modified organisms in foodstuffs are adequate.

The third challenge is to the narrow consumerist notion of choice. Do people really choose their diets? The hypermarket contains 20 000 or more items, but we use only a few. The veneer of choice is well understood in environmental health – climate change for instance. Few people believe they can control their air or on their own repair the ozone layer, yet the modern era has implied that diet is an individual responsibility. The new public health analysis suggests that the factors that determine what we eat, let alone its health impact, are more given and moulded than chosen. We might believe we all choose our diet, but it is remarkable how birth, genes, culture, and class differentiate between us. Did John Snow give the citizens of Southwark a choice to draw polluted water from the pump? Seemingly no politician today will give public health agencies the power to introduce tough pro-active food and health policies unless there is a crisis – as there loomed with AIDS in the 1980s or happened with BSE-CJD in 1996. Has the pendulum been swung too far away from control in favour of choice? Consumerism is not the same thing as citizenship.

References

1. Cockett R. *Thinking the unthinkable: think-tanks and the economic counter-revolution 1931–1983.* HarperCollins, 1994.
2. Hirst P, Thompson G. *Globalisation in question.* Cambridge: Polity Press, 1996.
3. Mulgan G. *Connexity.* London: Chatto and Windus, 1997.
4. Ritzer G. *The McDonaldization of society.* Thousand Oaks, CA: Pine Forge Press, 1993.
5. Vidal J. *McLibel: burger culture on trial.* London: Pan, 1997.
6. Drewnoski A, Poplin K. The nutrition transition: new trends in the global diet. *Nutr Rev* 1997; 55: 31–43.
7. Longfield J. Advertising and labelling – how much influence? In: National Consumer Council, ed. *Your food: whose choice?* London: HMSO, 1992.
8. World Health Organisation. *Communicable diseases won't stop at a border crossing.* World Health Organisation Regional Office for Europe, 1996.
9. Kaeferstein FK, Motarjemi Y, Bettcher DW. Foodborne disease control: a transitional challenge. *Emerging Infectious Diseases* 1997; 3: 503–10.
10. Paxton A. *The food miles report.* London: Sustainable Agriculture, Food and Environment Alliance, 1994.
11. World Trade Organisation. *Major companies to participate in WTO trade facilitation symposium.* Press Release 3 March 1998, 98–0847.
12. Avery N, Drake M, Lang T. *Cracking the Codex, report for 50 consumer NGOs.* London: National Food Alliance, 1993.

This edited extract comes from an editorial originally published in 1998 under the same title: 'The new globalisation, food and health: is public health receiving its due emphasis?' in the *Journal of Epidemiology and Community Health*, 52: 538–9. The author, Tim Lang, is Professor of Food Policy in the Wolfson Institute of Health Sciences, Thames Valley University, London, UK.

67 | Global AIDS epidemic: time to turn the tide

PETER PIOT

HIV/AIDS is catastrophic both from a public health perspective and in terms of its impact on economic and social stability in many of the most severely affected nations, including virtually all of southern Africa. A public health response alone is insufficient to address this devastating epidemic. Political leadership at the highest levels is needed to mobilize a multisectoral response to the impact of HIV/AIDS on educational systems, industry, agriculture, the military, and other sectors. With a few notable exceptions, political response was slow to mobilize in the early years of the epidemic, but response has dramatically improved [since 1999]. The Joint United Nations Programme on HIV/AIDS (UNAIDS) is involved in ongoing efforts to encourage political leaders to make a multisectoral response to the epidemic a major focus of their national plans.

The AIDS epidemic is not only pushing biomedical research to its frontiers but is also taking public health into uncharted territories in the national and global political arenas. It is sometimes argued that AIDS is treated unnecessarily as a special issue rather than as another disease added to the long list of old and new health problems plaguing the developing world. Such a view does not take into account the full extent and nature of the pandemic.

1. In contrast to most health problems, it primarily affects young adults. This age factor results in at least two of the major consequences of HIV/AIDS, including the unusually high impact on the economy through lost productivity and the large number of orphans left behind, creating a generation of desocialized youth- and child-headed households.
2. Unlike most other infectious diseases, HIV also affects the educated and skilled, further accentuating its economic impact. In the worst-affected countries, AIDS is single-handedly wiping out decades of investments in education and human resource development.
3. AIDS brings with it a stigma unprecedented in modern times, which is a major impediment in responding to the epidemic.

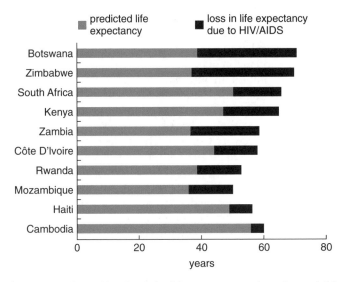

Figure 67.1 The impact of HIV/AIDS on the life expectancy of newborn children in 10 developing countries. Source: *U.S. Bureau of the Census*, 2000.

The year 2000 opened with a debate in the United Nations (UN) Security Council that recognized AIDS as an issue of human security, redefining security to mean not just the presence or absence of armed conflict. Although history offers other examples of destabilizing epidemics, such as Europe's bubonic plague, the speed and scope of HIV transmission worldwide are unprecedented. That AIDS has gone from a disease unknown to the global community to an epidemic infecting 50 million people and killing 19 million to date worldwide offers a clearer lesson on globalization and the interconnectivity of the world than does any media report on the global economy.

Indeed, unchecked, AIDS may become the first example of a massive nonconventional threat to worldwide security, illustrating not only the globalization of problems but the accompanying increase in vulnerability of all countries. Already, in southern Africa, AIDS is devastating the ranks of the most productive members of society with an efficacy history has reserved for great armed conflicts. In the first 10 months of 1998, for example, Zambia lost 1300 teachers – the equivalent of about two-thirds of all new teachers trained annually.[1] Life expectancy at birth in southern Africa, which rose from 44 years in the early 1950s to 59 in the early 1990s is set to recede to just 45 years between 2005 and 2010. (Figure 67.1 shows the predicted diminished life expectancy of children born in 2000 in several AIDS-affected countries.)

Conversely, all-too-frequent armed conflicts and associated population movements are themselves a fertile ground for the spread of HIV and an obstacle to an effective response to the epidemic. The dilemmas raised by AIDS are thus not simply limited to the field of health and science but fall squarely into the political arena: namely, whether world leadership will meet the global threat with a global political response.

Whether we conceptualize AIDS as a health issue only or as a development and human security issue is not just an academic exercise. It defines how we respond to the epidemic, how much money is allocated to combating it, and what sectors of government are involved in the response. Given all we now know about AIDS and its implications for development and security, is the world responding appropriately to AIDS today? With some early notable exceptions, particularly Thailand, Brazil, Uganda, and Senegal, global political leadership is late in responding to the wakeup call. In 1998, long after AIDS had emerged as the leading threat to countries in the Southern Hemisphere, only $300 million in international assistance funds was available for HIV/AIDS activities. Although this figure shows signs of a sharp upward rise, it is estimated that between $1.6 billion and $2.6 billion is needed annually just to mount an effective response in sub-Saharan Africa.

The groundbreaking UN Security Council debate, the high-level political momentum developing in the United States, and the announcement by other industrialized donor countries of increased interest and supply of funds signal the emergence of a new and welcome international response. But the front line of the epidemic is in southern countries themselves, where positive evidence of the impact of all actors coming together under national political leadership is mounting. Indeed, an unprecedented increase [has occurred since 1999] in political commitment from leaders throughout the world in addressing the epidemic. This not only takes the form of statements by heads of state and other leaders, but such actions as the formation of high-level AIDS councils with a mandate well beyond public health issues, and often chaired by the president or his deputy.

This is a complex epidemic. Simple solutions are unlikely to be effective, notwithstanding our collective desire for such simplicity. The response to the epidemic is therefore not just about best practice (in public health, for example) but about new practice. Access to care for people living with HIV is undoubtedly one of the most complex development challenges that the world currently faces, raising ethical, political, economic, and social issues that most of us would prefer not to have to face.

The wide availability of highly effective anti-retroviral therapy in high-income countries has greatly increased the gap between the North and South. It is fueling growing anger against the pharmaceutical industry and international development and financing agencies and is confronting governments in heavily affected countries with tough, if not impossible, choices regarding the allocation of meager public resources. Even considering the effects of poor infrastructure and the absence of sustainable financing for health care, the current price of HIV-related medicines is a major factor in the affordability of care for the majority of those who need it. AIDS once more uncovers a conflict in contemporary society – in this particular case, in how it deals with the protection of intellectual property. Although such protection brings important gains in the discovery of new technologies for affluent societies, it can be an obstacle to making these technologies and drugs widely accessible at affordable prices in poor societies.

However, complexity should never be a barrier to action. Lifesaving prevention efforts are not exclusively the domain of the industrialized world. Several countries in Africa and Asia, even as they face sharp budgetary restrictions, devastation of their economic base, and sharp decreases in skilled labor, have mounted productive responses to HIV, for example, prevention efforts in Uganda, Thailand, and Senegal.

Successful national programs appear to be characterized by at least seven features:

- the impact of all actors coming together under one powerful strategic plan;
- visibility and openness about the epidemic, including involving people with AIDS, as a way of reducing stigma and shame;
- addressing core vulnerabilities through social policies;

- recognizing the synergy between prevention and care;
- targeting efforts to those who are most vulnerable to infection;
- focusing on young people; and, last but not least,
- encouraging and supporting strong community participation in the response.

It is an accepted wisdom that responses to the epidemic must be based on solid scientific evidence. Unfortunately, too often science is neutralized by ideology when it comes to issues that are difficult for some members of society to accept. For example, harm reduction among injecting drug users, including needle exchange programs, has been shown in numerous studies to reduce the risk of HIV infection, and yet in most countries of the world such programs are not supported by the government or are even against the law. Another critical area is sex education for school-aged children. Again, there is sound evidence from numerous studies that sex and life-skills education not only results in safer sexual behaviour but also does not lead to earlier onset of sexual intercourse nor to increased sexual activity. So why do many school authorities deny their children access to life-saving sex education?

The challenge now is to be highly strategic, highly skillful, highly coordinated, and highly disciplined in applying what we know and to catalyze a social movement against AIDS, fully involving those living with HIV. We should offer nothing less than whole-hearted support. Our partners in developing countries should accept nothing less.

Note

1. UNAIDS, *Report on the Global HIV/AIDS Epidemic – June 2000* (UNAIDS, Geneva, Switzerland, 2000). This report is available 27 June 2000 at www.unaids.org (see also B. Schwartlander *et al.*). More statistical information on the AIDS epidemic is available at the UNAIDS Web site at www.unaids.org.

This edited extract comes from an article with the same title originally published in *Science*, 2000, **288**: 2176–8. The author, Dr Peter Piot, is Executive Director of the Joint United Nations Programme on HIV/AIDS (UNAIDS) and assistant secretary general of the United Nations. He was formerly a professor of microbiology at universities in Belgium, Uganda and the USA.

68 | Doctor in the house: the Internet as a source of lay health knowledge and the challenge to expertise

MICHAEL HARDEY

The Internet constitutes a new and unique medium in which expert knowledge is accessible to anyone with a computer linked to a network or modem. Medical dominance is challenged not only by exposing exotic knowledge to the public gaze but also by the presence of a wide range of information about and approaches to health. At the heart of medical autonomy is exclusive access to 'expert knowledge' (Giddens 1991) and the ability to define areas of expertise and practice. The Internet provides a possible threat to this situation. Anyone with a few technical skills and access to a suitable computer can add to the mass of health information on the Internet (McKenzie 1997). Users need only know of a convenient starting point that is likely to have a link to the desired resource or use any one of a number of search engines as well as various specialist health resources (*e.g.* Medical matrix, CliniWeb, OMNI) that provide annotated hierarchical links. Pallen, writing in the *British Medical Journal*, describes a search for the unusual condition of Recklinghausen's neurofibromatis which

> . . . was completed in two minutes and provided links to seven web pages at four sites. One particularly informative site at the Massachusetts General Hospital provided a description of the condition, complete with magnetic resonance scans, information about clinical services, research, conferences, and self-help groups (1995: 1552).

The challenge presented by self-help groups to medical dominance can be traced back to the late 1960s. Since then they have grown to such an extent that few chronic illnesses are not represented by a national if not international group. A search for information about cancer, for example, will provide links to sites that range from centres of clinical excellence to individuals advocating unconventional approaches to treatment. Commonly used search engines do not discriminate between material provided by those with clinical expertise and those for instance advocating astral healing. The search may also find OncoLink[1] which provides up to date clinical trial and treatment information, as well as acting as an educational resource for cancer patients and their families. This has hyperlinks to the British based Cancer Web which provides a range of material for patients and practitioners as well as links to support groups.[2] Pressure groups of all kinds have quickly colonised the Internet and warn users of threats that range from global ecological dangers to the consumption of genetically modified food.

This paper draws on a qualitative case study of people who use the Internet as a source of knowledge about health. It is probably the first attempt to examine in depth how people with no persistent chronic illness use the Internet as a source of information about health.

Reading the Internet

Using the Internet is an inherently interactive process that involves users in a continual process of decision making. Participants in the case study were familiar with the use of Web browsers and routinely used search engines to identify information. The process of finding information is anchored in experiences of print media:

> Even the kids know how to search for stuff they're interested in. The only frustration is the time it takes sometimes. Though if you think about how long and difficult it can be to find something in a book or a library the Internet is far more efficient. Of course you also know that whatever it is you are looking for it is bound to be there somewhere.

This perception of the inclusiveness of information on the Internet means that unfruitful or overlong searches for information are regarded as due to the users' failure to define appropriate key words or use search-relevant resources. A little ingenuity may be required:

> It can take a bit of lateral thinking to come up with the right terminology. It is also important to use the right search engine. I've found the Home Doctor page really simple and helpful.

The Home Doctor web site allows users to enter or browse through symptoms that are linked to products available from pharmacists in Britain.[3] A research project in the United States designed a Web site that provided information on the recognition and treatment of cardiac arrhythmias (Widman and Tong 1997). The site included an interactive demonstration and explanation of complex cardiac rhythms and allowed users to send questions to the site's authors. Over a month in 1995 the site received 10,732 visits for information from some 50 countries. The authors also received and responded to enquiries from users that were almost always appropriate to the clinical nature of the site. This demonstrates that users can not only identify material relevant to them but also use it as a resource to make further appropriate enquiries. The researchers also note that they usually responded to such enquiries within 24 hours, which points to a further advantage of Internet-based consultation for users.

As texts pass seamlessly across different readership groups they are subject to different interpretive strategies. For example, a research scientist may write a paper for a medical audience that is published in the electronic version of a medical journal and is available to anyone with access to the Internet. Furthermore, users may arrive at the paper from a hyperlink within a different source and depart from it in a similar manner. A participant explained the process:

It's not like reading a magazine. You can slip into a skimming mentality which is what the kids tend to do. . . . Unlike a book, you choose what you see and put things together as you go along. One quickly learns to reject the rubbish as you go along. When I'm looking for something specific I usually feel fairly confident when I have got what I wanted.

The struggle over expertise

The equity of presentation offered by the Internet dissolves the boundaries around areas of expertise upon which the professions derived much of their power. Furthermore the illusion of authority given to computer-mediated material may benefit non-orthodox medicine which lacks the symbols of power and authority routinely available to orthodox medicine. This diversity and the resulting uncertain nature of Internet health information has provided grounds for dismissing the Internet as a 'serious tool' for professionals (Information Market Observatory 1995), and for others to represent it as dangerously confusing to clients. At the heart of the debate about the unity and impact of the Internet lies the question of the quality of the material that is available on it. The issue of quality can be used to illustrate how lay users define and cope with the problem and the way it is used by the medical profession to attempt to retain and redefine boundaries around medical expertise.

There are two main dimensions to this problem of quality. The first relates to Web material that is authored by health professionals and the second concerns the boundary between medical and other approaches to health. A recent study of Internet advice for the home care of feverish children made a comparison between medical guidelines and the Internet advice (Impicciatore *et al.* 1997). It was found that only four out of 41 sites studied matched medical guidelines in the management of childhood fever. However, as the researchers note, 'fever in children is rarely harmful, and treatment may not always be necessary'. Part of the problem here is the global nature of the Internet that is highly subversive of national boundaries and guidelines to clinical treatment. It should be remembered that users from countries other than the originating site may experience problems related to the different labels used for proprietary drugs as well as national differences in the recognition of treatments. This raises the question of how and whether lay users are able to manage contradictory or misleading information. One user said:

> I think there is room for people to be misled. Some of the things you find simply contradict each other. Actually it only needs a little common-sense to make your mind up about what is useful . . . At the end of the day you have to rely on your own judgement.

Another respondent was similarly confident in her ability to discern reliable material:

> If you are a bit doubtful about something it is a simple matter to ask a slightly different question to get more information. I mean, one thing about the Net is that you only have to think about what you are looking for . . . so one piece of information makes you think a little differently so you get a different slant on what you want . . . I would say that it (contradictory or misleading information) was not a problem any more than it is on TV or a magazine.

These quotations suggest that users were aware of the quality problem and that they felt they could resolve the difficulty. Furthermore, direct comparisons can be made with the medical consultation:

> My GP is very busy and does not have time to answer questions fully. Actually it is much easier to think about what you want to ask when you look things up on the Net. I don't get that nagging feeling that I'm needlessly taking up his time.

Several participants mentioned how beginning a search to look for information about prescription drugs or symptoms had led them to information about non-orthodox approaches to health:

> I was given these anti-biotics but they gave me thrush and I couldn't sleep. My GP wasn't terribly helpful but when we looked up anti-biotics we found a lot about what they could do to you . . . you know, side effects that they don't bother explaining to you. Anyway we also found a lot about natural treatments that did not involve drugs as such . . . Allergies are probably a lot to do with my problem so I'm trying this diet we found out about and I'm seeing a homeopath.

As the quotation above suggests, the Internet may act as a conduit to non-orthodox therapy. It can also be instrumental in challenging a course of treatment:

> I was diagnosed as having high blood pressure and they gave me these pills. OK I was told I might get some side effects but I felt pretty bad sometimes after taking them. Anyway I found this place in the States [USA] that had a whole lot of information about this drug. Turns out that my symptoms happen to some people and there was this other pill that works better. When I got to see my GP she was surprised about what I knew about the prescription and put me on this other drug which works fine. I actually showed her some print outs from the Web that clearly show these tests that had been run on the drug and the symptoms that people in my circumstances had as a result. She was a bit taken aback, but took me seriously and spent longer than I have ever had going through the details with me.

A number of participants reported that they had renegotiated treatment for themselves or their children with their GP on the basis of information they had found on the Internet.

Participants in the study accessed the Internet in the familiar space of home with only self-imposed limits on time. This is a very different venue from the consulting room. Embarrassing or difficult questions can be asked and answers may only be shared with the computer. Furthermore, physical location is largely irrelevant to users of the Internet. This provides scope for minority communities to seek information about Ayurvedic, Unani and other approaches to health which may not be easily available where they are resident or not be encouraged by GPs. Those who live in rural areas or in parts of the globe with less developed services for particular conditions can participate in support groups and read information about their health problem.

Conclusion

The potential of the Internet as a source of health information has yet to be widely recognised. The Internet as a global market that offers new opportunities for consumerism continues to attract much media attention and considerable investment in electronic commerce. Access to the global health market enables users to undergo, for example, cosmetic surgery in Eastern Europe or visit India for hip replacements. Advice and advertising about diets, exercise plans, muscle building drugs and so forth continue to proliferate on the Internet. The capacity of the Internet to reassure people anxious about the 'external' and 'internal' health of their bodies is central to this process and the Internet provides a unique resource for users to cultivate their bodies. Such tendencies challenge the efforts of national governments' attempts to erect barriers to the importation of drugs that are not licensed locally or, as in the recent case of Viagra, have an uncertain status in local health care systems.

At one level the information available transcends established scientific, political and professional boundaries and at another interactive resources create the space for the construction of new narratives about health and lifestyle. Within newsgroups, chat rooms and other interactive resources people 'open up' to others in an environment where anonymity promotes trust in strangers. Such electronic communities offer new opportunities for people with chronic or debilitating conditions to participate on an equal basis in community life. Global self-help groups provide a space for strangers who are bound within an environment that minimises the 'gamble' (Giddens 1991) involved in sharing intimate feelings. The anonymity of such places provides fertile ground for giving meaning to life crises. This reflects the roots of electronic health information which can be traced back to the email-based on-line support groups that emerged in the 1980s and were often originated by people with HIV/AIDS. Such resources have developed into sophisticated collaborations between health professionals and user groups.

In line with the original idea behind the design of the browser it is *the users* of information rather than authors or professional experts who decide what is delivered to them. This represents a break with the print-based tradition of health information that is devised by health professionals and often delivered by them so that they can control the content and flow of information (Buckland and Gann 1997). The basic design of the Internet therefore represents a challenge to previously hierarchical models of information giving. This shift in control may be seen as contributing to the decline in awe and trust in doctors. The provisional nature of medical knowledge and the division between experts is evident in the debate about the quality of Internet health information. Lay challenges to medical expertise produced a renegotiation of treatment and in some instances the use of non-orthodox therapies. The blurring of boundaries between orthodox and non-orthodox beliefs encourages a definition of health that embraces spiritual and emotional dimensions often marginal in conventional medicine.

References to Internet sites

1. www.oncolink/upenn/edu
2. www.graylab.ad.uk/cancerweb.html
3. www.medetail.co.uk/home-doc

References

Buckland, S. and Gann, B. (1997) *Disseminating Treatment Outcomes Information to Consumers: Evaluation of Five Pilot Projects*. London: King's Fund Publishing.

Giddens, A. (1991) *Modernity and Self-Identity*. Cambridge: Polity Press.

Impicciatore, P., Pandolfini, C., Casella, N. and Bonati, M. (1997) Reliability of health information for the public on the world wide web: systematic survey of advice on managing fever in children at home, *British Medical Journal*, **314**, 1875–9.

Information Market Observatory (IMO) (1995) The quality of information products and services. Luxembourg, September, *IMO Working Paper 95/4*. http://www2.echo.lu/impact/imo/9504.html.

McKenzie, B.C. (1997) Quality standards for health information on the Internet, *Society for the Internet in Medicine*: Quarterly, Issue 3.

Pallen, M. (1995) The world wide web, *British Medical Journal*, **311**, 1552–6.

Widman, L.E. and Tong, D.A. (1997) Requests for medical advice from patients and families to health care providers who publish on the World Wide Web, *Archives of Internal Medicine*, **157**, 209–12.

This edited extract comes from a much longer article, originally published under the same title in the *Sociology of Health and Illness*, 1999, **21**(6): 820–35. The author, Michael Hardey, is a lecturer in Sociology in the School of Nursing and Midwifery, University of Southampton, UK. A brief version of his subsequent research on the use of the Internet by lay people and its effect on lay/professional relationships can be found at http://www.welcome.ac.uk/en/1/homlibinfacthiiarc16.html (accessed April 2001).

69 | Ageing and medicine

JOHN GRIMLEY EVANS

Throughout the developed and developing world, populations are ageing. In anticipating the increasing numbers of older people in the first half of the 21st century, the health services of the Western world need to be informed by an understanding of the nature of human ageing and the principles of rational health care for older people.

The nature of human ageing

Immortality is unattainable. Even if we had the biological capacity to live for ever we would all still die eventually from disease, accident, predation, famine or warfare. But our risk of death would be constant with age or might even fall, as, by natural selection, those who are cleverest at avoiding hazards survive longest. The characteristic manifestation of ageing, in the sense of senescence, is a rise in risk of death with age. This is because the essence of ageing is a progressive loss of adaptability of an individual organism as time passes. As we become older, our homeostatic mechanisms become, on average, less sensitive, less accurate, weaker and less well sustained. Sooner or later, we meet a challenge from the external or internal environment to which we can no longer mount an adequate adaptive response and we die.

In the human species, death rates fall from birth to a low point around the age of 12–13, after which they turn upwards. After perturbations due mainly to violent and accidental deaths, mortality rates rise as a continuous and broadly exponential function of age. It is of interest that in the UK the point of lowest mortality has remained remarkably constant over the last 100 years[1], suggesting that it has underlying biological determinants. This would not be surprising, since evolutionary pressure will tend to maximize the fitness of members of a species at the onset of reproductive capacity. The prevalence of disability also increases exponentially from early adult life into old age. Ageing has to be seen, therefore, as a lifelong process, not as a state which emerges acutely at the age of 65.

A model for ageing

It used to be conventional to try to divide age-associated changes into those due to 'disease' and those due to 'normal ageing'. This is unhelpful, since diseases can be defined in many ways and there is no satisfactory way of defining normal ageing. Too often, categorization of a phenomenon as normal ageing has allowed doctors to abrogate responsibility for doing anything about patients' problems and it has also delayed medical progress. Dismissal of the changes of Alzheimer's disease as a 'normal' age-associated process of senile dementia, and the assumptions underlying 'correcting' blood pressure for its 'normal' regression on age, are historical cases in point.

It is important to recognize age-associated changes which will respond to specific interventions, but it is best to regard these 'diseases' as components in the range of interacting factors contributing to the loss of adaptability of an individual as time passes. At a conceptual level, it is useful to regard this loss as coming about through interactions between intrinsic (genetically determined) factors and extrinsic factors in environment and lifestyle.

Intrinsic ageing. Ageing is partly under the control of genetically determined processes. Lifespan is a species characteristic, and within a species, selective breeding can produce relatively long- and short-lived strains. Twin studies indicate that longevity is partly heritable in the human[2]. Over more than a century, theories have been advanced to account for the existence of genes that limit lifespan. The most likely explanation lies with the disposable soma theory of Kirkwood and Rose[3]. This starts from the reasonable postulate that ageing is due to the accumulation of damage and that rate of ageing will be determined by the effectiveness of systems of damage control through prevention, detection, and repair or replacement. The fact that the damage control systems themselves become damaged[4] provides an intuitively plausible model for ageing being exponential in pattern.

Extrinsic ageing. Extrinsic factors in ageing can be detected by epidemiological, interventive and physiological studies, and have been shown to modulate ageing processes throughout life. Although still controversial, epidemiological studies and some experimental evidence suggest that intra-uterine and early infancy environments can set metabolic patterns that affect susceptibility to disease in middle life.

The nature and magnitude of extrinsic influence on ageing depend on intrinsically determined susceptibility. Genes are thought to determine the effect of dietary salt intake on blood pressure, for example, and affluent lifestyle may particularly enhance the incidence of diabetes and cardiovascular disease in people carrying 'thrifty genes' originally selected for their benefit in surviving periods of famine[5]. Susceptibility to the ill effects of smoking and alcohol also probably has genetic determinants. As knowledge of the human genome progresses, more interactions will surely emerge, raising the eventual possibility of individualized lifestyle prescriptions for optimal ageing with maximal enjoyment.

Rational health care for older people

Medicine has been slow to adapt to the needs of the increasing numbers of older people, in terms of service design and clinical practice and of research.

Table 69.1 Characteristics of disease in later life

Rapid deterioration if untreated
High frequency of multiple disease
Cryptic or non-specific presentation
High incidence of secondary complications
Frequent need for active rehabilitation
Frequent need for help in resettling in the community

Table 69.1 sets out characteristics of disease in later life that health services need to be designed to meet. In essence, these indicate that an old person who falls ill needs rapid access to high-quality diagnostic facilities and appropriate treatment which must include provision for rehabilitation. A central issue is that treatment should be appropriate. Old people may have at least as much as the young to gain from treatments in terms of preventing immediate death; thrombolysis in acute myocardial infarction, for example, saves more lives if given to older than to younger patients[6]. Patients may, however, be more concerned about quality of survival than about death.

Nor is it any business of doctors to ration care for older patients in favour of younger ones. If politicians wish a low value to be put on the lives and well-being of older people, it is for them, as elected representatives of their nations, to say so, no doubt bearing in mind that more than 25% of a typical Western electorate are aged over 65.

There are many people in their 70s and 80s who function within the normal range for people in their 20s and 30s. In making judgements about the appropriateness or choice of treatment, it is important to assess older patients as individuals and not to assume that they are all average members of their age group. Age is merely a number that can have no direct effect on treatment outcome. It only appears in equations predictive of outcome because in population studies it correlates with the physiological true determinants of outcome that are missing from the equations. If we know enough about the physiology of our patients, age will lose its predictive value. This ideal state has only been approached in the field of intensive care medicine, but it is high time other medical and surgical specialities took up the issue.

Individual variation needs special emphasis in an age of so-called evidence-based medicine (EBM). Large randomized controlled trials (RCTs) and systematic overviews are valuable in the appraisal of the efficacy of treatments. Most treatments work by mechanisms that can kill as well as cure. A treatment that emerges as efficacious in a large RCT or systematic overview is one that kills fewer patients than it cures. What the individual patient considering a treatment wants to know is which group he is likely to fall into. Unfortunately, the phase of research on determinants of individual outcomes that should follow on from demonstrations of efficacy is largely unprovided for. This does not make good sense either from the point of view of the individual patient or in terms of the optimal deployment of limited health care resources. Warning of this comes from a subanalysis of the European Carotid Surgery Trial suggesting that its overall positive result was due to good results in a potentially predictable 16% and no benefit for the other 84%.[7]

Possible futures

The aim of modifying the pace and pattern of human ageing is now out of the realm of science fiction and, at least in the USA, firmly on the scientific research agenda for the 21st century. Whenever a means emerges for humankind to take charge of its biological destiny, issues become muddied by ethicists trying to stop it and lawyers trying to make money out of it. In practical terms, whatever the anxieties, if it becomes possible to retard ageing, some people at least will seek to do so. Again in practical terms, what matters is not how long we live but the extent to which our life becomes a burden to us and to others. One possible effect of manipulation of intrinsic ageing processes would be for human ageing to be played at a slower rate so that lifespan is lengthened but the time spent in pre-death disability also lengthens pro rata. But this is no more worrying than the present drift of clinical medicine into postponing death by lengthening periods of survival in illness.

Most of the human race, at least in the civilized world, has grown out of a fear of death. Older people have more dread of disability and the dependency and loss of dignity it often brings. As an aim, prevention of disability leads to an emphasis on identification of extrinsic influences on ageing, which include medical interventions such as control of high blood pressure or hyperlipidaemia. Extrinsic influences are, in principle, more readily manipulable than intrinsic, although if people are to be persuaded to adopt healthier lifestyles, we may need to focus more on incentives and opportunities than on exhortation and government pamphlets. Modification of extrinsic influences to delay the onset of chronic disease carries the promise of reducing the duration as well as the incidence of disability. One consequence of age-associated loss of adaptability is that the older we are when a potentially disabling disease strikes, the sooner we will die from it. Postponement is prevention.

A focus on disability reduction will require appropriate priority to be given to the deployment of effective and timely medical and social interventions. The need for timeliness should particularly be noted by politicians whose obsession with reducing health care costs leads to insufficient hospital resources and long waiting lists for hip replacements or coronary artery surgery.[8] It is also important not to allow politicians to draw the wrong conclusion from the reduction in age-specific prevalence of disability amongst older Americans in the last two decades.[9] We have no reason to assume that what is happening in the USA will necessarily happen spontaneously elsewhere – but it could be made to happen elsewhere.

Even without engineered extensions of lifespan, we ought to think about the long-term implications of what is already happening. Short of some worldwide environmental or economic disaster, the ageing of populations is permanent, and it would be sensible for social organizations to adapt. Most importantly, given the plague proportions that human populations have already reached, in a rational world birth rate would be tuned to lifespan within parameters, including retirement age, chosen to limit the prevalence of poverty. Sadly, the chances of attaining a rational world in the 21st century seem notably less than those of retarding human ageing.

References

1. Grimley Evans J. A correct compassion. The medical response to an ageing society. *J Roy Coll Phys (Lond)* 1997; **31**: 674–84.
2. McGue M, Vaupel JW, Holm N, Harvald B. Longevity is moderately heritable in a sample of Danish twins born 1870–1880. *J Gerontol* 1993; **48**: B237–44.
3. Kirkwood TBL, Rose MR. Evolution of senescence: late survival sacrificed for reproduction. *Phil Trans R Soc Lond* B 1991; **332**: 15–24.
4. Wei Q, Matanoski GM, Farmer ER, Hedayati MA, Grossman L. DNA repair and aging in basal cell carcinoma: a molecular epidemiology study. *Proc Natl Acad Sci USA* 1993; **90**: 1614–18.
5. Neel JV. Diabetes mellitus: a 'thrifty' genotype rendered detrimental by progress? *Am J Hum Genet* 1962; **14**: 353–62.
6. ISIS-2 Collaborative Group. Randomised trial of intravenous streptokinase, oral aspirin, both, or neither among 17,187 cases of suspected myocardial infarction: ISIS–2. *Lancet* 1988; ii: 349–60.
7. Rothwell PM, Warlow CP on behalf of the European Carotid Surgery Trialists' Collaborative Group. Prediction of benefit from carotid endarterectomy in individual patients: a risk-modelling study. *Lancet* 1999; **353**: 2105–10.
8. Grimley Evans J. Health care for older people: a look across a frontier. *J Am Med Assoc* 1996; **275**: 1449–50.
9. Manton KG, Corder L, Stallard E. Chronic disability trends in elderly United States populations: 1982–94. *Proc Natl Acad Sci* USA 1997; **94**: 2593–98.

This edited extract comes from a much longer article, originally published under the same title in the *Journal of Internal Medicine*, 2000, 247: 159–67. Professor Sir John Grimley Evans is Professor of Clinical Geratology in the Nuffield Department of Clinical Medicine, University of Oxford, UK. His research includes epidemiological studies into risk factors for stroke and dementia and clinical trials of treatments for dementia.

70 | Brave New World II

TOM SHAKESPEARE

During 1999, anti-GM demos replaced road protests as the direct action of choice. Headlines about Frankenstein foods, and crop-stomping peers of the realm and soap opera characters, have reflected a popular backlash against the application of genetic technology. The impact of all this opposition causes disabled people like me to ask: why aren't people equally worried about genetically-modified human beings?

Human genetics, as currently practised, seems as publicly acceptable as plant genetics is controversial. Most prospective parents are happy to use pre-natal testing to screen out congenital abnormality. Can you imagine activists trashing experiments in human genetics research institutes? If it were to happen, the media response to such actions would surely be very different to the current half-approving coverage of GM crop damage.

Why is there such a different response to intervening in childbirth than to intervening in the grocery department? Isn't our internal personal environment just as important as the external global environment? Perhaps the first difference is that much of the opposition to GM foods is based on a distrust of big business. Consumers oppose corporate power, feeling that 'they' are manipulating our food, exploiting developing-world farmers and trying to control the world – hence the Seattle protests.

But the public face of human genetics tends to be doctors in white coats dangling healthy babies. Whereas the GM food debate has revolved around the need to empower consumers and provide information so they can choose not to buy new products, the rationale for genetic intervention in reproduction has been parental demand for access to new tests and procedures.

Secondly, most people can't see the point of GM food. Why change products which seem perfectly adequate. Recently Wellcome Trust research showed the public found it much more difficult to understand *why* Dolly was cloned, than to understand *how* Dolly was cloned.

There are few perceived benefits to the modification of plant or animal genes. On the other hand, human genetics has the alibi of improving health. It operates on a mechanistic model of removing 'faulty' bits of the human being – or else preventing the birth of 'faulty' humans – and it has the rationale of 'reducing suffering'. Whereas there seems little public anxiety about genetic screening or even gene therapy, there is widespread disquiet about human cloning. This is where human genetics seems to connect to genetic modification. People find it difficult to connect cloning to the reduction of diseases or suffering. It seems unnecessary, and above all, unnatural.

But there are some important connections between food genetics and human genetics. For example, consumer choice in reproduction is much more limited than the rhetoric implies. Implicit pressure from medics to screen out genetic differences, and a lack of proper information about disability, mean that parental choices are not as free as they seem.

Moreover, human genetics is about big business and corporate profits too. Gene patenting will enable biotechnology companies to exploit the demands for testing. Companies with exclusive control over tests will be able to prevent other laboratories testing for genes associated with breast cancer or other conditions, or else demand payment of licensing fees. In Britain, NHS genetics services are very concerned about the cost implications of these diagnostic monopolies.

Economics also influences the direction which genetic research will take. Biotechs, despite the propaganda about health, are only interested in certain kinds of human diseases. Rare genetic conditions, for which the market in tests or therapies will be limited, are of little concern. The big money is in everyday health problems such as cancer, hypertension, obesity and depression. At the same time, access to new therapies – or new methods of creating designer babies – will come at a cost. Those countries who cannot afford modern pharmaceuticals, or those couples who cannot afford advanced embryo selection techniques, will be the genetic losers. Princeton embryologist Lee Silvers has talked about the development of a genetic underclass, restricted to reproducing traditionally, while the 'GenRich' choose cleverer, healthier, more beautiful offspring.

The long term consequences of releasing GM organisms into the environment are a source of deep concern to opponents. There is a similar need for caution in the extension of new methods of making babies, selecting embryos and experimenting with gene therapies. Again, while thousands of test-tube babies have been born world-wide, the technology is only two decades old. No one knows whether genetically modified human beings might face problems as they begin to age, or when they themselves come to reproduce.

There are three areas in which there might be a value consensus among those concerned about GM food and GM people. First, there is an anxiety about the exploitation of the natural world and the dignity of living beings. There is considerable concern about the application of cloning to use animals as 'living medicine factories', or the breeding of transgenic pigs to provide spare parts for humans. There is particular anxiety about cloning human embryos solely to provide material for experimental treatments.

Second, respect for nature means distinguishing between interventions to improve the quality of life, and interventions which are disruptive of normal processes. Reducing suffering is an important goal, but we should be concerned about doctors 'playing God'. While research to combat cancer seems a good idea, research to combat natural human ageing seems like hubris. We must draw a line between trying to cure disease, and trying to engineer a better human species. If it worked, somatic gene therapy to help individuals might be desirable, but germline gene therapy, affecting subsequent generations could cause real problems in the future.

Finally, science is not the real answer to human problems. After all, applications of science usually reinforce social inequalities rather than remedying them. Both environmental campaigners and disability rights activists suggest that the real causes of suffering are social barriers, not biology. After all, enough food is grown to feed the world, and global inequality is the real cause of famine.

Disabled people argue that our problems are not caused by our bodies, but by the discrimination and prejudice we face in society. Rather than seeking individual solutions – either by eliminating people with impairment, or engineering a better soya bean – we should campaign for structural and global changes.

Links are growing between those who protest against GM foods, and those who are concerned about disability rights and human genetic engineering. Personally, I do not believe that we should reject all that genetics has to offer. But there is an urgent need for informed debate and for democratic accountability. Society should set limits to the genetic modification of the human species, just as much as to that of plants and animals.

This article was originally published in this form in *The Guardian* newspaper in the UK, on 5 January 2000. Professor Tom Shakespeare is Director of the Policy, Ethics and Life Sciences Research Institute (PEALS), Newcastle University.

71 | Exits

SALLY VINCENT

Dying is our most catastrophic expectation. Not death itself, we hasten to add, but dying. People who have witnessed an agonised and protracted death tend not to develop their experience into a conversation piece. Like a generation of first-world-war soldiers, they maintain their trauma in a kind of shamed and unbelieving silence. To have observed a calm and painless passing, however, is often described as a privilege and an honour, as though something undeserved but immeasurably enriching has been bestowed upon us. At such times a sense of grief seems to be both ameliorated and suspended by the stark relief of knowing that the dreadful has happened and, hey, it wasn't that dreadful. The dying was easy. There is nothing to fear. If we could only be sure that we, too, could glide as smoothly from the terminal of our choice, how much better (in a curious way) life would be.

As quantum leaps go, it is only a small step to conclude that if we could have some measure of control over the manner of our dying we would also, by way of a handy bonus, have our lives in control. Dignity is the word that springs to mind. We would have dignity. If our existence was not punctuated at either end by the twin parentheses of pain, bewilderment, helplessness and incontinence, what we leave behind in the memory banks of those we sought to impress would never bear the taint of indignity. In contemplation of the desirability of an easy, self-controlled death, we have moved inexorably into the field of the possibility of voluntary euthanasia as a universal rite of passage.

For two and a half thousand years, the moral rectitude of the medical profession was adequately served by the Hippocratic Oath. The old Greek was unequivocal on the issue of voluntary euthanasia. 'I will give no deadly medicine to anyone if asked, nor suggest any such counsel', was what he wrote and what physicians have been content to avoid thereafter, or at any rate up until 1947. It was then that the World Medical Association was formed and the Hippocratic Oath retranslated into the modern idiom of the Declaration of Geneva, which entirely omits the no-deadly-medicine line along with various archaic references to Apollo, Aesculapius and All-Heal. Subsequent re-editings of the Declaration have moved further from the Hippocratic emphasis on the sanctity of life and towards a more trade union approach where a doctor's consecration of his life to the service of humanity becomes nicely balanced by a code of conduct designed to protect and preserve the sanctity of a doctor's professional security.

The English text of the International Code of Medical Ethics innocuously embraces the ethic of voluntary euthanasia in its 'easy death' connotation when it states, '[when] a physician provides medical care which might have the effect of weakening the physical and mental condition of the patient, he must do so only in the patient's interest'. By 1977, voluntary euthanasia no longer meant 'easy death'. In full recognition of common usage and its erosion of 'easy death' into 'mercy killing', the BMA was moved to affirm that, 'Practitioners who are in conscience opposed to euthanasia must be fully protected in future legislation'. In other words, over the past 47 years, the British medical ethos has abandoned the Hippocratic condemnation of euthanasia and taken up arms to protect conscientious objectors from the obligation of killing people. No matter how they beg and plead.

However they may advise the Government, [the House of Lords Select Committee on Medical Ethics] will be less concerned with the minutiae of moral philosophy attending the issue of voluntary euthanasia than they are with the anomalies of a legal system that comes down like a ton of bricks on doctors who conscientiously do not object. The most likely outcome will be to decriminalise the practice of voluntary euthanasia along the lines of the system operating in the Netherlands.

'If asked', a Dutch physician – or at any rate 78 per cent of Dutch physicians – will give his 'deadly medicine' and, assuming he has sought another's 'counsel', filled in a lot of forms and notified the coroner, he will not have to waste his time justifying his action in a court of law. It is hoped – or feared – that a similar exemption from prosecution will swell the ranks of British doctors currently amenable to the role of mercy killer, from a mere 48 per cent to better resemble the Dutch model. Thereafter, British citizens diagnosing their lives as not worth living, will have little trouble finding a doctor with the know-how and wherewithal to take them literally, and a consultant rheumatologist called Dr Nigel Cox will take his place in medical history as the very last martyr to the cause of voluntary euthanasia.

It is the Cox case upon which our present deliberations are based. There was never any argument about what happened. Mrs Lillian Boyes had been Dr Cox's patient for three years. They knew each other well. By all accounts, Mrs Boyes's rheumatoid arthritis had her on her knees. As her condition worsened, she was reported to have suffered the agonies of the damned, 'howling like a dog' and pleading to be released from her misery. Dr Cox prescribed morphine-based drugs in increasing doses until it became clear that the pain from the disease and from the bone-deep bed sores resulting from years in hospital had become intractable. The lady made it clear to all concerned that she wished to die. It was in direct response to her awareness of her own best interests that, in 1991, Dr Cox injected potassium chloride into the vein of Mrs Lillian Boyes, as a result of which she very quickly died. Dr Cox's choice of potassium chloride – a poison with no therapeutic qualities – over the conventional anaesthetic cocktail which hastens death as a secondary effect, gave unequivocal evidence of his primary intention.

The charge was attempted murder. Had Mrs Boyes's body not been swiftly cremated, the charge would have been murder, but since it was not possible for anyone to ascertain whether or not she would have died without the lethal injection, the lesser crime was nominated.

Several members of the jury shed tears when they brought in a guilty verdict. Dr Cox was given a suspended sentence of one year's imprisonment, reprimanded by the Disciplinary Committee of the General Medical Council for failing to observe established practices and went back to work, accompanied by the sympathy, good wishes and admiration of his peers. Public support of voluntary euthanasia reached an all-time high.

The popularity of the leniency of the Cox decision was predicated largely upon public imagination, bounded by our desire to abolish pain and to have the ultimate say in our own fate. It was clear to everyone that in the spirit, if not the letter of the law, Mrs Boyes was the best judge of her own predicament and her own salvation. We can comprehend that somebody with a terminal illness and unremitting pain would long for oblivion, if they had reason to believe there was no alternative. And since Mrs Boyes had that reason, the responsibility for her death was her own. Dr Cox was merely the merciful operative.

Which of us would not hope to be similarly merciful, given the opportunity to load the needle, hold the cup, crush the pills, do the decent thing? But what if the recipient of our best attentions is less helpful with his prognosis? What if he has no opinion on the matter whatsoever?

Anthony Bland was nineteen and a half years old when, like Mrs Boyes, he inadvertently became a test case for the legalisation of euthanasia. A victim of the Hillsborough Stadium disaster, Anthony was diagnosed as clinically brain dead and lay in a permanent vegetative state for two and a half years, with no prospect of a reversal for his lamentable condition. He could, however, breathe unaided, and presumably would have done so indefinitely if artificially fed and regularly medicated for the various infections that beset the unconscious body. It is inarguable that Anthony's life had no discernible meaning to himself and was the cause of considerable sadness and grief to those who loved him. Mr and Mrs Bland decided that 30 months of living death was probably enough for any one family and in common with thousands of grieving relatives before them, they felt that in the absence of their son's opinion as to what was best for him, they must make the decision for him.

Had we never heard of Anthony Bland, there would have been no further debate about his fate. But we did know about him. And we cared. The media saw to that.

This happened a month ago: the father of a friend – I'll call her Margaret – suffered a massive stroke and was admitted to a London hospital. There he was carefully examined and it was discovered that while he was otherwise in fine fettle for a man of his age, he was now effectively brain dead. Only two things distinguished Margaret's father from Anthony Bland. One, he was 92 years old, and two, the incident of his brain damage was not a matter of public record. Margaret sat at her father's bed-side and held his hand. Then she was called to the consultant physician's office, where it was given to her straight. The doctor explained that her father's case was irreversible. In the tones of one who knows of what he speaks, he gave Margaret the benefit of his best advice. He suggested that if, with her permission, the hospital were to refrain from feeding and medicating her father, he would be physically as well as mentally dead within 19 days.

Margaret went back to her father and took his hand. She knew what was involved. She thought of the bed shortage. She knew that in all probability a younger, worthier candidate for the care and resources that might be lavished upon her father was worsening in the wings. She knew that she wouldn't want to lie there, lingering on. She knew her father was never a chap to relish that kind of prospect either. She pressed his freckly old hand and strained every nerve to imagine a response from him. All that happened was that he sneezed. And then she said no. No, she did not want her father to starve to death, nor did she want him to drown in his own lung fluid. She knew she was being bolshie, but dammit all, what was the rush? Her father was a good citizen. He'd paid his dues.

Margaret felt the disapproval. There was nothing she could put her finger on, of course, just a general air of impatience, mainly exemplified by the consultant's swift and brisk departure from her sight.

The old man died seven days later, just 12 days short of the date predicted by the starving method. Those decisions are taken every day in our hospitals. Passive euthanasia – the withdrawal of life-sustaining systems, up to and including food, when those systems clearly have no therapeutic purpose – is not illegal. It was by virtue of the public nature of Anthony Bland's tragedy that his parents' decision on his behalf was considered insufficient. The decision had to be made by the President of the Family Division of the High Court, affirmed by the Court of Appeal and thereafter upheld by the Appellate Committee of the House of Lords. Anthony starved to death, or to put it more accurately, Anthony was starved to death. The moral stance taken by the learned Lords who doubtless debated long and hard over the Bland case, was no different to the one taken by Dr Cox. In both cases the patient was intended to die. Whether the execution is technically 'active' or 'passive', the end and the motive are identical.

Dame Cicely [Saunders] is synonymous with the hospice movement, with Macmillan nurses and the complete obviation of all further contemplation of euthanasia. Anyone who has ever visited a hospice comes away marvelling at the atmosphere of peace and dignity they found there. Terminal cancer, once the euthanatist's prime target, literally lost its sting. You'd think we'd leave it there.

But the euthanatists have moved their goal-posts. Leave cancer to the hospices, from now on the maximum dread buzz-word is mental incapacity. Senility. Confusion. Alzheimer's disease. Terminal ga-ga-ness. Ending up like a prize marrow in some obsessive gardener's plot. And since these conditions render us incapable of knowing what is good for us, we must foresee their possibility and second-guess ourselves with the compilation of a Living Will. In these documents, properly witnessed and with the soundness of our minds attested to, we may make it abundantly clear that when we cease to be of use to ourselves or to others, we would wish to be bumped off as soon as possible. It is the decent, citizenly thing to do.

Dr Herbert Cohen, a Dutch euthanatist who confines himself to one act of euthanasia per month on the grounds that he finds it emotionally burdensome work, has been at pains to point out that old people who wish to die in order to relinquish their hospital beds to worthier patients should be treated as national heroes, like soldiers who die for their country and mothers who give their last crust to their starving children.

The hidden agenda of the great euthanasia debate is precisely this. It places us at the vanguard of a demographic catastrophe. We are living too long. In the past 50 years, the section of the population with the temerity to survive beyond 65 has increased from 10 to 15 per cent. If something is not done about it, 25 years into the next millennium this unacceptable and unprecedented drain on our resources will have swelled to 19 per cent. A direct link between available resources and what we are prepared to afford for the general good is a vital aspect of the social contract of all primitive cultures. It is not necessarily admirable in its implementation. Today, if we choose not to afford to support the elderly, we must urge them to loose their hold on life. Not because they are ill, but because they no longer contribute to our own survival. The bear eats grannie, we eat the bear. Our modern social contract suggests an equivalent cycle of regeneration. Grannie volunteers for euthanasia, her savings are not frittered away in nursing home fees but go directly to her descendants.

Simple practicalities don't enter the equation. In fact only one in 20 pensioners is entirely dependent on the state benefits to which their contributions entitle them. And, according to an Age Concern survey, people of 65 and over consult doctors less frequently than any other age group.

With touching doctorly elitism, the medical profession takes full responsibility for its part in creating a society progressively impoverished by its elderly. Theirs was the initial miracle, with their spare parts and pacemakers, of life prolongation. Theirs must now be the duty to do something about it! In an article published by the journal of the Royal College of GPs, Dr Mary Bliss, consultant geriatrician and member of the Voluntary Euthanasia Society, has written, 'We cannot expect to enjoy unnatural life unless we are also prepared to accept unnatural death.'

Dr Bliss was more than happy to take me round her geriatric ward. 'It's about time,' she said, 'someone looked at it.' They call it the long-stay ward, because people who come here tend to stay a long time. Three, four, oh anything up to eight years. It's not like a hospice. Nobody stays in a hospice for longer than three weeks. That's one of the differences. People are dying of something to be in a hospice. Here people aren't dying. They've nothing to die from. By virtue of iron constitutions and, in some cases, the officious striving of a medical practitioner in the distant past, they have merely failed to pass away at what they and their relatives might consider a reasonable age. Now they must wait, at great expense, for their frail and decrepit bodies to go the same way as their youth and vigour.

The ward is long and semi-compartmentalised. As you move out of earshot of one television set, you walk into the orbit of another one. Health workers – nurses are too expensive to be wasted on geriatric care – watch Princess Diana announce to the nation her preference for privacy. Dr Bliss tells me that hardly anyone here gets any visitors. The gentleman over there has a daughter, but she doesn't come any more. She said there was no point since he doesn't really recognise her any more. The lady there, the one who seems to be sleeping, has a husband who reckons she should have been dead years ago. Dr Bliss thinks he was right.

Elizabeth, same age as the Queen Mother, sits in solitary silence upon her commode; her eyes bright with humour, she waves to us with the close-fingered economy for which her namesake is famed. Elizabeth tumbles from this position in the course of her stay. They've lost count of the arms and legs she's broken. Elizabeth is saying something. She whispers and we cannot hear. Dr Bliss catches one word. 'She says she's lonely,' says Dr Bliss. Elizabeth's case-notes are two inches thick. Nobody minds me looking through them. From time to time someone has written in tipsy capitals across the page NTBR. Not To Be Resuscitated. They've tried to persuade her to go into a nursing home, but she won't have it. Her only complaint seems to be something to do with a hearing aid. When she came here, three-and-a-half years ago, she seems to have mislaid it. She accepts everything. She accepts her legs won't hold her any more. She is content to be kept safe and warm in this awful place. All she wants, all she's ever asked, is for somebody to find her bloody hearing-aid.

This article is an edited extract from a much longer article with the same title, written by journalist Sally Vincent and published in *The Guardian Weekend*, 19 February, 6–10 and 52 (1994).

72 | The shadow of genetic injustice

BENNO MÜLLER-HILL

The effects of the inevitable discoveries emerging from the Human Genome Project will be catastrophic for some. Now is the time for preventative action to be taken.

Many knowledgeable people have a deep dislike of the Human Genome Project. If you ask them why, some may say that the money would be better spent on different, smaller projects. A few fear that the outcome could be harmful: they foresee a new underclass, unable to get jobs or insurance. These pessimists of course overlook that this underclass already exists: 37 million people have no health insurance of any kind in the United States. Could things become worse?

Proponents of the Human Genome Project imagine great progress in diagnosis of diseases and in their therapy. Some predict that eventually everyone will carry all the sequences of his genes on a compact disk. Others even claim that the present knowledge of man and his mind is nil and that real culture will arise only out of the knowledge of the sequence of human DNA. This, I think, is unlikely.

As pure scientists, these enthusiasts often do not imagine the consequences for society as a whole. My own view is that the project will be truly enlightening about the molecular structure of the human body and brain, and that this knowledge alone is exciting enough to justify the programme. Little is known in molecular biology and many unsuspected medical applications may emerge from this endeavour. As a molecular geneticist I have always defended the Human Genome Project as scientifically sound and important, and I continue to do so. But I have also tried to spread the knowledge of the past criminal misuse of human genetics in Nazi Germany. Until now I have abstained from commenting on the possible effects of the Human Genome Project on society in the future. But science after all consists of making, and testing, predictions. So I have decided to stick my neck out and to make some predictions for the next 30 years.

There is no doubt that the main medical progress will be in diagnostics. Therapeutics may lag behind, possibly for decades, so I will abstain from discussing these aspects here. What will be the main diagnostic results of the Human Genome Project that are relevant to society? I think there are two different areas: genetic ailments of the body and those of the mind.

There are many severe ailments of the body for which there are genetic predispositions. Most of these conditions are extremely rare: only a very few are as frequent as one per cent. At the moment it is in most cases just about possible to say that, according to a family history, a certain risk exists. The Human Genome Project, however, will lead to the identification of DNA defects in the relevant genes. Then, accurate predictions can be made from the blood (DNA): for example, one will be able to predict that a healthy child will die in his or her forties from Huntington's [disease] or from familial Alzheimer's disease. In Huntington's [disease], the timepoint of the outbreak of the first symptoms will vary considerably. In other diseases it may vary even more. The predictions will thus not be accurate in the sense that the severeness of the symptoms can be predicted for a particular time, but they will be statistically accurate. This concept is difficult to explain to patients and clients.

There are some similarities between this situation and that in the late nineteenth century, when infections were random and where no treatment was available. Then, many had the bad luck to be infected whereas here we are talking about only a few people. But the late nineteenth century was the time that general health insurance was introduced in countries like Germany. Bismarck's reform in that country had the effect of increasing the industrial output of Germany. Perhaps the time of molecular revelation of rare diseases would be the proper time to introduce general health insurance in the United States?

To continue my predictions for the future. Imagine four potential cases of genetic disablement. (1) When a haemophiliac wants to become a butcher it makes sense to discourage him. (2) When a colour-blind man wants to become a truck driver, he fails at a colour test: his DNA does not need to be tested. (3) When a healthy young man asks for employment and his employer wants to know whether his genotype indicates that he may die in his thirties or forties from Huntington's disease, this is unfair. (4) When a healthy black person seeks employment and is tested for sickle-cell anaemia gene, then is refused employment because there may be an extra risk under certain conditions, this is unfair.

Thus, in my view, practical ability tests are acceptable, but genetic tests for disabilities which may turn up later in life should not be made available to employers. Moreover, DNA testing for employment purposes should not be performed if a large ethnic group would suffer. But it goes without saying that a person presenting a potential employer or insurance company with unsolicited evidence that he does not carry the genes predisposing for various ailments will have a definite advantage.

One can imagine the development of protest movements among those who have decided not to reveal their genetic identity, and there will be fundamentalists who will never have themselves tested because they themselves do not want to know. All these groups will suffer grave social disadvantages. One can also imagine clubs for the 'healthy' that will demand proof of 'genetic fitness'. The turning point may come when the US supreme court decides that genetic injustice is so immense that it is within the law to show an employer or the insurance company falsified genetic identity. (In Germany the supreme court has just decided that pregnant women may lie about the pregnancy to an employer.) From then on, the interest of employers and insurance companies in the genetic identity of their employees or clients will wane.

I think all these developments will be painful but could come to a good end: the genetic bad luck of a very few may, eventually, be helped by many in that general health insurance and tough anti-discrimination laws could become reality. It is, of course, also possible that the genetically handicapped will be simply too few ever to influence the majority to come to their help.

The situation will be different with the genetic ailments of the mind, which I shall now discuss. Here, the percentage of the population involved is much larger and cannot easily be overlooked. Any current textbook of human genetics will contain the assertion that most differences of the human mind and soul (to use an old-fashioned word) are inherited. But in almost all these cases the respective genes have not been located or isolated, and the DNA defects are thus totally unknown. It is claimed that psychiatric diseases such as manic depression or schizophrenia, and also psychological disablements such as low intelligence, are somehow inherited. But the truth is that the extent of family influence or other environmental factors is unclear. Proof that these ailments are essentially genetically determined can come only through the knowledge of the DNA sequences of these genes and their variants. Knowledge of the DNA sequences of a person will then allow one to make statistically accurate predictions about that person's intelligence and mental stability, and thus about their possible fate.

In earlier times, such predictions were the business of charlatans. But belief increases the likelihood of a predicted outcome: placebos against psychic ailments work astonishingly well. The scientific prediction of a person's limitations, and thus his possible fate, has a very dangerous component in that it may lead the individual to inaction and despair. It may also lead the population at large to believe that, as there is no real chance, money should not be wasted to counteract genetic limitations. It could be forgotten that these limitations are also set by environmental factors.

Many medical scientists would like the fame of having isolated one of these genes. Some succumb to the pressure and claim they have obtained evidence where in fact there is little or none. The 'discovery' of genes determining alcoholism, schizophrenia, manic depression and Alzheimer's disease have been peer-reviewed and published in leading scientific journals. They were hailed in the media as breakthroughs – and then they were shown to be wrong either by their own authors or by others. These errors do not mean that the main qualities of the mind and the soul are not biologically inherited: they show simply that scientists are ordinary people. One can predict safely that many more such non-discoveries will be made. This will be confusing for scientists and painful for the particular patients involved. But eventually the truth will emerge in areas where now we can only make guesses.

Finally, I would like to imagine what may happen if it does turn out that mental health can be shown to have a genetic basis. Let us assume as an example that a gene is isolated which in several mutated forms predisposes for schizophrenia. It will take by then a matter of weeks to determine the complete DNA sequence of such a gene. Will the sequence reveal anything about schizophrenia? For a molecular biologist, knowledge of a sequence means that the function of the protein specified by that sequence is known – for example the protein may form an ion channel or be an enzyme metabolizing a particular molecule. Does this mean that we will understand schizophrenia if we know that it often occurs in people when a certain ion channel or a certain enzyme is damaged?

Many scientists or doctors would answer in the affirmative, but I would like to say, emphatically, that the answer is no. Understanding a biochemical defect brings us no nearer to understanding the thoughts and actions of the schizophrenic. Those opposed to my view would argue that knowledge of the gene will allow us to identify which lifestyles are dangerous for such a person. But we do not need any knowledge of the gene or its product to do this. Pharmacologists, on the other hand, will point out that they now can design rational drugs which may influence precisely the functioning of the relevant gene product. But it is not true that if we know which drug to prescribe, we know all that is necessary to know about schizophrenia. Although the molecular–genetic approach will certainly lead to a frenzy of new drugs on the market, in the end the suffering patients will be helped only partially. It is so much easier to prescribe a pill than to change the social conditions that may be responsible for the severity of the symptoms.

I have little faith in the notion that treatment of mental diseases will truly benefit from knowledge of the culprit genes and gene products. But I have no doubt that diagnosis will flourish. Cheap tests will be developed which will allow everyone to be tested for the variants of genes determining psychiatric ailments or psychic qualities outside the doctor's office. Those carrying the disabling genes of schizophrenia, manic depression and low intelligence may constitute ten or more per cent of the US or European population. Medical scientists will test anonymously all possible ethnic and social groups for these genes, and doubtless some ethnic differences will be found. Suddenly, genetic racial injustice will be a fact.

The isolation of the first gene involved in determining 'intelligence' (whatever that is) will be a turning point in human history. Will governments endorse the view of the eugenicists of the 1930s that the carriers of such genes are 'bad and inferior' and that they and their followers are 'good and superior'? Or will they stress privacy and cleverly leave the necessary selection to market forces? Or will they resort to legal measures to speed up the process of the 'physical disappearance of the unwanted'? And what will the geneticists themselves say? Perhaps they will simply be relieved to find that their own mental genotypes are 'healthy'. But will some of them propose ways to eliminate the 'bad' genes from others?

Anticipating such conflicts, many may conclude that we do not need or want this genetic knowledge. I disagree. The knowledge will simply unveil reality, emphasizing the injustice of the world. It is certainly not enough to face reality bluntly if the future develops as I describe it. It is not enough simply that the right of privacy is acknowledged. If those who have this right have no education, health insurance or jobs, the right is not enough. Laws are necessary to protect the genetically disadvantaged. Social justice has to recompense genetic injustice. The details of such legislation can be spelled out only when the genetic facts are known. Deep changes in attitudes are also required. All we can do now is to be prepared. Progress may be painfully fast or slow, and will be full of contradictions. To master it demands firm values. At the extremes, people will have to choose between the values of the Nazis and those of Moses – that is, racism or an appreciation of equal human rights. The choice for politicians of the world's governments will be between international fascism or, if science and justice are combined, a fundamentally improved social structure throughout the world.

I would like to conclude by citing a sentence from *Science and the Future*, published in 1924, written by the optimist J.B.S. Haldane, 'I think that the tendency of applied science is to magnify injustices until they become too intolerable to be borne, and the average man whom all the prophets and poets could not move, turns at last and extinguishes the evil at its source'.

Benno Müller-Hill is a molecular geneticist working at the Institute for Genetics, University of Cologne, Germany. This article was originally published in *Nature*, **362**, 8 April (1993) pp. 491–492.

73 | The evolution of Utopia

STEVE JONES

Most Utopian novels of the future ignore one of the few predictable things about evolution, which is its unpredictability. No dinosaur could have guessed that descendants of the shrew-like creatures playing at its feet would soon replace it: and the chimpanzees who outnumbered humans a hundred thousand years ago would be depressed to see that their relatives are now so abundant while their descendants are an endangered species.

Evolution always builds on its weaknesses, rather than making a fresh start. The lack of a grand plan is what makes life so adaptable and humans – the greatest opportunists of all – so successful. Life's utilitarian approach also means that speculating about the future of evolution is a risky thing to do as it is difficult to guess what a pragmatist will do next. In this [article], I will take the risk.

Humanity evolved by the same rules as those which propel less pretentious creatures. Humans are, of course, more than just apes writ large. We have two unique attributes: knowing the past and planning the future. Both talents guarantee that the outlook for humankind will depend on a lot more than genes. Nevertheless, it should be possible to make some guesses from the biological past as to what the evolutionary forecast might be. One pessimistic but probably accurate prediction is that it means extinction. Although about one person in twenty who has ever lived is alive today, only about one in a thousand of the different kinds of animal and plant has survived. Our species is in its adolescence, at about a hundred and fifty thousand years old (compared to several times this for those of our relatives whose fossil record is good enough to guess their age). Its demise is, one hopes, a long way away; and we can at least reflect about what might happen before then.

The rules which drive evolution are simple and are unlikely to change. They involve the appearance of new genes by mutation, natural selection, and random changes as some genes, by chance, fail to be passed on. To speculate about what will happen to each of these processes is to make predictions about human evolution. Will this biological Utopia be anything like its fictional equivalents (as I hope it will not); will we continue to evolve as rapidly as we have since our beginnings, or is human evolution at an end?

Human beings have interfered quite unknowingly with their biological heritage since they first appeared on earth. Stone tools, agriculture and private property all had an effect on society and in turn on evolution. Many people are concerned that the next phase of human history will be one in which genetics makes deliberate plans for the biological future. This is expecting too much of science. Inadvertent change – evolution by mistake – is much more likely to be important than is any conscious attempt to modify biology.

Even the most determined efforts of doctors, genetic counsellors or gene therapists will have only a small effect on future generations. About one British child in two thousand five hundred is born with cystic fibrosis – but a hundred times as many carry the gene without knowing it. Molecular biology makes it possible to advise people of their condition and perhaps, one day, will provide a cure. Even today's imperfect treatment means that the number of affected children surviving to reproductive age will double in the next thirty years. Nobody knows what the balance will be; whether the fact that more of those with cystic fibrosis pass on the gene will be outweighed by a decrease in the number of sufferers as genetical advice allows parents to plan their reproduction. Many people with phenylketonuria have had children. There was once strong social pressure against those with inborn disease marrying. In the 1950s only a minority of achondroplastic dwarves found a spouse, but in the United States more than eighty per cent of them are now married, often to another dwarf. No doubt, many genes which once disappeared quickly as their carriers died or remained single will now persist.

This is unlikely to have much influence on the biological future. Most inborn diseases which are susceptible to treatment or to pre-natal diagnosis are recessive, so that there are hundreds of times as many copies of the gene in healthy people as in sufferers. As everyone carries several hidden recessive mutations there is little prospect that medicine will pollute a once pure human gene pool by allowing a few more copies to survive.

Many inherited diseases appear anew each generation by mutation. Is the evolutionary future in danger because of an increase in the mutation rate? There are real concerns that modern civilisation – with its dubious benefits of nuclear radiation and poisonous chemicals – will lead to a dramatic increase in the number of mutations. In many science fiction worlds this is, in a few short generations, enough to degrade the human race. The obvious threats, including man-made radiation and chemicals, have a smaller effect than do natural mutagens such as radon gas leaking from granite. The Sellafield nuclear power station in the North of England is the most polluting in the western world and the North Sea the most radioactive body of water. Yet, compared to other sources of radiation, its effects are minor. Avid consumers of shellfish collected near the discharge pipe receive about as much excess radiation as do those who fly from London to Los Angeles and back four times a year and are exposed to cosmic radiation as a result.

The rate of mutation goes up greatly with age. The control of infection means that most people now live for far longer than in earlier times. Mutation can hence take its toll on a much higher proportion of the population. This is very obvious when looking at such changes in body cells, including those which give rise to cancer. The cancer epidemic in the modern world is largely confined to older people. A shift in the pattern of survival has had effects on genes as they reside in body cells.

A more subtle transformation is having a dramatic effect on the mutation rate. In the western world at least, a change in the age at which people have children means that the number of new mutations will probably drop.

Cells which give rise to sperm or eggs are also exposed to the destructive effects of old age. Older parents are more likely to have genetically damaged children than are those who reproduce early. Any change in the age of reproduction will hence have an effect on the mutation rate. If the average age of reproduction goes up, there will be more mutations; if it decreases, there will be fewer. Social progress has led to just such a shift. The general picture, world-wide – a picture which applies to most of the Third World as much as to Britain and the United States – is simple and a little surprising.

Before the improvements in public health over the past few centuries most children died young. Mothers started having babies when they were themselves youthful and continued to have them until they were biologically unable to do so, perhaps twenty-five years later. As infant mortality drops there is less pressure to have children as an insurance against one's own old age. People prefer to have smaller families. The availability of contraception means that parents can choose to delay their first child – sometimes, as in middle-class Britain, until their mid-twenties – but then complete their families quickly. This means that most people stop having children soon after they have started. As a result, the average age of reproduction for both males and females goes down as social conditions improve.

All this means that mothers are younger on the average than they have been for much of the evolutionary past. Fathers, too, are getting more youthful. At the moment, at least, it looks as if the human mutation rate is on the way down. Whether this trend will continue is not known, but it does put fears about a new race of mutated monsters into context.

If mutation is the fuel of evolution, natural selection is its engine. As selection is a more elusive process than mutation it is more difficult to forecast what its future might be. Nature is always liable to come up – as it has so often before – with a nasty surprise with which natural selection must cope. The emergence of the AIDS virus shows that there is an eternal risk of this happening again. However, in the western world at least some of the greatest selective challenges have gone, because of the control of infectious disease.

Once a disease has disappeared (as so many have) the fate of the genes involved in combating it will change. Cypriots carry the inherited anaemia [*thalassaemia*] because the gene once defended their ancestors against malaria. Malaria has now disappeared from Cyprus – as, in time, will thalassaemia, with the incidence of carriers likely to drop by as much as one per cent per generation from its present level of seventeen per cent. In time, and given success – still far distant – in the fight against malaria, the same will happen to the dozens of other genes involved in resisting it elsewhere in the world. Perhaps such genes will, in time, remain only as mute witnesses to their evolutionary past.

There are more subtle ways of looking at the future of selection. Natural selection can only act on differences. If everyone survived to adulthood, found a partner and had the same number of children there would be almost no chance for it to operate. We do not need to know what genes selection is working on to see how important it might be. Looking at changes in the patterns of birth and death reveals a lot about its actions in the past and in the future.

In affluent countries, the differences between families in how many people survive have decreased. This means that there is less opportunity for natural selection. Ten thousand years ago, the struggle for existence really meant something. Skeletons from cave cemeteries show that few people lived to be more than twenty. If ancient fertility was anything like that found in modern tribal groups each female had about eight children, most of whom died young. For nine tenths of human evolution, society was like a village school, with lots of infants, plenty of teenagers and a few – probably harassed – adult survivors. Almost every death was potential raw material for selection as it involved someone young enough to have had a hope of passing on their genes. Nowadays, things have changed. Ninety-eight out of every hundred new-born British babies live to the age of fifteen, so that selection acting through childhood deaths (once its main mode of operation) has almost disappeared.

There have been changes in the balance of birth and death which have other effects on the opportunity for natural selection. Few modern peoples are as fertile as they once were. The Hutterites in North America wish for the largest possible family for religious reasons but even they, living in a healthy society, rarely have more than ten children. For most of human history it seems that people had as many children as is biologically possible. Only recently has that number begun to decrease.

Only in the past few years have humans lived as long as they are able. In the West, average life expectancy has nearly doubled over the past century. For the first time in history, most people die old; perhaps as old as biology allows. Life expectancy has risen from forty-seven to seventy-five years since 1900. Progress has now stopped, for some social classes at least. In the USA in 1979, a white woman of sixty-five could expect to live for another eighteen and a half years. In 1991 the figure was exactly the same. Even if all infectious diseases and all accidental deaths could be eliminated, average life expectancy in the western world would now go up by only a couple of years. There is still room for progress in the average length of life because of class differences in health. A baby born to an unskilled worker in Britain can expect to live for eight years less than one born to a professional person, a difference which, to our national shame, is actually increasing. However, the prospects for any dramatic improvement in longevity are dim.

This is important for the evolutionary future. The increase in the number of old people means that more people die for genetical reasons than in earlier times (largely because fewer are killed violently or by infection). Paradoxically, it also means that selection is weaker. The genes that kill are now those for cancer or heart disease, which act late in life. Those who die have already reproduced, passing on their fatal inheritance. Natural selection is much less powerful when acting on genes such as these than it is on those which alter the chances of survival before their carriers have children.

The new pattern of human existence (with fewer children than ever before but most people lasting until the biological clock runs down) emerged only about twenty human generations ago, compared to the six thousand or so since we first appeared on earth. It means that natural selection has changed the way it works. What there is nowadays acts more on fertility than on survival.

Differences in fertility among families, and the opportunity which they give for selection, shot up as birth control became popular. The upper classes adopted the idea well before the lower orders. Now that birth control is widespread the differences between families have dropped again, but selection working through variation in the number of children born is still, for the first time in history, greater than that working on the number that survive. The evolutionary fate of our genes depends more on the number of children we choose to have than on their chances of staying alive.

Nearly all the best understood forces of selection – disease, climate or starvation – act on survival rather than on fertility. The shift in the balance of the two may bring in new and unpredictable evolutionary forces. Perhaps the age of reproduction will become important, as those who mature young can have more children. There has been a drop in the age at which girls become sexually mature. In opposition to this trend, western women now marry five years later than they did half a century ago. Any inherited tendency to marry earlier or later (or to limit family size) could become a potent agent of evolution.

What this will do to the biological future is hard to say. A good general rule in evolution is that nobody gets a free lunch: success in one walk of life must be paid for by failure in another. History gives little reason to hope that selection will act as the agent of human perfectibility. It may direct the future, but will never make humanity superhuman.

The number of new mutations and the intensity of natural selection are both declining. This certainly does not mean that evolution is over. There is another change in modern society which is bound to influence our biological prospects. It is one which most people scarcely consider. It has to do with the geography of mating.

For most of history, everyone more or less had to marry the girl (or the boy) next door, because they had no choice. Society was based on small bands or isolated villages and marriages were within the group. In many places, populations were stable and quite inbred. Almost nobody moved. The genes of American Indians, drowned in a peat bog in Florida, display the effect clearly. The DNA in the preserved brains of people who died a thousand years apart shows that their genes are almost the same. There was little migration and the Indians had no option but to marry their relatives.

This pattern persisted in the West until recently and still exists in many parts of the world. In some places it is changing quickly. An increase in mating outside the local group is the most dramatic change in the developed world's evolutionary history. The effect is getting stronger and stronger. The influence of outbreeding on genetical health will outweigh anything that medicine is able to do.

One way of illustrating changes in breeding pattern is to use a crude but effective measure of how closely related our ancestors may have been. All that one needs to know is how far apart they were born. If they come from the same village they may well be relatives, but if they were born hundreds of miles apart this is much less likely. For nearly everyone reading this the distance between the places where they and their own partner were born is greater than that separating their parents' birthplaces. In turn, today's fathers and mothers were almost certainly born further apart than were their own parents. In nineteenth-century Oxfordshire the distance between the birthplaces of marriage partners was less than ten miles. Now it is more than fifty. In the United States it is several hundred, so that most American couples are completely unrelated. All this shows how quickly the world's populations are beginning to mix together.

It will take a long time before the mixing is complete. One estimate is that it will take as much as five hundred years to even out the genetic differences between England and Scotland – and perhaps even longer to get rid of their cultural contrasts. Even if global homogeneity is a long way away, increased movement will certainly have a biological effect. No longer will large numbers of children be born who have two copies of defective genes because their parents are related. The most common damaged gene in whites is the one for cystic fibrosis, in blacks that for sickle-cell anaemia. Only if a child inherits two copies of either of these will it suffer from an inborn disease.

Because cystic fibrosis is unknown in Africans and sickle cell in whites the child of a black–white mating is safe from both illnesses.

This effect can be a strong one. In many societies in the modern world there are immigrant communities which are beginning to merge with the people already there. Imagine that ten per cent of the population of Britain were to immigrate from West Africa (where about one person in fifteen is a carrier of the gene for sickle-cell anaemia) and to mate freely with the locals. The number of sickle-cell carriers in the new mixed British population would go up by seven times. However, the incidence of sickle-cell disease – which demands two copies of the damaged gene, one from each parent – would drop by ninety per cent compared to the previous situation in the two groups considered together. This is because many children would be born to parents from the two different peoples, one of whom – the native British partner – does not carry the sickle-cell gene. There would also be an effect on the indigenous British disease, cystic fibrosis, whose incidence would drop by about a sixth. Although this model of race mixing is simplistic it is not completely unreasonable. In Britain now, about one marriage in thirty is between two people of non-European origin; but a third as many are between a non-European and someone whose ancestors were born in the British Isles.

This change in mating patterns may mark the beginning of a new age of genetic well-being. Increased outbreeding inevitably means that recessive genes will be partnered by a normal copy which masks their effects. This is enough to dwarf the efforts of scientists to improve genetic health.

Most social changes seem to be conspiring to slow down human evolution. Mutation, selection, and random change have all lost some of their effectiveness in the past few centuries. All this means that the biology of the future will not be very different from that of the past. It may even be that economic advance and medical progress mean that humans are almost at the end of their evolutionary road, that we are as near to our biological Utopia as we are ever likely to get. Fortunately, no one reading this will be around to see if I am right.

Steve Jones is Professor of Genetics at University College London. This is an edited version of Chapter 16 of his award-winning book *The Language of the Genes*, which was originally published in 1993 by HarperCollins, London. The order of two paragraphs has been changed.

74 | Spawn of Satan?

NICOLA GRIFFITH

Egg donation has begun to bias the new and controversial Raswani Social Intelligence scale and the more traditional Stanford-Binet IQ test. Nationwide testing has been prompted by what some educators are calling an exponential change in the behaviour of kindergarten children. 'We noticed a real big difference,' said Anita Cunnings, a teachers' assistant at a grade school in an upscale Chicago neighbourhood. 'When I first took this job in 2015 we'd sometimes get a kid who was not only smart, but smart all round, who really knew how to handle other kids. Now we have half a dozen or more every year. They're almost perfect. To tell you the truth, they're a little frightening.'

A local bus driver, who prefers to remain anonymous was less circumspect. 'Spawn of Satan,' he said. 'It ain't natural. These kids climb on the bus, say "please" and "thank you", and read all the way to school. Lord knows, I can't abide all the yellin' and runnin'-up-and-down of normal kids but this ain't natural.'

Demographics point to white, middle-class women in the 45–48 age range. 'So it's only to be expected,' said a harassed-looking Dr Judith Sternberg, returning from testimony to a congressional ethics sub-committee. 'Record numbers of career-orientated, well-educated women are now choosing, in their mid-forties and older, to have children. And they're choosing extremely smart, well-educated women in their twenties to be the donors. The rest is genetics.'

'Nonsense,' responds educational sociologist Mike Chattergee, 'the deciding factor is the child's upbringing. These older mothers tend to be more affluent, so they can give the infant everything it needs in the way of education and nurture. Better nurturing means a happier, healthier, more well-adjusted child.'

A corollary of the egg-donation boom is the change in behaviour noted in the spouses of married mothers. 'It's good old-fashioned competition,' said red-faced Jack Donatelli at the bowling alley in Midwich, Connecticut. 'Women get to pick the father so, if you can't hack it, move aside for someone who can.'

'There's nothing old-fashioned about it,' says his companion, who would only give his name as Bill. 'Look at me, see that muscle? Strong as an ox. Good job. But that's not enough any more. Now it's "Oh, Bill, why don't you do the laundry while I write that proposal for the UK office?" Because I don't want to, that's why, but do I say anything? No. Because if I do she'll get someone else to father her goddamn test-tube baby, and I'll be slaving to support a cuckoo child!'

Some Church leaders have long decried the commercialization of egg donation. 'Life is a gift from God,' said the Archbishop of Chicago. 'When one woman who is blessed with fertility can help bring joy to another, that gift should be given freely.' Unitarians, on the other hand, believe God is in everything, even the test-tube and the bank account. Other religions, such as Islam, forbid the procedure entirely.

But ethics have nothing to do with it, argues the director for reproductive health at the Women's Clinic. 'It's all very well wishing things were different,' says Dr Allison Toomin, 'but this is the real world. What healthy 22-year-old college senior in her right mind would go through a month of pain, daily injections, bloating, hormonal disturbance and the risk of medical complication, just for altruism? Especially when prospective mothers are offering $75,000 and a trip around the world if the donor has a SAT score of over 1,500, good looks and perfect health.'

Senator George W. Bush III believes people like Dr Toomin are wrong. 'It's not right,' he tells voters gathered at a rally in Texas. 'These women are *buying* smarts for their babies. They're *buying* fertility, love and a secure old age, just because they were too selfish to stop working and have babies when they were young and healthy, while God-fearing folks are so crippled by Big Government taxes that they can hardly scrape together the bread for their own little ones!'

Not far from where Bush is speaking lies Austin, one of the epicentres of the intelligence spike being observed all over the country. Others include Seattle, the San Francisco Bay Area, and certain neighbourhoods of larger cities such as Atlanta and Boston. 'With the exception of Atlanta, these are all very white cities,' points out M'Shelle N'dele Mbele, from the Urban Justice Center in St Louis. She grins sardonically: 'Wonder why that is?' She believes that, like most racial issues, this is at heart a money-based discrimination. Few would disagree: reproduction by egg donation is expensive but, with a first-time success rate now approaching 80 per cent, it's by far the most reliable of *in vitro* technologies.

Dr Sternberg believes that, as Americans approach the second half of the twenty-first century, egg donation is here to stay. 'What I told the ethics sub-committee is that we need to think about what this means for business. Global competition from emerging nations is threatening the ascendancy of American corporations. We need our female executives to remain focused on their jobs through their thirties and early forties and not be distracted by the idea of a biological clock. Egg donation lets us reset that clock, if not banish it all together. Right now America has the edge. Egg donation lets us keep it.' The sub-committee has declared that there will no longer be regulation of viable human ova at the federal level, and the debate is under way regarding tax credits for donors and clinics.

All parties expect controversy. For every egg donor and prospective mother there will be someone like old-timer Sam Underhill, overheard recently at the Green Dragon Inn, in Bywater, Maine. 'It's not natural,' he said, 'and no good will come of it.'

This short story was published in the 'Futures' section of the leading science journal *Nature*, 1999, 402: 585. The author, Nicola Griffith (www.sff.net/people/Nicola) has just finished writing *Red Raw*, the sequel to her latest novel, *The Blue Place*. She lives in Seattle, Washington.

75 | The flesh

J. DESMOND BERNAL

In the alteration of himself man has a great deal further to go than in the alteration of his inorganic environment. Man has altered himself in the evolutionary process, he has lost a good deal of hair, his wisdom teeth are failing to pierce, and his nasal passages are becoming more and more degenerate. But the processes of natural evolution are so much slower than the development of man's control over environment that we might, in such a developing world, still consider man's body as constant and unchanging. If it is not to be so then man himself must actively interfere in his own making and interfere in a highly unnatural manner. Biologists are apt, even if they are not vitalists, to consider [evolution] as almost divine; but after all it is only nature's way of achieving a shifting equilibrium with an environment; and if we can find a more direct way by the use of intelligence, that way is bound to supersede the unconscious mechanism of growth and reproduction.

In a civilized worker the limbs are mere parasites, demanding nine-tenths of the energy of the food and even a kind of blackmail in the exercise they need to prevent disease, while the body organs wear themselves out in supplying their requirements. On the other hand, the increasing complexity of man's existence, particularly the mental capacity required to deal with its mechanical and physical complications, gives rise to the need for a much more complex sensory and motor organization, and even more fundamentally for a better organized cerebral mechanism. Sooner or later the useless parts of the body must be given more modern functions or dispensed with altogether, and in their place we must incorporate in the effective body the mechanisms of the new functions. Surgery and biochemistry are sciences still too young to predict exactly how this will happen. The account I am about to give must be taken rather as a fable.

Take, as a starting point, the perfect man such as the doctors, the eugenists and the public health officers between them hope to make of humanity: a man living perhaps an average of a hundred and twenty years but still mortal, and increasingly feeling the burden of this mortality. Sooner or later some eminent physiologist will have his neck broken in a super-civilized accident or find his body cells worn beyond capacity for repair. He will then be forced to decide whether to abandon his body or his life. After all it is brain that counts, and to have a brain suffused by fresh and correctly prescribed blood is to be alive – to think. The experiment is not impossible; it has already been performed on a dog and that is three-quarters of the way towards achieving it with a human subject. But only a Brahmin philosopher would care to exist as an isolated brain, perpetually centred on its own meditations. Permanently to break off all communications with the world is as good as to be dead. However, the channels of communication are ready to hand. Already we know the essential electrical nature of nerve impulses; it is a matter of delicate surgery to attach nerves permanently to apparatus which will either send messages to the nerves or receive them. And the brain thus connected up continues an existence, purely mental and with very different delights from those of the body, but even now perhaps preferable to complete extinction. The example may have been too far-fetched; perhaps the same result may be achieved much more gradually by using of the many superfluous nerves with which our body is endowed for various auxiliary and motor services. We badly need a small sense organ for detecting wireless frequencies, eyes for infra-red, ultraviolet and X-rays, ears for supersonics, detectors of high and low temperatures, of electrical potential and current, and chemical organs of many kinds. We may perhaps be able to train a great number of hot and cold and pain receiving nerves to take over these functions; on the motor side we shall soon be, if we are not already, obliged to control mechanisms for which two hands and feet are an entirely inadequate number; and, apart from that, the direction of mechanism by pure volition would enormously simplify its operation. Where the motor mechanism is not primarily electrical, it might be simpler and more effective to use nerve-muscle preparations instead of direct nerve connections. Even the pain nerves may be pressed into service to report any failure in the associated mechanism. A mechanical stage, utilizing some or all of these alterations of the bodily frame might, if the initial experiments were successful in the sense of leading to a tolerable existence, become the regular culmination to ordinary life.

But this is by no means the end of [man's] development, although it marks his last great metamorphosis. Apart from such mental development as his increased faculties will demand from him, he will be physically plastic in a way quite transcending the capacities of untransformed humanity. Should he need a new sense organ or have a new mechanism to operate, he will have undifferentiated nerve connections to attach to them, and will be able to extend indefinitely his possible sensations and actions by using successively different end-organs.

The carrying out of these complicated surgical and physiological operations would be in the hands of a medical profession which would be bound to come rapidly under the control of transformed men. The operations themselves would probably be conducted by mechanisms controlled by the transformed heads of the profession, though in the earlier and experimental stages, of course, it would still be done by human surgeons and physiologists.

It is much more difficult to form a picture of the final state, partly because this final state would be so fluid and so liable to improve, and partly because there would be no reason whatever why all people should transform in the same way. Probably a great number of typical forms would be developed, each specialized in certain directions. If we confine ourselves to what might be called the first stage of mechanized humanity and to a person mechanized for scientific rather than aesthetic purposes – for to predict even the shapes that men would adopt if they would make of *themselves* a harmony of form and sensation must be beyond imagination – then the description might run roughly as follows.

Instead of the present body structure we should have the whole framework of some very rigid material, probably not metal but one of the new fibrous substances. In shape it might well be rather a short cylinder. Inside the cylinder, and supported very carefully to prevent shock, is the brain with its nerve connections, immersed in a liquid of the nature of cerebro-spinal fluid, kept circulating over it at a uniform temperature. The brain and nerve cells are kept supplied with fresh oxygenated blood and drained of de-oxygenated blood through their arteries and veins which connect outside the cylinder to the artificial heart–lung digestive system.

The brain thus guaranteed continuous awareness, is connected in the anterior of the case with its immediate sense organs, the eye and the ear – which will probably retain this connection for a long time. The eyes will look into a kind of optical box which will enable them alternatively to look into periscopes projecting from the case, telescopes, microscopes and a whole range of televisual apparatus. The ear would have the corresponding microphone attachments and would still be the chief organ for wireless reception. Smell and taste organs, on the other hand, would be prolonged into connections outside the case and would be changed into chemical testing organs, achieving a more conscious and less primitively emotional role than they have at present. The remaining sensory nerves, those of touch, temperature, muscular position and visceral functioning, would go to the corresponding part of the exterior machinery or to the blood supplying organs. Attached to the brain cylinder would be its immediate motor organs, corresponding to but much more complex than, our mouth, tongue and hands. This appendage system would probably be built up like that of a crustacean which uses the same general type of arm for antenna, jaw and limb; and they would range from delicate micro-manipulators to levers capable of exerting considerable forces, all controlled by the appropriate motor nerves. Closely associated with the brain-case would also be sound, colour and wireless producing organs. In addition to these there would be certain organs of a type we do not possess at present – the self-repairing organs – which under the control of the brain would be able to manipulate the other organs, particularly the visceral blood supply organs, and to keep them in effective working order. Serious derangements, such as those involving loss of consciousness would still, of course, call for outside assistance, but with proper care these would be in the nature of rare accidents.

The remaining organs would have a more temporary connection with the brain-case. There would be locomotor apparatus of different kinds, which could be used alternatively for slow movement, equivalent to walking, for rapid transit and for flight. On the whole, however, the locomotor organs would not be much used because the extension of the sense organs would tend to take their place. Most of these would be mere mechanisms quite apart from the body; there would be the sending parts of the television apparatus, tele-acoustic and tele-chemical organs, and tele-sensory organs of the nature of touch for determining all forms of texture. Besides these there would be various tele-motor organs for manipulating materials at great distances from the controlling mind. These extended organs would only belong in a loose sense to any particular person, or rather, they would belong only temporarily to the person who was using them and could equivalently be operated by other people. This capacity for indefinite extension might in the end lead to the relative fixity of the different brains;

and this would, in itself, be an advantage from the point of view of security and uniformity of conditions, only some of the more active considering it necessary to be on the spot to observe and do things.

The new man must appear to those who have not contemplated him before as a strange, monstrous and inhuman creature, but he is only the logical outcome of the type of humanity that exists at present. Although it is possible that man has far to go before his inherent physiological and psychological make-up becomes the limiting factor to his development, this must happen sooner or later, and it is then that the mechanized man will begin to show a definite advantage. Normal man is an evolutionary dead end; mechanical man, apparently a break in organic evolution, is actually more in the true tradition of a further evolution.

A much more fundamental break is implicit in the means of his development. If a method has been found of connecting a nerve ending in a brain directly with an electrical reactor, then the way is open for connecting it with a brain-cell of another person. Such a connection being, of course, essentially electrical, could be effected just as well through the ether as along wires. At first this would limit itself to the more perfect and economic transference of thought which would be necessary in the cooperative thinking of the future. But it cannot stop here. Connections between two or more minds would tend to become a more and more permanent condition until they functioned as dual or multiple organisms. The minds would always preserve a certain individuality, the network of cells inside a single brain being more dense than that existing between brains, each brain being chiefly occupied with its individual mental development and only communicating with the others for some common purpose. Once the more or less permanent compound brain came into existence two of the ineluctable limitations of present existence would be surmounted. In the first place death would take on a different and far less terrible aspect. Death would still exist for the mentally directed mechanism we have just described; it would merely be postponed for three hundred or perhaps a thousand years, as long as the brain cells could be persuaded to live in the most favourable environment, but not for ever. But the multiple individual would be, barring cataclysmic accidents, immortal, the older components as they died being replaced by newer ones without losing the continuity of the self, the memories and feeling of the older members transferring themselves almost completely to the common stock before its death. And if this seems only a way of cheating death, we must realize that the individual brain will feel itself part of the whole in a way that completely transcends the devotion of the most fanatical adherent of a religious sect. It is admittedly difficult to imagine this state of affairs effectively. It would be a state of ecstasy in the literal sense, and this is the second great alteration that the compound mind makes possible. Whatever the intensity of our feeling, however much we may strive to reach beyond ourselves or into another's mind, we are always barred by the limitations of our individuality. Here at least those barriers would be down: feeling would truly communicate itself, memories would be held in common, and yet in all this, identity and continuity of individual development would not be lost. It is possible, even probable, that the different individuals of a compound mind would not all have similar functions or even be of the same rank of importance. Division of labour would soon set in: to some minds might be delegated the task of ensuring the proper functioning of the others, some might specialize in sense reception and so on. Thus would grow up a hierarchy of minds that would be more truly a complex than a compound mind.

The complex minds could, with their lease of life, extend their perceptions and understanding and their actions far beyond those of the individual. Time senses could be altered: the events that moved with the slowness of geological ages would be apprehended as movement, and at the same time the most rapid vibrations of the physical world could be separated. As we have seen, sense organs would tend to be less and less attached to bodies, and the host of subsidiary, purely mechanical agents and perceptors would be capable of penetrating those regions where organic bodies cannot enter or hope to survive. The interior of the earth and the stars, the inmost cells of living things themselves, would be open to consciousness through these angels, and through these angels also the motions of stars and living things could be directed.

The new life would be more plastic, more directly controllable and at the same time more variable and more permanent than that produced by the triumphant opportunism of nature. Bit by bit the heritage in the direct line of mankind – the heritage of the original life emerging on the face of the world – would dwindle, and in the end disappear effectively, being preserved perhaps as some curious relic, while the new life which conserves none of the substance and all the spirit of the old would take its place and continue its development. Such a change would be as important as that in which life first appeared on the earth's surface and might be as gradual and imperceptible. Finally, consciousness itself may end or vanish in a humanity that has become completely etherialized, losing the close-knit organism, becoming masses of atoms in space communicating by radiation, and ultimately perhaps resolving itself entirely into light. That may be an end or a beginning, but from here it is out of sight.

J. Desmond Bernal was a writer, physicist and communist. He was involved, until his death in 1971, in the politics of science. The extract 'The Flesh' included here is drawn from *The World, the Flesh and the Devil: An Enquiry into the Future of the Three Enemies of the Rational Soul*, first published in 1929 by Cape, London, and republished by Indiana University Press, Bloomington.

76 | Enough already! The pervasiveness of warnings in everyday life

SHULAMIT REINHARZ

I would like to get through a day without being assaulted by warnings. I find this barrage of dire information intrusive, pervasive, and depressing. All day long, cashiers, gas station attendants, waitresses, dry cleaning clerks, bureaucrats, and strangers tell me to have a nice day. And yet, the signs, newspaper articles, radio reports, and labels tell me to watch out. They let me know that life is dangerous. It's almost foolhardy to be in the sun, to be in a car, or to take food (poison?) from a supermarket shelf. Do I buy margarine or butter, knowing, as I have learned, that both are bad?

Attention to these messages makes it clear that warning signs have become extraordinarily repetitive. Can't we assume that everyone already knows that 'smoking is dangerous to one's health'? Can't we assume that I know 'the 10 danger signs,' without having to open a cookbook sponsored by the American Cancer Association and find warnings related to many body parts? You can lose your appetite! You can lose pleasure. You can lose a sense of being comfortably in your body. Instead, your body becomes an enemy of your health.

In fact, I don't like walking outdoors past buildings because that is where I am forced to experience 'secondary smoke'. Do I have to automatically dislike and feel endangered by all these people just because they smoke? How about seat belts? Do I have to disparage everyone who doesn't wear them? And how can I feel good about someone who is obese when I know they are endangering themselves?

I don't believe I am the only person who feels invaded in this way. I remember casually asking a colleague in his late 50's how he was doing, and he said, 'Well, I'm usually obsessed with a cancer-of-the-week, but other than that, I'm fine.' Or once I heard a woman say that she is so terrified of getting breast cancer that she has had to train herself to reduce her breast self-examinations. She now has them down to one per day!

Should I eat salt or not; eggs or not? Should I read medical literature continuously to keep up with the latest information about which is the least dangerous way to eat/live? Yes, I did have my annual mammogram, pap smear, eye checkup, dental exam, and on and on. Now the newspapers are recommending an annual lung X-ray too. Yes, I know what the dangers are when I pass the age of 50, as I just have. But do I have to check my calendar for what's next to examine?

Lung cancer information is forced not only on those who buy cigarette packs, but on the rest of us, too, by warnings 'writ large' on billboards. Colon cancer information is forced on me when I sit down for breakfast cereal because of the national media campaign to promote bran cereal consumption. Does anyone care, however, if people are distressed by the messages? If people would prefer a less gloomy breakfast?

Today, I take my office mail out of my briefcase and there is a one-page issue of the monthly Health Newsletter put out by the Health Services in my university. It starts, 'What you can do to prevent cancer.' Answer: Eat right. Then it tells me how many portions of what to eat every day. Am I doing the right thing? Never having been heavy, I don't count calories, so I don't pay much attention to exactly what I am eating. Is this living dangerously? I attend a meeting of a women's volunteer group that I belong to, concerned with a particular political issue, and I learn that they have now taken on issues of special concern to women – domestic violence and breast cancer – neither of which was in their original mission.

I innocently walk into the bathroom of a large synagogue after a bar mitzvah celebration and find myself in a stall facing a poster that tells me what to do about rape, suicide, mental illness, AIDS, and more. I am in another city, using the bathroom of a restaurant, and a plastic sign hangs from the coat hook suggesting that I do monthly breast examinations, with detailed instructions about how to carry them out. I visit another university, and its bathroom walls have flyers offering help in many languages for domestic violence problems I might be having. I go to a manicurist and when she cuts my cuticle, there is a tiny bit of blood. Will I get AIDS?

The muzak is in the elevators, soothing us with musical syrup. What is on the outside? Continuous alarm. Pajamas might catch on fire; your stroller can get entangled in an escalator. And what's the first thing we see when we enter our hotel room? The way to deal with fire in the hotel is to memorize your exit, double-bolt your door, remember not to use the elevator, follow the instructions, put a wet towel on your face, and crawl along the floor, testing first to see if the door is hot.

If I stop on the way home from work and buy a pizza, I know that I will see smiling faces of children with leukemia urging me to put quarters in the special slots of a paper display. I pick up a package with photos of children who have been abducted and what their kidnapper might look like or the way the child might look after the passage of the intervening years. In the window of the store is a poster about a walk that will take place to support the fight against AIDS. My neighbor calls to say she is raising funds for the Crohn's and Colitis Society.

I come home from work, empty my mailbox, and find catalogs advertising books concerning women who have lost a breast, who are coping with chemotherapy, or who are suffering in some graphic, disturbing way. An ad for a fitness center has the photograph of a missing child on the reverse side. I reach into the refrigerator and take out a carton of orange juice. There on the side of the package is a sketch of a woman running – the text discusses the race for the cure against breast cancer. I put some leftover food in a plastic bag and am warned that the bag may suffocate a baby. But, if I pay attention to all of these warnings, I actually feel suffocated! What if it turns out that warnings are stressful and bad for one's mental health?

I open the newspaper and it tells me that women who are depressed are more likely to have heart attacks than are women who are not depressed. I do a quick mental checkup: Am I depressed? Am I a likely candidate for a heart attack? I turn on the radio, and I learn that one pharmaceutical company has produced a flu vaccine that is not quite as powerful as expected. Listeners who did have a flu shot this year are advised to ask their doctor if they need to be revaccinated. Then the radio news moves on to inform us that air bags are killing children.

This is the holiday season. I am getting appeals from many different organizations to make donations. Paralyzed veterans, homeless women, starving children, Chernobyl victims, abortion rights, Jewish women's breast cancer coalitions, and more. The more graphic the descriptions, I presume, the greater the effectiveness of the promotional materials.

Maybe I should take a trip. I expect to be lucky and not have fuel tanks blow up midflight. Of course there will be security checks with their signs about bombs on airplanes, terrorists smuggling in weapons, and other delightful thoughts. On every flight, I am told how to evacuate the plane if we land over water or if there is some other emergency. Have a nice flight!

After I finish my work at the end of the evening, I get ready for bed and turn on the television. Big mistake. Nightly entertainment consists of people being shot, tortured, arrested, punched, or perhaps simply becoming ill from some horrible illness or another. I switch to a comedy station. Rosanne Barr's children are talking about premenstrual syndrome and using it to explain their mother. I switch to the news. The newscaster offers us some additional gruesome medical news and, having had a 'nice day,' I drift off to sleep. Only to awaken the next day with new information. Every woman is subject to rape, I learned (and believe). So, always be fearful if you walk alone (an attitude I resist as a feminist). But, when my teenage daughters begin to date, what do I tell them, now that I have learned all about date rape?

In the spring, signs inform me that lawns are dangerous to walk on because of pesticides. I could go for a walk in a field instead, but then, there's Lyme disease. Try as we might to make things attractive and enjoyable and safe, they end up killing us or making us sick. Even when we are doing nothing at all, we may be in danger. Information about danger may be spoiling our interpersonal relations.

The dangers of prevention

As a modern human being, I am, of course, a believer in education, information, and prevention. So, one would think I would be pleased that there is so much relevant information out there. My sociological question is, can prevention become so overdone that it becomes deleterious in and of itself? We strive to find balance in our lives, between work and family, between earning and spending, between being alone and being with others, between pride and self-criticism. Is there a balance we need to achieve about warnings so that the warnings themselves don't become the problem? Do we need to prevent some of this ubiquitous prevention?

I wonder if I am oversensitive. Do other people notice this deluge of information about the most unpleasant experiences imaginable? Is anyone being desensitized because of an overload of messages? Have prevention of disease and advocacy for research dollars to combat disease gotten so out of hand that they themselves have polluted our environment?

How did people live in the past? How do they live elsewhere? Did everyone die young because there were no danger signs out there? What did people do before they learned to check all over their bodies for moles and changes in warts?

Obviously, some of the information I am receiving is related to selling me something or trying to persuade me to contribute to something or another. But, I think that only very little of it actually has that intention. Surely, when the label tells me that cigarettes have carcinogens, that information does not encourage me to buy cigarettes.

Rather, I think the pervasiveness of warnings might have four roots: a) the increased emphasis on litigation in our society, (b) the medicalization of everyday life, (c) the emergence of political advocacy around illnesses and social problems, and (d) the respect for science. Moreover, these four factors intersect with and reinforce one another. Given that these four factors can be expected to remain strong in society it is unlikely that I will find my environment less filled with warnings in the near future.

Ironically, the only way I can imagine seeing the 'danger-amplified environment' change is if a new social movement or advocacy group emerges to protect the environment from the overemphasis on frightening people with warnings. It is difficult to imagine a public space that does not tell me that I have to fear theft, suffocating others, becoming ill, or being blown to pieces, unless I join with others to demand such a space. I can only imagine succeeding if I can demonstrate scientifically that the current environment is making me sick and I can find someone to sue!

I don't want to give the impression that I don't care about people's troubles, public safety, and personal health – I do. I don't want to aggravate anyone's health by wearing perfume, or having a cat nearby, or doing anything that's troublesome. God forbid that I should smoke or breathe in anyone else's smoke. I'm not advocating recklessness or selfishness. Instead, I'm suggesting relaxation and pleasure.

This extract comes from Shulamit Reinharz's Chapter 4 (pp. 31–40) in *Qualitative Sociology as Everyday Life*, edited by Barry Glassner and Rosanna Hertz (Sage Publications, 1999). The author is Professor of Sociology and Director of the Women's Studies Program, at Brandeis University, Waltham, Massachusetts, USA.

Name index

Subject index